MW01249089

The United Nations,
The Evolution of Global Values
and International Law

SCHOOL OF HUMAN RIGHTS RESEARCH SERIES, Volume 47

The titles published in this series are listed at the end of this volume.

# The United Nations,
# The Evolution of Global Values
# and International Law

Otto Spijkers

intersentia

Cambridge – Antwerp – Portland

This study was made possible with financial support from the Netherlands
Organisation for Scientific Research (NWO).

Intersentia Ltd
Trinity House | Cambridge Business Park | Cowley Road
Cambridge | CB4 0WZ | United Kingdom
mail@intersentia.co.uk

Otto Spijkers
The United Nations, the Evolution of Global Values and International Law

Cover image: © Victor Spijkers

ISBN 978-1-78068-036-1
NUR 820

British Library Cataloguing in Publication Data. A catalogue record for this book is
available from the British Library.

# ACKNOWLEDGEMENTS

First of all, I wish to thank my two supervisors, Professor Nico Schrijver and Dr. Koos van der Bruggen. They set up the research project on the United Nations and the Evolution of Global Values of which this study is also a product. They urged me to meet the deadlines, focus on the research question, study the literature and delve into the archives of the United Nations Organization. It was a fascinating journey through sixty-something years of UN ideas. They have also given me the liberty to go out and explore the international academic community, not just by familiarizing myself with the literature, but also by encouraging me to present my cosmopolitan - and perhaps somewhat naïve - thoughts at conferences all around the world.

Over the years, I have come to consider my two supervisors as my academic fathers. And like any child, I often wanted to rebel against them. I have enjoyed our cooperation tremendously. Whenever I needed advice, I could always be sure to receive a reply, be it in conversations at Leiden or Oegstgeest, or in the form of short email messages coming from places such as Geneva, New York, Kuala Lumpur, and the Hainan Island in the South China Sea. And if either of them ever again forgets his keys and wallet after a fancy diner and needs a ride home in my minuscule car, he is free to call upon me.

Many of the ideas we developed were 'tested' in a course called World Law, which Professor Schrijver and I set up and taught at Leiden University's Law Faculty. I have benefited a great deal from the critical remarks of the World Law students. We also organized a national workshop at Leiden University and an international conference in the Peace Palace on the theme of the United Nations and global values. The reflections of the participants of both the workshop and the conference have been enlightening.

I also wish to express my appreciation to Professors Willem van Genugten, Andre Nollkaemper, Jan Pronk, Thomas Mertens and Alfred van Staden for serving as members of the thesis committee and raising pertinent questions. I acknowledge with gratitude the skilful editing of the text by Tony Langham and Plym Peters.

I want to thank all my colleagues at Leiden University's Grotius Centre, in particular the three people I had the pleasure of sharing an office with: Lennert Breuker, Daniëlla Dam-de Jong, and Anna Gouwenberg. I want to thank Professors Niels Blokker, John Dugard, Larissa van den Herik and all the other colleagues for the daily lunch talk. Professor Fred van Staden played his role as professor of international relations in the faculty of international law brilliantly, by reminding his colleagues – me included – of the importance of politics, power, and economic relations. And I want to thank my colleagues at the Peace Palace Library, especially its Director Jeroen Vervliet, for the time and encouragement they have given me.

The research project was made possible by the Netherlands Organization for Scientific Research (NWO). I want to thank the NWO, and Jasper Roodenburg especially.

I also wish to thank the professors that introduced me to the law of the United Nations and to international law. It was Professor André Nollkaemper of the University of Amsterdam who got me fascinated by international law in the first place. I would also like to thank Professor Martti Koskenniemi, who taught a course at New York University Law School about the rise and fall of international law. It was especially the last lecture, about the fall of international law, which motivated me to think about – and doubt – the purpose and use of the language of international law. Fortunately, Koskenniemi showed great sympathy for the "tragic heroes," like Lauterpacht, who continued to believe in international law against all odds and against better judgment. Perhaps one of these "tragic heroes" was my other teacher at NYU, Professor Thomas Franck, who taught a course about the Constitutional Law of the United Nations together with Simon Chesterman. It was during the time of the 2003 Iraq invasion, in which the authority of the UN was largely ignored by the USA. Professor Franck often stood up in the middle of our seminars to defend the United Nations against various accusations from his highly critical students. Needless to say that his ideas have greatly influenced this study.

And I want to thank Hanna Dreifeldt and Pierre Bodeau-Livinec, my supervisors, and all my other former colleagues at the Codification Division of the Office of Legal Affairs of United Nations Headquarters. Thanks also go to my former colleagues at the Appeals Chamber Support Unit of the International Criminal Tribunal for Rwanda, especially Roman Boed and Laetitia Husson, and judge Inés Mónica Weinberg de Roca. Finally, I would like to thank all my fellow interns, both in New York and The Hague, for showing me what it means to be a part of the global UN community.

Last but not least, I want to thank my family, and especially my parents, Peter and Betty. They have supported me from the day I was born, and they never stopped doing so. Special thanks go to my brother Victor. My gratitude to you all is so gigantic that it cannot really be translated into words, so I'd rather not try to do so here. But I wish to dedicate this study to all of you.

# TABLE OF CONTENTS

# PART I

> A man was passing near the site of a new cathedral. He asked one of the workmen what he was doing, and the man replied: "I am breaking stones." A second workman said: "I am earning my salary," and a third, to whom he put the same question, turned his eyes, bright with religious fervour, toward the half-finished cathedral, and answered, "I am building a cathedral."[1]

With this beautiful parable the Luxembourg delegate explained the importance of the "construction work" that the world was engaged in towards the end of the Second World War. He urged all his fellow delegates to acknowledge the almost sacred nature of the task they were carrying out. The cathedral under construction was the United Nations Organization, the blueprint of which, the United Nations Charter, was being drafted by delegates from fifty nations in San Francisco in 1945.

This study is essentially about that UN Charter. It describes what happened to the global values that inspired the drafting of that document. The drafting process of this "constitution of the world" is examined first. Although the proceedings of the San Francisco Conference have been researched many times before, they have never been interpreted from the perspective of global values. This study also analyses the evolution and crystallization of these values by the United Nations during the entire lifespan of this Organization up to its 65th anniversary in 2010.[2] The focus is on the resolutions and declarations of the General Assembly, since that plenary organ is the most authoritative candidate to lead such a discussion about values. The reasons why the General Assembly is such a suitable candidate are explored in detail in this study. We begin by clarifying the concept of "global value". Automatically, various pre-conditions for a "value-making procedure" come

---

[1] United Nations, *Documents of the United Nations Conference on International Organization* (22 volumes), vol. 1, p. 504. This collection is referred to as ´UNCIO´ in the rest of this study.

[2] This evolutionary interpretation of the Charter is preferred by a significant number of scholars. See *e.g.*, James Leslie Brierly, "The Covenant and the Charter" (1946), p. 83; Clark M. Eichelberger, "The United Nations Charter: A Growing Document" (1947), p. 98; Hambro Pollux, "The Interpretation of the Charter" (1946), p. 54; Nico Schrijver, "Les valeurs fondamentales et le droit des Nations Unies" (2006), pp. 85-88; Nico Schrijver, "the Future of the Charter of the United Nations" (2006) pp. 5-7; Simon Chesterman, Thomas M. Franck & David M. Malone, *Law and practice of the United Nations* (2008), p. 10; Georg Ress, "Interpretation" (2002), pp. 15-16; Nigel D. White, *The United Nations System* (2002), especially Chapter 2. Also see Yearbook of the International Law Commission, Vol. I (1963), p. 76 (on the law of treaties).

to the surface. After a further theoretical exploration of those conditions, they will be applied to the General Assembly. This deliberative organ is tested for its suitability as a global value-making organ.

This introductory chapter presents the subject matter of this study, as well as the exact research question and the methodology used to answer that question. It also provides a brief outline of the general argument of the study.

## 1 PRESENTATION OF THE PROBLEM

This study characterizes the work of the United Nations as a contribution to a global discussion about the evolution of global values. This is not how the work of the UN is usually examined. The United Nations is generally seen as a political organization with various highly ambitious tasks. The research then focuses on how the UN has coped in fulfilling those tasks.[3] Here the focus is on the development of ideas, or more specifically: the definition and evolution of a limited set of global values.

Why is there a need to approach the work of the United Nations from the perspective of values? This study aims to fill the gap in scholarship noted by Jan Pronk, a prominent Dutch politician and former Special Representative of the UN Secretary-General in the Sudan. He believed that the history of the United Nations as a community of values needed to be written as a matter of urgency:

> The [United Nations] is more than just an international deliberative organ [...]; more even than an organization which can intervene, by joining forces on the basis of consensus, whenever international peace and security is threatened; more even than a set of organizations running programs promoting peace, development and poverty reduction. The United Nations is also a community of values. Through intensive and continuous international dialogue, a global consensus has been achieved on principles, norms and values. The results are codified in charters, conventions and resolutions. Without all this, the United Nations could never have acted effectively, either in the implementation of programs, or when international intervention is deemed desirable. A history of the United Nations can be written from this perspective: a history about the development of values, in order to better cope,

---

[3] The keyword is always "effectiveness." See *e.g.*, Hironobu Sakai, "Legitimization of Measures to secure Effectiveness in UN Peacekeeping" (2009); Steinar Andresen, "The Effectiveness of UN Environmental Institutions" (2007); Joachim Müller, *Reforming the United Nations: the struggle for legitimacy and effectiveness* (2006); Emilio J. Cardenas, "The United Nations Security Council's Quest for Effectiveness" (2004); Andy Knight, "Improving the effectiveness of UN arms embargoes" (2004); Guglielmo Verdirame, "Testing the effectiveness of international norms: UN humanitarian assistance and sexual apartheid in Afghanistan" (2001); Meaghan Shaughnessy, "The United Nations Global Compact and the continuing debate about the effectiveness of corporate voluntary codes of conduct" (2001); Fred Grünfeld, "The effectiveness of United Nations economic sanctions" (1999); Patrick James Flood, *The effectiveness of UN human rights institutions* (1998); and so on.

together, with the [global] challenges. The foundation [of such a history] is enshrined in the Charter of the United Nations and the Declaration of Human Rights. These texts are about peace, human rights, human dignity, international economic and social cooperation, respect for the principle of equal rights and self-determination of peoples, territorial integrity of all States, and other basic values.[4]

There are essentially three reasons for writing the history of the evolution of global values in the work of the United Nations. First of all, as Pronk pointed out, the UN's contribution to the evolution of values and ideas has been undervalued, and should be demonstrated.[5] Secondly, a study of UN ideas shows how powerful ideas can be as (rhetorical) tools to influence global politics. The emphasis on the UN's failure to act in some cases – Rwanda and Srebrenica are examples which spring to mind – does not do justice to the UN's success in the development of new and highly influential ideas. Thirdly, in recent times some highly influential politicians have used global values to describe their foreign policy objectives.[6] Global values have also become a popular object of study for many scholars, particularly in the disciplines of international law, political science and philosophy. Many international lawyers ask themselves whether international law has moved from an essentially value-free order of sovereign and independent States [7] to a more cosmopolitan order, based on universal values and common interests.[8] Political scientists ask themselves a similar question; the words "international law" can simply be replaced by "the world".[9] Since ancient times cosmopolitan philosophers

---

[4] Jan Pronk, "Een nieuwe jas voor de Verenigde Naties" (2007), p. 187 (translation from Dutch by the author of this study).

[5] The United Nations Intellectual History Project has studied the role of the United Nations in the creation and evolution of ideas, but not values. See their website (www.unhistory.org), and the numerous books published in the series. These books are referred to frequently in this study.

[6] See e.g., Barack Obama, President of the United States of America, Responsibility for Our Common Future, statement delivered at the 64th session of the General Assembly, 23 September 2009; Dmitry Medvedev, President of the Russian Federation, statement delivered on the same day at the same session; Kofi Annan, Global Values: The United Nations and the Rule of Law in the 21st Century (2000); Tony Blair, "A Battle for Global Values" (2007); and statement by Jan-Peter Balkenende, Prime Minister of the Netherlands, at the 62nd session of the General Assembly, 27 September 2007.

[7] This description of the "old" legal order is based on what is generally known as the Lotus principle: "International law governs relations between independent States. The rules of law binding upon States therefore emanate from their own free will as expressed in conventions or by usages generally accepted as expressing principles of law and established in order to regulate the relations between these coexisting independent communities or with a view to the achievement of common aims." (The Case of the S.S. "Lotus', Judgment, No. 9, 1927, P.C.I.J., Series A, No. 10, p. 18.)

[8] See e.g., Bruno Simma, "From Bilateralism to Community Interest" (1994). Many more examples will be discussed in subsequent chapters of this study.

[9] The literature will be referred to extensively in the next chapter of this study. See, e.g., Richard A. Falk and Saul H. Mendlovitz (eds.), Studies on a Just World Order, especially No. 3 in the series: Richard A. Falk, Samuel Kim & Saul H. Mendlovitz, The United Nations and a Just World Order (1991).

have advocated a world based on common interests and values. In recent years cosmopolitanism has experienced a revival, boosted by globalization: a cosmopolitan world view is now an accepted description of reality.[10] All these trends in political rhetoric and academic research also justify a renewed interest in the creation of values by the United Nations.

The aim of this study is to contribute to this interdisciplinary discourse on global values by looking in more detail at the link between global values, international law and the United Nations. The main assumption is that the international legal order, for which the United Nations Charter provides the "constitution,"[11] no longer aims to exclusively ensure the peaceful coexistence of independent States – if indeed, it ever did. Instead, it aims to realize a set of internationally shared, fundamental values. The question then, is how these values have been "incorporated" into the language of international law. This study suggests that this was primarily done through the adoption of the United Nations Charter, which therefore plays a crucial role in this "new," value-based, international legal order.

## 2 RESEARCH QUESTION

The aim of this study is to look at the United Nations documents from the perspective of values. It describes the "birth" of the most important post-World War II values and examines the subsequent evolution of these fundamental values of the international community, through the work of the UN General Assembly. However, the study does not limit itself to a mere description of this evolution. It also analyses the influence of the UN on the philosophical global values discourse, and conversely, the influence of philosophical notions on the UN's work. It is the cross-fertilization of the United Nations and the philosophical discourse on global values which is examined, together with the evolution of these values within the United Nations itself.

The research question may therefore be described as follows:

How, and to what extent, have moral points of view, defined in the language of values, determined the founding of the United Nations and the evolution of its purposes, principles and policies? How has the United Nations influenced these moral views through its own contributions to the debate on values and to the

---

[10] Many modern cosmopolitan philosophers were inspired by John Rawls' most recent book, *The Law of Peoples* (1999), which is itself not a cosmopolitan book. See, *e.g.*, Charles Beitz, *Political Theory and International Relations* (1999); Thomas Pogge, *Realizing Rawls* (1989); Thomas Pogge, "An Egalitarian Law of Peoples," (1995); Andrew Kuper, "Rawlsian Global Justice: Beyond The Law of Peoples to a Cosmopolitan Law of Persons," (2000).

[11] For the use of this qualification, see especially sections 2 and 3 of Chapter III below.

"translation" of these values into the language of international law, especially by means of adopting general resolutions, declarations, treaty texts, etc.?

To answer these questions, the study delves into the archives of the United Nations. The global values that defined the birth of the United Nations are presented, and a description is provided of how these values evolved over time, especially in declarations of the General Assembly. The Assembly is the only organ of the United Nations that can legitimately claim to speak on behalf of the entire world.

This historical, descriptive overview is preceded by some more theoretical reflections on the relationship between global values, international law and the United Nations. This is not only to justify the emphasis on the General Assembly, and the value-based approach to the work of the United Nations, but also to show the potential of the United Nations as a true "value-making machine."

## 3 METHODOLOGY

How are the research questions examined in this study? What is the chosen methodology, and why is that particular methodology adopted? Part I adopts a conceptual perspective, whilst Part II uses a more descriptive perspective. The conceptual part tests the hypotheses on which this study is based, in terms of their academic rigor. How does this research build on previous research, carried out in the fields of philosophy, international relations and international law? Do the hypotheses correspond to the scholarship of those disciplines? The descriptive part (Part II) tests the hypotheses against reality.

The working hypothesis is that global values guide international affairs, and that the United Nations General Assembly, aided by scholarship, should play a leading role in the evolution of these values. Does this make academic sense? Part I analyses the literature on global values. First, it examines a number of definitions of the term "value". These definitions come from various disciplines. They have been proposed by psychologists, philosophers, sociologists and international relations scholars. The aim is to compare all these definitions, and see which one comes closest to the intuitive notion of value which is the starting point of this study. The next step is to show that global values theoretically have the potential to influence global affairs.

When an academically sound definition of global values has been found, the following working hypothesis is tested: that a global plenary organ ought to play the leading role in the evolution of these global values. This hypothesis, which is not at all self-evident, is first examined from a purely scholarly perspective. Various theories, mainly of a cosmopolitan nature, are analysed. These theories all argue that there is no better place for the evolution of global values than a deliberative organ which somehow represents the views of all the world's citizens. According to these theories, a democratic organization of global society is the preferred type of organization.

The next step is to look for candidates in the present world to play the role of the global deliberative organ. The United Nations is presented as the sole candidate to play such a role. The suitability of the United Nations as a sufficiently authoritative value-making process is examined in Part I of this study. The focus is on the question as to what the role of the United Nations, and in particular the UN General Assembly, is, and what it was intended to be. Primary documents, as well as scholarly literature are examined. The aim is to find out what the "founding fathers" themselves had in mind when they established the United Nations, and, subsequently, how the representatives of various States perceived their role in the UN General Assembly. Did they see the UN as a source of ideas, or merely as a vehicle for political cooperation? And has the world's view of the role of the UN in global affairs changed with time? The focus in this part of the study is not on discussions about the potential of the United Nations in scholarship, but on discussions about such potential in the United Nations' assemblies themselves. These highly abstract questions were actually discussed at the highest inter-State level. The reason the focus is on the debates inside the assembly halls, instead of on the debates in the lecture halls of universities, is that discussions in assembly halls carry much more weight than similar discussions which take place in scholarship. After all, at the UN level, the views of the entire world are formally represented in these discussions, at least in theory. Moreover, once the State representatives have defined the characteristics of their work as precisely as possible, they immediately have the responsibility of carrying out their self-imposed tasks.[12]

Part II of this study constitutes the descriptive or historical part of this study. The focus is even more on UN documents and UN discussions. The methodology is identical in all the chapters, each of which is devoted to a discussion of a particular global value. First, the *travaux préparatoires* of the UN Charter are examined to give an overview of the ideas which were discussed in 1945 relating to a certain value. Secondly, the resolutions and declarations of the General Assembly are used as the "backbone" for the description of the evolution of each value. Wherever this is appropriate, the scientific literature on a certain value is also used to compare the scholarly treatment of a particular value with the way in which that same value is interpreted in the Assembly's documents. When the cross-fertilization between the ideas contained in the UN documents and those contained in the philosophical discourse was particularly successful, or where there is great potential for such successful cross-fertilization, the relevant literature is discussed in more detail.

The aim of this study is not to find out what the relevant norms of international law are for each particular global value. In this sense, this study is not a purely legal exercise. The products of the General Assembly are analysed as

---

[12] Also see the Fifth Plenary Session, 30 April 1945, UNCIO, vol. 1, pp. 368-369.

contributions to the evolution of global values, not as global legislation. For this reason, no rigid distinction is made between declarations of the General Assembly and texts of multilateral treaties. It is also for this reason that the *travaux préparatoires* of the UN Charter are studied in great detail, even though, according to the Vienna Convention on the Law of Treaties, the *travaux* can only be used as supplementary means for the interpretation of a treaty.[13] Strictly speaking, the *travaux* are therefore not decisive, according to the Vienna Convention, when it comes to the interpretation of a treaty. All this suggests that the UN General Assembly's work in the evolution of global values, and the evolution of the norms of international law, are two separate worlds. This is not entirely accurate. The first part of this study already shows that, according to scientific discourse, global values can only guide international affairs when someone or something is made responsible for promoting and safeguarding these global values. It will be shown that the ideal language for allocating this responsibility is the language of law. When it comes to realizing and promoting global values, the appropriate language is global – or international - law. Therefore the role of the General Assembly in allocating responsibilities for the continuous promotion of respect for global values and value-based norms does fall within the scope of this study. However, it becomes clear that some legally non-binding – or "political" – declarations are just as effective in promoting global values as widely ratified multilateral treaties.

## 4 OUTLINE OF THE ARGUMENT PER CHAPTER

### 4.1 Global values

Part I begins by providing a definition of the subject under discussion:

> A global value is an enduring, globally shared belief that a specific state of the world, which is possible, is socially preferable, from the perspective of the life of all human beings, to the opposite state of the world.

This is a working definition which helps to clarify the topic of this study. After finding a suitable definition for this limited purpose, some of the elements of this definition are analysed in more detail. First, the idea that one can refer to "all human beings" as together constituting some kind of community is analysed. An appropriate method for finding global values is proposed: a global discussion about values which is sufficiently inclusive and action-oriented. International law is presented as the ideal language to define obligations which are based on values.

---

[13] See Article 32, *Vienna Convention on the Law of Treaties*, signed in Vienna on 23 May 1969; entry into force on 27 January 1980. See *United Nations, Treaty Series*, vol. 1155, p. 331.

Finally, a first attempt is made at answering the question: what are the world's values?

## 4.2 Global values and the United Nations

When the San Francisco Conference started in 1945, the Second World War was nearly over. The main challenge of the United Nations was to find something better than a common enemy to keep the nations of the world united. [14] This study suggests that what replaced the common enemy and kept the United Nations united in the post-war period, was a set of global values.

The principal inspiration for the list of global values ultimately enshrined in the UN Charter was a list of "evils" that had dominated the world stage before the spring of 1945. The devastations of war inspired the delegates to strive for peace and security. The way in which individuals had been treated during the war was the basis for the delegates' motivation to pursue respect for human dignity for all people. In 1945, colonial oppression was not yet seen by the founding States as one of the world's evils, but a modest precursor to the right to self-determination did find a place in the Charter. The need for social progress and development after the devastating war formed the basis for the last value, even though it was only cursorily referred to in the Charter.

All these values found their place in the UN Charter, most of them in the list of purposes of Article 1. A comparison of the UN Charter's list with the list produced by the philosophical discourse on values reveals a significant overlap. It is very difficult to come up with a different list of global values if one uses the term as defined in this study. Therefore it is unfortunate that the UN Charter does not use the concept of "values." Instead, the UN Charter refers primarily to "purposes" and "principles." The principles were defined as rules of action, whereas the purposes were defined as the aims of action. The link between the concepts used in the Charter and this study's concept of "value" is explained in Part I of this study.

One of the basic assumptions of this study is that when describing the evolution of the UN Charter's values since 1945, the General Assembly is the closest thing we have to a "global conscience." Since the term global conscience is controversial, a section is devoted to explaining and justifying its use. Other sections look in more detail at the characteristics of the Assembly. Can it really be characterized as the "town meeting of the world," where all the world's citizens come together to discuss problems that have arisen in their global neighbourhood?

---

[14] Anne O'Hare McCormick, "San Francisco: Battlefield for Peace" (1945). To honour the war bond, the name "United Nations" was chosen, as a reference to the coalition that was fighting Nazi Germany and Japan. See Secretary of state for foreign affairs (UK), *A commentary on the Dumbarton Oaks proposals* (1944), p. 2.

## 4.3 The role of the United Nations in the evolution of global values

Part II examines the role that the United Nations actually played in the evolution of global values in great detail.

The UN Charter and the resolutions of the UN General Assembly are used as the "backbone" for this research. They constitute the essential documents. Because there are so many General Assembly resolutions – approximately 15,000 – it was necessary to decide on a method of selection. On the whole, reference is only made to resolutions in which the Assembly has declared certain general principles. Such resolutions are generally called "declarations" by the Assembly itself. Many of these declarations have been accompanied by a programme of action, the implementation of which was often the subject of subsequent General Assembly resolutions, adopted on an annual basis. Since this study is interested mainly in the evolution of ideas, these resolutions, which deal purely with the implementation of the general principles declared earlier, are not discussed in great detail. Many resolutions have been adopted, also on an annual basis, presumably to emphasize the continuing relevance of the ideas they contain, and/or to indicate any further development of these ideas. When the content of such resolutions is not substantially different from the resolutions adopted in previous years, the follow-up resolutions are not referred to.

The cross-fertilization of the UN's resolutions and the most influential literature is also examined, whenever this is relevant.

The value of peace and security is dealt with first (Chapter IV). Immediately after the Second World War, armed conflict was considered to be the greatest evil, and peace the most important value. Attempts to define the value of peace and security in positive terms are analysed. It soon becomes apparent that peace and security can be defined much more easily as the "absence" of international conflict, civil war, terrorism, etc. The "humanization" of the value of peace and security is also examined.

The second value is social progress and development (Chapter V). It appears that the UN has never attempted to provide a general definition or description of this value. Instead, the Assembly has repeatedly adopted various strategies and action plans for development. These are compared with philosophical theories of global social and distributive justice. An attempt is also made to distil a general description of social progress and development from all these Assembly declarations. Special sections are devoted to sustainable development and to a rights-based approach to development.

The third value is human dignity (Chapter VI). The promotion and development of this value in the language of human rights has been the United Nations' biggest success. The UN has been very consistent in presenting the value of human dignity as the foundation of all human rights. However, the Assembly has not been all that clear about the meaning of "human dignity". Therefore some philosophical theories are presented to fill that gap.

The last value treated in this study is the value of the self-determination of peoples (Chapter VII). In 1945, the world was largely blind to the oppression and exploitation of peoples through foreign domination. The Charter was therefore hesitant about adopting the alternative to this evil, *i.e.,* the self-determination of all peoples, as a value. As soon as the UN corrected this mistake, it became very successful in promoting this value. The UN's resolutions played a major role in the process of decolonization. With that process largely completed, the need arose for a more general definition of the self-determination of peoples. The search for such a definition is the subject of this last chapter. It examines both philosophical and UN discussions and ideas. Are minority groups entitled to determine their own future? What about the entire population of an existing State? Finally, a human rights-based approach to this value is discussed.

This study ends with a general assessment of the UN's role in the evolution of global values, and a brief look into the future.

# GLOBAL VALUES

This chapter provides a definition of "global values" and briefly examines various aspects of this definition (1). It analyses the notion, underlying the concept of global values, that there is such a thing as a "global community" (2). A separate section is devoted to the discussion of the need for and rules of a global discourse to determine a set of global values. The reason why international law is the language *par excellence* to define values-based obligations is also explained, as well as the role of the international lawyer in using the norms of international law, especially the law based on the UN Charter, as an instrument for the promotion and protection of global values (3).

This chapter further makes some general comments on the substantive content of the list of global values. It provides an initial answer to the question: what are the world's values? It also explains what is generally considered to inspire such a list and examines the way in which it is evolving (4). There are some comments on the allocation of responsibilities for action (5). Who is responsible for achieving global values, and how should this be done? This is followed by a conclusion (6).

## 1 A DEFINITION OF GLOBAL VALUES

There are many definitions of values, but no global or even widespread consensus on any of them. Therefore, although it is best not to rely too heavily on one particular definition of values, a definition may nevertheless serve as a starting point to explain the meaning of the concept as used in this study.[1]

Before presenting a definition of global values it is necessary to define the context in which global values operate.[2] Many books on values start by making a distinction between the concept of value in a normative sense and the use of the word "value" in a more economic sense. When the word "value" is used in the latter

---

[1] Hart always suggested his students (including Michael Walzer) to "never define your terms", with which he meant that one should not overemphasize the importance of definitions. See Marcel Becker, "In gesprek met Michael Walzer" (2008), p. 36.

[2] The concept of "values" derives its meaning from the way it is used in a particular discourse, and since there are many value-discourses, the word has many definitions. See *e.g.*, Nicolas Rescher, *Introduction to Value Theory* (1969). See also Schneider Report, *A la recherche d'une sagesse pour le monde: quel rôle pour les valeurs éthiques dans l'éducation?* (1987), p. 43.

sense, it simply refers to how much certain objects or goods are appreciated, and this is often measured in terms of *monetary* value.[3] This study is not concerned with the latter use of the term "value," but rather with its normative use. Normative values constitute the core of global morality. They are based on a shared vision of an ideal world. All sorts of obligations are defined on the basis of this vision of an ideal world, and these must be seen to bring that ideal world closer to the real world.

The context in which values operate can be narrowed down even further. Some values are concerned with the way in which individuals should act in their daily lives, and prescribe or prohibit certain forms of behaviour. However, the values which constitute the object of this study are concerned not so much with the behaviour of individuals in their everyday lives, but rather with the behaviour of the actors responsible for international politics and decision making. The aim of this study is to find a set of global values which guide global decision making.

One suitable definition of values was proposed by Rokeach, a professor of social psychology, in his treatise on the nature of human values. This treatise was used as the conceptual basis for the Rokeach Value Survey (RVS), an elaborate classification system of values. Rokeach began by setting out certain criteria that any proposed definition of values should meet to be "scientifically fruitful."[4] First, the definition must be "intuitively appealing yet capable of operational definition." Secondly, it should clearly distinguish values from other concepts with which this concept is confused. Thirdly, any definition of values should avoid "circular terms that are themselves undefined." Fourthly and finally, it should "represent a value-free approach to the study of values," meaning that it should allow "independent investigators to replicate reliably one another's empirical findings and conclusions despite [personal] differences in values".[5] These are essential criteria or benchmarks for any meaningful definition of the concept of values.

Rokeach's own definition of a value, which meets all these criteria, is as follows:

> A value is an enduring belief that a specific mode of conduct or end-state of existence is personally or socially preferable to an opposite or converse mode of conduct or end-state of existence.[6]

In order to modify this general definition of values in such a way that it accurately describes the specific kind of values that are the subject of this study, some of the key words in this definition are analysed in more detail.

---

[3] See, *e.g.*, Aligarh Muslim University, *Man, Reality, and Values* (1964), pp. 50-51.
[4] Milton Rokeach, *The Nature of Human Values* (1973), p. 3.
[5] *Idem*, p. 3.
[6] *Idem*, p. 5.

Values are presented as "beliefs." It is not uncommon in the literature to consider that ethical thought consists of beliefs. For example, Isaiah Berlin described ethical thought – principally a set of values – as an expression of "beliefs about how life should be lived, what men and women should be and do."[7] Such beliefs are by definition human inventions. To say that values are "beliefs" is basically to distinguish them from "facts". Values, as a subcategory of beliefs, cannot be falsified in the way that facts can be falsified.[8] If someone decides not to share a certain belief, he or she is not *per se* mistaken.[9] Therefore it is difficult to reach a consensus on the definition of global values and the consequent obligations. After all, it is perfectly reasonable for there to be different views of the ideal world and different value systems. Disagreements about values cannot be settled, and there will have to be a dialogue on these values until some kind of consensus is achieved. Alternatively, one could agree to disagree.

Secondly, values are *enduring* beliefs. Rokeach added this word to his definition because he believed that "any conception of human values, if it is to be fruitful, must be able to account for the enduring character of values as well as for their changing character."[10] In other words, values both last forever and continue to evolve all the time. It is because values change, rather than ever reaching the goal (the realization of all values), that "we seem to be forever doomed to strive for these ultimate goals without quite ever reaching them."[11] The global values of the international community have evolved over time. At the same time, this evolution has not affected the essence of these values. This makes them "enduring" in the sense of the term as used by Rokeach.

Another interesting aspect is the inclusion of values both as a "mode of conduct" and as an "end-state of existence" in Rokeach's definition. A distinction if often made between instrumental values, *i.e.* values referring to a desirable mode of conduct, and terminal values, values describing desirable end-states of existence.[12] This distinction is not without its opponents. Many critics point out that even end-state values are often defended as a means of achieving something else.[13] Moreover, the expression "end-state" is unfortunate because it gives the impression of a static

---

[7] Isaiah Berlin, "On the Pursuit of the Ideal" (1988).
[8] Hilary Putnam, The Collapse of the Fact/Value Dichotomy and Other Essays (2002); Henry Margenau, Facts and Values (1955).
[9] See also Bernard Williams, "Consistency and Realism" (1973).
[10] Milton Rokeach, *The Nature of Human Values* (1973), p. 6.
[11] *Idem*, p. 14.
[12] *Idem*, p. 7.
[13] For example, if someone does not agree that "peace" is a desirable end-state, one can try to convince this person by explaining that a peaceful world makes it possible for people to live in freedom, without the fear that whatever they construct might be destroyed the next day by rebel groups or the army. But if this person does not believe that to live in freedom is valuable, you have to find something that this person does find valuable and explain how the value of "peace" is a means to realizing that value. See also Richard Robinson, *An Atheist's Values* (1964), pp. 33-35.

and unchanging state, which is contrary to the evolving character of values emphasized above. For these reasons, this distinction is not made in the present study.

Rokeach's definition refers to values as beliefs that a particular end-state is either "personally" or "socially" preferable to its alternatives. There are values with a "personal" focus and others with a "society-centred" focus. Another way to make that distinction is to divide values into "intrapersonal" and "interpersonal" values. While peace of mind may be a desirable intrapersonal end-state, world peace is an interpersonal end-state.[14] In the same vein, Oyserman made a distinction between values operating at the individual level and values operating at the group level. The latter set of values were defined as "scripts or cultural ideals held in common by members of a group: the group's "social mind"."[15] Robinson made a similar distinction when he divided values into personal and political values. Robinson's personal values included beauty, truth, reason and love; his political values included equality, freedom, tolerance, peace and justice, and democracy.[16] Since this study is concerned with the global values that guide global decision making, the focus is on the latter type, *i.e.* the political or "interpersonal" values.

Another important keyword in the definition is the word "preferable". The concept of "value" is presented in the definition as a relative concept, in the sense that values do not describe a perfect world in a void (a perfect idea in the Platonic sense), but rather it involves a preference between two or more actual possibilities. McDougal and Lasswell noted that "a value is a preferred event";[17] it cannot be put more simply than that. For example, there is a choice between peace and war, or between sustainable development and unsustainable development.[18] The preferred option is the one that is valued. Therefore "peace" is a value, and "war" is not, simply because peace is preferable. The global values that guide global affairs are often directly inspired by serious disasters and deprivation in the modern world. In that case, the values are not so much descriptions of an ideal, but are rather based on efforts to remove the most obvious evils from the present state of affairs, or at least to prevent such evils from happening again in the future.

As some of the values identified by Rokeach are excluded from the present discussion (such as personal values), the definition can be slightly modified:

---

[14] Milton Rokeach, *The Nature of Human Values* (1973), pp. 7-8.
[15] Daphna Oyserman, "Values : Psychological Perspectives" (2004), p. 16151. Individual values are defined, on the same page, as "internalized social representations or moral beliefs that people appeal to as the ultimate rationale for their actions."
[16] Richard Robinson, *An Atheist's Values* (1964).
[17] Myres McDougal, *Studies in World Public Order* (1987), p. 11. The part of this book that is referred to was written together with Harold Lasswell.
[18] Milton Rokeach, *The Nature of Human Values* (1973), pp. 9-10.

> A value is an enduring belief that a specific state of existence is socially preferable to an opposite state of existence.[19]

After removing some of the words from the definition, it is now necessary to add a few new words. The aim is not to correct Rokeach's definition in any way, but to define more specifically the kind of values that are the subject of the present discussion.[20]

First, this study deals only with those values that guide global decision making. Therefore reference should be made to the state of existence of "the world," rather than that of one specific individual or of specific communities. This is a marked difference compared to the approach adopted by Rokeach. He focused his research on individual values, although he did include a world of beauty and a world at peace in his list. The fact that the focus is on the state of existence of the world does not mean that the health and well-being of the planet itself is at the heart of global values. It is the human inhabitants of the world who compare various states of existence of the world, and the criterion for preferring one possible end-state to another is the standard of living of all human beings in that world. The world is looked at from a "human perspective."[21] This perspective has actually been adopted by those in charge of global decision making. Whether this choice of perspective can be morally justified is another matter.[22]

Secondly, the definition should explicitly state that global values must be "globally shared." If the set of global values presented in this study were based on the beliefs of the author of this study, a small group of experts or a small group of nations, they could never actually guide global affairs.[23]

Thirdly, the definition should explicitly state that the values refer to "possible" worlds and not to options that are simply unattainable, like heaven on earth. Kekes defined values as "possibilities whose realization may make lives good."[24] The word "possibilities" is appealing, because it emphasizes that values describe a state of affairs which can be achieved. This aspect of values is often

---

[19] The words "or converse" were deleted because these words add nothing to the word "opposite".

[20] None of the changes in the definition is meant as an "improvement." Instead, it is meant to narrow down the values under discussion, and to give further clarification.

[21] Indeed, this is a form of "speciesism", meaning that animals, plants and the planet as a whole are looked at from a human-centered perspective. See Richard Ryder, "All beings that feel pain deserve human rights" (2005). However, that does not mean they are morally irrelevant. After all, it may be better, from a human perspective, to live in a world where animals are not mistreated and "tortured."

[22] The consequences of such a choice of perspective are most clearly visible when it comes to the environment (see Chapter V on Social Progress and Development, below).

[23] See further section 3 of Chapter II, below.

[24] John Kekes, *The Morality of Pluralism* (1993), p. 27. This is also the definition of values that is chosen by the Netherlands Scientific Council for Government Policy in their report on *Waarden, normen en de last van het gedrag* (2003) [values, norms and the burden of behaviour], p. 54 and p. 65. One assumption that is not made explicit in the definition is the interpersonal aspect of values.

emphasized. For example, elsewhere it is suggested that values are "not abstract ideals beyond our reach but determinate, desirable actions anchoring on the process of the movement from the actual to the ideal stage."[25] As the present discussion is about values guiding actual politics and decision making, the search for *attainable* preferences is essential.

Kekes' definition is also interesting for another reason. It suggests that achieving all values results in a "good life." The reference to the "good life" in the definition of global values provides a standard for comparing two states of the world and choosing the preferred one, i.e., that world in which the "good life" is guaranteed, or at least in which there is a better guarantee than in any alternative state of the world. Therefore it is helpful to take a closer look at what Kekes meant by a "good life":

> A life will be called here "good" only if it is both personally satisfying and morally meritorious. Either component alone would not be sufficient to make a life good. For personal satisfaction may be obtained at the cost of causing much evil, and the price of moral merit may be the frequent frustration of reasonable desires, and neither evil nor frustrated lives should be supposed to be good.[26]

Kekes applied his definition to human beings in their daily interaction with other human beings. For that purpose, it is perfectly justifiable to base a definition of values on the search for a "good life." However, the definition that serves to guide the present discussion should include a guiding criterion for moral behaviour, not in the relationship between two individual human beings, but in global, political decision making. The term "good life," as described by Kekes, is helpful only if the ultimate purpose of global decision making is to teach people how to live in such a way that all the world's citizens are both "satisfied" and "morally meritorious." But this sounds almost as if the ultimate purpose of the global ethic is a global "civilizing mission," and that is not the intention.

It could also be argued that international decision making is about ensuring a "normal life" for all the world's citizens.[27] But what is a "normal" life? One can look at what all human beings value simply because they are humans. Kekes referred to primary values as values that "derive from the universal aspect of human nature."[28] An analysis of human nature can focus on what human beings need simply to stay alive. In his search for a complete list of human values, Rokeach noted that "[i]t can be argued that the total number of values is roughly equal to or

---

[25] Aligarh Muslim University, *Man, Reality, and Values* (1964), p. 59.
[26] John Kekes, *The Morality of Pluralism* (1993), p. 8.
[27] Bart Landheer, "Ethical Values in International Decision-making: Remarks around the Conference" (1960), p. 8.
[28] *Idem*, p. 32-33. See also p. 38 onwards.

limited by man's biological and social make-up and most particularly by his needs."[29] Basic needs can be seen as the absolute minimum that is necessary for physical well-being. Miller similarly tried to define human values by looking, first of all, at biological needs. In his view,

> Some needs are biologically derived: every living person needs food and shelter as a minimum and therefore places a basic value on securing them. Beyond the bare survival values come a host of those intended to provide the greater and greater realization of human potential.[30]

Although some of the higher values mentioned by Miller (such as poetry) may be less important than others, more is expected of a normal life than the fulfilment of the most basic needs, or "bare survival values". But what exactly constitutes a "normal life" differs from person to person, and depends only to a limited extent on the state of the world.

Descriptions of a good or normal life essentially consist of a set of values. For example, a normal life is defined as a life in which food, shelter and security are guaranteed. To define a normal life, it is necessary to define food, shelter and security. An approach which defines the set of values by referring to these general terms then becomes a circular approach.

There is another objection to using the terms "good life" or "normal life" in a definition of "global value." They both suggest that there is an end-stage, and that the aim is to reach that end-stage as quickly as possible. The use of these words suggests that as soon as all human beings lead a "good" or "normal" life, all global values have been realized and that should be the end of it. In actual fact, "[e]very good is not a final resting place but a stage in the never ceasing struggle for social progress."[31] It is thus preferable not to use an end-stage and instead to stick to a more relative notion of values. The search for global values is more like a never-ending comparison between the actual situation and "better" alternatives. In other words: the world's effort to strive for progress should not be seen as an attempt to achieve one supreme value ("a good life for all"), but rather as an attempt to achieve various different values, which together lead to a state of the world that is preferable to the current state of the world from the perspective of the human being. This search will never be completed. The state of the world can always be better than it is at the moment. Our beliefs about what can make the world a better place also evolve continuously. They do not focus on one super standard, such as a "good life" for everyone.[32]

---

[29] Milton Rokeach, *The Nature of Human Values* (1973), p. 11.
[30] Lynn H. Miller, *Global Order* (1990), pp. 10-11. Examples of such higher values are poetry (mentioned by Miller), and one may add such values as beauty, or love.
[31] Aligarh Muslim University, *Man, Reality, and Values* (1964), p. 59.
[32] See section on evolution of global values (4.3 of Chapter II), below.

All these insights lead to the following definition of global values:

A global value is an enduring, globally shared belief that a specific state of the world, which is possible, is socially preferable, from the perspective of all human beings, to the opposite state of the world.

Many other questions remain. For example, the question arises whether the definition suggests that global values should be seen from the perspective of individual human beings and not from the perspective of collectives, such as States or peoples. To avoid having to choose between the two perspectives, the intention was to define global values in such a way that both approaches are permissible. Another question is what the ideal language might be to express these "globally shared beliefs," ensuring that the beliefs motivate the responsible actors to strive for the realization and promotion of these beliefs. What are the world's values? What role do these global values actually play in global politics? All these questions are dealt with in subsequent sections in this chapter.

## 2 VALUES AS PREFERENCES OF THE INTERNATIONAL COMMUNITY

The first of these remaining questions is the choice of perspective. According to the definition, a global value describes a preference from the "perspective of all human beings." Does this mean that all individual citizens of the world have to share an identical set of preferences? Or is the reference to "all human beings" to be understood in a vaguer sense, as referring to the general preference of some kind of global community?

This study chooses the latter option. The world does not consist of isolated individuals. At least, that is not a viewpoint which is universally accepted. It is not necessary to interview every single person in the world. Instead, it is necessary to find those places where authoritative decisions are made on behalf of the global community as a whole. It is there that the world chooses between different possible futures. It is there that global values are defined.

This view suggests that the fate of the world is not decided as a result of a conflict between opposing value systems and interests. Instead, the assumption is that there is a collective and genuine attempt to look at the state of the world from a global perspective. Such a view makes great demands on the participants in this process. They must show consideration, not only for themselves and their own lives, but also for others, for the global community as a whole. The assumption here is not that such a viewpoint *ought* to be adopted, but that it actually *is*. This assumption clearly has its opponents. For example, according to Landheer, there is only one principle that *actually* operates at a global level, and that is the principle –

it is not a value – of coexistence.[33] He argues that values only operate within smaller communities.

As the assumption that values also operate at a global level is therefore not generally shared, an attempt is made to make it plausible. The following subsections examine the scope of values. They try to discover exactly what constitutes the community in which the values introduced in this chapter guide the search for a better world. As the definition of global values proposed above already shows, the suggestion is that this community is the community of all the world's citizens. To substantiate this claim, cosmopolitan ideas are examined (subsection 2.1), as well as the facts of globalization (2.2). Finally, the relevance of local communities in this global community is examined (2.3).

## 2.1 The global community as an ideal: cosmopolitanism

The assumption that there is a need for a set of global values, together depicting a preferred world from the perspective of all human beings in that world, corresponds well with the cosmopolitan discourse. This discourse might have European roots,[34] but Ribeiro is certainly right to state that "[t]he sentiments cosmopolitanism evokes are not restricted to the western world."[35] They are universal. And in the end, cosmopolitanism is more of a sentiment than a fully-fledged theory.

The origin of "cosmopolitanism" can be traced back to Ancient Greece.[36] In the ancient world, there were two strands of cosmopolitanism: the Stoic version and the Cynic version.[37] Depending on whether one was a stoic cosmopolitan or a cynic cosmopolitan,[38] one believed in a solid world community or in a world of free individuals with no attachment to any community whatsoever.

---

[33] Bart Landheer, "Ethical Values in International Decision-making: Remarks around the Conference" (1960), p. 7.
[34] This fact is often highlighted. For example, the first sentence of an introductory article about the term in the International Encyclopedia of the Social & Behavioral Sciences reads: "Cosmopolitanism is a western notion." See Antonio Sousa Ribeiro, "Cosmopolitanism" (2004), p. 2842.
[35] *Idem*, p. 2843.
[36] For a general introduction to cosmopolitanism, see Pauline Kleingeld, *Cosmopolitanism: entry for the Internet Stanford Encyclopedia of Philosophy* (2006).
[37] *Idem*. See also Pauline Kleingeld, "Wereldburgers in eigen land: Over kosmopolitisme en patriottisme" (2005).
[38] In late eighteenth-century Germany alone, many thinkers have expressed many different (Stoic) cosmopolitan views. For an overview, see Pauline Kleingeld, "Six Varieties of Cosmopolitanism in Late Eighteenth-Century Germany" (1999).

The cynics, led by Diogenes of Sinope, claimed to be completely detached from any particular community.[39] When asked what *polis* he came from, Diogenes replied: *"kosmopolitês"* (citizen of the cosmos); thereby not only denying his ties to his hometown Sinope - the town from which he was banished - but at the same time emphasizing his ties to the universe.[40] This makes Diogenes a (self-professed) cosmopolitan. At the same time, Diogenes' lifestyle and aphorisms do not show he believed that being a cosmopolitan involved universally shared solidarity and universally shared responsibility.[41] His idea of cosmopolitanism focused more on the *negative* aspect: a cosmopolitan is someone who has no national attachments or prejudices. This is why Diogenes can be called a *cynic* cosmopolitan. According to this version of cosmopolitanism, being a citizen of the world means being free and (officially) unbound. An examination of Diogenes' life shows that being a cynic cosmopolitan can be a lonely business.[42] This cynic version of cosmopolitanism has not inspired many political philosophers, because it is more of an anti-theory, rather than a very constructive theory.[43] However, the sense of freedom at the heart of it can be found in the spirit of many cynical world travellers and cynical novelists.

Recent examples of cosmopolitan sentiments expressed by novelists can be found in the work of the Dutch novelist Gerard Reve, and the French author Michel Houellebecq. In *Op Weg naar het Einde*, Reve writes:

> See here, to start at the beginning, the truth that made me free, but not at all contented. I suspected it for a long time, but now I know for certain: that I will never, no matter where, no matter how old I have become, find peace, and that I shall never see a region or city, which is not exhaustive because of its familiarity, since I will have seen everything, without exception, once before.[44]

---

[39] As most cynics, Diogenes of Sinope did not write much. His philosophy *is* his life style, and we know about his lifestyle because it has been described by others, especially by Diogenes Laertius in his book *The Lives and Opinions of Eminent Philosophers* (first half of the third century AD).

[40] Diogenes Laertius, *The Lives and Opinions of Eminent Philosophers*, Book VI: Life of Diogenes.

[41] Diogenes shows a complete disregard for official ties, such as taxes, respect for authority, etc. However, he shows a genuine concern for the fate of other human beings, especially (fellow) outsiders, regardless of their position etc. This is what makes him a cosmopolitan. See also Pauline Kleingeld, *Cosmopolitanism: entry for the Internet Stanford Encyclopedia of Philosophy* (2006).

[42] The following anecdote may serve as an example of his loneliness: once Diogenes of Sinope was going into a theatre while everyone else was coming out of it; and when asked why he did so, he said: "It is what I have been doing all my life." Diogenes Laertius, *The Lives and Opinions of Eminent Philosophers*, Book VI: Life of Diogenes. A similar combination of melancholy and endless travels one can find in the letters of Petrarch.

[43] This fact was cause for considerable anti-cosmopolitan sentiments. Pauline Kleingeld, "Wereldburgers in eigen land: Over kosmopolitisme en patriottisme" (2005), p. 4 quotes the French philosopher Jean-Jacques Rousseau and the *Dictionary of the Académie Française* 4th Edition (1762) as examples of negative attitudes towards cosmopolitanism. In the latter, one can find the following definition of "cosmopolite": "Celui qui n'adopte point de patrie. Un Cosmopolite n'est pas un bon citoyen." Clearly this is a definition of a cynic, not stoic cosmopolitan.

[44] The translation is my own. Gerard Reve, *Op weg naar het einde* (1963).

In *Plateforme*, Houellebecq writes:

> Qu'avais-je, pour ma part, à reprocher à l'Occident ? Pas grand-chose, mais je n'y étais pas spécialement attaché (et j'arrivais de moins en moins à comprendre qu'on soit attaché à une idée, un pays, à autre chose en général qu'à un individu). [...] Je pris soudain conscience avec gêne que je considérais la société où je vivais à peu près comme un milieu naturel – disons une savane, ou une jungle – aux lois duquel j'aurais dû m'adapter. L'idée que j'étais solidaire de ce milieu ne m'avait jamais effleuré; c'était comme une atrophie chez moi, une absence.[45]

A society based on freedom and detachment alone is a very unhappy one.

According to the stoic version of cosmopolitanism, all the people in the world share a common rationality, common values and a common fate, despite their different cultural backgrounds, and this formally binds them, or ought to do so. This version of cosmopolitanism is *positive*, in the sense that it requires all men and women to do something, namely to create and sustain a common life and order.[46] The ideas of Zeno, the founder of the Stoics, are summarized as follows by Plutarch:

> All the inhabitants of this world of ours should not live differentiated by their respective rules of justice into separate cities and communities, but [..] we should consider all men to be of one community and one polity, and [..] we should have a common life and an order common to us all, as a herd that feeds together and shares the pasturage of a common field.[47]

The stoic version of cosmopolitanism has flourished in political philosophy. Immanuel Kant is often seen as a cosmopolitan in this more positive, stoic sense.[48] In his lectures on anthropology, Kant wrote:

> The character of the [human] species, as it is indicated by the experience of all ages and of all peoples, is this: that, taken collectively (the human race as one whole), it is a multitude of persons, existing successively and side by side, who cannot do without associating peacefully and yet cannot avoid constantly offending one another. Hence they feel destined by nature to [form], through mutual compulsion under laws that proceed from themselves, a coalition in a cosmopolitan society – a coalition which, though constantly threatened by dissension, makes progress on the whole.[49]

---

[45] Michel Houellebecq, *Plateform : au milieu du monde* (2001), p. 339.
[46] See, *e.g.*, Martha C. Nussbaum, "Kant and Stoic Cosmopolitanism" (1997), p 6.
[47] Plutarch, *De Fortuna Alexandri*, First Oration, Paragraph 6.
[48] Martha C. Nussbaum, "Kant and Stoic Cosmopolitanism" (1997), pp. 1-25.
[49] Immanuel Kant, *Anthropology from a Pragmatic Point of View* (1798), para. 331. Kant hastens to add that the idea of a cosmopolitan society is "unattainable", but that it is an ideal that can guide us.

This describes a cosmopolitan society which ultimately includes all human beings. In our own time, cosmopolitans are calling for even more intense solidarity and cooperation, like a minimalist welfare State structure operating on a global level,[50] based on universal principles.[51]

Underlying all these suggestions is the idea that all human beings are equal and that they all relate to each other. In a sense, any cosmopolitan theory argues above all for the application, within that cosmopolitan society, of Kant's categorical imperative: "act as if your maxims were to serve at the same time as a universal law (for all rational beings)."[52] This imperative is basically the principle of reciprocity, and a cosmopolitan version suggests that you should treat others, *i.e.* all other world citizens, as you want to be treated yourself. Kant never suggested that this imperative was a philosophical invention. Rather, he presented it as a rule of thumb, or as an intuitive principle which most people already adopt in everyday life.[53]

As Railton noted, this intuition forms the basis of all law and legal reasoning. He rephrased the categorical imperative as follows:

> Like ideal legislators, we [...] authorize ourselves to act by "making law," aware of the condition that we ought to be – even when we would prefer otherwise – subject to the very same law (the imperative is categorical).[54]

This type of solidarity and reciprocity is the positive aspect of cosmopolitanism, proposed by the stoic version. The challenge is to combine the cynic's sense of freedom with the stoic's sense of global solidarity, without completely ignoring the special bonds that people have with those close to them.

---

[50] Most present-day cosmopolitan philosophers use John Rawls' latest book, *The Law of Peoples* (1999), to argue against. In that book, Rawls decides not to apply his (domestic) theory of justice, *mutatis mutandis*, to the global community of individuals. There are many philosophers, some of them students of Rawls, who do apply Rawls' theory on a global level. See *e.g.*, Roland Pierik and Wouter Werner, "Cosmopolitism, Global Justice, and International Law" (2005); Thomas W. Pogge, "An Egalitarian Law of Peoples" (1994); Andrew Kuper, "Rawlsian Global Justice: Beyond a Law of Peoples to a Cosmopolitan Law of Persons" (2000).

[51] Roughly speaking, these are the assumptions/principles: 1) the equality of all individuals; 2) the freedom of all individuals to choose how to live their life (restricted only by respect for the freedom of others); 3) the acknowledgment of personal accountability and responsibility of all individuals for the consequences of their decisions made in freedom; 4) consent and meaningful participation of individuals in collective decision-making processes that affect them; 5) some basic form of global solidarity. See *e.g.*, David Held, "Law of States, Law of Peoples" (2002).

[52] Immanuel Kant, *Grundlegung zur Metaphysik der Sittenn* (1785). Lynn H. Miller, *Global Order* (1990), p. 206 writes that this imperative can be applied both on an interpersonal as well as an interstate level.

[53] See Matthias Kaufmann, "Kantian Ethics and Politics" (2004), p. 8075.

[54] Peter Railton, "Ethics and Values" (2004), p. 4786.

An attempt to do this can be found in the ideas of humanism.[55] This clearly advocates a respect for the freedom of the individual, complemented by an appeal for global solidarity, organized in a global community. This combination is expressed in the Humanist Manifesto of 1973, as follows:

> We deplore the division of humankind on nationalistic grounds. We have reached a turning point in human history where the best option is to transcend the limits of national sovereignty and to move toward the building of a world community in which all sectors of the human family can participate. Thus we look to the development of a system of world law and a world order based upon transnational federal government. This would appreciate cultural pluralism and diversity. It would not exclude pride in national origins and accomplishments nor the handling of regional problems on a regional basis. Human progress, however, can no longer be achieved by focusing on one section of the world, Western or Eastern, developed or underdeveloped. For the first time in human history, no part of humankind can be isolated from any other. Each person's future is in some way linked to all. We thus reaffirm a commitment to the building of world community, at the same time recognizing that this commits us to some hard choices.[56]

A cosmopolitan attitude essentially comes down to the belief that all human beings together constitute a community. This is not something one can argue for or against. It is more of a "cosmopolitan sentiment," an intuition which can be shared – or not.

Cynical cosmopolitans demonstrate a feeling of detachment from any particular community, *i.e.* the sense that the world does not end at the border of one's local community. These cynical cosmopolitans often travelled around the world. But even someone like Kant, who never left his local community, can share this cosmopolitan sentiment and feel that there is no reason to be particularly attached to a particular local community and see the "outside world" as being alien.

The stoic cosmopolitans believe that, since the outside world is part of one's own world, one also has various responsibilities to the individuals living in that world. The Greeks did not elaborate much on how this sense of responsibility should influence behaviour, since their opportunities to influence global affairs were rather limited. These opportunities have grown exponentially since that time,

---

[55] Humanism also suffers from the fact that, like cosmopolitanism, it has a Western origin. The manifestos that will be referred to below are made in the USA. And, according to the first words of the European Treaty, the universal values of the inviolable and inalienable rights of the human person, freedom, democracy, equality and the rule of law have all developed from the cultural, religious and humanist inheritance of Europe. *Consolidated Version of the Treaty on European Union*, published in the Official Journal of the European Union, C 115/15 (9 May 2008).

[56] *Humanist Manifesto II* (1973), 12th principle. See also *Humanist Manifesto III* (2003). The first Humanist Manifesto was written in 1933 by Roy Sellars and Raymond Bragg. The second Manifesto was written in 1973 by Paul Kurtz and Edwin Wilson. The third Humanist Manifesto was published in 2003 by the American Humanist Association. See Edwin H. Wilson, *The genesis of a humanist manifesto*, and Paul Kurtz, *Humanist manifesto 2000: a call for a new planetary humanism*.

and therefore it has become necessary to consider some organized or institutional ways of implementing the global responsibilities arising from the cosmopolitan sentiment.

These institutions have been referred to as a "cosmopolitan society" (Kant), a "world community" (Humanist Manifesto), or a "global community." The two fundamental ideas of any such cosmopolitan order are that all human beings are equal and that their commonality leads to a set of rights and obligations which are universal, and are thus best expressed in universally valid laws (or "world law," the term used in the Humanist Manifesto).[57]

## 2.2 The reality of the global community: globalization

In the previous section, cosmopolitan sentiments and theories were invoked to justify the global application of a value-based system of decision making. Philosophical exposés and theories were used to support the idea that the state of the world should be viewed from the perspective of all human beings in that world. The central question in this section is whether we *actually* look at the world from this sort of a cosmopolitan perspective.

In 2003, Kofi Annan, the former Secretary-General of the United Nations, explained the need for global values as follows:

> Every society needs to be bound together by common values, so that its members know what to expect of each other, and have some shared principles by which to manage their differences without resorting to violence. That is true of local communities and of national communities. Today, as globalization brings us all closer together, and our lives are affected almost instantly by things that people say and do on the far side of the world, we also feel the need to live as a global community. And we can do so only if we have global values to bind us together.[58]

Nowadays, as the world is getting smaller and many individuals actually interact with people from all over the world, the cosmopolitan view of the world as "a herd that feeds together and shares the pasturage of a common field" becomes more and more persuasive, to the point where it is being transformed from an idea into fact.

The common field is no longer divided into various parts. Individuals no longer have to justify their behaviour only to those who share the particular part of the field where they are grazing. Global cooperation has gone beyond the principle of coexistence, *i.e.* simply tolerating other herds being in fields elsewhere. In Peter Singer's words:

---

[57] For the notion of "world law," see Otto Spijkers, "De notie van wereldrecht vóór, tijdens en na de oprichting van de Verenigde Naties" (2010).
[58] Kofi Annan, "Do we still have Universal Values?" (2003). See also Kofi Annan, *Global Values: The United Nations and the Rule of Law in the 21st Century* (2000).

Ethics appears to have developed from the behaviour and feelings of social mammals. [...] If the group to which we must justify ourselves is the tribe, or the nation, then our morality is likely to be tribal, or nationalistic. If, however, the revolution in communications has created a global audience, then we might feel a need to justify our behaviour to the whole world. This change creates the material basis for a new ethic that will serve the interests of all those who live on this planet in a way that, despite much rhetoric, no previous ethic has ever done.[59]

The revolution in communications referred to by Singer is only one aspect of the globalization that necessitates this new ethic. The world is flat, wrote Thomas Friedman,[60] and the fences that used to divide one grazing herd from another have weakened considerably. This is not a development of the last ten years. It began to take serious shape at the end of the Second World War. There is now a need to work out the global values to guide this flat world with its feeble fences, and to give globalization a human face.[61] The idea is clear: the world has become a global community not because of shared cosmopolitan sentiments, but because people actually interact with each other at a global level. And wherever and whenever people interact, they need a common set of values to guide their interaction.

As early as 1955, the American political scientist Quincy Wright foresaw the importance that this process of globalization would have on ethics. He distinguished four stages in the development of the "international ethic". [62] Together, these four stages describe a kind of evolution from various irreconcilable and isolated local cultures into one universally shared culture. According to Wright, this evolution had to be completed for an international ethic to be established. In the initial stage of this evolution, "the value systems of the principal nations of the world differ, and are, in varying degree, inconsistent with one another." This inconsistency is not problematic as long as these nations "coexist" and do not interact with each other. However, "the conditions of the modern world, by increasing the contacts between persons and social systems guided by divergent value systems, have developed these inconsistencies into conflicts of interest, of more or less intensity" (second stage). When nations with differing value systems *do* interact, conflicting value systems become apparent and problematic. Some common ground has to be found. As Wright wrote, "these contacts have resulted in

---

[59] Peter Singer, *One World: The Ethics of Globalization* (2002), p. 12.
[60] Thomas L. Friedman, *The World Is Flat: a Brief History of the Twenty-first Century* (2005).
[61] Willem van Genugten, Kees Homan, Nico Schrijver & Paul de Waart, *The United Nations of the Future: Globalization with a Human Face* (2006).
[62] International ethics is "the science relating the standards and values which individuals, governments, and international organizations believe they ought to observe in their decisions intended to influence international relations." Philip Quincy Wright, *The Study of International Relations* (1955), p. 438.

the emergence of an embryonic, universal culture and of institutions and organizations for its interpretation and application, seeking to resolve inconsistencies and conflicts" (third stage). In the final stage of this evolution, "social observation and analysis indicate that value systems can be synthesized, and that philosophical insight and analysis can develop and continually reinterpret universal values to facilitate such synthesis."[63] This last stage is the stage we find ourselves in at the moment. The biggest challenge in global decision making is therefore to find such a synthesis of values. Both Singer and Wright agreed on this in principle.[64]

Increasingly one can see references in the literature to the idea that we are all individuals living together in a "global village". This term is not meant to convey a cosmopolitan ideal or even a metaphor. It is meant to be a description of reality. Mendlovitz, the director of the World Order Models Project, wrote in 1975:

> As I see it, it is necessary to accept seriously not only the rhetoric but the reality of the term "global village." The fact that the overwhelming majority of humankind understands for the first time in history that human society encompasses the entire globe is a phenomenon equivalent to humankind's understanding that the globe is round rather than flat.[65]

This idea is also the starting point for Kofi Annan's *We the Peoples*, a report he named after the first words in the United Nations Charter. In an attempt to answer the questions "who are we, the peoples?" and "what are our common concerns?," Annan suggested that we all "imagine, for a moment, that the world really is a 'global village' — taking seriously the metaphor that is often invoked to depict global interdependence."[66] After listing the problems this village (the world) has to cope with, Annan openly asked himself:

> Who among us would not wonder how long a village in this state can survive without taking steps to ensure that all its inhabitants can live free from hunger and safe from violence, drinking clean water, breathing clean air, and knowing that their children will have real chances in life?[67]

---

[63] *Idem*, pp. 445-448.

[64] Wright did not believe that when he wrote the book, in 1955, the final stage of the evolution was already reached.

[65] Saul Mendlovitz, *On the Creation of a Just World Order* (1975), p. xvi. This language reminds one of the Copernican revolution, and indeed, in another article, Mendlovitz explicitly makes that comparison. See Saul Mendlovitz & Thomas Weiss, "The Study of Peace and Justice: Toward a Framework for Global Discussion" (1975), p. 155.

[66] Kofi Annan, *We, the Peoples: the Role of the United Nations in the Twenty-first Century* (2000), paras 51-52.

[67] *Idem*, para. 57.

It is difficult to see the world as a global village if one stays in a particular village for all of one's life. Not every human being has Kant's imagination. Only the truly privileged can live their lives as though the whole world were their oyster.[68]

Astronauts, some of the most privileged people in this world, are unique in the sense that they have actually *seen* the "global village" in its entirety with their own eyes. Astronauts have described their profound feelings when they first saw the earth from a distance. The first Dutch astronaut, Wubbo Ockels, expressed this as follows:

> I remember that after ten minutes, we folded and put away our chairs. I had to go again, so I floated to the toilet. I passed by the door and looked through the round window. For the first time, I saw the world from outside. Well, that was a shock. It gives such impact. You have that huge perspective. It's really a shock. Gigantic. [...] During the trip, the more you look at the earth, the more you begin to love the earth. In a very deep sense. Our planet is in fact fascinatingly beautiful. But you also realize that a lot of mess is made on earth, which is also a spacecraft as it were. People do not realize how fragile spaceship earth really is.[69]

Almost all astronauts had this profound sensation when they first saw the earth in its entirety.[70] For those less fortunate, the idea that we live in a "global village" remains more abstract than for the astronaut. But if the people of Ancient Greece were capable of feeling part of a "common herd," it should also be possible for our own generation.[71]

If one accepts that we live in a "global village," or that the world is flat,[72] or, in less metaphorical terms, that globalization is a fact, then does this mean that values must be applied at a global level? The globalization of the media makes it possible for specific incidents occurring in a remote village to be broadcast all over the world, not infrequently causing a global outrage. The whole world sympathizes and to a certain extent identifies with the victims.[73] But others have pointed out that

---

[68] This expression is inspired by William Shakespeare, *The Merry Wives of Windsor* (1602), at the beginning of Scene II (A room in the Garter Inn).

[69] Keizer, "Het Grote Wubbo Ockels Interview," p. 57. The translation is my own.

[70] For other descriptions of such sensations, see a book called *The Home Planet*, which is essentially a collection of pictures from earth, some of them accompanied by quotes from astronauts describing the way they felt when they first saw the earth from outer space. See Kevin W. Kelley, *The Home Planet* (1988).

[71] We can refer to René-Jean Dupuy as an example of an international lawyer imagining looking at the world from the moon. See René-Jean Dupuy, *La communauté internationale entre le mythe et l'histoire* (1986), p. 177.

[72] For a counterargument to Friedman's argument, see *e.g.*, Pankaj Ghemawat, "Why the World Isn't Flat" (2007). This debate is essentially about facts, not theories.

[73] A gruesome example is the global outrage after a 17-year-old girl was stoned to death in Iraq, an incident that was filmed. The story (and the footage) was all over the "blogosphere" and appeared in

globalization may have brought people closer together, only to make them realize how different they really are.[74] In response, one could point to Wright's theory and argue that a full synthesis of values has not yet been achieved, and that there are still some value conflicts that need to be resolved. But is this any different in a local community?

Recently, a survey of global values studied the actual existence of feelings of global solidarity. An examination of the extent to which there is a concern for other people's living conditions results in the following picture: 83% of the world population is concerned with the living conditions of their immediate family.[75] Only 29% are concerned with the living conditions of the people in their neighbourhood.[76] 25% are concerned about their fellow countrymen,[77] and 26% about all their fellow human beings.[78] It is clear that the biggest drop actually occurs when we move away from the family to the neighbourhood, not, as might be imagined, when State borders are crossed. When the State borders are crossed, we actually gain a percentage point. Therefore the conclusion is that State boundaries have very little impact on people's sense of solidarity. However, some of the data suggest that people do feel that they "belong" more to their nation than to the world in its entirety. For example, when asked to which geographical group they belong first of all, 41% of the world's citizens responded that it was their own locality, 34% said it was their country, 7% the world.[79] Furthermore, 56% of the world population was very proud of their own nationality,[80] and 75% would be willing to fight for their country (but not necessarily die for it!).[81] Therefore it must be concluded – if such surveys justify any conclusion at all – that national sentiments are strong, even in a globalized world. The existence of nationalist sentiments is not *per se* a reason to refute cosmopolitanism. The next and final section explains how cosmopolitanism and nationalism can coexist.

For those who do not share the cosmopolitan sentiment or intuition, the choice between cooperating with distant others in an effort to solve global problems, or not trying to solve them at all by avoiding all contact with other communities, becomes a choice between two evils. To make this point, we refer to the grazing herd of the Stoics one last time. This time the metaphor comes from

---

newspapers all over the world. Muller, "Jihad in Koerdistan na steniging van meisje", *de Volkskrant*, 10 May 2007 (frontpage).

[74] See Fred Halliday, "Global Governance : Prospects and Problems" (2000).

[75] E153 (Table), in Ronald Inglehart, *Human Beliefs and Values* (2004). Denmark (34), Finland (34) and the Czech Republic (30) are the exceptions.

[76] E154 (Table). Finland (8%) and Turkey (7%) are at the very bottom.

[77] E156 (Table).

[78] E158 (Table).

[79] G1 (Table). Jordan is the exception: 68% say the world, first of all.

[80] G006 (Table). At the bottom, we find the Netherlands (20%), South Korea (17%), Germany (17%), and Taiwan (15%).

[81] E012 (Table). Only 25% in case of Japan, but that is the exception.

Schopenhauer and the cosmopolitan sheep are replaced by slightly less cosmopolitan porcupines:

> A company of porcupines crowded themselves very close together one cold winter's day so as to profit by one another's warmth and so save themselves from being frozen to death. But soon they felt one another's quills, which induced them to separate again. And now, when the need for warmth brought them nearer together again, the second evil arose once more. So that they were driven backwards and forwards from one trouble to another, until they had discovered a mean distance at which they could most tolerably exist.[82]

Of course, the porcupines prefer to form little groups consisting solely of those fellow porcupines they feel more closely related to. After all, love softens the pain of the quills. But as the world gets colder, and global problems get bigger, the need for all porcupines to stick together in one big group increases, whether they want to or not.

## 2.3 Local communities in the global community

When cosmopolitans call for a certain detachment from the local community, they do not mean to disregard the importance of communities altogether; they do not think of the world literally as one big family, or as a collection of detached and lonely individuals, like the 6,768,181,146[83] children of Diogenes, each and every one in their own barrel, without any community to belong to. It may be possible to find an "unhappy compromise," as the porcupines did. As both the Stoics of Ancient Greece and many present day philosophers have often pointed out, one can be a cosmopolitan citizen and still find warmth outside the abstract "global neighbourhood."[84] Even in a fenceless field sheep (or even porcupines) may choose to form little herds to find warmth, without disregarding the fact that they are sheep grazing in a field that belongs to all and needs to be shared by all.[85] Therefore, although this sounds contradictory, cosmopolitanism does not conflict with the existence of local communities.[86]

---

[82] One of the parables in Arthur Schopenhauer, *Parerga und Paralipomena* (1851), cited at Elizabeth Monroe Drews & Leslie Lipson, *Values and Humanity* (1971), p. 8. The translation is to be found in this book.

[83] The estimate is for July 2010, see *CIA Factbook*.

[84] The term was borrowed from Commission on Global Governance, *Our Global Neighborhood* (1995).

[85] For a legal outline of cosmopolitanism as applied to the community of states, see Bruno Simma, "The Contribution of Alfred Verdross to the Theory of International Law" (1995), pp. 6-11. For a more philosophical discussion, see Kok-Chor Tan, *Justice Without Borders* (2004); David Miller, "Reasonable Partiality Towards Compatriots" (2005).

[86] Ribeiro remarks on p. 2842 of "Cosmopolitanism" (2004) that "[m]uch of the malaise and misunderstanding cosmopolitanism may provoke are related to its ambiguity, that is, its unique way of

Those proclaiming an institutional arrangement for a global community, do not discard the existence and moral relevance of local communities. According to Kant's Perpetual Peace, the cosmopolitan society should consist of a voluntary league of sovereign, republican states,[87] which he later called a permanent congress of states.[88] Kant believed that people were first and foremost citizens of their own particular State, [89] and supported the principle of non-intervention by one State in the affairs of another.[90] By prescribing a conditional form of universal hospitality as the central principle of the law of world citizenship ("*Weltbürgerrecht*"), Kant did allow the cynical cosmopolitan to wander around the globe and to exercise his right to visit ("*Besuchsrecht*") any place on this planet, but only to a limited extent.[91] Therefore the global community prescribed by Kant was based both on cosmopolitan solidarity and on the need for local communities to coexist.

This focus on peaceful coexistence meant that Kant was much more realistic than the more idealist cosmopolitans of Ancient Greece. However, according to some it was still not realistic enough. In response to Kant's ideas, Hegel wrote that Kant's *voluntary* League of Nations would be too fragile, as it would be ultimately based on agreements between all States' "own particular will." Therefore "if no agreement can be reached between particular wills, conflicts between States can be settled only by *war*."[92] Hegel did give cosmopolitans some hope: cooperation within a State was so successful because it was based on both common laws and a common culture (based upon family, civil society and the nation state). Together these constituted a shared ethical life, or "*Sittlichkeit*".[93] Without a shared culture, international legal obligations would remain too abstract

---

uniting difference and equality, an apparent paradox of wishing to reconcile universal values with a diversity of culturally and historically constructed subject positions."

[87] Kant, *Zum Ewigen Frieden* (1795). On the interpretation of this treatise (*Zum Ewigen Frieden* mainly consists of a number of articles), much has been written. See *e.g.*, Pauline Kleingeld, "Approaching Perpetual Peace: Kant's Defence of a League of States and his Ideal of a World Federation" (2004). See also, James Bohman & Matthias Lutz-Bachmann (editors), *Perpetual Peace: Essays on Kant's Cosmopolitan Idea* (1997).

[88] Kant, *Die Metaphysik der Sitten*, Part II (Die Metaphysischen Anfangsgründe der Rechtslehre), published in 1797, para. 61. These ideas have influenced the establishment of the League of Nations, which may be seen as the realization of Kant's ideas. For an assessment of this assumption, see, *e.g.*, Samuel Rozemond, *Kant en de Volkenbond* (1930).

[89] See the second part of Pauline Kleingeld, "Wereldburgers in eigen land: Over kosmopolitisme en patriottisme" (2005).

[90] See Section 1 (Containing the Preliminary Articles for Perpetual Peace among States), Article 5, of Kant, *Zum Ewigen Frieden* (1795).

[91] See Kant, *Zum Ewigen Frieden* (1795), Third Definitive Article for a Perpetual Peace. See Pauline Kleingeld, "Kant's Cosmopolitan Law" (1998); Martha C. Nussbaum, "Patriotism and Cosmopolitanism" (1994); Lynn H. Miller, *Global Order* (1990), p. 14.

[92] See Georg Wilhelm Friedrich Hegel, *Grundlinien der Philosophie des Rechts* (1821), paras. 333-334.

[93] *Idem*, paras. 330-360. One could specifically refer to the last sentence in Georg Wilhelm Friedrich Hegel, *Grundlinien der Philosophie des Rechts* (1821): "In the state, the self-consciousness finds the actuality of its substantial knowledge and volition in organic development."

to form the basis of a world community.[94] Therefore, according to Hegel, it is only when all States develop a similar ethical life from within – and Hegel saw the German *Sittlichkeit* as the ideal – that a world league can be successful.[95] This is also reminiscent of Wright and Singer's ideas: all that is needed in order for there to be a true global community is some kind of global synthesis of values, based on global laws and a global culture.

If one accepts that a global community is – and must be – more than just a patchwork quilt of communities tolerating one another's existence, and cooperating only out of necessity, the question is whether a globally shared ethical life, as defined by Hegel, is actually possible, Can this develop, despite the existence of local communities?[96] It is a factual, not a conceptual question that constantly recurs in this study. According to some of the stoic cosmopolitans, the fact that we are all (rational) human beings, which no one can deny, is enough to bind us together.[97] But as Nussbaum explained, this abstract bond lacks the warmth of more traditional bonds:

> Becoming a citizen of the world is often a lonely business. It is, in effect, as Diogenes said, a kind of exile - from the comfort of local truths, from the warm nestling feeling of patriotism, from the absorbing drama of pride in oneself and one's own. […] If one begins life as a child who loves and trusts its parents, it is tempting to want to reconstruct citizenship along the same lines, finding in an idealized image of a nation a surrogate parent who will do one's thinking for one. Cosmopolitanism offers no such refuge; it offers only reason and the love of humanity, which may seem at times less colourful than other sources of belonging.[98]

The abstract nature of the global community and the concrete character of local communities mean that ordinary people become more attached to the latter. But even when the focus is on the local, the abstract bond based on a sense of common

---

[94] Hegel did believe that all human beings are identical as human beings, but he also believed that this idea needed the concretization in the State. See Georg Wilhelm Friedrich Hegel, *Grundlinien der Philosophie des Rechts* (1821), para. 209.

[95] Georg Wilhelm Friedrich Hegel, *Enzyclopädie der philosophischen Wissenschaften im Grundrisse (1817), Book 3,* Para. 548. See also Georg Wilhelm Friedrich Hegel, *Grundlinien der Philosophie des Rechts* (1821), para. 340. On Hegel and cosmopolitanism, see also Steven V. Hicks, *International Law and the Possibility of a Just World Order* (1999), especially pp. 21-26, and Chapter Four: Hegel and Cosmopolitanism.

[96] Habermas has some doubts. See Jürgen Habermas, *The Postnational Constellation* (2001). See especially Chapter 4 on The Postnational Constellation and the Future of Democracy, pp. 58-112.

[97] But even if this fact alone would indeed be strong enough to bind us, it seems unlikely that a world state can be based solely on that. Even Kant says that the world can only get as far as a permanent congress of states, and this is mainly because it is impossible to point out or create a global central authority, without risking the danger of global despotism. Immanuel Kant, *Die Metaphysik der Sitten*, Part II (Die Metaphysischen Anfangsgründe der Rechtslehre), published in 1797, para. 61.

[98] Martha C. Nussbaum, "Patriotism and Cosmopolitanism" (1994).

humanity could be a solid enough basis for some type of global cooperation and global solidarity. It is always possible to view the fate of fellow human beings in other places from the warmth of the family and local communities. A certain bias is acceptable, as long as we – all human beings – do not behave "as if our separate nations housed separate species."[99]

It is in the concrete local communities that the abstract values of the global community can be fleshed out. If different cultural traditions express the same core values in different ways, this will lead to a kind of cultural diversity that must be celebrated and cherished, since it allows local communities to learn from the way in which the same values are implemented by others in different ways.[100] Cosmopolitan sentiments will be satisfied if the global community is allowed to monitor from afar whether all human beings are treated adequately from the perspective of the global synthesis of values. It is precisely because this is a global synthesis, that it is by definition of a vague and general nature, and must be elaborated and interpreted at a local level.

## 2.4 Conclusion

These philosophical reflections were intended to clarify the idea that a global value is a belief that a specific state of the world is preferable, *from the perspective of all human beings*, to an opposite state of the world. The italicized phrase should not be interpreted to mean that all individual citizens of this world have to share an identical set of preferences. Instead, the idea was that all human beings were in a sense united in a global community, and that this global community operated on the basis of a shared global ethic. The above subsections merely showed that it was intuitively plausible that there really is such a global community, and that there really is such a global ethic. What has not yet been explored is the content of this global ethic, and the way in which the global community expresses itself, and "acts out" this global ethic. This is explained below.

### 3 A GLOBAL DISCUSSION TO DETERMINE GLOBAL VALUES

According to the definition used in this study, global values are globally shared beliefs about a better world. Does that mean all individuals in this world must actually share a certain belief before it can be regarded as such? Or does it mean that a majority of all the world's citizens must do so? A process of representative and authoritative global decision making must be found. Wherever it takes place,

---

[99] Lynn H. Miller, *Global Order* (1990), p. 14.
[100] Kofi Annan, *Farewell speech as UN Secretary-General*, delivered at the Truman Library in the United States of America on 11 December 2006.

this process is the source of the international community's beliefs. This section contains some philosophical reflections on this process.

## 3.1 The need for a discussion that involves the entire global community

As values are beliefs and not facts, these values cannot be "found" in any particular place.[101] Therefore, when determining the values of the global community, it is useless to send a group of respected scientists into the world to examine the world's values in an objective and definitive way. Rather, a global discussion should be organized to endeavour to find universal agreement, *i.e.* a synthesis of values.

For it to be successful, this discussion should involve the whole of the international community. In the past, there were many examples of particular groups claiming to have found values that applied universally. Even today, Europe, as organized in the European Union, claims to have identified values that apply to everyone.[102] It is possible that the values that are most vividly expressed in a particular history and way of thinking are nevertheless universally applicable, and are or come to be universally shared.[103] Be that as it may, instead of taking for granted the universal validity of a group of values promoted by particular people, it is preferable to come up with a process for defining global values which is sufficiently inclusive. In that case, a particular value is a global value, not when a particular philosopher argues that the value ought to be adopted by all the world's citizens, but when the value can be shown, in fact, to be universally shared.[104] This is also the view of the Ghanaian philosopher Appiah, who states:

> I want to hold on to at least one important aspect of the objectivity of values: that there are some values that are, and should be universal, just as there are lots of values that are, and must be, local. We can't hope to reach a final consensus on how to rank and order such values. That's why the model I'll be returning to is that of conversation – and, in particular, conversation between people from different ways of life.[105]

Who participates in this global conversation which determines our global values? If the inclusiveness of the process for determining global values is acted upon, the

---

[101] On the objectivity of values, see also the fact/value debate, for example, Hilary Putnam, *The Collapse of the Fact/Value Dichotomy and Other Essays* (2002).
[102] See the first words of the *Consolidated Version of the Treaty on European Union*, Official Journal of the European Union, C 115/15 (9 May 2008).
[103] See Martti Koskenniemi, "International Law in Europe: Between Tradition and Renewal" (2005).
[104] See *e.g.*, Thomas Hobbes, *Leviathan* (1651), Chapter XIII: Of the Natural Condition of Mankind as Concerning their Felicity and Misery.
[105] Kwame Anthony Appiah, *Cosmopolitanism: Ethics in a World of Strangers* (2006), p. xxi.

answer surely is everybody.[106] It is sometimes argued that the participation of all the world's citizens in defining and realizing values, and their participation in both local and global governance, is a value in itself, a value sometimes labelled as "participation" and sometimes as "democracy."[107]

The importance of this kind of inclusiveness, to the extent that it is practically feasible, cannot be overemphasized. One would have to agree with Robinson that it is strange to suggest that the layman needs professional philosophers to tell him or her what is valuable in his or her own life.[108] Although important people may serve as an inspiration, it is old-fashioned to state that "historically situated outstanding figures or institutions," such as "great moral personalities, prophets, philosophers, ideologists, intellectuals, scientists, artists, novelists, film directors, and institutions such as Churches, clubs, learned societies, research centres, universities, etc." serve as the exclusive "value producers."[109]

### 3.2  The need for rules of communication to ensure a genuine discussion

To ensure a genuine discussion about values, it is important to have rules of communication. This section describes these rules in very general terms. In subsequent chapters, especially the equivalent section in the chapter about the United Nations (Chapter III), these general rules are applied to existing political institutions.

A global discussion about values can only succeed if the participants understand that it is in their interest to voluntarily follow certain general rules, and accept the legitimacy of these rules. If everybody always agrees on the *outcomes* of the discussion, then the process by which the outcome was achieved will not be criticized very much. However, if no universal agreement on the outcome is guaranteed in advance, the legitimacy of the rules of the discussion becomes essential, in order for a small dissenting minority to nevertheless accept the outcome of the global discussion as an expression of a global consensus.[110]

---

[106] Some global referenda on values have in fact been organized. For European values, see Loek Halman, Ruud Luijkx & Marga van Zundert, *Atlas of European Values* (2005). For global values, see the World Values Survey: http://www.worldvaluessurvey.org.

[107] Falk referred to a discussion among the participants of WOMP on the issue "as to whether the goal of democratizing participation in authority structures within states and in the world system should be emphasized through the device of formulating a fifth value of participation or by being incorporated in the interpretation of the agreed four." See Richard A. Falk, "Contending Approaches to World Order" (1982), p. 161. See also Rajni Kothari, "World Politics and World Order" (1975), p. 50; this WOMP author does mention participation as a distinct value. Within the United Nations system, White regards "self-determination and democracy" as a distinct value. See Nigel D. White, *The United Nations system* (2002).

[108] Richard Robinson, *An Atheist's Values* (1964), p. 10.

[109] Rodilf Rezsohazy, "Sociology of Values" (2004), p. 16155.

[110] Thomas Risse, "Global Governance and Communicative Action" (2004).

In his article in which he applied the rules of communicative action on a global level with great insight, Risse argued that in order for a global conversation to work, the participants should not put forward one sole aim, i.e., "to maximize or to satisfy their given interests and preferences." Instead, they should be more open-minded and be "prepared to change their views of the world or even their interests in light of the better argument."[111] The aim of the discussion is not to bargain for compromises in an attempt to secure one's own self-interests, but to reach a reasoned consensus based on sound arguments.[112]

These rules alone do not guarantee that a reasoned consensus on global values will actually be achieved. As human beings are social beings, agreement may be facilitated by the fact that we *want* to reach such universal agreement. It is something we strive for. As Robinson noted, "[t]o find good what everyone else finds bad is apt to be uncomfortable or worse."[113] This particularly applies when a lack of consensus means a lack of global action to tackle the world's major problems and alleviate the worst human miseries.

At the same time, Robinson warned against an excessively strong response to unusual points of view. They should not be rejected without proper consideration:

> Suppose a man to say that flowers are out of place in a garden, which should contain only trees and grass. Even if he gives no reason for this judgment we may be glad to hear it. It may strike us as a novelty worth considering. We may like to imagine ourselves maintaining such a garden and rejecting flowers, and to ask ourselves whether that would be a change for the better.[114]

Robinson's point, *i.e.* that any contribution to the global conversation is valuable, is at least intuitively plausible. One could imagine a world without armies, or a world without international criminal courts and tribunals, or a world without state boundaries, or a world without the United Nations. In a global discussion, everything is worth considering. That is the idea.

---

[111] *Idem*, p. 294. Many of these ideas on communicative action are based on Jürgen Habermas, *Theorie des kommunikativen Handelns* (1981).

[112] The difference between the two forms of negotiation is succinctly explained as follows: "Bargaining compromises refers to cooperative agreements through the give and take of negotiations based on fixed interests and preferences. Reasoned consensus refers to the voluntary agreement about norms and rules reached through arguing and persuasion." Thomas Risse, "Global Governance and Communicative Action" (2004), p. 310.

[113] Richard Robinson, *An Atheist's Values* (1964), p. 45.

[114] *Idem*, pp. 45-46.

## 3.3 Values and interests

These rules of global communication and decision-making can be criticized. One criticism is that the "rules of the game" should not be defined in terms of the rules for a fair and inclusive global discussion. That is not the aim of the conferences and other meetings where international decisions are made. These meetings are about finding ways to prevent conflicts between competing interests and some common interests which can be jointly realized. These discussions are not about values. Instead, they are – and ought to be – about interests. Even if decision makers claim to be guided by values, they are, in fact, guided by interests. For example, Mendlovitz wrote that "[o]f course, we know that national leaders more often than not pursue State *interests* (that is, the material and security goals of a given State) even when talking about global *values* (that is, ethically beneficial goals that pertain to humanity as a whole), and that moral claims are often made in a self-serving fashion by geopolitical rivals."[115]

At first, it may appear that whenever politicians make a decision (*e.g.* to sign a treaty, or to go to war, or to do nothing), they are guided by particular interests, especially the national interest. The philosopher may be like a "poet who reflects in tranquillity upon past experience (or other people's experience), thinking about political and moral choices already made."[116] The politician does not have time for that. The politician must act, and act now. The reference to values, philosophy, ethics and legal theories is an *ex post facto* rationalisation for a particular decision. It is argued that it is not these ideas that determine the politician's behaviour, but actually the interests at stake.[117]

Seeing interests and values as conflicting in this way is the result of a misunderstanding of what caused the conflict. The two conflicting elements are the local and the global aspects: the *national* interest versus the *global* interest, or the *national* values versus the *global* values.[118] It is possible to define the global interest, or the "human interest," in terms of values, and in a goal-oriented way.[119] For example, Johansen defined the human interest as "the collection of goals and strategies that are consistent with and will advance the values of global

---

[115] Richard A. Falk, Samuel S. Kim & Saul H. Mendlovitz, "General Introduction" (1982), p. 2. Emphasis in the original.

[116] Michael Walzer, *Just and Unjust Wars: A Moral Argument with Historical Illustrations* (2006, original 1977), p. xix.

[117] See Martti Koskenniemi, "By their Acts you shall know them... (And not by their Legal Theories)" (2004), pp. 839-851.

[118] See Robert C. Johansen, *The National Interest and the Human Interest : An Analysis of U.S. Foreign Policy* (1980), in which the author assesses US foreign policy on the basis of the human interest, defined in terms similar to those of global values. See also Lynn H. Miller, *Global Order* (1990), pp. 74-75.

[119] On the importance of seeing values as goal-oriented, see also Christian Tomuschat, "Die internationale Gemeinschaft" (1995), p. 20.

humanism."[120] What appears to be a conflict between values and interests, between philosophy and action, is in reality a dispute about the reach of one's value system: do values apply equally to all the world's citizens, or is the duty to act morally applicable only in relation to certain groups of people? For example, the "realist" accounts of international relations often adopt a rather restricted reach (Hobbes famously saw man acting as a wolf to other men), while "idealists" often give value systems a global reach, sometimes even extending to animals and plants.[121] The conflict occurs because politicians act from a *nationalist* perspective, while trying to justify their actions to the rest of the world from a *global* perspective.[122] This does not explain away the criticism, but it shows that the conflict is not between values and interests, but between a nationalist and global approach to international decision making. There is no reason to reject the nationalist approach. Even according to most cosmopolitans, it is perfectly justifiable for a decision maker to devote particular attention to the interests of his or her own group, as long as this does not lead to unreasonable costs for the rest of the international community.

## 3.4 The need for a discussion as a motivation for action

To prevent the global discussion about values from becoming an academic or philosophical discussion, the political relevance of the discussion must be ensured. It must be able to motivate action, in order to bring the real world closer to the ideal world, the ideal being defined by the totality of global values.

One of the principal ideas underlying this study is that, if the discussion about global values is phrased in the language of international law, the outcome of the discussion, a continuously growing collection of international legal norms and principles, can actually serve as an instrument to both define global values *and* encourage their global realization.[123] The most important international legal document resulting from this discussion is the United Nations Charter.

When value-based norms, such as the norms in the Charter, are considered to be instruments for the promotion of global values, they have to be interpreted in such a way that the instruments work as effectively as possible to achieve this. This has significant consequences for the study and practice of international law. Lawyers cannot be mere technicians, in the sense Kelsen that used the term. Just after the adoption of the UN Charter, Kelsen wrote that "it is not superfluous to

---

[120] Robert C. Johansen, *The National Interest and the Human Interest* (1980) (emphasis in the original). See also Bruno Simma, "From Bilateralism to Community Interest" (1994), p. 233.

[121] See Richard Ryder, "All beings that feel pain deserve human rights" (2005).

[122] See Richard A. Falk, Samuel S. Kim & Saul H. Mendlovitz, "General Introduction" (1982), p. 2.

[123] This was also Tomuschat's point of departure in Christian Tomuschat, "International law: ensuring the survival of mankind on the eve of a new century (general course on public international law)", see esp. p. 23. See also Antônio Augusto Cançado Trindade, "International law for humankind: towards a new jus gentium (I): general course on public international law", p. 84.

remind the lawyer that as a 'jurist' he is but a technician whose most important task is to assist the law-maker in the adequate formulation of the legal norms."[124] As Walzer pointed out, this restricted view of what the lawyer is and what he does "has become in the age of the United Nations increasingly uninteresting."[125] Such "technicians" fail to grasp the political context in which they operate. By restricting themselves to technicalities, "[t]he lawyers have constructed a paper world, which fails at crucial points to correspond to the world the rest of us still live in."[126]

Confronted with value-based norms such as those of the UN Charter, some lawyers adopt a more interdisciplinary approach. These policy-oriented lawyers interpret the law in accordance with the values and goals the laws are made to protect. The most influential is Myres McDougal.[127] To put it briefly, McDougal believed that international law should not be studied as a collection of legally binding norms and their enforcement mechanisms. Instead of focusing on whether a certain norm is binding or non-binding, and on whether a certain enforcement mechanism is strong enough to secure compliance with binding norms, international law should be studied and used as an *authoritative language*, used by the international community as a whole, to discuss values and to come up with means to implement those values at the global level. International law is a *value-oriented jurisprudence*, a language which is used by chosen representatives of the international community (governments, diplomats, international judges and arbitrators, elements of the "UN family," etc.), to make difficult choices based on shared values. This process of making choices is not restricted to the legal realm. It takes place in the larger context of international relations.[128]

Walzer noted that this interpretation of international law requires some imagination, "for the customs and conventions, the treaties and charters that constitute the laws of international society do not invite interpretation in terms of a single purpose or set of purposes."[129] The United Nations Charter, by clearly listing its main purposes in value-based language, could be the exception to this rule.

---

[124] p. xiii, Hans Kelsen, *The Law of the United Nations: A Critical Analysis of its Fundamental Problems* (1950).
This "rule of thumb" constitutes the basis of Kelsen's pure theory of law, which aims to remove from (international) legal doctrine all extra-juridical elements. See Hans Kelsen, *Pure Theory of Law* (1967).
[125] p. xx of Michael Walzer, *Just and Unjust Wars: A Moral Argument with Historical Illustrations* (Fourth Edition, 2006; original is of 1977).
[126] *Idem*, p. xxi.
[127] Myres S. McDougal, "Law School of the Future: From Legal Realism to Policy Science in the World Community" (1947), p.1352. Also cited on p. 565 of Frederick S. Tipson, "The Laswell-McDougal Enterprise: Toward a World Public Order of Human Dignity" (1973), no. 3.
[128] See also pp. 80-82 of Patrick Capps, *Human dignity and the foundations of international law* (2009), where the McDougal school is described.
[129] *Idem*.

Some of the policy-oriented lawyers go even further. They argue that the values are themselves part of international law. According to Walzer, these "policy-oriented lawyers are in fact moral and political philosophers,"

> And it would be best if they presented themselves that way. Or, alternatively, they are would-be legislators, not jurists or students of the law. They are committed, or most of them are committed, to restructuring international society – a worthwhile task – but they are not committed to expounding its present structure.[130]

The best approach to the practice of law lies between the two extreme positions: the lawyer as technician and the lawyer as philosopher. This study certainly leans towards the policy-oriented approach. At the same time, Walzer's warning has been taken to heart: the aim is not to describe an ideal framework, but rather to describe the actual law as recognized by the international community, in the context of the United Nations Organization.

There is nothing controversial about the idea of distinguishing a certain body of norms from the rest of international law on the basis of the fact that these norms aim to protect global values, and to give them a more prominent place because of that link.[131] At the same time, Danilenko rightly pointed out that community interests and moral values cannot be regarded as part of law, let alone part of "higher law," without some form of approval within the recognized normative processes.[132] In a sense, the aim is therefore to look both at the "*substratum* of legal norms ," *i.e.* at "the beliefs, values, ethics, ideas and human aspirations" that form the foundation of international law,[133] and at the legal norms that have emerged through the formal and universally accepted rules of law-making.[134] The challenge is not to choose between a value-based international law and a State consent-based international law, but rather to reconcile the two approaches. Many scholars have already attempted such reconciliation. For example, in his treatise on international law Cassese made it his goal to

> Combine the strictly legal method with the historical and sociological approach, to expound the dynamic of international law: in particular, to illustrate the tension between traditional law, firmly grounded in the rock of State sovereignty, and the

---

[130] *Idem.*

[131] Antônio Augusto Cançado Trindade, "International law for humankind: towards a new jus gentium (I): general course on public international law" (2005), p. 35, and footnote 91 (page 56), and p. 57. See also Alfred Verdross, "Le fondement du droit international" (1927).

[132] Gennady M. Danilenko, 'International Jus Cogens: Issues of Law-Making' (1991), p. 46. See also Michael J. Glennon, 'De l'absurdité du droit impératif (*Jus cogens*)' (2006), p. 531.

[133] Antônio Augusto Cançado Trindade, "International law for humankind: towards a new jus gentium (I): general course on public international law" (2005), p. 177.

[134] See also Michael Byers, "Conceptualising the Relationship between *Jus Cogens* and *Erga Omnes* Rules" (1997), p. 212.

new or nascent law, often soft and hazy as a cloud, but inspired with new, community values. [135]

The next chapter (especially sections 2.4 and 3.5 of Chapter III) explains why the type of international law that is the subject of this study, *i.e.* the norms of the United Nations Charter and those contained in declarations of the United Nations General Assembly, can be considered as meeting the formal requirements of law making. However, the formal rules should not be applied too restrictively, as this would stand in the way of an effective use of international law as an instrument for the promotion and protection of fundamental values.

## 3.5 Conclusion

As beliefs are not facts, a globally shared belief cannot be "discovered" by scientists. Therefore any list of global values proposed by a single scientist must be treated with suspicion. Instead, it is important to organize a discussion which is as inclusive as possible, in the sense that the entire international community can participate. Furthermore, this discussion should be a genuine search for a synthesis of values. If it is merely a discussion in which various actors try to persuade others to adopt their particular beliefs, the discussion will never reach its goal: a set of globally shared values to guide global decision making. Finally, the discussion should have a sense of urgency. It should be action-oriented. An inclusive and genuine character and the capacity to act as a motivation for action; these are the essential requirements of any global discussion.

## 4 A DESCRIPTION OF THE "PREFERABLE" WORLD

For the sake of clarity and to gain a better idea of the subject of this study, a tentative list is provided of global values, based solely on an examination of the philosophical discourse (4.2). This is followed by some general remarks about the enduring nature of these values (4.3), and about the possibility of progress in our thinking about values (4.4). First, a few words will be devoted to the source of inspiration for these values (4.1).

---

[135] Antonio Cassese, *International law* (2nd ed, 2005), Preface.

## 4.1 Perceived shortages as the primary source of global values

According to the definition used in this study, a global value is a belief that a specific state of the world, which is possible, is preferable to an opposite state of the world. Therefore values are attempts to distinguish an ideal world from an opposite, less ideal, world. To describe the ideal world, it is necessary to have a good sense of what it is that is lacking in the present world. Only then is it possible to imagine a better, or "preferable," alternative.

This exercise is motivated by an urgent sense of what is lacking, a sense that the state of the world could – and should be – better than it is now.[136] In order to define what is lacking in our world most clearly, the priority is to listen to those who directly experience this, because they are in the best position to define it.[137]

It is only possible to improve the actual state of the world by first defining exactly what is lacking.[138] It is much easier to reach universal agreement on what is lacking than on the more positive formulation of what the alternative ought to be.[139] The easiest way to find global values is to compare the current state of the world, focusing on what can be considered to be its major problems, with a world in which all these major problems have been solved – to the extent that this is possible. Kluckhohn and Strodtbeck noted that there is a limited variation in value systems because "there is a limited number of common human problems for which all peoples at all times must find some solution."[140] Friedrich von Weizsäcker made the same point. He wrote that

> The more [values] indicate the absence of an evil, the clearer they become. In wartime the desire for peace, in hunger the desire of satiation, under foreign domination the will to emancipation – all these are immediately comprehensible.[141]

Tag referred to Moore's list of social causes of all human misery: the ravages of war, poverty, hunger and disease, injustice and oppression, and persecution for holding dissident beliefs. This list provides a fruitful basis for a list of values, because it is difficult – though not impossible - to find a human being who does not

---

[136] See also Bruno Simma, "From Bilateralism to Community Interest" (1994), p. 235.

[137] This includes "listening to the voices of the oppressed." See Richard A. Falk, Samuel S. Kim & Saul H. Mendlovitz, "Voices of the Oppressed" (1982), p. 13.

[138] For such a problem-related approach to values, see Hilary Putnam, *The Collapse of the Fact/Value Dichotomy and Other Essays* (2002).

[139] See also Martti Koskenniemi, *The Gentle Civilizer of Nations* (2001), pp. 504-505.

[140] Florence Kluckhohn & Fred Strodtbeck, *Variations in Value Orientations* (1961).

[141] Carl-Friedrich von Weizsäcker, "A Sceptical Contribution" (1975), pp. 113-114. See also Saul Mendlovitz, *On the Creation of a Just World Order* (1975), p. xii-xiii.

believe that these are the sources of human misery that need to be urgently eradicated, to the extent that this is possible.[142]

At the same time, a certain state of the world can only be described as being "non-ideal" because it is possible to imagine what the ideal is. If one cannot imagine a peaceful world, then war cannot be considered an evil. Therefore an assessment of the major problems in this world is only half of the job. What is crucial is the capacity to imagine a better alternative. But one must start somewhere, and the best strategy is to start with a perceived lack, a vivid example of human misery, and continue by thinking of alternatives, adding details along the way. Many people respond emotionally when they are exposed to suffering and misery. This is the case even when the misery occurs in distant lands, and is only seen on television or read about in newspapers. These gut reactions are a good starting point for a positive quest for values.[143]

To summarize what has been said so far, reference is made to the work of Beres. He described the first part of the value finding process as follows:

> After experiencing the realization that this [i.e. the actual world] is not "the best of all possible worlds," scholars must begin to probe underneath their judgment. This brings them to specific values. Self-consciously or otherwise, these values spark the initial feeling of dissatisfaction. Without them, there can be no criteria by which to assess the adequacy of the extant system.[144]

How do we proceed when the world's most pressing problems have been exposed and an intuitive alternative is imagined? If a world at war is generally perceived not to be the best possible world, and if there is a universal desire for a peaceful world, how can this lead to a definition of peace in more positive terms, rather than simply as "a world without war"? How can this serve as the inspiration for global strategies to implement this global value of peace in global politics and law-making?

As all human beings are used to looking at the world from a particular perspective, finding a positive formulation of global values requires a rather artificial way of looking at the world. It is necessary to look at the world like the astronaut who literally sees the earth as a "global village". Most people cannot fly into space, and therefore need to use their imagination before they can adopt such a

---

[142] Harry Targ, "Constructing Models of Presents, Futures, and Transitions" (1975), pp. 132-133. Reference is made to Barrington Moore, *Reflections on the Causes of Human Misery* (1973), p. 2. In this essay the argument is made that it is impossible to achieve universal agreement on a definition of happiness, but we can agree on what constitutes unhappiness. Falk refers to this essay approvingly in a footnote on p. 30 of Richard A. Falk, *A Study of Future Worlds* (1975).

[143] The term "gut reactions" was taken from Daphna Oyserman, "Values : Psychological Perspectives" (2004), p. 16150.

[144] Louis Beres, "Reordering the Planet" (1975), p. 52.

global point of view. This can be called a "philosophical enterprise". Walzer described this enterprise with the help of a beautiful metaphor:

> One way to begin the philosophical enterprise – perhaps the original way – is to walk out of the cave, leave the city, climb the mountain, fashion for oneself (what can never be fashioned for ordinary men and women) an objective and universal standpoint. Then one describes the terrain of everyday life from far away, so that it loses its particular contours and takes on a different shape.[145]

Only then is it possible to find global solutions to global problems, *i.e.* to find ways to bring the real world closer to the ideal world. However, as no global culture exists yet, Walzer's "shape" is an abstraction, and therefore different from the way one is used to looking at more local forms of coexistence and cooperation.

Walzer wrote: "Our common humanity will never make us members of a single universal tribe" and "the crucial commonality of the human race is particularism: we participate, all of us, in thick cultures that are our own."[146] This explains why people often have a tendency to use the way in which problems are solved in their own community to solve global problems. It also explains why people compare the institutional configuration of the international order with the constitutional order of their own State, even though the world will probably never be transformed into a State-like structure. But there is another way. When people from various local communities gather together frequently to discuss global problems and come up with global solutions, and such gatherings become institutionalized, a new, global culture can emerge slowly but surely, with a truly global perspective.[147] This is the basis of the global ethic, and of the list of global norms arising from that ethic.

## 4.2 A list of global values

The World Order Models Project (WOMP) drew up a list of the major problems confronting the world, which were used to produce a list of global values, or "world order values" as they were termed by that project. The concept of "world order" is based on Bull's definition of that term:

---

[145] Michael Walzer, *Spheres of Justice* (1983), p. xiv. Walzer does not wish to adopt such a viewpoint, since he immediately adds: "But I mean to stand in the cave, in the city, on the ground."
[146] Michael Walzer, *Thick and Thin: Moral Argument at Home and Abroad* (1994), p. 83.
[147] See also Philip Quincy Wright, *The Study of International Relations* (1955), pp. 445-448. According to Walzer, we are not at this stage yet. In 1994, Walzer wrote that "[global] encounters are not – not now, at least – sufficiently sustained to produce a thick morality [of their own]. Minimalism leaves room for thickness elsewhere; indeed, it presupposes thickness elsewhere." Michael Walzer, *Thick and Thin: Moral Argument at Home and Abroad* (1994), p. 19.

The order which men look for in social life is not any pattern or regularity in the relations of human individuals or groups, but a pattern that leads to a particular result, an arrangement of social life such that it promotes certain goals or values.[148]

The WOMP project then went on to look for these values. Mendlovitz, the Director of WOMP, explained the approach of the project as follows:

We were able to agree that humankind faced five major problems: war, poverty, social injustice, environmental decay and alienation. We saw these as social problems because we had values  - peace, economic well-being, social justice, ecological stability and positive identity – which no matter how vaguely operationalized, we knew were not being realized in the real world. Our task then was to develop an analytic frame of reference that would provide us analytical tools for coming to grips with these problems so as to realize our values, which are termed world order values.[149]

Like Bull, the WOMP authors defined the concept of "world order" in terms of values, *i.e.* the values listed above.[150] Another book in the WOMP series by Falk contains the most detailed list and description of the WOMP-values. This list includes four of the five values mentioned in the quotation above; the value of positive identity was not on Falk's list. The list is as follows:

The minimization of large-scale collective violence (calls for ending interstate war, nuclear deterrence and calls for disarmament);

The maximization of social and economic well-being (calls for the general improvement of the quality of life, above all, the elimination of poverty);

The realization of fundamental human rights and conditions of political justice (calls for the realization of individual and group dignity, and therefore including both the protection of human rights and group rights such as the elimination of colonial regimes);

The maintenance and rehabilitation of ecological quality in terms of pollution and resources (embraces both the containment of pollution and the conservation of resources for future generations).[151]

---

[148] Hedley Bull, *The Anarchical Society* (1977), p. 4.
[149] Saul Mendlovitz, *On the Creation of a Just World Order* (1975), pp. xii-xiii. See also Saul Mendlovitz & Thomas Weiss, "The Study of Peace and Justice: Toward a Framework for Global Discussion" (1975), p. 150.
[150] See also Saul Mendlovitz & Thomas Weiss, "The Study of Peace and Justice" (1975), p. 157.
[151] Richard A. Falk, *A Study of Future Worlds* (1975), pp. 11-30.

The list is based on "the most severe inadequacies in the present world order system: war, poverty, oppression, and ecological decay."[152] Although not all the participants in the project immediately agreed with the list of values, and although there was at times a slight variation in the list,[153] it has not changed fundamentally in the many books published by the project over the course of three decades.[154]

Apart from the WOMP project, reference can also be made to lists of global values proposed by various individual scholars. Miller's list, for example, included minimizing cases in which violence is resorted to, the search for economic well-being, the enhancement of human dignity and respect for the environment.[155] White's list included peace and security, justice and law, human rights, self-determination and democracy, the environment, and economic and social well-being.[156] McDougal and Lasswell's list contained the following values: security, the allocation of wealth, respect for human dignity in terms of the articulation and implementation of human rights, enlightenment by increasing and sharing scientific and technological skills and know-how, well-being by maintaining optimum standards of safety, health and comfort, rectitude, and affection in the form of global solidarity.[157] Anne-Marie Slaughter listed greater peace and prosperity for all peoples, improvement of their stewardship of the earth and the achievement of minimal standards of human dignity.[158]

It is a problem to rely too much on lists of global values drawn up by individuals, even though the scholars referred to above all based their lists on thorough - and in some cases brilliant – reflection and research. Some scholars admitted that their list of values was only one of many possible end-states, based on preferences that were influenced by their own particular environment, culture and political preferences. For example, in his *Global Covenant*, David Held proposed a

---

[152] *Idem*, p. 30.

[153] Von Weizsäcker refers to "peace, freedom, social justice, and prosperity" as WOMP values. See Carl-Friedrich von Weizsäcker, "A Sceptical Contribution" (1975), p. 111. Sakamoto refers to ecological balance, economic well-being, communication development, human development, and peaceful change. See Yoshikazu Sakamoto, "Toward Global Identity" (1975), pp. 191-192. Falk refers to peace, economic well-being, environmental quality, and social and political justice. See Richard A. Falk, "Toward a New World Order" (1975), p. 257. Johansen refers to "peace without national military arsenals", "economic well-being for all inhabitants on the earth ", "universal human rights and social justice", and "ecological balance". See Roben Johansen, "The Elusiveness of a Humane World Community" (1982), p. 202.

[154] Especially in the last series, called *Studies on a Just World Order*, this list of values determines the skeleton of all the books in the series. See Richard A. Falk, Samuel S. Kim & Saul H. Mendlovitz (editors), *Toward a Just World Order* (vol. 1, 1982), Falk, Friedrich Kratchowil & Mendlovitz (editors), *International law* (vol. 2, 1985), and Falk, Kim, Donals McNemar & Mendlovitz, *The United Nations and a Just World Order* (vol. 3, 1991).

[155] Lynn H. Miller, *Global Order* (1990).

[156] Nigel D. White, *The United Nations system* (2002).

[157] See, *e.g.*, Myres McDougal, *Studies in World Public Order* (1987), pp. 17-19 and pp. 32-36.

[158] Anne-Marie Slaughter, *A New World Order* (2004), p. 15.

list of global values explicitly based on social democracy: the rule of law, political equality, democratic politics, social justice, social solidarity and economic efficiency.[159] As a social-democratic model may not be universally shared, other promoters of global values preferred to express themselves in more general terms, in the hope that their list would be considered to be politically neutral. For example, in one of his speeches on foreign policy, Tony Blair spoke about the need for the globalization of the economy to be accompanied by a globalization of politics, which was a "common global policy based on common values."[160] Even though he suggested that his values were "the values universally accepted across all nations, faiths and races, though not by all elements within them," Blair's choice of global values, and the absence of others, was not politically neutral. His values together defined a body of *freedom values*, values strongly inspired by the ideas of the enlightenment: the focus was on liberty, democracy, tolerance and justice.[161]

Certain manifestos or declarations can also be mentioned. According to Küng, the scholar behind the Global Ethic, this ethic provided "a minimal consensus relating to binding values, irrevocable standards and moral attitudes, which can be affirmed by all religions despite their "dogmatic" differences and should also be supported by non-believers."[162] As his ethic met these demands for universality, it could be seen as a "consensus of values [which] will be a decisive contribution to overcome the crisis of orientation which has become a real problem worldwide."[163]

The *Humanist Manifesto* is like a secular version of Küng's global ethic. It could be described as a minimal consensus, affirmed by all non-religious people, which should also be supported by believers. The *Humanist Manifesto II* (1973), stated that "[w]e will survive and prosper only in a world of shared humane values,"[164] these values being, first of all, the "preciousness and dignity of the individual person,"[165] "renounc[ing] the resort to violence and force as a method of solving international disputes,"[166] the "cultivation and conservation of nature,"[167]

---

[159] David Held, *Global Covenant* (2004), p. 16.

[160] Tony Blair, "Clash about Civilizations" (2006). He said: "The defining characteristic of today's world is its interdependence; that whereas the economics of globalization are well matured, the politics of globalization are not; and that unless we articulate a common global policy based on common values, we risk chaos threatening our stability, economic and political, through letting extremism, conflict or injustice go unchecked."

[161] Tony Blair, "PM's foreign policy speech - third in a series of three" (2006). For a critical response by an Islamic scholar, see Mohd Kamal Hassan's lecture in Hans Küng, *Towards a Common Civilization: Public Lectures by Hans Kueng and Mohd Kamal Hassan* (1997), pp. 27-29.

[162] *Idem*, p. 7. See also Hans Küng, *Declaration toward a Global Ethic* (1993). The term "non-believers" sounds rather odd.

[163] Idem.

[164] *Humanist Manifesto II* (1973), "In Closing".

[165] *Idem*, 5th principle.

[166] *Idem*, 13th principle,

and the reduction of "extreme disproportions in wealth, income, and economic growth [...] on a worldwide basis."[168]

It is also possible to refer to global surveys, which ask a representative part of the world's population about their list of global values.[169] It should be noted that no such survey has ever been conducted. Neither the Global Values Survey, nor any other survey, has ever asked the citizens of the world for a list of global values that guide global affairs. Some findings may be indirectly relevant. For example, 68% of the world population strongly agreed that their government should reduce environmental pollution, and 66% would use part of their income for the protection of the environment (56% would like to see an increase in taxes to prevent environmental pollution).[170] This suggests that the attainment of an ecological balance is a globally shared concern. 57% believed that more economic aid should be given to poorer countries, which indicates a call for social justice.[171]

These are just some of the examples of possible sources of global values. The similarities between all the lists is striking. In any case, the list of global values presented in this study is not based on a common denominator of all the lists of values referred to in the literature, but on United Nations resolutions and documents.

The suggested list of global values is the following: peace and security, social progress and sustainable development, human dignity, and the self-determination of peoples.[172] This list of values is based on the work of the United Nations, whose Charter identified these values as constituting the fundamental basis

---

[167] *Idem*, 14th principle.

[168] *Idem*, 15th principle. Other values relate to the use of technology and communication (16th and 17th principle).

[169] Robinson has an interesting description of what the reader of a book on human values goes through. First of all, the reader discovers he already had his own list of values, and these values are simply reaffirmed by the philosopher. However, exactly because no such reader truly has a mind that resembles a *tabula rasa*, it is unavoidable that at some point the reader disagrees with what he reads. As this happens, "[f]rom being an earnest pupil [the reader] is liable to become an infuriated teacher" (P. 11, Richard Robinson, *An Atheist's Values* (1964)). And the reader then "comes to see that what he really wanted from philosophers was not that they should lead him, but that they should lead others to adopt his convictions" (*idem*). See also Will Kymlicka, "Introduction: The Globalization of Ethics" (2007), p. 2.

[170] See B001, B002, and B003 (Tables), in Ronald Inglehart, *Human Beliefs and Values* (2004).

[171] *Idem*, E129 (Table).

[172] For the sake of coherence in this list of values, it might be better to replace "sustainable development" with "the well-being and dignity of the planet". Then you would have the well-being and dignity of the individual, the well-being and dignity of the community (State), and the well-being and dignity of the planet. Such an approach is often suggested, for example, in the Earth Charter - see Mikhail Gorbachev, "The Third Pillar of Sustainable Development" (2005) - or in the Global Ethic – see Hans Küng, *Declaration toward a Global Ethic*, declaration adopted at the Parliament of the World's Religions, Chicago 1993. However, the "well-being of the planet" is generally viewed as valuable from a human-centered perspective: it is valuable as our home, as our source for food and natural resources. The (philosophical) debate on our relationship with the planet is far from over.

49

of all its work. [173] The list is therefore not necessarily complete, in the sense that other potential candidates, such as democracy, the rule of law, and the preservation of the global commons, to name but a few suggestions, cannot be qualified at all as such. It all depends on one's definition of "value," and on one's focus. In this study, the focus of the United Nations, guided by its constitutive Charter, has been followed.

The next chapter argues that the United Nations provides a suitable forum for the kind of global conversation about values that was referred to above. The following chapters show that the outcome of that global discussion is a list of global values, *i.e.* a set of enduring, globally shared beliefs that a specific state of the world, which is possible, is socially preferable, from the perspective of the life of all human beings, to an opposite state of the world. It is argued that a world at peace, in which respect for human dignity and the self-determination of peoples is guaranteed, and in which the needs of the present generation are satisfied without compromising the ability of future generations to meet their own needs, is an ideal – but possible – world.

## 4.3 The evolution of global values

Global values were referred to in the definition as "enduring" beliefs. This referred both to the enduring character of values, and to their changing character. The list of global values is not static, in the sense that a particular list of values has guided global affairs since the beginning of time, and will do so until the end of time. In fact, the opposite is true. Global values evolve over time.[174] Some behaviour which is now generally considered to be a violation of the moral code was very common, and was openly defended, only a few decades ago.[175] As Florini pointed out in her article on the evolution of international norms, the changes have sometimes been stunning:

---

[173] The WOMP project looked extensively at the work of the United Nations Organization, but it was very much future oriented. The formulation of its "world order values" is not based on opinions expressed in authoritative documents of the past, such as UN resolutions. WOMP does not have philosophers as participants to the project, and it is difficult to find a chapter, in all of the WOMP-literature, discussing the concept of "value". This was also noted by Elisabeth Gerle in her study, *In Search of a Global Ethics: Theological, Political, and Feminist Perspectives based on a Critical Analysis of JPIC and WOMP* (1995), see especially p. 131. JPIC stands for Justice, Peace and Integrity of Creation; this is a religion-based project.

[174] See also Aligarh Muslim University, *Man, Reality, and Values* (1964), p. 52.

[175] In 1950, one of the colonial powers (Belgium) defended colonialism at the United Nations General Assembly as a "systematic action taken by an advanced people with a view to helping the backward indigenous populations in their efforts towards political, economic, social and cultural progress." A/PV.392 (General Assembly plenary meeting of 10 November, 1950). The Belgian representative explained to the General Assembly what his country was doing in the Congo at that time.

Slavery, common for millennia, has virtually disappeared. Colonialism has given way to agreement on the right of self-determination. Aggression across recognized national borders, once a standard tool of state policy, now meets with international condemnation.[176]

One could go on: *sustainable* development, the equality of men and women, democratic government... these are all relatively modern value-based ideas, now considered to be self-evident. How can these drastic changes be explained? One way would be to refer to the fact that the balance of power has changed, *i.e.* the powerless and the oppressed have become powerful and have claimed their dignity, as part of an effort to enhance their power and security in international relations.[177] Even though the research into the balance of power goes a long way to explain changes in the discourse on global values, it does not provide the full answer to the question of why and how global values evolve. For example, can the change from colonialism to the self-determination of peoples be explained solely in terms of shifts in military and economic power? Many people do not think it can.[178] It is clear that a change in the hearts and minds of the powerful also played a role. Some scholars referred to the debate itself as the primary reason for change, even change in the real world.[179] Florini provided an unorthodox theory by comparing the evolution in international relations, guided by norms, with the biological form of evolution, guided by genes.[180] By describing in detail *how* global values have evolved over time in the framework of the United Nations, this study also aims to give an implicit answer to the question *why* such an evolution is possible.[181]

---

[176] Ann Florini, "The Evolution of International Norms" (1996), p. 363. See also Lynn H. Miller, *Global Order* (1990), pp. 12-13, who remarks, in relation to slavery, that "what had been accepted by earlier generations as an economic necessity and therefore excluded from the moral agenda became unthinkable to their descendants" (p. 13).

[177] This focus in power and the perpetual search for security as determinative of how ideas and policies change is typical of the (neo)realist school. See Hans J. Morgenthau, *Politics among Nations: The Struggle for Power and Peace* (1948); and Kenneth Waltz, *Theory of International Politics* (1979).

[178] See James Crawford, *Argument and Change in World Politics: Ethics, Decolonization, and Humanitarian Intervention* (2002).

[179] According to the constructivists, a look at shifts in the balance of power does not explain all changes in global values and norms, and thus one must look beyond power, to the argumentative discourse, and how ideas, norms and values determine state behavior. See, *e.g.*, Alexander Wendt, *Social Theory of International Politics* (1999), who goes as far as to conclude that "it is through ideas that states ultimately relate to one another", and that "these ideas help define who and what states are." (p. 372)

[180] Ann Florini, "The Evolution of International Norms" (1996). This theory is somewhat more subtle than the "survival of the fittest."

[181] See Part II of this study.

## 4.4. Global values and the belief in progress

Related to the issue of evolving values is the idea of progress. Although this is not always stated explicitly, one cannot help thinking, for example, when the prohibition of slavery is mentioned or the process of decolonization, that the world's ideas about values and international relations in general are not just *evolving*, but are *progressing* towards the ideal. We are making progress not only in the realization of our values, but also in our thinking about values. This belief in progress is very strong in the United Nations. For example, at a world conference on racism organized in 2001, all States acknowledged that "slavery and the slave trade are a crime against humanity and should always have been so."[182] Nowadays, there are very few people who would argue otherwise. It is now generally believed that our ancestors behaved in ways that cannot be justified and should be condemned retrospectively. This not only applies to slavery. It also applies to *apartheid* and genocide. [183] History is generally viewed with a sense of embarrassment. In the study of history, there is a tendency to wonder every now and again, how our forefathers could have committed such terrible acts.

Some philosophers have recently warned against this way of thinking. One of the most important is John Gray. He reminded us that we should not think that we are slowly going through a checklist of things to do to improve the world (such as abolishing slavery, prohibiting torture, prohibiting war, etc.), and that what is removed from the list will never reappear. He warned us that "[t]he gains that have been achieved in ethics and politics are not cumulative" and that "what has been gained can also be lost, and over time surely will be."[184] Therefore progress is an illusion, and like all illusions, we turn to it, not to understand the way the world works, but to give our own life meaning. In short: to write about global values as a story of progress, and to promote the realization of global values in the illusory belief that it is a way of perfecting the world, is essentially a way to give meaning to one's own life by giving one's own work a mythical or even missionary character.[185] The belief in progress and the realization of the human potential "in the here and now" then replace religious beliefs.[186]

---

[182] Declaration, included in the *Report of the World Conference against Racism, Racial Discrimination, Xenophobia and Related Intolerance*, held in Durban (South Africa), between 31 August and 8 September 2001. UNDoc. A/CONF.189/12, para. 13.

[183] For *apartheid* and genocide, see *idem*, para. 15.

[184] John N. Gray, *Heresies: Against Progress and Other Illusions* (2004), p. 3.

[185] *Idem*, pp. 4-5.

[186] For example, in the *Humanist Manifesto* I of 1933, we can read that "Religious Humanism considers the complete realization of human personality to be the end of man's life and seeks its development and fulfillment in the here and now."

Such belief in progress is naïve.[187] This is not only because new evils continuously emerge, but also because values change, and what is generally believed to be a better world now will not automatically be considered as such by the next generation. A review of Gray's book in the British newspaper *The Guardian* started with the following description of a cartoon:

> [One can see] a field of sheep all grazing peacefully, all, that is, save one wise ovine, who has lifted its head in appalled astonishment to cry out: "Wait! This is grass - this is grass we're eating!"[188]

One can easily picture the next angry young man to be the ovine (according to the reviewer, Gray is the ovine), calling for change at a time when it is generally believed that all shared values have been realized. Carl-Friedrich von Weizsäcker made a similar point when he remarked that "when after frightful periods of war a generation, with the help of technology, has achieved a situation that it conceives to be peaceful, prosperous, with freedom and some degree of justice, the next generation finds in it manipulation instead of freedom, injustice, hunger, and war." This leads the author to conclude that the "[b]attle is joined not over the verbally formulated values themselves, not really even over their order of priorities, but over their meaning and their content."[189] Not only does reality continue to evolve, but the content of the world's values evolve with it. And this will never end. Values are like the carrot on a stick, always placed a few centimetres in front of the donkey's nose. The donkey will forever chase the carrot, and this will make it move forward. But the donkey will never manage to grab and eat it.

## 5 RESPONSIBILITY FOR THE REALIZATION OF GLOBAL VALUES

Although this study focuses on defining global values, questions relating to the responsibility for realizing these values cannot simply be dismissed. After all, as noted above, the definition of values is not an academic exercise. It is intended to be action-motivated. It is meant to allocate responsibilities, and to oblige relevant actors to act.

---

[187] The first *Humanist Manifesto* was written in 1933, just before the Second World War. Clearly this has led the humanist movement to become more realistic. In 1973, a new Manifesto (*Humanist Manifesto* II) was written, with a preface in which it noted that "[e]vents since then [*i.e.* since the adoption of the Humanist Manifesto in 1933] make that earlier statement seem far too optimistic."

[188] John Banville, "Beyond dentistry" (2004). In this new Manifesto, one still finds the same idea, *i.e.* that we must strive for a good life for all, here and now.

[189] Carl-Friedrich von Weizsäcker, "A Sceptical Contribution" (1975), pp. 113-114.

## 5.1 Who is responsible for promoting and safeguarding global values?

The question which has to be addressed at the end of this first chapter is: who is responsible for promoting and safeguarding global values? Participating in the process of defining values is – or should be – a responsibility for realizing these values, and an accountability towards those on whose behalf and in whose interest this is done.[190] It is partly for these reasons that it is not helpful to include values that are impossible to attain. For example, it makes no sense to derive from a list of values norms such as "there shall be no earthquakes," or "human beings must not be allowed to die at all." Human beings cannot prevent earthquakes entirely and cannot avoid death.[191]

The simple answer to the question of responsibility for the realization of global values is that the global community, however constituted, is responsible. This does not mean that everybody is responsible for the welfare of everybody else. People are first of all responsible for their own welfare, for the welfare of their own family, community, and so on. It was Nagel who gave this argument a sound philosophical basis. Nagel distinguished two moral standpoints:

From an *impersonal* standpoint, all lives matter equally; this means those lives that are immediately threatened must be immediately saved, and everybody has an immediate obligation to do so. Everybody always has the responsibility to save the lives of all his or her fellow human beings whenever these lives are endangered.

From a *personal* standpoint, one's own life is more important than anyone else's life. This is true for every human being. People should understand and respect that not only they themselves, but others too, prefer their own interests over those of others, and that they are morally entitled to do so. [192]

These two standpoints are equally valid, and, even though they seem contradictory, they must be adopted simultaneously. The easiest way to avoid conflicting obligations from arising each and every day is to delegate the duties arising from the impersonal standpoint to the collective, so that the individual can focus on the personal standpoint. This means that the collective must be given the resources to do so. At the national level, individuals delegate certain duties (and certain resources) to their State. In this way, the State can use the individual's resources to care for all other citizens residing within that State, on that individual's behalf. In the world as it is constituted today, it is clear that the main responsibility for

---

[190] See also Richard A. Falk, *On Humane Governance* (1995), pp. 246-247. Falk sees (criminal) accountability of individuals as one of ten key dimensions of humane governance.

[191] On the example of the earthquake, Aligarh Muslim University, *Man, Reality, and Values* (1964), p. 57.

[192] Thomas Nagel, *Equality and Partiality* (1991). In Chapter 2 he focuses on the national level.

realizing global values lies with States. After all, that is the way in which the world order is constituted. It is a world of States, acting in international affairs on behalf of their own populations, together acting on behalf of all the world's citizens. Although the literature rightly recognizes a shift in responsibility away from the State to a plurality of actors, it generally also emphasizes the central role of the State.[193] One can imagine that in the future, States will delegate some of the global duties (and resources) to international organizations, such as the United Nations. However, that has not happened yet to any great extent. This also explains why the United Nations can be much more accurately characterized as a global deliberative organization, rather than as a global executive.

Despite the central role of the State, and despite the delegation of responsibilities from the individual to the State, individuals will always continue to have some responsibilities towards all other citizens themselves.[194] These responsibilities include taking a critical look at what the State is doing on their behalf and in their name. Individuals must find alternative ways of fulfilling their responsibilities towards all the world's citizens, if the State does not do so to a sufficient extent,[195] or if it makes the wrong choices.[196]

## 5.2 Global values as the driving force for global governance

A global value system helps global policy makers choose between alternative goals. A clear choice will in turn help to resolve conflicts and facilitate global decision making.[197] Global values "help us to define the state of the world, to evaluate the

---

[193] The project became more and more modest in its suggestions for change as time moved on. First, the project based itself on the rather grandiose suggestions for constitutional change to be found in Grenville Clark & Louis Sohn, *World peace through world law* (1958), which aimed basically to vigorously revise the UN Charter so as to turn the United Nations into a world government. Then more modest suggestions were made in the second series of "preferred worlds". In the final series, instead of suggesting grand designs suggested by the elite, it was decided to focus instead on the voices of the oppressed, and to help them achieve modest changes from below.

[194] See Declaration of Human Duties and Responsibilities, adopted by a High Level Group chaired by Richard J. Goldstone under the auspices of the city of Valencia and UNESCO, 1999.

[195] For example, the rich nations of the world promised to spend 0.7 per cent of their gross domestic product (GDP) for official development assistance (see, *e.g.*, UN General Assembly Resolution 1524(XV) of 15 December 1960; resolution 2626(XXV) of 24 October 1970, and the 2005 World Summit Outcome Document, para. 23), but only five countries complied so far: Denmark (0.84%), Luxembourg (0.81%), Netherlands (0.80%), Norway (0.92%), and Sweden (0.79%).

[196] Perhaps the State does not make the same choices as the individual would make. See *e.g.* Thomas Pogge, "Priorities of Global Justice" (2003). On the decision to bomb Kosovo (by NATO in 1999) and not alleviate millions of people from poverty, Pogge wonders: "If it makes sense to spend billions and to endanger thousands of lives in order to rescue a million people from Serb oppression, would it not make more sense to spend similar sums, without endangering any lives, on leading many millions out of life-threatening poverty?"

[197] See Milton Rokeach, *The Nature of Human Values* (1973), p. 14.

meaning of the world so defined, to explain the human condition, and to prescribe a correct line of action."[198]

As global values are based on ideas of what constitutes a better world from the perspective of all the world's citizens, they are above all about the humanization of global affairs. They are about the desire to actively build a future based on human needs. It is a natural development that whenever people interact frequently and as equals, a body of values to humanize this interaction emerges. For example, it is striking that with the increasing (economic) integration of Europe came the desire to formulate and formalize a list of European values that are in a sense distilled from various cultures and traditions within Europe.[199] The idea is not to wipe out the cultural differences that exist in Europe, but to value both Europe's differences and common characteristics at the same time, and to humanize the European economy by injecting some common values into it. The slogan was: "Europe united in diversity". This could be the global slogan too.[200]

Since it is generally believed that the global politics of the past have not been dominated by a search for a reasoned consensus, but rather by bargaining for compromises to secure particular interests, a former Dutch Minister for Development Cooperation summarized this suggested change in global policy (from bargaining on the basis of self-interest to a reasoned consensus on global values) in an attractive slogan: "less *laissez-faire* and more globalization with a human face."[201] As the next chapter shows, the United Nations could provide some

---

[198] Samuel S. Kim, *The Quest for a Just World Order* (1984), p. 22.

[199] Of this European abstraction exercise, Bernard-Henri Levy said: "European nations are bound within by history, by language, by culture, sometimes by skin color. The idea of Europe is to lift above all of that, to abstract from all the qualities that caused hate and war. It is very similar to the American identity, whose achievement is to unify all the disparate parts: people with different backgrounds, ideas, races and religions." See Bernard-Henri Levy, ""Europe Has Lost Confidence" (2007).

[200] In the Berlin Declaration of 2007, one can read both that "we are enriched by open borders and a lively variety of languages, cultures and regions", and that "European unification has made peace and prosperity possible [and] it has brought about a sense of community and overcome differences." *Declaration on the occasion of the fiftieth anniversary of the signature of the Treaties of Rome*, adopted by EU leaders in Berlin, on the 25 March 2007.

[201] Speech by Bert Koenders, at the Society for International Development's 50th Anniversary International Congress on 5 July 2007 in The Hague, Netherlands. See also, Willem van Genugten, Kees Homan, Nico Schrijver & Paul de Waart, *The United Nations of the Future: Globalization with a Human Face* (2006).

minimal formal leadership in this process,[202] not as a world government, but as a focal point in a process generally referred to as global governance.[203]

# 6 CONCLUSION

A definition of global value was sought in the academic literature of various disciplines, including philosophy, sociology and psychology. A suitable definition was found, which reflected the hypotheses on which this study is based. Global values were defined as a set of enduring, globally shared beliefs that a specific state of the world, which is possible, is socially preferable, from the perspective of the life of all human beings, to an opposite state of the world. This was based on a definition proposed by Rokeach, a social psychologist. As Rokeach used the definition in a different context, some modifications were proposed. These modifications led to some reflections on the sort of value we had in mind. Subsequently various elements of this definition were examined more closely. An attempt was made to make the idea that there is a global community which shares a limited set of beliefs at least intuitively plausible, and that the only way to "discover" such beliefs was through a discussion which was as inclusive as possible, in the sense that it involved the entire international community.

The following list of values was proposed: human dignity, the self-determination of peoples, peace and security, and social progress and development. It was explained that this list of values was mainly a result of a universally felt "lack of something" *i.e.* an urgent sense that there was something wrong with the world we actually live in. Attempts to define values are ways to imagine improvements of the present world conditions. This approach to the list of values also allows for it to constantly evolve. It could even be argued that the list of values serves to motivate the world to continuously "improve" itself, and that it therefore helps the world to continuously progress. Responsibility for implementing these ideas of progress in the actual world cannot be assigned to the world as a whole, because the world is without arms and legs. Therefore the responsibility must be distributed evenly over all the participants.

---

[202] In determining what was required to keep the world together, the Commission on Global Governance called for two things: (1) "the broad acceptance of a global civic ethic to guide action within the global neighbourhood," and (2) "courageous leadership infused with that ethic at all levels of society." The Commission added that "without a global ethic, the frictions and tensions of living in the global neighbourhood will multiply; without leadership, even the best- designed institutions and strategies will fail." Commission on Global Governance, *Our Global Neighborhood* (1995), p. 47.

[203] Rosenau very clearly explained the difference between a global government and global governance: "Government suggests activities that are backed by formal authority, by police powers to insure the implementation of duly constituted policies, whereas governance refers to activities backed by shared goals that may or may not derive from legal and formally prescribed responsibilities and that do not necessarily rely on police powers to overcome defiance and attain compliance." James N. Rosenau, "Governance, Order, and Change in World Politics" (1992), p. 4.

This chapter had a modest aim: the introduction of a few ideas and concepts, ensuring that they could be intuitively grasped and could be used in the rest of this study. Many of the topics addressed in general terms in this chapter resurface in the chapters on the United Nations.

# UNITED NATIONS DECISION MAKING AS VALUE-BASED DECISION MAKING

## 1 INTRODUCTION

Global values have been described as globally shared beliefs about a better world. Beliefs are not facts. Beliefs exist only in the world of ideas, and therefore a small group of scientists researching the state of the world and looking for improvements cannot simply draw up a list of global values. Global values can only be discovered through a global discussion which is sufficiently inclusive, in the sense that the entire global community participates in some way. The participants should not all focus on safeguarding their own particular interests, but rather on defining and safeguarding the global interest, defined in terms of globally shared values. The discussion should also be action-oriented. It should inspire those responsible for action to act.

Does the United Nations, and more in particular the UN General Assembly, provide a forum for this global discussion? That is the central question of this chapter. It reveals how the key features of value-based decision making, outlined in rather abstract terms in the previous chapter, have been fleshed out in the framework of the United Nations. The drafting process of the UN Charter (2) and the subsequent continuation of the decision-making process by the General Assembly (3) are analysed and the way in which United Nations allocates the responsibility for realizing the pledges made in this global discussion is examined (4).

## 2 THE UNITED NATIONS CHARTER: THE RESULT OF GLOBAL DISCUSSION

### 2.1 Introduction

There was a general sense among the 1,500 participants at the San Francisco Conference that history was being made.[1] Evatt, the leader of the Australian delegation, referred to the conference as "an unforgettable experience for those who

---

[1] For a list of names of all participants, see Delegates and Officials of the United Nations Conference on International Organization, UNCIO, vol. 1, pp. 13-54.

had the privilege of participating in it."[2] But what was so unforgettable about it? The following sections present the San Francisco Conference as a key discussion about values. The criteria for this discussion, which were outlined in the previous chapter, are applied to the Conference. These are the inclusive and genuine character of the discussion and its capacity to motivate action.

## 2.2 The drafting of the UN Charter as a global discussion

Where did the drafting of the UN Charter begin?[3] The starting point of the prehistory of the UN Charter is always rather arbitrary. Reference could be made to the drafting of the League of Nations Covenant at the end of the First World War in 1919. However, the delegates in San Francisco hardly mentioned the League.[4] The representatives of the League who were invited to San Francisco were largely ignored and went home after only one month, no more than halfway through the Conference.[5] Their dismissal had great symbolic significance. The aim in San Francisco was to build something new, not to create a successor for the League, which had failed to prevent the Second World War.

But why not go back even further? Was it a coincidence that the UN Charter was signed on the 150th anniversary of the publication of Kant's *Zum Ewigen Frieden*, which described the structure of a world federation similar to the United Nations system?[6] One could go back even further to the Stoics of Ancient Greece, who preached a kind of international community, and claim that the United Nations helped put these ancient philosophical ideas into practice. Referring to the United Nations era and the international community established by it, Tomuschat said that "what was a philosophical postulate in the past, has become a living reality, albeit with many flaws and weaknesses."[7] If Kant's ideas and the ideas of the Stoics influenced the founding fathers of the UN Charter, then this influence was only of a very general nature. Nothing indicates that the drafters of the Charter had any profound knowledge of Kant's work, let alone that they were heavily

---

[2] Herbert Vere Evatt, *The United Nations* (1948), p. 14.

[3] For a detailed history, see Ruth B. Russell, *A History of the United Nations Charter* (1958).

[4] The name of the founding father of that League, the American President Wilson, was also hardly mentioned in San Francisco. See James, "Wilson Forgotten at San Francisco" (1945). He wrote that "[e]ven though forgotten by the delegates here assembled, who can doubt that the spirit of Wilson hovers over San Francisco?"

[5] *New York Times*, "Old League" Chief Quits Conference" (1945).

[6] See Carl J. Friedrich, "The Ideology of the United Nations Charter and the Philosophy of Peace of Immanuel Kant 1795-1945" (1947).

[7] Christian Tomuschat, "International law: ensuring the survival of mankind on the eve of a new century" (1999), pp. 75.

influenced by it when they drafted the Charter.[8] On the other hand, the delegates were motivated by a cosmopolitan sentiment, *i.e.* a shared intuition that States were not isolated from each other, but lived together like sheep grazing in one and the same field.

The following documents can be considered as *immediate* precursors of the United Nations Charter:

> The Atlantic Charter of August 1941;
> The United Nations Declaration of January 1942;
> The Moscow Declaration of October 1943.[9]

The Atlantic Charter contained a set of principles subscribed to by the United Kingdom and United States of America. These principles included the duty to respect the right of all peoples to choose their own form of government, the duty to promote the access for all States, on equal terms, to trade and to the world's raw materials, and the duty to refrain from the use of force.[10]

Other States subscribed to these principles by signing the United Nations Declaration. In that declaration, the "United Nations," *i.e.* the States united in the fight against the common enemy, stated that "complete victory over their enemies [was] essential to defend life, liberty, independence and religious freedom, and to preserve human rights and justice in their own lands as well as in other lands."[11]

The Moscow Declaration, signed only by the Soviet Union, the UK, the US, and China, essentially contained a pledge to continue the "united action." For this purpose, it proposed establishing a general international organization to maintain international peace and security.[12]

The efforts of the States to coordinate their actions at the international level were motivated, more than anything else, by the Second World War.[13] Without this

---

[8] About "l'influence effective de Kant sur les négociateurs de la Charte de San Francisco" Dupuy remarks that "rien ne dit qu'ils en aient eu une connaissance approfondie." However, despite the lack of any profound knowledge of Kant's philosophy among the San Francisco delegates, Kant may nonetheless have had considerable influence on the drafting of the Charter. After all, "[l]e propre d'une grande philosophie est cependant d'influencer au-delà du cercle, toujours restreint, de ses lecteurs attentifs." Pierre-Marie Dupuy, "L'unité de l'ordre juridique international" (2002), p. 267 (footnote 493).

[9] Almost all overviews of the drafting history start with these declarations. See *e.g.*, United Nations, *Guide to the United Nations Charter* (1947). See also Yearbook of the United Nations 1946-47, pp. 1-51; and Emmanuelle Jouannet, "Les travaux préparatoires de la Charte des Nations Unies" (2005), pp. 3-5.

[10] Yearbook of the United Nations 1946-47, p. 2.

[11] *Idem*, p. 1.

[12] *Idem*, p. 3.

[13] See the Canadian report on the San Francisco Conference, where we can read that "[t]andis que le feu de la guerre brûle encore, la possibilité est donnée à cette Conférence de forger et de façonner, sur ce

war, the distrust and differences between the "United Nations," which were certainly present, would have made it impossible to come to an agreement on essentially all the fundamental problems of international relations.[14]

The declarations listed only some general principles and put forward the idea that an international organization should be established to defend at least some of these principles. They did not contain an actual plan for the post-war world that was fully worked out. Such a plan was first presented in 1943, when a draft charter for a new international organization was presented by the United Kingdom, China, the Soviet Union and the United States of America.[15] As this draft was mainly written at Dumbarton Oaks, a mansion in Washington, it is referred to as the Dumbarton Oaks proposals. The US presented these proposals as a "basis for discussion."[16] They were published and widely disseminated to allow the general public to comment on them.[17] Some non-governmental groups, and even some individuals took advantage of this opportunity.[18] Only States could *formally* submit amendment proposals.[19] Some of these State amendments were implemented by the four sponsors in the *revised* Dumbarton Oaks proposals.[20]

---

feu même, l'instrument de la sécurité mondiale." Ministère des affaires ètrangères (Canada), *Rapport sur les travaux de la conférence des Nations Unies* (1945), p. 10.

[14] This is not so say that there was no distrust in San Francisco and before. James B. Reston nicely described these suspicions among the major powers: "[t]he British fear of American 'economic imperialism' is equally as great as our [*i.e.* the American] ancient bogy that in these international deals we always get 'hornswoggled'; and the Russian fear of the capitalistic alliance is equally as real to them as the fear of the Communist bogy is to some Americans." James B. Reston, "Light on Foreign Policy Awaited," in *New York Times* of February 11, 1945.

[15] France only joined the ranks of the Big Powers in San Francisco. See James B. Reston, "France Lining up with Big Powers," in *New York Times* of April 25, 1945.

[16] See James B. Reston, "U.S. Retains Right to Alter Oaks Plan," in *New York Times* of April 7, 1945.

[17] They were published as Department of State (USA), *Dumbarton Oaks documents on international organization* (1944).

[18] For an example of an influential individual commentary, see Hans Kelsen, "The Old and the New League: The Covenant and the Dumbarton Oaks Proposals" (1945). See also some Letters to *The Times*, such as Coudert's "Hope for World Peace," and Kunstenaar's "Revised Morals Urged," which both appeared in the *New York Times* of April 22, 1945. For comments by NGO's, see James B. Reston, "Changes Offered in Oaks Proposals," in *New York Times* of April 23, 1945, and "Jewish Group Asks World Rights Bill," an article in the *New York Times* of April 30, 1945, and "Human Rights Seen Safe in Conference," an article that appeared in the *New York Times* of June 4, 1945.

[19] The Netherlands was one of the few nations to actually publish its amendment proposals. See Netherlands, *Nederland en Dumbarton Oaks*. As a consequence, the Dutch proposals were discussed extensively in the *New York Times*. See *e.g.*, James B. Reston, "Dutch Oppose Idea of Oaks Big 5 Veto," in *New York Times* of February 8, 1945, and James B. Reston, "Dutch to Ask Veto for Small Nations," in *New York Times* of April 24, 1945.

[20] For an overview of the amendments accepted by the sponsors, see James B. Reston, "Oaks Amendments Speed New Charter," in *New York Times* of May 6, 1945.

The last and most important stage in the drafting history of the United Nations Charter was the San Francisco Conference of 1945.[21] The States met and drew up the UN Charter there. No NGOs or other non-State entities were formally invited, but they did influence the drafting from the side-lines. This was a good compromise for the dilemma of including as many people as possible in the drafting process and ensuring an orderly conference, consistent with the rules of international law-making. The aim was "to give the impression that [the people of the world] could come to [the conference] yet not invite them – a difficult thing to do."[22]

Not all the States were invited. Only the "United Nations," *i.e.* States officially at war with the Axis powers, were invited to come to San Francisco.[23] This basically meant that neutral countries,[24] and the Axis nations themselves,[25] were not allowed to participate. The American continent was well represented.[26] There were also a number of delegations from Europe, both Eastern and Western Europe.[27] Europe, the old centre of international affairs, was embarrassed about the Second World War, and was not as outspoken as one might have expected it to be.[28] There were also delegations from Asia, the Middle East and Africa.[29] Poland was

---

[21] For an overview, see Grayson Kirk & Lawrence Chamberlain, "The Organization of the San Francisco Conference" (1945), and Wilhelm G. Grewe & Daniel-Erasmus Khan, "Drafting History" (2002).
[22] Minutes of Second Meeting (Executive Session) of the United States Delegation, March 23, 1945, in United States Department of State, *Foreign relations of the United States diplomatic papers* ("FRUS"), *1945. General*, Volume I, p. 150.
[23] See Yearbook of the United Nations 1946-47, p. 12.
[24] When the US told Iceland that it had to declare war in order to participate, the Prime Minister of Iceland replied that "such a declaration at this late date would be ridiculous." See Telegram from the Acting Secretary of State to the Minister in Iceland, May 7, 1945, in FRUS, General, Volume I, p. 641.
[25] Italy wanted to join, but the US did not allow it. See James B. Reston, "Italians Protest Parley Exclusion," in *New York Times* of April 26, 1945.
[26] North-America was represented by Canada and the United States of America. From South- and Central-America came Bolivia, Argentina, Brazil, Chile, Colombia, Costa Rica, Cuba, Dominican Republic, Ecuador, El Salvador, Guatemala, Haiti, Honduras, Mexico, Nicaragua, Panama, Paraguay, Peru, Uruguay and Venezuela.
[27] Belgium, France, Greece, Netherlands, Luxembourg, Norway, and the United Kingdom sent delegations, and so did the Byelorussian Soviet Socialist Republic, Czechoslovakia, Turkey, Ukrainian Soviet Socialist Republic, Union of Soviet Socialist Republics and Yugoslavia.
[28] Anne O'Hare McCormick, "San Francisco: Voice of Europe is Muted at Conference." McCormick points to Belgium and the Netherlands as the leaders of the little countries of Europe during the San Francisco Conference. See also William T. R. Fox, "The Super-Powers at San Francisco" (1946), p. 116.
[29] Asia was represented by China, India, and the Philippine Commonwealth. Of the Middle East came Egypt, Iran, Iraq, Lebanon, Saudi Arabia, and Syria. There were only three African nations in San Francisco: Ethiopia, Liberia, and the Union of South Africa. And then there were Australia and New Zealand.

the only nation that signed with the founding fathers, but did not participate in the Conference.[30]

Most of the delegates of the United Nations came from impoverished and war-torn lands to the peaceful and extravagant city of San Francisco, described by a British delegate as "a fantastic world of glitter and light and extravagant parties and food and drink and constantly spiraling talk."[31] As a contribution, the Soviet Union sent an entertainment ship, loaded with caviar and vodka.[32] The delegates made and signed the constitutive document of the UN in this environment, a long way away from the devastation in most of the rest of the world. The Latin American nations were the most self-confident and influential of the smaller States.[33] The Big Powers, and especially the United States, generally had the most influence.[34]

The *revised* Dumbarton Oaks proposals were the starting point for the San Francisco Conference. Amendments that had not been implemented in these proposals now had to be accepted by a two-thirds majority of the conference's participants.[35] This did not mean that the San Francisco Conference mainly served to fill in the gaps in the revised Dumbarton Oaks proposals.[36] As Molotov, the People's Commissar for Foreign Affairs of the Soviet Union, remarked, "[i]f we did

---

[30] This was caused by a "Cold War-type" dispute about which Government should represent Poland. The dispute "hung like a shadow over all deliberations." That quotation is from McNeil, "New Security Charter Seems to be Assured," in *New York Times* of June 24, 1945. And indeed, this dispute was covered extensively in the press, and sometimes took away the attention from what was happening in San Francisco itself. For the coverage of this issue by the *New York Times*, see *e.g.*, James B. Reston, "Pacific War Role for Soviet Hinted"; James B. Reston, "Six Problems Facing Security Conference"; James B. Reston, "46 Nations Ready to Organize Peace: Only Poles Absent"; Porter, "Soviet Action Hit" (all published in 1945). See also Evan Luard, *A History of the United Nations* (1982), pp. 41-42.

[31] Stephen S. Schlesinger, *Act of Creation* (2003), p. 116. For a nice description of the long and perilous journey from Europe to San Francisco, see Jean Dupuy, *San Francisco et la Charte des Nations Unies* (1945), pp. 3-4, and 13-17.

[32] James B. Reston, "Party Ship is Sent to Parley by Soviet," in *New York Times* of April 21, 1945. When Molotov was asked the question, by an American journalist, whether vodka was "safe for Americans to drink it without internal danger," Molotv replied: "I like your accent. Permit me to take leave." See "Transcript of Molotoff Interview," which appeared in the *New York Times* of April 27, 1945.

[33] Anne O'Hare McCormick, "San Francisco: Voice of Europe is Muted at Conference," in *New York Times* of May 14, 1945. See also William T. R. Fox, "The Super-Powers at San Francisco" (1946), p. 116.

[34] President Roosevelt (US) unfortunately died only a few days before all delegates came to San Francisco. Smuts, the leader of the South AfricaSouth African delegation, wrote to his son Japie that with the loss of Roosevelt, the conference was 'no one's baby' anymore." See Jan Christiaan Smuts, "Letter to Japie Smuts", on p. 529 of Jean van der Poel, *Selections from the Smuts Papers*, Volume VI (1973).

[35] In practice, the Big Powers could also veto any amendment to their proposals. See Evan Luard, *A History of the United Nations* (1982), pp. 43, 49; and Leland M. Goodrich and Edvard Hambro, *Charter of the United Nations* (1946), pp. 14-15.

[36] This was suggested in James B. Reston, "Dumbarton 'Gaps' Big Parley Issue," in *New York Times* of April 16, 1945.

not intend to make any amendments, it would be useless to hold the San Francisco Conference."[37] Various amendments to the revised Dumbarton Oaks proposals, proposed by the smaller States, were adopted.[38]

During the first few days of the conference, plenary sessions were held in the San Francisco Opera House, where representatives delivered speeches of a general nature.[39] These speeches, although eloquently worded, were not of any particular use to the drafting of the Charter.[40] The main work took place in the Veterans Building next door to the Opera.[41] There, four commissions, each subdivided into various committees and sometimes-even subcommittees, busied themselves drafting particular sections of the UN Charter.[42] The work was guided by a healthy mix of realism and idealism. The "Little Forty-Five" focused on the idealism, whilst the "Big Five" focused on the realism.[43]

When the delegates of all fifty States unanimously approved the text of the UN Charter on 25 June 1945, the audience "jumped to its feet to cheer and applaud for a full minute."[44] As the local printing shops and bookbinders had not yet managed to publish the Charter in all five of the Organization's official languages, the actual signing took place a day later.[45] At the end of the signing ceremony, where "[g]reat spotlights, focused on the signers and their surroundings, made the scene in the Veterans Building look like a Hollywood movie set," Stettinius, the leader of the US delegation, finally brought the San Francisco Conference to a close

---

[37] See "Report of V.M. Molotov's Press Conference at San Francisco, on April 26, 1945," published in an official booklet called *Soviet Union at the San Francisco Conference* (1945), p. 19.

[38] See Herbert Vere Evatt, *The United Nations* (1948), p. 4.

[39] In the beginning, there weren"t that many people present to listen to these speeches. See Lawrence E. Davies, "Small Nations Set Goals for Parley," in *New York Times* of April 29, 1945.

[40] Grayson Kirk & Lawrence Chamberlain, "The Organization of the San Francisco Conference" (1945), p. 333. The leader of the Dutch delegation wrote in his diary on the last day of the sequence of plenary sessions: "sick and tired of so much empty rhetoric I went to bed." See: Cees Wiebes, "De oprichting van de Verenigde Naties" (1995), p. 80. Dupuy had a more favourable opinion of the plenary speeches. He saw them as constituting "travail préparatoire." See Jean Dupuy, *San Francisco et la Charte des Nations Unies* (1945), p. 29.

[41] See "Conference Talks Stress Unity Plea," an article in the *New York Times* of May 2, 1945.

[42] See Yearbook of the United Nations 1946-47, p. 13, for an overview. See also Organization, Functions, and Officerships: United Nations Conference on International Organization (Chart), UNCIO, vol. 1, p. 79; Emmanuelle Jouannet, "Les travaux préparatoires de la Charte des Nations Unies" (2005), pp. 5-6.

[43] Betty Jane Davis, *Charter for Tomorrow: the San Francisco Conference* (1945), p. 35. See also Jan Christiaan Smuts' "Letter to Hofmeyr," in Jean van der Poel, *Selections from the Smuts Papers*, Volume VI (1973). The "Big Five" were the four sponsors of the Conference, plus France, which was also allotted a permanent seat at the Security Council.

[44] Lawrence E. Davies, "Historic Plenary Session Approves World Charter," in *New York Times* of June 26, 1945.

[45] Idem.

"with a single heavy rap of the gavel."[46] Because the United Nations did not have a building or Secretariat at the time the Charter was signed, it was agreed that President Truman would keep the document in a safe in the White House for the time being.[47]

Can the drafting of the UN Charter be considered as a form of value-based decision making? Was the San Francisco Conference an example of a discussion between people from different ways of life, with significant authority to speak on behalf of those they claimed to represent?[48] Most of the world was still colonized in 1945 and many oppressed peoples were not represented in San Francisco. For obvious reasons the Axis Powers were not invited and States which refused to declare war against the Axis Powers were not welcome either. Nevertheless, at least some representatives from regions all over the world were present at the conference. The influence of the United States was substantial, but Europe, Latin America, the Arab world, Africa and Asia also played a significant part.

The United States was most concerned with ensuring an inclusive drafting process and it believed that this aim was actually achieved. When President Truman opened the San Francisco Conference, he reminded all the participants that they "represent[ed] the overwhelming majority of all mankind," and that they "h[e]ld a powerful mandate from [their] people."[49] This idea of a people's mandate was expressed in the text of the Charter by the use of the words "we the peoples" at the very beginning. These words suggested that the UN Charter reflected the ideas of the peoples of the world.[50] They "express[ed] the democratic basis on which rests our new Organization."[51] The words "we the peoples" are reminiscent of the first words in the US Constitution. The US made this comparison,[52] but other States did too, either in a general sense,[53] or to criticize certain elements in the UN Charter.[54]

---

[46] The first quote is from Lawrence E. Davies, "Nation after Nation Sees era of Peace in Signing Charter," in *New York Times* of June 26, 1945. There, we also read that the US was supposed to sign last, but this did not happen because President Truman had to leave early. The last quote comes from an extract of Stettinus" Diary, entry for June 26, 1945, as published in FRUS, *1945. General*, Volume I, pp. 1432.

[47] See Lawrence E. Davies, "Charter is Flown to Washington," in *New York Times* of June 29, 1945, and Sutterlin, "Interview with Alger Hiss" (1990), p. 48. There, Hiss tells the famous anecdote of the parachute: Hiss, who personally took the Charter by airplane from San Francisco to Washington, was not given a parachute, whilst a parachute was attached to the UN Charter. See also Nico Schrijver, "The Future of the Charter of the United Nations" (2006).

[48] See section 3.1 of Chapter II, above.

[49] Verbatim Minutes of Opening Session, April 25, 1945, UNCIO, vol. 1, p. 113.

[50] See Report of Rapporteur of Committee 1 to Commission I, UNCIO, vol. 6, p. 391. See also Report of Rapporteur of Committee 1 to Commission I, UNCIO, vol. 6, p. 450.

[51] First Session of Commission I, June 14, 1945, UNCIO, vol. 6, p. 19. See also Fifth Meeting of Commission I, June 23, 1945, UNCIO, vol. 6, p. 203, and Report of Rapporteur of Commission I to Plenary Session, UNCIO, vol. 6, p. 245.

[52] President Truman made this comparison when he spoke during the Final Plenary Session, June 26, 1945, UNCIO, vol. 1, pp. 680-683 (see also pp. 715-717). Earlier, US delegate Stettinus had already

The Netherlands pointed out that not all governments represented in San Francisco derived their power directly from the people, and that they could therefore not formally claim to speak in their name.[55] In response, it was suggested that the phrase "we the peoples" should be read in conjunction with another phrase in the preamble, viz. "[t]hrough our representatives assembled at San Francisco."[56] This was considered to be a satisfactory solution, and a more realistic depiction of what was going on at the conference.

Was it a genuine discussion? Did the participants seek to define and protect the global interest, and were they prepared, as Risse believed was essential for a genuine discussion, to change their views in the light of the better argument? There are many indications that the drafters were concerned with the global interest and global values.

According to Dupuy, the intentions of the founding fathers went beyond drawing up a new treaty. They even went beyond the establishment of a new international organization. The UN Charter marked a fundamental break with the system of international relations that existed in the past. It constituted the basis for a new international order.[57] A delegate from Luxembourg even compared the "building" of the United Nations with the building of a new cathedral, as though the

---

made the same comparison, during the First Plenary Session, April 26, 1945, UNCIO, vol. 1, p. 127. See also Pierre-Marie Dupuy, "L'unité de l'ordre juridique international" (2002), p. 218.

[53] There are some examples. See *e.g.* the speech of the Chinese delegate in the Final Plenary Session, June 26, 1945, UNCIO, vol. 1, p. 660 (see also p. 692). And see Cuba's speech during the Seventh Plenary Session, May 1, 1945, UNCIO, vol. 1, p. 499.

[54] Australia used this comparison to criticize the rigidity of the UN Charter's amendment procedure. The US Constitution was amended very shortly after it was made, and this seemed impossible when it came to the UN Charter. See First Plenary Session, April 26, 1945, UNCIO, vol. 1, p. 178 (see also Corrigendum to Summary Report of Eighteenth Meeting of Committee III/I, June 12, 1945, UNCIO, vol. 11, p. 492). New Zealand did exactly the same during the Fifth Meeting of Commission III, June 20, 1945, UNCIO, vol. 11, pp. 171-172, and once again during the Eighteenth and Nineteenth Meetings of Committee III/1, June 12, 1945, UNCIO, vol. 11, p. 472. Greece is another example, see Corrigendum to Summary Report of Eighteenth Meeting of Committee III/I, June 12, 1945, UNCIO, vol. 11, p. 490. And so is Turkey, see Fourth Meeting of Commission I, June 19, 1945, UNCIO, vol. 6, p. 175. And Mexico, see Twentieth Meeting of Committee III/1, June 13, 1945, UNCIO, vol. 11, p. 531.

[55] The Netherlands, for example, did not. See Thirteenth Meeting of Committee I/1, June 5, 1945, UNCIO, vol. 6, p. 366, and Fifteenth Meeting of Committee I/1, June 11, 1945, UNCIO, vol. 6, p. 421. See also Jean-Pierre Cot & Alain Pellet, "Préambule" (2005), pp. 306-307.

[56] Report of Rapporteur, Subcommittee I/1/A, Section 3, to Committee I/1, June 5, 1945. UNCIO, vol. 6, p. 358. The Coordination Committee agreed. See the Coordination Committee's Summary Report of Seventeenth Meeting, June 13, 1945, UNCIO, vol. 17, pp. 105-106. See also the Minutes of the Seventy-Sixth Meeting of the United States Delegation, June 19, 1945, in FRUS, General, Volume I, pp. 1363-1367.

[57] Pierre-Marie Dupuy, "L'unité de l'ordre juridique international" (2002), p. 217.

delegates at the San Francisco Conference were establishing some kind of a new global religion.[58]

The drafting of the UN Charter was more than an exercise in the codification of existing international law.[59] The drafters therefore had to look elsewhere for their inspiration. Welles suggested that to create the post-war international order the world needed "men who have their eyes on the stars but their feet on the ground."[60] What was achieved was more than merely drafting yet another treaty that codified the existing norms or the existing *status quo*.

## 2.3 The UN Charter as a value-based document

The text of the UN Charter does not make its value-based character explicit. The word "value" is not found anywhere.[61] The UN Charter refers primarily to "purposes" and "principles." According to the Dumbarton Oaks proposals, the Organization and its members should act in accordance with certain principles in their pursuit of certain purposes.[62] The idea, as explained by Pasvolsky (USA), who was very influential in drafting the Charter, was that "the principles were rules of action, whereas the purposes were the aims of action."[63] This was also how the delegates in San Francisco distinguished the purposes from the principles.[64] This clear and straightforward distinction between purposes and principles, and the very neat description of both these terms, is not reflected in the text of the Charter itself.

---

[58] Seventh Plenary Session, May 1, 1945, UNCIO, vol. 1, p. 504.

[59] Not everyone seems to agree with that assessment. For example, according to Dutch Member of Parliament Mr. Beaufort, the aim of the United Nations was "to turn the natural community of nations into a legal community," in other words, to "legalize" the *status quo*. See p. 125, Dutch Parliament, "Meeting of Tuesday 30 October, 1945," in *Handelingen der Staten-Generaal: Tijdelijke Zitting 1945* (II).

[60] Sumner Welles, *The United Nations: their creed for a free world* (1942), p. 3. Welles spoke these words before the Conference, so it was a prescription of what kind of men were needed to put the world back on track, not a description of who in fact did bring the world back on track.

[61] It can be found in the Treaty of Lisbon amending the Treaty on European Union and the Treaty establishing the European Community: "The Union is founded on the values of respect for human dignity, freedom, democracy, equality, the rule of law and respect for human rights."

[62] Dumbarton Oaks Proposals for a General International Organization, UNCIO, vol. 3, p. 3.

[63] See Minutes of Fifth Meeting of the United States Delegation, April 9, 1945, in FRUS, *1945*, Vol. I, p. 224.

[64] A rather complex definition of the terms can be found in the Report of Rapporteur, Subcommittee I/1/A, to Committee I/1, June 1, 1945, UNCIO, vol. 6, pp. 698-699. See also Report of Rapporteur of Committee 1 to Commission I, UNCIO, vol. 6, p. 388. The text is reproduced on p. 17, of Yearbook of the United Nations 1946-47. In that Yearbook, the difference is summarized as follows: "(...) the Purposes constitute the *raison d"être* of the United Nations, and the Principles serve as the standards of international conduct."

The purposes can be found in Articles 1 and 55 of the UN Charter. The principles are formulated in Articles 2 and 56. The purposes of Article 1 consist of one general purpose and three value-based purposes. The general purpose is Article 1(4):

> [One of the purposes of the United Nations is] to be a centre for harmonizing the actions of nations in the attainment of these common ends.

These "common ends" are defined in the value-based purposes of paragraphs 1 to 3 of Article 1:

> To maintain international peace and security, and to that end: to take effective collective measures for the prevention and removal of threats to the peace, and for the suppression of acts of aggression or other breaches of the peace, and to bring about by peaceful means, and in conformity with the principles of justice and international law, adjustment or settlement of international disputes or situations which might lead to a breach of the peace;

> To develop friendly relations among nations based on respect for the principle of equal rights and self-determination of peoples, and to take other appropriate measures to strengthen universal peace;

> To achieve international co-operation in solving international problems of an economic, social, cultural, or humanitarian character, and in promoting and encouraging respect for human rights and for fundamental freedoms for all without distinction as to race, sex, language, or religion.

These purposes reflect the values of peace and security, self-determination of peoples, social progress and development, and human dignity. Purposes can also be found in Article 55 of the UN Charter:

> With a view to the creation of conditions of stability and well-being which are necessary for peaceful and friendly relations among nations based on respect for the principle of equal rights and self-determination of peoples, the United Nations shall promote:

> Higher standards of living, full employment, and conditions of economic and social progress and development;

> Solutions of international economic, social, health, and related problems; and international cultural and educational cooperation; and

> Universal respect for, and observance of, human rights and fundamental freedoms for all without distinction as to race, sex, language, or religion.

This list reiterates most of the value-based purposes already mentioned in Article 1, including self-determination of peoples, social progress and development, and respect for human dignity and rights.

The list of principles or "rules of action" is more varied. The first principle states that "the Organization is based on the principle of the sovereign equality of all its Members."[65] This should be interpreted to include an obligation for all States to respect the sovereign equality of all other States. In that sense, it is a rule of action.

The other six principles are formulated as rules of action or "norms." Four of those norms bind all Member States. Within that category of norms a distinction can be made between those norms that are directly related to the promotion of a particular purpose/value, and those of a more general character. The general norms are 2(2) and 2(5) UN Charter:

> All Members, in order to ensure to all of them the rights and benefits resulting from membership, shall fulfil in good faith the obligations assumed by them in accordance with the present Charter.

> All Members shall give the United Nations every assistance in any action it takes in accordance with the present Charter, and shall refrain from giving assistance to any state against which the United Nations is taking preventive or enforcement action.

The value-based norms are 2(3) and 2(4):

> All Members shall settle their international disputes by peaceful means in such a manner that international peace and security, and justice, are not endangered.

> All Members shall refrain in their international relations from the threat or use of force against the territorial integrity or political independence of any state, or in any other manner inconsistent with the Purposes of the United Nations.

Both these norms relate to the value of peace and security. Article 2 does not contain any principles obliging the Member States to protect and defend any of the other purposes outlined in Article 1. This is done by a general principle in Article 56:

> All Members pledge themselves to take joint and separate action in co-operation with the Organization for the achievement of the purposes set forth in Article 55.

As Article 55 contains a reference to most of the global values, this principle effectively complements the principles and norms in Article 2.

---

[65] Article 2(1), UN Charter. See Albrecht Randelzhofer, "Article 2" (2002).

The remaining two norms in Article 2 bind the Organization, and not the Member States. One of those norms can be directly related to a particular value/purpose. This is Article 2(6):

The Organization shall ensure that states which are not Members of the United Nations act in accordance with these Principles so far as may be necessary for the maintenance of international peace and security.

Once again, the value is peace and security. The other norm binding the Organization has a more general character. This is Article 2(7):

Nothing contained in the present Charter shall authorize the United Nations to intervene in matters which are essentially within the domestic jurisdiction of any state or shall require the Members to submit such matters to settlement under the present Charter; but this principle shall not prejudice the application of enforcement measures under Chapter VII.

This norm can be linked to sovereignty. It obliges the Organization to respect the sovereign independence of its Member States.

To avoid variation in the list of principles, it was suggested that the general principles be separated from the norms,[66] or that all the principles be rephrased as a combination of norm and principle.[67] These suggestions were not adopted.

During the San Francisco Conference a Preamble was added.[68] Smuts, the leader of the South African delegation who drafted this preamble, referred to it as a "statement of ideals and aspirations which would rally world opinion in support of the Charter."[69] To ensure that the Preamble would fulfil its purpose, Gildersleeve (USA) suggested that it "should be hung up in every peasant's cottage throughout

---

[66] See Eighth Meeting of Committee I/1, May 17, 1945, UNCIO, vol. 6, p. 310.

[67] Revision of Technical Committee Text Suggested by the Secretariat as Submitted to the Coordination Committee, June 14, 1945, UNCIO, vol. 18, p. 117.

[68] The US wanted a preamble from the beginning, but never submitted a draft. See Minutes of the Fifth Meeting of the United States Delegation, April 9, 1945, in FRUS, *1945, General:* Volume I, p. 219.

[69] Second Meeting of Committee, I/1, May 7, 1945, UNCIO, vol. 6, p. 277. See also Sixth Plenary Session, May 1, 1945, UNCIO, vol. 1, p. 425. Scholars have always been puzzled by the fact that Smuts defended these lofty words in San Francisco, but when he returned to South Africa he continued to support the policies of racial segregation. See *e.g.,* Christof Heyns, "The Preamble of the United Nations Charter" (1995); David Tothill, "Evatt and Smuts in San Francisco" (2007), especially a quote from Smuts himself on p. 186, in which he basically admits that he is both a "humanist" and proud of the "clean society" built by Europeans in South Africa, which should not be "lost in the black pool of Africa." However, on p. 289 of Jean-Pierre Cot & Alain Pellet, "Préambule" (2005), Smuts is detached from the apartheid system.

the world."[70] The Preamble had an ideological rather than a legal importance.[71] It was not intended to legally bind the signatory States.[72] It served as a guideline for the interpretation of the Charter, and to "explain ambiguous statements in the articles which do impose obligations."[73]

Most of the purposes in Articles 1 and 55 can be qualified as expressions of the world's most fundamental values.[74] The purposes are "aims of action"; they oblige the Organization and its members to take action in an attempt to realize certain fundamental values. If peace and security constitute a value, then the *maintenance* of peace and security is a purpose. If human dignity is a value, then the promotion of universal respect for human rights and fundamental freedoms is a purpose. And so on. The principles, or at least most of them, can be considered as value-based norms. If human dignity is a value, then the obligation for all States to take joint and separate action to achieve universal respect for human rights is a principle. These principles can be worked out in more detail in specific legal obligations or "rules." Rules are specific obligations based on a fundamental principle. In this sense, "principles [could] be seen as the link between ideals and duties, between the morality of aspiration and the morality of duty, between values and rules."[75] For example, if human dignity is a value, and the protection of human rights is a principle, then the universal bill of rights contains the specific rules.

Because the United Nations Charter does not clearly and explicitly list the values on which it is based, other values could be added to the list. There are particularly good reasons for adding justice, and perhaps international law itself. The promotion of justice and international law is mentioned in Article 1, as a means to maintain the peace. Moreover, the Preamble states that the United Nations was created, *inter alia*, "to establish conditions under which justice and respect for the obligations arising from treaties and other sources of international law can be maintained." This phrase ended up in the Preamble, instead of Article 1, because

---

[70] Minutes of Twenty-First Meeting of the United States Delegation, April 27, 1945, in FRUS, *1945, General:* Volume I, p. 478. See also First Session of Commission I, June 14, 1945, UNCIO, vol. 6, p. 19.

[71] Hans Kelsen, "The Preamble of the Charter - A Critical Analysis" (1946), p. 143. See also George A. Finch, "The United Nations Charter" (1950). For a different view, see Mintauts Chakste, "Justice and Law in the Charter of the United Nations" (1948), pp. 594 and 600.

[72] There was some dispute on the legal character of the Preamble in San Francisco. See *e.g.*, the Thirteenth Meeting of Committee I/1, June 5, 1945, UNCIO, vol. 6, p. 367. A Rapporteur gave the impression that the Preamble was binding. See Report of Rapporteur of Committee 1 to Commission I, UNCIO, vol. 6, pp. 388-389.

[73] Summary Report of Sixteenth Meeting of Advisory Committee of Jurists, June 19, 1945, UNCIO 17, p. 435. See also Edward R. Stettinius, *Charter of the United Nations* (1945), p. 35; Ministerie van Buitenlandse Zaken (Netherlands), *Het ontstaan der Verenigde Naties* (1950), p. 17; and Alfred Verdross, "Idées directrices de l'Organisation des Nations Unies" (1955), p. 8.

[74] See also Sandra Szurek, "La Charte des Nations Unies constitution mondiale?" (2005), p. 45.

[75] Jonathan M. Verschuuren, *Principles of Environmental Law* (2003), p. 25.

the founding fathers of the UN wanted to establish a new legal order, a United Nations order, as opposed to the traditional order based on traditional international law.[76] In order not to obstruct this metamorphosis in international relations, it was stressed during the drafting of the Charter that the reference to respect for international law should not lead to a "negation of healthy international evolution" or "the crystallization or the freezing of the international *status quo.*"[77] Thus the *travaux préparatoires* do not strongly support the addition of justice and particularly international law to the list of values. However, that does not settle the debate once and for all.

In any case, in this study the promotion of justice and international law, and related purposes like the promotion of the rule of law, are not treated as based on a separate value. In this study, international law is treated as the framework and language in which the discussion about values is phrased. This choice is perhaps somewhat arbitrary, and it still does not explain why justice – as opposed to international law – should not be a value. Franck rightly pointed out that international law is a language in which various opinions are expressed, but that justice is not morally neutral, and that "the principles and rules of justice are a moral community's response to perceptions of distributive unfairness, inequality, or lack of compassionate grace."[78] Is justice thus a value? Defined in Franck's broad terms, justice could also be considered as an "umbrella value," in the sense that if the international legal order is based on the values of peace and security, social progress and development, human dignity, and self-determination of peoples, it is a just order.

## 2.4 The United Nations Charter as a document to motivate action

Although the UN Charter does not use the word "value," and although only part of the world was represented in San Francisco, the conference was as good as it could be at that time. There were objections to the fact that various parts of the world were not represented in San Francisco, but this situation was rectified in later years. Many peoples, unrepresented in San Francisco, later signed and ratified the final outcome of the San Francisco dialogue, the UN Charter.

The one aspect of the global discussion held in San Francisco that has as yet not been assessed is its capacity to motivate action. As law is by definition

---

[76] See also Witenberg, "New Set of Rules Acceptable to All Nations is Proposed," in *New York Times* of May 13, 1945.
[77] Report of Rapporteur, Subcommittee I/1/A, Section 3, to Committee I/1, June 5, 1945, UNCIO, vol. 6, p. 359. See also Report of Rapporteur of Committee 1 to Commission I, UNCIO, vol. 6, p. 451 and p. 461.
[78] p. 239 of Thomas M. Franck, *The Power of Legitimacy among Nations* (1990). See also Thomas M. Franck, *Fairness in International Law and Institutions* (1995).

action-oriented,[79] this criterion can be easily satisfied. The obligations to act, arising from the Charter's values, purposes and principles, were meant to override all other conflicting obligations.

This superiority of the Charter inspired scholars to refer to it as the world's constitution, even in its very early days,[80] and this notion has experienced a revival in recent times. For example, according to Alvarez, the Charter could be considered as constituting the world's "basis for a system of hierarchically superior legal norms and values," and therefore as the world's constitution.[81] According to Fassbender, the UN Charter is a constitution, *inter alia,* because it "has a substantive part, in which common values, goals and principles are set out." [82] Although this qualification of the UN Charter as a "constitution" is popular in the literature,[83] it does not always explain what that qualification entails.[84] The word constitution may mean different things to different people. At the very least it indicates, when reference is made to the UN Charter, that there is something special about that document. One of the special characteristics is its formulation of a set of hierarchically superior values, purposes and principles.

---

[79] See section 3.4 of Chapter II, above.

[80] See *e.g.*, Hans Kelsen, "The Preamble of the Charter" (1946), pp. 134-159; p. 307, Georges Kaeckenbeeck, "La Charte de San-Francisco dans ses rapports avec le droit international" (1948); Louis B. Sohn, "The impact of the United Nations on international law" (1952), pp. 106-107. See also p. 187, of Dissenting Opinion of Mr. de Visscher, in ICJ, International Status of South-West Africa, Advisory Opinion of July 11th, 1950.

[81] José E. Alvarez, "Legal Perspectives" (2007), pp. 58-59.

[82] Bardo Fassbender, "The United Nations Charter as Constitution" (1998), p. 589. These two characteristics are most often referred to. See also Bruno Simma, "From Bilateralism to Community Interest" (1994), p. 262 (already quoted above), and Pierre-Marie Dupuy, "The Constitutional Dimension of the Charter of the United Nations Revisited" (1997).

[83] See *e.g.*, André Nollkaemper, *Kern van het Internationaal Publiekrech (2007)*, p. 116; Bruno Simma, "From Bilateralism to Community Interest" (1994), pp. 258-262; Bardo Fassbender, "The United Nations Charter as Constitution" (1998); Thomas M. Franck, "Is the UN Charter a Constitution?" (2003); James Crawford, "Multilateral Rights and Obligations in International Law" (2006), pp. 371-391; Nigel D. White, *The United Nations system* (2002), pp. 14-17; Christian Tomuschat, "Foreword", p. ix; Regis Chemain & Alain Pellet, *La Charte des Nations Unies, constitution mondiale?* (2006); Gaetano Arangio-Ruiz, "The normative role of the General Assembly" (1972), p. 633; Francis Aime Vallat, "The competence of the United Nations General Assembly" (1959), pp. 248-250; Bruno Simma and Andreas L. Paulus, "The "International Community" (1998), p. 274; Krzysztof Skubiszewski, "Remarks on the interpretation of the United Nations Charter" (1983); Blaine Sloan, "The United Nations Charter as a constitution" (1989); Ronald Macdonald, "The Charter of the United Nations in constitutional perspective" (1999); Pierre-Marie Dupuy, "L'unité de l'ordre juridique international" (2002), pp. 215-244; Sandra Szurek, "La Charte des Nations Unies constitution mondiale?" (2005); Michael W. Doyle, "The UN Charter: a Global Constitution?" (2009), and so on.

[84] And thus, as Dupuy pointed out, if we would ask an international lawyer whether the UN Charter is the world's constitution, he might be inclined to answer: "Yes, of course! But, by the way, what was the question?" Pierre-Marie Dupuy, "The Constitutional Dimension of the Charter of the United Nations Revisited" (1997), p. 2.

The Dumbarton Oaks Proposals had no provision stating that obligations under the UN Charter would prevail over all other obligations under "ordinary" international law in the case of a conflict between the two. Certain States proposed amendments to clarify that the UN Charter had precedence over the rest of international law.[85]

In San Francisco it was decided that when an obligation under the UN Charter was inconsistent with previously existing obligations under international law, these existing obligations should either be automatically abrogated, or States should be obliged to take immediate steps to secure their release from these prior obligations.[86] With regard to future obligations inconsistent with the UN Charter, it was simply decided that States should not undertake such obligations.[87] This sounds reasonable, but as the Soviet Union pointed out, "in some cases a treaty which, considered in the abstract, might seem compatible with the Charter, in practice might be actually incompatible with it."[88] Consequently there was a need to address the important question "how [to] determine[..] that a given obligation was contrary to the Charter."[89] It was suggested that "the Charter should state not only the principle of invalidity of obligations inconsistent with the Charter," but that it should also describe "a procedure by which organs of the Organization, such as the Assembly or the Security Council, could determine in practice what obligations were inconsistent with the Charter."[90] The International Court of Justice was referred to as a potential candidate to resolve such constitutional disputes.[91] In the end "[t]he question of what organ should determine issues of inconsistency […] was raised but not considered."[92]

---

[85] See *e.g.*, Australian Amendments, UNCIO, vol. 3, p. 553; Belgian Amendments, UNCIO, vol. 3, pp. 343-344; Egyptian Amendments, UNCIO, vol. 3, p. 463; Ethiopian Amendments, UNCIO, vol. 3, p. 561; Norwegian Amendments, UNCIO, vol. 3, p. 371; Philippines Amendments, UNCIO, vol. 3, p. 540; Venezuelan Amendments, UNCIO, vol. 3, p. 223 and p. 226.

[86] Fourth Meeting of Committee IV/2, May 12, 1945, UNCIO, vol. 13, p. 592. In a later meeting, one delegate summarized the view of the Committee as follows: "that all inconsistent obligations contained in treaties between member states would be abrogated *ipso facto*, the necessary consent having been obtained here at San Francisco." Sixth Meeting of Committee IV/2, May 17, 1945, UNCIO, vol. 13, p. 603.

[87] Fourth Meeting of Committee IV/2, May 12, 1945, UNCIO, vol. 13, p. 592. See also the remarks by the Rapporteur of Committee IV/2 during the First Meeting of Commission IV, May 19, 1945, UNCIO, vol. 13, p. 20.

[88] Fifth Meeting of Committee IV/2, May 15, 1945, UNCIO, vol. 13, p. 598.

[89] Fourth Meeting of Committee IV/2, May 12, 1945, UNCIO, vol. 13, p. 593.

[90] Fifth Meeting of Committee IV/2, May 15, 1945, UNCIO, vol. 13, p. 598.

[91] Sixth Meeting of Committee IV/2, May 17, 1945, UNCIO, vol. 13, p. 603.

[92] Department of External Affairs (Canada), *Report on the United Nations conference on international organization* (1945), p. 61. According to the same report, one suggestion was to make use of advisory opinions of the International Court of Justice.

A Subcommittee was established to consider the issue of inconsistent obligations in more detail.[93] With regard to the obligation of Member States not to sign treaties inconsistent with the UN Charter after its entry into force, it was believed that this rule was so "evident that it would be unnecessary to express it in the Charter."[94] With regard to the more problematical issue of conflicts with already existing treaties, the Subcommittee remarked that there was "a general disposition to accept as evident the rule according to which all previous obligations inconsistent with the terms of the Charter should be superseded by the latter."[95] This did not mean that treaties inconsistent with the UN Charter would automatically be nullified. Rather, it was felt that a practical problem needed a practical solution. If the obligations under the Charter and another norm of international law were in conflict with each other in a specific situation, the latter could be ignored for the time being.[96] In the end, the Subcommittee suggested the following provision:

> In the event of any conflict arising between the obligations of Members of the Organization under the Charter and their obligations under any other international agreement the former shall prevail.[97]

This provision was adopted by the Committee.[98] When the provision came before the Conference Secretariat, the Advisory Committee of Jurists, and the Coordination Committee, a problem arose as to the exact meaning of the term "international agreement." It was suggested that treaties and agreements were two different things, and that this formulation therefore excluded treaties, which was certainly not the intention.[99] Golunsky (USSR), who was both a member of the Subcommittee and the Advisory Committee of Jurists, explained that the term

---

[93] To assist the Subcommittee in its work, a number of States proposed new formulations of the desired provision. See Obligations Inconsistent with the Charter: Texts Proposed for Consideration by Subcommittee IV/2/A, May 31, 1945, UNCIO, vol. 13, pp. 800-801. The US, for example, suggested that "[t]he obligations of the Charter shall take precedence over any inconsistent obligation between members."

[94] Report of Subcommittee IV/2/A on Obligations Inconsistent with the Charter, UNCIO, vol. 13, p. 806 (see also p. 812).

[95] *Idem*, p. 805 (see also p. 811).

[96] *Idem*, p. 806 (see also p. 812).

[97] *Idem*, p. 807 (see also p. 813).

[98] See Fourteenth Meeting of Committee IV/2, June 7, 1945, UNCIO, vol. 13, p. 654, and Report of the Rapporteur of Committee IV/2, as Approved by the Committee, UNCIO, vol. 13, pp. 707-708.

[99] See Revision of Technical Committee Text Suggested by the Secretariat as Submitted to the Coordination Committee, June 12, 1945, UNCIO, vol. 18, p. 341; Coordination Committee's Summary Report of Eighteenth Meeting, June 13, 1945, UNCIO, vol. 17, p. 112; Text Revised by the Advisory Committee of Jurists at its Seventh Meeting, June 13, 1945 and Approved by the Coordination Committee at its Eighteenth Meeting, June 13, 1945, UNCIO, vol. 18, p. 342; Summary Report of Seventh Meeting of Advisory Committee of Jurists, June 13, 1945, UNCIO, vol. 17, p. 415; and Second Meeting of Commission IV, June 15, 1945, UNCIO, vol. 13, p. 104.

"agreements" could be used both in a technical sense, in which case it meant "special instruments other than treaties," and in a general sense, in which case it meant "all sorts of international agreements." In this provision it was used in the general sense.[100]

In the end, the following Article (Article 103) was adopted:

> In the event of a conflict between the obligations of the Members of the United Nations under the present Charter and their obligations under any other international agreement, their obligations under the present Charter shall prevail.

This Charter's self-proclamation of being hierarchically superior to other treaties was later accepted in other treaties and legal documents, most notably in the Vienna Convention on the Law of Treaties and the ILC Articles on State Responsibility.[101]

It can be concluded from the text and remarks made during the drafting in San Francisco, that Article 103 proclaims that legal obligations conflicting with obligations arising from the Charter are not automatically annulled. Article 103 UN Charter only becomes relevant when, in an actual situation, a State has to choose between abiding by its obligations under the Charter and those under other legal norms. In that case, the State has to act as prescribed by the Charter.[102] This rule guarantees that the Charter is not regarded as "just another treaty," in the words of Stettinius, but as something hierarchically superior to other legal documents.[103] In this sense it is the world's constitution.[104]

To explain exactly how Article 103 functions, the best comparison is with the rules on non-derogability as codified in the Vienna Convention on the Law of Treaties. Article 53 of that treaty states that "a treaty is void if, at the time of its

---

[100] See the Coordination Committee's Summary Report of Eighteenth Meeting, June 13, 1945, UNCIO, vol. 17, p. 112.

[101] See Article 30 of the Vienna Convention on the Law of Treaties, which was drawn up in Vienna on 23 May 1969, and entered into force on 27 January 1980; and Article 59 of the ILC Articles on the Responsibility of States. The latter document simply states that "[t]hese articles are without prejudice to the Charter of the United Nations", which means, according to the ILC Commentary, that "the Articles [on State Responsibility] cannot affect and are without prejudice to the Charter of the United Nations. The Articles are in all respects to be interpreted in conformity with the Charter of the United Nations." See International Law Commission, Draft Articles on Responsibility of States for Internationally Wrongful Acts with commentaries, p. 365. To appear in Yearbook of the International Law Commission, 2001, vol. II, Part Two.

[102] This is how the Dutch Government interpreted the intentions of the drafters. See Ministerie van Buitenlandse Zaken (Netherlands), *Het ontstaan der Verenigde Naties* (1950),p. 139.

[103] Edward R. Stettinius, *Charter of the United Nations* (1945), pp. 156-157. See also Department of External Affairs (Canada), *Report on the United Nations conference on international organization* (1945), p. 61.

[104] Some authors did not think the qualification of "constitution" could be based solely on Article 103, but others gave the article a prominent place in their "constitutional" theories. For a more skeptical view, see Jean-Marc Thouvenin, "Article 103" (2005).

conclusion, it conflicts with a peremptory norm of general international law." Article 103 UN Charter does not nullify treaties if they conflict with the UN Charter, but functions more like a traffic regulation. When two cars approach an intersection, and one of them happens to be a police car with both its siren sounding and its emergency lights flashing, then the traffic regulation provides that the police car has priority. The ordinary car has to wait, even when this upsets the normal course of events and causes hindrance, or even damage, to other drivers. Article 103 functions in exactly the same way. Whenever there is a conflict between norms, the UN Charter norm has to be given priority, and the ordinary norms have to wait.[105]

It has been suggested that if a particular State objects to the hierarchically superior nature of the Charter, it can simply leave the Organization altogether and "de-ratify" the Charter. The UN Charter does not explicitly provide for the possibility for Member States to leave the organization.[106] According to Article 56 of the Vienna Convention on the Law of Treaties, a treaty which "does not provide for denunciation or withdrawal is not subject to denunciation or withdrawal unless [..] it is established that the parties intended to admit the possibility of denunciation or withdrawal [or] a right of denunciation or withdrawal may be implied by the nature of the treaty." In San Francisco there was an understanding that it was the sovereign right of States to withdraw in certain cases.[107] States have not done so much in practice. To express its outrage at the election of Malaysia to the Security Council, Indonesia announced that it wished to withdraw from the organization on 20 January 1965. It is generally believed that this was not a good reason to withdraw, but the withdrawal was never formally identified as being either legal or

---

[105] See also Robert Kolb, *Théorie du ius cogens international* (2001), p. 132. See also *e.g.* Pierre-Marie Dupuy, "L'unité de l'ordre juridique international" (2002), p. 305; Michel Virally, "Réflexions sur le « jus cogens »" (1966), pp. 26-27; Andreas L. Paulus, "Jus Cogens in a Time of Hegemony and Fragmentation" (2005), pp. 317-319 ; Erik Suy, "Article 53" (2006, p. 1913. See also Special Committee on Principles of International Law concerning Friendly Relations and Co-operation among States, Report, A/6230, adopted 27 June 1966, para. 563. And see para. 41, of the Conclusions of the work of the Study Group on the Fragmentation of International Law: Difficulties arising from the Diversification and Expansion of International Law, adopted by the International Law Commission at its Fifty-eighth session, in 2006. These conclusions are based on Martti Koskenniemi, *Fragmentation of international law: difficulties arising from the diversification and expansion of international law (Report of the Study Group of the International Law Commission)*, 13 April 2006, UN Doc. A/CN.4/L.682, especially pp. 328-360. See also Sandra Szurek, "La Charte des Nations Unies constitution mondiale?" (2005), p. 39. It must be pointed out that Szurek believed that ultimately most of the UN's purposes and principles were *jus cogens*, and that this – instead of Article 103 - was what made them truly hierarchically superior. See especially pp. 45-49.
[106] Thomas M. Franck, "Is the UN Charter a Constitution?" (2003), pp. 95-97.
[107] See Egon Schwelb, "Withdrawal from the United Nations: The Indonesian Intermezzo" (1967), p. 663.

illegal.[108] Indonesia re-joined voluntarily at the end of September 1966, and the international community simply pretended that nothing had happened.[109]

The values, purposes and principles are therefore both hierarchically superior, and inescapable. This means that they are ideally suited to serve as a vehicle which motivates States to act in pursuance of the principles in their efforts to achieve the value-based purposes for which the UN was established.

## 2.5 The evolution of the United Nations Charter

Schachter believed that the law of the United Nations should "not be approached as a set of autonomous norms which dictate decisions but as a process through which States and peoples pursue their interests and undertake joint action in accordance with felt necessities and values."[110] The Charter provided the foundation for this process. The provisions of the UN Charter were intended to guide global decision making for hundreds of years. This is what the delegates had in mind when they drafted them. The aim was to draft provisions that were both enduring and at the same time capable of evolution. This is also an important characteristic of global values.[111]

This aim was most clearly described in a report of the Canadian Government about the San Francisco Conference, published around the time of the conference. This suggested that "[a]n international body such as the United Nations cannot work effectively if the constitutional document on which it is based is subject to frequent serious alteration."[112] On the other hand, "the constitution should not be too rigid [and] it must be capable of growth and of adaptation to changing conditions."[113] The Charter was drafted during the Second World War. At that extraordinary moment in world history it was hard to predict what the world would look like in the future.[114] According to the Canadian government: "It was therefore important that the Charter [...] should be flexible – capable of growth from within by the development of custom and precedent and by the adoption of regulations – capable of change by formal constitutional amendment when the world had returned

---

[108] According to one commentator, "with no stretch of the imagination" could the admittance of Malaysia to the Council be regarded as warranting withdrawal. p. 641, Frances Livingstone, "Withdrawal from the United Nations: Indonesia" (1965).
[109] See Egon Schwelb, "Withdrawal from the United Nations: The Indonesian Intermezzo" (1967), pp. 665-670.
[110] Oscar Schachter, "The relation of law, politics and action in the United Nations" (1964), p. 169.
[111] See especially section 4.3 of Chapter II.
[112] Department of External Affairs (Canada), *Report on the United Nations conference on international organization* (1945), p. 66.
[113] Idem.
[114] See also Leland M. Goodrich, "San Francisco in retrospect" (1969), especially p. 240.

to a more normal state."[115] It was necessary to find a compromise between its enduring quality and flexibility.

Van Kleffens, the leader of the Dutch delegation in San Francisco, later described this uncertainty about the future with the help of a beautiful metaphor:

> When, in the early summer of 1945, the United Nations Charter was drawn up in San Francisco, it was like the launching of a ship, a ship which a little later put to sea, laden with the hopes and the aspirations for peace of the whole world. She is now sailing the stormy waters she was expected to encounter, and it does not seem probable that most of the time she will run before a light wind.[116]

States chose to board this new ship by signing and ratifying the Charter. The destination of this ship was the realization of a set of generally defined values, which had the capacity to evolve. The States accepted "an entire system which is in constant movement, not unlike a national constitution whose original texture will be unavoidably modified by thick layers of political practice and jurisprudence."[117] This is exactly what has happened since 1945. Despite the virtual impossibility of amending the UN Charter,[118] the UN system has proved that it is able to "grow from within," as described in the Canadian report, and that it is flexible enough to cope with the continuous change of international society.[119] In the Declaration on the Occasion of the Fiftieth Anniversary of the United Nations, the General Assembly proclaimed that "the Charter [still gave] expression to the common values and aspirations of humankind."[120]

A constitution like the UN Charter is not a static set of norms. It is a living and growing document, a "living tree."[121] To interpret such an instrument, it is

---

[115] Department of External Affairs (Canada), *Report on the United Nations conference on international organization* (1945), p. 66.

[116] Eelco N. van Kleffens, "The United Nations and Some Main Trends of Our Time" (1947), p. 71. See also p. 53 of Dissenting opinion of M. Alvarez to the International Court of Justice, Reservations to the Convention on the Prevention and Punishment of the Crime of Genocide, Advisory Opinion of 28 May 1951; and p. 18 of the Dissenting Opinion by M. Alvarez, in the Competence of the General Assembly for the Admission of a State to the United Nations, Advisory Opinion of March 3rd, 1950.

[117] Christian Tomuschat, "Obligations arising for states without or against their will" (1993), p. 251. See also James Leslie Brierly, "The Covenant and the Charter" (1946), p. 83.

[118] On Charter amendment, see Articles 108 and 109 of the UN Charter, and Emile Giraud, "*La revision de la Charte des Nations Unies*" (1956), pp. 340-399.

[119] See Nico Schrijver, "The Future of the Charter of the United Nations" (2006); Nico Schrijver, "Les valeurs fondamentales et le droit des Nations Unies" (2006), p. 88.

[120] Declaration on the Occasion of the Fiftieth Anniversary of the United Nations, General Assembly resolution 50/6, adopted 24 October 1995.

[121] The expressions "living document" and "growing document" come from Clark M. Eichelberger, "The United Nations Charter: A Growing Document" (1947), p. 98 and title. See also Hambro Pollux, "The Interpretation of the Charter" (1946), p. 54. The "living tree" metaphor is taken from Thomas M. Franck, "Is the UN Charter a Constitution?" (2003). For a very early example, see F. B. Schick, "Towards a living constitution of the United Nations" (1948).

necessary to look not only at the "ordinary meaning to be given to the terms of the treaty in their context and in the light of its object and purpose," as the Vienna Convention on the Law of Treaties prescribed.[122] One must also take into account the history of ideas and values, as they have evolved within the UN framework set up by the UN Charter.[123]

## 2.6 Conclusion

The drafting history of the United Nations Charter was characterized as a global discussion about global values. The discussions held in San Francisco were considered to be sufficiently inclusive. Many parts of the world did not send representatives for various reasons. Nevertheless, most regions were included in the discussions in some way. They were also sufficiently genuine. The representatives were concerned with the world's future, not just that of their own particular State. This sense of a common destiny was very strong at the time. All the States had just gone through a horrific collective experience, and there was a strong collective desire to prevent such a thing from recurring in the future. There was also a strong sense of urgency, a shared awareness that there was a need to define global values and global obligations to act on them.

## 3 GENERAL ASSEMBLY RESOLUTIONS AS THE RESULT OF GLOBAL DISCUSSION

## 3.1 Introduction

After 1945, the discussion of San Francisco moved to the General Assembly. Thakur described the General Assembly as "the unique forum of choice for articulating global values and norms and the arena where contested norms can be

---

[122] Article 31, Vienna Convention on the Law of Treaties.
[123] See especially Oscar Schachter, "The relation of law, politics and action in the United Nations" (1964), p. 193 and pp. 196-198. See also Georg Ress, "Interpretation" (2002), pp. 15-16 ; Emmanuelle Jouannet, "Les travaux préparatoires de la Charte des Nations Unies" (2005), especially pp. 21-24. This evolutionary interpretation of the Charter is preferred by a substantial number of scholars. See *e.g.*, James Leslie Brierly, "The Covenant and the Charter" (1946); Benedetto Conforti, "Le rôle de l'accord dans le système des Nations Unies" (1974), p. 210; Clark M. Eichelberger, "The United Nations Charter: A Growing Document" (1947), p. 98; Hambro Pollux, "The Interpretation of the Charter" (1946), p. 54; Nico Schrijver, "Les valeurs fondamentales et le droit des Nations Unies" (2006), pp. 85-88; Nico Schrijver, "The Future of the Charter of the United Nations" (2006), pp. 5-7; Simon Chesterman, Thomas M. Franck & David M. Malone, *Law and Practice of the United Nations* (2008), p. 10; Nigel D. White, *The United Nations system* (2002), especially Chapter 2. See also Yearbook of the International Law Commission, Vol. I (1963), p. 76. For a very short overview of that history, see Jan Pronk, "Een nieuwe jas voor de Verenigde Naties" (2007), pp. 9-11.

debated and reconciled."[124] These global values are articulated in the resolutions of the General Assembly, especially in its so-called "declarations." In contrast with other types of resolutions adopted by the Assembly, such as specific recommendations relating to a particular issue, these declarations contain general norms and principles. The Assembly's declarations read like treaty texts. Both contain rules that elaborate on the general purposes and principles in the Charter.[125] These declarations can therefore justifiably be described as "one of the principal instrumentalities of the formation of the collective will and judgment of the community of nations represented by the United Nations."[126]

It is certainly true that the General Assembly does not generally describe its own work as a discussion about values. Only one specific project, the dialogue between civilizations, has been presented as such. According to the General Assembly's Global Agenda for Dialogue among Civilizations,

> Dialogue among civilizations is a process between and within civilizations, founded on inclusion, and a collective desire to learn, uncover and examine assumptions, unfold shared meaning and core values and integrate multiple perspectives through dialogue.[127]

The list of objectives of this dialogue included the "development of a better understanding of common ethical standards and universal human values" and the "identification and promotion of common ground among civilizations in order to address common challenges threatening shared values, universal human rights and achievements of human society in various fields."[128] There is no reason to suggest that these objectives apply only to that one particular project, and that the remaining activities of the General Assembly have little or nothing to do with addressing common challenges threatening shared values.

The following sections explain why the Assembly is the "unique forum of choice" for the continuation of the global discussion about global values which started in San Francisco in 1945. Focusing on the General Assembly does not mean that other organs of the United Nations are irrelevant in the creation and interpretation of global values and the norms of the United Nations. This is

[124] Ramesh Thakur, *The United Nations, Peace and Security* (2006), p. 162. See also Bruno Simma, "From Bilateralism to Community Interest" (1994), pp. 262-263; Vekateshwara Subramanian Mani, "The Friendly Relations Declaration and the International Court of Justice" (1998), p. 532.
[125] See also Jorge Castaneda, "Valeur juridique des résolutions des Nations Unies" (1970), pp. 223-225, who distinguished various types of non-recommendatory resolutions.
[126] Separate Opinion of Judge Lauterpacht, p. 122, to International Court of Justice, Voting Procedure on Questions relating to Reports and Petitions concerning the Territory of South West Africa, Advisory Opinion of 7 June 1955.
[127] Article 1, Global Agenda for Dialogue among Civilizations, General Assembly resolution 56/6, adopted 9 November 2001.
[128] *Idem*, Article 2.

certainly not the case.[129] Global conferences organized by the United Nations play a key role in this process.[130] In a way, the Assembly itself is such a global conference. It is a "standing international conference in which any UN member State can raise any international issue it regards as deserving global attention."[131]

## 3.2 The Assembly's competence to discuss UN values, purposes and principles

To continue the global dialogue started in San Francisco, the Assembly first needed a mandate to discuss all global values, purposes, and principles in the UN Charter. The Assembly has such a mandate. According to Article 10 of the Charter, "the General Assembly may discuss any questions or any matters within the scope of the present Charter," and it "may make recommendations to the Members of the United Nations […] on any such questions or matters."

The drafting history of this Article is unusual. At first the text passed without problems from Dumbarton Oaks, through the various Commissions, Committees and Subcommittees, into the Charter. Then at a rather late stage in the drafting process, the Soviet Union intervened, and a new provision had to be made.

According to the Dumbarton Oaks proposals, "[t]he General Assembly should have the right to consider the general principles of cooperation in the maintenance of international peace and security, including the principles governing disarmament and the regulation of armaments."[132] The general description of the Assembly's mandate included only peace and security, and not the other UN purposes. This provision was intended to be interpreted in the broadest terms. After all, in subsequent articles in the Dumbarton Oaks proposals, the Assembly was given tasks that were not directly linked to the maintenance of international peace and security.[133]

Certain amendments proposed broadening the general functions and powers of the Assembly. Australia believed that the competence of the Assembly

---

[129] On the Security Council as promoter of the global interest (world peace), see Jean d'Aspremont, *Contemporary International Rulemaking and the Public Character of International La* (2006), pp. 24-25; and Pierre-Marie Dupuy, "The Constitutional Dimension of the Charter of the United Nations Revisited" (1997). Somewhat surprisingly, both authors do not mention the role of the General Assembly in defining and promoting the global interest.

[130] For an overview of all the global conferences on development organized by the United Nations since the 1990s, see The United Nations Development Agenda: Development for all (Goals, commitments and strategies agreed at the United Nations world conferences and summits since 1990). Many of the outcomes of these conferences are endorsed in an Assembly resolution.

[131] M. J. Peterson, "General Assembly" (2007), p. 98. See also Jorge Castaneda, "Valeur juridique des résolutions des Nations Unies" (1970), pp. 313-314.

[132] Dumbarton Oaks Proposals for a General International Organization, UNCIO, vol. 3, pp. 4-5.

[133] See *idem*, pp. 6 and 19.

should extend to "any matter affecting international relations."[134] Other delegations did not go that far. They had more modest proposals about what the Assembly's mandate should extend to, often related to the promotion of justice, as well as peace and security.[135]

Australia continued to play a leading role in the debates in San Francisco.[136] Evatt, the Australian delegate, suggested that the Committee dealing with the functions and powers of the General Assembly should address the following question of principle: "Should the Assembly have general power to discuss and make recommendations in respect to any matter affecting international relations?"[137] The Committee's answer to this question was unanimous and affirmative.[138] According to the Rapporteur of the Committee: "There should be no limitation whatsoever upon the right of the General Assembly to discuss any matter in the sphere of international relations at any time [and] the only limitation on the Assembly's power to make recommendations should be in respect of matters relating to the maintenance of peace and security during the period when the Security Council was dealing with such matters."[139] Furthermore, "the

---

[134] Amendments to the Dumbarton Oaks Proposals Submitted on Behalf of Australia, UNCIO, vol. 3, p. 544. Australia suggested that "[t]he General Assembly may consider, and may make such recommendations as it thinks fit with regard to, any matter affecting international relations." Australia's neighbour, New Zealand, made an identical suggestion. Amendments Submitted to the Dumbarton Oaks Proposals (Document 1 G/1) Submitted by the Delegation of New Zealand, UNCIO, vol. 3, p. 487: "The General Assembly shall have the right to consider any matter within the sphere of international relations." See also Seventh Plenary Session, May 1, 1945, UNCIO, vol. 1, p. 510.

[135] See e.g., Amendments to the Dumbarton Oaks Proposals Presented by the Delegation of Mexico, UNCIO, vol. 3, p. 180: "[t]he General Assembly should be competent to deal with any questions affecting international peace and security." This included (UNCIO, vol. 3, p. 181) the obligation "to examine any principles governing disarmament and the treaties proving inapplicable and any international situation having become unjust." See also the Proposals of the Delegation of the Republic of Bolivia for the Organization of a System of Peace and Security, UNCIO, vol. 3, p. 583. Bolivia suggested that "[t]he General Assembly should have the right to consider the general principles of cooperation in the maintenance of international peace, security, and justice."

[136] See also David Tothill, "Evatt and Smuts in San Francisco" (2007), especially p. 178.

[137] Fourth Meeting of Committee II/2, May 10, 1945, UNCIO, vol. 9, p. 29. A Subcommittee tasked with formulating a list of principle questions that needed to be addressed by the Committee included this general question at the very end of its list, and rephrased it slightly: "Subject to any exceptions specifically provided, should the Assembly have general power to discuss and make recommendations in respect of any matters affecting international relations?" Report of Subcommittee II/2/A, May 11, 1945, UNCIO, vol. 9, pp. 335-336. Almost all the other questions in this list were about the relationship between the Council and the Assembly in the maintenance of peace and security. See also Eighth Meeting of Committee II/2, May 16, 1945, UNCIO, vol. 9, pp. 50-53, where these questions are addressed. See also McCormack, "H.V. Evatt at San Francisco : a lasting contribution to international law."

[138] Ninth Meeting of Committee II/2, May 18, 1945, UNCIO, vol. 9, p. 60.

[139] Idem.

interpretation of the expression 'international relations' should be the widest possible."[140]

The Soviet Union objected to this summary of the discussion.[141] It agreed that the question was answered in the affirmative, but felt that this did not have all the implications suggested by the Rapporteur.[142] Attempts were made in a Subcommittee to redraft the provision so that it was satisfactory to everyone, including the Soviet Union.[143] This Subcommittee started with a redrafted proposal of the UK as the basis for discussion. According to this proposal, the General Assembly "should have the right [...] to discuss any matter within the sphere of international relations which affects the maintenance of international peace and security."[144]

At the Soviet Union's insistence, the Subcommittee put aside the UK redraft, and used the draft of the Sponsors and France as the basis for discussion.[145] This draft stated that "[t]he General Assembly should have the right to consider the general principles of cooperation in the maintenance of international peace and security."[146] In response, Australia again suggested that "[t]he General Assembly shall have the right to discuss any matter within the sphere of international relations."[147] The discussion was back where it started. The drafting subcommittee could not agree on how to proceed, so it proposed two possible formulations to the committee: the first alternative was that "[t]he General Assembly should have the right to discuss any matter within the sphere of international relations"; the second possibility was that the "[t]he General Assembly should have the right to discuss any matter within the sphere of international relations which affects the maintenance of international peace and security."[148]

---

[140] Ninth Meeting of Committee II/2, May 18, 1945, UNCIO, vol. 9, p. 60.

[141] See also Ministerie van Buitenlandse Zaken (Netherlands), *Het ontstaan der Verenigde Naties* (1950), pp. 45-47.

[142] See Communication from Delegate of U.S.S.R. concerning Summary Report of Ninth Meeting of Committee II/2, May 25, 1945, UNCIO, vol. 9, pp. 64-65. See also the Third Meeting of Subcommittee B of Committee II/2, May 23, 1945, UNCIO, vol. 9, pp. 388-389.

[143] See First Meeting of Subcommittee B of Committee II/2, May 21, 1945, UNCIO, 9, p. 375.

[144] See Second Meeting of Subcommittee B of Committee II/2, May 22, 1945, UNCIO, vol. 9, pp. 378-380, and Draft of Chapter V, Section B, Paragraph 1 Agreed upon as Basis for Further Discussion, UNCIO, vol. 9, p. 384. Belgium believed that the additional phrase at the end was welcome, because "[i]t safeguarded the domestic jurisdiction of states, which [was] a matter of capital importance for the small powers just as much as for the great powers." Second Meeting of Subcommittee B of Committee II/2, May 22, 1945, UNCIO, vol. 9, p. 379.

[145] See Fourth Meeting of Subcommittee B of Committee II/2, May 24, 1945, UNCIO, vol. 9, p. 393.

[146] Working Paper for Committee II/2/B: Redraft of Chapter V, Section B, Paragraph 1, UNCIO, vol. 9, p. 371.

[147] Suggestion by the Representative of Australia on Redraft of Chapter V, Section B, Paragraph 1, UNCIO, vol. 9, p. 397. Fifth Meeting of Subcommittee B of Committee II/2, May 25, 1945, UNCIO, vol. 9, pp. 401-402.

[148] Report of Subcommittee B to Committee II/2, UNCIO, vol. 9, p. 407.

The first alternative was defended in the committee with the argument that "the clear authorization to discuss 'any matter within the sphere of international relations', without any limitation, was important in order that the Assembly might truly become the 'town meeting of the world'."[149] Other delegates "objected to the vagueness of the powers which would be given to the Assembly by the unqualified use of the words 'within the sphere of international relations', and held that in practice the result would be to swamp the Assembly with more business than it could discharge at its rare meetings."[150] Nevertheless, the first alternative was preferred.[151] The fact that the General Assembly could now truly be considered as a real "town meeting" in which no subjects related to international affairs would be barred from discussion" was presented as a big victory for the small States over the Big Five.[152]

Almost three weeks later, the Soviet Union once again suggested that the Assembly could only discuss matters "which affect the maintenance of international peace and security."[153] In a meeting of the Executive Committee, Gromyko, the Soviet delegate, remarked that in its attempt at liberalism, the paragraph "concealed an element of danger to the effectiveness of the Organization as a whole, in that it made it possible for any country to raise for discussion in the General Assembly any act of another country which it did not like."[154] According to Evatt, the Soviets

---

[149] Fifteenth Meeting of Committee II/2, May 29, 1945, UNCIO, vol. 9, p. 108. See also Blaine Sloan, "The binding force of a "recommendation" of the General Assembly of the United Nations" (1948), pp. 1 and 32.

[150] *Idem*, p. 109.

[151] *Idem*, pp. 109-110. When the two possibilities were put to the vote, the first got 27 affirmative votes and 11 negative votes, while the second possibility got 9 affirmative votes and 27 negative votes: this meant that the first possibility was adopted. The draft then went successfully through the Coordination Committee and the Advisory Committee of Jurists. The former only discussed the difference between "has the right" and "may", and decided to stick to the latter. Summary Report of Fifteenth Meeting, June 12, 1945, UNCIO, vol. 17, pp. 92-93. For the Advisory Committee of Jurists, see Summary Report of Ninth Meeting of Advisory Committee of Jurists, June 16, 1945, UNCIO, vol. 17, p. 421.

[152] John H. Crider, "Assembly to Act as "Town Meeting"," in *New York Times* of May 30, 1945. US delegate Vandenberg "invented" this expression. Vandenberg used the expression on various occasions. An example can be found in the Minutes of the Twenty-First Five-Power Informal consultative Meeting on Proposed Amendments, June 13, 1945, in FRUS, *General*, Volume I, pp. 1285. See also John Foster Dulles, "The United Nations: A Prospectus (The General Assembly)" (1945), p. 1; and Fernand Dehousse, *Cours de politique international* (1945), p. 103.

[153] Twenty-Fourth Meeting of Committee II/2, June 16, 1945, UNCIO, vol. 9, pp. 221-222. Earlier, the USSR already raised this issue in a Five-Power meeting. In response, the US told the Soviets that to reopen the debate would be a "terrific error." See Minutes of the Twenty-First Five-Power Informal consultative Meeting on Proposed Amendments, June 13, 1945, in FRUS, *General*, Volume I, pp. 1284-1286. It was especially the timing of the Soviet objection which caused a situation qualified by the *New York Times* as "awkward, but not serious." See James B. Reston, "Russians Demand Curb on Assembly or They Won"t Sign" (1945).

[154] Summary Report of Ninth Meeting of Executive Committee, June 17, 1945, UNCIO, vol. 9, p. 522. Later, the Soviet Union described the attempt to widen the powers of the General Assembly as an attempt "to water it down, to doom it to floods of eloquent prattle to the detriment of speedy and

were most concerned with the interference of the Assembly in the domestic affairs of States; such interference was already prohibited elsewhere in the Charter.[155] The Rapporteur of the Committee in which the draft was first adopted, stood up to defend the text of "his" Committee. He said that the "representatives of the small nations of the Conference ha[d] given up many things they came to the Conference to fight for because they wanted to show that they trusted the big powers."[156] Now the big powers had an opportunity to show they trusted the smaller ones not to abuse the extensive powers of the Assembly. A subcommittee was established, consisting of Evatt, Gromyko, and Stettinius. Evatt came up with the following solution:

> The General Assembly should have the right to discuss any matters covered by the purposes and principles of the Charter or within the sphere of action of the United Nations or relating to the powers and functions of any of its organs or otherwise within the scope of the Charter.[157]

When Evatt presented his draft to the Executive Committee, he explained that the intention was to "[l]et the Charter itself [...] be the field over which discussions in the Assembly can and should range."[158] Gromyko was still not satisfied. In his view, the provision "should say that the General Assembly should have the right to discuss any matters relating to the maintenance of peace and security and matters relating to economic, social, and educational cooperation among the nations" because that statement "would properly emphasize the main purpose of the

---

decisive actions of the organization as a whole." See p. 5 of the "Introduction" to the booklet the *Soviet Union at the San Francisco Conference* (1945).

[155] Summary Report of Ninth Meeting of Executive Committee, June 17, 1945, UNCIO, vol. 9, pp. 523-525. See also Seventh Meeting of Steering Committee, June 17, 1945, pp. 264-266.

[156] Seventh Meeting of Steering Committee, June 17, 1945, p. 266.

[157] Tenth Meeting of Executive Committee, June 18, 1945, UNCIO, vol. 5, p. 533. According to James B. Reston, this was a Soviet suggestion. See James B. Reston, "Truce is Offered by Soviet on Issue of Assembly Talk." In the Minutes of the Seventy-third Meeting of the United States Delegation, June 16, 1945, in FRUS, *General*, Volume I, p. 1310, we find a US suggestion, which reads somewhat like a compromise between the old and the new: "Within the purposes and in accordance with the principles laid down in the Charter, the General Assembly should have the right to discuss any matter within the sphere of international relations." See also the Minutes of the Twenty-First Five-Power Informal consultative Meeting on Proposed Amendments, June 16, 1945, in FRUS, *General*, Volume I, pp. 1319-1323, where the Russians reject this US proposal because, in view of the Russians, it does not change anything. See further the Minutes of the Seventy-fifth Meeting of the United States Delegation, June 18, 1945, in FRUS, *General*, Volume I, pp. 1340-1343, where delegates express their concern about a newspaper article by James B. Reston, "Russians Demand Curb on Assembly or They Won"t Sign," which appeared in the *New York Times* of June 18, 1945, and in which all details of the discussion are described.

[158] Summary Report of Tenth Meeting of Executive Committee, June 18, 1945, UNCIO, vol. 5, p. 536.

Organization."[159] The Australian suggestion was sent to the Steering Committee, which then sent it back to the Committee it came from.[160] At that moment, it was the only outstanding issue on the agenda, and all the delegates wanted the conference to come to a close.[161] The Committee therefore swiftly and unanimously adopted the Australian draft.[162] To appease the Rapporteur, the US offered him the gavel he had used to chair his meetings, an offer which he gratefully accepted.[163]

When he presented his report to the Commission the Rapporteur referred to the Assembly as "the fortress where human aspirations are going to be defended." He also explained how the Assembly would do this:

> It will not have armies at its disposal, it will not have cannon or prisons; it will instead have something which, though incorporeal, has, in the course of human history, shown itself to be stronger and more invincible than brute force: the power of thought.[164]

Evatt believed that the Assembly's "right of discussion [was] free and untrammelled."[165] The Assembly could therefore justifiably be considered to be the "Town Meeting of the United Nations of the World,"[166] where the "everyday relations" of nations, as described by China, could be discussed.[167] Tunkin, one of

---

[159] *Idem*, p. 537. In response, Vandenberg (US) suggested that the Assembly should have the right to discuss any "matter relating to the maintenance of international peace and security, or any other matters covered by the purposes and principles of the United Nations or pertaining to the functions of its organs." See Minutes of the Twenty-Fourth Five-Power Informal Consultative Meeting on Proposed Amendments, June 18, 1945, in FRUS, *General*, Volume I, pp. 1351.

[160] Summary Report of Tenth Meeting of Executive Committee, June 18, 1945, UNCIO, vol. 5, p. 537. See also the discussion in the Steering Committee, where no new arguments were brought forward. When the Steering Committee voted on the decision to send the provision back to Committee II/2, Bolivia cast the only negative vote. This vote was cast by the Rapporteur of that Committee, Andrade. Summary Report of Eighth Meeting of Steering Committee, June 18, 1945, UNCIO, vol. 5, pp. 273-274.

[161] See the article in the *New York Times* entitled "Success at San Francisco" (1945). See also the Minutes of the Twenty-Eighth Five-Power Informal Consultative Meeting on Proposed Amendments, June 20, 1945, in FRUS, *General*, Volume I, pp. 1397-1398.

[162] Twenty-Fifth Meeting of Committee II/2, June 20, 1945, UNCIO, vol. 9, pp. 233-235.

[163] *Idem*, p. 235. The entire drafting history of the provision is summarized in the Report of the Rapporteur of Committee II/2, UNCIO, vol. 9, pp. 242-243.

[164] Fourth Meeting of Commission II, June 21, 1945, UNCIO, vol. 8, p. 196.

[165] Fourth Meeting of Commission II, June 21, 1945, UNCIO, vol. 8, p. 208. As Dulles later pointed out, all this "is enough to make apparent that the Assembly is given a tempting invitation to chase rainbows." See John Foster Dulles, "The United Nations: A Prospectus (The General Assembly)" (1945), p. 2.

[166] Fourth Meeting of Commission II, June 21, 1945, UNCIO, vol. 8, p. 209.

[167] When explaining the importance of the General Assembly, the Chinese delegate pointed out that while the Security Council essentially deals with emergencies in international relations, the Assembly deals with "everyday relations." Fourth Meeting of Commission II, June 21, 1945, UNCIO, vol. 8, p. 196. See also Clyde Eagleton, "The Charter Adopted at San Francisco" (1945), p. 940: "The Security

the most influential Soviet scholars, later admitted that the Assembly's "competence include[d] practically all the most important questions of international relations."[168] This would satisfy the small States, and the term "town meeting of the world" could be – and was – used to sell the Charter at home.[169]

Evatt later stressed the importance of the general mandate of the Assembly. In his view, "Th[e] broadening of the scope of the General Assembly's powers [was] one of the most important achievements of the San Francisco Conference and one of the main democratic safeguards of the United Nations Organization."[170] Since 1945 the Assembly has used its *compétence générale* to the full.[171] It has dealt with all global matters – even at the time that the Security Council was occupied with the same issues – always linking its resolutions to (parts of) the UN Charter.[172]

## 3.3 The General Assembly as a forum for global discussion

Now that the competence of the Assembly to discuss all the values, purposes and principles proclaimed in the UN Charter has been affirmed, it is time to assess the inclusive and genuine character of the Assembly's discussions and their capacity to motivate action.

Dehousse once referred to the Assembly as "*l'organe démocratique par excellence*."[173] That is an exaggeration,[174] but it is clear that, of all the principal organs of the United Nations, the Assembly comes closest to a World Parliament in

---

Council operates only for crises; the General Assembly has a hand in all the current activities of international life."

[168] Grigory I. Tunkin, "The legal nature of the United Nations" (1969), p. 18. According to Tunkin, the emphasis was nonetheless on peace and security.

[169] The expression was used to characterize the General Assembly in the Report of the Foreign Relations Committee of the US Senate. See Foreign Relations Committee (US Senate), "Foreign Relations Committee's Report Urging Ratification of the United Nations Charter" (1945). It was also used in the Dutch Government's "Memorie van Toelichting bij de Goedkeuringswet van het Handvest der Verenigde Naties" (1945), p. 20. There it was translated into "den gemeenteraad der Wereld," or the "city council of the world."

[170] Herbert Vere Evatt, *The United Nations* (1948), p. 20.

[171] Georges Kaeckenbeeck, "La Charte de San-Francisco dans ses rapports avec le droit international" (1948), p. 146. See also p. 251.

[172] See Kofi Annan, *We, the Peoples: the Role of the United Nations in the Twenty-first Century* (2000), para. 319, and, of course, the UN Charter (especially Article 1 and Chapter IV). See also Oscar Schachter, "United Nations law" (1994), p. 2.

[173] Fernand Dehousse, *Cours de politique international* (1945), p. 101. See also Oscar Schachter, "United Nations law" (1994), p. 2, who referred to the "democratization" of the treaty-making process by the Assembly.

[174] See Alain Pellet, "La formation du droit international dans le cadre des Nations Unies" (1995), p. 14, for some objections to seeing the Assembly as a democratic organ.

which the voices of the entire world population are represented,[175] and that the interpretation and elaboration of the constitutional norms of the UN Charter should therefore be concentrated in this organ of the United Nations.[176] In line with his "constitutional" perspective on the work of the principal United Nations organs, Fassbender referred to this on-going process of interpreting the norms of the UN Charter, sometimes *re*interpreting them to accommodate changes in international life, as the "constitutional history" of the international community. Fassbender wrote that this "constitutional history" took place primarily in the UN General Assembly:

> As far as we can speak of a "constitutional history" of the international community since 1945, it has been shaped, and taken place, in the United Nations and, in particular, in its General Assembly. It is sufficient to mention a few key words to make the reader recall the great debates which have profoundly influenced, if not changed, global life: self-determination of peoples, decolonization, human rights, fight against racial discrimination, definition of aggression, nuclear arms, utilization of outer space and the sea-bed ("common heritage of mankind"), global environmental problems, especially the use of non-renewable resources and the protection of particularly vulnerable areas (Antarctica, tropical forests). In all these discussions, the U.N. regarded itself as the "natural forum"; and, indeed, no other body could have claimed a similar legitimacy.[177]

Why can the General Assembly claim to be the "natural forum" for shaping the constitutional history of the United Nations? The most important answer to this question is the inclusive character of the Assembly's discussions. Representatives of virtually all States, each representing the views of a particular population, come together at the United Nations General Assembly to adopt declarations of principles and ideas. In this way they "collaboratively engage each other and other sectors of society in the multilateral management of global affairs."[178] This inclusiveness means that the stream of UN resolutions and declarations is the "closest we are able to get to an authentic voice of humanity."[179]

This inclusiveness, in terms of the participation of States, was not shared by its predecessor, the League of Nations. For a long time the "global discussion"

---

[175] Bruno Simma, "From Bilateralism to Community Interest" (1994), pp. 262-263.

[176] This is in fact what happened. Only in recent years has the Security Council contributed to the evolution of global values. See Nico Schrijver, "De Verenigde Naties in de 21ste eeuw" (2007), p. 154. However, as was noted before, this is not to suggest that other organs of the "UN family" are irrelevant when it comes to global value-making.

[177] Bardo Fassbender, "The United Nations Charter as Constitution" (1998), p. 580. In Part II of this study, this "constitutional history" will be looked at in great detail.

[178] See Chapter 1 – A New World, the Concept of Global Governance, in Commission on Global Governance, *Our Global Neighborhood* (1995).

[179] *Idem*, p. 9.

excluded most of the international community by formally distinguishing between civilized and uncivilized nations.[180] The League of Nations explicitly excluded from independent membership nations "inhabited by peoples not yet able to stand by themselves under the strenuous conditions of the modern world".[181] This distinction also surfaced in the infamous dispute between Ethiopia and Italy, a dispute which showed that the League was in fact irrelevant and which eventually led to its end. When Ethiopia notified the League of the Italian aggression committed against it, Italy did not defend its actions. Instead, it claimed that "Italy's dignity as a civilized nation would be deeply wounded were she to continue a discussion in the League on a footing of equality with Ethiopia."[182] This statement suggested that some States were more equal than others, even among those fortunate enough to be admitted to League membership.

Instead of leaving the global leadership to an elite group of "civilized nations," this leadership and the creation of global values that comes with it is now in the hands of the General Assembly of the United Nations, which welcomed the entire world.

Admittedly the UN Charter itself does not reflect this aim of universal membership. The Charter proclaimed that the original Members of the United Nations should be those States that participated in the San Francisco Conference, and that "other peace loving States" could be invited to join later.[183] At San Francisco it was agreed that "peace loving" essentially meant "that a nation [was] ready to accept and fulfil the obligations of the Charter and that it [was] able to accept and fulfil them."[184] In a sense, this requirement of being "peace loving" was therefore rather meaningless. It essentially meant subscribing to the purposes and principles of the Charter. By acceding to the UN Charter a State had already declared its acceptance of these purposes and principles. As time passed, universality of membership became the ultimate goal, and references to being "peace loving" faded into the background.[185]

---

[180] See Jean d'Aspremont, *Contemporary International Rulemaking and the Public Character of International Law* (2006), pp. 7-11; and Bert Röling, *International law in an expanded world* (1960).

[181] See Article 22 of the Covenant of the League of Nations, which constituted Part I of the Versailles Peace Treaty, signed on June 28, 1919, to end the First World War.

[182] Situation in Ethiopia, Memorandum by the Italian Government dated September 4th, 1935, and Documents relating thereto, in League of Nations Official Journal, volume 16, issue 11 (November 1935), p. 1137.

[183] Article 3 and 4, UN Charter.

[184] Report of the Rapporteur of Committee I/2 on Chapter III (Membership) (Incorporating Changes Submitted by Delegation for the Approval of Commission I), UNCIO, vol. 7, p. 326 (emphasis added).

[185] Indeed, as Robinson rightly pointed out, since 1945: "The membership of the United Nations has developed from a wartime coalition on the eve of victory against the common Axis enemy, through an organization of 'like-minded' States, to a near-universal but heterogeneous society of nations, presumed to be at peace." Jacob Robinson, "Metamorphosis of the United Nations" (1958), p. 500.

The universal membership of the United Nations, and therefore of the Assembly, is considered crucial, especially by the peoples who were marginalized in the past. As one third world scholar pointed out, it is the dominance of a certain world view, rather than overwhelming military or economic power, that most concerns the marginalized voices. The dominance of ideas is often the result, not of better arguments, but of military power, used to sustain that ideological dominance.[186] The General Assembly aims to remedy this situation by giving one vote to each country, instead of basing voting power on economic or military power, as some other international organizations do.[187] As Morgenthau pointed out, the fact that States have to convince a large majority of their fellow States, rather than only a limited group of the most powerful nations, to have a certain common foreign policy approved, means that different arguments need to be used, appealing to a new perception of common interest.[188] At the same time, it was suggested as early as 1947 that the Assembly should follow the example of the economic organizations and replace its one State, one vote system with a system of "weighted voting under which each member of the United Nations is given in the Assembly an influence and an authority in consonance with its actual influence and authority in the world of today."[189] The one State, one vote system was never without its opponents.

The global discussions of the Assembly are public[190] and are observed and scrutinized by non-governmental organizations, academics, bloggers,[191] global pollsters,[192] and so on.[193] The Member States of the United Nations are reluctant to

---

[186] Chimni said in his Manifesto for a third world approach to international law: "[p]owerful states [..] exercise dominance in the international system through the world of ideas and not through the use of force. But from time to time force is used both to manifest their overwhelming military superiority and to quell the possibility of any challenge being mounted to their vision of world order." B. S. Chimni, "Third World Approaches to International Law: A Manifesto" (2006), p. 19. This critique may sound convincing, but when Chimni explains how international law is based on a worldview inconsistent with that of the third world, his main objections are to the rules of the international economic system. These rules were established largely outside the UN framework (in fact, UN's Economic and Social Council was supposed to add some values into that largely valueless economic framework).

[187] The IMF and World Bank are examples of international organizations where economic power directly influences the voting-power.

[188] Hans J. Morgenthau, "The New United Nations and the Revision of the Charter" (1954), pp. 12-13.

[189] Sir Carl Berendsen, "The United Nations and international law" (1947), p. 123. Interestingly, at San Francisco, the one-State-one-vote arrangement of the Assembly was hardly discussed. Apparently, it was the self-evident thing to do. See also Francis Aime Vallat, "Voting in the General Assembly of the United Nations" (1954), p. 279.

[190] See rule 60 of the Rules of Procedure of the General Assembly (embodying amendments and additions adopted by the General Assembly up to September 2006), UNDoc. A/520/Rev.16.

[191] For a good example, see: www.invisiblecollegeblog.com (this is my own weblog). See also Global Voices Online (www.globalvoicesonline.org), a project that aims to give the non-Western blogger a bigger audience.

[192] A good example is www.worldpublicopinion.org.

[193] See Mary Kaldor, "The Idea of Global Civil Society" (2003), p. 590.

accept the influence of all these non-State actors. In a 2004 report on this topic the problems were described as follows:

> Governments do not always welcome sharing what has traditionally been their preserve. Many increasingly challenge the numbers and motives of civil society organizations in the United Nations — questioning their representivity, legitimacy, integrity or accountability. Developing country Governments sometimes regard civil society organizations as pushing a "Northern agenda" through the back door. At the same time, many in civil society are becoming frustrated; they can speak in the United Nations but feel they are not heard and that their participation has little impact on outcomes.[194]

The same report suggested that global civil society was here to stay. Instead of regretting or even denying this reality, the Member States ought to look for ways to benefit from the new situation. "The question is not how would the United Nations like to change? But, given how the world has changed, how must the United Nations evolve its civil society relations to become fully effective and remain fully relevant?"[195]

It is not only the formal participants in the debate, *i.e.* the representatives of all Member States, who provide the ideas for discussion. These ideas also come, for example, from the United Nations Secretary-General and the Expert Panels established by him, or from the International Law Commission, or from other (subsidiary) organs and institutions of the United Nations.[196] These new ideas, values and norms can be discussed and adopted by the Assembly.[197] In every case it is the resolutions of the Assembly that must be examined to discover which ideas, whatever their exact origin, were embraced by the United Nations membership as a whole.

This rather optimistic account of the inclusiveness of the Assembly discussions could be viewed with some scepticism. First, the global discussions do not take place during the public sessions of the General Assembly. Only the end results of the discussions can be found in the records of the Assembly.[198] The actual

---

[194] We the peoples: civil society, the United Nations and global governance, Report of the Panel of Eminent Persons on United Nations–Civil Society Relations, UNDoc. A/58/817, distributed 11 June 2004, p. 7.

[195] *Idem.*

[196] For example, the Millennium Declaration, resolution adopted by the UN General Assembly, 18 September 2000. UNDoc. A/RES/55/2, is inspired by Kofi Annan, *We, the Peoples: the Role of the United Nations in the Twenty-first Century* (2000). See Ramesh Thakur, Andrew F. Cooper & John English, *International Commissions and the Power of Ideas* (2005).

[197] The power to put something on the agenda for discussion (agenda-setting) is important. See Rule 13 of the Rules of Procedure of the General Assembly, UNDoc. A/520/Rev.15.

[198] Only the majority opinion ends up in an Assembly resolution, whilst dissenting views end up in the record of the Assembly as explanations of the (abstaining or dissenting) vote, if this is the wish of the dissenting state(s).

Chapter III

debates often take place in various committees, or outside the conference halls altogether.[199] The Assembly's public sessions are mainly used to ensure that members' opinions appear in the records, and not to exchange ideas and engage in a discussion on the spot. Obviously this has an effect on the attendance record, which is generally not very impressive.[200]

One could also be sceptical about the representative character of some of the representatives in the Assembly. Those representing dictatorial regimes do not represent anyone and are accountable to no one. Therefore their opinions should not be taken very seriously in the global discussions.[201] When global civil society scrutinizes the Assembly's global discussions, it can challenge the representative character of such a representative, even when he or she is formally mandated to speak on behalf of his or her people. That is at best an *ad hoc* solution. Because of the domestic – and not global – lack of democratic accountability, it is sometimes suggested that a new UN type of international organization should be established, consisting solely of democratic nations: a community of democracies.[202] As this would automatically exclude the voice of a vast number of the world's citizens – those who live in undemocratic countries – other suggestions have also been made to have the voice of all the world's citizens heard. One suggestion is to conduct global polls instead, as a method to find out what "the people" value most, or to establish a General Assembly where the world's citizens are represented by persons directly elected by them.[203] Because of the wide variety of cultures and political preferences, it is impossible to have a representative representation unless an Assembly is created with thousands of representatives.[204] Even if such an immense

[199] Johan Kaufmann, *United Nations Decision Making* (1980), pp. 32-40. On pp. 119-129, Kaufmann, a former representative of the Netherlands at the United Nations, describes in detail how General Assembly resolutions come into being. There is nothing surprising about this process: it particularly involves looking for support among friends and among the major powers. States usually do this in private, not during the Assembly meetings.
[200] Kaufmann noted: "attendance at the general debate tends to be poor, except when a speech is made by the head of delegation of a major power, or when somebody deemed to be a celebrity takes the floor." p. 27 of Johan Kaufmann, *United Nations Decision Making* (1980).
[201] See, *e.g.*, John McCain, speech delivered on the first of May 2007 at the Hoover Institution, Stanford University in Stanford, California. (http://news-service.stanford.edu/news/2007/may2/mccain-050207.html.) See also G. John Ikenberry and Anne-Marie Slaughter, *Forging A World Of Liberty Under Law* (2006).
[202] Such a community actually exists already. This is a brief description of the Community of Democracies: "a global gathering of 106 governments committed to democracy came together to develop and pursue a common agenda. This community of states – drawn from a diverse mix of regions, cultures, and religions – dedicated itself to a core set of democratic principles and to support cooperation among democracies worldwide." Source: http://www.ccd21.org. For more information about this movement, see this website.
[203] In April 2007, a Campaign for the Establishment of a United Nations Parliamentary Assembly was launched. See: http://en.unpacampaign.org/events/index.php.
[204] See M. J. Peterson, "General Assembly" (2007), p. 113.

construction were possible at an affordable price, the "European experience" shows that the establishment of a world parliament does not necessarily solve the problem.[205] The existing institutional arrangement, *i.e.* to have all States represented in the Assembly, may not be so bad after all. The focus should be on promoting democracy *within* States.

The world's population should feel that it is involved in the work of the United Nations in some way, irrespective of the official procedures and institutional rules. In the words of the second United Nations Secretary-General, Dag Hammarskjöld from Sweden: "Everything will be all right [...] when people, just people, stop thinking of the United Nations as a weird Picasso abstraction and see it as a drawing they made themselves." Recent surveys show that if this is the goal, the Organization still has work to do. For example, the Global Values Survey of 2004 concluded that the confidence in the United Nations was as low as 54%.[206] This is still better than the confidence people have in their own governments (50%).[207] With regard to various problems of international concern, the survey asked who could handle the problem better, the United Nations, the respective national governments, or both together? In all cases (international peacekeeping, protection of the environment, international development assistance, refugees and the protection of human rights) it was felt that national governments would handle the problem better on their own, without the involvement of the United Nations.[208] According to a Gallup Poll of 2005, nearly half of the people of the world who were aware of the existence of the United Nations had a positive opinion of it (48%), whilst a third (35%) held a neutral and 13% had a negative opinion.[209]

These polls suggest that the world's population as a whole does not identify with the discussions going on at the Assembly. But these are just a few polls, and sweeping conclusions should be avoided. However, if the impression people have of the UN is as negative as these polls suggest, the United Nations must find new ways to reach ordinary people, and make them feel involved in some way. As was the case in the San Francisco Conference in 1945, the aim should once again be to ensure that the people of the world can participate in the Assembly's work, without formally granting them any powers to influence the debates.

---

[205] As the former Minister for Foreign Affairs of the Netherlands, Maxime Verhagen, put it: "European citizens view European integration as an elite project, which controls their daily lives but over which they have no control." Verhagen, *Norbert Schmelzer lecture* (2007).

[206] E088 (Table), in Ronald Inglehart, *Human Beliefs and Values* (2004).

[207] *Idem*, E79 (Table). See also E125.

[208] *Idem*, E135-E139 (Table).

[209] Gallup International Association – Voice of the People 2005, poll conducted for BBC World Service by the international polling firm GlobeScan together with the Program on International Policy Attitudes (PIPA) at the University of Maryland. It showed that on average 59 per cent rated the United Nations as having a positive influence, while just 16 per cent rated it as having a negative influence.

## 3.4 The Assembly's rules of communication to ensure genuine discussion

This section examines the genuine character of the Assembly's discussions. Again, there is room for scepticism in this respect. The United Nations, with its General Assembly, has been described as "a battle-ground of particular interests,"[210] or as "simply a meeting place, where the nations of the world attempt to conduct their business in the same competitive, self-serving, and (dare we say it) even deceitful way that they always have and surely always will."[211] This is a sobering thought, and Peterson added that "though a truism, it bears repeating that governments, even more than individuals in domestic political systems, evaluate decisions in terms of what is in the outcome for them," and that a government generally "focus[es] on the interests of [its] own State or of its closest allies."[212] The behaviour of States in the Assembly is above all based on the outcome of a cost-benefit analysis, which includes, but is certainly not restricted to, defending their own principles and values. It is often suggested that only if a State feels very strongly about certain values and principles, that these values and principles could determine the behaviour of that State. For example, the proposal for a New International Economic Order, presented by a large group of developing nations, was claimed to be above all, about values.[213] Western States defeated this proposal by pointing out that it was not based on values at all, but that the developing States were simply disguising a demand for more money in these idealistic proposals.[214] Arguably this effectively shut the door on any value-based discussion of the proposals. In response, reference can be made to the remarks made earlier, that it is pointless to oppose values and interests in this way.[215] Discussions about values and their relative importance are by definition also about the allocation of limited resources. Moreover, no State can persuade another State to join a particular project by

---

[210] Jacob Robinson, "Metamorphosis of the United Nations" (1958), p. 514.

[211] John Tessitore, "The UN at 60: Still Misunderstood" (2007).

[212] M.J. Peterson, *The General Assembly in World Politics* (1986), p. 208. See also M. J. Peterson, "General Assembly" (2007), p. 102.

[213] Declaration on the Establishment of a New International Economic Order, General Assembly resolution 3201 (S-VI), adopted without a vote during a special session in 1974. It was adopted by the Assembly against the wishes of the Western States, which made the ideas enshrined in these resolutions somewhat unrealistic. See p. 199-211 of Louis Henkin, *How Nations Behave: Law and Foreign Policy* (1979). Henkin remarked that "one can conclude with some confidence [..] that although the developed world holds most of the cards today, the influence of numbers, of rhetoric, of ideas whose time have come – if slowly – will be strongly felt in the politics of economics; and the international economic order at the end of the century, if not new, will be substantially different from what we know today." We have now reached that point, the change of the millennium, and one can judge for oneself.

[214] Andrew F. Cooper and John English, "International Commissions and the mind of Global Governance" (2005), p. 3.

[215] See section 3.3 of Chapter II.

referring to its own self-interest. As Jessup pointed out, to convince other States it is necessary to translate self-serving motives into an argument about values:

> [States] are of course responsive each to [their] own national interest but they recognize and respect a moral stand; you cannot secure the sympathetic support of the General Assembly by ignoring moral values. Pure opportunism and the absence of an underlying theory or principle is not persuasive. The sophisticated outsider mocks at the high-sounding principles enunciated in the United Nations Charter but no competent delegate does so within the United Nations.[216]

The General Assembly's debates cannot be accurately characterized as an abstract, academic or "philosophical" discussion about global values. However, describing them as being opportunistic and self-serving is also a caricature. One of the biggest supporters of the United Nations, Sir Richard Jolly, referred to the process of making resolutions as "UN hypocrisy." As an example of such hypocrisy, he referred to one of the resolutions the United Nations is most proud of – the Universal Declaration of Human Rights – and explained that even though the result was a glorious document protecting the human dignity of all men and women, the resolution was formulated with the greatest hypocrisy, and with various political tensions and provocations.[217] Jolly thought it was an ideal task for global civil society, which he called the "third UN," to constantly remind States of their hypocritical promises.[218]

This "hypocrisy warning" reveals the need for clear rules of communication and realistic expectations about the outcomes of the discussions. In 1957, Jessup made an attempt to do so by comparing the Assembly's rules of procedure with those of domestic parliaments.[219] He concluded that the Assembly's work could

---

[216]Philip C. Jessup, "Parliamentary diplomacy" (1957), p. 236. See also Oscar Schachter, "The relation of law, politics and action in the United Nations" (1964), p. 173; Oscar Schachter, "United Nations Law" (1994), p. 9.

[217] Sir Jolly made these remarks as panelists at the 50th Anniversary International Congress of the Society for International Development, Reconciling the Dichotomies of Development: Ways Forward, held 4-7 July 2007, in The Hague, The Netherlands. The summary is based on my own notes; a very brief outline of his remarks can be found in the SID 50th Anniversary Congress Report, p. 6-7 (available on the website of SID: http://www.sidint.org).

[218] *Idem.* Jolly distinguished three different UNs: (1) the United Nations of all Member States combined; (2) the United Nations of all global civil servants; and (3) the United Nations of the ngos, academics, and other "outsiders" checking on the UN from the sidelines, in order to ensure that the Member States genuinely respect the promises they made, even if they generally make them in a state of hypocrisy.

[219] He did not believe that the rules of procedure of domestic parliaments should simply be applied also in the Assembly. Instead, Jessup believed that there were some "general principles of parliamentary law," which were inherent in all such systems, and that the Assembly could adapt them to the international situation with its own peculiarities. See especially p. 225 of Philip C. Jessup, "Parliamentary diplomacy" (1957).

aptly be characterized as a form of "parliamentary diplomacy," a term he borrowed from Rusk, a US representative to the UN. The process of parliamentary diplomacy was characterized by a number of factors, such as:

> On-going discussions, not limited to a specific issue;
> Discussions which are exposed to and scrutinized by world public opinion;
> Discussions governed by clear rules of procedure;
> Formal conclusions as the concrete results of the discussions, adopted by a majority vote.[220]

These rules would not in any way turn the representatives of the self-serving States into cosmopolitan philosophers. That would be an unreasonable expectation in any case. This process, in which various regional value systems and interests meet, sometimes conflicting and sometimes converging, provides the best foundation for defining global values, precisely because States have an interest in the outcome of these discussions. The politics of the discussions therefore add a sense of urgency to the debates. The process increases their relevance in global decision making in a way that a purely philosophical debate about values could never do. At the United Nations General Assembly, at least all States are more or less obliged to participate and vote in all the debates on a wide range of global issues. They are obliged to take these discussions seriously, and take account of their political implications.[221] The Assembly's discussions fall somewhere between a debate based primarily on a struggle for power and the realization of particular interests, and a debate about global values and the realization of the global interest.

Throughout the history of the United Nations it has been the United States that has dominated international relations in terms of power, although its power was to some extent balanced by that of the Soviet Union during the Cold War.[222] At the General Assembly, it is apparent that it is not power that determines dominance, but rather the voice of the majority – the developing States – over a "Western" minority.[223] This is a typical consequence of a democratic system in which every

---

[220] Philip C. Jessup, "Parliamentary diplomacy" (1957), p. 185.

[221] Judge Alvarez: "The General Assembly of the United Nations is the meeting place where States discuss political matters of general interest (open diplomacy); in doing so, the Assembly is in a good position to reconcile Law and Politics." Alvarez, Separate Opinion in the International Court of Justice's Reservations to the Genocide Convention Advisory Opinion, ICJ Reports of 1951, p. 52.

[222] This balance of power led to an almost complete paralysis of the Security Council. The relationship between the United Nations and the United States since the end of the Cold War has been the subject of many books. For two examples written by senior United Nations civil servants, see Boutros Boutros-Ghali, *Unvanquished: A U.S. - U.N. Saga* (1999), and Ramesh Thakur, *The United Nations, Peace and Security* (2006).

[223] See Louis Henkin, *How Nations Behave: Law and Foreign Policy* (1979), p. 177. He notes that only in the early stages it was the West that dominated. After a wave of decolonization, the majority shifted to those new states.

State was given one vote. [224] The Assembly often called upon the overruled "Western" minority to carry out the wishes of the majority of developing States.[225] It was partly for this reason that the United States increasingly turned its back on the Assembly, which could, in a worst case scenario, turn the Assembly into a practically irrelevant debating society.[226] The important thing to learn from this was neatly phrased by Peterson:

> The full impact of Assembly resolutions has always depended upon the relation between the ability to muster votes inside the Assembly and the control of resources for taking effective action outside.[227]

The Assembly itself has always been very conscious of this. The affirmative votes of the economic and military superpowers have always been valued more than the one nation, one vote system formally requires.

## 3.5 The General Assembly resolutions as a motivation for action

### 3.5.1 Introduction

The language of international law is *par excellence* the language which motivates action in the international community.[228] When a State is bound by a certain legal norm, it is obliged to act in accordance with that norm. Moreover, international law provides various ways to ensure a State's future compliance with the legal principles and provisions it voluntarily subscribed to in the past. Do General

---

[224] The one state, one vote principle gives Nauru and China both one vote in that Assembly, despite the fact that the latter country has 100,000 times more inhabitants than the former. This is not very democratic. See also p. 113 of M. J. Peterson, "General Assembly" (2007), and Bruno Simma, "From Bilateralism to Community Interest" (1994), p. 263.

[225] Peterson: "The Third World majority was hobbled by a serious disjuncture between its control of votes inside and lack of resources for action outside, exposing all the weaknesses of a deliberative body that commands no effective and coercive institutions." p. 109 of M. J. Peterson, "General Assembly" (2007). See also p. 51 of M.J. Peterson, *The General Assembly in World Politics* (1986).

[226] However, it must be emphasized that the debate in the US on what to do with the UN General Assembly - to ignore it or to use it for political advantage - has always been a heated debate, and it is not yet settled. See p. 110-112 of M. J. Peterson, "General Assembly" (2007).

[227] M. J. Peterson, "General Assembly" (2007), p. 109.

[228] See also section 3.4 of Chapter II, above. Of course, one might think that divine obligations would be even more action-motivating than legal obligations. Many Dutch politicians were annoyed by the fact that the Netherlands delegation had not managed, in San Francisco, to include an explicit reference to God as ultimate source of the purposes and pledges made into the United Nations Charter. See "Voorloopig Verslag Algemeene Beschouwingen bij de Goedkeuringswet van het Handvest der Verenigde Naties," in Handelingen der Staten-Generaal, Tweede Kamer, Bijlagen Tijdelijke Zitting 1945, Bijlage no. 7, p. 45. For the response of the Dutch Government, see "Memorie van Antwoord," in Bijlage no. 8, p. 49.

Assembly resolutions also have this effect? Do they oblige States to act in a certain way? To what extent are States actually invited or compelled to do more than pay lip service to certain values in the General Assembly, and act on them only if convenient and on a piecemeal basis? The legal nature of commitments made by States through the adoption of General Assembly resolutions is assessed below.

Resolutions of the General Assembly do not have the same status as the provisions of the United Nations Charter. Assembly resolutions do not contain constitutional or hierarchically superior law of the international community. The text of the Charter and the *travaux préparatoires* show that it was certainly not the intention to grant the Assembly such extraordinary legislative powers.[229] The Charter does not explicitly give the Assembly any legislative powers.[230] And if an Assembly resolution does not fit the description of any of the recognized sources of international law – treaty, custom, or general principle – it cannot be considered as a source of international law.

Although that is the end of the story according to the most basic legal doctrine, the reality is always much more complex than any doctrine.[231] The central question is not whether Assembly resolutions can be formally qualified as a source of international law, but whether they contain commitments by States to behave in a particular way in the future, and whether these commitments are such that they can be legitimately and justifiably relied upon.[232] In the international legal order, the consequences of the violation of a norm of international law on the one hand, and the breaking of a political pledge on the other hand, are generally not all that different. Therefore it would be artificial to assume that only legal norms have the capacity to motivate behaviour and ensure compliance with certain principles and values.[233]

The debates of the San Francisco Conference in 1945 are examined first. Three discussions are summarized. First, the discussion about whether or not the Organization should have a general purpose to promote international law. Secondly, the discussion about the role of the General Assembly in promoting the progressive development of international law, and thirdly, the discussion about the role of the Assembly in promoting the progressive development of the law of the United Nations.

---

[229] See also Gaetano Arangio-Ruiz, "The normative role of the General Assembly" (1972), pp. 445-452. It is also clear that over time no custom has developed in the sense that the Assembly's lawmaking powers are recognized in practice (pp. 452-460).
[230] See also Christopher C. Joyner, "U.N. General Assembly resolutions and international law" (1981), p. 452; Oscar Schachter, "United Nations law" (1994), p. 1.
[231] See also Gaetano Arangio-Ruiz, "The normative role of the General Assembly" (1972), pp. 434. See also Alain Pellet, "La formation du droit international dans le cadre des Nations Unies" (1995), especially pp. 3-4.
[232] See also Samuel A. Bleicher, "The Legal Significance of Re-Citation of General Assembly Resolutions" (1969), p. 446.
[233] See also Jorge Castaneda, "Valeur juridique des résolutions des Nations Unies" (1970), p. 220.

## 3.5.2    The development of international law as a purpose of the United Nations

Despite the US suggestions to authorize the Organization "to strengthen and develop the rule of law in international relations,"[234] and despite China's suggestions to establish an International Law Codification Commission "to study problems of international law," "propose conventions," and "codify existing international law,"[235] the Dumbarton Oaks proposals did not include the promotion of justice and international law in their list of purposes.[236] The Dumbarton Oaks proposals focused on international peace and security. It was the belief, especially of the Soviet delegation, that "any suggestion of [adding] principles of international law as a possible provision in the future Charter seemed to be a deviation from this primary emphasis on security."[237] International law was not necessary to prevent future wars. The united power of the victors of the Second World War would deter any future outbreak of war. Robinson concluded that "the Dumbarton Oaks proposals were based on the principle of security through power, rather than of peace through law."[238]

Some States were not convinced. They suggested adding a reference to justice and/or international law to the list of purposes.[239] Ecuador proposed that the name of the new Organization be changed to "International Juridical Association," or "Juridical Community of States."[240] Egypt believed that it was the Organization's purpose to "determine, define, codify and develop the rules of international law and international morality,"[241] and also to enforce respect for these laws.[242] During the San Francisco conference many States proposed that the list of purposes should contain a reference to international law and justice.[243] Most importantly, as one of

---

[234] Plan for the Establishment of an International Organization for the Maintenance of International Peace and Security, published in FRUS, *1944, General:* Volume I, p. 616.

[235] Tentative Chinese Proposals for a General International Organization, in FRUS, *1944, General:* Volume I, p. 722. See also Progress Report on Dumbarton Oaks Conversations – Thirty-eighth Day, *idem*, p. 864.

[236] See also Guenter Weissberg, "United Nations movements toward world law" (1975), pp. 460-463.

[237] Yuen-li Liang, "The Progressive Development of International Law and its Codification under the United Nations" (1947), p. 28. Liang was the Director of the UN Secretariat's Division on the Development and Codification of International Law. See also Robert C. Hilderbrand, *Dumbarton Oaks* (1990), p. 88.

[238] Jacob Robinson, "Metamorphosis of the United Nations" (1958), p. 563.

[239] See *e.g.*, The Amendments Submitted by Uruguay, UNCIO, vol. 3, p. 34; Guatemala, *idem*, p. 256; Brazil, *idem*, p. 243; Venezuela, *idem*, p. 224; Mexico, *idem*, p. 179; Cuba, *idem*, p. 494; Australia, *idem*, p. 543; Bolivia, *idem*, pp. 577 and 580.

[240] Amendments submitted by Ecuador, UNCIO, vol. 3, p. 397.

[241] Amendments submitted by Egypt, UNCIO, vol. 3, p. 453. See also Lebanon, *idem*, p. 473.

[242] *Idem*, p. 448.

[243] See the Third Meeting of Committee, I/1, May 9, 1945, UNCIO, vol. 6, p. 282; Fourth Meeting of Committee, I/1, May 11, 1945, UNCIO, vol. 6, p. 286; Fifth Meeting of Committee I/1, May 14, 1945, UNCIO, vol. 6, p. 291; Sixth Meeting of Committee I/1, May 14, 1945, UNCIO, vol. 6, p. 296.

the Organization's purposes, Egypt proposed to "establish the fundamental principles and rules of international law." [244] When it was suggested that international law "evolved partly through codification but largely through jurisprudence" and that it was therefore "unnecessary to imply the codification of it as one of the specific purposes of the Organization," Egypt proposed that the Assembly be mandated to achieve international cooperation in the solution of international problems of a "juridical" character.[245] This compromise proposal was also rejected.[246]

Consequently all the amendments proclaiming the promotion of justice and international law as a general purpose of the Organization were rejected. This did not mean that there were no references at all to international law in the UN Charter. The Preamble's reference to international law is very carefully phrased and proclaims a shared determination of all Member States to "establish conditions under which justice and respect for the obligations arising from treaties and other sources of international law can be maintained." [247] Following an amendment submitted by Bolivia, Article 2(3) UN Charter obliges all States to "settle their disputes by peaceful means in such a manner that international peace, security, *and justice* are not endangered."[248] Despite objections that "justice" was too vague a term, this reference to justice was finally included in the UN Charter.[249] According

---

[244] Fourteenth Meeting of Committee I/1, June 7, 1945, UNCIO, vol. 6, p. 382.

[245] *Idem.*

[246] *Idem.*

[247] See Draft Preamble (as Approved by Committee I/1/A), UNCIO, vol. 6, p. 694. See also Draft Preamble to the Charter of the United Nations Proposed by the Union of South Africa, UNCIO, vol. 3, p. 475. It was Belgium that suggested referring in the Preamble to "obligations arising from treaties and other sources of international law." Thirteenth Meeting of Committee I/1, June 5, 1945, UNCIO, vol. 6, p. 367. This text was adopted and became part of the Preamble, despite the fact that the Coordination Committee apparently believed that the phrase was "intricate, complicated, and legalistic, [a phrase] which only lawyers would understand." Summary Report of Eleventh Meeting of Steering Committee, June 23, 1945, UNCIO, vol. 5, p. 307.

[248] Amendments Submitted by Bolivia, UNCIO, vol. 3, p. 582. The Dumbarton Oaks proposals lacked the reference to justice here. See Dumbarton Oaks Proposals for a General International Organization, UNCIO, vol. 3, p. 3. There were also some suggestions to refer to international law, as opposed to justice. See e.g, Amendments Submitted by Ethiopia, UNCIO, vol. 3, p. 558; Chile, *idem*, p. 283; China, *idem*, p. 25; Cuba, *idem*, p. 498.

[249] See Report of Rapporteur of Subcommittee I/1/A, to Committee I/1, UNCIO, vol. 6, p. 720, and Eleventh Meeting of Committee I/1, June 4, 1945, UNCIO, vol. 6, p. 333. See also Report of Rapporteur of Committee 1 to Commission I, UNCIO, vol. 6, p. 458, where we read that "[t]he Committee felt, in the light of past experience of some unjust adjustments or settlements, that it is not sufficient to assure that peace and security are not endangered. It added "justice"." Mr. Manuilsky, the Coordination Committee member of the Soviet Union, once again suggested that the word "justice " was a vague term, and that it should be deleted. Summary Report of Twenty-Fourth Meeting, June 16, 1945, UNCIO, vol. 17, p. 164.

to this amendment, disputes endangering the peace have to be settled in accordance with principles of justice.[250]

Although the promotion of principles of justice and international law was not included in the list of the Organization's purposes, there is a reference to international law in Article 1. This reference obliges the Organization "to bring about by peaceful means, *and in conformity with the principles of justice and international law*, adjustment or settlement of international disputes or situations which might lead to a breach of the peace."[251] The Organization is therefore required to apply principles of justice and international law when maintaining peace and security. In this way it indirectly promotes international law. It is worth looking at the drafting history of this reference to law, and the consequences it has for the work of the Security Council and International Court of Justice. At an early stage in the drafting process of the Charter, it was suggested that the Organization itself should be bound by some standards of justice when settling disputes, even when maintaining the peace through enforcement measures.[252] The Netherlands, like many other States, believed that the Charter should stipulate the standards which applied to the Organization when it acted to maintain the peace.[253] The Netherlands did not believe that a reference to international law would suffice, as this would "exclude relevant considerations of another nature," and "it may also be doubted whether international law, in spite of its being subject to change and evolution, may be relied upon at all times and in all circumstances to provide a completely satisfactory standard."[254] This distrust of international law was widely shared in San Francisco, but it was difficult to find an alternative yardstick. The Netherlands wondered "whether a reference to those feelings of right and wrong, those moral principles which live in every human heart, would not be enough."[255] In response to these and similar, but less imaginative proposals, the Big Powers accepted that the Organization should be bound by some standard of "justice" when settling

---

[250] According to Tomuschat, the article just discussed actually introduced a general duty for all States to settle their international disputes, or at least to try and do so. See Christian Tomuschat, "Article 2(3)" (2002), p. 106. Tomuschat speaks of an "obligation of conduct," as opposed to an "obligation of result."
[251] Article 1(1) UN Charter.
[252] Tentative Chinese Proposals for a General International Organisation, August 23, 1944, in FRUS, *1944, General:* Volume I, p. 718. See also Amendments Submitted by France, UNCIO, Vol. 3, pp. 377 and 383; Belgium, *idem*, p. 336; Greece, *idem*, p. 531; Norway, *idem*, pp. 355 and p. 373; Bolivia, *idem*, p. 582; Ecuador, *idem*, p. 410; Egypt, *idem*, pp. 447 and 453; Iran, *idem*, p. 554; Mexico, *idem*, p. 178; Panama, *idem*, p. 265; Turkey, *idem*, pp. 481 and 484. For an overview of this debate, see Department of External Affairs (Canada), *Report on the United Nations conference on international organization* (1945), pp. 16-17.
[253] Amendments Submitted by the Netherlands, UNCIO, vol. 3, p. 312.
[254] *Idem*, p. 313.
[255] *Idem.*

disputes.[256] They did not believe, however, that the Organization should be bound in this way when maintaining the peace through enforcement.[257]

The rejection of all the proposals suggesting "to add after 'peace and security' words which indicate[d] that justice [was] an end that [went] hand in hand with peace and security," was explained by the Rapporteur, as follows:

> None wanted to contend the importance of "justice" as a fundamental element of the purposes of the Organization, or to contend that real and endurable peace can be based on anything other than justice. On the contrary, all affirmed the above-mentioned conception. But it was held by the subcommittee that adding "justice" after "security" brings at that juncture a notion which lacks in clarity after the clearer notion of peace and security, and would thus charge the text by welding together the two notions.[258]

The rather modest role for principles of justice and international law caused Sohn to remark that "international law thus gained an official entrance into the United Nations, but it was clear from the beginning that it should repose quietly in a corner, ready to serve when called upon, but that it was not entitled to play any leading role of its own."[259]

That may be true for enforcement measures, but when it comes to the role of the Organization, and especially its Security Council and Court of Justice, in the maintenance of peace through the facilitation of the peaceful settlement of international disputes, "justice" does have a prominent place. Although the major powers believed that parties to a dispute should first of all try to settle it themselves,[260] they also suggested that the Council "should be empowered, at any stage of a dispute [likely to endanger the peace] to recommend appropriate procedures or

---

[256] Amendments Submitted by the United States, the United Kingdom, the Soviet Union and China, UNCIO, vol. 3, p. 622. Somewhat confusingly, a reference to such an obligation was added to the peace-purpose, and not to the list of principles. See Text of Chapter I, as Agreed upon by the Drafting Committee of Committee I/1, UNCIO, vol. 6, p. 684, Text of Paragraph 1, Chapter I, as Agreed upon by the Drafting Committee, UNCIO, vol. 6, p. 654. See also James B. Reston, "46 Nations Ready to Organize Peace; Only Poles Absent," in *New York Times* of April 25, 1945.

[257] The Soviet Union believed that "if it were possible for a state to appeal from the Council to the International Court of Justice [...] the Council would find itself handicapped in carrying out its functions." See Seventh Meeting of Committee III/2, May 17, 1945, UNCIO, vol. 12, p. 49. The UK added that "the procedures proposed by the amendment would cause delay, at a time when prompt action by the Security Council was most desirable." See Ninth Meeting of Committee III/2, May 21, 1945, UNCIO, vol. 12, p. 65.

[258] Report of Rapporteur, Subcommittee I/1/A, to Committee I/1, June 1, 1945, UNCIO, vol. 6, p. 702.

[259] Louis B. Sohn, "The impact of the United Nations on international law" (1952), p. 105. See also the Dutch Government's "Memorie van Toelichting bij de Goedkeuringswet van het Handvest der Verenigde Naties," in Handelingen der Staten-Generaal, Tweede Kamer, Bijlagen Tijdelijke Zitting 1945, Bijlage no. 3, p. 18.

[260] See UNCIO, vol. 3, p. 13.

methods of adjustment."[261] Australia believed that if the parties could not settle their disputes, the Council would do it for them and also ensure the implementation of its settlement, acting both as judge and executioner.[262] Australia also suggested that "in general the Security Council shall avail itself to the maximum extent of the services of the Court in the settlement of disputes of a legal character, in obtaining advice on legal questions connected with other disputes, and in the ascertainment of disputed facts."[263] The Court therefore had a role as the Council's legal adviser.

Not all States were equally happy with the central role envisaged for the Council, and this merely advisory role for the Court.[264] Turkey proposed that the Council should not interfere when a dispute had been presented to a judicial body.[265] Many others also believed that the settlement of disputes was usually carried out by judges. To some extent, the major powers agreed. According to the Dumbarton Oaks Proposals, the Security Council "normally" had to refer "justiciable disputes" to the International Court of Justice.[266] In the view of Peru, the word "normally" should be replaced by "obligatorily," leaving the Council no room for discretion.[267] The Security Council could then focus on settling political disputes.[268] Venezuela believed that "an increase of the attributions of the Court as against those of the Council would appear as a strengthening of the principle of law and of the sentiment of international solidarity."[269] Venezuela therefore suggested that "a distinction should be drawn between legal controversies, which the States would bind themselves to refer to the International Court, and the other disputes which the States would refer to the Security Council, with the express and important reservation that, in case of failure to agree, the Court should determine the nature of the dispute."[270]

Other States were not so enthusiastic about this division of labour. Brazil proposed that "non-justiciable disputes," or political disputes, be referred to a Court of Arbitration, and not to the Council.[271] Costa Rica believed that "[s]ome thought might perhaps be given to the possibility of there being submitted to [the International Court] not only questions of a juridical nature but all questions; even

---

[261] *Idem.*
[262] Amendments to the Dumbarton Oaks Proposals Submitted on Behalf of Australia, UNCIO, vol. 3, p. 551.
[263] *Idem.*
[264] Amendments and Observations on the Dumbarton Oaks Proposals, Submitted by the Norwegian Delegation, May 3, 1945, UNCIO, vol. 3, p. 370. Norway also suggested an advisory role for the Court.
[265] Turkish Amendments, UNCIO, vol. 3, p. 482. See also p. 485.
[266] UNCIO, vol. 3, p. 14.
[267] Motions of the Peruvian Delegation on the Dumbarton Oaks Proposals, UNCIO, vol. 3, p. 597.
[268] See also the Bolivian Amendments, UNCIO, vol. 3, p. 584.
[269] Venezuelan Amendments, UNCIO, vol. 3, p. 208.
[270] *Idem*, p. 210.
[271] Brazilian Amendments, UNCIO, vol. 3, p. 233. This was also the suggestion of Uruguay, UNCIO, vol. 3, p. 47.

those of a political character, that might affect the general security or peace."[272]
Uruguay strongly opposed the distinction between justiciable and non-justiciable –
or "legal" and "political" – disputes, and also believed that all international disputes
should be decided by the Court:

> [Uruguay] thinks that it should be established that any difference, opposition or
> conflict between nations, of any character whatever, ought obligatorily to be
> submitted to the International Court of Justice, if it should not first have been settled
> by good offices or arbitral procedure. The thesis is based on the assurance that all
> international differences are matter for a decision by law, and on the fear that the
> distinction between legal disputes and political disputes, and the exclusion of the
> latter from the competence of the International Court of Justice, could reinstate
> intervention by force in the conflicts between peoples.[273]

Similarly, Paraguay believed that if States failed to settle any dispute through other
means, they were obliged to go to the International Court of Justice.[274]
    For the Court to play such a prominent role, it was necessary that all States
recognized its compulsory jurisdiction in all future international disputes.[275]
Belgium proposed that

> Members of the Organization should recognize the obligatory jurisdiction of the
> Permanent Court of International Justice as regards any question of law for which
> they have not made use of another method of peaceful settlement: they should
> acknowledge themselves bound by the decisions of the Court.[276]

In 1946, not all States were ready to accept the Court's compulsory jurisdiction.
Therefore it was agreed that the States could "at any time [after 1945] declare that
they recognize[d] as compulsory *ipso facto* and without special agreement, in
relation to any other State accepting the same obligation, the jurisdiction of the
Court."[277]
    What could the role of the Council be, if the Court were granted such a
prominent place in the settlement of international disputes? Perhaps the Council

---

[272] Comments of the Government of Cost Rica, May 4, 1945, UNCIO, vol. 3, p. 275.

[273] Uruguayan Amendments, UNCIO, vol. 3, p. 29.

[274] See Paraguayan Amendments, UNCIO, vol. 3, p. 346.

[275] It is important to emphasize that the Council can only get involved in the settling of an international
dispute when that particular dispute threatens international peace and security. See Report of
Rapporteur of Subcommittee I/1/A, to Committee I/1, UNCIO, vol. 6, p. 720, and positive response by
Czechoslovakia (UNCIO, vol. 3, p. 468).

[276] Suggestions of the Belgian Government, UNCIO, vol. 3, p. 334. See also *e.g.*, Guatemala, *idem*, pp.
254-255; Netherlands, *idem*, p. 321; Paraguay, *idem*, p. 346.

[277] Article 36(2), Statute of the International Court of Justice (annexed to the UN Charter). In 2011, 66
States have accepted the Court's compulsory jurisdiction.

should act not so much as a judge – that would be a task for the Court – but rather as an enforcer of the law. This is what Venezuela suggested:

> The ideal […] would be to entrust the solution of international controversies to the International Court or an independent arbitration agency, and entrust to the Council the mission of executing such decisions and of imposing on any States in conflict the intervention of the agency mentioned.[278]

According to the Dominican Republic, a UN army, led by the Security Council, could act rather like a global enforcer of the rule of law.[279] Egypt underlined the need for such an enforcer. It pointed out that "[t]he weakness of International Law was that, contrary to all other branches of Law, its rules could not be enforced."[280] This situation would change with the creation of the United Nations:

> Now, finally, military power is put at the disposal of a World Organization which is the latest expression of the Law of Nations, and the climax of a long process of international thought. It is more than ever necessary to determine and define these rules of International Law, now that they are being given that essential element of authority which hitherto they have lacked.[281]

As these discussions show, the role of the Organization, and especially that of the Court and Security Council, was to promote a "just" settlement of any dispute threatening the peace. In this sense, the idea of a "just peace" achieved through a procedure which was itself considered as "just" was defined very precisely. At the same time, these references to "justice" do not mean that the development of international law can be considered to be included in the general list of purposes of the Organization. In fact, the work of the Security Council and of the International Court of Justice only promotes and further develops principles of justice and international law indirectly.[282] Their work cannot be qualified as legislation, drawn up in the name of the international community as a whole, or as a direct contribution to the global discussion about values.

    The explanation for this modest role of principles of justice and international law is that there was little faith in public international law in 1945. Perhaps, as a United States delegate commented, the world was "fed up" with international law.[283] The reason for establishing the United Nations was to bring to

---

[278] Venezuelan Amendments, UNCIO, vol. 3, p. 208 (see also p. 209).
[279] Amendments submitted by the Dominican Republic, UNCIO, vol. 3, p. 568.
[280] Suggestions of the Egyptian Government, UNCIO, vol. 3, p. 448.
[281] *Idem.*
[282] See also section 3.6 of Chapter III, below.
[283] See Minutes of Fifth Meeting of the United States Delegation, April 9, 1945, in FRUS, *1945, General:* Volume I, p. 221. The damaged reputation of international law had not affected that of "justice." When American President Harry Truman opened the San Francisco Conference on 25 April,

life a "new" international law, a United Nations legal order to replace the traditional order based on traditional international law. [284] This also explains why the discussions in San Francisco stressed that the reference to treaties and other traditional sources of international law in the Preamble should not be interpreted as a "negation of healthy international evolution" or "the crystallization or the freezing of the international *status quo*."[285]

### 3.5.3 *The development of international law as a purpose of the General Assembly*

As the promotion of international law was not included in the list of purposes of the Dumbarton Oaks proposals, it cannot come as a surprise that there was nothing about the role of the Assembly in promoting the development of international law in those proposals.[286] Again, certain States wanted this to be changed, so that the Assembly could be more than a debating society, and truly become a global legislator or a true "parliament of the world."[287]

In its amendments China suggested that "[t]he Assembly should be responsible for initiating studies and making recommendations with respect to the development and revision of the rules and principles of international law." [288]

---

1945, he focused his speech on promoting justice and saw the achievement of a "just and lasting peace" as the ultimate aim of the new Organization. See Verbatim Minutes of Opening Session, April 25, 1945, UNCIO, vol. 1, pp. 111-113. See also James B. Reston, "Justice Put First," in *New York Times* of April 26, 1945. As Wolfrum explained, the reference to justice was really a reference to natural law type principles, while the reference to international law referred primarily to treaty law. See Rüdiger Wolfrum, "Preamble" (2002), p. 36.

[284] See also Witenberg, "New Set of Rules Acceptable to All Nations is Proposed," in *New York Times* of May 13, 1945. One of the most prominent international lawyers in the 1940s even considered the UN Charter to be inconsistent with international law. See Hans Kelsen, *The Law of the United Nations* (1950), p. 110, cited in Bardo Fassbender, "The United Nations Charter as Constitution" (1998), p. 573. This idea that the UN Charter introduced a "new" international law was also embraced by the President of the ICJ. See p. 13 of the Dissenting Opinion by M. Alvarez, in the Competence of the General Assembly for the Admission of a State to the United Nations, Advisory Opinion of March 3rd, 1950. Alvarez later elaborated on this idea of a "new international law," for example on pp. 175-176, Dissenting Opinion of Mr. Alvarez, in International Status of South-West Africa, Advisory Opinion of July 11th, 1950; pp. 132-133, Dissenting Opinion of Judge Alvarez, in the Anglo-Iranian Oil Co. Case (United Kingdom v. Iran), Preliminary Objection, Judgment of July 22nd, 1952.

[285] Report of Rapporteur, Subcommittee I/1/A, Section 3, to Committee I/1, June 5, 1945, UNCIO, vol. 6, p. 359. See also Report of Rapporteur of Committee 1 to Commission I, UNCIO, vol. 6, p. 451 and p. 461.

[286] Dumbarton Oaks Proposals for a General International Organization, UNCIO, vol. 3, p. 6.

[287] Porter, "Smaller Countries Rush Amendments," in *New York Times* of May 5, 1945.

[288] Chinese Proposals on Dumbarton Oaks Proposals, UNCIO, vol. 3, p. 25. See also Yuen-li Liang, "The General Assembly and the Progressive Development and Codification of International Law" (1948), p. 66.

Liberia believed that "the General Assembly [should] also initiate studies which should lead to the Codification of International Law." [289] Similarly, in San Francisco, the Egyptian delegate believed that "a new channel or agency [was] needed to accomplish [the development and clarification of international law], either through the General Assembly or through the Economic and Social Council." [290]

Not all States believed this to be a task for the General Assembly itself. Iran, for example, suggested that "[a] Committee of qualified jurists should be established to draw up a code of International Law." [291] Similarly, Lebanon proposed "to create a permanent Committee of Jurists whose function [should] be the periodic codification or consolidation of existing principles of international law together with the modifications thereof which shall be deemed necessary from time to time." [292]

Some States went much further than proposals to grant the Assembly, or some special committee, the right to initiate studies on international law. They essentially suggested that the General Assembly should become a global legislator. The most far-reaching proposal came from the Philippines. It suggested the following law-making procedure:

> The General Assembly should be vested with the legislative authority to enact rules of international law which should become effective and binding upon the members of the Organization after such rules have been approved by a majority vote of the Security Council. Should the Security Council fail to act on any of such rules within a period of thirty days after submission thereof to the Security Council, the same should become effective and binding as if approved by the Security Council. In the exercise of this legislative authority the General Assembly may codify the existing rules of international law with such changes as the Assembly may deem proper. [293]

This was a bit too ambitious for most fellow delegates. Stettinius, the leader of the US delegation in San Francisco, later wrote that, "[i]n the present state [...] of world opinion, an international legislative body is out of the question, since several

---

[289] Memorandum of the Liberian Government on the Dumbarton Oaks Proposals, UNCIO, vol. 3, p. 465.

[290] Third Plenary Session, April 28, 1945, UNCIO, vol. 1, p. 6.

[291] Amendments Presented by the Delegation of Iran to the Dumbarton Oaks Proposals, UNCIO, vol. 3, p. 556. It is not clear what the relationship is between this committee and the General Assembly. The amendment was withdrawn, see Sixteenth Meeting of Committee III/3, May 30, 1945, UNCIO, vol. 12, pp. 400-401.

[292] Lebanon's Suggestions, UNCIO, vol. 3, p. 473.

[293] Proposed Amendments to the Dumbarton Oaks Proposals Submitted by the Philippine Delegation, UNCIO, vol. 3, pp. 536-537.

nations are not willing to sacrifice their sovereignty to the extent of permitting an international legislature to enact laws binding upon them or on their peoples."[294]

Belgium suggested that "[t]he General Assembly may submit general conventions for the consideration of States which form part of the United Nations Organization [...] with a view to securing their approval in accordance with the appropriate constitutional procedure."[295] That suggestion was not controversial. The second part of the Belgian suggestion, however, was more in line with that of the Philippines. Belgium proposed:

> If the General Assembly is of the opinion that the obligations involved in any draft general convention are mere corollaries of principles it already recognizes as compulsory, or that the general observance of these obligations is necessary for the maintenance of international peace and security, it may decide that the convention in question will come into force for all States Members of the Organization and, should occasion arise, for third-party States, as soon as it has been ratified under the conditions contemplated for the coming into force of amendments to the Charter.[296]

Ecuador proposed the following "law-making procedure":

> The power to establish or progressively amend the principles and rules of law which are to govern the relations between the States lies with the General Assembly, through a two-third majority of its members. The instruments embodying those principles and rules shall only come into compulsory effect for all members of the Organization when they are ratified by a number equivalent to two-thirds thereof.[297]

Ecuador therefore suggested a two-stage process. First, the Assembly would adopt a certain treaty text with a large majority. Secondly, the States could decide on an individual basis whether to ratify these texts. The radical element of Ecuador's proposal was that a majority could impose a treaty on a reluctant minority. Ecuador later explained that, in its view, the General Assembly, being the "organ directly representing all the States composing it," should be "enabled to lay down the principles and rules of international law or to amend them progressively, thus becoming in a way an international legislative power."[298] Although this procedure was never explicitly adopted in the text of the UN Charter, most of the treaties have

---

[294] Edward R. Stettinius, *Charter of the United Nations* (1945), p. 54.

[295] Dumbarton Oaks Proposals concerning the Establishment of a General International Organization: Amendments Submitted by the Belgian Delegation, UNCIO, vol. 3, p. 339 (see pp. 339-340 for the grounds on which this suggestion was based).

[296] Idem.

[297] Delegation of Ecuador to the United Nations Conference on International Organization, UNCIO, vol. 3, p. 427. See also pp. 403-405.

[298] Fifth Plenary Session, April 30, 1945, UNCIO, vol. 1, p. 369.

come into existence with the help of Ecuador's two-stage process.[299] There is one marked difference between Ecuador's ideas and the reality: no State can be bound by any treaty against its consent.

The only thing that the sponsors accepted before the start of the San Francisco Conference, was China's more modest proposal, *viz.* that the Assembly could initiate studies and make recommendations for "the encouragement of the development of international law."[300] The other amendments, including the Belgian proposal, were not dropped completely, but reappeared in San Francisco. The relevant Subcommittee compiled a list of questions which were later used as the basis for the discussion of the Belgian amendment and all related amendments.[301] The San Francisco proceedings only provide the answers to some of those questions, and not the reasons or justifications for those answers. A list of the questions that were answered follows below:

> Q: Should the Assembly be empowered to initiate studies and make recommendations for the *codification* of international law?
> A: Yes.
> Q: Should the Assembly be empowered to initiate studies and make recommendations for promoting the *revision* of the rules and principles of international law?
> A: Yes.
> Q: Should the Assembly be authorized to enact rules of international law which should become binding upon members after such rules shall have been approved by the Security Council?
> A: No. [302]

Thus the Belgian suggestion was clearly and explicitly rejected. Sloan concluded from this that it "was clearly decided [in San Francisco] that the General Assembly should not be given the function of international legislation."[303]

---

[299] This quasi-legislative role of the Assembly in codifying global norms was also applauded in scholarship. See *e.g.*, p. 198, Borris M. Komar, "A Code of World Law Now" (1966); Oscar Schachter, "International law in theory and practice" (1982), pp. 111-112; and Grigory I. Tunkin, "International law in the international system" (1975), pp. 144-146.

[300] Third Meeting of Committee II/2, May 9, 1945, UNCIO, vol. 9, pp. 21-22. It was thus due to the insistence of the Chinese that even the most modest proposal about international law, initially also supported by the USA, made it into the Charter. See Louis B. Sohn, "The impact of the United Nations on international law" (1952), p. 105.

[301] See also Ministerie van Buitenlandse Zaken (Netherlands), *Het ontstaan der Verenigde Naties* (1950), pp. 47-48.

[302] Second Report of Subcommittee A, UNCIO, vol. 9, pp. 346-347. The answers to these questions were given during the Tenth Meeting of Committee II/2, May 21, 1945, UNCIO, vol. 9, pp. 69-70. See also Yuen-li Liang, "The General Assembly and the Progressive Development and Codification of International Law" (1948), p. 67.

There was a discussion about what the correct word would be to describe the Assembly's role in promoting international law. Should the Assembly engage in the "codification," "development" or "revision" of the norms of international law?[304] The difference between the "development" and "revision" of international law was explained as follows: development meant "adding to existing rules," whilst revision meant "modifying" existing rules. The term "progressive development" was suggested as a compromise, as this term "would establish a nice balance between stability and change, whereas 'revision' would lay too much emphasis on change."[305] The Committee adopted this latter view, and chose to use "progressive development" and "codification."

The word "revision" was not used in the UN Charter.[306] The Assembly is authorized to "initiate studies and make recommendations for the purpose of [...] encouraging the progressive development of international law and its codification."[307] To assist it in its work, the Assembly established the International Law Commission (ILC).[308] To ensure that the Commission was as representative of the international community as the Assembly itself, the Assembly proclaimed that the ILC should be "composed of persons of recognized competence in international law and representing as a whole the chief forms of civilization and the basic legal systems of the world."[309] Therefore as it was the ILC which was granted the prime task of promoting the "progressive development" and "codification" of international law on behalf of the Assembly, it does come as a surprise that this Commission has

---

[303] See also Blaine Sloan, "The binding force of a "recommendation" of the General Assembly of the United Nations" (1948), p. 6.

[304] About the discussion, see also the Seventh Meeting of Subcommittee B of Committee II/2, June 5, 1945, UNCIO, vol. 9, pp. 423-424; and Third Report of Subcommittee II/2/B, UNCIO, vol. 9, pp. 419-420.

[305] Twenty-First Meeting of Committee II/2, June 7, 1945, UNCIO, vol. 9, pp. 177-178.

[306] France later stressed the importance of the fact that "revision" was "brushed aside." According to France: "If the Assembly were competent to revise treaties at any time, you might have agitation for revision of this or that treaty, and there would never be any stability in the treaties." In response, Egypt remarked that it was exactly the opposite: "if you allow some sort of readjustment by peaceful means, you are really respecting the spirit of this Charter." Fourth Meeting of Commission II, June 21, 1945, UNCIO, vol. 8, p. 202 and p. 212, respectively.

[307] Article 13(1)(a), UN Charter. See also Texts Passed through May 17, 1945, UNCIO, vol. 18, p. 9; Twelfth Meeting of Committee II/3, May 25, 1945, UNCIO, vol. 10, p. 101; Draft Report of the Rapporteur of Committee II/3, UNCIO, vol. 10, p. 233, and p. 239; Provisions Text of Report of the Rapporteur of Committee II/2, UNCIO, vol. 9, p. 204; Report of the Rapporteur of Committee II/2, UNCIO, vol. 9, p. 249

[308] Establishment of an International Law Commission, General Assembly resolution 174(II), adopted 21 November 1947.

[309] Article 8, Statute of the International Law Commission, annexed to General Assembly resolution 174(II).

been struggling with the difference between the two since its very establishment. [310] In an early report the Committee responsible for establishing the ILC described "progressive development" as "the drafting of a convention on a subject which has not yet been regulated by international law or in regard to which the law has not yet been highly developed or formulated in the practice of States." [311] "Codification," on the other hand, was described as "the more precise formulation and systematization of the law in areas where there has been extensive State practice, precedent and doctrine." [312] Even in 1947 it was understood that the two tasks were not "mutually exclusive," in the sense that the ILC had to do both things simultaneously when working on any topic of international law. [313] These views were later reflected in the ILC's constitution. [314]

The UN Charter's *travaux* and its immediate follow-up show that the Assembly's mandate explicitly included guiding the evolution or progressive development of international law. The delegate from Haiti stressed the importance of promoting this evolution. In his view, "it [did] not seem superfluous to us to add here that international law cannot remain static," rather that "it must be capable of adapting itself to the changing conditions of life of the peoples of the world." [315] The Assembly was intended to play the leading role in this development. China, the most important supporter of the quasi-legislative role of the Assembly, also applauded its adoption, calling it of "very great significance to our future." [316] The explanation for China's enthusiasm was interesting. It believed that "while the maintenance of international peace and security [was] a very important task entrusted to the Security Council, it, after all, [could] only constitute an incident or an accident in the course of international life, whereas the normal course of international life [was] bound to be everyday relations," and "if we desire to promote those relations, there can be no better basis than the promotion of respect

---

[310] For an early article, see Yuen-li Liang, "The General Assembly and the Progressive Development and Codification of International Law" (1948). For a more recent example, see Alain Pellet, "Between Codification and Progressive Development of the Law" (2004).

[311] *Report of the Committee on the Progressive Development of International Law and its Codification on the Methods for Encouraging the Progressive Development of International Law and its Eventual Codification* (1947), para. 7 (p. 20).

[312] *Idem.*

[313] *Idem.* See also para. 10, where the Committee acknowledged that "in any work of codification, the codifier inevitably has to fill in gaps and amend the law in the light of new developments," and that sounds more like progressive development.

[314] Article 15, Statute of the International Law Commission, annexed to General Assembly resolution 174(II). See also Guenter Weissberg, "United Nations movements toward world law" (1975), pp. 461-470.

[315] Sixth Plenary Session, May 1, 1945, UNCIO, vol. 1, p. 443.

[316] Fourth Meeting of Commission II, June 21, 1945, UNCIO, vol. 8, p. 204.

for international law and for its development. It is only thus that we can hope to develop our relations and place them always under the rule of law."[317]

### 3.5.4 The development of UN norms and values as a purpose of the General Assembly

So far the discussion has focused on the powers of the Assembly to affect the evolution of international law in general. The principal aim of this study is to look at the role of the General Assembly in the evolution, not of international law in general, but of the norms and values of the UN Charter, especially in Articles 1, 2, 55 and 56.

In San Francisco, Belgium proposed that "the General Assembly [should have] sovereign competence to interpret the provisions of the Charter."[318] After an interesting debate about this, it was agreed that each organ should be entitled to interpret its own part of the Charter:

> In the course of the operations from day to day of the various organs of the Organization, it is inevitable that each organ will interpret such parts of the Charter as are applicable to its particular functions. This process is inherent in the functioning of any body which operates under an instrument defining its functions and powers. It will be manifested in the functioning of such a body as the General Assembly, the Security Council, or the International Court of Justice. Accordingly, it is not necessary to include in the Charter a provision either authorizing or approving the normal operation of this principle.[319]

This meant that the General Assembly, the mandate of which covered all principles and purposes, was the main organ to interpret the UN Charter as a whole. Most parts of the Assembly's mandate were also partly included in the mandates of the Councils, *i.e.* the Trusteeship Council, the Economic and Social Council, and/or the Security Council. Thus the drafters correctly foresaw potential disputes among these principal organs relating to the correct interpretation of certain provisions.[320] Some suggestions were given for means to settle disputes between UN organs, but the idea was basically that all sorts of dispute settlement mechanisms were available to solve disputes about interpretation .[321]

---

[317] *Idem.*

[318] Supplement to Annex 2 to Report by the Officers of the Committee on Grouping of Suggested Modifications to Dumbarton Oaks Proposals, UNCIO, vol. 9, p. 319. See also Gaetano Arangio-Ruiz, "The normative role of the General Assembly" (1972), p. 504.

[319] Report of Special Subcommittee of Committee IV/2 on the Interpretation of the Charter, UNCIO, vol. 13, p. 831.

[320] *Idem*, pp. 831-832.

[321] *Idem.*

Another important issue was the question of dissenters. What would happen if the Assembly decided, with a large majority, to interpret the UN Charter in a particular way, but a small group of States disagreed?[322] To say that General Assembly resolutions are legally non-binding is beside the point, because the binding character of the norm derives from the UN Charter itself. The matter at issue is the extent to which the Assembly's *interpretation* of the norm as contained in the Charter is binding. The Assembly was explicitly granted the authority to interpret the document by the drafters of the UN Charter. So what should be done about the dissenting minority? This is what the drafters had to say:

> It is to be understood, of course, that if an interpretation made by any organ of the Organization [such as the General Assembly] is not generally acceptable it will be without binding force. In such circumstances, or in cases where it is desired to establish an authoritative interpretation as a precedent for the future, it may be necessary to embody the interpretation in an amendment to the Charter. This may always be accomplished by recourse to the procedure provided for amendment.[323]

The aim is to come up with an interpretation of the Charter which is "generally acceptable," and the most suitable organ to do so is the General Assembly, assisted by its subsidiary organs, such as the International Law Commission.[324] The remark quoted above is rather vague, but does suggest that if the Assembly's interpretation is not accepted by consensus, then the best way to overrule the dissenting minority is to follow the formal route of UN Charter amendment. This means, first of all, that two thirds of the members of the General Assembly have to vote in favour of the interpretative declaration. Secondly, two thirds of the Members of the United Nations, including all the permanent members of the Security Council, have to ratify the interpretative declaration as if it were a separate multilateral treaty. This formal process is so cumbersome that it has never been used as a means to interpret the Charter.[325] The Subcommittee only suggested this cumbersome procedure to deal effectively with a very stubborn minority that has to be bound to a particular interpretation of the Charter against its own will. Such a situation was considered to be rare. In practice, however, it has often happened that a minority of States

[322] See also Oscar Schachter, "International law in theory and practice" (1982), pp. 118-123.
[323] Report of Special Subcommittee of Committee IV/2 on the Interpretation of the Charter, UNCIO, vol. 13, p. 832.
[324] Oscar Schachter, "United Nations law" (1994), p. 7.
[325] The only amendments ever adopted expanded the membership of the Security Council (once) and ECOSOC (twice). See Question of equitable representation on the Security Council and the Economic and Social Council, General Assembly resolution 1991(XVIII), adopted 17 December 1963; Enlargement of the Economic and Social Council, General Assembly resolution 2847(XXVI), adopted 20 December 1971; and Amendment to Article 109 of the Charter of the United Nations, General Assembly resolution 2101(XX), adopted 20 December 1965. The last amendment was needed to make Article 109 consistent with the amended Articles.

objected to a particular resolution adopted by a majority in the Assembly, challenging that resolution's "constitutionality." No supranational organ has the authority to overrule such dissenters.[326] The International Court of Justice later noted that such dissent was of particular importance if the dissenters had a specific interest in the norms being discussed. [327] The Court's ruling was about the prohibition of nuclear weapons, but the same could be said any other topic. States with the relevant resources to carry out the norm – or violate it – have a special interest in the recognition – or rejection – of that norm, and this special interest ought to be recognized and respected.[328]

This discussion of the San Francisco proceedings leads to the conclusion that the Assembly's powers to promote the progressive development of international law are restricted to recommending treaty texts and interpreting the Charter in a binding way. The San Francisco proceedings do not explain whether the Assembly could interpret the Charter merely on its own behalf, or also on behalf of all Member States, binding them in this way. In 1945 nothing was said about the role of Assembly resolutions in the development of customary international law. Therefore a few questions remained to be answered. Subsequent practice and discussions in the UN about the legal relevance of Assembly resolutions are examined below, with the aim of finding out whether the conclusions reached in San Francisco are still valid, and to see if some of the open questions have been answered since that time.

### 3.5.5    Debates during the drafting of the Friendly Relations Declaration

The issue of the legal relevance of Assembly resolutions, especially those interpreting the provisions in the UN Charter, was most intensely discussed in the 1960s when the Assembly busied itself drafting the Declaration on Principles of International Law concerning Friendly Relations and Co-operation among States in accordance with the Charter of the United Nations ("Friendly Relations Declaration"). According to Schachter, the resolution was "the international

---

[326] See Benedetto Conforti, "Le rôle de l'accord dans le système des Nations Unies" (1974), especially pp. 220-235.

[327] Legality of the Threat or Use of Nuclear Weapons, paras. 70-74, ICJ Advisory Opinion of 8 July 1996. Before the Court reached its decision, Henkin already noted the importance of the fact that the US and other nuclear powers (except the Soviet Union, which did vote in favour) never subscribed to these resolutions. See p. 180, 182 of Louis Henkin, *How Nations Behave: Law and Foreign Policy* (1979).

[328] Schachter thus rightly noted that "resolutions [adopted] by majorities on economic matters are likely to remain "paper" declarations without much effect unless genuinely accepted by states with the requisite resources to carry them out." Oscar Schachter, "United Nations law" (1994), p. 4.

lawyer's favourite example of an authoritative UN resolution."[329] It authoritatively interpreted most of the principles in the United Nations Charter.[330]

Drafting the Declaration took almost ten years. It took so long because the drafters wanted a consensus on every single paragraph in the declaration, and ultimately they achieved this. Therefore they avoided the problem of dissenters that was discussed above. A Special Committee was established by the General Assembly in 1963. It was mandated to look at four essential principles of the United Nations Charter, chosen by the Assembly itself. These were :

1. The prohibition on the use of force;
2. The principle that States should settle their disputes peacefully,
3. The non-intervention principle, and
4. The principle of sovereign equality of States.[331]

During the second session of the Committee, three more principles were added to the list: (5) the duty to cooperate, (6) the principle of good faith, and (7) the principle of self-determination of peoples.[332] The global values identified in this study were therefore well represented, except for human dignity. [333] The lack of references to this last value led to serious criticism by the Dutch delegation. Houben, a member of that delegation, believed that the Committee was more concerned with "preserving a country's own [...] system as a closed unit" than with "joint efforts for the promotion of human dignity and the freedom and well-being of mankind."[334]

---

[329] *Idem*, p. 3.

[330] Declaration on Principles of International Law concerning Friendly Relations and Co-operation among States in accordance with the Charter of the United Nations, General Assembly resolution 2625 (XXV), adopted 24 October 1970. See also Sir Ian Sinclair, "The Significance of the Friendly Relations Declaration" (1994). Sinclair was the UK representative in the Special Committee that drafted the Friendly Relations Declaration.

[331] Consideration of principles of international law concerning friendly relations and co-operation among states in accordance with the Charter of the United Nations, General Assembly resolution 1966 (XVIII), adopted 16 December 1963. For the list of principles, see General Assembly resolution 1815 (XVII), adopted 18 December 1962.

[332] *Idem.*

[333] See also Dominic McGoldrick, "The principle of non-intervention: human rights" (1994), p. 91, who described the Declaration as "rather conservative and cautious" because of its sparse reference to human rights. The same conclusion, this time on the sparse references to the environment, was reached in Alan Boyle, "The principle of co-operation" (1994), pp. 120-121. Generally, see Robert Rosenstock, "The Declaration of Principles of International Law Concerning Friendly Relations" (1971), p. 735.

[334] Piet-Hein Houben, "Principles of International Law Concerning Friendly Relations and Co-Operation Among States" (1967), pp. 731-732. Houben pointed out that the idea of peaceful co-existence was essentially a communist idea, embraced by the "new" States because it emphasized self-determination and independence of peoples and States. See also Special Committee, Sixth Report, para. 166.

The Assembly explicitly asked States to nominate "jurists" as representatives in the Committee. It is not clear what exactly was meant by the word "jurists." It certainly did not result in only academic experts on international law taking a seat in the Committee. Because of its political importance, the Assembly gave the task of drafting the declaration to its own Sixth Committee, which was composed of State representatives. The International Law Commission, which consisted of independent legal experts, was ignored.[335] As McWhinney pointed out, if the Assembly meant academics when it referred to "jurists," it must have been disappointed to see that, at least during the first session, "academic lawyers were a rarity in the final composition of the various national delegations."[336] At the same time, some of the delegates were – or later became – renowned international law scholars. Michel Virally, Gaetano Arangio-Ruiz, Hisashi Owada, Willem Riphagen, Hans Blix and Mohammed el-Baradei all participated in the work of the Committee.

The legal relevance of the declaration was discussed even before the establishment of the Special Committee. The Sixth Committee of the General Assembly suggested that a declaration annexed to a General Assembly resolution would not be binding as a multilateral treaty. However, it would be more than a mere recommendation. It could be considered as the *opinio juris* of the international community as a whole, binding all States whose practice was consistent with the text of the declaration.[337] Alternatively, the Sixth Committee suggested that the declaration could be seen as an authoritative interpretation of the norms of the UN Charter.[338]

Many of the delegates in the Special Committee understood their task to be that of a legislator. Therefore they set out to draft general rules, applicable in as many concrete situations as possible in the future. In the Committee's first report the declaration was envisaged to be like other declarations interpreting parts of the Charter, such as the Universal Declaration of Human Rights, and the Declaration on the Granting of Independence to Colonial Peoples, which were all recognized as having some law-making power.[339] Like those previous declarations, the new declaration should not repeat what was already in the Charter, but should reflect the

---

[335] See Report of the Sixth Committee, UNDoc, A/5671, adopted 13 December 1963, para. 110.

[336] Edward McWhinney, "The 'New' Countries and the 'New' International Law" (1966), p. 4.

[337] Report of the Sixth Committee, UNDoc, A/5671, adopted 13 December 1963, para. 38. See Rosalyn Higgins, *The development of international law through the political organs of the United Nations* (1963), especially pp. 2, 4-5. This book was published in 1963, and it has clearly had an influence on the debates at the Committee. According to Grigory I. Tunkin, "International law in the international system" (1975), pp. 146-149, the General Assembly resolution should be seen as the first expression of a new norm, but not as *opinio juris* or as part of State practice; it was thus only the first step in the formation of customary law.

[338] *Idem*, para. 46.

[339] Special Committee on Principles of International Law concerning Friendly Relations and Co-operation among States, Report, A/5746, adopted 16 November 1964 ("First Report"), para. 21.

evolution in international law since the adoption of the constitutive document. It should therefore give new meaning to the UN Charter's principles.[340] At the same time, the delegates realized that the Committee, and the Assembly itself, formally lacked legislating power.[341] It was the generally shared belief that Assembly resolutions, if adopted by a large majority or by consensus,[342] could be seen as being binding on all States, not as independent sources of international law, but as authentic interpretations of the UN Charter. In this way, they could contribute to the law-making process.[343] Some delegates objected to this view. In their opinion, General Assembly resolutions were meant to be political statements and could not be automatically interpreted as law-making resolutions, or as authoritative interpretations of the Charter.[344]

An issue that also came up was whether the General Assembly itself was bound by its previous resolutions. Interestingly, when discussing the principle of non-intervention, the Committee was faced with the question to what extent it was bound by the Declaration on the Inadmissibility of Intervention, adopted earlier by the General Assembly.[345] The sponsors of that resolution, which was not adopted by consensus but with a majority vote, believed that the Assembly could not "undo" a resolution adopted only a few years before. In the end, the Special Committee's definition of the principle of non-intervention in the Friendly Relations Declaration was almost identical to that contained in the Declaration on the Inadmissibility of Intervention, which indicates that the Committee did believe that the Assembly was "bound" to follow its own previous resolutions.[346]

In their final comments submitted after the adoption of the Friendly Relations Declaration by the Special Committee, many States stressed the legal importance of what was soon to become an Assembly declaration. For example, Argentina believed that the Declaration ought to be regarded as "the most up-to-date expression of the scope and interpretation of the Charter of the United Nations, the basis of international law as it was understood and practiced by the civilized

---

[340] Special Committee on Principles of International Law concerning Friendly Relations and Co-operation among States, Report, A/7326, adopted 30 September 1968 ("Fourth Report"), para. 20.
[341] See *e.g.*, Special Committee, Fourth Report, para. 34.
[342] The non-intervention declaration was adopted by a large majority (almost all States voted in favour, one State abstained from voting), but it was, strictly speaking, not adopted by consensus. Special Committee on Principles of International Law concerning Friendly Relations and Co-operation among States, Report, A/6799 ("Third Report"), paras. 323.
[343] Special Committee, Third Report, para. 324.
[344] *Idem*, paras. 328-329.
[345] *Idem*, paras. 321-331.
[346] A similar debate took place about the legal force of the Declaration on the Granting of Independence to Colonial Countries and Peoples, General Assembly Resolution 1514 (XV), adopted 4 December 1960. See Special Committee, Fourth Report, para. 147.

nations of the world today."[347] Rosenstock, the representative of the USA in the Special Committee, referred to the Declaration as "the most important single statement representing what the Members of the United Nations agree to be the law of the Charter."[348] It was generally believed that the legal nature of the declaration derived from the fact that it was an authoritative interpretation of the norms of the UN Charter, as they had evolved with the changes in the international community, but was not an amendment of these norms.[349] Therefore their authority was based on a combination of two arguments: first, the Declaration constituted an interpretation of the UN Charter, and secondly, it was a reflection of customary international law. The first argument was generally considered to be more convincing. The customary law argument only served to strengthen the first argument.

Not all Assembly resolutions were considered to authoritative interpretations of provisions in the UN Charter. In his lectures delivered at The Hague Academy, Sahović, the delegate from Yugoslavia in the Special Committee, explained what distinguished the Friendly Relations Declaration from ordinary resolutions. He noted three aspects which generally determined the importance that should be attached to declarations adopted by the General Assembly.[350] The first was the historical aspect, the process by which the declaration had been drawn up and the political importance of this process.[351] Secondly, Sahović referred to the aspect of legal technique, by which he meant the importance of the particular methodology adopted by the drafters – research into the Charter principles and their evolution – and the ultimate aim of these drafters. It was important to know whether the declaration was *meant* to be an interpretation of existing norms of international law, or whether it was meant to provide suggestions for norms to be adopted in the future.[352] The third and final aspect mentioned by Sahović was the procedural

[347] Special Committee on Principles of International Law concerning Friendly Relations and Co-operation among States, Report, A/8018, adopted 1 May 1970 ("Sixth Report"), paras. 102 and 109. Argentina even referred to the principles as *jus cogens*, but this was later denied by the USA (para. 254).

[348] Robert Rosenstock, "The Declaration of Principles of International Law Concerning Friendly Relations" (1971), p. 714. Rosenstock emphasized that it was not a complete statement, since it only discussed a number of the UN Charter's principles, not all of them.

[349] See especially the remarks by the Romanian delegate, at Special Committee, Sixth Report, para. 119, Yougoslavia, at para. 162, and India (para. 213). See also remarks by the Italian delegate, at para. 142, and Australia, at para. 199, and USA, at para. 254.

[350] Milan Sahovic, "Codification des principes du droit international des relations amicales et de la coopération entre les Etats" (1974), p. 250. Compare with C. Don Johnson, "Toward self-determination" (1973), pp. 154-156, who distinguished four factors: intention of the drafters, consensus, legal foundation, and realistic acceptability.

[351] *Idem*, pp. 255-284. In discussing the history, Sahović mainly summarized the drafting history of the declaration.

[352] *Idem*, pp. 285-299. Bleicher made an interesting proposal. He suggested that the Assembly should explicitly state if a certain resolution was intended to reflect customary international law, or, one might

aspect.[353] This referred simply to the formal legal character of the resolution. In Sahović's view, there was general agreement that the principles contained in the Friendly Relations Declaration were legally binding because they constituted authoritative interpretations of some fundamental principles contained in the UN Charter. However, this was only the case for a limited number of General Assembly resolutions.[354]

A fourth aspect could be added to these three: the importance of consensus. Many delegates noted that for the first time in the history of the United Nations, the developing nations had been given a chance to express themselves on the most fundamental principles on which the work of the Organization was based. Their participation in the drafting process did not happen automatically. It was only after the first session of the Special Committee that the Assembly added a number of developing nations to the Committee, to provide a better guarantee of proper geographical representation, or inclusiveness.[355] This inclusiveness was universally applauded. Cameroon, for example, remarked that "the Committee's work had given the emergent nations an opportunity to play a part in the progressive development of international law, and the problems and aspirations of those countries were amply reflected in the text."[356] Similarly, Rosenstock remarked that one of the reasons for making the declaration in the first place was "a felt need on the part of some of those who had not been present at San Francisco in 1945 to put their views on record." [357] Mani (India) later wrote that "the Declaration constitute[d] one of the corner-stones of contemporary international law, in whose creation the Third World and the Socialist countries consciously participated, for the first time in the history of the world, alongside the 'old' States of the West."[358] Finally, Sinclair (UK) remarked that it "provided an ideal opportunity for the representatives of some newly independent States to flex their muscles in the international arena, and to pursue their quest for a 'new' international law which would be responsive to their needs and which would be freed from the constraints

---

add, an authoritative interpretation of the UN Charter. See Samuel A. Bleicher, "The Legal Significance of Re-Citation of General Assembly Resolutions" (1969), especially p. 448.

[353] *Idem*, pp. 300-308.

[354] *Idem*, pp. 302 and 307. See also p. 73, S.K. Roy Chowdhury, "The status and norms of self-determination in contemporary international law" (1977). Grigory I. Tunkin, "International law in the international system" (1975), pp. 149-152 did not agree; he believed the Friendly Relations Declaration went much further than merely interpreting certain Charter provisions.

[355] Consideration of principles of international law concerning friendly relations and co-operation among states in accordance with the Charter of the United Nations, General Assembly resolution 2103 (XX), adopted 20 December 1965. The results were immediately apparent, as the Committee started to discuss the principle of self-determination and decolonization from that second session onwards.

[356] Special Committee, Sixth Report, para. 155.

[357] Robert Rosenstock, "The Declaration of Principles of International Law Concerning Friendly Relations" (1971), p. 716.

[358] Vekateshwara Subramanian Mani, *Basic principles of modern international law* (1993), p. 5.

of what they perceived to be outmoded, Euro-centric and inevitably 'colonialist' concepts."[359] The universal participation in the drafting of the text also ensured that it would be taken seriously by all States once it was adopted. The delegate of the United Arab Republic noted that "all the members of the Committee were authors of the text, and that fact alone should carry it towards ultimate success."[360]

The influence of the smaller nations resulted in the Declaration expressing a new, or evolved interpretation of the UN Charter's principles, which reflected the changes in the international community. The Western States, on the other hand, acted much more conservatively. Bearing in mind that the UN Charter was a "living constitution," Houben, the Dutch delegate, even blamed some of his Western colleagues for "adhering too rigidly to their conviction that in creating international law in this field one must not venture beyond the boundaries of the Charter."[361] Similarly, McWhinney blamed one of the Western States (the United States of America) for teaching the policy-oriented approach at its most prestigious universities, whilst defending the positivist, black-letter law approach in the Special Committee.[362] In any case, it was generally felt that the authority of the Friendly Relations Declaration was significantly enhanced because it was adopted by consensus, and because the drafting process was as inclusive as it was.[363]

What did these discussions add to the conclusions reached in San Francisco? Once again, it was suggested that the authority of Assembly resolutions was primarily derived from the fact that they constituted authoritative interpretations of the UN Charter, shared by the (majority of) States party to that treaty. This interpretation could bind the States themselves, and not just the Assembly.[364] In this sense, a State representative played two roles at the same time when voting for a certain Assembly resolution. He influenced both the legal obligations of the Assembly itself, and those of the State he represented.[365] It was suggested, not only in the Special Committee but also beyond, that a resolution containing an interpretation of the Charter had a certain value, not just because it was an Assembly resolution, but because certain Assembly resolutions showed that

---

[359] Sir Ian Sinclair, "The Significance of the Friendly Relations Declaration" (1994), p. 28.
[360] Special Committee, Sixth Report, para. 242.
[361] Piet-Hein Houben, "Principles of International Law Concerning Friendly Relations and Co-Operation Among States" (1967), p. 734.
[362] See Edward McWhinney, "The 'New' Countries and the 'New' International Law" (1966), pp. 30 and 33.
[363] Special Committee on Principles of International Law concerning Friendly Relations and Co-operation among States, Report, A/6230, adopted 27 June 1966 ("Second Report"), para. 37.
[364] See Francis Aime Vallat, "The competence of the United Nations General Assembly" (1959), p. 231.
[365] Max Sørensen, "Principes de droit international public" (1961), p. 105. He spoke of "dédoublement fonctionnel."

all States party to that treaty approved of a certain interpretation of the Charter.[366] In 1948 Sloan pointed out that the most authoritative description of the sources of international law, *i.e.* Article 38 of the Statute of the International Court of Justice did not yet mention General Assembly resolutions as a subsidiary means for the determination of rules of law, let alone as an independent source of law. [367] However, as Sloan and literally all the scholars who refer to Article 38 immediately admit, things are not that simple, and they can change.[368]

### 3.5.6 *The true meaning of votes cast at the General Assembly*

If General Assembly resolutions can be regarded as authoritative interpretations of the UN Charter, binding both the Organization and its Member States, they may very well be qualified, in the spirit of the Vienna Convention on the Law of Treaties, as "subsequent agreement[s] between the parties regarding the interpretation of the treaty or the application of its provisions."[369] As resolutions of the Assembly are not generally presented as such, the intention of the drafters must be determined for every single resolution. Was the resolution meant to interpret the relevant provisions in the Charter? The criteria proposed by Sahović may prove to be helpful here. The fact that a particular interpretation of the Charter is repeated in resolutions adopted in subsequent years is also relevant. Such repetition can be considered as proof that a certain interpretation really "stuck."[370] Arangio-Ruiz, however, believed that "it would be too easy if the 'shouting out' of rules through

---

[366] *Idem,* p. 512. See also Gaetano Arangio-Ruiz, "The normative role of the General Assembly" (1972), p. 512. On one occasion, the ICJ even used a declaration of the General Assembly as proof of the *jus cogens* character of a particular norm. See para. 188 of the ICJ, Case Concerning Military and Paramilitary Activities in and against Nicaragua (Nicaragua v. United States of America), Merits, Judgment of 27 June 1986.

[367] Many scholars started by pointing this out, and then continued to present more imaginative arguments. See *e.g.*, Blaine Sloan, "The binding force of a 'recommendation' of the General Assembly of the United Nations" (1948), p. 2; Jorge Castaneda, "Valeur juridique des résolutions des Nations Unies" (1970), p. 212.

[368] Blaine Sloan, "The binding force of a 'recommendation' of the General Assembly of the United Nations" (1948), pp. 21-22. See also p. 212 of Jorge Castaneda, "Valeur juridique des résolutions des Nations Unies" (1970); Christopher C. Joyner, "U.N. General Assembly resolutions and international law" (1981), pp. 453-455 and p. 477; Oscar Schachter, "International law in theory and practice" (1982), p. 111; Oscar Schachter, "United Nations law" (1994), p. 3. Gaetano Arangio-Ruiz, "The normative role of the General Assembly" (1972), p. 461, had some problems with this argument.

[369] Article 31(3)(a), Vienna Convention on the Law of Treaties. See also Robert Rosenstock, "The Declaration of Principles of International Law Concerning Friendly Relations" (1971), p. 715; Oscar Schachter, "The relation of law, politics and action in the United Nations" (1964), p. 186 (this was published before the Convention entered into force).

[370] Samuel A. Bleicher, "The Legal Significance of Re-Citation of General Assembly Resolutions" (1969).

General Assembly resolutions were to be law-making simply as a matter of 'times' shouted and size of the choir."[371]

Is it fair to suggest that any State casting an affirmative vote for a particular General Assembly resolution, interpreting certain provisions in the Charter, is always consciously expressing its opinion about the proper interpretation of that Charter provision? Or is it fair to suggest that a negative vote should always be interpreted as the rejection of the proposed interpretation of the Charter? It has been suggested that this seriously misconstrues the intention of such votes.[372] It is important to look beyond the affirmative vote itself, and try to find out the true motive behind the vote. Or, in the words of Arangio-Ruiz, one must find out "whether members of the General Assembly 'meant it' or not."[373] After all, "a vote cast in favour of a resolution of the General Assembly is not [by definition] the manifestation of that State's conviction that it is legally bound by the terms of the resolution."[374] In contrast with actually signing and ratifying a treaty, a "yes" vote to a non-binding resolution has little legal significance in itself. It may serve as an expression of a certain opinion, but then it is necessary to know what opinion is actually expressed.[375] At the very least, without evidence to the contrary, it may be assumed that when a State adopts an Assembly resolution, it agrees with the interpretation of the Charter proposed in that resolution.

---

[371] Gaetano Arangio-Ruiz, "The normative role of the General Assembly" (1972), p. 476.

[372] See Benedetto Conforti, "Le rôle de l'accord dans le système des Nations Unies" (1974), pp. 239-246; Oscar Schachter, "International law in theory and practice" (1982), pp. 115-118.

[373] Gaetano Arangio-Ruiz, "The normative role of the General Assembly" (1972), p. 457. As Arangio-Ruiz pointed out, sometimes States vote in a certain way because they wish to keep their good "image" intact.

[374] S. Prakash Sinha, "Has self-determination become a principle of international law today?" (1974), p. 349. See also Gaetano Arangio-Ruiz, "The normative role of the General Assembly" (1972), pp. 485-486.

[375] A former state representative at the UN summarizes the difficulty in interpreting the votes as follows: "countries often have a tendency to cast their votes in a way obscuring their real intentions: a yes vote can mean anything from enthusiastic support at one end of the range, to: I do not like this text at all, but find it inconvenient to distinguish myself by voting against it. An abstention can signal: yes, but…, or: no, but… Only a no vote has kept most of its unambiguity: it is rare for a country to vote no although it really likes the text. However, this may occur if a country aligns itself with a no vote of other members of its group." p. 129 of Johan Kaufmann, *United Nations Decision Making* (1980). For a similar description, see p. 102 of M. J. Peterson, "General Assembly" (2007). See also p. 179 of Louis Henkin, *How Nations Behave: Law and Foreign Policy* (1979). The explanations of the vote may be of assistance here. If a State representative wishes to explain why it voted the way it did, it is given the opportunity to do so. The explanations are often very illuminating. See, for example, the objections some (Soviet) states had against the Universal Declaration of Human Rights when it was adopted in 1948 (UN Doc. A/PV. 183), or the objections of the United States of America to the Declaration on the Right to Development when it was adopted in 1986 (UNDoc. A/41/PV.97).

### 3.5.7    Conclusion

Some Assembly resolutions can be regarded as authoritative interpretations of the UN Charter *and* as a reflection of customary international law. [376] As such, they bind Member States of the United Nations and create justified expectations as to their future behaviour. [377] The Assembly therefore has enormous influence when interpreting the general provisions of the UN Charter. This is limited only by the need for consistent State practice. When the Assembly declares new rules that are not followed in practice, it cannot be said to have changed the legal obligations of the Organization and its Member States. Speaking about the Friendly Relations Declaration, Lowe warned about the potential for abuse of the Assembly's interpretative freedom if State practice were ignored:

> Once articulation [of a certain principle] was attempted, there was a tendency to establish a definition of the principle which cohered with other principles [...] which together constitute the understanding of the international legal order. Coherence with other principles tended to be more important [than] the conformity of the putative principle with State practice. And once a coherent formulation of the legal principle had been adopted, the further elaboration of that principle became a matter of exegesis – the explanation of the meaning and significance of earlier "authoritative" texts, rather than an exercise based upon a return to State practice and the inference of rules therefrom. [378]

Thus Assembly resolutions derive their legal force from the fact that they are adopted by:

> An organ authorized to interpret the most fundamental principles of the international legal order as codified in the UN Charter;
> And (a majority of) all the States in the world.

---

[376] According to the ICJ: "Opinio juris may, though with all due caution, be deduced from, *inter alia*, the attitude of the Parties and the attitude of States towards certain General Assembly resolutions [...]." Pp. 99-100, International Court of Justice, Case concerning Military and Paramilitary Activities in and against Nicaragua (Nicaragua v. United States of America), Merits, Judgment of 27 June 1986. However, Assembly resolutions have no more value as evidence of a custom than any other evidence of State practice or *opinio juris*. It is clearly not the case that the Assembly has formalized the custom-making process, in the sense that a vote in favour of a certain resolution would serve as evidence of an *opinio juris*, an abstention as tacit agreement, and a vote against as a persistent objection. Gaetano Arangio-Ruiz, "The normative role of the General Assembly" (1972), pp. 471-486. See also pp. 254-256, ICJ, Legality of the Threat or Use of Nuclear Weapons, Advisory Opinion of 8 July 1996. See also p. 180, 182 of Louis Henkin, *How Nations Behave: Law and Foreign Policy* (1979); and Jorge Castaneda, "Valeur juridique des résolutions des Nations Unies" (1970), pp. 317-318.

[377] See also Samuel A. Bleicher, "The Legal Significance of Re-Citation of General Assembly Resolutions" (1969), especially pp. 446-451, and p. 447.

[378] Vaughan Lowe, "The principle of non-intervention" (1994), p. 73.

Assembly declarations thus serve principally as constitutional interpretations of the UN Charter, but they also serve as "evidence" of customary international law, if States show, by acting accordingly, that they really meant it when they adopted the Assembly's declaration.[379]

## 3.6 The contribution of other UN organs to the global discussion

The focus in this study is on the role of the General Assembly in the evolution of the Charter's norms and values. As the Assembly is the only organ in which the procedural rules and substantive mandate comply with the criteria of a global discussion, the focus is on that organ. This is not to suggest that other organs of the United Nations have played no role whatsoever in the evolution of global values since 1945. Many organs, including the Trusteeship Council, the Economic and Social Council, the Human Rights Council, and the International Law Commission, in a sense work for the Assembly. This means that their work is "rubber-stamped" by the General Assembly in the form of a resolution. Two other organs deserve a special mention: the Security Council and the International Court of Justice. These organs operate largely independently of the Assembly.[380]

### 3.6.1 The Security Council

The UN Charter gives the Security Council immense powers to maintain international peace and security.[381] To ensure international peace and security, the Council can issue binding decisions on all Member States, including ordering them to temporarily ignore, or even violate their international legal obligations.[382] Such resolutions are not intended to be contributions to the progressive development of international law. Instead, they authorize emergency measures that apply for a short time, and only with regard to a particular dispute. The drafters of the Charter in San Francisco were very clear about their intention not to grant the Security Council any legislative powers. At best, it was believed that "[t]he Security Council, although not intended to be a legislative body, might conceivably build up a body of international common law through its reasoned action in dealing with international disputes."[383] The Security Council resolutions could then be considered to be

---

[379] The use of the word "evidence" to characterize the role of Assembly resolutions in the development of custom was taken from Oscar Schachter, "International law in theory and practice" (1982), p. 117.

[380] See also section 3.5 of Chapter III, above.

[381] The latter additional phrase is essential: the Council only has such broad powers when responding to a threat to international peace and security, invoking Chapter VII of the UN Charter.

[382] See Article 103 of the UN Charter, in relation with Chapter VII and Articles 24, 25 and 48.

[383] John Foster Dulles, "The United Nations: A Prospectus (The General Assembly)" (1945), p. 4.

judgments adjudicating particular disputes. The way in which one international dispute was settled by the Council could then set a precedent for the settlement of future disputes of a similar nature.

However, that is already going one step too far. The Security Council was not meant to have such a judicial function at all. It had – and still has – an action-oriented, essentially political character. [384] According to Stettinius, the Security Council was supposed to be "hardly even 'quasi-judicial' in its conciliatory function because of the latitude permitted for the play of political considerations." [385] In practice, the Council has made good use of this latitude.

And so it must be concluded that the resolutions of the Security Council should not be considered to have any sort of legislative function. In San Francisco the major powers suggested that the Council would operate largely outside the realm of the law. This frightened the smaller nations. Egypt proposed an amendment that explicitly stated that the maintenance of international peace and security, which was the prime task of the Council should be "in conformity with the principles of justice and international law." [386] The Soviet Union disagreed. The Soviets believed that the Organization was established to effectively prevent the repetition of a new war, and that the smaller countries simply had to trust the superpowers. [387] The response of the USA was that the Security Council had two very important functions, and that

> These might be characterized somewhat as being the functions of a policeman and the functions of a jury. [...] It is our view that the people of the world wish to establish a Security Council, that is, a policeman who will say, when anyone starts to fight, "stop fighting". Period. And then it will say, when anyone is all ready to begin

---

[384] On the Security Council as promoter of the global interest (world peace), see p. 24-25 of Jean d'Aspremont, *Contemporary International Rulemaking and the Public Character of International La* (2006), pp. 574-575 of Bardo Fassbender, "The United Nations Charter as Constitution" (1998), Pierre-Marie Dupuy, "The Constitutional Dimension of the Charter of the United Nations Revisited" (1997), and Bruno Simma, "From Bilateralism to Community Interest" (1994), pp. 264-283. Somewhat surprisingly, the first three authors hardly mention the role of the General Assembly in defining and promoting the global interest, while the last author devotes barely two pages to the Assembly as "World Parliament", which contrasts with the 20 pages devoted to the Council as the "World Government".

[385] Edward R. Stettinius, *Charter of the United Nations* (1945), p. 80.

[386] UNCIO, vol. 6, p. 23. All of the following delegates made a similar point in their proposed amendments to the Dumbarton Oaks proposal: France (UNCIO, Vol. 3, p. 383. See also, UNCIO, Vol. 3, p. 377); Greece (Vol. 3, p. 531); Netherlands (Vol. 3, p. 323); Norway (vol. 3, p. 355); Uruguay (vol. 3, p. 34); Venezuela (vol. 3, p. 224); Bolivia (Vol. 3, p. 582); Ecuador (vol. 3, p. 398); Egypt (vol. 3, p. 447); Iran (vol. 3, p. 554); Mexico (vol. 3, p. 178); Panama (vol. 3, p. 265); Chili (vol. 3, p. 284). About this amendment and what became of it, see also Mohammed Bedjaoui, "Article 1" (2005), p. 315, and Manfred Lachs, "Article 1, paragraphe 1" (2005), p. 331.

[387] Speech by Molotov (UNCIO, vol. 1, p. 135): "The point at issue is whether other peace-loving nations are willing to rally around these leading powers to create an effective international security organization, and this has to be settled at this Conference in the interests of the future peace and security of nations." See also: UNCIO, vol. 1, p. 662-666.

to fight, "you must not fight". Period. That is the function of a policeman, and it must be just that short and that abrupt; that is, unless at that place we add any more, then we would say "Stop fighting unless you claim international law is on your side". That would lead to a weakening and a confusion in our interpretation.[388]

Uruguay agreed that "the world [was] sick of wars," but then asked the rhetorical question: must the threat of all wars be reduced at any price? Payssé, the Uruguayan delegate, answered the question himself:

> The mere police function, which pursues the materiality or formality of the order, and which in the popular language of my country is translated into the meaningful expression "You are right, but you are under arrest," cannot attract our sympathies nor our hopes in the panorama of the reconstruction of the world. The day when there occurs anew the illusion that by sacrificing the rights of the weak in the face of threats by the strong the peace would be saved, on that day the fuse will have been lighted which sooner or later would set off the explosion of war. Injustice is not a propitious atmosphere for peace.[389]

After this discussion the Egyptian amendment was put to the vote. The result was 21 for, 21 against. Amendments required a two-thirds majority to be adopted in San Francisco.[390] The amendment was therefore rejected. This meant that the Security Council was not to be hindered by constraints of law when maintaining international peace and security. This discussion is often characterized as a struggle for power between the Big Five, who preferred to give the maintenance of security complete freedom, and the "small" Forty-Five, who wanted this freedom to be constrained by principles of justice. However, Uruguay had already rejected this characterization in San Francisco when the Uruguayan delegate warned that this debate should not be seen as "a duel between David and Goliath, in which the small countries [...] throw the stone of justice at the great powers," because "that would be quite contrary to the truth."[391]

The Rapporteur of the relevant Commission hastened to explain this surprising result. He said that none of the delegates were against justice, but they felt that "adding 'justice' after 'peace and security' brings in at that juncture of the text a notion which lacks in clarity."[392] The United States, regretting the tone of the previous statement, tried to reassure the smaller States a few days later in a subsequent meeting of the Commission:

---

[388] UNCIO, vol. 6, p. 29. The US delegate then explained the "jury function".
[389] UNCIO, vol. 6, p. 31.
[390] *Idem*, p. 34. See also pp. 229-230.
[391] First Session of Commission I, 14 June 1945, UNCIO, vol. 6, p. 31.
[392] *Idem*, p. 394 (already cited in section 3.5 of Chapter III, above).

> We are here [in San Francisco], first of all, to find ways and means to maintain international peace and security throughout the world. But above and beyond that most desirable objective, we are here to lay the first foundation of a new world civilization which in its international relations shall be based upon law and justice and brotherhood, rather than upon brute force.[393]

There is something hypocritical about this statement, considering that it was made after the Egyptian amendment had been rejected. The relevant article in the UN Charter does not have the desirable reference to international law. This is largely due to US resistance. When maintaining international peace and security, the Security Council can take measures obliging Member States to act in violation of international agreements. [394] An organ which is itself not even bound by international law cannot be expected to contribute to its evolution, either as international judge, or as an international legislator. Nevertheless, the Council did create for itself, at least during a few years after the Cold War, a "quasi-legislative role."[395] Understandably, these resolutions proved to be highly controversial. The Council's "legislation" is discussed in the next chapter on peace and security.

### 3.6.2   The International Court of Justice

The other organ that deserves a special section is the International Court of Justice. It is possible to imagine a role for the Court in assisting States and the General Assembly with the legally correct interpretation of the UN Charter. However, this role for the Court as the "legal guardian" of the UN Charter was explicitly rejected. [396] This can best be shown by referring to the proposal made in San Francisco that the International Court should ensure that the Security Council would act in accordance with the values, purposes, and principles of the UN Charter. The immense powers given to the Council, and the fact that these powers could be exercised outside the realm of the law, worried the delegates of the smaller nations in San Francisco.[397] They therefore attempted to create some kind of judicial control

---

[393] *Idem*, p. 118.

[394] See Article 103 of the UN Charter, in relation with Chapter VII and Articles 24, 25 and 48. When the Security Council acts outside Chapter VII, it is bound by international law and agreements. See Articles 24 and 1.

[395] Nico Schrijver, "The Future of the Charter of the United Nations" (2006)," p. 23.

[396] Judge Lachs referred to the Court as the "guardian of legality for the international community as a whole, both within and without the United Nations," but then failed to explain the consequences of such a qualification. P. 26, Separate Opinion of Judge Lachs, in Case Concerning Questions of Interpretation and Application of the 1971 Montreal Convention arising from the Aerial Incident at Lockerbie (Libyan Arab Jamahiriya v. United Kingdom), Request for the Indication of Provisional Measures, Order of 14 April 1992.

[397] The Dutch delegate leader, Eelco van Kleffens, wrote in his diary: "De Belgen maken zich evenals wij ongerust over het van de conferentie te verwachten resultaat: bezegeling van de hegemonie der

over the Security Council. As the Council was not immediately bound by international law in general, exercising "judicial control" essentially meant checking whether the Council's resolutions were in accordance with the UN Charter. Contrary to most other international law, the Charter had the power to limit the competence of the organ – the Security Council – it had itself established.

The Netherlands suggested leaving this judicial scrutiny up to a "body of eminent men."[398] The Netherlands believed that "it clearly could not be left to the Security Council to decide, for if that were done this Council would be allowed to sit in judgment on its own proposals."[399] A more obvious candidate to exercise judicial control over Security Council decisions, rather than this body of eminent men, was the International Court of Justice. This is what Belgium proposed as an amendment to Dumbarton Oaks:

> Any State, party to a dispute brought before the Security Council, shall have the right to ask the [International] Court of Justice whether a recommendation or a decision made by the Council or proposed in it infringes on its essential rights. If the Court considers that such rights have been disregarded or are threatened, it is for the Council either to reconsider the question or to refer the dispute to the [General] Assembly for decision.[400]

It does not come as a surprise that the Soviet Union was the most outspoken opponent of this proposal. According to the Soviet Union, "if it were possible for a state to appeal from the Council to the International Court of Justice [...] the Council would find itself handicapped in carrying out its functions."[401] The UK

---

groote mogendheden ten koste van de kleinere, gepaard aan een ronflant verdrag zonder inhoud." [Translation: "The Belgians are just as worried as we are about the expected results of this conference: sealing of the hegemony of the big powers at the cost of the smaller nations, through a treaty without much content."]. Kleffens" Diary, published in Cees Wiebes, "De oprichting van de Verenigde Naties" (1995), p. 84.

[398] The Netherlands (UNCIO, vol. 3, p. 313): "[The Netherlands] offer as a solution the appointment of an independent body of eminent men from a suitable number of different countries, men known for their integrity and their experience in international affairs, who should be readily available to pronounce upon decisions of the Security council whenever an appeal to that effect were addressed to them, either by the Council or by a party to the case in question. This body, it should be emphasized, should pronounce upon the matter solely from the point of view of whether the Council's decision is in keeping with the moral principles [...], and should render its decision within a set number of days so as to avoid an undue delay."

[399] UNCIO, vol. 3, p. 313.

[400] UNCIO, vol. 3, p. 336. Belgium also said, in relation to the hypothetical situation that the recommended procedure of the Security Council for the peaceful settlement of disputes is not successful, that "before a project for the settlement of a difference, drawn up by the Council or by any other body became final, each of the States concerned should be able to ask an advisory opinion from the International Court of Justice as to whether the decision respected its independence and vital rights." (UNCIO, vol. 14, p. 446.)

[401] UNCIO, vol. 12, p. 49.

added that "the procedures proposed by the [Belgian] amendment would cause delay, at a time when prompt action by the Security Council was most desirable."[402] The Belgian proposal was ultimately withdrawn.[403]

This meant that the Court lost its role as legal guardian of the Charter altogether. A subcommittee was established in San Francisco to answer the following question: "How and by what organ or organs of the Organization should the Charter be interpreted?"[404] The answer was as follows: "Each organ will interpret such parts of the Charter as are applicable to its particular functions."[405] Therefore the International Court of Justice was not the organ to check whether the Council, or any other UN organ, was acting within its constitutional scope of competence (*intra vires*).

The "founding fathers" did not give the International Court of Justice the competence to check the binding resolutions of the Security Council on their constitutionality. But the UN Charter is a "living tree." The interpretation of the text evolves over time.[406] However, since 1945 the judges of the International Court of Justice have consistently denied themselves the authority to exercise judicial control over the Council. As early as 1962, the Court noted in the Certain Expenses Opinion that:

> In the legal systems of States, there is often some procedure for determining the validity of even a legislative or governmental act, but no analogous procedure is to be found in the structure of the United Nations. Proposals made during the drafting of the Charter to place the ultimate authority to interpret the Charter in the International Court of Justice were not accepted.[407]

A little less than ten years later, the Court reiterated its standpoint in the Namibia Opinion.[408] In the 1990s the Court was asked to deal with the issue of judicial

---

[402] UNCIO, vol. 12, p. 65.

[403] See UNCIO, vol. 12, p. 66; see also: vol. 13, p. 645.

[404] UNCIO, vol. 13, p. 668. The Subcommittee (Subcommittee IV-2-B) consisted of representatives from Belgium, France, Norway, the UK and the USA.

[405] UNCIO, vol. 13, p. 668, 709. See also section 3.5 of Chapter III, above. The Committee added that "two organs may conceivably hold and may express or even act upon different views. Under unitary forms of national government the final determination of such a question may be vested in the highest court or in some other national authority. However, the nature of the Organization and of its operation would not seem to be such as to invite the inclusion in the Charter of any provision of this nature."

[406] Thomas M. Franck, "Is the UN Charter a Constitution?" (2003).

[407] See International Court of Justice, Certain Expenses of the United Nations (Article 17, paragraph 2, of the Charter), Advisory Opinion of 20 July 1962. I.C.J. Reports 1962, p. 168.

[408] There the Court said: "Undoubtedly, the Court does not possess powers of judicial review or appeal in respect of the decisions taken by the United Nations organs concerned." International Court of Justice, Legal Consequences for States of the Continued Presence of South Africa in Namibia (South West Africa) notwithstanding Security Council resolution 276 (1970), an Advisory Opinion of 1971. I.C.J. Reports 1971, p. 45.

control in a contentious case. The Security Council imposed economic sanctions on Libya in an attempt to force it to comply with requests from the USA and the United Kingdom to surrender Libyan nationals accused of blowing up an airplane above Lockerbie, Scotland.[409] Libya claimed the sanctions were illegal and, as it could not bring the Security Council itself before the Court, it instead initiated proceedings against the UK and the US.[410]

Two decisions of the Court in the Lockerbie Case are discussed briefly to show what the Court said about its competence of constitutional review: first, the order on the request by Libya for an indication of provisional measures ("Lockerbie Order"),[411] and secondly, the judgment on preliminary objections ("Lockerbie Judgment").[412]

First, Libya asked the Court to order the US and the UK, as a provisional measure, not to compel it to surrender the individuals accused of the Lockerbie bombing.[413] This was exactly what the relevant Security Council resolutions compelled Libya to do.[414] The Court did not grant Libya's request, because such a provisional measure would undermine the rights which the US and the UK appeared to have by virtue of a Security Council resolution.[415] The Court did not assess the legality of the Council's resolution in the order, nor did it address the issue of judicial control in any detail.

---

[409] The relevant resolutions: Security Council 731 (1992) of 21 January 1992, 748 (1992) of 31 March (1992), and 883 (1993) of 11 November 1993. In the first resolution, Libya was urged to surrender the suspected individuals; in the second, adopted after Libya went to the ICJ, the Council invoked Chapter VII and ordered Libya to surrender the suspects, already imposing sanctions. On the 31st of January 2001, an essentially Scottish court, set up in the Netherlands especially for the trial, sentenced one man to life, another was set free.

[410] Case Concerning Questions of Interpretation and Application of the 1971 Montreal Convention Arising from the Aerial Incident at Lockerbie (Libyan Arab Jamahiriya v. United States of America). Similar proceedings were started against the UK, with similar orders and similar judgments as the result.

[411] Order on the Request for the Indication of Provisional Measures, 14 April 1992, in the Case Concerning Questions of Interpretation and Application of the 1971 Montreal Convention Arising from the Aerial Incident at Lockerbie (Libyan Arab Jamahiriya v. United States of America) ("Lockerbie Order").

[412] Judgment (Preliminary Objections), 27 February 1998, in the Case Concerning Questions of Interpretation and Application of the 1971 Montreal Convention Arising from the Aerial Incident at Lockerbie (Libyan Arab Jamahiriya v. United States of America) ("Lockerbie Judgment").

[413] Lybia asked the Court "to enjoin the United States from taking against Libya measures calculated to exert coercion on it or compel it to surrender the accused individuals to any jurisdiction outside of Libya; and to ensure that no steps are taken that could prejudice in any way the rights of Libya with respect to the proceedings instituted by Libya's Application." Lockerbie Order, para. 20.

[414] Security Council resolutions 731 (1992) of 21 January 1992, and 748 (1992) of 31 March (1992).

[415] Lockerbie Order, Para. 42-44. The Court relied on Article 25 and 103 of the UN Charter in reaching its decision.

However, the separate and dissenting opinions did. [416] In his separate opinion one judge asked "If there are any limits [to the competence of the Security Council], what are those limits and what body, if other than the Security Council, is competent to say what those limits are?"[417] In addressing their colleague's question, the other judges mainly discussed two issues: "constitutional relations,"[418] and the *legal versus political* dichotomy.[419] Bluntly stated, the conclusion was, that contrary to many domestic constitutions, the UN constitution did not contain any system of checks and balances, and that the Council and the Court did not need to interfere in each other's work, even when dealing with the same situation, because they operated in different fields (politics and law, respectively). Some academics followed in their footsteps, many others criticized them. [420]

The demand for provisional measures was therefore rejected. Subsequently, the Court had to decide whether it had jurisdiction in principle. The answer in the Lockerbie Judgment was affirmative. But the Court reserved the question on the Council's resolution for the discussion on the merits of the case.[421] The Court never reached that point, because the Lockerbie Case was ultimately removed from the Court's list at the joint request of the Parties. [422]

Again, the most elaborate discussions on judicial control can be found not in the actual judgment, but in the separate and dissenting opinions. The American judge Schwebel wrote a strong dissenting opinion on the judgment. He wrote that "the conclusions to which the *travaux préparatoires* and text of the Charter lead are that the Court was not and was not meant to be invested with a power of judicial

---

[416] For a discussion of these separate opinions, see also Thomas M. Franck, "The "powers of appreciation"" (1992).

[417] Separate Opinion of Judge Shahabuddeen to the Lockerbie Order.

[418] See (almost) all opinions to the Lockerbie Order. Some judges compared the relationship between the main UN organs with those of a State. See, *e.g.*, the Dissenting Opinion by Judge Bedjaoui, para. 7; and the Dissenting Opinion of Judge Weeramantry.

[419] The judges believed that the Court had to adopt a *legal* standpoint, whilst the Council could consider the same issue from a *political* standpoint. See, *e.g.*, the Declaration of Judge Ni to the Lockerbie Order.

[420] There are many articles on the Lockerbie case, focusing on "constitutional relations". See, *e.g.*, Vera Gowlland-Debass, "The Relationship Between the International Court of Justice and the Security Council in the Light of the Lockerbie Case" (1994), p. 643-677; Jose E. Alvarez, "Judging the Security Council" (1996).

[421] For a discussion on the Security Council resolutions, see especially paras. 36-38 and 42-44 (jurisdiction and admissibility had to be considered at a time when the main resolutions were not yet passed). The Court did not want to respond at the stage of preliminary objections to the argument that Libya's claims became moot because Security Council resolutions rendered them without object, because it would then have to make a decisions on two issues which formed the subject-matter of the case: a decision establishing that the rights claimed by Libya under the Montreal Convention were incompatible with its obligations under the Security Council resolutions; and, on the other hand, a decision that those obligations prevailed over those rights by virtue of Articles 25 and 103 of the Charter. (see para. 49).

[422] Lockerbie Order of 10 September 2003.

review of the legality or effects of decisions of the Security Council."[423] According to Schwebel, even if the UN Charter is considered to be a living instrument, with an interpretation which evolves over time, the Court could still not exercise a judicial review of Security Council resolutions, because that would be a "revolutionary," as opposed to an "evolutionary," interpretation of the Charter. "It would be not a development but a departure, and a great and grave departure."[424]

After the Lockerbie Judgment was published, some authors argued that the only check on the Security Council's actions arose from *realpolitik*. The limit of the Council's powers would be reached when it ordered sanctions or military intervention and no one was willing to respond.[425] In response to this pessimistic view, others argued that judicial control was meant to prevent exactly that: by preventing the Council from ordering unconstitutional measures, the Court could ward off illegitimate orders that no State in the world would obey.[426]

For different reasons then, the roles of the Security Council and the International Court of Justice are limited in the global conversation about values. The Security Council is a political organ, dealing only with emergencies. The role of the International Court of Justice in the evolution of the Charter's values and norms has weakened because the Court has not yet accepted for itself in an unambiguous way the power to check the acts of the other organs on their constitutionality.

## 3.7 Conclusion

The General Assembly's discussions that were examined were a continuation of the discussions started in San Francisco in 1945.

First, it was shown that the Assembly had the competence to discuss all values, purposes and principles of the UN Charter. Then the Assembly's discussions were assessed on the basis of the three essential conditions of a discussion suitable for determining and evolving global values: its inclusive and genuine character, and the capacity to motivate action.

With regard to its inclusive character, it was noted that all States had the opportunity to participate in the discussion. Although there are some objections to the one State, one vote rule, this rule is the best of all possibilities to ensure universal representation.

---

[423] Dissenting Opinion of Judge Schwebel to the Lockerbie Judgment.

[424] *Idem.*

[425] José E. Alvarez, "Judging the Security Council", p. 2, and the literature cited there. See also Thomas M. Franck, "The 'powers of appreciation'" (1992), p. 523; Oscar Schachter, "United Nations law" (1994), p. 8.

[426] José E. Alvarez, "Judging the Security Council," p. 3, and the literature cited there.

With regard to its genuine character, some remarks were made about the sincerity of the representatives in the Assembly. Why do States *really* vote the way they do? The fact that the State's national interest plays an important role here does not, so it was argued, mean that the discussions are carried out insincerely.

As international law is the language *par excellence* to motivate action, the Assembly's resolutions were assessed in terms of their legal power or binding character. There are generally two ways in which Assembly resolutions could reflect legal obligations: as interpretations of the provisions in the UN Charter, and as authoritative declarations of existing customary law.

Finally, the role of other organs was examined, especially the Security Council and the International Court of Justice. It was not suggested that the other organs of the United Nations played no role whatsoever in the global discussions, but that the General Assembly was the organ that best satisfied the general criteria any global discussion should meet, and that other organs could consequently only play a secondary role.

## 4 RESPONSIBILITY FOR THE REALIZATION OF THE NORMS AND VALUES OF THE UN CHARTER

### 4.1 Introduction

Who better to accept responsibility for the realization of global values and the defence of the community interest than the international community itself?[427] The United Nations Organization is often mentioned as the most suitable candidate to serve as the active limbs of the international community.[428] However, the Organization and its organs cannot realize the global values on their own.[429] The States need to do most of the work.

---

[427] See Andre de Hoogh, *Obligations Erga Omnes and International Crimes* (1996); Pierre-Marie Dupuy, "L'unité de l'ordre juridique international" (2002), pp. 373-374, p. 391; p. 272, Christian Hillgruber, "The Right of Third States to Take Countermeasures" (2006); Jochen Frowein, "Reactions by not directly affected states to breaches of public international law" (1994), p. 423; Christian Tomuschat, "Obligations arising for states without or against their will" (1993), pp. 364-365; Christian Tomuschat, "International law: ensuring the survival of mankind on the eve of a new century" (1999), p. 377; Antônio Augusto Cançado Trindade, on p. 108, Annuaire de l'Institut de droit international, vol. 71-II (2006); p. 200, Martti Koskenniemi, *Fragmentation of international law: difficulties arising from the diversification and expansion of international law (Report of the Study Group of the International Law Commission)*, 13 April 2006, UN Doc. A/CN.4/L.682.

[428] For the moment, the term "international community," which is often left undefined in the literature, can be defined as the collective of all the world's citizens, organized in various States.

[429] See *e.g.*, p. 287-288, Christian Hillgruber, "The Right of Third States to Take Countermeasures" (2006); Santiago Villalpando, *L'émergence de la communauté internationale dans la responsabilité des Etats* (2005), pp. 79-83.

This section discusses two possibilities for collective action. The "institutionalized" alternative is examined first. The principal organs of the United Nations are assessed in terms of their capacity to realize the values proclaimed in the Charter and in General Assembly resolutions (4.2). Secondly, the role of the States themselves, acting in concert, is assessed (4.3).

## 4.2 The United Nations Organization

The UN Charter has often been called a "constitution." This label is particularly relevant in the present context. The similarities between the UN Charter and domestic constitutions are most obvious when the principal organs of the Organization, and the powers accorded to them in the UN Charter, are compared with the principal organs of domestic systems of government.[430]

The United Nations machinery is quite similar to the way in which things are organized domestically. The General Assembly can be seen as the world's parliament. The executive branch of the "world government" is made up of a collection of specialized councils: the Security Council for peace and security; the Economic and Social Council for social progress and development; the Human Rights Council for human dignity; and the Trusteeship Council for self-determination of peoples. These councils are comparable to the ministries that jointly constitute the government at the domestic level. There is a "world court," the International Court of Justice.[431] In addition, there is a system of checks and balances in the Charter, although this is much less developed than the checks and balances in most domestic systems.[432]

A closer look leads to the conclusion that there are substantial differences between the UN machinery and domestic constitutional systems. One of these differences is that in the UN, every organ interprets its own mandate. Access to the Court to decide on constitutional questions is limited, if there is such access at all.[433] The main organs of the United Nations have hardly any powers to compel

---

[430] See also Bardo Fassbender, "The United Nations Charter as Constitution" (1998), p. 589. See also Bruno Simma, "From Bilateralism to Community Interest" (1994), p. 262, and Pierre-Marie Dupuy, "The Constitutional Dimension of the Charter of the United Nations Revisited" (1997).

[431] This comparison was already made in San Francisco. For example, Stettinus referred to the UN's main organs as "the enforcement officer" (Security Council), "the Court" (ICJ), "the public meeting" (General Assembly), and "the center of science and of knowledge" (Economic and Social Council). Edward R. Stettinius, *Charter of the United Nations* (1945), pp. 13-118 (quote can be found on p. 17).

[432] See, *e.g.*, Thomas M. Franck, "The 'powers of appreciation'" (1992); James Crawford, "Multilateral Rights and Obligations in International Law" (2006), pp. 379-388.

[433] The most often discussed of these checks and balances is the check by the International Court of Justice, and, to a lesser extent, by the General Assembly, on the powers of the Security Council. The Court has pronounced itself on this issue in a few occasions: See International Court of Justice, Certain Expenses of the United Nations (Article 17, paragraph 2, of the Charter), Advising Opinion of 20 July 1962. I.C.J. Reports 1962, p. 168; International Court of Justice, Legal Consequences for States of the

Member States to act in compliance with the UN's purposes and principles. The Court has no compulsory jurisdiction. The General Assembly cannot impose binding legislation on the Member States, and the Security Council can only act against the wishes of States by imposing sanctions or when authorizing the use of force to maintain international peace and security. Such measures are – and should be – exceptional measures. The other Councils, responsible for the implementation of the other values, have no such sweeping powers. The situation is very different at the domestic level, where the government is constantly imposing obligations on its "clientele," *i.e.* the population. Therefore the slight similarities between the UN machinery and domestic organs of government should not lead to the conclusion that the United Nations was intended to be a world government, or ever will be. This was already pointed out by the International Court of Justice in 1949, when it stated that the Organization was not a "super-State;" and there is nothing to indicate that this view is out of date now.[434]

This does not mean that the Organization has no means at its disposal to defend the values it proclaims and develops. Slowly but surely, the United Nations has become "a machine that runs by itself."[435] It has become increasingly independent from its creators. The UN Charter provides the skeleton of that machine. The UN's international civil servants provide the machine with a soul.[436] It is noticeable that this machine is generally studied by looking at the intention of its makers, not by looking at the machine itself. In less metaphorical terms, looking at international organizations as instruments made and controlled by States may not necessarily be the best way to look at them. As Klabbers commented on international organizations in general, "[t]he very thing that is subjected to control tends to escape from control and instead ends up in control (not unlike Frankenstein's creation)."[437] Instead of studying Doctor Victor Frankenstein to understand the monster, it may be better to study the monster itself. This monster then independently sets out to pursue the purposes and principles it was set out to pursue. As it only seeks to accomplish certain noble purposes, the monster has some moral authority and legitimacy that a mere instrument of powerful States can never

---

Continued Presence of South Africa in Namibia (South West Africa) notwithstanding Security Council resolution 276 (1970), an Advisory Opinion of 1971. I.C.J. Reports 1971, p. 45; and the Lockerbie case discussed above.

[434] See International Court of Justice, Reparation for Injuries suffered in the Service of the United Nations, Advisory Opinion of 11 April 1949, especially p. 179.

[435] Thomas M. Franck, "Is the UN Charter a Constitution?" (2003), pp. 98 - 101.

[436] In Dupuy's own words: "Il faut lui insuffler une âme." See Jean Dupuy, *San Francisco et la Charte des Nations Unies* (1945), p. 69. Similarly, van Kleffens remarked that "[t]he United Nations, if left alone, is nothing but a disused piece of machinery," and that "[i]t will do nothing unless handled." Eelco N. van Kleffens, "The United Nations and Some Main Trends of Our Time" (1947), p. 74.

[437] Jan Klabbers, "Constitutionalism Lite" (2004), p. 37. Klabbers borrowed this metaphor from Dan Sarooshi.

have.[438] As soon as the monster is out in the open, the constitutive document (the UN Charter) becomes more of a constraining force, limiting the monster's powers in the pursuance of its purposes, and in this way protecting the creator from his creation.[439] Thus, like all constitutions, the UN Charter contains both ambitious principles, and rules that serve to restrain the powers of the organs of that very same Organization. The most important of those rules is the rule that prohibits the organization from interfering in essentially domestic affairs, *i.e.* Article 2(7) UN Charter.

How exactly does this monster operate? If it does not operate exactly in the same way as a domestic government, how far does this comparison apply? It is certainly true that not a single organ or subsidiary body of the United Nations has the mandate to defend the values and norms of the United Nations on behalf of all member States. The organ that is most often mentioned as a potential "enforcer" of the norms in the UN Charter is the Security Council. For a long time the Council could not be considered a serious candidate for the role of enforcer of United Nations values and norms because of the extensive use of the veto and the failure to create a "UN Army," as envisaged in Article 43 of the Charter. [440] These two Cold War facts together "at once paralyzed and disarmed" the Council. The direct consequence of this was that the Charter's intentions in the field of collective security essentially "came to nothing." [441] After the recent "*résurrection spectaculaire*" of the Security Council,[442] it did, at least for a few years, truly act as the defender of United Nations values and norms, by considering any serious violation of such norms and values as constituting a "threat to the peace, breach of

---

[438] See Michael Barnett and Martha Finnemore, *Rules for the World: International Organizations in Global Politics* (2004), p. 5. This is the gist of the argument: "IOs [international organizations] act to promote socially valued goals such as protecting human rights, providing development assistance, and brokering peace agreements. IOs use their credibility as promoters of "progress" toward these valued goals to command deference, that is, exercise authority, in these arenas of action. In addition, because they are bureaucracies, IOs carry out their missions by means that are mostly rational, technocratic, impartial, and nonviolent. This often makes IOs appear more legitimate to more actors than self-serving states that employ coercive tactics in pursuit of their particularistic goals. Their means, like their missions, give IOs authority to act where individual states may not."

[439] This is a characteristic all constitutions share, be it domestic or international. On the UN Charter's constraining powers, see also Grigory I. Tunkin, "The legal nature of the United Nations" (1969), p. 22.

[440] In 1948, Kaeckenbeeck still believed that is was the Council's command over the "UN Army," which constituted "l'embryon dun pouvoir exécutif." Georges Kaeckenbeeck, "La Charte de San-Francisco dans ses rapports avec le droit international" (1948), p. 131.

[441] Rosalyn Higgins, "International law and the avoidance, containment and resolution of disputes" (1991), p. 229. See also Francis Aime Vallat, "The competence of the United Nations General Assembly" (1959), p. 251.

[442] Alain Pellet, "La formation du droit international dans le cadre des Nations Unies" (1995), p. 6. See also p. 296 of Jean-Pierre Cot & Alain Pellet, "Préambule" (2005), and Manfred Lachs, "Article 1, paragraphe 1" (2005), p. 333. Simma and Paulus speak of the "revitalization" of the Council. See p. 274, Bruno Simma and Andreas L. Paulus, "The International Community" (1998).

the peace, or act of aggression." [443] Some scholars agreed with this extensive interpretation of the Council's mandate. Hannikainen, for example, believed that "according to current interpretation of the Charter, those obligations which are most essential for the maintenance of international peace and security are the same as the basic obligations arising from the main purposes of the UN in Art. 1 of the Charter: the prohibition of acts of aggression, the respect for self-determination of peoples and the (elementary) respect for human rights without distinction, especially without distinction of race." [444] Tomuschat did not have any problem either with an expanded interpretation of a "threat to the peace" so that whenever other values were violated "to such a degree that outbursts of violence may be expected," [445] the Security Council should use far-reaching means to act in the general interest. [446] If the Council interpreted its own mandate in this way, it would become the *primus inter pares* among the UN's councils. It could make full use of its authority to impose obligations on all States. The other councils lacked this authority.

Other scholars were less enthusiastic. According to Dupuy, an organ like the Security Council could not replace the decentralized way of upholding global values, [447] primarily because of the arbitrary nature of its actions. [448] If the Council was to fulfil a role as a global enforcer, its actions should be based on objective terms (values) that all States can accept, at least in principle, and which can be applied objectively. [449] This raises the question of control over the Council. The call, often heard during the Cold War, to find ways to make the Council more active was recently suddenly replaced by a call for (legal) restraints on that very same Council.

The Security Council still does not have its own army, and has to rely on Member States to respect and carry out its resolutions. This is why Simma and Paulus have referred to the "authorization model," in which "individual States assume the role of agents of the international community represented by the Security Council." [450] In that case the actions taken by individual States on the authority of the Council are not all that different from counter measures taken in the collective interest. The main difference is a prior authorization to act – or in the

---

[443] Article 39 of the UN Charter.

[444] Lauri Hannikainen, *Peremptory Norms (jus cogens) in International Law* (1988), p. 284.

[445] Christian Tomuschat, "Obligations arising for states without or against their will" (1993), p. 342.

[446] *Idem*, pp. 333-346, and pp. 355-356.

[447] Pierre-Marie Dupuy, "L'unité de l'ordre juridique international" (2002), pp. 377.

[448] The genocide in Rwanda and in Srebrenica can be considered as examples. See Samantha Power, *"A problem from hell": America and the age of genocide* (2002), Romeo Dallaire, with Brent Beardsley, *Shake Hands with the Devil* (2003); Otto Spijkers, "Legal Mechanisms to Establish Accountability for the Genocide in Srebrenica" (2007).

[449] See also Ian Johnstone, "Legislation and adjudication in the UN Security Council" (2008), pp. 275-308.

[450] Bruno Simma and Andreas L. Paulus, "The International Community" (1998), p. 275.

case of sanctions: a legal obligation to act – stemming from a collective organ established by all members of the international community together.[451]

Apart from the Council, there are many other, "softer" means available to the United Nations to ensure compliance on behalf of the international community as a whole, with the norms and values proclaimed in the UN Charter and developed by the General Assembly. The powers of the other Councils are discussed in the chapters dealing with the particular value they were established to protect.[452] The Assembly's resolution-making "power" could also be included in this list. Even though the Assembly has no means to enforce compliance with its resolutions, the violation of an essential norm adopted by the Assembly may be followed by public condemnation, "naming and shaming," which is sometimes, as a judge of the Court already pointed out as early as 1951, more powerful than more legalistic methods of "enforcement".[453] The drafters of the Charter foresaw that its influence on world public opinion would become the Assembly's most powerful weapon. Evatt, for example, believed it was crucial for the Assembly to have "the widest possible powers of discussion and recommendation, so that the pressure of world public opinion could be brought to bear upon countries not living up to their international obligations."[454] If "public opinion" was a powerful weapon in the 1950s, it is certainly a powerful weapon today, with the globalization of the media and the impressive mushrooming of NGOs specializing in scrutinizing international affairs.

The exact qualification of the role of the United Nations and its principal organs, in the promotion and codification of value-based norms is not yet clear. It is certainly not a world government, but how then can its role be qualified? Earlier, global values were described as the driving force behind global governance.[455] It was suggested that the United Nations was the focal point in the global realization of certain shared goals. These goals, as Rosenau explained, could be derived from legal norms, but they do not necessarily need a global police force to ensure compliance.[456] Recently the Assembly itself started researching its own role and that of the Organization as a whole in global governance. It "acknowledg[ed] the vital importance of an inclusive, transparent and effective multilateral system in order better to address the urgent global challenges of today."[457] This is the general challenge of global governance. The Assembly "recogniz[ed] the universality of the

---

[451] See also Jochen Frowein, "Reactions by not directly affected states to breaches of public international law" (1994), p. 433.

[452] See the relevant chapters in Part II of this study.

[453] See Alvarez, Separate Opinion in the ICJ's Reservations to the Genocide Convention Advisory Opinion, 28 May 1951, p. 52.

[454] Herbert Vere Evatt, *The United Nations* (1948), p. 19.

[455] See section 5.2 of Chapter II, above.

[456] James N. Rosenau, "Governance, Order, and Change in World Politics" (1992), p. 4.

[457] The United Nations in global governance, General Assembly resolution 65/94, adopted 8 December 2010.

United Nations [and] reaffirm[ed] the role and authority of the General Assembly on global matters of concern to the international community, as set out in the Charter."[458] Although the debate on the role of the United Nations in global governance has only just begun, this contribution already indicates that the Assembly accepts for itself a central role in global attempts to address the most urgent global challenges.

## 4.3 United Nations Member States

It is clear that as the prime actors of the international community, States have the primary responsibility for realizing the global values proclaimed by the United Nations. In doing so, they act on behalf of their citizens. The United Nations Organization merely provides the framework in which the States are required to fulfil their responsibilities. But global civil society,[459] and even individuals, have a responsibility too.[460]

Most importantly, States have a duty to implement the values to which they subscribed by ratifying the UN Charter and by voting in favour of General Assembly resolutions, within their jurisdiction. Therefore they are required to ensure that their territory is not used as a basis for activities that threaten international peace and security. The State must also respect the human dignity of all individuals residing within its jurisdiction and under its effective control. Furthermore, it is required to ensure sustainable development and social progress, and to show respect for the self-determination of all peoples – including minorities – who find themselves within its jurisdiction. Almost all the declarations adopted by the Assembly stress this primary responsibility of States.[461]

States also have an obligation to assist each other in these domestic efforts. One of the principal roles of the United Nations is to coordinate and institutionalize this international assistance. Article 2(5) UN Charter states that "all Members shall give the United Nations every assistance in any action it takes in accordance with the present Charter." This principle is an expression of the general *legal* duty of all States to cooperate in promoting the values, purposes and principles of the UN. Arangio-Ruiz referred to this principle as a "sort of procedural super-principle,"

---

[458] *Idem.*

[459] See *We the peoples: civil society, the United Nations and global governance, Report of the Panel of Eminent Persons on United Nations–Civil Society Relations*, UNDoc. A/58/817, distributed 11 June 2004. This report explores various ways in which global civil society can help the United Nations realize their values. The most important recommendation is to establish partnerships including ngos, states, and businesses to undertake specific tasks. The UN can do the coordination.

[460] See the Declaration of Human Duties and Responsibilities, adopted by a High Level Group chaired by Richard J. Goldstone, 1999.

[461] See especially the concept of the responsibility to protect, discussed in section 5.4 of Chapter VII.

which could be given substance by the shared goals to be achieved through cooperation.[462]

The general duty for all Member States to cooperate with the Organization in its efforts to achieve its purposes was discussed in great detail when the Friendly Relations Declaration was being drafted. Before that, not much attention was devoted to it. As Mani pointed out about the discussion of this principle in the 1960s: "It [was] probably for the first time that the concept of international co-operation was considered juridically by the United Nations and formulated in an international instrument alongside other basic principles of international law."[463]

The first discussions took place during the second session of the Special Committee that drafted the declaration. There it was suggested that the UN Charter, especially Article 56, had created a legal, as opposed to political or moral, duty to cooperate in realizing the purposes of the United Nations.[464] According to Mani, "all delegations – the Socialist, the Western, and the Third World – ha[d] agreed that the duty of States to co-operate in accordance with the Charter [was] a legal obligation."[465] The only remaining disagreement was on the exact content of this obligation. It was suggested that the United Nations Charter had established a duty of "active coexistence," as opposed to a situation in which "States [..] merely tolerate[d] the existence of other States."[466] The most interesting element was whether such a duty to cooperate introduced some kind of global distributive justice into world politics.[467] Some suggestions indicated that this was indeed the case. The USA and some other States, for example, suggested that each State should "contribute to the acceleration of economic growth and the equitable elevation of standards of living throughout the world and the economic and social progress and development of other States."[468] The most obvious way to do this was to provide development aid to developing States, or at least to remove all trade barriers.[469] No definition of the principle could be agreed upon by all States represented in the Committee.

---

[462] See also Gaetano Arangio-Ruiz, "The normative role of the General Assembly" (1972), p. 572.

[463] Vekateshwara Subramanian Mani, *Basic principles of modern international law* (1993), p. 168.

[464] Special Committee on Principles of International Law concerning Friendly Relations and Co-operation among States, Report, A/6230, adopted 27 June 1966 ("Second Report"), para. 435. See also Vekateshwara Subramanian Mani, *Basic principles of modern international law* (1993), pp. 174-180.

[465] Vekateshwara Subramanian Mani, *Basic principles of modern international law* (1993), pp. 175-180.

[466] Special Committee, Second Report, para. 420. Abi-Saab distinguished between the law of "co-existence" and the law of "cooperation." The latter can be compared with the law of "active co-existence." See Georges Abi-Saab, "Whither the international community?" (1998).

[467] Vekateshwara Subramanian Mani, *Basic principles of modern international law* (1993), pp. 186-192.

[468] Special Committee, Second Report, para. 416.

[469] *Idem*, paras. 427-429, and para. 442.

The third session again discussed the principle of cooperation. It was suggested that the principle could serve as a "catalyst," without which other, more substantive principles, would not have any effect.[470] The universal application of this principle was stressed. It meant that all States should have an opportunity to participate in global efforts to jointly realize shared goals, on equal terms and without discrimination, and that they all had an obligation to do so.[471] Once again, development aid, granted without any political conditions or restrictions, was suggested as part of global cooperation in economic affairs.[472] One representative (USA) suggested that the Friendly Relations Declaration should at least refer to global cooperation in the promotion of human rights, if only because Article 55 UN Charter also did so.[473]

At the end of the third session, the Special Committee adopted, with a consensus, the definition of the principle of cooperation as it later appeared in the Friendly Relations Declaration. It described a general duty of all States to "co-operate with one another, irrespective of the differences in their political, economic and social systems, in the various spheres of international relations, in order to maintain international peace and security and to promote international economic stability and progress, the general welfare of nations and international co-operation free from discrimination based on such differences." This was followed by a list of substantive goals, viz. peace and security, human rights, sovereign equality and non-intervention, the realization of which required global cooperation. This list was followed by a reiteration of Article 56 UN Charter. The suggestions relating to development cooperation ended up in the final paragraph, which, *inter alia*, stated that, "States should co-operate in the promotion of economic growth throughout the world, especially that of the developing countries."[474]

The duty to cooperate was mentioned again in the Millennium Declaration, which stressed that the Organization and its Members should act in "solidarity". This meant that "global challenges must be managed in a way that distributes the costs and burdens fairly in accordance with basic principles of equity and social justice [and that] those who suffer or who benefit least deserve help from those who benefit most". [475] The Declaration also introduced the idea of "shared responsibility," which was described as follows:

---

[470] Special Committee on Principles of International Law concerning Friendly Relations and Co-operation among States, Report, A/6799, adopted 26 September 1967 ("Third Report").
[471] Special Committee, Third Report, paras. 146-149.
[472] *Idem*, para. 156.
[473] *Idem*, paras. 158 and 164.
[474] Friendly Relations Declaration.
[475] Millennium Declaration, resolution adopted by the UN General Assembly, 18 September 2000. UNDoc. A/RES/55/2 para. 6 (see also para. 2).

Responsibility for managing worldwide economic and social development, as well as threats to international peace and security, must be shared among the nations of the world and should be exercised multilaterally. As the most universal and most representative organization in the world, the United Nations must play the central role.[476]

Although these ideas were not presented as such, they can be interpreted as giving more substance to the principle of global cooperation.

States have a legal duty to cooperate and take joint and separate action in cooperation with the Organization to achieve the UN's purposes. But what are the means available to the Member States to take such action? There is a great deal of uncertainty about this. First, the UN Charter itself does not give Member States any special rights to actively promote the values of the United Nations. It is presumed that such action should be taken collectively, or at the initiative of the Organization itself. However, because of the frequent failure of the UN organs to accept their responsibility in the past, many efforts have been made to create an alternative mechanism to uphold the UN's values, a mechanism which allows States to act independently of the UN.[477] This development does not change the fact that States have an obligation to cooperate and play their part in the work of the Organization. Any discussion of the means available to States, acting individually but on behalf of the international community, would take us outside the framework of the United Nations.[478]

## 4.4 Conclusion

The means available to the international community to collectively defend its values and norms, as defined in the UN Charter and further elaborated by the General Assembly, are limited. The general idea is that States themselves bear the primary responsibility for ensuring respect for human dignity, sustainable development and social progress within areas under their own jurisdiction and control. States are also responsible for respecting the self-determination of peoples in their internal and international affairs, and they are prohibited from threatening international peace and security. The role of the United Nations Organization is "only" to remind States

---

[476] *Idem.*

[477] See especially, "Seventh report by Arangio-Ruiz," UNDoc. A/CN.4/469 and Add.1-2. See also pp. 48-49, "Third report by Willem Riphagen," in the Yearbook of the International Law Commission 1982, vol. II, Part I; and p. 22, "Fourth report by Willem Riphagen," in the Yearbook of the International Law Commission 1983, vol. II, Part I. For a discussion of these proposals, see Pierre Klein, "Responsibility for Serious Breaches of Obligations Deriving from Peremptory Norms of International Law and United Nations Law" (2002), p. 1246.

[478] For an overview of these alternative means to defend global values, outside the UN context, see Otto Spijkers, "What's running the world" (2010).

of their responsibilities, and to provide international assistance. Only in exceptional cases can the Organization intervene in the domestic affairs of States.

## 5 CONCLUSION

This chapter characterized the decision making of the United Nations, especially during the drafting of the UN Charter in 1945 and in all subsequent debates in the General Assembly, as value-based authoritative decision making. It examined the inclusive and genuine character, and the capacity to motivate action of both these global discussions.

In 1945, representatives of nearly fifty States came together to draft the blueprint of the post-war legal order. The horrors of the Second World War made them aware of the urgency of their work. All cultural and political differences faded into the background. The purposes and principles adopted in San Francisco were considered to be so important that all other legal norms had to be ignored if they obliged States to violate the newly agreed post-war principles. These purposes and principles can be linked to a set of fundamental values shared by all the States present in San Francisco. Therefore the discussion was about values, and satisfied the criteria of genuineness and the capacity to motivate action. But was it a truly "global" discussion? Many peoples were absent in San Francisco: colonial peoples, the Axis powers, and those States that refused to declare war against these powers. All these peoples later adhered to the UN Charter, and thus they also subscribed to the principles contained in that blueprint, ensuring their "global" relevance.

Once the Charter entered into force and the United Nations Organization was established, the discussions continued in the General Assembly. Representatives of a growing number of States came – and still come – together every year to discuss international affairs and to find global solutions to global challenges. As all the States in the world are represented in the Assembly, the criterion of inclusiveness has been met. The important thing is that the world's citizens feel sufficiently involved in the work of the Organization, and this has been achieved to a great extent. The ideal would be for everyone to see the UN as *their* organization, even though they have little direct influence on UN decision making. What about the other two criteria? Is the discussion about values a genuine discussion? Sir Jolly referred to the Assembly's practice of adopting resolutions with lofty goals, values and principles as "hypocrisy." He suggested that not all States represented in the Assembly intended to practise what they preached. Increasingly, States are reminded of the "promises" they made in General Assembly resolutions by non-State actors that closely observe what is going on at UN Headquarters in Manhattan, New York. No State is entirely insensitive to such public naming and shaming. The resolutions are also frequently invoked, for example, in academic circles and by the International Court of Justice, as "evidence" of the existence of a norm of customary law. Once established with the help of the Assembly's resolutions, a norm can be applied to any State, especially those that voted in favour of the norm and generally acted in accordance with it. When it comes to resolutions that interpret the value-based principles of the UN Charter itself, things get even more serious. The Assembly has the authority to interpret those principles in a binding way, speaking on behalf of the Organization's Members. Thus the Assembly plays a central role in the continued evolution of the Charter's value-based principles. This makes the Assembly the most relevant Organization for this study, and a true successor to the San Francisco Conference.

# PART II

# PEACE AND SECURITY

## 1 INTRODUCTION

In Part II of this study, the UN Charter and the declarations of the UN General Assembly form the backbone for each chapter. Where relevant, these UN texts are compared with the scholarly literature about the same value. The cross-fertilization between the work of the United Nations and the scholarship is examined only when there has actually been such cross-fertilization. The following values are discussed: peace and security (Chapter IV), social progress and development (Chapter V), human dignity (Chapter VI), and self-determination (Chapter VII).

There is an important *Leitmotif* which runs through the entire work of the United Nations. The evolution of values can be characterized as an attempt to improve the world, primarily by avoiding a repetition of the evils of the past. From the beginning the main idea was to base a new world order on the solidarity revealed in the efforts to fight the common enemy during the war.[1] When the UN Charter was drafted, the war was nearly over. The common enemy was about to be defeated. The main challenge for the victorious States was to find "something better than an enemy to unite and hold them."[2] As Dulles had suggested as early as 1945, the UN Charter provided the solution to this problem by "propos[ing] to its members that they stay united to wage war against [abstract] evils," such as "intolerance, repression, injustice and economic want," as those were the "common enemies of tomorrow."[3] After the war the former enemy States also joined the fight against these new evils.

The evils of the Second World War were the main inspiration for the list of values on which the United Nations Charter is based. It has often been pointed out that evils can serve as a good source for defining values. For example, Friedrich von Weizsäcker wrote that "[t]he more [values] indicate the absence of an evil, the

---

[1] See *e.g.*, Commission to Study the Organization of Peace, *The United Nations and the organization of peace: third report* (1943), p. 22, and James B. Reston, "U.S Foreign Policy Set by Stettinus for Secure Peace," in *New York Times* of May 29, 1945.

[2] Anne O''Hare McCormick, "San Francisco: Battlefield for Peace" (1945). To honor the war-bond, the name "United Nations" was chosen, as a reference to the coalition that was fighting Nazi Germany and Japan. See Secretary of state for foreign affairs (UK), *A commentary on the Dumbarton Oaks proposals* (1944), p. 2.

[3] John Foster Dulles, "The United Nations: A Prospectus (The General Assembly)" (1945), p. 7. See also Porter, "Charter Stronger than Expected," in *New York Times* of June 17, 1945.

clearer they become. In wartime the desire for peace, in hunger the desire of satiation, under foreign domination the will to emancipation."[4] The only thing that needs to be done once the fundamental evils have been identified, is to imagine the alternative. It is not unrealistic to see the United Nations Charter as exactly that: a description, or blueprint, of a world that is almost exactly the opposite of the world at the time of the Second World War. Contemporary evils have continued to serve as an inspiration for the definition of the world's values, and have proved to be the most immediate inspiration for the subsequent evolution of these values.

The value of peace and security is the clearest example. In San Francisco, war was considered to be the greatest evil, and peace the primary purpose of the United Nations. This has not changed since that time. Peace and security are still considered to be the UN's "but des buts."[5] This chapter examines the value of peace and security as defined by the United Nations. First, there is a survey of the debates on this value during the San Francisco Conference of 1945. This shows how the value of peace and security ended up in the preamble and in the list of purposes and principles of the Organization. Secondly, it examines the evolution of this value, as well as the accompanying purposes and principles. Initially, peace was defined as a situation in which States do not use force against other States. Later, other threats to the peace were identified, such as domestic conflicts, the arms race, hijackers, hostage takers, mercenaries and terrorists. The United Nations came to realize that when maintaining peace and security, it should also deal with the root causes of threats to the peace, such as diseases of mass destruction, *apartheid*, natural disasters and environmental threats, poverty and underdevelopment, and genocide. Finally, the humanization of the value of peace and security is examined. In recent times, the value of peace and security has also been examined from the perspective, not of the State, but of the individual. The section on the human right to security discusses the approach to peace and security as a legal entitlement, the right of all individual human beings.

## 1.1 The Security Council's role in the evolution of the value of peace and security

The main organ of the United Nations responsible for the maintenance of international peace and security is the Security Council.[6] Since the "Members [of

---

[4] See Carl-Friedrich von Weizsäcker, "A Sceptical Contribution" (1975), pp. 113-114. See also Richard A. Falk, Samuel S. Kim & Saul H. Mendlovitz, "General Introduction" (1982), pp. 2-3. See also Florence Kluckhohn & Fred Strodtbeck, *Variations in Value Orientations* (1961).
[5] Mohammed Bedjaoui, "Article 1" (2005), p. 314.
[6] See also Vaughan Lowe (editor), *The United Nations Security Council and war: the evolution of thought and practice since 1945* (2008).

the UN] confer on the Security Council primary responsibility for the maintenance of international peace and security, and agree that in carrying out its duties under this responsibility the Security Council acts on their behalf," one might expect the Security Council to have played the leading role in the evolution of the value of peace and security.[7] That is not exactly what happened. There are two main reasons for this. First, in contrast with the General Assembly, the Council does not customarily adopt resolutions or have a mandate to do so, on abstract or "constitutional" issues, such as the interpretation of values. Secondly, the Security Council has basically been paralyzed for most of its existence by the two main rivals in the Cold War: the United States of America and the Soviet Union.[8] As early as 1948 the General Assembly considered that it was necessary to remind the great powers with seats in the Security Council of their pledges made in the UN Charter and in the declarations they signed during the war, such as the Atlantic Charter and the United Nations Declaration.[9] As the Cold War continued, the Assembly reiterated its appeal to the Security Council, and particularly its permanent members, to accept their responsibilities and act accordingly. In 1986, the Assembly "stresse[d] the necessity for the members of the Security Council, in particular its permanent members, to take appropriate and effective measures in carrying out their primary responsibility for the maintenance of international peace and security in accordance with the Charter."[10] But this was to no avail.

This stalemate, or "ice age of confrontation," as President Yeltsin so aptly described the situation, was only resolved in the early 1990s, when the Cold War came to an end.[11] This happy development was celebrated with the convening of the first ever Security Council meeting at the level of heads of State in 1992.[12] President Yeltsin, the first President of the new Russian Federation, referred to this unique meeting as "the first of its kind on the political Olympus of the contemporary world [and] a historic and unprecedented event."[13] Sitting on the political Olympus, many of the heads of State referred to the new opportunities for

---

[7] Article 24, UN Charter.
[8] See also Hans J. Morgenthau, "The New United Nations and the Revision of the Charter" (1954), especially p. 7; Nico Schrijver, "Article 2, paragraph 4" (2005), p. 454.
[9] See Appeal to the Great Powers to renew their efforts to compose their differences and establish a lasting peace, General Assembly resolution 190(III), adopted 3 November 1948.
[10] Need for result-oriented political dialogue to improve the international situation, General Assembly resolution 41/91, adopted 4 December 1986.
[11] Verbatim Records of the 3046th meeting of the Security Council, 31 January 1992, UNDoc. S/PV.3046, p. 46.
[12] Not all States were represented on the highest level. President Mugabe of Zimbabwe, for example, could not come to New York because his wife, Sally Hayfron, had just passed away.
[13] Verbatim Records of the 3046th meeting of the Security Council, 31 January 1992, UNDoc. S/PV.3046, p. 43.

the Council resulting from the end of the Cold War.[14] The French President Mitterrand commented:

> Past experience has shown that nothing can be done without the determination of States, particularly the major Powers, to reject the law of the jungle and the principle that might is right. That determination is reflected in the Charter of the United Nations. For a long time, the Charter was hobbled, but today all its provisions are usable, and we must implement them immediately.[15]

Jeszenszky of Hungary even suggested finally establishing a UN army, as envisaged in Article 43 of the UN Charter. The Security Council had never managed to do so before. According to the Hungarian Prime Minister: "Due consideration should be given to the idea of the United Nations instituting a force readily and constantly available that could be mobilized on very short notice, at any given time, and deployed without delay in accordance with the purposes and principles of the United Nations Charter to any conflict-stricken region of the world."[16]

Similarly, the representative of Zimbabwe suggested that the Security Council should take a fresh look at Article 47 UN Charter, another of those provisions that had never been invoked before, and "put in place a system for the regulation of armaments."[17] Zimbabwe also suggested that "this could very well be the time to revive the idea of an international criminal code and to create an international criminal court."[18] A few years later, an international criminal court was established, but Zimbabwe has not become a party.

Other State leaders agreed that this meeting marked the true beginning of the Security Council. President Bush of the United States believed that it was "[f]or perhaps the first time since that hopeful moment in San Francisco [that] we can look at our Charter as a living, breathing document."[19] Similarly, Miyazawa of Japan noted that "[t]he cold war that divided East and West throughout the post-war period ha[d] finally ended," and that "the United Nations has [finally] begun to play, both in theory and in practice, a central role in efforts to achieve and maintain world peace."[20] Miyazawa did not fail to mention the potential of the UN Charter in this new world:

---

[14] See also the Presidential Statement, adopted at the end of the meeting. *Idem*, pp. 141-142.

[15] *Idem*, p. 18.

[16] *Idem*, p. 119.

[17] *Idem*, p. 128.

[18] *Idem*, p. 133. Article 47 called for the establishment of a Military Staff Committee.

[19] *Idem*, 54-55.

[20] *Idem*, pp. 104-105.

> In securing a peaceful world order, the ideals and purposes of the United Nations Charter, which represent fundamental and universal values, will be of even greater relevance than ever before. It is incumbent on Member States to strive, constantly, to ensure that each of these values is respected in practice.[21]

Japan was one of the enemy States in 1945. This makes it even more significant that it now wholeheartedly adopted the principles and values of the Charter.

At this historic meeting, a Presidential statement was adopted on the responsibility of the Security Council in the maintenance of international peace and security. The UK, presiding the meeting, emphasized the potential of the Council in the maintenance of the peace, and encouraged all Members to start using the Council for the purpose it was set up.[22]

Since 1992, the Security Council has contributed to the further evolution of the value of peace and security. According to Schrijver, since the end of the Cold War, the "Council [was] taking on a quasi-legislative role, which hitherto was considered the prerogative of the General Assembly only."[23] The products of this quasi-legislative period of the Council, of which there are relatively few, are discussed below. It will be difficult for the Council to catch up with the Assembly, which has been adopting quasi-legislative declarations since 1945, also on the value of peace and security. The question arises whether it would be appropriate for the Council to compete with the Assembly in this way, considering that it only represents the views of a handful of countries, primarily those of the "Big Five."[24]

## 2  PEACE AND SECURITY IN SAN FRANCISCO

### 2.1 The Preamble

The evolution of the value of peace and security within the United Nations started with the drafting of the UN Charter in 1945. First, the *travaux préparatoires* are examined, beginning with the Preamble, and followed by the Purposes and Principles.

---

[21] Idem.

[22] Presidential Statement, adopted at the end of the meeting. See Verbatim Records of the 3046th meeting of the Security Council, pp. 141-142.

[23] Nico Schrijver, "The Future of the Charter of the United Nations" (2006), p. 23.

[24] In the literature, the quasi-legislative action of the Council has often been criticized for the reason stated above. See e.g, Paul C. Szasz, "The Security Council Starts Legislating," (2002); Axel Marschik, "The Security Council as world legislator?" (2005); Keith Harper, "Does the United Nations Security Council have the competence to act as Court and legislature?" (1994); Björn Elberling, "The *ultra vires* character of legislative action by the Security Council" (2005); Martti Koskenniemi, "The Police in the Temple Order, Justice and the UN: A Dialectical View" (1995).

According to Smuts' first draft of the Preamble, the United Nations was established, *inter alia*, "to prevent a recurrence of the fratricidal strife which has twice in our generation brought untold sorrows and losses on mankind." [25] This was a clear reference to the two world wars, and the message was: "never again." The relevant subcommittee of the San Francisco Conference rephrased this paragraph, so that the Organization was established "to save succeeding generations from the scourge of war, which twice in our lifetime has brought untold sorrow to mankind." [26] The Rapporteur of that committee emphasized that this paragraph did not imply that the Organization would only prevent such catastrophic wars as the First and Second World Wars. It would also concern itself with wars on a much smaller scale. [27] The Commission approved the text, [28] and this is how it ended up in the Charter. The "scourge of war" was thus recognized as the biggest evil, and "peace and security" as the most important value.

## 2.2 The Purpose

According to the Dumbarton Oaks proposals, the first – and most important – purpose of the UN was "[t]o maintain international peace and security." [29]

Unsurprisingly, very few amendments criticized this primary purpose. If the Second World War had shown anything, it was that there was nothing civil or sophisticated about modern wars; war had become an "all-consuming juggernaut." [30] Instead of being directed at this primary purpose, many smaller States suggested in their amendments that peace was not the only value worth striving for, and that in striving for peace, certain principles should be respected at all times. The major powers believed that the peace should be maintained, more or less at all costs. Of the big powers, the Soviet Union was the strongest defender of the idea that the United Nations was an "International Security Organization," concerned solely with

---

[25] Draft Preamble to the Charter of the United Nations Proposed by the Union of South Africa, 26 April, 1945, UNCIO, vol. 3, pp. 474-475. See also Preamble to the Charter of the United Nations Submitted by the South African Delegation in Revision of Draft of April 26, 1945, May 3, 1945, *idem*, pp. 476-477.

[26] Draft Preamble (as Approved by Committee I/1/A), UNCIO, vol. 6, p. 694.

[27] Report of Rapporteur, Subcommittee I/1/A, Section 3, to Committee I/1, June 5, 1945, UNCIO, vol. 6, p. 359. See also Report of Rapporteur of Committee 1 to Commission I, *idem*, p. 450.

[28] First Session of Commission I, June 14, 1945, UNCIO, vol. 6, p. 20.

[29] Dumbarton Oaks Proposals for a General International Organization, UNCIO, vol. 3, p. 2. The terms "peace" and "security" are always used together, with "peace and security" a single concept. Wolfrum attempted to explain the difference between "peace" and "security" in Rüdiger Wolfrum, "Purposes and Principles" (2002), pp. 40-42.

[30] This expression was used in Senator Vandenberg, "Plea for Charter as the Only Hope of Averting Chaos in World," Text of Senator's Report to Congress, as reproduced in the *New York Times* of June 30, 1945.

maintaining international peace. It maintained this position even after the end of the San Francisco Conference, when many other purposes were added.[31]

The discussion as to how the peace was to be maintained continued when a decision was made on the powers of the Organization with regard to the maintenance of peace and security. The primary role was assigned to the Security Council.

According to the Dumbarton Oaks proposals, the way for the United Nations, and especially its Security Council, to help achieve international peace and security was

> To take effective collective measures for the prevention and removal of threats to the peace and the suppression of acts of aggression or other breaches of the peace, and to bring about by peaceful means adjustment or settlement  of international disputes which may lead to a breach of the peace.[32]

The first part of the sentence was not significantly changed in San Francisco, where it was explained that the addition of the words "other breaches" was necessary, because a "breach of the peace" was a much broader term than aggression alone. It was "an all-inclusive term which implie[d] the use of any means of coercion or undue external influence, which, through exertion or threat to security of a state, amounts to a breach of the peace."[33]

The Security Council had two principal tasks. One was of a "quasi-judicial" nature, and the other of an "executive" nature.[34] First, it was to assist Member States to settle disputes that threatened the international peace. Secondly, it was to take measures to maintain international peace and security. In a sense, even though the Dumbarton Oaks provision stated them in the reverse order, it is clear that the executive task became relevant only after the Council failed in its quasi-judicial task, *i.e.* when it failed to settle a dispute considered to be a threat to the peace. This was made clear in subsequent provisions. According to the Dumbarton Oaks proposals,

---

[31] See "Introduction" to the booklet the *Soviet Union at the San Francisco Conference* (1945), p. 3.

[32] United Nations: Dumbarton Oaks Proposals for a General International Organization, UNCIO, vol. 3, p. 2. Both tasks of the Council, *i.e.* the settlement of disputes and the supervision of collective measures, are further elaborated upon in Sections A and B, respectively, of Chapter VIII. See United Nations: Dumbarton Oaks Proposals for a General International Organization, UNCIO, vol. 3, pp. 11-17.

[33] Report of Rapporteur, Subcommittee I/1/A, to Committee I/1, June 1, 1945, UNCIO, vol. 6, p. 703. See also Report of Rapporteur of Committee 1 to Commission I, UNCIO, vol. 6, p. 395.

[34] These terms were used in the Amendments to the Proposals for the Maintenance of Peace an Security Agreed on at the Four Powers Conference of Dumbarton Oaks Supplemented as a Result of the Conference of Yalta, Submitted by the Netherlands Delegation to the San Francisco Conference, UNCIO, vol. 3, p. 326. The Netherlands made this comment in the context of the Council's voting arrangement.

> Should the Security Council deem that a failure to settle a dispute [...] constitutes a threat to the maintenance of international peace and security, it should take any measures necessary for the maintenance of international peace and security in accordance with the purposes and principles of the Organization.[35]

It was up to the Council to decide whether or not a particular dispute threatened the peace,[36] and if it did, the Council had to take the necessary measures.[37] This two-step procedure was complemented by a more general provision, stating that "[i]n general the Security Council should determine the existence of any threat to the peace, breach of the peace or act of aggression and should make recommendations or decide upon the measures to be taken to maintain or restore peace and security."[38]

When the Council considered something a threat to the peace or an act of aggression, it could take – or authorize – far-reaching measures. There were essentially two types of such measures, which had to be considered in a specific order. As a first step,

> The Security Council should be empowered to determine what diplomatic, economic, or other measures not involving the use of armed force should be employed to give effect to its decisions, and to call upon members of the Organization to apply such measures. Such measures may include complete or partial interruption of rail, sea, air, postal, telegraphic, radio and other means of communication and the severance of diplomatic and economic relations.[39]

Then, if necessary, the Council could take the second and final step:

> Should the Security Council consider such measures to be inadequate, it should be empowered to take such action by air, naval or land forces as may be necessary to maintain or restore international peace and security. Such action may include demonstrations, blockades and other operations by air, sea or land forces of members of the Organization.[40]

---

[35] Dumbarton Oaks Proposals for a General International Organization, UNCIO, vol. 3, p. 14.

[36] Some nations suggested to make this first step more explicit: Amendments to the Dumbarton Oaks Proposals Submitted by the Texts Adopted at Yalta, Submitted by the Greek Delegation, May 3, 1945, UNCIO, vol. 3, pp. 532-533, Amendments submitted by the Netherlands Delegation to the San Francisco Conference, UNCIO, vol. 3, p. 326.

[37] Comment of the Norwegian Government on the Dumbarton Oaks Proposals, UNCIO, vol. 3, p. 361. Norway wanted to avoid all ambiguity, and suggested that it be made clear that "the Council should not have only the right, but also the duty to take the necessary military measure against an aggression or a threat of aggression."

[38] Dumbarton Oaks Proposals for a General International Organization, UNCIO, vol. 3, pp. 14-15.

[39] Idem, p. 15.

[40] Idem.

Because these were far-reaching measures, Iran proposed that the Charter should make clear exactly what constituted a "threat to the peace," so that States would know what to do – and not to do – to avoid these measures. Iran gave its own definition:

> Any threat to the territorial integrity or independence of a Member State constitutes a threat to the maintenance of peace and international security.[41]

Bolivia focused more on defining "aggression." According to Bolivia, "[t]he efficacy of the security machinery is directly related to the need of designating the aggression as such and defining what is meant by aggressor state, a point which should be considered in the Charter of the General Organization."[42] Both the Iranian and the Bolivian suggestion gave the impression that the Security Council measures should be seen as a kind of punishment, a response to the violation of a legal principle, and not as the work of an international police force maintaining peace in the world.

This idea of enforcement measures as punishment was foremost in the minds of the drafters. One of the central ideas of the collective security arrangement was that any threat to the peace or act of aggression would be followed by overwhelming collective measures, taken by the international community as a whole, under the supervision of the Security Council. It was thought that the fear of such overwhelming force would scare off any potential aggressor. Therefore, like criminal sanctions in domestic systems, the collective security mechanism was meant as a deterrent. In the words of the Bolivian delegate:

> World security is founded on the principle that a mere attempt at aggression is a policy contrary to good understanding, good neighbourliness, and the purposes of lasting peace. This principle can be put into practice only if all nations, great and small, admit that an act of violence on their part should be immediately countered by collective measures.[43]

This is reminiscent of the principle of the musketeers: all for one, and one for all. Many of the small powers understood that not all musketeers had equally big swords and were equally proficient swordsmen. It was understood that the world

---

[41] Amendments Presented by the Delegation of Iran to the Dumbarton Oaks Proposals, UNCIO, vol. 3, p. 556.
[42] Proposals of the Delegation of the Republic of Bolivia for the Organization of a System of Peace and Security, UNCIO, vol. 3, p. 578.
[43] *Idem.*

needed to rely on the military might of the great powers, and it was necessary simply to trust them.[44]

It is clear that the Security Council had the most prominent role in the maintenance of peace and security. It acted on behalf of the entire UN membership. To avoid any ambiguity, this principal responsibility of the Security Council was outlined as follows:

> In order to ensure prompt and effective action by the Organization, members of the Organization should by the Charter confer on the Security Council primary responsibility for the maintenance of international peace and security and should agree that in carrying out these duties under this responsibility it should act on their behalf.[45]

Many of the smaller nations, who had little influence over the Security Council, were not very happy that it was so dominant.[46] Uruguay spoke on behalf of many smaller nations when it said that it "d[id] not share the idea of creating a super-state with its own police force and other attributes of coercive power."[47] Venezuela believed that "the intention of concentrating all powers in a small number of nations with prejudice to the legitimate interests of the others [was] the fundamental defect that is found in the Dumbarton Oaks draft."[48]

To solve this problem, many of the smaller States attempted to strengthen the role of the Assembly in the settlement of disputes and the maintenance of peace and security.[49] The central idea of those amendments was that the General Assembly,

---

[44] However, many of these acknowledgements were followed immediately by a big "but," *i.e.* some form of "conditional trust." See *e.g.*, Suggestions of the Belgian Government, UNCIO, vol. 3, p. 331; Proposals of the Delegation of the Republic of Bolivia for the Organization of a System of Peace and Security, UNCIO, vol. 3, p. 577; Suggestions of the Egyptian Government on the Tentative Proposals of Dumbarton Oaks under Examination a the United Nations Conference at San Francisco, UNCIO, vol. 3, p. 448.

[45] Dumbarton Oaks Proposals for a General International Organization, UNCIO, vol. 3, p. 8.

[46] When commenting on the Dutch amendment proposals, the *New York Times* believed that the fundamental criticism of the Netherlands was the small role of the smaller nations in maintaining peace and security. See James B. Reston, "Dutch Oppose Idea of Oaks Big 5 Veto."

[47] Position of the Government of Uruguay Respecting the Plans of Postwar International Organization for the Maintenance of Peach and Security in the World, UNCIO, vol. 3, p. 29.

[48] Observations of the Government of Venezuela on the Recommendations Adopted at the Dumbarton Oaks Conferences for the Creation of a Peace Organization, UNCIO, vol. 3, p. 190.

[49] For such general amendments, see *e.g.*, the amendments proposed by Chile, UNCIO, vol. 3, p. 287; Cost Rica, *idem*, pp. 275 and pp. 278-279; Czechoslovakia, p. 467; Dominican Republic, pp. 567-568 and 572; Ecuador, pp. 403-408; Egypt, p. 450 and p. 456; Guatemala, pp. 256 and 258; Iran, p. 555; Mexico, pp. 134-135 and p. 160 and p. 175; Paraguay, p. 346; Turkey, pp. 481 and 484; and Venezuela, pp. 202 and 208. Venezuela believed that "such a delegation of powers [to the Council] can be admitted if there are attributed to the central organization, that is, the General Assembly, the necessary powers of control and if the member States are given the remedy of an appeal thereto; all the more because there will be represented in the Assembly all the members of the Council."

the "world town council," [50] could assert political control over the Security Council's activities in a way that was similar to the control that a domestic parliament has over the cabinet. In the Dumbarton Oaks proposals, the General Assembly had very few powers of its own. One observer called the Assembly "a mere 'rubber stamp' of the wishes of the Security Council."[51] The smaller States attempted to change the situation in San Francisco. Czechoslovakia suggested a prominent role for the "town meeting of the world"[52] whenever the maintenance of international peace and security required the Security Council to act in violation of international law.[53] This was to give at least some legitimacy to an illegal act. Egypt, Ecuador and others, made a similar point.[54] It was suggested that the General Assembly should have a mandate to "discuss any matter within the sphere of international relations," including the maintenance of international peace and security. Although the proposal was adopted with the required two-thirds majority,[55] an effective campaign of the Soviet Union led to a "reconsideration" of the proposal. Eventually, after a cumbersome procedure, an Australian amendment was unanimously accepted,[56] which stated that the General Assembly could not discuss a particular security issue when the Security Council was already doing so.[57] This rule ended up in Article 12 of the UN Charter.

---

[50] Gerrit Jan de Voogd & Cornelis Willem van Santen, *Volkenbond en Vereenigde Naties* (1946), p. 24.

[51] Betty Jane Davis, *Charter for Tomorrow: the San Francisco Conference* (1945), p. 13.

[52] This expression for the General Assembly was coined by Arthur Vandenberg of the US Delegation (Fifteenth Meeting of Committee II/2, May 29, 1945, UNCIO, vol. 9, p. 108; Ninth Plenary Session, June 25, 1945, UNCIO, vol. 1, p. 621). See also: Leland M. Goodrich and Edvard Hambro, *Charter of the United Nations* (1946), p. 94. Nowadays, most General Assembly meetings can be followed "live" on the internet.

[53] Observations of the Czechoslovak Government on the Dumbarton Oaks Proposals, UNCIO, Vol. 3, p. 467.

[54] See the Third Plenary Session, April 28, 1945, UNCIO, vol. 1, p. 237 and the Amendments to the Dumbarton Oaks Proposals Presented by the Egyptian Delegation, UNCIO, vol. 3, p. 460; Fifth Plenary Session, April 30, 1945, UNCIO, vol. 1, pp. 369-370 and the Delegation of Ecuador to the United Nations Conference on International Organization, UNCIO, vol. 3, p. 403-404; Logical Arrangements of Amendments Relating to Chapters VIII, B and XII of Dumbarton Oaks Proposals, UNCIO, vol. 12, p. 637 (Report by Committee III-3). New Zealand, Mexico, Canada and Egypt also suggested that the General Assembly participated in decisions on enforcement action.

[55] Fifteenth Meeting of Committee II/2, May 29, 1945, UNCIO, vol. 9, pp. 108-110. A two-thirds majority was obtained, but all superpowers (USA, China, France, the Soviet Union and the United Kingdom) cast a negative vote.

[56] Revised Text of Paragraph 1, Chapter V, Section B, as Proposed to be Amended by Dr. Evatt of Australia following upon Action by a Subcommittee of the Executive Committee Composed of Mr. Stettinius, Mr. Gromyko, and Dr. Evatt, UNCIO, vol. 9, p. 230.

[57] See Articles 10 and 12 of the UN Charter. For a summary of the cumbersome procedure and the final adoption, see Twenty-Fifth Meeting of Committee II/2, June 20, 1945, UNCIO, vol. 9, p. 233-235. The Australian delegate said in a meeting of the Commission (Fourth Meeting of Commission II, June 21, 1945, UNCIO, vol. 8, pp. 208-209), that after "a long struggle in the committee and subcommittees" "[w]e have agreed upon a formula. It is established, I think, that this right of discussion [of the General

Therefore the small States had lost this battle. Venezuela defended the superpowers to some extent, by noting that an increasing influence of the small and medium countries in the maintenance of international peace and security meant that countries which could not take responsibility and act in accordance with their intentions, would still have a say. After all, the small countries had little military strength to maintain world peace.[58] Davis put forward the same argument in 1946, when she noted that the success of the collective security arrangement depended entirely on the great powers. It would be "their troops and planes and guns which [would] be used to maintain the security of the world."[59] The smaller States only acquiesced because the superpowers accepted their enormous responsibilities and agreed to act on them.[60] At San Francisco, the Dutch delegate remarked:

> The Netherlands Delegation fully realizes that in the present state of the international community, it may be necessary to invest certain powers with special rights if a new organization for the maintenance of peace and security is to be established at all. Such a position the great powers have in fact always enjoyed in the past. Now, however, this special status is going to be officially recognized and sanctioned. We believe this to be regrettable. Why? Because this new system legalizes the mastery of might which in international relations, when peace prevailed, has been universally deemed to be reprehensible. If, nevertheless, we acquiesce in giving the great powers this special status, we can only do so in the expectation that they will demonstrate in practice that they are conscious of the special duties and responsibilities which are now placed upon them.[61]

The Big Powers and their troops, planes and guns were to give the Organization the teeth it needed.[62] Both France and Iraq cited the famous French writer Pascal, who once said that "strength without justice is tyrannical, and justice without strength is

---

Assembly] is so broad, that so long as the matter referred to comes within the scope of the Charter or any of its provisions, there will be no attempt on the part of anybody to block discussion or free criticism at the meeting of the Assembly."

[58] Observations of the Government of Venezuela on the Recommendations Adopted at the Dumbarton Oaks Conferences for the Creation of a Peace Organization, UNCIO, vol. 3, p. 208.

[59] Betty Jane Davis, *Charter for Tomorrow: the San Francisco Conference* (1945), p. 10. See also Paul Kennedy, *The Parliament of Man* (2006), p. 28.

[60] See *e.g.*, the UK Secretary of state for foreign affairs, *A commentary on the charter of the United Nations* (1945), p. 16, where the UK acknowledges that "the principle on which the Charter is based is that power must be commensurate with responsibility, and it is on the Great Powers that the Charter places the main responsibility for the maintenance of international peace and security."

[61] Fifth Meeting of Commission III, June 20, 1945, UNCIO, vol. 11, pp. 163-164.

[62] The "teeth" metaphor was often used in this context. See Keith R. Kane, "The United Nations: A Prospectus (The Security Council)" (1945), p. 18, and the article "UNCIO's Charter: The Final Tasks," in *New York Times* of June 17, 1945. See also Edward R. Stettinius, *United Nations will write charter for World Organization* (1945), p. 7. He said: "The only hope of the small countries, as of the large countries, lies in a world so organized that the industrial and military power of the large nations is used lawfully for the general welfare of all nations."

a mockery."[63] The League of Nations had been exactly that: a mockery. This had to be prevented at all costs.

The Assembly cannot control the Council when it maintains international peace and security.[64] What if the Council refrains from acting? Could there be a role for the General Assembly, or a group of States, to intervene? Not all amendments were aimed at controlling an overly *active* Security Council. Some delegations also considered the possibility of an overly *passive* Council. France (itself a future permanent member of the Council) suggested an amendment that "should the [Security] Council not succeed in reaching a decision, the members of the Organization reserve the right to act as they may consider necessary in the interest of peace, right and justice." [65] This amendment was not accepted. As the Netherlands realized,[66] the possibility of an inactive Council would be most relevant when one of its permanent members was itself causing a threat to international peace and security.[67] In such a case the relevant superpower could simply veto any Security Council action which it regarded to be against its interests. During the Cold War the Soviet Union and the United States of America used their veto extensively to prevent many potentially helpful interventions. Furthermore, the superpowers hardly ever sent troops abroad themselves.[68] Some commentators in San Francisco foresaw disaster as a result of the veto. In 1946, Davis wrote that a "connotation accompanied its two syllables [ve-to] which became suggestive of tyranny, of dark shadows and clouds of disaster, of an eternal curse thrust upon all that it concerned."[69]

There was no disagreement in San Francisco about the importance of maintaining international peace and security. The only thing that caused serious debate was the manner in which the international peace and security was to be maintained. The dominant role of the Big Powers was particularly controversial. But in the end this dominance was tolerated as long as the Big Powers accepted their heavy responsibilities. The Cold War prevented the Big Powers from keeping the promises they made in San Francisco. This changed only with the end of the Cold War.

---

[63] Final Plenary Session, June 26, 1945, UNCIO, vol. 1, pp. 668-669. See also Iraq at the Seventh Plenary Session, May 1, 1945, UNCIO, vol. 1, p. 503.

[64] "General Assembly Powers Voted: It Loses Rigid Rule over Council," in *New York Times* of May 27, 1945.

[65] Comments of the French Ministry of Foreign Affairs, UNCIO, Vol. 3, p. 385.

[66] The Netherlands circulated a statement on this issue in Committee III-1. See Statement of Delegate of the Netherlands at Ninth Meeting - May 17, 1945, UNCIO, vol. 11, p. 329.

[67] Proposals to make it impossible for a permanent member to use the veto in case the member was himself involved in a threat to international peace and security were rejected, mainly because of the Soviet Union. See Evan Luard, *A History of the United Nations* (1982), pp. 28-29 (Dumbarton Oaks), and pp. 45-47 (San Francisco: the issue almost made the entire conference collapse).

[68] Paul Kennedy, *The Parliament of Man* (2006), p. 58.

[69] Betty Jane Davis, *Charter for Tomorrow: the San Francisco Conference* (1945), p. 5.

## 2.3 The Principle

One of the most important principles in the Dumbarton Oaks proposals is that "[a]ll members of the Organization shall refrain in their international relations from the threat or use of force in any manner inconsistent with the purposes of the Organization."[70]

The exact meaning of the word "force" was not immediately obvious. Brazil suggested that the provision prohibiting the use of force should be rewritten, so as to include a prohibition on "any interference that threatens the national security of another member of the Organization, directly or indirectly threatens its territorial integrity, or involves the exercise of any excessively foreign influence on its destinies."[71] Such a comprehensive interpretation would turn the prohibition on the use of force into a general prohibition on intervention, with whatever means, be it military or economic, in the affairs of other States.[72] Such a principle had more to do with protecting the sovereign independence of States than with protecting international peace and security. An Australian amendment proposed that "[a]ll members of the Organization shall refrain in their international relations from the threat or use of force *against the territorial integrity or political independence of any member or State*."[73] This amendment was adopted unanimously by the Subcommittee,[74] but it did not clarify the meaning of the word "force," which remained undefined.

Interstate aggression is the least controversial example of the use of force. However, no authoritative definition of inter-State aggression could be agreed upon.[75] Certain States attempted to define aggression,[76] but no definition was acceptable to all the participants.

---

[70] Dumbarton Oaks Proposals for a General International Organization, UNCIO, vol. 3, p. 3. For an overview of the *travaux* of this provision, see also Nico Schrijver, "Article 2, paragraph 4" (2005), pp. 442-445.

[71] Brazilian Comment on Dumbarton Oaks Proposals, November 4, 1944, UNCIO, vol. 3, p. 237.

[72] Amendments Submitted by Brazil, UNCIO, vol. 3, p. 253. Brazil suggested, as an amendment, that "[a]ll members of the Organization shall refrain in their international relations from the threat or use of force and from the threat or use of economic measures."

[73] Amendments Submitted by Australia, UNCIO, vol. 3, p. 543. Australia's suggested additions are in italics.

[74] See Text of Chapter II, as Agreed upon by the Drafting Committee, UNCIO, vol. 6, p. 687, and Report of Rapporteur of Subcommittee I/1/A, to Committee I/1, UNCIO, vol. 6, p. 720.

[75] A number of States emphasized the need for a definition. See *e.g.*, Amendments Submitted by Bolivia, UNCIO, vol. 3, p. 578; Egypt, *idem*, p. 459; Iran, *idem*, p. 557.

[76] See *e.g.*, Amendments Submitted by Bolivia, UNCIO, vol. 3, p. 582; Ecuador, UNCIO, *idem*, p. 399. See also James B. Reston, "Hemisphere Peace Sought at Parley," in *New York Times* of February 24, 1945. Bolivia, and a few other nations, also proposed a list of aggressive acts, as opposed to a general definition. See again Amendments Submitted by Bolivia, UNCIO, vol. 3, p. 579; and Czechoslovakia, UNCIO, *idem*, p. 469; and Philippines, *idem*, p. 538.

New Zealand suggested a new principle, obliging all Member States "collectively to resist every act of aggression against any member."[77] Once again, this is reminiscent of the motto of the musketeers: *un pour tous, tous pour un*.[78] If one member of the group is attacked, this is an attack on all the members of the group. Thus all the members have an obligation to respond.[79] The amendment was rejected by the subcommittee, because "[t]he amendment limit[ed] itself to the collective resistance of every act of aggression, aggression not being defined."[80] The amendment was then discussed in the full Committee.[81] There, New Zealand defended its amendment by arguing that "aggression" had been defined in various legal documents, and was used elsewhere in the Charter. More to the point, according to the New Zealand delegate, it was important to add a principle obliging States to respond collectively to an act of aggression, because "if nations in the past had been prepared to guarantee security collectively there would have been no war."[82] Therefore it was necessary to include a clear obligation for all States to respond to acts of aggression: "If it were left to an *ad hoc* decision to decide whether or not to take action, even after the Security Council had decided that an act of aggression had taken place, the door would be open to evasion, appeasement, weaselling and sacrifice on the part of small nations." [83] The New Zealand amendment was considered to be "the minimum obligation which would guarantee the success of the Organization in the maintenance of peace and security."[84] In support, the Belgian delegate said that the amendment "did not require each member to give the same kind of aid [to curb aggression], but simply to participate in measures which would protect the political independence and territorial integrity of the members."[85] The New Zealand amendment did get a substantial majority, but not the two-thirds majority required for its adoption.[86]

The Dumbarton Oaks principle stating that "[a]ll members of the Organization shall settle their disputes by peaceful means in such a manner that international

---

[77] Amendments Submitted by New Zealand, UNCIO, vol. 3, p. 487.

[78] This motto can be found in Chapitre IX: d'Artagnan se Dessine, in Alexandre Dumas, *Les Trois Mousquetaires* (1844).

[79] Many amendments made this idea more explicit. See *e.g.*, Amendments Submitted by Bolivia, UNCIO, vol. 3, p. 582; Ecuador, *idem*, p. 399; Mexico, *idem*, p. 127; Colombia made such a suggestion in the Documentation for Meetings of Committee I/1, UNCIO, vol. 6, pp. 528-529; Amendments Submitted by Chile, UNCIO, vol. 3, p. 293.

[80] Report of Rapporteur of Subcommittee I/1/A, to Committee I/1, UNCIO, vol. 6, p. 721.

[81] Twelfth Meeting of Committee I/1, June 5, 1945, UNCIO, vol. 6, pp. 342-346.

[82] *Idem*, p. 343.

[83] *Idem*.

[84] Twelfth Meeting of Committee I/1, June 5, 1945, UNCIO, vol. 6, p. 343. The UK and US spoke against the amendment. See Twelfth Meeting of Committee I/1, UNCIO, vol. 6, p. 344.

[85] *Idem*, p. 345.

[86] *Idem*, p. 346. The amendment got 26 votes in favour, 18 against. See also Report of Rapporteur of Committee 1 to Commission I, UNCIO, vol. 6, p. 400.

peace and security are not endangered" should also be mentioned.[87] The link between this provision and peace and security is clear: if disputes are settled peacefully, they do not threaten the peace.[88] The provision did not trigger much debate, and was not changed significantly in San Francisco.[89]

## 3 THE SEARCH FOR A SUBSTANTIVE DEFINITION OF INTERNATIONAL PEACE AND SECURITY

### 3.1 Introduction

In San Francisco, the maintenance of international peace and security was considered to be the most important purpose of the United Nations.[90] But what does "international peace and security" mean? This section examines attempts to define peace and security in positive, substantive terms.

### 3.2 Peace and security defined in positive terms

The Assembly generally refers to "peace *and* security" as a single notion. There are some reports in which "peace" is distinguished from "security." For example, in his Agenda for Peace, former Secretary-General Boutros-Ghali wrote that "[t]he concept of peace is easy to grasp," but that the concept of international security is "more complex."[91] "Security" was presented as a more comprehensive concept than "peace." The latter was mainly used to refer to some of the collective mechanisms,

---

[87] Dumbarton Oaks Proposals for a General International Organization, UNCIO, vol. 3, p. 3. In their amendments, the sponsors added the word "international" before "disputes." See Amendments Submitted by the United States, the United Kingdom, the Soviet Union and China, UNCIO, vol. 3, p. 623.

[88] Some States also pointed this out. See *e.g.*, Amendments Submitted by Chile, UNCIO, vol. 3, p. 293.

[89] The main addition was a reference to "justice." During a Committee meeting, it was suggested that the text of the provision was repetitive, in the sense that "since members were to settle their disputes by peaceful means, international peace and security could not thus be endangered." See Seventh Meeting of Committee I/1, May 16, 1956, UNCIO, vol. 6, p. 305. The Rapporteur of the relevant Subcommittee explained – but not too convincingly - why it was not repetitive: see Report of Rapporteur of Subcommittee I/1/A, to Committee I/1, UNCIO, vol. 6, pp. 719-720.

[90] See *e.g.*, Leland M. Goodrich, *The United Nations and the maintenance of international peace and security* (1955); Evgheny V. Bougrov, *The United Nations and the maintenance of international peace and security* (1987); Nigel D. White, *Keeping the peace: the United Nations and the maintenance of international peace and security* (1997); Vaughan Lowe (editor), *The United Nations Security Council and war : the evolution of thought and practice since 1945* (2008).

[91] An Agenda for Peace: Preventive diplomacy, peacemaking and peace-keeping, Report of the Secretary-General, UNDoc. A/47/277, distributed 17 June 1992, p. 3.

such as peacekeeping. The former was mainly defined by presenting a long list of causes for insecurity, including "the proliferation of weapons of mass destruction [and] conventional arms," "racial tensions," "ecological damage, disruption of family and community life, greater intrusion into the lives and rights of individuals," "unchecked population growth, crushing debt burdens, barriers to trade, drugs and the growing disparity between rich and poor," "[p]overty, disease, famine, oppression and despair," "[a] porous ozone shield," and "[d]rought and disease."[92]

This is not the Assembly's approach. Generally the Assembly does not distinguish at all between peace and security. When it does, it does exactly the opposite of what Boutros-Ghali suggested. It uses "security" to refer to the collective security mechanism of the UN Charter. Peace is used in more general, non-technical, contexts.[93] Although none of the other main UN organs have ever distinguished peace from security in a general sense, there are some indications that the Security Council shares the Assembly's view that if a distinction must be made between the two, security is used in a more technical sense, and peace in a more "philosophical" sense.[94]

The Assembly never defined the value of peace and security. The Essentials of Peace, the earliest declaration of the General Assembly on peace and security, does not provide any definition.[95] Instead, the declaration reiterated the Charter's basic principles, compliance with which was considered necessary for an enduring peace. In another resolution, adopted at about the same time, the Assembly gave the impression that peaceful relations among States was very similar to peaceful relations among neighbours in an apartment complex.[96] As long as neighbours leave one another alone, they live at peace with each other. Therefore it is necessary to tolerate the unusual habits of neighbours, and refrain from

---

[92] *Idem.*

[93] There are some exceptions to this general rule. See, for example Creation of a global culture of cybersecurity, General Assembly resolution 57/239, adopted 20 December 2002, and Creation of a global culture of cybersecurity and the protection of critical information infrastructures, General Assembly resolution 58/199, adopted 23 December 2003.

[94] See *e.g.*, the minutes of the first meeting of the Council, UNDoc. S/PV.1(1). This first meeting was held in Westminster, London, on 17 January 1946. It was only in April 1952 that the Council first convened in its current location. We read, *e.g.*, that it is the UN's ultimate purpose to "build[…] the kind of world in which lasting peace will be possible" (Stettinus, USA), or that the Council should be regarded as the "guardian of world peace" (Koo, China), or that it is the Council's task to "ensure lasting peace among nations" (Gromyko, USSR), that the Council is the "safeguard of lasting peace" (Badawi, Egypt). None of the delegates saw the establishment of security as the ultimate aim of the Security Council.

[95] Essentials of Peace, General Assembly resolution 290(IV), adopted 1 December 1949.

[96] Peaceful and neighborly relations among States, General Assembly resolution 1236(XII), adopted 10 December 1957. See also Measures aimed at the implementation and promotion of peaceful and neighborly relations among States, General Assembly resolution 1301(XIII), adopted 10 December 1958.

interference. The idea was to "develop peaceful and tolerant relations among States, in conformity with the Charter, based on mutual respect and benefit, non-aggression, respect for each other's sovereignty, equality and territorial integrity and non-intervention in one another's international affairs."[97]

Most resolutions on peace and security require a more proactive attitude from the neighbours. In Peace through Deeds, the General Assembly recognized "the profound desire of all mankind to live in enduring peace and security," and expressed its confidence that "if all governments faithfully reflect this desire and observe their obligations under the Charter, lasting peace and security can be established."[98] The Assembly added that "for the realization of lasting peace and security it [was] indispensable [that] prompt united action be taken to meet aggression wherever it arises," and that every State should agree to "regulate all armaments and armed forces under a United Nations system of control and inspection, with a view to their gradual reduction," and that all States should use the resources that would otherwise be spent on weapons "for the general welfare, with due regard to the needs of the under-developed areas of the world."[99] This time, the neighbours were obliged to actively cooperate to secure peace and security.

This more comprehensive approach to peace and security was promoted for a while under the heading of a "culture for peace." The Assembly defined the culture for peace as consisting of a "set of values, attitudes, traditions and modes of behavior and ways of life."[100] This "transdisciplinary" approach to peace and security was inspired by the work of the United Nations Educational, Scientific and Cultural Organization (UNESCO).[101] The Director of UNESCO explained that the fundamental principle of this culture of peace was the "transformation from conflict to cooperation through a process of dialogue leading to cooperation for shared goals of human development." [102] After all, in UNESCO's view, "the most effective means to end or avoid a conflict is the engagement of the contending parties in collaboration for a shared higher goal."[103] Thus the culture of peace reflected this higher goal, which was basically to make the world a better place. This culture of peace, *i.e.* this set of values, attitudes, traditions, *et cetera*, encompassed everything: it included respect for life, respect for the principles of sovereignty, territorial integrity and political independence, respect for human rights, the obligation to

---

[97] *Idem.*

[98] Peace through Deeds, General Assembly resolution 380(V), adopted 17 November 1950.

[99] Idem.

[100] Declaration on a Culture of Peace, part one of General Assembly resolution 53/243, adopted 13 September 1999.

[101] The word "transdisciplinary" is used by UNESCO. See *e.g.*, Report of the Director-General of the United Nations Educational, Scientific and Cultural Organization on educational activities under the project "Towards a culture of peace", UNDoc. A/51/395, distributed 23 September 1996, p. 5.

[102] *Idem*, p. 4.

[103] *Idem.*

settle disputes peacefully and the obligation to meet the developmental and environmental needs of both present and future generations. [104] Such an all-encompassing definition of peace is hard to work with. In any case, UNESCO's "culture for peace" did not have a major impact on the work of the United Nations, or on scholarship.[105]

## 3.3 Conclusion

From the very few resolutions that did deal with peace and security in a more general sense, it is possible to distil two approaches to the value, which are both adopted by the General Assembly. One approach sees a peaceful world as a world in which States merely tolerate each other's presence, and leave each other alone. The other sees a peaceful world as an ideal world, a world in which all global values are realized through joint efforts.

## 4 THE USE OF FORCE AS A THREAT TO INTERNATIONAL PEACE AND SECURITY

## 4.1 Introduction

The Assembly has clearly stated what it means by *threats to* peace and security. Presumably then, peace and security can be defined as a situation in which all such threats are absent. The most direct threat, the one which was hotly debated in San Francisco, was the use of (military) force by one State against another.

## 4.2 The prohibition on the use of force

According to Article 2(4) UN Charter: "All Members shall refrain in their international relations from the threat or use of force against the territorial integrity or political independence of any state."[106] This provision does not explicitly define such threats or uses of force as threats to peace and security, but this can be

---

[104] See also UNESCO, *Mainstreaming the Culture of Peace* (2002), p. 5. The ensuing obligations are equally comprehensive, and include the promotion of sustainable development, respect for all human rights, the equality of men and women, democracy, tolerance, solidarity, the free flow of information, and international peace and security.

[105] In 2010, the Assembly attempted to revitalize the culture of peace. See Implementation of the Declaration and Programme of Action on a Culture of Peace, General Assembly resolution 65/11, adopted 23 November 2010.

[106] See Taslim Olawale Elias, "Scope and meaning of article 2(4) of the United Nations Charter" (1988); Nico Schrijver, "Article 2, paragraphe 4," (2005).

assumed when the provision is read in conjunction with Chapter VII of the Charter, especially Article 39.

The United Nations never really dealt with the rules of warfare (*jus in bello*). Traditionally this has been a subject regulated outside the UN framework, primarily in the series of Conventions adopted in Geneva.[107] In recent times, this has changed to some extent.[108]

The United Nations does concern itself with the prohibition on going to war in the first place (*jus ad bellum*). Some efforts have been made, especially by the General Assembly, to interpret and elaborate on the prohibition on the use of force as prescribed in Article 2(4) UN Charter in more detail.[109] The Declaration on the Duties of States in the Event of the Outbreak of Hostilities is an interesting early example.[110] The Assembly recommended that all States, if they became "engaged in armed conflict with another State or States," should "take all steps practicable in the circumstances and compatible with the right of self-defence to bring the armed conflict to an end at the earliest possible moment," and "make a public statement wherein [they] proclaim [their] readiness, provided that the States with which [they] are] in conflict will do the same, to discontinue all military operations and withdraw all [their] military forces which have invaded the territory." Apparently, the duty to stop an armed conflict as soon as possible was part of the prohibition on the use of force in international relations.

In 1965, the Assembly adopted the Declaration on the Inadmissibility of Intervention in the Domestic Affairs of States and the Protection of Their Independence and Sovereignty.[111] This Declaration dealt with both armed intervention, as well as economic or political pressure. It suggested that any "violation of the principle of non-intervention [could] pose a serious threat to the maintenance of peace." This is consistent with a broad interpretation of the

---

[107] The most important by far are the Geneva Convention (I) for the Amelioration of the Condition of the Wounded and Sick in Armed Forces in the Field, the Geneva Convention (II) for the Amelioration of the Condition of Wounded, Sick and Shipwrecked Members of Armed Forces at Sea, the Geneva Convention (III) relative to the Treatment of Prisoners of War, and the Geneva Convention (IV) relative to the Protection of Civilian Persons in Time of War. All four were adopted in Geneva, on 12 August 1949. On 8 June 1977, three additional protocols were adopted, of which the Protocol relating to the Protection of Victims of International Armed Conflicts (Protocol I), and the Protocol relating to the Protection of Victims of Non-International Armed Conflicts (Protocol II) are the most important.

[108] In Security Council resolution 1674, adopted 28 April 2006, the Council reaffirmed the need to comply with international humanitarian law and stressed that ending impunity was essential. In a Presidential Statement made on 14 January 2009, the Council condemned all violations of international humanitarian law and called for an end to impunity. See also S.PV/6066, where the Council discussed the protection of civilians, with a central role for international humanitarian law.

[109] As Schrijver rightly pointed out, the Security Council has never defined in general terms what constitutes a prohibited use of force. Nico Schrijver, "Article 2, paragraph 4" (2005), p. 451.

[110] General Assembly resolution 378(V), adopted 17 November 1950.

[111] General Assembly Resolution 2131(XX), adopted 21 December 1965.

prohibition on the use of force, including interventions not involving the use of military force. [112]

By far the most authoritative and best-known interpretation of the prohibition on the use of force can be found in the Friendly Relations Declaration adopted in 1970.[113] As this is such an important interpretation of the prohibition on the use of force, the *travaux préparatoires* of the declaration are examined below. [114] The declaration was essentially drafted by a Special Committee, working for the General Assembly. [115] Most of the debates in this Special Committee focused on defining the prohibition on the use of force.

The main issue, which had already been discussed during the Special Committee's first session, was the search for the correct interpretation of the word "force" as used in Article 2(4) of the UN Charter.[116] The smaller States believed that it included non-military force, such as political pressure and economic sanctions. This would have been consistent with the resolution on the inadmissibility of intervention adopted in 1965, and with the views of many smaller States in San Francisco. Other States, mainly from the West, believed that the framework of the UN Charter, and especially the relationship between Articles 2(4), 51 and Chapter VII, as well as the *travaux préparatoires* of the Charter, showed that "force" should be interpreted as referring to military force alone. [117] The discussion about the definition of the word "force" continued during the second session. [118] During the third session, it was once again suggested that a broad definition of the word "force" was required, as economic coercion was just as devastating as the use of armed force. The counter-argument was, once again, that the intention of the UN Charter was to prohibit only armed force, and that any other

---

[112] See also section 5.4 of Chapter VII, on the general prohibition for States to intervene in the affairs of other States.

[113] Declaration on Principles of International Law Concerning Friendly Relations and Co-operation among States in accordance with the Charter of the United Nations, General Assembly resolution 2625(XXV), adopted 24 October 1970 ("Friendly Relations Declaration").

[114] See also Vekateshwara Subramanian Mani, *Basic principles of modern international law* (1993), pp. 9-48.

[115] See also section 5.5 of Chapter III.

[116] Special Committee on Principles of International Law concerning Friendly Relations and Co-operation among States, Report, A/5746, adopted 16 November 1964 ("First Report"), paras. 47-63. See also Gaetano Arangio-Ruiz, "The normative role of the General Assembly" (1972), pp. 529-530; and p. 9 of Edward McWhinney, "The 'New' Countries and the 'New' International Law" (1966); Vekateshwara Subramanian Mani, *Basic principles of modern international law* (1993), pp. 11-16.

[117] Mani, *Basic principles of modern international law* (1993), pp. 12-14. This was also the more traditional view. See *e.g.*, Alfred Verdross, "Idées directrices de l'Organisation des Nations Unies" (1955), pp. 12-13.

[118] Special Committee on Principles of International Law concerning Friendly Relations and Co-operation among States, Report, A/6230, adopted 27 June 1966 ("Second Report"), paras. 64-76. See also Piet-Hein Houben, "Principles of International Law Concerning Friendly Relations and Co-Operation Among States" (1967), pp. 707-708.

interpretation would upset the system of the UN Charter.[119] During the fourth session of the Special Committee, the discussion about the meaning of the word "force" in Article 2(4) UN Charter continued.[120] There was now general agreement that the prohibition on the use of force also prohibited "indirect aggression," *i.e.* armed assistance to irregular forces causing civil strife in another State, and assistance to terrorist groups operating on another State's territory.[121] Once again it was suggested that other forms of coercion, such as certain political and economic pressure, should also be regarded as "force," but this view was still not universally accepted.[122] During the fifth session of the Special Committee, a compromise was sought. According to this proposed compromise, a statement on the prohibition of undesirable forms of political or economic pressure should be included in the principle on non-intervention, not as part of the prohibition on the use of force.[123] During the sixth and last session of the Committee, the debate on the interpretation of the word "force" had to be settled in some way. The delegates simply agreed to disagree. No definition of the word "force" was to be found in the final declaration. However, the Preamble states that it is the duty of States to refrain from military, political, economic or any other form of coercion aimed against the political independence or territorial integrity of any State.[124] So that is where an extensive definition of "force" can be found.[125] In their final comments many representatives wanted to clarify what they believed the word "force" meant as used in Article 2(4) UN Charter. According to Argentina, "the use of force referred only to armed or physical force." But this "did not of course mean that other kinds of pressure should be accepted, since they were contrary to the principle of non-intervention."[126] Thus Argentina had chosen to join the Western States. Nigeria, on the other hand, regretted that the Committee could not reach a consensus on the idea that the term force "denoted economic and political prejudice as well as every kind of armed force."[127]

---

[119] Special Committee on Principles of International Law concerning Friendly Relations and Co-operation among States, Report, A/6799, adopted 26 September 1967 ("Third Report"), paras. 51-57.

[120] Special Committee on Principles of International Law concerning Friendly Relations and Co-operation among States, Report, A/7326, adopted 30 September 1968 ("Fourth Report"), paras. 49-54.

[121] Special Committee, Fourth Report, para. 47. See also Vekateshwara Subramanian Mani, *Basic principles of modern international law* (1993), pp. 31-33.

[122] Special Committee, Fourth Report, para. 52.

[123] Special Committee on Principles of International Law concerning Friendly Relations and Co-operation among States, Report, A/7619, adopted 19 September 1969 ("Fifth Report"), para. 93.

[124] Special Committee on Principles of International Law concerning Friendly Relations and Co-operation among States, Report, A/8018, adopted 1 May 1970 ("Sixth Report"), p. 63.

[125] Vekateshwara Subramanian Mani, *Basic principles of modern international law* (1993), p. 16.

[126] Special Committee, Sixth Report, para. 106. See also UK, para. 227, and USA, para. 256.

[127] Special Committee, Sixth Report, para. 187. See also Czechoslovakia, para. 194, and Mexico, para. 210.

The Friendly Relations Declaration as finally adopted, uses a restrictive definition of the use of force. The Declaration also explicitly prohibits the use of force as a "reprisal," *i.e.* as a means to respond to a wrongful act committed by another State. In addition, the declaration makes it clear that "every State has the duty to refrain from organizing or encouraging the organization of irregular forces or armed bands including mercenaries, for incursion into the territory of another State." This is interesting because it is not evident that the prohibition of Article 2(4) also covers such assistance to armed bands acting abroad. The same can be said of the duty "to refrain from organizing, instigating, assisting or participating in acts of civil strife or terrorist acts in another State or acquiescing in organized activities within its territory directed towards the commission of such acts, when [these acts] involve a threat or use of force." Finally, the Declaration emphasized that "no territorial acquisition resulting from the threat or use of force shall be recognized as legal;" this cannot be found in Article 2(4) either.

The Declaration on the Inadmissibility of Intervention and Interference in the Internal Affairs of States was, as the title suggests, mainly about the non-intervention principle.[128] However, it also dealt with the prohibition on intervening with the use of armed force. The distinction between the general non-intervention principle and the prohibition on the use of force in international relations became blurred.[129]

In 1987, the Assembly adopted the Declaration on the Enhancement of the Effectiveness of the Principle of Refraining from the Threat or Use of Force in International Relations.[130] This Declaration was much more detailed than the Friendly Relations Declaration. The first part contained a list of prohibitions that followed from Article 2(4) UN Charter. First, the Declaration reaffirmed the duty, also stated in the Friendly Relations Declaration, that "States shall […] refrain from organizing, instigating, or assisting or participating in paramilitary, terrorist or subversive acts, including acts of mercenaries, in other States, or acquiescing in organized activities within their territory directed towards the commission of such acts." The Declaration also broadened the interpretation of the prohibition, or at least linked it to the general non-intervention principle in the same way as the 1981 Declaration on the Inadmissibility of Intervention and Interference in the Internal Affairs of States had done. It referred to a prohibition for all States on the use or encouragement of "the use of economic, political or any other type of measures to

---

[128] General Assembly resolution 36/103, adopted 9 December 1981.
[129] This dual nature of the Declaration is nicely summarized in the Preamble, as follows: "any violation of the principle of non-intervention and non-interference in the internal and external affairs of States poses a threat to the freedom of peoples, the sovereignty, political independence, territorial integrity of States to their political, economic, social and cultural development, and also endangers international peace and security."
[130] General Assembly resolution 42/22, adopted 18 November 1987.

coerce another State in order to obtain from it the subordination of the exercise of its sovereign rights and to secure from it advantages of any kind." In San Francisco, many States denied that such coercion fell within the scope of Article 2(4) UN Charter, which was said to be only about armed or military force.

Although some issues were left unresolved, these declarations give a general idea of what constitutes a prohibited use of force. The use of force probably has to involve military measures, and must be directed at a target across the State boundary. It is not entirely clear whether non-military intervention, such as economic sanctions and pressure, can also be said to constitute force, and thus a threat to the peace. There are various indications that "force" should not be defined so broadly, and consequently that peace and security should also be interpreted as describing a situation in which States refrain from intervening in each other's affairs through military measures.

The prohibition on the use of force, as defined in the UN Charter, is one of the most important norms of international law.[131] In the view of the community of States, it was a popular example of a peremptory norm .[132] When Waldock, the Rapporteur of the International Law Commission on the Law of Treaties, suggested adding some examples to the provision on *jus cogens* in the Vienna Convention on the Law of Treaties, the first example he suggested including was "the use or threat of force in contravention of the principles of the Charter of the United Nations".[133] The International Court of Justice referred to this view, without adopting it.[134] Judge Schwebel pointed out that "[w]hile there [was] little agreement on the scope of *jus cogens*, it is important to recall that in the International Law Commission and at the Vienna Conference on the Law of Treaties there was general agreement that, if *jus cogens* has any agreed core, it is Article 2, paragraph 4 [of the UN

---

[131] See *e.g.*, Bernard Victor Aloysius Röling, "On the prohibition of the use of force" (1983). For a critical view, see Nicholas Rostow, "International Law and the Use of Force: a Plea for Realism" (2009).

[132] For Bulgaria, see UNDoc. A/Conf.39/5 (Vol. II), p. 298; Cyprus, *idem*, p. 301, Czechoslovakia, p. 304, Iraq, p. 310, Pakistan, p. 312, Poland, p. 315, Ukraine, p. 319, USSR, p. 321; USSR, p. 294 of UNDoc. A/Conf.39/11[A], Greece, p. 295, Kenya, p. 296, Uruguay, p. 303, United Kingdom, p. 304, Cyprus, p. 306, Byelorussian Soviet Socialist Republic, p. 307, Italy, p. 311, Romania, p. 312, Federal Republic of Germany, p. 318, Ukraine, p. 322, Philippines, p. 323, Canada, p. 323.

[133] Yearbook of the International Law Commission, Vol. II (1963), p. 52. In his view, "the principles stated in the Charter are generally accepted as expressing not merely the obligations of Members of the United Nations but the general rules of international law of today concerning the use of force." *Idem*, p. 53.

[134] Reference can be made to para. 190 of International Court of Justice, Case Concerning Military and Paramilitary Activities in and against Nicaragua (Nicaragua v. United States of America), Merits, Judgment of 27 June 1986, in which an ILC Report is cited (p. 247 of the Yearbook of the International Law Commission, 1966, Volume II, A/CN.4/SER. A/1966/Add. 1), which labels the prohibition on the use of force as *jus cogens*.

Charter]."[135] Judge Elaraby referred to it as the "most important principle that emerged in the twentieth century," one which was "universally recognized as a *jus cogens* principle."[136] This strong support for the provision contrasts with the lack of agreement regarding exactly what kind of behaviour constitutes a violation of the prohibition on the use of force.

## 4.3 Aggression and the prohibition on the use of force

The Assembly considered aggression to be the "the most serious and dangerous form of the illegal use of force, being fraught, in the conditions created by the existence of all types of weapons of mass destruction, with the possible threat of a world conflict and all its catastrophic consequences."[137] This suggests that there is a "normal" type of illegal use of force, as well as a more serious and dangerous type, which is qualified as aggression. Aggression was considered to be the worst thing one State could do to another, but it was not so easy to define this "evil" in legal or technical terms.[138]

Article 2(4) UN Charter does not use the word "aggression." However, the word is used in Article 39. When that article was discussed during the San Francisco Conference, it was suggested that a more specific definition of aggression should be found, so that States would know what not to do to be free from Security Council sanctions and force.[139] In 1974, the Assembly finally came up with a definition of aggression:

> Aggression is the use of armed force by a State against the sovereignty, territorial integrity or political independence of another State, or in any other manner inconsistent with the Charter of the United Nations […].[140]

---

[135] See p. 615, Dissenting Opinion of Judge Schwebel, in the Case Concerning Military and Paramilitary Activities in and against Nicaragua (Nicaragua v. United States of America), Jurisdiction of the Court and Admissibility of the Application, Judgment of 26 November 1984.

[136] Separate Opinion of Judge Elaraby, Legal Consequences of the Construction of a Wall in the Occupied Palestinian Territory, International Court of Justice, Advisory Opinion of July 9, 2004. See also Dissenting Opinion of the same judge in the Case Concerning Oil Platforms (Islamic Republic of Iran v. United State of America), Judgment of 6 November 2003, where he remarked that it was "the most important principle in contemporary international law to govern inter-State conduct" and "the cornerstone of the [UN] Charter."

[137] Definition of Aggression, General Assembly Resolution 3314 (XXIX), adopted 14 December 1974.

[138] See also Special Committee responsible for the drafting of the Friendly Relations Declaration, Third Report, paras. 58-61. See also Special Committee, Second Report, paras. 77-81.

[139] See section 2.3 of Chapter IV, above.

[140] Article 1, Definition of Aggression, General Assembly Resolution 3314 (XXIX), adopted 14 December 1974. For the coming into being of this definition, see Bengt Broms, "The definition of aggression" (1977), pp. 315-335. See also Stephen M. Schwebel, "Aggression, intervention and self-defence in modern international law" (1972), for a comment on the earlier drafting stages.

Thus aggression was seen as a violation of the prohibition on the use of armed force. The difference between the prohibition on the use of force of Article 2(4) UN Charter and the prohibition on aggression was, first of all, that reference was made explicitly to "armed force" in the definition of aggression. This effectively prevented a repetition of the debates on a more extensive interpretation of the word "force." Secondly, the *threat* of the use of force was not sufficiently grave to be labelled aggression.[141] The Assembly gave some examples of potential acts of aggression, which differed, though only slightly, from the examples of the prohibition on the use of force provided earlier in the Assembly's Friendly Relations Declaration. The use of the Assembly's list of examples of aggression is limited, as the Assembly itself presented the list as non-exhaustive. It was up to the Security Council to decide whether a particular use of armed force by one State against another constituted an act of aggression. The Assembly merely recommended that the Security Council "should, as appropriate, take account of th[e] Definition as guidance in determine[ing], in accordance with the Charter, the existence of an act of aggression."[142]

The word "aggression" has criminal connotations.[143] However, suggestions to explicitly include an *animus aggressionis*, or an "aggressive intent," in the definition were rejected.[144] The issue resurfaced when the International Criminal Court was authorized to "exercise jurisdiction over the crime of aggression once a provision is adopted [...] defining the crime and setting out the conditions under which the Court shall exercise jurisdiction with respect to this crime."[145] This has

---

[141] When the definition was being drafted, some States suggested including economic aggression in the definition, but this was clearly not done. See Bengt Broms, "The definition of aggression" (1977), p. 342.

[142] Definition of Aggression, General Assembly Resolution 3314 (XXIX), adopted 14 December 1974.

[143] This is why it was the prototype of a State crime, at least until the notion was abandoned. It then became the prototype of an international crime. See *e.g.*, International Court of Justice in the Case Concerning the Barcelona Traction, Light and Power Company, Limited (Belgium v. Spain), Judgment of 5 February 1970, paras. 33-34; "Fifth report on State responsibility by Mr. Roberto Ago," in the Yearbook of the International Law Commission 1976, vol. II (Part I), p. 26; "Summary records of the twenty-eighth session (3 May-23 July 1976)," in Yearbook of the International Law Commission 1976, vol. I, p. 239; "Report of the International Law Commission on its twenty-eighth session," in the Yearbook of the International Law Commission, 1976, Volume II (Part Two), pp. 95-96; State responsibility: Comments and observations received from Governments, UNDoc. A/CN.4/515, 19 March 2001, p. 44; Report of the Ad Hoc Committee on the Establishment of an International Criminal Court, General Assembly Official Records, Fiftieth Session, Supplement No. 22 (A/50/22), distributed on 6 September 1995, pp. 11-18; and, finally, Article 5, Rome Statute of the International Criminal Court.

[144] See Bengt Broms, "The definition of aggression" (1977), pp. 344-346.

[145] Article 5, Rome Statute of the International Criminal Court.

led to an immense amount of literature on the crime of aggression.[146] In 2010, the parties to the Rome Statute of the International Criminal Court finally adopted a definition of the international crime of aggression. It used the Assembly's definition of 1974 as a starting point. The crime of aggression is defined as

> The planning, preparation, initiation or execution, by a person in a position effectively to exercise control over or to direct the political or military action of a State, of an act of aggression which, by its character, gravity and scale, constitutes a manifest violation of the Charter of the United Nations.[147]

An act of aggression is then defined as "the use of armed force by a State against the sovereignty, territorial integrity or political independence of another State, or in any other manner inconsistent with the Charter of the United Nations."[148] This is an exact copy of the Assembly's definition of 1974.

## 4.4 Conclusion

How can the efforts to define the prohibition on the use of force help to create an understanding of the value of peace and security? The Charter itself suggests that the threat or use of force, as prohibited in Article 2(4) UN Charter, disturbs international peace and security. A world without "force" is therefore a more peaceful world. This raises the question as to what is meant by "force". Aggression can certainly be qualified as the use of force. But what about non-military interference by one State in another State's affairs? Should this also be qualified as the use of "force," and a disturbance of international peace and security?[149] The answer to this question indirectly defines what is meant by a peaceful world. Is it a world without military force? Or is it a world without economic interference and other types of unwelcome intervention by one State in the internal affairs of another?

---

[146] See *e.g.*, Larry May, *Aggression and crimes against peace* (2008); Niels Blokker, "The Crime of Aggression and the United Nations Security Council" (2007).

[147] The Crime of Aggression, resolution RC/Res.6, adopted at the 13th plenary meeting, on 11 June 2010, by consensus. The ICC can exercise jurisdiction over the crime of aggression after 1 January 2017, and only if at least two-thirds of the States party to the Rome Statute confirm such exercise of jurisdiction at that time. For a discussion of the ICC meeting, see the contributions in the *Leiden Journal of International Law*, vol. 23 (2010), no. 4.

[148] *Idem*.

[149] Instead, it will be seen as a violation of the sovereign independence of States. See especially section 5.4 of Chapter VII.

## 5 OTHER THREATS TO INTERNATIONAL PEACE AND SECURITY

### 5.1 Introduction

The use of force, whether defined broadly or restrictively, is not the only possible way in which peace and security can be disrupted. Threats to peace and security not caused by a State violating the principle prohibiting the use of force in international relations are discussed below. Domestic conflicts (civil war) are examined, as well as the arms race. Threats posed by hijackers, hostage takers, mercenaries and terrorists are also analyzed. An examination of these "evils" provides a better understanding of what is entailed by the value of peace and security.

### 5.2 Domestic conflicts and genocide

The Security Council has qualified various domestic conflicts as threats to international peace and security, particularly since the early 1990s.[150] It has consistently justified its interference in domestic conflicts with two arguments, summarized by the representative of Cape Verde:

> National conflicts are sometimes as destructive as the fiercest international conflicts. The enormous loss of life and the human tragedy they produce demand no less attention and appeal for no less speedy a response from the international community. Apart from the loss of human lives, every national conflict has an international dimension, for it generates massive numbers of refugees, thus creating enormous social pressure in neighbouring countries, threatening their peace and stability.[151]

It is (1) the gravity of the situation and (2) the flow of refugees that turn a domestic conflict into a threat to *international* peace and security.[152]

One of the worst domestic conflicts in recent history was the genocide in Rwanda.[153] In May 1994, the Council for the first time "determin[ed] that the situation in Rwanda constitute[d] a threat to peace and security in the region," and

---

[150] It can be argued that the Council already did so when responding to the minority regime in Rhodesia (1966-1979) and the *apartheid* regime in South Africa. See sections below.

[151] Verbatim Records of the 3046th meeting of the Security Council, 31 January 1992, UNDoc. S/PV.3046, p.81.

[152] See Thomas M. Franck, *Recourse to Force* (2002), pp. 43-44.

[153] For a definition of genocide, see Prevention and punishment of the crime of genocide, General Assembly resolution 260 (III), adopted 9 December 1948. See further Draft convention on genocide, General Assembly resolution 180(II), adopted 21 November 1947; Status of the Convention on the Prevention and Punishment of the Crime of Genocide, General Assembly resolution 40/142, adopted 13 December 1985; Fiftieth anniversary of the Convention on the Prevention and Punishment of the Crime of Genocide, General Assembly resolution 53/43, adopted 2 December 1998.

invoked Chapter VII. [154] The "situation" was considered to be a threat to the peace, not the fact that genocide was being committed. [155] A month later, the Council referred to "the magnitude of the humanitarian crisis in Rwanda [as] a threat to peace and security in the region." [156] A few weeks earlier, the Council had already "underscor[ed] that the internal displacement of some 1.5 million Rwandans facing starvation and disease and the massive exodus of refugees to neighbouring countries constitute[d] a humanitarian crisis of enormous proportions." [157] Therefore the flow of refugees was part of the humanitarian crisis which posed a threat to the peace.

In the resolution that established the International Criminal Tribunal for Rwanda at a time when the genocide was effectively over, the Council "express[ed] its grave concern at the reports indicating that genocide and other systematic, widespread and flagrant violations of international humanitarian law ha[d] been committed in Rwanda," and "determin[ed] that this situation continue[d] to constitute a threat to international peace and security." [158] It is not clear what "this situation" referred to exactly this time. In any case, the Council did not adopt the view that genocide had been committed, leaving it to the International Criminal Tribunal, which it had just established, to determine this instead. Therefore it can be concluded that the Council never qualified the situation in Rwanda as genocide, and did not identify genocide as a threat to the peace. Instead, it was the gravity of the humanitarian crisis, combined with the international flow of refugees, which turned the domestic conflict in Rwanda into a threat to international peace and security. [159]

---

[154] Security Council resolution 918 (1994), adopted on 17 May 1994.

[155] There was an implicit mention of genocide in the preamble. Later on, reference was made to reports indicating that genocide was committed. See Security Council resolution 925 (1994), adopted on 8 June 1994, and Security Council resolution 935 (1994), adopted 1 July 1994, and, most importantly, Security Council resolution 955 (1994), adopted 8 November 1994, which established the International Tribunal for Rwanda.

[156] Security Council resolution 929 (1994), adopted 22 June 1994.

[157] Security Council resolution 925 (1994), adopted on 8 June 1994.

[158] Security Council resolution 955, adopted 8 November 1994. See also Larissa Jasmijn van den Herik, *The contribution of the Rwanda Tribunal to the development of international law* (2005).

[159] The violent break-up of a State might also be so destructive, that it constitutes a threat to international peace and security. See: The maintenance of international security - prevention of the violent disintegration of States, General Assembly resolution 51/55, adopted 10 December 1996. See also Marc Weller, "The international response to the dissolution of the Socialist Federal Republic of Yugoslavia," (1992).

## 5.3 Apartheid

The United Nations labelled *apartheid* as a root cause of conflict.[160] But is it not also a direct threat to international peace and security? In 1960, the Security Council referred to the "situation in the Union of South Africa" as one that "led to international friction and if continued might endanger international peace and security."[161] The Council referred to the "situation," and not to the policies of *apartheid*. The Assembly was much more direct. In 1961, it noted that the policies of *apartheid* had led to "international friction" and that "their continuance endanger[ed] international peace and security."[162] In a resolution in 1962, the Assembly reaffirmed this view, and requested States to take certain economic measures in order "to bring about the abandonment of those policies."[163] The Assembly also "request[ed] the Security Council to take appropriate measures, including sanctions."[164]

In response, the Council referred to the Assembly's resolution as a reflection of "world public opinion," and expressed its conviction that "the situation in South Africa [was] seriously disturbing international peace and security," and imposed a non-mandatory arms embargo.[165] The Council still referred to the "situation" as opposed to *apartheid*. In 1970, the Council expressed its belief that the "continued application of the policies of *apartheid* and the constant build-up of the South African military and police forces [...] constitute[d] a potential threat to international peace and security."[166] It considerably strengthened the arms embargo, without, however invoking Chapter VII. This time, the "situation" was a combination of an arms build-up and the policies of *apartheid*.

---

[160] For example, in 1991, the Assembly labelled apartheid as the "root cause of the conflict in southern Africa. Status of the International Convention on the Suppression and Punishment of the Crime of Apartheid, General Assembly resolution 46/84, adopted 16 December 1991.

[161] See Security Council resolution 134 (1960), adopted on 1 April 1960.

[162] Question of race conflict in South Africa resulting from the policies of apartheid of the Government of the Union of South Africa, General Assembly resolution 1598 (XV), adopted 13 April 1961. Earlier, a Commission had referred to apartheid as "constitut[ing] a grave threat to the peaceful relations between ethnic groups in the world." See Question of race conflict in South Africa resulting from the policies of apartheid of the Government of the Union of South Africa, General Assembly resolution 820 (IX), adopted 14 December 1954.

[163] The policies of apartheid of the Government of the Republic of South Africa, General Assembly resolution 1761(XVII), adopted 6 November 1962.

[164] Idem.

[165] Security Council resolution 181(1963), adopted 7 August 1963. It was not mandatory in the sense that the Council did not invoke Chapter VII of the UN Charter, and could thus not bind the Member States. One year later, the Council expressed its conviction that "the situation in South Africa [was] continuing seriously to disturb international peace and security." Security Council resolution 191(1964), adopted 18 June 1964.

[166] Security Council resolution 282(1970), adopted 23 July 1970. See also Security Council resolution 311(1972), adopted 4 February 1972.

In 1977, the Council stated that "the policies and acts of the South African Government [were] fraught with danger to international peace and security," and invoked Chapter VII for the first time, imposing mandatory sanctions.[167] This suggests that the Security Council considered *apartheid* as a threat to the peace, but the Council invoked Chapter VII after "determin[ing], having regard to the policies and acts of the South African Government, that the acquisition by South Africa of arms and related *matériel* constitute[d] a threat to the maintenance of international peace and security."[168] Thus the Council emphasized the danger of the arms build-up.

One can conclude that, in contrast with the Assembly, the Council, hesitated to refer explicitly to the policies of *apartheid* as in themselves constituting a threat to the peace,[169] although it can be argued that the Council at least did so indirectly. This view was certainly expressed by States when a convention was drafted on the subject. The preamble to the Apartheid Convention states that the States party to that convention "observe[d] that the Security Council ha[d] determined that *apartheid* and its continued intensification and expansion seriously disturb[ed] and threaten[ed] international peace and security."[170] Moreover, all States party to the Apartheid Convention expressly agreed that *apartheid* ought to be seen as "constituting a serious threat to international peace and security."[171] In other contexts, *apartheid* was also consistently considered as a threat to peace and security.[172] Together with the Assembly's resolutions, this leads to the conclusion that *apartheid* in and of itself constitutes a threat to peace and security. A world in which one State imposes an *apartheid* regime on (parts of) its population is therefore not a world in which the value of peace and security is upheld.

---

[167] Security Council resolution 418(1977), adopted 4 November 1977.

[168] *Idem.*

[169] In 1976, the Security Council explicitly referred to apartheid as "seriously disturb[ing] international peace and security," but it did not refer to Chapter VII. See Security Council resolution 392(1976), adopted 19 June 1976.

[170] International Convention on the Suppression and Punishment of the Crime of Apartheid, General Assembly resolution 3068 (XXVIII), adopted on 30 November 1973.

[171] Idem.

[172] Apartheid was especially mentioned, also as threat to the peace, in the discussions about whether States can commit crimes. See *e.g.*, "Fifth report on State responsibility by Mr. Roberto Ago," in the Yearbook of the International Law Commission 1976, vol. II (Part I), p. 26; "Draft Code of Offences against the Peace and Security of Mankind", in Yearbook of the International Law Commission 1984, vol. II(1), p. 91; Report of the Preparatory Committee on the Establishment of an International Criminal Court, vol. 1, pp. 25-27.

## 5.4 The arms race

During the Cold War the arms race was considered to be one of the most important threats to international peace and security. This led to various calls for disarmament and the prohibition of many different kinds of weapons.[173] In the Declaration on the Preparation of Societies for Life in Peace, the Assembly stated that "[a] basic instrument of the maintenance of peace is the elimination of the threat inherent in the arms race, as well as efforts towards general and complete disarmament."[174] Thus it explicitly stated that there was a link between the arms race and the value of peace and security. In 1986, the Assembly was "deeply concerned at the tense and dangerous situation in the world and the danger of continuing down the path of confrontation and the arms race towards the abyss of the nuclear self-destruction of mankind."[175] The Assembly considered this arms race to be a "consequent threat posed to the security of all States."[176]

The Security Council was paralyzed by the Cold War and could not take action to combat the arms race. Two of its permanent members were directly responsible for the threat. At the same time, the Assembly continued to be very active, and adopted a large number of resolutions on the topic, both during and after the Cold War.[177]

Many conventions calling for the elimination or reduction of various types of weapons were adopted or recommended by the Assembly, both during and after the Cold War. Most of those conventions had been prepared by the UN Conference on Disarmament.[178] Sometimes the actual drafting took place at a global conference

---

[173] See *e.g.*, Keith Krause, "Disarmament" (2007); United Nations Centre for Disarmament Affairs, *The United Nations and disarmament since 1945* (1996).

[174] Declaration on the Preparation of Societies for Life in Peace, General Assembly resolution 33/73, adopted 15 December 1978.

[175] Establishment of a comprehensive system of international peace and security, General Assembly resolution 41/92, adopted 4 December 1986.

[176] *Idem.*

[177] See *e.g.*, the Declaration on the Strengthening of International Security, General Assembly resolution 2734(XXV), adopted 16 December 1970; the Friendly Relations Declaration; and the Declaration on de Occasion of the Twenty-fifth Anniversary of the United Nations, General Assembly resolution 2627 (XXV), adopted 24 October 1970.

[178] On the conference, see Toma Galli, "The Conference on Disarmament: its Glorious History, Non-existent Present and Uncertain Future" (2010). The conventions included the Convention on the Prohibition of the Development, Production and Stockpiling of Bacteriological (Biological) and Toxin Weapons and on their Destruction, General Assembly resolution 2826 (XXVI), adopted on 16 December 1971; the Convention on the Prohibition of Military or Any Other Hostile Use of Environmental Modification Techniques, General Assembly resolution 31/72, adopted 10 December 1976; and the Convention on the Prohibition of the Development, Production, Stockpiling and Use of Chemical Weapons and on Their Destruction, General Assembly resolution 47/39, adopted 30 November 1992.

organized outside the UN framework.[179] A substantial number of those convention texts related specifically to nuclear weapons.[180]

    The General Assembly also adopted a number of non-binding declarations on disarmament, mainly in response to and during the Cold War.[181] The 1970s, 1980s, and 1990s were all "baptized" as Disarmament Decades.[182] In addition, the Assembly endorsed certain declarations made elsewhere, such as the Hague Code of Conduct against Ballistic Missile Proliferation.[183]

---

[179] On 19 December 1977, the Assembly adopted a resolution on Incendiary and other specific conventional weapons which may be the subject of prohibitions or restrictions of use for humanitarian reasons, General Assembly resolution 32/152, which was followed by General Assembly resolution 33/70, adopted 14 December 1978, in which the Assembly suggested to convene a Conference on the topic. During this conference, the Convention on Prohibitions or Restrictions on the Use of Certain Conventional Weapons which may be deemed to be Excessively Injurious or to have Indiscriminate Effects was made (the conference took place in Geneva, on 10 October 1980). Subsequently, the Assembly continued to adopt resolutions on this topic. See further the Convention on the Prohibition of the Use, Stockpiling, Production and Transfer of Anti-personnel Mines and on Their Destruction, General Assembly resolution 52/38[A], adopted 9 December 1997; and the Convention on Cluster Munitions, General Assembly resolution 63/71, adopted 2 December 2008. This convention was adopted at the Convention on Cluster Munitions, held in Dublin on 30 May 2008. In its resolution, the Assembly merely "not[ed] that the Convention [would] be opened for signature."

[180] See the Treaty on the Prohibition of the Emplacement of Nuclear Weapons and other Weapons of Mass Destruction on the Sea-Bed and the Ocean Floor and in the Subsoil Thereof, General Assembly resolution 2660 (XXV), adopted 7 December 1970; Treaty on the Non-Proliferation of Nuclear Weapons, General Assembly resolution 2373(XXII), adopted 12 June 1968; and the Comprehensive Nuclear-Test-Ban Treaty, General Assembly resolution 50/245, adopted 10 September 1996. The text can be found in an Annex to a Letter dated 22 August 1996 from Australia to the Secretary-General, UNDoc. A/50/1027. See already The Urgent Need for a Treaty to Ban Nuclear Weapons Tests under Effective International Control, General Assembly resolution 1649(XVI), adopted 8 November 1961

[181] See *e.g.*, the Declaration on the Conversion to Peaceful Needs of the Resources Released by Disarmament, General Assembly resolution 1837 (XVII), adopted 18 December 1962; Declaration on the Deepening and Consolidation of International Detente, General Assembly resolution 32/155, adopted 19 December 1977; Declaration on International Co-operation for Disarmament, General Assembly resolution 34/88, adopted 11 December 1979; Declaration on the Prevention of Nuclear Catastrophe, General Assembly resolution 36/100, adopted 9 December 1981; and the Principles that Should Govern Further Actions of States in the Field of the Freezing and Reduction of Military Budgets, annexed to Reduction of military budgets, General Assembly resolution 44/114[A], on 15 December 1989.

[182] Question of General and Complete Disarmament, General Assembly resolution 2602 (XXIV)[E], adopted 16 December 1969, proclaimed the 1970's as the First Disarmament Decade (without a disarmament declaration); Declaration of the 1980s as the Second Disarmament Decade, General Assembly resolution 35/46, adopted 3 December 1980, proclaimed the 1980s as the Second Disarmament Decade; Declaration of the 1990s as the Third Disarmament Decade, General Assembly resolution 45/62[A], adopted 4 December 1990, proclaimed the 1990s as the Third Disarmament Decade.

[183] The Code was introduced to the Assembly by the Netherlands. See Annex to Letter dated 30 January 2003 from the Netherlands to the Secretary-General, UNDoc. A/57/724. In The Hague Code of Conduct against Ballistic Missile Proliferation, General Assembly resolution 60/62 of 8 December

The Assembly adopted general resolutions on essentially all aspects of disarmament. Through its resolutions, the Assembly has encouraged a multilateral approach in the field of disarmament and non-proliferation.[184] It also adopted a series of resolutions on compliance with non-proliferation, arms limitation and disarmament agreements and commitments. [185] Furthermore, the Assembly adopted resolutions on the relationship between disarmament and development [186] and on the economic and social consequences of the armaments race and its extremely harmful effects on world peace and security. [187] Finally, the Assembly called for objective information and transparency on States' activities relating to armaments and military expenditure. [188]

Apart from the adoption of these general resolutions on disarmament, the Assembly also concerned itself with more specific issues, including some for which no convention had been drawn up. For example, the Assembly called for the adoption of an arms trade treaty for conventional arms, [189] and on control mechanisms relating to these arms at the regional and subregional levels. [190] In addition, it adopted a series of resolutions on the problems arising from the accumulation of conventional ammunition stockpiles. [191] It also adopted a series of resolutions on global efforts to curb the illicit traffic in small arms, [192] and finally, the Assembly called for a prohibition on the development and manufacture of new types of weapons of mass destruction. [193]

---

2005, the Assembly invited all States that had not yet subscribed to the Hague Code of Conduct against Ballistic Missile Proliferation to do so, and since then the item has been on its agenda.

[184] Promotion of multilateralism in the area of disarmament and non-proliferation, General Assembly resolution 57/63, adopted 22 November 2002, and subsequent resolutions (only the first such resolution will be referred to here and in the following footnotes).

[185] Compliance with arms limitation and disarmament agreements, General Assembly resolution 44/122, adopted 15 December 1989.

[186] Relationship between disarmament and development, General Assembly resolution 38/71, adopted 15 December 1983.

[187] Economic and Social Consequences of Disarmament, General Assembly resolution 1516 (XV), adopted 15 December 1960.

[188] See Transparency of military expenditures, General Assembly resolution 46/25, adopted 6 December 1991; and Objective information on military matters, including transparency of military expenditures, General Assembly resolution 49/66, adopted 15 December 1994.

[189] Towards an arms trade treaty: establishing common international standards for the import, export and transfer of conventional arms, General Assembly resolution 61/89, adopted 6 December 2006.

[190] Conventional arms control at the regional and subregional levels, General Assembly resolution 61/82, adopted 6 December 2006.

[191] Problems arising from the accumulation of conventional ammunition stockpiles in surplus, General Assembly resolution 61/72, adopted 6 December 2006.

[192] Assistance to States for curbing the illicit traffic in small arms and collecting them, section H of General and complete disarmament, General Assembly resolution 50/70, adopted 12 December 1995.

[193] Prohibition of the Development and Manufacture of New Types of Weapons of Mass Destruction and New Systems of Such Weapons, General Assembly resolution 3479 (XXX), adopted 11 December 1975.

An examination of resolutions dealing specifically with the threat of nuclear weapons reveals a series of resolutions on decreasing the operational readiness of nuclear weapons systems, [194] and on the conclusion of effective international arrangements to safeguard non-nuclear weapon States against the use or threat of use of nuclear weapons. [195] More ambitious resolutions include those on the renewed determination to totally eliminate nuclear weapons, [196] and those aimed at a world free of nuclear weapons.[197]

Reference should be made to resolutions aimed at the prevention of an arms race in outer space.[198] In 1963, the Assembly "solemnly call[ed] upon all States to refrain from placing in orbit around the earth any objects carrying nuclear weapons or any other kinds of weapons of mass destruction, installing such weapons on celestial bodies, or stationing such weapons in outer space in any other manner."[199] This obligation later ended up in the Treaty on Principles Governing the Activities of States in the Exploration and Use of Outer Space, including the Moon and Other Celestial Bodies, adopted by the Assembly in 1966.[200]

As noted above, the Security Council's contributions started only after the end of the Cold War, though there are some exceptions. As early as 1947, the Council "recognize[d] that the general regulation and reduction of armaments and

---

[194] Decreasing the operational readiness of nuclear weapons systems, General Assembly resolution 62/36, adopted 5 December 2007.

[195] Conference of Non-Nuclear-Weapons States, General Assembly resolution 2456 (XXIII), 20 December 1968; Implementation of the results of the Conference on Non-Nuclear Weapon States, General Assembly resolution 2664 (XXV), adopted 7 December 1970; and Conclusion of an international convention on the strengthening of the security of non-nuclear-weapon States against the use or threat of use of nuclear weapons, General Assembly resolution 36/94, adopted 9 December 1981. In 1986, the Assembly ceased to refer to a Convention, and instead only referred to international agreements. See Conclusion of effective international arrangements on the strengthening of the security of non-nuclear-weapon States against the use or threat of use of nuclear weapons, General Assembly resolution 41/51, adopted 3 December 1986.

[196] A path to the total elimination of nuclear weapons, General Assembly resolution 57/78, adopted 22 November 2002.

[197] Towards a nuclear-weapon-free world: the need for a new agenda, General Assembly resolution 57/59, adopted 22 November 2002 .

[198] Conclusion of a treaty on the prohibition of the stationing of weapons of any kind in outer space, General Assembly resolution 36/99, adopted 9 December 1981. The idea of a treaty was changed into a more general strategy in subsequent years: see Prevention of an arms race in outer space, General Assembly resolution 37/83, adopted 9 December 1982.

[199] Question of General and Complete Disarmament, General Assembly resolution 1884 (XVIII), adopted 17 October 1963.

[200] Treaty on Principles Governing the Activities of States in the Exploration and Use of Outer Space, Including the Moon and Other Celestial Bodies, General Assembly resolution 2222 (XXI), adopted 19 December 1966. See especially article IV. The obligation to use outer space for peaceful purposes only was also included in the Declaration of Legal Principles Governing the Activities of States in the Exploration and Uses of Outer Space, General Assembly resolution 1962 (XVIII), adopted 13 December 1963.

armed forces constitute[d] a most important measure for strengthening international peace and security," but did not take any significant measures in this respect.[201] In 1968, the Council "recognize[d] that aggression with nuclear weapons or the threat of such aggression against a non-nuclear weapon State would create a situation in which the Security Council, and above all its nuclear-weapon State permanent members, would have to act immediately."[202]

Despite some activity during the Cold War, it was the end of the Cold War that opened up an enormous window of opportunity for the Council when it came to disarmament. This was noted by many of the speakers during the summit of 1992. Rao of India, for example, said that "[t]he Cold War [was] now over: the nuclear stand-off [was] a thing of the past [and] the doctrine of nuclear deterrence [was] no longer relevant."[203] This gave the world a "historic opportunity to exercise statesmanship and move, quickly, to eliminate nuclear weapons altogether from the face of the Earth."[204]

According to the Zimbabwean representative, the focus of disarmament should not be on nuclear weapons alone. Instead, it should cover all aspects of arms:

> The route we should take in the area of disarmament is to demilitarize consistently both the domestic and the international situations. The manufacturers as well as the recipients and users of dangerous weapons should be stopped from trading in death. We should demilitarize our societies in the new world order.[205]

One of the most successful demilitarization efforts was the conclusion of the Chemical Weapons Convention. The Assembly proposed such a convention in 1992.[206] With regard to these efforts to prohibit chemical weapons, King Hassan II of Morocco said that

> The progress achieved by the United Nations in the nuclear sphere should not prevent us from redoubling our efforts to ensure the success of the Geneva negotiations on the prohibition of chemical weapons and their destruction in order to rid ourselves of a devastating weapon that constitutes a negation of civilization and noble human values.[207]

---

[201] Security Council resolution 18(1947), adopted 13 February 1947.
[202] Security Council resolution 255(1968), adopted 19 June 1968.
[203] Verbatim Records of the 3046th meeting of the Security Council, 31 January 1992, UNDoc. S/PV.3046, p. 101.
[204] *Idem.*
[205] *Idem*, p. 128.
[206] Convention on the Prohibition of the Development, Production, Stockpiling and Use of Chemical Weapons and on Their Destruction, General Assembly resolution 47/39, adopted 30 November 1992.
[207] *Idem*, p. 37.

The two former Cold War rivals did not go as far as to call for complete disarmament, or the complete abolition of nuclear weapons. Nevertheless their ambitions were impressive.[208] Yeltsin, for example, outlined his post-Cold War disarmament plan:

> The new political situation in the world makes it possible not only to advance new, original ideas but also to make even the most ambitious of them practicable. [...] Russia believes that the time has come to reduce considerably the presence of means of destruction on our planet. [...] Today there are real opportunities for implementing deep cuts in strategic offensive arms and tactical nuclear weapons; resolutely moving towards significant limitations on nuclear testing and even towards its complete cessation; making anti-ballistic-missile defences less complicated and costly and eliminating anti-satellite systems; considerably reducing conventional armaments and armed forces; ensuring practical implementation of international agreements on the prohibition of chemical and bacteriological weapons; and enhancing the reliability of barriers to the proliferation of weapons of mass destruction.[209]

President Bush of the United States also devoted a large part of his speech to disarmament.[210] So too did Li Peng of China, who believed that "[e]fforts should be stepped up to attain the complete prohibition and thorough destruction of nuclear and chemical weapons at an early date and to ban the development of space weapons," and that "[a]ll nuclear-weapon States should undertake not to be the first to use nuclear weapons and not to use or threaten to use such weapons against non-nuclear-weapon States or nuclear-free zones."[211]

Some of the smaller countries also expressed their hope that with the end of the Cold War, the Council could promote disarmament as one of its key objectives. For example, Vranitzky of Austria saw "a more active involvement in the areas of arms control, non-proliferation and disarmament" as "one of the most important future tasks of the Security Council."[212]

---

[208] In 2003, the Council adopted a Declaration on the Proliferation of Small Arms and Light Weapons and Mercenary Activities, which was particularly concerned with the situation in West Africa. Security Council resolution 1467 (2003), adopted on 18 March 2003, has the declaration annexed to it. See also Resolution 1209(1998), adopted by the Security Council on 19 November 1998, in which the Council "expresses its grave concern at the destabilizing effect of illicit arms flows, in particular of small arms, to and in Africa and at their excessive accumulation and circulation, which threaten national, regional and international security and have serious consequences for development and for the humanitarian situation in the continent."

[209] Verbatim Records of the 3046th meeting of the Security Council, 31 January 1992, UNDoc. S/PV.3046, p. 43.

[210] *Idem*, pp. 51-53.

[211] *Idem*, p. 93.

[212] *Idem*, pp.64-65.

At the end of the 1992 Summit, the Security Council adopted a Presidential Statement.[213] The following text on disarmament was added to that statement:

> The members of the Council underline the need for all Member States to fulfil their obligations in relation to arms control and disarmament; to prevent the proliferation in all its aspects of all weapons of mass destruction; to avoid excessive and destabilizing accumulations and transfers of arms; and to resolve peacefully in accordance with the Charter any problems concerning these matters threatening or disrupting the maintenance of regional and global stability.[214]

In the same statement, the Council proclaimed that "[t]he proliferation of all weapons of mass destruction constitutes a threat to international peace and security," and thus becomes a matter the Security Council can legitimately consider.[215] In 2004 the Council considered that the "proliferation of nuclear, chemical and biological weapons, as well as their means of delivery, constitute[d] a threat to international peace and security," and, acting under Chapter VII, adopted measures binding on all States.[216]

Some years later, during the third high-level summit, President Kirchner of Argentina noted that "[t]he proliferation of weapons of mass destruction and the danger of their falling into the hands of terrorists [was] one of the greatest threats to international peace and security."[217] Similarly, the Prime Minister of Denmark, Rasmussen, believed that "[t]he threat of terrorists or irresponsible dictators armed with weapons of mass destruction [was] a shared nightmare for all mankind," and that the "Council ha[d] the obligation to ensure that the nightmare never materialize[d]."[218]

What conclusion can be drawn from all these Assembly resolutions, conventions, and statements made in the Security Council? What does this mean for the value of peace and security? What is of most concern here is whether the existence of weapons can be considered an "evil" which threatens the value of peace. Does the existence of various weapons itself pose a threat to the peace? If that is the case, it must be concluded that, as the United Nations submits, a world in peace and security would be a weapon-free world. It is not possible to reach such a

---

[213] This has also been issued separately, as Note by the President of the Security Council, UNDoc. S/23500, distributed on 31 January 1992.

[214] Verbatim Records of the 3046th meeting of the Security Council, 31 January 1992, UNDoc. S/PV.3046, p. 145.

[215] *Idem.* This view was reiterated in the Statement by the President of the Security Council, UNDoc. S/PRST/1998/12. distributed 12 May 1998.

[216] Resolution 1540 (2004), adopted by the Security Council on 28 April 2004. See also Resolution 1673 (2006), adopted by the Security Council on 27 April 2006.

[217] Verbatim Records of the 5261st meeting of the Security Council, 14 September 2005, UNDoc. S/PV.5261, p. 7.

[218] *Idem*, p. 15.

general and sweeping conclusion on the basis of the many conventions, declarations, resolutions and statements referred to. Although the use and possession of various weapons has been restricted, and an increasing number of such restrictions have been imposed over the years, it is difficult to see why this process would ultimately lead to the complete prohibition of all weapons. The UN's efforts in maintaining peace and security do not require a weapon-free world.

## 5.5 Hijackers, hostage takers, mercenaries and terrorists

The General Assembly and the Security Council of the United Nations have regarded a number of activities of particular groups of individuals as threats to peace and security.

For example, in 1970, the Security Council was "gravely concerned at the threat to innocent civilian lives from the hijacking of aircraft" by the Popular Front for the Liberation of Palestine.[219] The Council "appeal[ed] to all parties concerned for the immediate release of all passengers and crews." To prevent such hijacking in the future, the Council "call[ed] on States to take all possible legal steps to prevent further hijackings or any other interference with international civil air travel."[220] One month later, States responded by signing the Convention for the Suppression of Unlawful Seizure of Aircraft.[221]

In 1979, the General Assembly adopted the text of an International Convention against the Taking of Hostages.[222] The taking of hostages was considered to be "an offence of grave concern to the international community," and a "manifestation[…] of international terrorism."[223] A hostage taker was defined as "any person who seizes or detains and threatens to kill, to injure or to continue to detain another person […] in order to compel a third party, namely, a State, an international intergovernmental organization, a natural or juridical person, or a group of persons, to do or abstain from doing any act as an explicit or implicit condition for the release of the hostage."[224] All States pledged to make this a punishable offence within their jurisdiction.

Ten years later in 1989, the General Assembly adopted the text of an International Convention against the Recruitment, Use, Financing and Training of

---

[219] Security Council resolution 286, adopted 9 September 1970.

[220] *Idem.*

[221] The Convention for the Suppression of Unlawful Seizure of Aircraft was signed in the Hague, Netherlands, on 16 December 1970.

[222] International Convention against the Taking of Hostages, annexed to General Assembly resolution 34/146, adopted 17 December 1979.

[223] Idem.

[224] *Idem*, Article 1.

Mercenaries.[225] A mercenary was defined as "any person who [was] motivated to take part in the hostilities essentially by the desire for private gain."[226] In 1986 the Assembly had already "recogniz[ed] that mercenarism [was] a threat to international peace and security." [227] The topic has been on the Assembly's agenda ever since. Mercenaries are frequently employed, especially in Africa. In 2008, the Assembly expressed its "alarm[…] and concern[…] at the danger that the activities of mercenaries constitute to peace and security in developing countries, in particular in Africa and in small States."[228]

The most pertinent of this category of threats is certainly that caused by terrorists.[229] It is also the threat that the United Nations has paid most attention to. Although it had been on the UN's agenda before, it was in the 1990s that the United Nations first came up with a comprehensive response to terrorism. In 1995, the General Assembly adopted a Declaration on Measures to Eliminate International Terrorism.[230] In that declaration, the General Assembly said it was

> Deeply disturbed by the world-wide persistence of acts of international terrorism in all its forms and manifestations, including those in which States are directly or indirectly involved, which endanger or take innocent lives, have a deleterious effect on international relations and may jeopardize the security of States.[231]

Using Security Council language, the Assembly also expressed its conviction that "the suppression of acts of international terrorism [was] an essential element for the maintenance of international peace and security." [232] In addition, the Assembly stated that "criminal acts intended or calculated to provoke a state of terror in the general public, a group of persons or particular persons for political purposes [were] in any circumstance unjustifiable, whatever the considerations of a political, philosophical, ideological, racial, ethnic, religious or any other nature that may be

---

[225] International Convention against the Recruitment, Use, Financing and Training of Mercenaries, annexed to General Assembly resolution 44/34, adopted 4 December 1989. See also Marie-France Major, "Mercenaries and international law" (1992).

[226] *Idem*, Article 1. As Article 1 makes clear, the hostilities referred to could be qualified as a war between two nations, but also as an armed conflict between a secessionist movement and a local government.

[227] Use of mercenaries as a means of violating human rights and to impede the exercise of the right of peoples to self-determination, General Assembly resolution 41/102, adopted 4 December 1986.

[228] General Assembly resolution 63/164, adopted 18 December 2008.

[229] See also Jane Boulden & Thomas G. Weiss, *Terrorism and the UN: before and after September 11* (2004).

[230] Measures to eliminate international terrorism, General Assembly resolution 49/60, adopted 9 December 1994.

[231] Declaration on Measures to Eliminate International Terrorism, annexed to General Assembly resolution 49/60, adopted 9 December 1994.

[232] Idem.

invoked to justify them." [233] Although not presented as such, this is a good definition of acts of terrorism. It was reiterated two years later, in a declaration calling for the drafting of a variety of conventions on different legal aspects of terrorism. [234] The texts of these conventions were adopted by the General Assembly in the years that followed. In 1997, the Assembly adopted the International Convention for the Suppression of Terrorist Bombings. [235] In 1999, it adopted the text of an International Convention for the Suppression of the Financing of Terrorism. [236]

One day after the terrorist attacks in New York, the Security Council finally followed the Assembly's suggestion, and labelled all acts of terrorism as a threat to international peace and security. [237] Two weeks later, it invoked its powers under Chapter VII to essentially oblige all States to accept as binding the obligations under the above-mentioned terrorism conventions, which most States had not yet ratified. [238] The Council also adopted a Declaration on the Global Effort to Combat Terrorism. [239] In that declaration the Council "declare[d] that acts of international terrorism constitute[d] one of the most serious threats to international peace and security in the twenty-first century." [240] It "reaffirm[ed] its unequivocal condemnation of all acts, methods and practices of terrorism as criminal and unjustifiable, regardless of their motivation, in all their forms and manifestations, wherever and by whomever committed." In January 2003, the Council adopted yet another declaration on terrorism. [241] In this the Council reaffirmed that "terrorism in all its forms and manifestations constitutes one of the most serious threats to peace and security," and that "any acts of terrorism are criminal and unjustifiable, regardless of their motivation, whenever and by whomsoever committed and are to be unequivocally condemned, especially when they indiscriminately target or injure

---

[233] Idem.

[234] See the Declaration to Supplement the 1994 Declaration on Measures to Eliminate International Terrorism, annexed to General Assembly resolution 51/210, adopted 17 December 1996.

[235] International Convention for the Suppression of Terrorist Bombings, General Assembly resolution 52/164, adopted 15 December 1997.

[236] International Convention for the Suppression of the Financing of Terrorism, General Assembly resolution 54/109, adopted 9 December 1999.

[237] See Security Council resolution 1368, adopted on 12 September 2001. In earlier resolutions, the Council did come close. For example, in 1999, it noted that "the suppression of acts of international terrorism [was] an essential contribution to the maintenance of international peace and security." See Security Council resolution 1269, adopted 19 October 1999, and Security Council resolution 1267, adopted 15 October 1999.

[238] Security Council resolution 1373, adopted on 28 September 2001. The Council also established a Counter-Terrorism Commitee.

[239] Declaration on the global effort to combat terrorism, Security Council resolution 1377, adopted on 12 November 2001.

[240] *Idem.*

[241] Declaration on the issue of combating terrorism, annexed to Security Council resolution 1456, adopted 20 January 2003.

civilians."[242] In line with this tough approach to terrorism, the Security Council once again determined, in its response to the terrorist bombing that killed the former Lebanese Prime Minister Hariri, "that [a] terrorist act and its implications constitute a threat to international peace and security."[243]

Terrorism was also one of the two main themes during the third high-level summit of the Security Council held in 2005.[244] The UN Secretary-General Annan addressed the Security Council at that summit. In his view, "[t]errorism constitute[d] a direct attack on the values for which the United Nations stands."[245] All Member States agreed with the Secretary-General that the Council should take the lead in combating terrorism. According to Putin, the President of the Russian Federation, the Council should become the "headquarters for the international antiterrorist front."[246] The Secretary-General set out a counter-terrorism strategy which consisted of five pillars:[247]

First, the Security Council and all its members should "dissuade disaffected groups from choosing terrorism as a tactic," essentially by clearly prohibiting all forms of terrorism;

Secondly, the Council should "deny terrorists the means – above all, weapons of mass destruction – to carry out their attacks;"

Thirdly, the Council should make sure that "all States [...] know that if they provide support for terrorists in any form, this Council will not hesitate to take coercive measures against them;"

Fourthly, the Council should "develop State capacity to prevent terrorism,"
Fifthly and finally, the Council should "defend human rights."[248]

---

[242] *Idem.*

[243] Security Council resolution 1757, adopted 30 May 2007.

[244] See the Verbatim Records of the 5261st meeting of the Security Council, 14 September 2005, UNDoc. S/PV.5261. The second topic of that meeting was conflict prevention, particularly in Africa.

[245] Verbatim Records of the 5261st meeting of the Security Council, 14 September 2005, UNDoc. S/PV.5261, p. 3.

[246] *Idem*, p. 4.

[247] These five pillars had guided the Secretary-General's thinking for quite some time. See also *A more secure world: our shared responsibility*, Report of the High-level Panel on Threats, Challenges and Change, distributed 2 December 2004, UNDoc. A/59/565, para. 148 (*"A more secure world"*) ; *In larger freedom: towards development, security and human rights for all*, Report of the Secretary-General, distributed 21 March 2005, UNDoc. A/59/2005, para. 88 (*"In larger freedom"*); and especially Uniting against terrorism: recommendations for a global counter-terrorism strategy, report of the Secretary-General, distributed 27 April 2006, UNDoc. A/60/825.

[248] Verbatim Records of the 5261st meeting of the Security Council, 14 September 2005, UNDoc. S/PV.5261, p. 3.

The President of the People's Republic of China, Hu Jintao, believed there was something missing in this list, namely the Council's obligation to tackle the root causes of terrorism. He believed that it was essential "to earnestly address problems such as poverty, ignorance and social injustice in order to eliminate the breeding grounds for terrorism."[249] Similarly, De Villepin, the French Prime Minister at that time, said that "resolute action with respect to everything that fuels terrorism" was necessary, "including inequality, on-going violence, injustice, conflict and cultural misunderstanding."[250] The French considered that, "[f]orce alone [would] never defeat terrorism, for it does not address people's frustrations or go to the roots of evil." [251]

This is a truism. So why not address the root causes of terrorism in the Counter-terrorism Strategy? Blair of the United Kingdom gave a reason why this aspect should not be addressed:

> [Terrorism] will not be defeated until we [*i.e.* the Members States of the Security Council] unite not just in condemning the acts of terrorism, which we all do, but in fighting the poisonous propaganda that the root cause of this terrorism somehow lies with us around this table and not with them. [The terrorists] want us to believe that, somehow, it is our fault and that their extremism is somehow our responsibility. They play on our divisions; they exploit our hesitations. This is our weakness, and they know it. We must unite against this ghastly game with our conscience. There are real injustices in our world: poverty, which it is our duty to eradicate; conflicts […], which it is our duty to help resolve; and nation-building, […] which it is our responsibility to help deliver. But none of this has caused this terrorism. The root cause [of terrorism] is a doctrine of fanaticism, and we must unite to uproot it by cooperating on security, […] by taking action against those who incite, preach or teach this extremism, wherever they are in whichever country; and also by eliminating our own ambivalence by fighting not just the methods of this terrorism, but also the terrorists' motivation, twisted reasoning and wretched excuses for terror.[252]

At the end of this third high-level meeting, unusually strong words were used in a Security Council resolution on terrorism.[253] The Council "condemn[ed] in the strongest terms all acts of terrorism irrespective of their motivation, whenever and by whomsoever committed, as one of the most serious threats to peace and

---

[249] *Idem*, p. 8.

[250] *Idem*, p. 14.

[251] *Idem*.

[252] *Idem*, p. 10.

[253] Security Council resolution 1624, adopted 14 September 2005. In this resolution the Council called upon all States, *inter alia*, to "prohibit by law incitement to commit a terrorist act or acts," "prevent such conduct," and "deny safe haven to any persons with respect to whom there is credible and relevant information giving serious reasons for considering that they have been guilty of such conduct."

security." [254] It also condemned "in the strongest terms the incitement of terrorist acts and repudiating attempts at the justification or glorification (*apologie*) of terrorist acts that may incite further terrorist acts." This indicates that Blair's approach was followed here.

It was now the Assembly's turn to come up with its own strategy to combat terrorism. In 2006, the Assembly adopted the comprehensive United Nations Global Counter-Terrorism Strategy. [255] First, the Assembly "[r]eiterated its strong condemnation of terrorism in all its forms and manifestations, committed by whomever, wherever and for whatever purposes, as it constitute[d] one of the most serious threats to international peace and security." [256] The Assembly also reaffirmed that "terrorism cannot and should not be associated with any religion, nationality, civilization or ethnic group." This was to counterbalance the fact that many people associated terrorism with Islam. In addition, the Assembly included a paragraph to appease those States that believed the United Nations should not ignore the root causes grounds of terrorism.[257] In general, the Assembly's strategy consisted mainly in a resolve of all States to "consider becoming parties […] to the existing international conventions and protocols against terrorism," and to cooperate with the Council and implement its resolutions.[258] The actual strategy was based on a revised version of the strategy of the Secretary-General. [259] It addressed the "conditions conducive to the spread of terrorism," for example, by promoting a culture of peace, by eradicating poverty and by promoting sustained economic growth, sustainable development and global prosperity for all. At the same time, the Assembly emphasized that nothing could "excuse or justify acts of terrorism." The Strategy also included a long list of preventive measures; means to

---

[254] *Idem.*

[255] The United Nations Global Counter-Terrorism Strategy, General Assembly resolution 60/288, adopted 8 September 2006.

[256] *Idem.* See also para. 81 of the 2005 World Summit Outcome, resolution adopted by the General Assembly on 16 September 2005, UNDoc, 60/1 ("2005 World Summit Outcome").

[257] The Assembly thus "affirm[ed] Member States" determination to continue to do all they can to resolve conflict, end foreign occupation, confront oppression, eradicate poverty, promote sustained economic growth, sustainable development, global prosperity, good governance, human rights for all and rule of law, improve intercultural understanding and ensure respect for all religions, religious values, beliefs or cultures." The United Nations Global Counter-Terrorism Strategy, General Assembly resolution 60/288, adopted 8 September 2006.

[258] By that time, the General Assembly had proposed yet another treaty text on terrorism to the UN Member States. See International Convention for the Suppression of Acts of Nuclear Terrorism, annexed to General Assembly resolution 59/290, adopted 13 April 2005. In that convention text, the Assembly "not[ed] that acts of nuclear terrorism may result in the gravest consequences and may pose a threat to international peace and security [but that] existing multilateral legal provisions [did] not adequately address those attacks."

[259] It was based on Uniting against terrorism: recommendations for a global counter-terrorism strategy, report of the Secretary-General, distributed 27 April 2006, UNDoc. A/60/825.

strengthen all States' efforts to fight terrorism; and it included a list of obligations for all States to respect human rights whilst fighting terrorism.[260]

It can be concluded from the above-mentioned conventions, declarations and resolutions that the United Nations has recognized that non-State actors can pose a threat to international peace and security. When it comes to terrorists and mercenaries, the United Nations has explicitly labelled their actions as threats to international peace and security. A world with active terrorists and mercenaries is not a peaceful world.

## 5.6 Conclusion

The approach of the General Assembly, when it comes to the value of peace and security, has been to recognize various threats to this value, define them as accurately as possible, and ensure universal agreement on measures to contain them. This has been the approach with regard to domestic conflict, *apartheid*, the arms race, and threats posed by hijackers, hostage takers, mercenaries and terrorists. By clearly defining these threats, the Assembly has indirectly defined the value of peace and security. It can now be concluded that a peaceful world is not just a world in which States do not go to war with each other, but also requires the absence of domestic conflicts, the absence of certain weapons, and the absence of individuals and groups of individuals who pose a threat to international peace.

## 6  THE ROOT CAUSES OF THREATS TO INTERNATIONAL PEACE AND SECURITY

## 6.1 Introduction

It is often suggested that the Security Council has considerably broadened its interpretation of threats to peace and security in recent times. Some "new" threats have already been discussed, such as domestic conflicts and terrorist threats. These do not fit easily into the framework of the UN Charter. Other, more "imaginative" threats have also been mentioned in the literature. A closer look at the Council's resolutions shows that it is rather conservative. Some of the more imaginative threats are seen by the Council as root causes of conflict, not as threats to the peace. The Assembly is more flexible, but the difference between the two principal organs of the United Nations is not all that great. This difference can be explained by the fact that a qualification by the Council of a particular situation as a threat to the

---

[260] The Secretary-General himself noticed that his five-pillar edifice was replaced by a four pillar version in para. 2 of United Nations Global Counter-Terrorism Strategy: activities of the United Nations system in implementing the Strategy, Report of the Secretary-General, distributed 7 July 2008, UNDoc. A/62/898.

peace has legal consequences, while a similar qualification by the Assembly does not. After all, as soon as the Security Council determines that a certain situation is a threat to the peace, it can impose sanctions and authorize the use of armed force.[261] This section examines some of the root causes of conflict which have been addressed by the General Assembly and the Security Council. None of these root causes has been qualified as a threat to the value of peace and security.

## 6.2 Diseases of mass destruction

The typhus epidemic was one of the main preoccupations of the Council of the League of Nations.[262] The League Council considered that "the matter [was] one of such magnitude and [bore] on the welfare of so many countries that it seem[ed] eminently one with which the League of Nations should deal."[263] The epidemic soon spread across the whole of Central and Eastern Europe, including Russia.[264] The arguments that supported the pledge for assistance made by the Council to all members of the Assembly of the League combined references to self-interest, common interest and moral values.[265] In the end, it was decided to organize a Global Health Conference to find worldwide support to fight the disease. The experts assembled at this conference reiterated that both self-interest, common interest, and moral values required a joint effort to combat typhus.[266] Unfortunately, the League Council could not contribute all that much to combatting the epidemic. It could only ask States to provide goods, such as food, clothes and medicine. These goods were distributed in Poland and elsewhere by the League of Red Cross Societies, not the League of Nations.[267]

The disease of mass destruction facing the Security Council of the United Nations is a different disease. It is the human immunodeficiency virus which causes the immunodeficiency syndrome (HIV/AIDS).[268] Even this disease was never considered as a threat to peace and security. Instead, the Security Council did

---

[261] This follows from Article 39 UN Charter and the remainder of Chapter VII, UN Charter.

[262] For an overview of the events, see League of Nations, *Report of the Endemic Commission of the League of Nations* (1921).

[263] League of Nations Official Journal, volume 1, issue 2 (March 1920), p. 67. Resolution adopted 13 March 1920.

[264] League of Nations Official Journal, volume 1, issue 6 (September 1920), p. 367.

[265] Letter from Balfour containing a further appeal from the Council to the Members of the League, in the League of Nations Official Journal, volume 1, issue 6 (September 1920), p. 367.

[266] Letter by Viscount Astor, Chairman of the Conference, League of Nations Official Journal, volume 1, issue 3 (April-May 1920), p. 91.

[267] League of Nations Official Journal, volume 1, issue 4 (June 1920), p. 122.

[268] See also Kenneth Marvin Manusama, *The United Nations Security Council in the post-cold war era: applying the principle of legality* (2006), p. 33.

"stress[…] that the HIV/AIDS pandemic, if unchecked, may pose a risk to stability and security."[269] Stability and security is not the same as peace and security.

At about the same time, the General Assembly adopted a Declaration of Commitment on HIV/AIDS. In that declaration the Assembly said that it was

> Deeply concerned that the global HIV/AIDS epidemic, through its devastating scale and impact, constitutes a global emergency and one of the most formidable challenges to human life and dignity, as well as to the effective enjoyment of human rights, which undermines social and economic development throughout the world and affects all levels of society – national, community, family and individual.[270]

The Assembly was particularly concerned about the situation in sub-Saharan Africa, "where HIV/AIDS [was] considered a state of emergency which threaten[ed] development, social cohesion, political stability, food security and life expectancy and impose[d] a devastating economic burden, and that the dramatic situation on the continent need[ed] urgent and exceptional national, regional and international action." [271] To tackle this threat, the General Assembly came up with a comprehensive plan which focused on prevention.[272]

Even though the gravity of the issue was recognized, the Assembly and the Security Council did not qualify the global HIV/AIDS epidemic as a threat to international peace and security.[273]

## 6.3 Poverty and underdevelopment

The link between poverty and peace is often emphasized. Vranitzky of Austria said in the Council that "[o]ur search for peace cannot be separated from the need to

---

[269] Security Council resolution 1308, distributed 17 July 2000. Five years later, the Security Council debated the issue of HIV/AIDS awareness among peacekeeping personnel. See the Statement by the President of the Security Council, distributed 18 July 2005, UNDoc. S/PRST/2005/33, and the Verbatim Records of the 5228t[th] meeting of the Security Council, 18 July 2005, UNDoc. S/PV.5228, pp. 2-23.

[270] Declaration of Commitment on HIV/AIDS, resolution adopted by the General Assembly on 27 June 2001, UNDoc. S-26/2.

[271] *Idem.*

[272] Nowhere in this comprehensive document was there any mention of the Security Council, or of the idea that it might be considered, by the Security Council, as a threat to the peace in the sense of Article 39 UN Charter.

[273] In the Political Declaration on HIV/AIDS: Intensifying our Efforts to Eliminate HIV/AIDS, General Assembly resolution 65/277, adopted 10 June 2011, the disease was described as a "global emergency, pos[ing] one of the most formidable challenges to the development, progress and stability of our respective societies and the world at large" (para. 4). But the words " peace" and " security" were not at all used in the lengthy declaration. In Security Council resolution 1983 (2011), adopted 7 June 2011, the Council "recognize[ed] that the spread of HIV can have a uniquely devastating impact on all sectors and levels of society," but that was as far as it went.

improve economic and social conditions everywhere in the world."[274] Rao of India remarked that "[l]asting peace and security necessarily require comparable levels of human happiness across the globe," and that it was therefore "impossible to think of a United Nations functioning usefully or harmoniously while humankind continues to be riddled with ever-increasing disparities and while the world's natural resources [were] getting fast depleted by thoughtless acts of overexploitation and environmental degradation."[275] However, the fact that the two are related does not mean that poverty should be regarded as an immediate threat to the peace.

Some States did suggest that poverty should be seen as a threat to the peace. In the words of President Boria of Ecuador:

> We must be clear about the idea that behind poverty there lurk serious threats to the peace because – as they had not in times gone by – the peoples of today have passed value judgments on poverty. People used to view poverty as a household object and with the familiarity with which one views a household object, but they do not do so today. The conviction that poverty can be avoided leads to rebellion, and thus a dangerous and explosive political equation has now arisen: poverty plus a value judgment on it plus rebellion equal the breaking of the peace.[276]

King Hassan II of Morocco noted that "[w]e must not forget that underdevelopment has been and remains the greatest threat to world peace and security and that at the present time it represents the greatest challenge the international community must meet."[277] Despite labelling poverty and underdevelopment as a potential threat to the peace, none of these speakers had any suggestions about what the Council should do to tackle this "new" threat, on the basis of the mandate in Chapter VII.

In the Presidential Statement adopted at the 1992 High-level summit, the Council "recognize[d] that peace and prosperity are indivisible and that lasting peace and stability require effective international cooperation for the eradication of poverty and the promotion of a better life for all in larger freedom."[278] This statement does not suggest that poverty is considered to be a threat to the peace, let alone something the Council can respond to with the use of its powers under Chapter VII of the UN Charter.

The same issue arose during the second high-level meeting of the Security Council. There the Jamaican President, Patterson, stated that "[p]overty and social injustice constitute[d] the greatest threat to global peace and international

---

[274] Verbatim Records of the 3046th meeting of the Security Council, 31 January 1992, UNDoc. S/PV.3046, p. 67.
[275] *Idem*, pp. 96-97.
[276] *Idem*, p. 31.
[277] *Idem*, p. 37.
[278] *Idem*, p. 147.

security."[279] At the end of this debate on the role of the Council in tackling the root causes of conflict the Security Council adopted a Declaration on Ensuring an Effective Role for the Security Council in the Maintenance of International Peace and Security, particularly in Africa.[280] In that declaration, the Council "[p]ledge[d] to enhance the effectiveness of the United Nations in addressing conflict at all stages from prevention to settlement to post-conflict peace-building," and "[s]trongly encourage[d] the development within the United Nations system and more widely of comprehensive and integrated strategies to address the root causes of conflicts, including their economic and social dimensions."[281] What the Council did *not* do was to see itself as the focal point of the United Nations when it comes to tackling the root causes of conflict. It also refrained from labelling poverty as a threat to peace and security.

Some States, particularly Latin American States, persisted. At the third high-level meeting, President da Silva of Brazil remarked that "there [would] be no peace or security in the world as long as a billion people are oppressed by hunger." He explained as follows:

> I insist that that evil [*i.e.* hunger] can be considered the most devastating of all weapons of mass destruction. Hunger and poverty affect people's capacity to work, as well as their health, their dignity and their hopes; they also break down families, tear apart societies and weaken economies. Hunger and poverty fuel a vicious circle of frustration and humiliation that sets the stage for violence, crises and conflicts of all sorts.[282]

Poverty is a great evil. It affects not only peace and security, but the realization of all other values as well. The Assembly and the Council are therefore correct to label poverty as a root cause of conflict, rather than as an immediate threat to peace and security.

---

[279] Verbatim Records of the 4194th meeting of the Security Council, 7 September 2000, UNDoc. S/PV.4194, p. 16.

[280] Declaration on ensuring an effective role for the Security Council in the maintenance of international peace and security, particularly in Africa, declaration attached to Security Council resolution 1318 (2000), adopted on 7 September 2000.

[281] Idem.

[282] Verbatim Records of the 5261st meeting of the Security Council, 14 September 2005, UNDoc. S/PV.5261, p. 13.

## 6.4 Climate change

Does climate change constitute a threat to international peace and security? The possibility was already suggested in 1989.[283] Christopher Penny believed that the Council had begun to address "emerging non-traditional security challenges" in the 1990's, and that it would be part of its "evolving institutional practice" if the Council were to take measures, invoking Chapter VII of the UN Charter, to tackle the threat posed by climate change.[284] Knight agreed, especially when climate change could be linked to a particular State policy, such as a policy of deforestation or massive pollution.[285] In such cases, the responsible State or non-State actor could be identified, and the Council could impose legally binding sanctions, invoking Article 41 UN Charter.[286] Authorizing the use of force was not an option, said Knight.[287]

In the 1992 statement on the responsibility of the Security Council in the maintenance of international peace and security, the Council already noted that "the non-military sources of instability in the economic, social, humanitarian *and ecological fields* ha[d] become threats to peace and security." [288] And in 2007, at the initiative of the United Kingdom, the Security Council held its first-ever debate on the impact of climate change on peace and security.[289] However, the General Assembly and Security Council have not determined until now that climate change constitutes a threat to international peace and security. The Assembly recently "recognize[d] that climate change poses serious risks and challenges to all countries." [290] Around the same time, the Security Council debated the relationship between climate change and international peace and security. At the end of the debate, the President of the Council made a statement, in which the Council "expresse[d] its concern that possible adverse effects of climate change may, in the long run, aggravate certain existing threats to international peace and security," and that

---

[283] See Nico Schrijver, "International Organization for Environmental Security" (1989).

[284] Christopher K. Penny, *Climate change and the Security Council: a preliminary framework for implementing remedial measures through Chapter VII of the UN Charte* (2007), p. 7.

[285] Alexandra Knight, "Global Environmental Threats: can the Security Council protect our Earth?" (2005).

[286] *Idem*, pp. 1575-1577, and p. 1585.

[287] *Idem*, pp. 1563-1564.

[288] Emphasis added. Presidential Statement, adopted at the end of the meeting. See Verbatim Records of the 3046th meeting of the Security Council, pp. 141-142.

[289] Letter dated 5 April 2007 from the United Kingdom, 5 April 2007, UNDoc. S/2007/186. For the debate, see Verbatim Records of the 5663rd meeting of the Security Council, 17 April 2007, UNDoc. S/PV.5663.

[290] Protection of global climate for present and future generations of humankind, General Assembly resolution 65/159, adopted 20 December 2010.

In matters relating to the maintenance of international peace and security under its consideration, conflict analysis and contextual information on, *inter alia*, possible security implications of climate change [was] important, when such issues [were] drivers of conflict, represent[ed] a challenge to the implementation of Council mandates or endanger[ed] the process of consolidation of peace.[291]

For some States, this careful statement was clearly a disappointment. The President of Nauru, representing the Pacific small island developing States, had come especially to New York to address the Council. He explained that rising sea levels actually threatened the very existence of Nauru. He suggested that the Council "formally recogniz[ed] that climate change is a threat to international peace and security," or at the very least that it constituted one of the "root causes of conflict," and that the Council should deal with the "security implications" of climate change effectively.[292]

## 6.5 Conclusion

It is difficult to accept that in theory a world with diseases of mass destruction and mass poverty can nonetheless be qualified as a peaceful world. This conclusion appears to trivialize the impact of diseases and poverty on people's lives. On the other hand, it is important to distinguish issues that directly threaten international peace from other, equally urgent, global challenges. This results in a more specific and therefore more useful definition of peace and security.

When addressing the Security Council in 2000, the former US President Bill Clinton remarked that AIDS, malaria, tuberculosis, poverty and climate change were all issues the Security Council should concern itself with. In response to potential critics of this new approach,[293] he remarked:

> Now let me just say in closing that some people will listen to this discussion [about these new threats to the peace] and say, "Well, peacekeeping has something to do with security, but these other issues do not have anything to do with security and do not belong in the Security Council." […] I just have to say that I respectfully disagree. These issues will increasingly be considered by the Security Council. Until we confront the iron link between deprivation, disease and war, we will never be able to create the peace that the founders of the United Nations dreamed of. […] I hope

---

[291] Statement by the President of the Security Council, 20 July 2011, UNDoc. S/PRST/2011/15.
[292] Verbatim records of the 6587th meeting of the Security Council, 20 July 2011, UNDoc. S/PV.6587, pp. 22-24.
[293] President Bush, his predecessor, had a more traditional approach. See *e.g.*, Verbatim Records of the 3046th meeting of the Security Council, 31 January 1992, UNDoc. S/PV.3046, p. 50.

that the Security Council increasingly will have a twenty-first century vision of security that we can all embrace and pursue.[294]

There was a great deal of support for this comprehensive approach. Supporters included France, Namibia, Ukraine, Bangladesh and Mali.[295] Similarly, the Prime Minister of the United Kingdom, Blair believed that the Council

> Cannot deal with these problems of security and conflict without dealing with the causes of conflict too. Whether it is poverty, debt, aid and development, infectious diseases or Governments and the rule of law, we need a far broader concept of how we deal with these security issues for today's world. We cannot isolate a conflict from its root causes.[296]

It is striking that Tony Blair emphasized the importance of tackling the root causes of conflict here, whilst he criticized the idea that terrorism had to be fought by tackling its root causes in his address to the Council five years later.[297] In any case, the problem is that the Security Council was never set up to deal with these root causes. It does not even have the competence to deal with them. The fight against poverty and the promotion of development are more suitable tasks for the UN system as a whole, supervised by the General Assembly.

Not everything is by definition a threat to peace and security. The term "international peace and security," as used in the Security Council's mandate, has a technical meaning. It defines the scope of activity of the Security Council. Therefore it is confusing that in its Presidential Statement adopted at the very end of the 1992 meeting, the Council stated that "[t]he non-military sources of instability in the economic, social, humanitarian and ecological fields have become threats to peace and security," but that it did not believe the Security Council should deal directly with such threats. Instead, the Statement said that "[t]he United Nations membership as a whole, working through the appropriate bodies, need[ed] to give the highest priority to the solution of these matters."[298] The General Assembly can play a crucial role here. However, even for the Assembly it is important to make a meaningful distinction between promoting international peace and security, and promoting social progress and development, or universal respect for human rights.

An overstretched interpretation of the value of peace and security only leads to confusion. Diseases of mass destruction, poverty and underdevelopment,

---

[294] Verbatim Records of the 4194th meeting of the Security Council, 7 September 2000, UNDoc. S/PV.4194, p. 5.
[295] *Idem*, pp. 8, 10, 13, 14, 21.
[296] *Idem*, p. 18.
[297] See section 5.5 of Chapter IV, above.
[298] Verbatim Records of the 3046th meeting of the Security Council, 31 January 1992, UNDoc. S/PV.3046, p. 143.

and climate change can be seen as "root causes" of armed conflicts rather than as threats to peace and security. This was neatly explained by the representative of Cape Verde:

> The Council's role will be facilitated when, and only when, the root causes of instability and conflicts are properly addressed. Therefore, if we, Members of the United Nations, are to succeed in creating a safer and more stable world, we should be prepared to couple the efforts of the Security Council with those of the United Nations system and the international community in general to help find an urgent and satisfactory answer to poverty, underdevelopment and social problems, all of them natural ferments that brew frustration and violence and spawn constant instability in world affairs.[299]

This is the most helpful approach.[300] A peaceful world can then be defined in narrow terms, namely as a world without inter-State wars, without domestic conflict, without the arms race and various weapons of mass destruction, and without mercenaries and terrorists.[301] But a peaceful world is not the same as an ideal world. There are other global values that also need to be achieved. An ideal world is a peaceful world, *and* a world without poverty, climate change, disease and underdevelopment. It is a world in which universal respect for the dignity of all individuals is guaranteed, as well as the right of all peoples to freely determine their own future.

## 7 THE HUMAN RIGHT TO PEACE AND SECURITY

### 7.1 Introduction

At one point or another, the UN proposed a human rights approach to all the global values dealt with in this study. The consequences of this approach in terms of concepts are examined in separate sections in each chapter on a particular value. This section analyzes the human rights approach to the value of peace and

---

[299] *Idem*, pp. 82-85.

[300] There is evidence of such a view also in some General Assembly resolutions. See *e.g.*, Articles 10 and 11, Declaration on de Occasion of the Twenty-fifth Anniversary of the United Nations, General Assembly resolution 2627 (XXV), adopted 24 October 1970.

[301] Apartheid is already something that might better be characterized as a root cause of conflict, rather than a threat to the peace itself. The Council and the Assembly appear to disagree when it comes to the appropriate categorization of apartheid in this distinction between threats and root causes.

security.[302] The following sections are devoted to a discussion of the "right to peace" and the concept of "human security."

## 7.2 The right to peace

According to the Declaration on the Preparation of Societies for Life in Peace, "[e]very nation and every human being [had] the inherent right to life in peace."[303] Peace was presented both as a right of States, and as a human right. The right to peace as a human right was affirmed in a number of subsequent resolutions.[304] States had the corresponding obligation to secure a life of peace for all their citizens. The Declaration also referred to peace as "mankind's paramount value, held in the highest esteem by all principal political, social and religious movements."[305] According to the Assembly, peace was a global value, and all States had a direct duty to their citizens to achieve this.

A few years later, the General Assembly also presented peace as a peoples' right. The Assembly did so in its Declaration on the Right of Peoples to Peace.[306] It proclaimed that "the peoples of our planet have a sacred right to peace," and that the "preservation of the right of peoples to peace and the promotion of its implementation constitute a fundamental obligation of each State."[307] In more concrete terms, this required that "the policies of States be directed towards the

---

[302] For the other values, see section 6 of Chapter V (social progress and development) and section 6 of Chapter VII (self-determination of peoples). The global value of human dignity (chapter VI) is all about human rights.

[303] Declaration on the Preparation of Societies for Life in Peace, General Assembly resolution 33/73, adopted 15 December 1978.

[304] In a subsequent resolution, the General Assembly reaffirmed that peace was an "inalienable right of every human being." See Right of peoples to peace, General Assembly resolution 40/11, adopted 11 November 1985. This same idea, *i.e.* that the right to a life in peace is a human right, was reiterated in a follow-up resolution of 1987. See the Implementation of the Declaration on the Preparation of Societies for Life in Peace, General Assembly resolution 42/91, adopted 7 December 1987.

[305] Declaration on the Preparation of Societies for Life in Peace, General Assembly resolution 33/73, adopted 15 December 1978. The tenth anniversary of the declaration was celebrated with a reaffirmation of its "lasting validity." See the Tenth anniversary of the adoption of the Declaration on the Preparation of Societies for Life in Peace, General Assembly resolution 43/87, adopted 7 December 1988.

[306] Declaration on the Right of Peoples to Peace, General Assembly resolution 39/11, adopted 12 November 1984. In Right of Peoples to Peace, General Assembly resolution 43/22, adopted 11 November 1988, the Assembly emphasized the Declaration's "lasting importance and validity." See also Implementation of the Declaration on the Right of Peoples to Peace, General Assembly resolution 45/14, adopted 7 November 1990.

[307] Declaration on the Right of Peoples to Peace, General Assembly resolution 39/11, adopted 12 November 1984. See also Promotion of the Right of Peoples to Peace, Human Rights Commission resolution 2002/71, adopted 25 April 2002; and see Promotion of the right of peoples to peace, Human Rights Council resolution adopted 10 June 2011.

elimination of the threat of war, particularly nuclear war, the renunciation of the use of force in international relations and the settlement of international disputes by peaceful means on the basis of the Charter of the United Nations."[308]

This "right to peace" approach has had some success. Most importantly, the African Charter on Human and Peoples' Rights, adopted by the Organization of African Unity (now the African Union) on 27 June 27 1981, reflected this idea of peace as a peoples' right.[309] In recent times, the General Assembly has moved away from the idea of peace as a human and people's right. Instead, the Assembly emphasized that "peace [was] a vital requirement for the promotion and protection of all human rights for all."[310] Peace and human rights were then seen as separate but related issues.[311]

## 7.3 Human security

In the United Nations it is often noted that international armed conflicts are increasingly rare.[312] This is good news, of course. It is a clear sign that the UN's collective security mechanism, which basically started to operate as intended in the early 1990s, is working properly as a deterrent. However, it does not mean that all people live their lives in security. Annan pointed this out as follows:

> How far we have moved from a strictly international world is evidenced by the changed nature of threats to peace and security faced by the world's people today. The provisions of the Charter presupposed that external aggression, an attack by one State against another, would constitute the most serious threat; but in recent decades far more people have been killed in civil wars, ethnic cleansing and acts of genocide, fuelled by weapons widely available in the global arms bazaar. Technologies of mass

---

[308] *Idem.* In a subsequent resolution, the focus was more on obligations relating to disarmament. Promotion of the right of peoples to peace, General Assembly resolution 57/216, adopted 18 December 2002.

[309] In Article 23 of that Charter, it is stated that "all peoples shall have the right to national and international peace and security." Note that the Charter does not refer to a right to peace, but to a right to peace and security.

[310] Promotion of peace as a vital requirement for the full enjoyment of all human rights by all, General Assembly resolution 58/192, adopted 22 December 2003. See also General Assembly resolution 62/163, adopted 18 December 2007.

[311] Nevertheless, in General Assembly resolution 60/163, adopted 16 December 2005, the Assembly went back to its previous approach, and affirmed that the right to peace was a human right, and declared "that the peoples of our planet have a sacred right to peace."

[312] For some statistics, see *A more secure world*, paras. 1-16; and the "Overview" in Human Security Centre, *Human Security Report* (2005). Both reports rely on the Uppsala Conflict Database of the Department of Peace and Conflict Research, Uppsala University (http://www.pcr.uu.se/database/).

destruction circulate in a netherworld of illicit markets, and terrorism casts shadows on stable rule. We have not yet adapted our institutions to this new reality.[313]

These are threats of a traditional, military nature.[314] But there are other threats and root causes as well. There are natural disasters, and the spread of HIV/AIDS and other diseases of mass destruction.[315] And there is poverty. It is suggested that none of these threats has a place in the paradigm of an inter-State order. The deprivation caused by all these threats, often threatening the existence of large groups of individuals rather than the existence of the State, shows "the need to reframe security in human terms."[316] In the past, it was believed that poverty had little to do with security, and that it was simply a fact of life. Nowadays it is intellectually and morally indefensible to regard threats such as poverty and disease as "a sad but inescapable aspect of the human condition."[317]

The problem is that these threats do not have a place in the UN paradigm. The classic interpretation of the UN rules on the use of force, which is based on the idea that security is about securing the State and not the individual, is out-dated.[318] The question therefore arises whether a paradigm shift is necessary. Should the focus of the world's efforts to maintain a more secure world remain on the State, or

---

[313] Kofi Annan, *We, the Peoples: the Role of the United Nations in the Twenty-first Century* (2000), para. 31. For data to substantiate this remark, see *e.g.*, Commission on Human Security, *Human security now* (2003), Chapter 2; and Human Security Centre, *Human Security Report* (2005). According to the latter report, "during the last 100 years far more people have been killed by their own governments than by foreign armies," thereby suggesting that this phenomenon is not so new after all.

[314] The statistics show a sharp increase in the number of civil wars from 1950 up to the end of the eighties/early nineties (the end of the Cold War and the beginning of an impressive increase in the number of UN peacekeeping missions), and then starts a significant decline in civil wars, a trend that continues up to the present day. Human Security Centre, *Human Security Report* (2005) also shows a decrease in the number of battle deaths, although these deaths sometimes include only 6% of the total number of deaths during a certain conflict. See p. 128.

[315] See the Address on behalf of the European Union by the Minister of Foreign Affairs of the Kingdom of the Netherlands, H. E. Dr. Bernard Bot, at the 59th session of the General Assembly of the United Nations, on 21 September 2004.

[316] Ramesh Thakur, *The United Nations, Peace and Security* (2006), p. 71. MacFarlane and Khong list six factors in the field of international relations that explain the historic shift from state security to human security. See S. Neil MacFarlane and Yuen Foong Khong, *Human Security and the UN* (2006). See also Commission on Human Security, *Human security now* (2003), pp. 2 and 5.

[317] *In larger freedom*, para. 27.

[318] The human security debate is not the first effort to introduce a new view on security. Commission on Global Governance, *Our Global Neighborhood* (1995), has gathered various types of "security": people security, planet security, common security, collective security, comprehensive security and human security. And then, of course, there's always the "old-fashioned" concept of national security.

should it shift to the individual? This has been one of the central questions in modern debates about security.[319]

This section attempts to define what is meant by "human security." To do so, it examines the most influential reports and declarations on the issue of security of the last two decades, focusing on the publications and declarations made within the UN system.[320] This debate is analyzed in some detail, because it provides an example of a discussion in which there is cross-fertilization between the scholarly community, Non-Governmental Organizations, and the United Nations.

What is human security? It is not the kind of security that sees individuals as pawns of the State, required to make the ultimate sacrifice, often involuntarily.[321] Security should no longer be seen solely as security of the State, *i.e.* as "security of territory from external aggression, or as protection of national interests in foreign policy or as global security from the threat of a nuclear holocaust."[322] The State-centred approach to security is not a given. It is a product of a particular historical context and type of thinking: the consolidation of the nation State and the ideological hegemony of nationalism.[323] Thus there is room for change.

It is not that there is no definition of human security, as was the case with the more traditional "international peace and security." The problem is rather that there are too many definitions of human security.[324] One of the first descriptions of human security – one can hardly call it a definition – can be found in the Human Development Report of 1994:[325]

---

[319] For a very convincing argument that the concept of human security, or the theory that underlies it, is not a recent invention, see S. Neil MacFarlane and Yuen Foong Khong, *Human Security and the UN* (2006).

[320] These are (in chronological order): Mahbub ul-Haq, *People's participation* (human development report 1993); Mahbub ul-Haq, *New dimensions of human security* (human development report 1994); Kofi Annan, *We, the Peoples: the Role of the United Nations in the Twenty-first Century* (2000); Millennium Declaration, resolution adopted by the UN General Assembly, 18 September 2000. UNDoc. A/RES/55/2 ("Millennium Declaration"); International Commission on Intervention and State Sovereignty (ICISS), *Responsibility to Protect* (2001); Commission on Human Security, *Human security now* (2003); High-level Panel on Threats, Challenges and Change, *A more secure world: Our shared responsibility* (2004); Kofi Annan, *In larger freedom: towards development, security and human rights for all* (2005); Human Security Centre, *Human Security Report* (2005); 2005 World Summit Outcome, General Assembly resolution 60/1, adopted 16 September 2005.

[321] Presumably, that was how things were seen in the past. See *e.g.*, Ramesh Thakur, *The United Nations, Peace and Security* (2006), p. 72.

[322] Mahbub ul-Haq, *New dimensions of human security* (human development report 1994), p. 22.

[323] S. Neil MacFarlane and Yuen Foong Khong, *Human Security and the UN* (2006), p. 15. See also Chapter 1 of this book.

[324] An overview of some of these definitions can be found in Table 1: Selected Descriptions of Human Security, annexed to Sabina Alkire, *A Conceptual Framework for Human Security* (2003).

[325] The Report of 1993 already prepared the world for next year's report. See especially Mahbub ul-Haq, *People's participation* (human development report 1993), pp. 1-2.

[Human security means] first, safety from such chronic threats as hunger, disease and repression. And second, it means protection from sudden and hurtful disruptions in the patterns of daily lives – whether in homes, in jobs or in communities.[326]

As this description shows, human security is people-centered. It is "concerned with how people live and breathe in society, how free they are to exercise their many choices, how much access they have to market and social opportunities – and whether they live in conflict or in peace."[327] This shift is made more explicit in later literature. For example, Thakur wrote that

By contrast [to state security], human security puts the individual at the centre of the debate, analysis and policy. He or she is paramount, and the State is a collective instrument to protect human life and enhance human welfare. The fundamental components of human security – the security of *people* against threats to personal safety and life – can be put at risk by external aggression, but also by factors within a country, including "security" forces.[328]

That is essentially what human security entails. It means putting the individual at the centre of security.[329]

This shift in focus is sometimes called a paradigm shift.[330] The most important consequence of this paradigm shift is that threats to security become much more diverse. After all, the life of an individual can be threatened by nuclear catastrophe, but also by ordinary crime, pollution, starvation, or even suicide.[331]

To bring some order into this wide range of potential threats to security, a distinction is made, following the former US President Roosevelt, between threats to the individual's freedom from fear and threats to his or her freedom from want.[332]

---

[326] Mahbub ul-Haq, *New dimensions of human security* (human development report 1994), p. 23.
[327] *Idem.*
[328] Ramesh Thakur, *The United Nations, Peace and Security* (2006), p. 72.
[329] Surprisingly, the Commission on Global Governance, *Our Global Neighborhood* (1995), does not use the concept of human security. It chose to use the concepts of people security and planet security instead. See Chapter 3.
[330] See Sadako Ogata, *State Security – Human Security* (2001), pp. 8 and 10. See also Thomas Kuhn, *The Structure of Scientific Revolutions* (1962). He introduced the idea of "paradigm shifts": one scientific paradigm is suddenly replaced by another, thereby creating a scientific revolution and a whole new way of thinking.
[331] Mahbub ul-Haq, *New dimensions of human security* (human development report 1994), chapter 2.
[332] *Idem*, p. 24. The origin of these freedoms is the speech "The Four Freedoms", delivered by Franklin Delano Roosevelt on January 6, 1941, to the members of the 77th US Congress. This distinction has proven to be very influential, and resurfaces in many of the human security literature that followed, albeit sometimes under different headings. See, *e.g.*, Commission on Human Security, *Human security now* (2003), p. 10; Kofi Annan, *We, the Peoples: the Role of the United Nations in the Twenty-first Century* (2000), and *In larger freedom* (although these reports do not refer to "human security" explicitly); MacFarlane and Khong refer to the "development dimension" and the "protection

Some reports use a narrow concept of human security, focusing on freedom from fear. [333] Others prefer a broad concept of human security, which includes – and often focuses on – freedom from want. [334]

Essentially, the freedom from fear component of human security is about the right of the individual to be protected against military violence. The traditional rules protecting the security of the State, *i.e.* the prohibition on the use of force and the rules of the collective security mechanism, are useful here, as they indirectly also protect the individual from aggression by a foreign State. State security is therefore a derivative of human security: "The notion of human security is based on the premise that the individual human being is the only irreducible focus for discourse on security," and consequently "the security claims of other referents, including the State, draw whatever value they have from the claim that they address the needs and aspirations of the individuals who make them up." [335] There is no better way of guaranteeing human security than an effective State. [336]

The freedom from fear does not stop there. It also aims to protect the individual from military violence committed against him by his own State. [337] This second aspect is generally connected to the human rights tradition, "which sees the State as the problem and the source of threats to individual security." [338] It is this second component which creates tensions and frictions with the classical, purely State-based, concept of security. The UN has tried to explain away such frictions. Attempts are made to explain why threats to human security could be characterized as threats to peace and security, interpreted in the traditional sense. The human security concept then remains faithful to that of its predecessor, "international peace

dimension" of human secuirty in their book: S. Neil MacFarlane and Yuen Foong Khong, *Human Security and the UN* (2006).

[333] The two influential reports that are based in Canada have deliberately been restricted to dealing with the "freedom from fear" component of human security. For an explanation of this restriction, see the section on "What is Human Security?" in Human Security Centre, *Human Security Report* (2005). International Commission on Intervention and State Sovereignty, *The responsibility to protect* (2001), does mention – and embraces – a broader concept of human security (p. 15), but the report is about humanitarian interventions, which explains the emphasis on the "freedom from fear" in the report.

[334] The Human Development Reports and the Report of the Commission on Human Security focus on the freedom from want.

[335] S. Neil MacFarlane and Yuen Foong Khong, *Human Security and the UN* (2006), pp. 2 and 5.

[336] A well-functioning State can best guarantee human security; and in that case State security and human security do not contradict one another at all. See Ramesh Thakur, *The United Nations, Peace and Security* (2006), p. 90. As MacFarlane and Khong point out, even Hobbes acknowledged that when a State fails to protect its citizens, these citizens no longer owe obedience to their State (S. Neil MacFarlane and Yuen Foong Khong, *Human Security and the UN* (2006), pp. 39-40 and pp. 58-59).

[337] See Human Security Centre, *Human Security Report* (2005) (in Section on "What is Human Security?"); Commission on Human Security, *Human security now* (2003), p. 4; Ramesh Thakur, *The United Nations, Peace and Security* (2006), p. 90. See also Neil MacFarlane and Yuen Foong Khong, *Human Security and the UN* (2006), pp. 2 and 5.

[338] Ramesh Thakur, *The United Nations, Peace and Security* (2006), p. 72.

and security." The reasoning is usually that some acts are so gruesome, that even if committed against a limited group of individuals, they nevertheless destabilize the entire international legal order, causing a threat to international peace and security.[339] The advantage of this approach is that it does not require the old legal framework of collective security to be revised. But is it feasible to perceive threats to human security as international threats in that traditional sense? Is it plausible to argue that the mistreatment of a group of individuals constitutes a threat to international peace and security? Additional criteria have been proposed, other than the gruesome character of the treatment concerned, to justify qualifying essentially domestic conflicts as threats to international peace and security. It has been suggested that the threat must affect a significant number of people.[340] However, focusing on the scale of misery is a way of avoiding rather than solving the issue. Human security requires a different theory from the theory of common interest that supports the interstate approach to security. Human security is based more on the principle of global solidarity rather than on the collective interests of all human beings in effectively tackling all threats to human security wherever they occur.[341]

The Responsibility to Protect Report is more traditional in its approach. It sees poverty, political repression and the uneven distribution of resources, both within a State and at the global level, essentially as causes of threats to security, where the resulting military conflict is the direct threat to security.[342] However, in the literature on human security, this is a minority position. Emma Rothschild called for a considerable expansion of the concept of security, downwards (focusing on the individual, with a secondary role for the State) and upwards (focus on the global order), and horizontally (to include a varied horizon of different security threats), as well as an expansion in terms of responsibilities.[343] The concept of human security, as used in the Human Development Reports and the report of the Commission on Human Security, certainly reveals the horizontal extension of the

---

[339] *Idem*, para. 203. See also *In larger freedom*, paras. 122-126; and the 2005 World Summit Outcome, paras. 77-80 and paras. 138-140. For insightful commentary, see Nico Schrijver, "The Future of the Charter of the United Nations" (2006), pp. 23-25.

[340] See Sabina Alkire, *A Conceptual Framework for Human Security* (2003), p. 4.

[341] This crucial issue is underappreciated in the reports. The last part of Commission on Human Security, *Human security now* (2003), only mentions this question, very briefly and succinctly, under the heading Clarifying the need for a global identity, p. 141. See also *In larger freedom*, paras. 18 and 220.

[342] See especially the Chapter on the Responsibility to Prevent (Chapter 3), in International Commission on Intervention and State Sovereignty (ICISS), *Responsibility to Protect* (2001). Unfortunately the Commission did not add a research essay on the concept of security, or human security, to the report (there are three research essays: one on "sovereignty", one on "intervention", and one on "prevention".) See also *A more secure world*, para. 22.

[343] Rothschild, "What is security?", p. 53. For references to the idea of "extensive security", see *e.g.*, Ramesh Thakur, *The United Nations, Peace and Security* (2006), p. 72; S. Neil MacFarlane and Yuen Foong Khong, *Human Security and the UN* (2006), pp. 1-2.

concept of security. According to these reports, threats to human security come in many shapes and sizes. For example, the Commission believes that human security is threatened, not only by violent conflicts, but also by hunger, scarcity of (unpolluted) fresh water, the ageing of the world population, the degradation of natural resources and environmental crises.[344]

The horizontal broadening of the concept of security in every direction has often led to the criticism that it has caused a conceptual overstretch, *i.e.* that "the concept has been stretched to cover almost every imaginable malady affecting human beings," [345] and that it has become "so vague that it verges on meaninglessness." [346] The Human Security Centre, itself using a narrow interpretation of human security, wrote that "a concept that lumps together threats as diverse as genocide and affronts to personal dignity may be useful for advocacy, but it has limited utility for policy analysis."[347]

There is some truth in these objections. The concept of security, as traditionally used by the United Nations, had a specific, technical meaning: it was used to refer to the collective security mechanism. It is not immediately apparent that this mechanism should also be used to respond to certain human security threats such as poverty, famine, etc. This kind of criticism can be countered by pointing out, first of all, that international peace and security is just as hard to define as human security.[348] Secondly, it can be argued that this broadening of security has not created a new dilemma in world politics, but it has forced an already existing dilemma to emerge from the shadows. Statistics show that most people do not consider the traditional threats to State security, such as nuclear war and interstate aggression, to be the most urgent or pertinent threats they face in their lives.[349] Therefore we should look at the entire range of security threats, rather than stubbornly focusing on the same threat. At first this new view may be overwhelmingly confusing. Thakur summarized the new situation as follows:

> The militarized and statist concept of security serves to disguise the reality of intervalue competition; a multidimensional concept highlights the need for

---

[344] Commission on Human Security, *Human security now* (2003), pp. 14-19.

[345] S. Neil MacFarlane and Yuen Foong Khong, *Human Security and the UN* (2006), p. 237.

[346] Roland Paris, "Human Security: Paradigm Shift or Hot Air?" (2001), pp. 87-102.

[347] The authors immediately add that "it is no accident that the broad conception of human security articulated by the UN Development Programme in its much-cited 1994 Human Development Report has rarely been used to guide research programs." See section: What is Human Security? in Human Security Centre, *Human Security Report* (2005).

[348] The concept of "human security" is often criticized for its vagueness. "State security", however, is also rather vague. There is no agreed definition of this classic concept. See Neil MacFarlane and Yuen Foong Khong, *Human Security and the UN* (2006), p. 12.

[349] See Human Security Centre, *Human Security Report* (2005), p. 51. Less than 10% of the people interviewed said they considered war to be the greatest single threat to their personal security; criminal violence (27%) is what people fear the most.

integrative strategies that resolve or transcend values conflicts. Most individuals, societies and countries hold core values in addition to territorial integrity and there are domains of social activity in addition to the military which should be factored into the concept of security. As well as trade-offs, there are opportunity costs: allocation of resources to cope with military security is at the cost of promoting socio-economic security. A multidimensional conceptualization of security compels scholars and policymakers alike to explicate value trade-offs.[350]

What is the point of conceptual clarity if it does not accord with reality? The number of lives threatened by poverty and hunger dwarfs the number of lives threatened by military conflict.[351] The number of deaths caused by (easily) preventable diseases, given the world's existing knowledge, technologies and health resources, is equally alarming.[352]

What has been the UN's response to these new approaches to the value of peace and security? A brief summary of how the value ended up in the most influential documents of the United Nations follows below. First of all, A More Secure World, a report published by a high-level panel, did not explicitly embrace the shift from inter-State security to human security. It combined both approaches to security in the concept of "international security."[353] According to the report, "any event or process that leads to large-scale death or lessening of life chances and undermines States as the basic unit of the international system is a threat to international security."[354] As the UN Charter already makes many references to international security and allows this concept to be interpreted in accordance with contemporary circumstances and perceptions, the high-level panel did not suggest any drastic changes specifically intended to adapt the United Nations system to deal with human security.[355] Nor did it suggest that the Security Council drastically change its interpretation of the concept of security."[356] Even before the report was

---

[350] Then Thakur referred to the damage and loss of life caused by hurricane Katrina in relation to the war in Iraq. Ramesh Thakur, *The United Nations, Peace and Security* (2006), p. 83. See also International Commission on Intervention and State Sovereignty (ICISS), *Responsibility to Protect* (2001), p. 15.

[351] See Commission on Human Security, *Human security now* (2003), p. 73.

[352] 26 million deaths could be avoided annually. See *idem*, p. 95.

[353] The report interpreted state security in terms of human security. See, *e.g.*, A *more secure world*, para. 29-30.

[354] *Idem*, para. 25.

[355] That may be surprising, considering that in Part 1: Towards a new security consensus, the report remarks that "although the United Nations gave birth to the notion of human security, it proved poorly equipped to provide it." See *idem*, para. 12.

[356] The main conclusion of A *more secure world*, is that "the Security Council is fully empowered under Chapter VII of the Charter of the United Nations to address the full range of security threats with which States are concerned." (*idem*, para. 198.) Yes, but what about human security? In the report human security is always mentioned together with State security, as if there really is no distinction to be made (see *e.g.*, *idem*, paras. 165, 184, 197, 207).

published, it was already clear that the Security Council and other security organs had extended their interpretation of security.[357] The report simply suggested that the Council continue on this path.

A few months after A More Secure World was published the Secretary-General published his own report on security, In Larger Freedom.[358] Annan embraced the broad list of threats to international security of the high-level panel report.[359] Annan emphasized that a broad interpretation of security was in line with the UN Charter:

> In setting out to save succeeding generations from the scourge of war, [the framers of the UN Charter] understood that this enterprise could not succeed if it was narrowly based. They therefore decided to create an organization to ensure respect for fundamental human rights, establish conditions under which justice and the rule of law could be maintained, and "promote social progress and better standards of life in larger freedom". [...This larger freedom] implies that men and women everywhere have the right to be governed by their own consent, under law, in a society where all individuals can, without discrimination or retribution, speak, worship and associate freely. They must also be free from want — so that the death sentences of extreme poverty and infectious disease are lifted from their lives — and free from fear — so that their lives and livelihoods are not ripped apart by violence and war.[360]

In addition to the freedom from fear (security in the narrow sense) and the freedom from want (referred to as development), Annan added the freedom to live in dignity, which in his view included the rule of law, democracy, and respect for human rights. He did not explicitly refer to human security.[361] Nevertheless, considering all the previous reports, the above citation describes the logical conclusion of the concept of human security: a life lived in larger freedom is a life lived in security. The concept of human security could be criticized for having become so broad that it could vanish into thin air without anyone even noticing. From a non-critical perspective, it could be argued that the concept of human security has come to

---

[357] See the Secuirty Council resolutions mentioned at Nico Schrijver, "the Future of the Charter of the United Nations" (2006), p. 17. Thakur referred among other examples to the Security Council's discussions on HIV/AIDS and the rights of the child. See Ramesh Thakur, *The United Nations, Peace and Security* (2006), pp. 85-86.

[358] The aim of the report was to assist the General Assembly with establishing an agenda for the 2005 World Summit.

[359] *In larger freedom*, para. 78.

[360] *Idem*, paras. 13–15. As Schrijver rightly pointed out, the founding fathers of the UN Charter were ahead of their time by already making the link between peace and security and socio-economic development and respect for human rights. See Nico Schrijver, "The Future of the Charter of the United Nations" (2006), p. 10.

[361] Interestingly enough, Annan wanted to return to a clear division between security, development, and respect for human rights, without however denying the interconnectedness. See *e.g.*, *In larger freedom*, paras. 17, 81 and 140.

dominate our way of thinking in such a way that it is no longer necessary to refer to it explicitly every time we discuss security issues.

Many of the report's recommendations and ideas were adopted by the Member States of the United Nations in the 2005 World Summit Outcome Document. They "acknowledge[d] that peace and security, development and human rights are the pillars of the United Nations system and the foundations for collective security and well-being."[362] One paragraph dealt explicitly with human security:

> We stress the right of people to live in freedom and dignity, free from poverty and despair. We recognize that all individuals, in particular vulnerable people, are entitled to freedom from fear and freedom from want, with an equal opportunity to enjoy all their rights and fully develop their human potential. To this end, we commit ourselves to discussing and defining the notion of human security in the General Assembly.[363]

It is worth pointing out here that this paragraph is not in the section on peace and security, but in the section on human rights. One important consequence of the shift in the thinking about peace and security from the State to the individual is the change of language that necessarily accompanies this change. Now that the individual has become the focus of security, it is logical to formulate security demands in the language of human rights.[364] Most of the reports on human security explicitly suggest this change in the language.[365] Furthermore, they suggest that existing human rights documents may help define the new concept of security.[366] The dominance of human rights in modern international discourse is evidence of an emerging human approach to security.[367] However, the two should not blur into each other too much. Not all human rights violations constitute a threat to human security. Human security is defined by MacFarlane and Khong as the "freedom from threat to the core values of human beings, including physical survival, welfare, and identity."[368] This reference to "core values" is also found in the definition of the Commission on Human Security, which defines human security as the protection of

---

[362] Annexed to *In larger freedom* is a draft resolution, following the structure of the report (using the headings "freedom from want", "freedom from fear", etc.) The 2005 World Summit Outcome did not adopt this language, and used more objective headings: development; peace and collective security; human rights and the rule of law. Collective security is clearly an interstate interpretation of security, as para. 72, 2005 World Summit Outcome, showed.
[363] 2005 World Summit Outcome, para. 143.
[364] See Commission on Human Security, *Human security now* (2003), p. 10.
[365] In the International Commission on Intervention and State Sovereignty (ICISS), *Responsibility to Protect* (2001), p. 15, human security is defined as "the security of people – their physical safety, their economic and social well-being, respect for their dignity and worth as human beings, and the protection of their human rights and fundamental freedoms."
[366] See Bertrand G. Ramcharan, *Human Rights and Human Security* (2002), p. 3.
[367] S. Neil MacFarlane and Yuen Foong Khong, *Human Security and the UN* (2006), pp. 62-63.
[368] *Idem*, p. 14.

the vital core of all human lives in ways that enhance human freedom and human fulfillment.[369] One of the principal difficulties of this human rights based approach to security is to determine which human rights violations affect these core values and in this way constitute a threat to human security. Various attempts have been made to distinguish a "vital core" of human rights from the rest. In any case, even a very strict interpretation of this "vital core" leads to a considerable broadening of security threats, to include things above and beyond military-type threats to the individual's life.[370]

## 7.4 Conclusion

Instead of looking only at peaceful relations between States, it is also worth looking at what it means for individuals to live a life in peace and security. This approach comes with a significant broadening of the meaning of peace and security. After all, it is suggested that the biggest threat to the security of most individual human beings is not inter-State war, nor domestic conflict, nor the arms race. Although this "humanization" of the value of peace and security is popular, it is not clear where this definition of "human security" will lead, and it is equally unclear what consequences this new approach to the value of peace and security could have for the UN's efforts to promote it.

## 8 CONCLUSION

In San Francisco the maintenance of international peace and security was seen as the most important purpose of the post-war order. This was the reason that all the States assembled there in 1945. The value of peace and security was based on a strong universally shared sentiment that war was the greatest evil and that a collective attempt was required to avoid its reoccurrence. In 1945, many States were represented in the discussion on how to prevent such a new global war, and how exactly to define the alternative: a peaceful world. Since 1945, the Assembly has continuously searched for ways and strategies to achieve a peaceful world. New threats to peace and security have emerged over time, and the Assembly has adapted its strategies accordingly. This process has affected the meaning of the value of peace and security. It has continuously evolved.

Although the Assembly focused on defining the threats to peace, rather than on the value of peace and security itself, there are some exceptions. UNESCO's attempt to develop a culture for peace, acknowledged by the Assembly,

---

[369] Commission on Human Security, *Human security now* (2003), p. 4.
[370] See also Ramesh Thakur, *The United Nations, Peace and Security* (2006), pp. 83-84.

is an example. UNESCO aimed to come up with a positive definition of peace. But the Assembly's main contribution to the debate was a list of threats to the value of peace and security. These threats, taken together, give a good idea of what a world in which the value of peace and security is realized, is like. If inter-State wars, domestic conflict, attacks by mercenaries and terrorists, the arms race and the development of various weapons of mass destruction are all considered as threats to peace, then it must be assumed that a peaceful world is a world in which there is no place for any of these things. Other potential threats, such as diseases of mass destruction and poverty, have also sometimes been labelled as threats to peace. However, most of the time they are seen as root causes of threats to peace. Is this a correct and defensible view? On the one hand, it could be considered a bit harsh to say that diseases and mass poverty do not constitute a threat to peace and security. It suggests that these global challenges are somehow considered to be "less important" than the more traditional threats to peace, such as inter-State aggression. On the other hand, including everything that is as important as the prevention of armed aggression in the list of threats to the realization of the global value of peace and security, implies that the value is all-encompassing, with little specific meaning. It is important to stress the fact that peace and security is but one value in a collection of equally important values. Social progress and development, as well as human dignity and the self-determination of peoples, are all equally deserving of the world's attention.

Seen from an inter-State point of view, this discussion can been settled in favour of a more restrictive approach to the value of international peace and security. This is in line with the text and the *travaux* of the United Nations Charter. It also ensures conceptual clarity. When the same value is approached from a human-centered point of view, it is more difficult to maintain the restrictive approach. From that perspective, the rigid distinction between State aggression and other forms of military force (by mercenaries and terrorists), on the one hand, and diseases of mass destruction and poverty, on the other hand, is hard to justify. What is the difference? Is it the presence of weapons, of some form of violence, in the case of the former types of threats? The two categories of threats are equally deadly from the point of view of the individual victim. Therefore calls for a human-centered approach to security have generally been accompanied by calls to expand the range of potential security threats. The problem is that adopting the human security approach quickly takes us outside the framework of the UN Charter. It is difficult to envisage the exact role the United Nations Organization, and especially its Security Council, could play in such a new framework.

# SOCIAL PROGRESS AND DEVELOPMENT

## 1 INTRODUCTION

Article 55 of the United Nations Charter allows the Organization to promote, *inter alia*, "higher standards of living, full employment, […] conditions of economic and social progress and development, solutions of international economic, social, health, and related problems and international cultural and educational cooperation." This chapter deals with the background and drafting of this article, as well as the way in which the United Nations, especially the General Assembly, has clarified, modernized and elaborated upon the purpose as defined in Article 55.

The UN General Assembly has adopted more declarations on social progress and development than on any of the other global values examined in this study. This suggests that the General Assembly devoted more energy and time to the promotion of social progress and development than to the promotion of the other values. This was probably the case, at least for a large group of developing States, but the number of declarations on a particular topic does not tell the full story. Relatively few of the declarations on social progress and development have ended up as multilateral treaties, or have been recognized as authoritative statements of existing customary international law. Many declarations on social progress and development have essentially remained no more than political declarations. They have not added any new legal obligations for the Organization or its Member States. Consequently they have also had relatively little influence on actual State behaviour. Thus they lack the authority which some of the declarations relating to other values have acquired.

A summary of the General Assembly's general declarations on social progress and development is given below. These declarations generally contain strategies and action plans for development. The meaning of the global value of social progress and development can be deduced from those plans. These UN resolutions are compared with philosophical ideas about a fair distribution of resources and responsibilities at the global level. In philosophy a distinction is often made between responsibilities relating to an equitable distribution of goods and responsibilities relating to immediate needs. In line with this distinction, a separate section of this chapter is devoted to the UN's strategy for responding to immediate needs. There is also a special section on the series of declarations about *sustainable* development, as well as those introducing a human rights based approach to development.

Chapter V

## 1.1 Putting the role of the UN into perspective

Most of the principal international institutions promoting the global value of social progress and development were not established by the United Nations Charter. The International Bank for Reconstruction and Development, a specialized agency of the United Nations, and the World Trade Organization, both play a much more significant role in regulating trade than any of the main organs of the UN. These international financial institutions are at best rather loosely linked to the UN system.

When the UN and these financial institutions were established in the 1940s, it was not the intention to separate them so drastically. The International Bank for Reconstruction and Development and the International Monetary Fund were established in 1945,[1] and the General Agreement on Tariffs and Trade was signed in 1947.[2] The intention was also to establish an International Trade Organization to oversee the implementation of that agreement. The Havana Charter for an International Trade Organization was adopted at the end of the United Nations Conference on Trade and Employment, held in Havana (Cuba) in 1947-1948. This was intended to be the constitution for this new trade organization.[3] Article 1 of that Charter showed that the primary purpose of this new Organization was the "realiz[ation of] the aims set forth in the Charter of the United Nations, particularly the attainment of the higher standards of living, full employment and conditions of economic and social progress and development, envisaged in Article 55 of that Charter."[4]

The Havana Charter never entered into force. The World Trade Organization was established only in 1995.[5] In contrast with the Havana Charter, there was no reference at all to the purposes of the UN Charter in the Agreement establishing the World Trade Organization. Therefore when the declarations of the United Nations on the issue of development are examined, it is important to bear in mind that "we live with a global economic governance system in which discussion

---

[1] See the Bretton Woods Agreements, which consist of the Articles of Agreement of the International Monetary Fund and the Articles of Agreement of the International Bank of Reconstruction and Development, both signed at Washington, on 27 December 1945, entry into force on the same day. See *United Nations Treaty Series* vol. 2 (1947), pp. 40-132 and pp. 134-204, respectively.

[2] The Final Act of the second session of the Preparatory Committee of the United Nations Conference on Trade and Employment, the General Agreement on Tariffs and Trade, and the Protocol of Provisional Application of the General Agreement on Tariffs and Trade, were all signed at Geneva, on 30 October 1947.

[3] Havana Charter for an International Trade Organization, pp. 9-115 of the Final Act of the United Nations Conference on Trade and Employment, adopted 24 March 1948. UNDoc. E/Conf. 2/78.

[4] *Idem*, Article 1.

[5] Marrakesh Agreement establishing the World Trade Organization (with final act, annexes and protocol), concluded at Marrakesh on 15 April 1994. See *United Nations Treaty Series*, volume 1867 (1995), pp. 154-164, for the agreement itself.

and implementation are the responsibility of different international organizations."[6] The United Nations serves as a forum for discussion and for the adoption of non-binding declarations on global economic policy, with a strong focus on the element of global justice and duties of assistance to developing States. The international financial institutions, on the other hand, function as centres for the implementation of economic policy. However, what they implement is not necessarily UN policy.

## 1.2 The role of the Economic and Social Council

According to the Charter, the Economic and Social Council (ECOSOC) is the main organ specialized in social progress and development.[7] In reality, ECOSOC acts more like a subsidiary organ of the General Assembly. Most of the declarations adopted by ECOSOC were later also adopted by the General Assembly. Moreover, the General Assembly and ECOSOC both include the promotion of social progress and development in their mandate, and thus it is not a task primarily given to ECOSOC.

The UN Charter had already clearly referred to this subordinate role of ECOSOC. According to Article 62 of the UN Charter, the Economic and Social Council had the following tasks:

> To make or initiate studies and reports with respect to international economic, social, cultural, educational, health, and related matters and [to] make recommendations with respect to any such matters to the General Assembly, to the Members of the United Nations, and to the specialized agencies concerned.

> To prepare draft conventions for submission to the General Assembly, with respect to matters falling within its competence.

> To call, in accordance with the rules prescribed by the United Nations, international conferences on matters falling within its competence.

According to the Dumbarton Oaks proposals, the Economic and Social Council was meant to "make recommendations, on its own initiative, with respect to international economic, social and other humanitarian matters," and to coordinate

---

[6] Richard Jolly, Louis Emmerij & Thomas G. Weiss, *UN Ideas that Changed the World* (2009), p. 108. The failure of the Havana Charter was perceived as a major defeat for the United Nations. See *e.g.*, Walter M. Kotschnig, "The United Nations as an Instrument of Economic and Social Development" (1968), p. 18.

[7] For the "prehistory" of the Economic and Social Council, and its relationship with the other economic institutions, see Nico Schrijver, "International Organization for the Management of Interdependence: Alternative Ideas in Pursuit of Global Decision Making" (1988), especially pp. 175-176.

the work of all kinds of organizations working in the socio-economic field.[8] Expert commissions could be established to assist the Council in its work.[9]

Many of the States which suggested broadening the socio-economic purpose of the UN also suggested amendments to broaden the mandate of the "first international agency in the history of man designed to coordinate the activities of the nations in the solution of social and economic problems," *i.e.* ECOSOC.[10] Great things were expected of this Council in 1945. Some experts, who saw socio-economic development as the main tool to eliminate the causes of war, even suggested that "[i]f the Economic and Social Council succeeds in its broad objectives [...] it should finally reduce the Security Council to the status of the human appendix, which [...] is an organ with a history but no remaining functions."[11]

The same group of States also suggested broadening ECOSOC's powers. For example, Bolivia suggested that the Economic and Social Council of the United Nations (ECOSOC) be mandated:

> To achieve concerted action destined to promote the economic development, the industrialization, and the raising of the standard of living of the less favoured nations as well as the protection of the international rights of man, the perfecting of social security and the provision of the material opportunities for work, the solution of problems of health and population and others of a similar nature.[12]

Bolivia did not explain how ECOSOC could achieve such concerted action. This would require more than just recommendatory powers. Australia proposed that ECOSOC be allowed "to initiate, for promoting the economic and social objectives declared in this Charter, the making of conventions (subject always to ratification by the members of the United Nations in accordance with their constitutional processes)."[13]

Other States, which proposed ambitious new socio-economic purposes, believed that it would be too much for one Council to promote them all. Brazil

---

[8] United Nations: Dumbarton Oaks Proposals for a General International Organization, UNCIO, vol. 3, pp. 20-21.
[9] *Idem*, p. 21.
[10] John H. Crider, "World Economic Council Emerging," in *New York Times* of May 27, 1945. References to "culture" can be found in the Amendments to the Dumbarton Oaks Proposals Submitted on Behalf of Australia, UNCIO, vol. 3, p. 547; Proposed Amendments to the Dumbarton Oaks Proposals Submitted by the Philippine Delegation, UNCIO, vol. 3, p. 540; Amendments Proposed by the Governments of the United States, the United Kingdom, the Soviet Union and China, UNCIO, vol. 3, p. 627.
[11] Porter, "Economic Council is Key Peace Aid," in *New York Times* of June 12, 1945.
[12] Proposals of the Delegation of the Republic of Bolivia for the Organization of a System of Peace and Security, UNCIO, vol. 3, p. 586.
[13] UNCIO, vol. 3, p. 547.

therefore suggested the establishment of a Council of Cultural Relations, working independently from ECOSOC, to promote education and culture worldwide. [14] Similarly, the French Delegation called for the establishment of a separate "international Organization on intellectual and educational questions." [15] Lebanon, Costa Rica and Ecuador made similar proposals. [16] There were also ideas about establishing specialized organizations under the umbrella of the Council. [17]

Belgium suggested changing the name of the Economic and Social Council to "International Cooperation Council," because the old name no longer covered all the tasks assigned to it. [18]

Morales of Guatemala, the Rapporteur of the relevant Committee in San Francisco, stressed the importance of ECOSOC's ambitious goals:

> […] international cooperation in any of the many fields of human concern brought within the purview of the Social and Economic Council will be – to the extent that it is successful – of practical significance in itself in improving the conditions of human existence. But it will do more. It will contribute to the attainment of peace in this world by substituting the method of joint action for unilateral action, and by progressively shifting the emphasis of international cooperation to the achievement of positive ends in lieu of the negative purpose of preventing the outbreak of war by way of organized security measures. [19]

France also saw the potential of ECOSOC's work as a way of maintaining peace and security. In its enthusiasm, the French delegate explained that if ECOSOC carried out its task effectively, the Security Council would have nothing left to do. After all, "[i]f the Economic and Social Council is successful in its task of preparing the future basis of peace by securing effective international cooperation to insure the rights of man and to insure the essential freedoms, then we consider that we will never need the coercive measures which are provided under other parts of the Charter through the Security Council." [20]

But ECOSOC never became the International Cooperation Council. It never became the centre of all social, cultural and economic cooperation between States.

---

[14] Addition to Chapter XII Submitted by the Brazilian Delegation, UNCIO, vol. 3, p. 252.

[15] Dumbarton Oaks Proposals for the Establishment of a General International Organization, Chapter IX, Sections A and C: Draft Amendments Submitted by the French Delegation, UNCIO, vol. 3, p. 391.

[16] See Lebanon's Suggestions on the Dumbarton Oaks Proposals, UNCIO , vol. 3, p. 473; Cuba, pp. 506-508; Ecuador, p. 402 (see also pp. 417, 424); Haiti, p. 53.

[17] See *e.g.*, Comments of the French Ministry of Foreign Affairs, UNCIO, vol. 3, p. 388 (see also Sixth Plenary Session, May 1, 1945, UNCIO, vol. 1, p. 436); Netherlands, p. 321; Brazil, p. 249; Haiti, p. 53; Philippines, p. 540; Uruguay, p. 42.

[18] Propositions of the Belgian Delegation, UNCIO, vol. 10, p. 209. See also Fernand Dehousse, *Cours de politique international* (1945), p. 60.

[19] UNCIO Selected Documents, p. 642-643.

[20] Second Meeting of Commission II, June 11, 1945, UNCIO, vol. 8, p. 62.

It did not reduce the Security Council to an appendix in the corpus of the United Nations Organization. Article 7 of the UN Charter included ECOSOC among the principal organs of the United Nations, but it is clear from Article 62 UN Charter, as well as from subsequent practice, that ECOSOC was merely meant to assist the General Assembly in its work, particularly that on social progress and development.[21]

## 2 SOCIAL PROGRESS AND DEVELOPMENT IN SAN FRANCISCO

This chapter continues by addressing the value of social progress and development itself. Like all the chapters on values, it begins by examining the *travaux préparatoires* of the UN Charter.

### 2.1 The Preamble

According to Smuts' first draft of the Preamble, the United Nations was established, *inter alia*, to re-establish faith "in the enlargement of freedom and the promotion of social progress and the possibility of raising the standards of life everywhere in the world."[22] Smuts himself later changed the wording to "to promote social progress and better standards of life in larger freedom."[23] This phrase ended up unchanged and without discussion in the Preamble of the UN Charter.[24]

### 2.2 The Purpose

The Dumbarton Oaks plan was essentially a plan to prevent all future wars. As Egypt rightly pointed out, it focused on the "negative side of the international problem."[25] It focused on what States ought *not* to do. At the same time, it did not neglect the positive side, which, according to the Egyptian delegate, "consist[ed] in the development of international solidarity and cooperation."[26] The Dumbarton Oaks plan listed as one of the purposes of the Organization the "achieve[ment of]

---

[21] ECOSOC has been criticized, more than any other of the principal organs of the United Nations, for a lack of relevance. See *e.g.*, Gert Rosenthal, "Economic and Social Council" (2007).

[22] Draft Preamble to the Charter of the United Nations Proposed by the Union of South Africa, 26 April, 1945, UNCIO, vol. 3, pp. 474-475.

[23] See Preamble to the Charter of the United Nations Submitted by the South African Delegation in Revision of Draft of April 26, 1945, 3 May 1945, UNCIO, vol. 3, pp. 476-477, and Documentation for Meetings of Committee I/1, UNCIO, vol. 6, p. 530.

[24] Thirteenth Meeting of Committee I/1, June 5, 1945, UNCIO, vol. 6, p. 367. Colombia wanted to add to this phrase a reference to the Atlantic Charter, but that motion failed. See Report of Rapporteur of Committee 1 to Commission I, UNCIO, vol. 6, p. 452.

[25] Third Plenary Session, April 28, 1945, UNCIO, vol. 1, p. 234.

[26] *Idem.*

international cooperation in the solution of international economic, social and other humanitarian problems."[27]

This provision did not specify the ultimate aim of all this cooperation.[28] Australia suggested that it was "[t]o promote human welfare in all lands."[29] According to Guatemala, the aim of all this socio-economic cooperation was to "enable all the countries of the world to raise the standard of living of their people, and to banish misery from the face of the earth."[30] Other States saw socio-economic cooperation as a means to maintain international peace and security,[31] or as a means to a more sustainable and more comprehensive peace, or "positive peace."[32] The issue of solidarity also came to the fore here. Bolivia believed that poorer people had a right to socio-economic assistance simply because they were part of the human race.[33] The Philippines pointed out that it was no longer defensible not to care about the plight of fellow human beings in other parts of the world. In the words of the Philippines delegation, "[u]ntil the weakest link in our human chain is made safe, not one of us is safe."[34] These considerations were also the basis for suggestions to have the UN promote fair and equitable international trade.[35]

Despite all these interesting amendments, very little happened to the Dumbarton Oaks provision in San Francisco. The provision had called for "international cooperation in the solution of international economic, social and other humanitarian problems." The relevant Subcommittee only slightly rephrased

---

[27] Dumbarton Oaks Proposals for a General International Organization, UNCIO, vol. 3, p. 2.

[28] Other additions were also suggested. The most popular additions were references to "cultural," "educational," or "intellectual" problems. The sponsors decided to add only "cultural" problems. See Amendments Submitted by the United States, the United Kingdom, the Soviet Union and China, UNCIO, vol. 3, p. 622.

[29] Amendments Submitted by Australia, UNCIO, vol. 3, p. 543. Similarly, Canada (*idem*, p. 591) believed that "attaining higher standards of living and economic and social progress and development" should be a purpose of the Organization.

[30] Sixth Plenary Session, May 1, 1945, UNCIO, vol. 1, p. 441. See also the views of the delegates from the Philippines (Fourth Plenary Session, April 28, 1945, *idem*, p. 293), Norway (Eighth Plenary Session, May 2, 1945, *idem*, p. 554), and Uruguay (Fourth Plenary Session, April 28, 1945, *idem*, p. 299).

[31] See *e.g.*, Amendments Submitted by Chile, UNCIO, vol. 3, p. 294; Panama, *idem*, pp. 259-260; Czechoslovakia, *idem*, p. 470.

[32] See *e.g.*, Amendments Submitted by Bolivia, UNCIO, vol. 3, pp. 577 and 581, and First Plenary Session, April 26, 1945, UNCIO, vol. 1, pp. 186-187; Norway, UNCIO, vol. 3, pp. 355 and 366; Uruguay, *idem*, p. 43.

[33] First Plenary Session, April 26, 1945, UNCIO, vol. 1, p. 187.

[34] Fourth Plenary Session, April 28, 1945, UNCIO, vol. 1, p. 293. The Philippines used a nice metaphor to stress the interdependence of nations in the modern world. According to the Philippines, "[t]he mountain of man's progress is great and terrible, and they who climb must adjust their pace to the weakest or the entire chain of climbers will go down."

[35] See *e.g.*, Amendments Submitted by Cuba, UNCIO, vol. 3, p. 498; Dominican Republic, *idem*, pp. 564, and 571; Uruguay, *idem*, p. 43.

the provision, correcting "the defective use of adjectives." [36] The UN Charter provision now reads that it is one of the Organization's purposes "[t]o achieve international co-operation in solving international problems of an economic, social, cultural, or humanitarian character."[37]

In addition to this provision in the list of purposes, there was also a "purpose in disguise" slightly further down in the list of the Dumbarton Oaks proposals, which stated that "[w]ith a view to the creation of conditions of stability and well-being which are necessary for peaceful and friendly relations among nations, the Organization should facilitate solutions of international economic, social and other humanitarian problems."[38] This is a purpose in disguise because it is not included in the list of purposes, but does read like a purpose.[39] In contrast with the genuine purpose referred to earlier, this purpose in disguise *did* explicitly refer to the link between socio-economic cooperation and the maintenance of peace,[40] in which the former appears to be subordinate to the latter. At the same time, socio-economic cooperation was also considered as a purpose in and of itself.[41] Some of the amendments to this provision echo those made to the genuine purpose.[42] It was also felt that the phrase "to facilitate solutions" was too weak, and it was therefore replaced with the word "promote."[43] Other than that, no significant changes were made to the Dumbarton Oaks provision that listed different types of cooperation.[44]

---

[36] Report of Rapporteur, Subcommittee I/1/A, to Committee I/1, June 1, 1945, UNCIO, vol. 6, p. 704.

[37] UN Charter, Article 1(3). The French version refers to "intellectual" as opposed to "cultural" problems.

[38] Dumbarton Oaks Proposals for a General International Organization, UNCIO, vol. 3, p. 19. Bedjaoui later suggested that the order of this sentence should be reversed, *i.e.* that friendly relations among nations would facilitate the solution of various international problems. See Mohammed Bedjaoui, "Article 1" (2005), p. 318.

[39] Canada suggested moving the text of this purpose-in-disguise to the list of purposes. Amendments Submitted by Canada, UNCIO, vol. 3, p. 591. See also the Coordination Committee's Summary Report of Thirty-First Meeting, June 18, 1945, UNCIO, vol. 17, pp. 228-232.

[40] This link was emphasized in the Report of the Rapporteur Committee II/3, Approved by Committee II/3, June 8, 1945, UNCIO, vol. 10, p. 279.

[41] It thus, as Kaeckenbeeck pointed out, treated socioeconomic cooperation "à la fois comme fins et comme moyens." Georges Kaeckenbeeck, "La Charte de San-Francisco dans ses rapports avec le droit international" (1948), p. 253.

[42] For example, more or less the same countries made more or less the same suggestions to add references to "culture". The sponsors adopted this reference to "culture" in their amendments. See Amendments Submitted by the United States, the United Kingdom, the Soviet Union and China, UNCIO, vol. 3, p. 626. See also the Tenth Report of Drafting Subcommittee II/3/A , UNCIO, vol. 10, p. 409. See also Fourteenth Meeting of Committee II/3, May 29, 1945, UNCIO, *idem*, p. 127, and Report of the Rapporteur Committee II/3, Approved by Committee II/3, June 8, 1945, UNCIO, *idem*, p. 280.

[43] Report of the Rapporteur Committee II/3, Approved by Committee II/3, June 8, 1945, UNCIO, vol. 10, p. 271.

[44] Working Draft of Paragraphs Approved by Committee II/3, UNCIO, vol. 10, p. 181 (this text is already identical to what was to become article 55 of the UN Charter); Fifth Report of Drafting

One suggestion for a new field of international cooperation, which was ultimately rejected, is particularly interesting. According to the French delegate, "[w]ars do not arise simply because two rival armies want to match their strength against each other." [45] In fact, "[t]hey arise from a number of other causes, including economic rivalries and rivalries over raw materials." [46] According to France, "the inequality in the distribution of raw materials among the various countries was one of the great causes of war."[47] The country therefore proposed "ensuring access, on equal terms, to trade, raw materials, and to capital goods" as a new purpose of the Organization, and of the Economic and Social Council in particular.[48] The Netherlands objected. It believed that "the French amendment took account only of the interests of consumers of raw materials [and] any mention of raw materials in the Charter should provide for protection of producers as well as consumers."[49] New Zealand stated that if the French proposal meant "that nations pledged themselves to abandon tariffs, exchange controls, quotas, and trade agreements," then the New-Zealand delegation would be hesitant to accept it.[50] Peru believed that to abandon such trade barriers was the only effective way to achieve higher standards of living and full employment.[51] In response to the French amendment, Peru also pointed out that "specific reference to the question of raw materials was unnecessary, as international raw material problems are clearly within the sphere of international economic problems."[52] In its report the Committee explicitly stated that the wording used in the article should be interpreted very broadly, and covered the international problems relating to the distribution of raw

---

Committee of Committee II/3, *idem*, p. 390; Tenth Report of Drafting Subcommittee II/3/A, *idem*, p. 409; Twentieth Meeting of Committee II/3, June 6, 1945, *idem*, p. 212.

[45] Second Meeting of Commission II, June 11, 1945, UNCIO, vol. 8, p. 62.

[46] *Idem*. The importance of providing access to the world's raw materials was already pointed out in the Atlantic Charter, adopted on the 14th of August 1941, by President Roosevelt (USA) and Churchill (UK)

[47] Minutes of the Fifteenth Five-Power Informal Consultative Meeting on Proposed Amendments, June 4, 1945, in FRUS, *1945, General:* Volume I, p. 1149.

[48] Fourteenth Meeting of Committee II/3, May 29, 1945, UNCIO, vol. 10, p. 128. See also Mexico, during the Fifteenth Meeting of Committee II/3, May 30, 1945, *idem*, p. 141. See also Lawrence E. Davies, "Ask World Rights to Raw Materials," in *New York Times* of May 27, 1945.

[49] Fourteenth Meeting of Committee II/3, May 29, 1945, UNCIO, vol. 10, p. 129. See also the Minutes of the Sixtieh Meeting of the United States Delegation, May 31, 1945, in FRUS, *1945, General:* Volume I, p. 1027, and Ministerie van Buitenlandse Zaken (Netherlands), *Het ontstaan der Verenigde Naties* (1950), p. 100.

[50] Fourteenth Meeting of Committee II/3, May 29, 1945, UNCIO, vol. 10, p. 130.

[51] Second Meeting of Commission II, June 11, 1945, UNCIO, vol. 8, p. 63.

[52] Fifteenth Meeting of Committee II/3, May 30, 1945, UNCIO, vol. 10, p. 141.

materials.[53] The French delegation could not claim a victory, but it was not a defeat either.[54]

Canada suggested adding "attaining higher standards of living and economic and social progress and development" as an entirely new element in the purpose in disguise.[55] The Ukraine wanted a "guarant[ee] for all the working people of the right to work."[56] Greece urged that the "Organization should be empowered to assist in the reconstruction of territories devastated by the war."[57] The Greek suggestion was not adopted, but the other two were basically combined into the following new purpose: to promote "higher standards of living, high and stable levels of employment and conditions of economic and social progress and development."[58] At New Zealand's request, the Committee changed "high and stable levels of employment" to "full employment." [59]

The Organization therefore promotes "higher standards of living, full employment, and conditions of economic and social progress and development," and "solutions of international economic, social, health, and related problems," and "international cultural and educational cooperation."[60] This shows that the purpose in disguise was significantly changed, compared to the original Dumbarton Oaks version.[61] Thus it was rightly referred to as "one of the best illustrations to date of what can happen to the language of the Dumbarton Oaks agreement at this [San Francisco] conference."[62] The adoption of all these new socio-economic purposes was of particular concern to the US, but there was little even the US could do to stop it.[63]

---

[53] Report of the Rapporteur Committee II/3, Approved by Committee II/3, June 8, 1945, UNCIO, vol. 10, p. 271.

[54] See also Jean Dupuy, *San Francisco et la Charte des Nations Unies* (1945), pp. 52-53.

[55] Amendments Submitted by Canada, UNCIO, vol. 3, p. 591.

[56] Fifth Meeting of Committee II/3, May 14, 1945, UNCIO, vol. 10, p. 27.

[57] Eleventh Meeting of Committee II/3, May 24, 1945, UNCIO, vol. 10, p. 84.

[58] First Report of Drafting Subcommittee, UNCIO, vol. 10, p. 373.

[59] Seventh Meeting of Committee II/3, May 16, 1945, UNCIO, vol. 10, p. 39. The subcommittee chose "high and stable" over "full" by a difference of just one vote.

[60] Article 55 UN Charter. In the French version, "cultural cooperation" is translated this time as "coopération internationale dans les domaines de la culture intellectuelle."

[61] For the provision on human rights, see Chapter VI on human dignity.

[62] "Widen Definition of Human Rights," an article that appeared in the *New York Times* of May 18, 1945.

[63] Mrs. Gildersleeve, the US representative in the Committee, remarked that "it was frightening to observe what the members of the Committee expected in the way of results," and that "this development [of adopting more and more socio-economic purposes] was alarming and would be difficult to hold in check." See Minutes of Fifty-third Meeting of the United States Delegation, May 25, 1945, in FRUS, *1945, General:* Volume I, pp. 886-887.

## 2.3 The Principle

In the Dumbarton Oaks proposals there was no principle that obliged the Member States or the Organization to cooperate on socio-economic issues. Australia saw the "fullest collaboration in the economic fields with the object of securing for all improved labour standards, economic advancement, and social security" as one of the three great starting points of the Organization.[64] It therefore suggested adding a brand new principle that "[a]ll members of the United Nations pledge themselves to take action both national and international for the purpose of securing for all peoples, including their own, improved labour standards, economic advancement, social security and employment for all who seek it."[65] This article became known simply as "the pledge."[66] In Australia's view, the central idea of the pledge was that it consisted of two types of obligations: first, all Member States had a duty to cooperate with each other in promoting socio-economic purposes at the international level. Secondly, each State should pursue the same socio-economic purposes at the national level "by its own action in its own way."[67]

The US was strongly opposed to the pledge.[68] Stettinius believed it was "dangerous," and Dulles suggested that the US would attempt to "have this clause ruled out of order because it constituted, in effect, a multilateral agreement – a pledge to take individual action."[69] The US was alone in its opposition, and was confronted by all the other nations, described by Pasvolsky as a "stampede under way," which could not be stopped.[70] When the relevant Subcommittee and Committee of the San Francisco Conference were looking at ways of redrafting the Australian provision in an attempt to please the Americans, Australia had to fight

---

[64] First Plenary Session, April 26, 1945, UNCIO, vol. 1, p. 170.

[65] Amendments Submitted by Australia, UNCIO, vol. 3, pp. 546-547. See also First Plenary Session, April 26, 1945, UNCIO, vol. 1, p. 177, where Australia defends the amendment in plenary session.

[66] See *e.g.*, Department of External Affairs (Canada), *Report on the United Nations conference on international organization* (1945), pp. 46-47.

[67] Twelfth Meeting of Committee II/3, May 25, 1945, UNCIO, vol. 10, p. 100. According to the UK, the pledge had not two, but three elements, namely a pledge "for separate action, for joint action, and for cooperation with the Organization." See Fifteenth Meeting of Committee II/3, May 30, 1945, UNCIO, vol. 10, p. 140.

[68] Evatt later described the attitude of the US and other major powers as "extremely unresponsive." Herbert Vere Evatt, *The United Nations* (1948), p. 31.

[69] See Minutes of Fifty-fourth Meeting of the United States Delegation, May 26, 1945, in FRUS, *1945, General:* Volume I, p. 893. See also Rüdiger Wolfrum, "Article 56" (2002), p. 942.

[70] *Idem*, p. 894. In order to at least slow down the stampede, the US proposed an alternative formulation, that "[a]ll members undertake to cooperate with the Organization and with each other and to take separate action, consistent with their own political and economic institutions, to the achievement of the [socioeconomic] purposes." See Minutes of Fifty-sixth Meeting of the United States Delegation, May 28, 1945, in FRUS, *1945, General:* Volume I, p. 945.

hard to ensure that this twofold nature of the pledge survived. [71] Australia was successful, and the pledge ended up in the Charter as follows:

> All Members pledge themselves to take joint and separate action in co-operation with the Organization for the achievement of the purposes set forth in Article 55 [*i.e.* the purpose in disguise]. [72]

When the work was finished, Stettinius referred to the pledge in surprisingly positive terms as "epoch-making in the history of international organization." [73] Australia later claimed credit for being the drafter of the pledge, and the records show they certainly deserved it. [74]

## 3   SOCIAL PROGRESS AND DEVELOPMENT

### 3.1 Introduction

This section examines the general ideas on social progress and development presented by the Assembly. Where relevant, these ideas are compared with suggestions from outside the UN framework, especially in the (philosophical) literature.

What can be expected from the General Assembly's declarations on social progress and development when they are examined from a value-based perspective? [75] First, we might expect some general ideas on what various actors should do to ensure the fair distribution of goods, opportunities and resources at the global level, [76] as well as something about global social justice or global distributive justice.

Before looking at the declarations, some of the more influential literature on this topic is presented, so that the ideas in the literature can be compared with those in the UN's declarations.

---

[71] See *e.g.*, the Fourteenth Meeting of Committee II/3, May 29, 1945, UNCIO, vol. 10, p. 130, and especially the Fifteenth Meeting of Committee II/3, May 30, 1945, *idem*, pp. 139-140.

[72] The pledge´s meaning is explained by the Rapporteur at the Ninth Plenary Session, June 25, 1945, UNCIO, vol. 1, p. 622.

[73] Edward R. Stettinius, "Human Rights in the United Nations Charter" (1946), p. 1.

[74] Herbert Vere Evatt, *The United Nations* (1948), p. 9.

[75] The cross-fertilization between economics and "UN ideas" has been studied elsewhere. See especially the work of the United Nations Intellectual History Project, *e.g.*, Richard Jolly, Louis Emmerij, Dharam Ghai & Frédéric Lapeyre, *UN Contributions to Development Thinking and Practice* (2004), and Richard Jolly, Louis Emmerij & Thomas G. Weiss, *UN Ideas that Changed the World* (2009).

[76] As examples of goods, one might think simply of money, but also of the most basic needs, such as food, health care, education, and a healthy environment.

Principles of social or distributive justice are normative principles designed to allocate goods that are limited in supply relative to demand, on the basis of a mechanism that is considered fair.[77] The problem is how to interpret the word "fair". According to a strictly egalitarian concept of fairness, the distribution is fair when all individuals receive an equal share of the goods.[78] But there are alternatives. John Stuart Mill suggested a deserts-based approach to social justice.[79] In general, these deserts refer to certain acts or qualities of the recipient.[80] For example, all humans are equally deserving because they are humans.[81] But certain acts by specific individuals may positively or negatively affect what they deserve.[82] In 1971, Rawls introduced the now famous difference principle: within a community, inequalities in the distribution of goods and opportunities are only morally acceptable if they are to everyone's advantage.[83] Most theories of social justice have in common that they require that all inequalities in the distribution of resources and opportunities must be justified in some way, and that any inequality that is unjustifiable by any standard of justice is an injustice.[84] The big question is whether such theories, most of which were originally applied at the national level or to some other clearly defined community, can be applied at the global level. Rawls

---

[77] "Distributive Justice", entry in the Stanford Encyclopedia of Philosophy, available online at http://plato.stanford.edu/. This definition should not give the suggestion that there is unanimous agreement on what global social/distributive justice is. It is actually rather difficult to give a definition of global social justice. Perhaps for that reason, David Miller wrote in the preface of his book Social Justice, that the reader should be warned he was not to be provided with a definition of social justice. Miller, *Social Justic* (1979).

[78] *Idem.* See also Kok-Chor Tan, "The Boundary of Justice and the Justice of Boundaries" (2006), pp. 319-344.

[79] Mill: "If it is a duty to do to each according to his deserts, returning good for good as well as repressing evil by evil, it necessarily follows that we should treat all equally well (when no higher duty forbids) who have deserved equally well of us, and that society should treat all equally well who have deserved equally well of it, that is, who have deserved equally well absolutely. This is the highest abstract standard of social and distributive justice; towards which all institutions, and the efforts of all virtuous citizens, should be made in the utmost possible degree to converge." This quote is from "On the Connection between Justice and Utility", chapter V of Mill, *Utilitarianism* (1863).

[80] On the problems of defining "desert" in this context, see Julian Lamont, "The Concept of Desert in Distributive Justice" (1994).

[81] They may deserve equally, but the needs of different people and States can be quite different: cold countries require heating, mountainous and landlocked countries require more expensive infrastructure, hot countries require air-conditioning, etc. The question one may raise is how a concept of global justice can take into account differences in the requirements to achieve a "common" level of living. Marx's adage comes to mind: "From each according to his ability, to each according to his needs!" Marx, *Critique of the Gotha Program*, Part I, first published in 1875.

[82] See Peter Vallentyne, "Desert and Entitlement: An Introduction" (2003); Alan Zaitchik, "On Deserving to Deserve" (1977).

[83] John Rawls, *A Theory of Justice (Revised Edition)* (1999, original of 1971), p. 55. Rawls" theory is generally seen as a form of egalitarianism, albeit not strict egalitarianism.

[84] This may seem like an unhelpful play with words, but the point is that inequality caused by chance or mere factual circumstances alone is unjust.

did not believe that his theory of justice could be applied to the international community.[85] Many disagree with him on this point.[86]

One of the main problems one encounters when transposing theories of national justice to the international level, is that it is difficult to speak of distributive justice if there is no "distributor." It has often been argued that if there is no global institution mandated to (re)distribute goods, it is probably impossible to speak about global social justice at all.[87] No international institution, not even the United Nations, has been given a mandate to distribute goods evenly over all Member States, let alone all the individual people in the world.[88]

None of the General Assembly declarations go so far as to introduce any system of global social/distributive justice. At best, the proposals aim to enable States to get what they need through participation in the international economic order.[89] Therefore the idea is to create a level playing field, but the game is still one of the survival of the fittest, a game in which States provide for themselves. Most people agree that there is something immoral about this system when it leads to extreme forms of misery in those communities that fail to provide for themselves. Even Charles Darwin, the champion of natural selection and of the "survival of the fittest" theory, believed this to be so. After all, he wrote that "if the misery of our poor be caused not by laws of nature, but by our own institutions, great is our sin."[90] At the very least, the world should provide a safety net for those who do not benefit from participating in the existing international economic order. If this is

---

[85] John Rawls, *The Law of Peoples* (1999), p. 83.

[86] See *e.g.*, Charles R. Beitz, *Political Theory and International Relations* (1999); Pogge, *Realizing Rawls* (1989). Many articles have also made this point: See *e.g.*, Thomas W. Pogge, "An Egalitarian Law of Peoples" (1994), pp. 195-224; Andrew Kuper, "Rawlsian Global Justice: Beyond a Law of Peoples to a Cosmopolitan Law of Persons" (2000), pp. 640-674; the contributions of Allen Buchanan and Charles Beitz in Ethics, Volume 110, Number 4, July 2000 (which contained a Symposium on John Rawls' *The Law of Peoples* (1999)). There are many others...

[87] See *e.g.*, Thomas Nagel, "The Problem of Global Justice" (2005); Charles R. Beitz, *Political Theory and International Relations* (1999), p. 194; Darrel Moellendorf, *Cosmopolitan Justice* (2002).

[88] As other candidates, one might think of the Bretton Woods institutions: the World Trade Organization (WTO), the World Bank and the International Monetary Fund (IMF). There has been a big debate about whether the Bretton Woods institutions should be reformed or rather be replaced by fundamentally different institutions or mechanisms at the international level. See *e.g.*, Anne O. Krueger, "Whither the World Bank and the IMF?" (1998); Christopher L. Gilbert & David Vines (editors), *The World Bank* (2006).

[89] That is also the main aim of official development assistance: it is not to (re)distribute the goods evenly over all participants, but it is intended to assist developing nations in being able to cope for themselves. Development aid is thus based on the idea that the rich have a duty to assist those that do not prosper in the economic world order. See Thomas W. Pogge, "Recognized and Violated by International Law: The Human Rights of the Global Poor" (2005); Pogge, "The International Significance of Human Rights" (2000); Pogge, *World Poverty and Human Rights* (2002).

[90] Cited in Thomas W. Pogge, *World Poverty and Human Rights* (2002), p. 67, who refers to Gould, "The Moral State of Tahiti", p. 19, who then refers to the original source: Charles Darwin, *Voyage of the Beagle* (1839).

implemented seriously, it is reminiscent of the very beginning of a rather minimalist global welfare system.[91]

Compared to theories calling for the equal or fair (re)distribution of global goods, theories calling for international duties of assistance are much more modest. The General Assembly has acknowledged that the poor nations should be given assistance, and not simply because they need help to survive. They *deserve* such assistance. They are entitled to it. In philosophy, a distinction is generally made between needs-based assistance, and assistance based on rights and duties. No one would argue that there is no duty to save people who are in desperate need when we have the ability to do so at a reasonable cost.[92] This duty to come to the rescue of the needy is an absolute duty. It is different from a duty to assist based on principles of social justice. In case of the absolute duty, those who are rescued are indebted to their rescuer. The rescuer can reclaim the emergency relief money at a later stage, or decide not to reclaim it on the basis of good will or charity. This does not apply in the case of the duty of social justice. This duty to assist is based on the idea that it is unfair and unjust for the poor to be poor while others are rich. For that reason alone, the misery of the poor must be remedied.[93] If global social justice could be described as a duty to remedy the most fundamental lack of basic needs in the world, then there is global social justice in the declarations of the General Assembly of the United Nations. The declaration that comes closest to setting out the rules and principles of a system of global social justice is the Millennium Declaration.

The absolute duty to help those who are in immediate danger, and some minimalist duties based on global social justice, are the two main themes of all General Assembly declarations on social progress and development. The two general purposes are:

> To win the fight against an absolute lack of development in certain parts of the world, *i.e.* to find ways to ban absolute poverty and the lack of basic services from all States in the world;

> To win the fight against unequal development, *i.e.* to repair the international economic order to halt and possibly reverse the growing inequality of opportunities for development, both between States and between individuals within States.[94]

---

[91] See also Thomas W. Pogge, *World Poverty and Human Rights* (2002), Chapter 8: Eradicating Systemic Poverty: Brief for a Global Resources Dividend. For a critique, see Tim Hayward, "Thomas Pogge's Global Resources Dividend (2005).

[92] For the practical consequences, see the article by Peter Singer in the *New York Times* of 5 September, 1999, "The Singer Solution to World Poverty".

[93] Thomas W. Pogge, *World Poverty and Human Rights* (2002), p. 23.

[94] The formulation of these two goals is consistent with the general tendency to use military language, such as the "fight against poverty," and the "strategy for development," when talking about development. See also Maurice Flory, "International Development Strategy for the Third United

These two main purposes constitute the common thread in the Assembly's list of general declarations on development.[95] The first is discussed in a special section devoted to programmes of assistance for the least developed nations of the world.[96] Most of this chapter deals with resolutions of the second category.

When it comes to the strategy for action, most – if not all – resolutions distinguish between obligations for States at the national level, and obligations at the international level. When it comes to the national aspect of the strategy, the United Nations General Assembly has continuously emphasized the primary responsibility of States – or Governments – for their own development. The Assembly set certain goals, and then advised States on how to achieve those goals. It subsequently examined the progress of developing States in achieving them.[97] In general, the results can be described as falling somewhere between "full achievement" and "total failure," but they come closer to the latter.[98]

When it comes to the international aspect of the UN strategy to promote the value of social progress and development, the Assembly has always been hesitant about obliging States to behave in a certain way in their economic relations. At best, the Assembly has suggested that developed States have a duty to assist the developing States in their development.[99] The Assembly has consistently focused on three types of obligations to assist:

An obligation for all States to help revise the rules of the international economic order so that preferential treatment is provided to developing States;

An obligation for developed States to spend a small part of their gross domestic product on official development assistance to developing States;

And an obligation for all States, and especially developing States, to facilitate foreign direct investment.[100]

These three obligations taken together represent a rather drastic change in international economic affairs. In contrast, the concrete obligations have

---

Nations Development Decade" (1982), pp. 69-70, where this trend was noticed already in the earlier days.

[95] For an overview of the UN's work on development, see Thomas G. Weiss, David P. Forsythe, Roger A. Coate & Kelly-Kate Pease, *The United Nations and Changing World Politics* (2009).

[96] See section 4 of Chapter V.

[97] See also Richard Jolly, Louis Emmerij & Thomas G. Weiss, *UN Ideas that Changed the World* (2009), pp. 87-88.

[98] *Idem*, p. 88.

[99] Unfortunately, even these rather weak duties of assistance have generally not been complied with. See *idem*.

[100] See also *idem*, p. 101.

consistently been drafted in more careful language. This careful formulation of the strategy in most resolutions can be explained in the same way as the language of Article 56 UN Charter. It is a direct result of the friction between the duty of all States to cooperate in the realization of certain common interests and values, and the duty of all States – and the United Nations itself – to respect the sovereign independence of all States and therefore to refrain from interference in their internal affairs. [101]

When it comes to international development cooperation, a problem arises which is in many ways unique to the realization of the value of social progress and development. This problem is the dominant role of non-State actors in this field, and the lack of control that States have over them. [102] The flow of capital and resources from private investors, often based in the developed States, to developing nations, dwarfs the flow of capital from developed States to developing States, *i.e.* official development aid.[103] The United Nations has an influence on the relations between States. But the United Nations has very few means to influence the behaviour of those non-State actors, whose role is much more substantial when it comes to the realization of the value of social progress and development.

## 3.2 The First United Nations Development Decade

The Assembly's work on defining and developing the value of social progress and development essentially started in the 1960s.[104] Since then, the developing world has had an almost automatic majority in the General Assembly.[105] Therefore it is not surprising that the declarations on development focused on the interests of the developing States. There is no definition for a "developing State". When the

---

[101] See section 2.1 and 4 of Chapter VII.

[102] As White rightly noted, "a major export of most developed nations has been technological information and know-how and quite obviously this is as important a "resource"in the international economic environment as raw materials such as oil or sugar." Robin C. A. White, "New International Economic Order" (1975), p. 550.

[103] As the US Legal Adviser rightly pointed out, "since World War II, ninety percent of the investment in the developing world has been from private sources; only ten percent has come from public sources." See Leigh, on p. 349 of Paxman (rapporteur), "Discussion" (1975).

[104] Earlier, some assistance programmes were initiated by the UN to assist developing States, such as the United Nations Expanded Program of Technical Assistance, and the United Nations Special Fund. For the first, see Technical assistance for economic development, General Assembly resolution 200 (III), adopted 4 December 1948. For the latter, see Establishment of the Special Fund, General Assembly resolution 1240(XIII), adopted 14 October 1958. For comments, see David Owen, "The United Nations Expanded Program of Technical Assistance - A Multilateral Approach" (1959); and Ronald A. Manzer, "The United Nations Special Fund" (1964).

[105] The United Nations had 82 Members in 1958, and 127 in 1970; nearly all the 45 nations that were welcomed to the UN family in the 1960s were developing nations.

Assembly refers to development, it is mainly concerned with the allocation of resources. According to this approach, a developing country is defined simply as a country in which most people have fewer resources and opportunities than those in developed countries. It is a relative term, and the distinction is rather arbitrary. Sometimes it is clear whether a State is relatively developed or developing, but the distinction becomes problematical near the borderline.

One of the earliest general declarations on the topic of social progress and development proclaimed the First United Nations Development Decade, an initiative launched by President Kennedy of the United States of America.[106] In this resolution, the Assembly set a specific target for the growth of developing States – 5% of average national income – and suggested various measures to support the developing States to reach that target.[107] The plan was essentially to make it easier for them to flourish in the international economic order, to increase official development aid, and to stimulate foreign direct investment. This is a clear example of the Assembly's general three-pronged strategy to achieve the value of social progress and development for everyone. This strategy might not sound all that extraordinary, but it actually was very different from the approach of the past. For example, with regard to the pledge of developed States to devote part of their domestic product to development assistance, the UN Secretary-General remarked that it "showed that the concept of shared resources is beginning to enter the philosophy of States in relation not simply to their own citizens but to other States as well."[108] The plan was not developed in great detail and was therefore, in Tinbergen's words, "a plan in embryo."[109]

One year later, the Assembly adopted the Declaration on Permanent Sovereignty over Natural Resources.[110] Although the resolution was initially meant to emphasize the exclusive and sovereign right of States to exploit their own natural resources, it imposes many conditions for this. It is these conditions that are the most interesting elements of the resolution.[111] Foreign direct investment was seen as one of three possible strategies for the development of developing States, although it also had a negative side: a foreign multinational corporation can exploit the

---

[106] United Nations Development Decade: A Programme for International Economic Co-operation, General Assembly resolutions 1710 (XVI) and 1715 (XVI), both adopted on 19 December 1961.

[107] All are quotes from para. 2, General Assembly resolution 1710 (XVI).

[108] The United Nations Development Decade at Mid-Point, UN Secretary-General's report, UNDoc. E/4071/Rev.1, p. 6, as cited on pp. 22-23, of Walter M. Kotschnig, "The United Nations as an Instrument of Economic and Social Development" (1968).

[109] Jan Tinbergen, "International Economic Planning" (1966), p. 538.

[110] Declaration on Permanent Sovereignty over Natural Resources, General Assembly resolution 1803(XVII), adopted 14 December 1962. For a detailed overview of the *travaux préparatoires* of this resolution, see Nico Schrijver, *Sovereignty over natural resources* (1997), pp. 57-76.

[111] For a similar view, see Stephen M. Schwebel, "The Story of the U.N.'s Declaration on Permanent Sovereignty over Natural Resources" (1963), p. 464. The resolution will also be discussed in Chapter VII on self-determination.

developing States' natural resources solely for its own benefit (to make a profit), and not for the benefit of the local population. Thus the resolution attempted to find a balance between respect for the rights of the foreign investor and the sovereign rights of States to exploit their own resources for the benefit of their population.[112] The result of this balancing act was the emergence of a conditional right of States to expropriate, for the public interest, the property rights of foreign investors.[113] Thus expropriation was not forbidden entirely, but was allowed only in certain exceptional cases. In all cases of expropriation, the foreign investor was entitled to "appropriate compensation." [114] According to Garcia-Amador, the resolution outlined the "basic principles of traditional international law which govern expropriation, nationalization, and compensation."[115] It could certainly be argued that this is still the case.

The Permanent Sovereignty Declaration also proclaimed certain principles to protect the interests of the foreign investor. Thus it was a balanced resolution, not wholly focused on improving the situation of developing States. Many of the resolutions that followed in the 1970s were primarily concerned with the interests of the developing States, although they continued to stress the responsibility of States for their own development. This can be explained by the fact that since the early 1960s, the developing States had not only gained a numerical majority in the Assembly, but they had also started to organize themselves. The developing nations first organized themselves formally by adopting the Joint Declaration of the Developing Countries in 1963. This declaration was not adopted by the General Assembly, but by a group of developing countries within the Assembly.[116] It was the precursor to the Joint Declaration of the Seventy-Seven Developing Countries, adopted by more or less the same group at the end of the first United Nations Conference on Trade and Development in 1964. This marked the establishment of

---

[112] The resolution sets out certain conditions which had to be fulfilled before a State could expropriate the property of foreign investors. See especially para. 4, Declaration on Permanent Sovereignty over Natural Resources, General Assembly resolution 1803(XVII), adopted 14 December 1962.

[113] See Karol N. Gess, "Permanent Sovereignty over Natural Resources" (1964).

[114] Declaration on Permanent Sovereignty over Natural Resources, General Assembly resolution 1803(XVII), adopted 14 December 1962, para. 4. The United States, who defended the interests of the foreign investor at the time, wanted the Assembly to state explicitly that "appropriate compensation" should be interpreted as "prompt, adequate and effective" compensation, but an amendment to make this explicit was withdrawn after the United States understood that the words "appropriate compensation" were to be interpreted in such a way. See Stephen M. Schwebel, "The Story of the U.N.'s Declaration on Permanent Sovereignty over Natural Resources" (1963), pp. 465-466. See also Karol N. Gess, "Permanent Sovereignty over Natural Resources" (1964), pp. 427-428.

[115] Francisco V. García-Amador y Rodriguez, "Proposed New International Economic Order: A New Approach to the Law Governing Nationalization and Compensation" (1980), p. 23.

[116] Joint Declaration of the Developing Countries, annexed to General Assembly resolution 1897(XVIII), adopted 11 November 1963.

the Group of 77.[117] The developing nations focused on the establishment of a new international economic order, friendly to developing nations, and much less on the reform of their own national development strategies. The G77 Declaration is itself a good example of this approach. It called for a "new and just world economic order," the basic premises of which "involve[d] a new international division of labour oriented towards the accelerated industrialization of developing countries."[118] It is striking that the declaration said very little about the responsibilities of developing nations themselves to improve their own domestic development policies.[119]

In 1969, the General Assembly adopted a Declaration on Social Progress and Development.[120] The declaration set specific goals[121] and objectives,[122] and described the means to achieve these goals and objectives. The Declaration also assigned the responsibility for achieving them. The Assembly stressed that "each Government ha[d] the primary role and ultimate responsibility of ensuring the social progress and well-being of its people."[123] The efforts of the international community were meant to "supplement, by concerted international action, national efforts to raise the living standards of peoples."[124] These international obligations of assistance included, as was the case in previous declarations, international development assistance, and the "expansion of international trade based on principles of equality and non-discrimination."[125]

## 3.3 The Second United Nations Development Decade

In 1970, the General Assembly came up with an International Development Strategy for the Second Development Decade, prepared by the UN Committee for Development Planning, chaired by the Dutch economist Jan Tinbergen.[126] In the

---

[117] The Group of 77 has its own website. See http://www.g77.org.

[118] Joint Declaration of the Seventy-Seven Developing Countries made at the Conclusion of the United Nations Conference on Trade and Development, Geneva, 15 June 1964, para. 2. See also Para. 5 of the Joint Declaration.

[119] See *idem*, paras. 7-10.

[120] Declaration on Social Progress and Development, General Assembly resolution 2542(XXIV), adopted 11 December 1969 ("Declaration on Social Progress and Development").

[121] *Idem*, Articles 10 and 11.

[122] *Idem*, Articles 12 and 13.

[123] *Idem*, Article 8.

[124] *Idem*, Article 9.

[125] *Idem*, Article 23. The Article furrther called for "the rectification of the position of developing countries in international trade by equitable terms of trade [and] a general non-reciprocal and non-discriminatory system of preferences for the exports of developing countries to the developed countries."

[126] International Development Strategy for the Second United Nations Development Decade, General Assembly resolution 2626(XXV), adopted 24 October 1970 ("International Development Strategy for the Second United Nations Development Decade").

Preamble, the Assembly acknowledged that during the First Development Decade, not much progress had been made in the fight against an absolute lack of development in many parts of the world, or in the fight against unequal development.[127] In the Assembly's view, "the level of living of countless millions of people in the developing part of the world [was] still pitifully low," and "while a part of the world live[d] in great comfort and even affluence, much of the larger part suffer[ed] from abject poverty, and in fact the disparity [was] continuing to widen."[128] Thus "the ultimate objective of development must be to bring about sustained improvement in the well-being of the individual and bestow benefits on all." [129] The Assembly emphasized that domestic Governments had primary responsibility, and that the international community had a secondary obligation to provide aid and assistance.[130] These international obligations of aid and assistance were stated in much more detail than had been the case earlier.[131] Included in the long list was a pledge by developed States to spend at least 0.7 per cent of their gross domestic product on official international development assistance.[132]

The first half of the Second United Nations Decade was not a success. A series of economic crises had worsened the situation in most developing nations.[133] Therefore there was a general feeling that more drastic measures were needed. In 1974 the Assembly adopted the very ambitious Declaration on the Establishment of a New International Economic Order. [134] This new order divided not only the community of States, but also the academic community.[135]

---

[127] This was also noted in the Declaration on the Occasion of the Twenty-Fifth Anniversary of the United Nations, General Assembly resolution 2627(XXV), also adopted on 24 October 1970, para. 9. Some authors see the First Development Decade as a success. See Richard Jolly, Louis Emmerij & Thomas G. Weiss, *UN Ideas that Changed the World* (2009), p. 105.

[128] International Development Strategy for the Second United Nations Development Decade, para. 3.

[129] *Idem*, para. 7.

[130] *Idem*, para. 11.

[131] *Idem*, paras. 21-78. They included pledges that are not normally considered to be the concern of the United Nations Organization, such as the pledge that "no new tariff and non-tariff barriers will be raised." See *idem*, para. 25.

[132] This paragraph is preceded by a paragraph in which the main responsibility of developing countries for their own development is emphasized. See *idem*, paras. 41-42.

[133] See the First Biennial Over-All Review and Appraisal of Progress in the Implementation of the International Development Strategy for the Second United Nations Development Decade, General Assembly resolution 3176(XXVIII), adopted 17 December 1973.

[134] Declaration on the Establishment of a New International Economic Order, General Assembly resolution 3201(S-VI), adopted 1 May 1974 ("Declaration on the Establishment of a New International Economic Order").

[135] In the 1970s alone, over 300 books and articles were published on the new international economic order (they were not necessarily all about the Assembly's declaration). For an overview, see Linus A. Hoskins, "The New International Economic Order: A Bibliographic Essay" (1981). See also Robert W. Cox, "Ideologies and the New International Economic Order: Reflections on Some Recent Literature" (1979).

In the Declaration, the Assembly acknowledged that "it ha[d] proved impossible to achieve an even and balanced development of the international community under the existing international economic order," and that "the gap between the developed and the developing countries continue[d] to widen in a system which was established at a time when most of the developing countries did not even exist as independent States and which perpetuate[d] inequality." [136] It therefore proposed to

> Work urgently for the establishment of a New International Economic Order based on equity, sovereign equality, interdependence, common interest and cooperation among all States, irrespective of their economic and social systems, which shall correct inequalities and redress existing injustices, make it possible to eliminate the widening gap between the developed and the developing countries and ensure steadily accelerating economic and social development and peace and justice for present and future generations. [137]

This proclaimed new order was based on a very strong respect for the sovereign independence and equality of States, especially of the newly independent States. A number of specific rights and obligations were derived from the principle of sovereign independence, such as the right of States to use their own natural resources for the benefit of the local population, and in this way supervise the activities of transnational corporations active within their territory, and, if necessary, expropriate the property of foreign investors. [138] Furthermore, the Assembly recognized a "right of all States, territories and peoples under foreign occupation, alien and colonial domination or *apartheid*, to restitution and full compensation for the exploitation and depletion of, and damages to, the natural resources and all other resources of those States, territories and peoples." [139] This gave the impression that one of the elements of the new international economic order was to rectify historic wrongs by means of expropriation. In the words of Boutros-Ghali, "generations of colonial exploitation made the development effort seem to be a debt owed by the post-imperial powers to the lands they had in the past sought to rule," and that "the only solution, it was thought, was to 'expropriate the expropriators.'" [140] This was not acceptable to the former colonizers. The Assembly also listed far-reaching obligations for all States to contribute to an international economic order that was friendly to developing States, based on "preferential and non-reciprocal treatment for developing countries, wherever feasible, in all fields of

---

[136] Declaration on the Establishment of a New International Economic Order, para. 1.

[137] *Idem*, Preamble.

[138] *Idem*, paras. 4(e) and (g).

[139] *Idem*, para. 4(f).

[140] Boutros Boutros-Ghali, "A New Departure on Development" (1995), p. 45. Boutros-Ghali was not referring to any General Assembly declaration in particular.

international economic co-operation whenever possible." [141] The Assembly suggested introducing a minimal form of distributive justice into the international legal order. The developed States, especially the United States, were rather overwhelmed by this resolution, which was adopted "by consensus," *i.e.* without a recorded vote.[142]

The distributive justice element of this economic order made it a truly "new" order. The new economic order was based on the principle that the developing States deserved some preferential treatment.[143] The principal flaw in the "old" international economic order was that, at a time when many States were experiencing tremendous economic growth, other States were lagging behind. As time passed it became increasingly difficult for the "laggards" to catch up with the successful States. The fact that they had lagged behind also negatively affected their ability to compete effectively in the global market.[144]

Contrary to what its title suggests, the Declaration on the Establishment of a New International Economic Order was presented merely as a prelude to, or as an "additional source of inspiration" for the Charter of Economic Rights and Duties of States.[145] This Charter was presented as the key document of the new economic order.[146] It was adopted by the Assembly in December 1974, approximately half a year after the adoption of its predecessor.[147] The developing States, which were the

---

[141] Declaration on the Establishment of a New International Economic Order, para 4(n).

[142] Many developed States made declarations expressing their reservations at the time of the vote. See Branislav Gosovic and John G. Ruggie, "On the Creation of a New International Economic Order" (1976), p. 314 (footnote 8). On the US position, see Clarence Clyde Ferguson, "The Politics of the New International Economic Order" (1977).

[143] See also John F. Dorsey, "Preferential Treatment: A New Standard for International Economic Relations" (1977), pp. 113-116; David R. Lindskog, "The New International Economic Order" (1986), p. 22; Francisco V. García-Amador y Rodriguez, "Proposed New International Economic Order: A New Approach to the Law Governing Nationalization and Compensation" (1980), pp. 17-20; and Nico Schrijver, "The Evolution of Sustainable Development in International Law" (2007), p. 249. Schrijver did not refer to preferential treatment, but focused more on the idea that the rules needed to be changed so that the "best cards would no longer automatically fall in the hands of the rich countries and multinational corporations."

[144] The word "laggards" was used by Fred Hirsch, "Is there a New International Economic Order?" (1976), p. 523. See also Hans W. Singer, "The New International Economic Order: An Overview" (1978), pp. 539-541. He argued that the new international economic order was more a response to the collapse of the old order in the early 1970s than a dissatisfaction with that old order.

[145] Declaration on the Establishment of a New International Economic Order, para. 6.

[146] Tiewul rightly warned not to draw too many conclusions from the use of the word "Charter," which reminds one of the UN Charter. It does not affect the non-binding nature of the resolution. See S. Azadon Tiewul, "The United Nations Charter of Economic Rights and Duties of States" (1975), pp. 655-658.

[147] Charter of Economic Rights and Duties of States, General Assembly resolution 3281(XXIX), adopted 12 December 1974 ("Charter of Economic Rights and Duties of States"). It was adopted by voting, and thus we can see that many (16) of the developed nations either voted against or abstained.

main supporters of the Charter, hoped that it would not be considered as just another non-binding declaration, but that it would genuinely "alter the rules of the game."[148] These new rules of the game were very similar to those in the Declaration that preceded it. The right to sovereign independence of States was once again emphasized, as well as the corresponding obligation of non-interference.[149] The Charter emphasized every State's "primary responsibility to promote the economic, social and cultural development of its people," but this did not constitute the main theme of the document.[150] Almost all the other articles were about international cooperation and assistance. They imposed obligations on developed countries.[151] The obligation to right historic wrongs, which had appeared in the Declaration on the Establishment of a New International Economic Order, was also included in the Charter.[152]

The most controversial part of the Charter, and the reason why most of the developed States either abstained from voting or voted against, was the article describing some of the supposed consequences of the right to sovereign economic independence of States in matters relating to the regulation of foreign investment.[153] The more general consequence, which was acceptable to most States, was that "every State ha[d] and sh[ould] freely exercise full permanent sovereignty, including possession, use and disposal, over all its wealth, natural resources and economic activities."[154] The more controversial consequences were those regarding the relationship between the foreign investor, often a national of a developed State,

---

However, since the developing nations constituted a majority in the Assembly, it was nonetheless adopted by overwhelming majority (120 in favour).

[148] Eduard Rozental, "Charter of Economic Rights and Duties of States and the New International Economic Order" (1975), p. 317.

[149] Charter of Economic Rights and Duties of States, Article 1.

[150] Only one Article was about the responsibilities of Governments for the development of their own State. See *idem*, Article 7.

[151] See especially *idem*, Articles 8, 9, 13, 14, 17, 18, 19, 22, and 25. See also S. Azadon Tiewul, "The United Nations Charter of Economic Rights and Duties of States" (1975), pp. 666-670, who referred to some of these articles.

[152] *Idem*, Article 16.

[153] This was Article 2. For the reasons – and justifications – why most developed States could not vote in favour of the resolution, see *e.g.*, S. K. Chatterjee, "The Charter of Economic Rights and Duties of States: An Evaluation after 15 Years" (1991), pp. 672-675; Alfred P. Rubin, "The Charter of Economic Rights and Duties of States: Remarks" (1975), p. 225; Eduard Rozental, "Charter of Economic Rights and Duties of States and the New International Economic Order" (1975), p. 319; G. W. Haight, "New International Economic Order and the Charter of Economic Rights and Duties of States" (1975), pp. 595-603; G. White, "A New International Economic Order?" (1975), pp. 330-335; and Robin C. A. White, "New International Economic Order" (1975), pp. 546-547. See also, Cerna (Rapporteur), "The Charter of Economic Rights and Duties of States," pp. 225-246. Tiewul attempted to show why the developed States need not worry. See S. Azadon Tiewul, "The United Nations Charter of Economic Rights and Duties of States" (1975), pp. 678-681.

[154] Charter of Economic Rights and Duties of States, Article 2.

and the State where the investment was made, often a developing State. [155] Compared with the rules adopted in the Permanent Sovereignty Declaration, the Charter did not contain a rule stating that expropriation must be in the public interest, and that compensation should be paid.[156] It treated the contract between the investor and the State essentially as a domestic affair, which meant that expropriation disputes had to be settled by local courts applying local law.[157] By proclaiming this new regime against the wishes of the economically powerful States of that period, the United Nations General Assembly missed its chance to influence State practice.[158] The relationship between foreign investor and host State was since regulated by the Convention on the Settlement of Investment Disputes between States and Nationals of Other States ("ICSID").[159]

The basic rules of this framework are almost exactly the opposite of those proclaimed in the Charter. The emphasis shifted from the domestic to the international level, as the US had proposed when the Charter on Economic Rights and Duties was being drafted,[160] and as proclaimed by the Assembly in its earlier Declaration on the Permanent Sovereignty over Natural Resources, and as suggested by many scholars.[161] Disputes between the host State and the foreign investor can be settled by international arbitration and not necessarily by the courts of the host State. International law can be chosen as the applicable law for the settlement of these disputes, and not – at least not exclusively – the domestic law of

---

[155] Since these consequences primarily dealt with expropriation, White referred to the controversy over these consequences as the "expropriation controversy." See G. White, "A New International Economic Order?" (1975), pp. 330-331.

[156] Weston argues that this might not be such a big change after all, since it was as yet unclear who determined the public good. See Weston, "Charter of Economic Rights and Duties of States and the Deprivation of Foreign-Owned Wealth," pp. 439-440 and p. 474.

[157] This had as consequence that all references to international law were also removed. See Weston, "Charter of Economic Rights and Duties of States and the Deprivation of Foreign-Owned Wealth," pp. 448-449; G. W. Haight, "New International Economic Order and the Charter of Economic Rights and Duties of States" (1975), pp. 598, and 599-602. For a supportive view of this new approach, see Eduardo Jimenez de Arechaga, "State Responsibility for the Nationalization of Foreign Owned Property," (1978), pp. 189-195.

[158] At the same time, it must be admitted that many expropriations took place in the 1970's, and ICSID had little influence on these expropriations. But it is doubtful whether these practices constituted the foundation of a legal regime, similar in sophistication to that of ICSID.

[159] The Convention on the Settlement of Investment Disputes between States and Nationals of Other States entered into force already in 1966, before the adoption of the Charter of Economic Rights and Duties of States, but it remained dormant in the beginning. In a discussion of the Charter of Economic Rights and Duties of States, a representative of Shell, the Dutch oil company, referred briefly to the ICSID framework as the way for the future. See MacLean, Swift, and Blair, "Commentaries" (1975), p. 349.

[160] For the US amendments, see e.g., "The Charter of Economic Rights and Duties of States: Remarks" (1975), p. 225 and pp. 233-234.

[161] See e.g., Francisco V. Garcia-Amador y Rodriguez, "Proposed New International Economic Order: A New Approach to the Law Governing Nationalization and Compensation" (1980), pp. 24-29.

the host State.[162] The Charter on Economic Rights and Duties thus shows that acquiring a majority of votes in the Assembly is important to introduce a new idea or policy, but it is equally important to have the economically powerful States on board.

## 3.4 The Third United Nations Development Decade

In 1980, the General Assembly once again adopted a new International Development Strategy, this time for the Third Development Decade.[163] In the Preamble, the Assembly acknowledged that "the goals and objectives of the International Development Strategy for the Second Development Decade remain[ed] largely unfulfilled," and that the situation had worsened.[164] The new strategy, not unlike the previous strategy, "aim[ed] at the promotion of the economic and social development of the developing countries with a view to reducing significantly the current disparities between the developed and developing countries, as well as the early eradication of poverty and dependency."[165]

The primary responsibility of States, including developing States, for their own development was once again emphasized. The role of the international community was to facilitate the efforts of the developing States, and to create "an environment that [was] fully supportive of the national and collective efforts of the developing countries for the realization of their development goals."[166] The pledge of developed States to spend at least 0.7 per cent of their gross domestic product on official international development assistance was reiterated.[167]

At the end of this Decade the Assembly adopted the Declaration on International Economic Cooperation.[168] There was no reference to any new international economic order in this declaration.[169] In the Assembly's view, although some developing countries had had relative success in developing, "for many developing countries, the 1980s have been viewed as a decade lost for

---

[162] These rules differ per country, since the relationship between the State and the foreign investor is primarily regulated in a bilateral investment treaty, signed by the host State and the State of which the investor is a national.

[163] International Development Strategy for the Third United Nations Development Decade, General Assembly resolution 35/56, adopted 5 December 1980.

[164] *Idem*, para. 3.

[165] *Idem*, para. 7.

[166] *Idem*, para. 9.

[167] *Idem*, para. 24.

[168] Declaration on International Economic Cooperation, in particular the Revitalization of Economic Growth and Development of the Developing Countries, General Assembly resolution S-18/3, adopted 1 May 1990 ("Declaration on International Economic Cooperation").

[169] R. St. John MacDonald, "Solidarity in the Practice and Discourse of Public International Law" (1996), pp. 266-269.

development."[170] The most pertinent problem was that the gap between developed and developing countries had widened further, and that this process was continuing.[171] In addition, absolute poverty was as urgent a problem as ever. Extreme poverty and hunger had escalated.[172] Despite all these negative trends, the Declaration did not contain many new or specific measures.[173] According to Schrijver, the Declaration was a disappointment, as the acknowledgment of "collective responsibility for development was considerably watered down by a substantial, one-sided stress upon the responsibility of developing countries for their own development and the lack, yet again, of binding commitments [...] with the result that the least developed countries – despite all the rhetoric – finished up with very little."[174]

## 3.5 The Fourth United Nations Development Decade

In 1990, the Assembly adopted the International Development Strategy for the Fourth United Nations Development Decade.[175] In this Strategy the Assembly admitted that "the goals and objectives of the International Development Strategy for the Third United Nations Development Decade were for the most part unattained," and that in fact "the decade of the 1980s saw a widening of the gap between the rich and the poor countries."[176] The Strategy was essentially the same as those that had preceded it, albeit formulated in stronger terms than before, to emphasize the increasing urgency of the situation. The Assembly stressed that "the developing countries themselves ha[d] the responsibility for the great effort needed to mobilize the potential of their people, to modernize and diversify their economies and to set themselves ambitious targets to build the foundation on which development rests."[177] As "developing countries [could] prosper only in a stable and progressive world economy," the developed States had the responsibility to ensure that the world economy became more friendly to the developing nations.[178]

---

[170] Declaration on International Economic Cooperation, para. 7.

[171] See *e.g.*, *idem*, paras. 5, 8 and 18.

[172] See *idem*, paras. 18 and 25.

[173] The obligation for the developed States to spend 0.7 percent of their gross national product on official development aid was there, as well as the more general obligations of cooperation. See *idem*, para. 27.

[174] See Nico Schrijver, "The Evolution of Sustainable Development in International Law" (2007), pp. 262-263.

[175] International Development Strategy for the Fourth United Nations Development Decade, General Assembly resolution 45/199, adopted 21 December 1990 ("International Development Strategy for the Fourth United Nations Development Decade").

[176] *Idem*, paras. 2 and 3.

[177] *Idem*, para. 15.

[178] *Idem*, paras. 16. More specific measures were outlined in paras. 21-107 of the Strategy.

This general Strategy for the 1990s also failed, and based on that sobering conclusion, one commentator suggested referring to this decade as the "decade of broken promises."[179]

In subsequent resolutions in the same decade, one of the UN's priorities was to combat the growing gap between rich and poor. In 1995, the Copenhagen Declaration on Social Development stated that the world was "witnessing in countries throughout the world the expansion of prosperity for some, unfortunately accompanied by an expansion of unspeakable poverty for others."[180] To remedy this situation, the States participating in the Social Summit pledged their commitment to a "political, economic, ethical and spiritual vision for social development that is based on human dignity, human rights, equality, respect, peace, democracy, mutual responsibility and cooperation, and full respect for the various religious and ethical values and cultural backgrounds of people."[181] The Declaration also contained a number of more specific commitments, including the commitment to accelerate "the economic, social and human resource development of Africa and the least developed countries."[182]

Two years later, the General Assembly adopted UN Secretary-General Boutros-Ghali's Agenda for Development, the companion to his Agenda for Peace.[183] Some developing nations had benefited from the increasing interdependence and interconnectedness of States, often referred to as the process of globalization, but others, particularly in Africa, failed to do so, and were becoming more marginalized than ever.[184] Thus "a primary objective of the implementation of the present Agenda should be to contribute in such a way that the benefits stemming from future growth and development [*i.e.* benefits stemming from the almost universal pursuit of increased economic openness and integration] are distributed equitably among all countries and peoples."[185]

As inequalities increased and the situation in many developing States continued to deteriorate, the United Nations started to distinguish one group of States as the "least developed." Least developed countries had already been recognized and defined as a group in the International Development Strategy for the Third United Nations Development Decade, as "the economically weakest and

---

[179] Jan Vandemoortele, "Are the MDGs Feasible?" (2003), p. 2.

[180] The Copenhagen Declaration on Social Development, which can be found in the Conference report: World Summit for Social Development (Copenhagen, Denmark, 6-12 March 1995), UNDoc. A/CONF.166/9, distributed on 19 April 1995 ("Copenhagen Declaration on Social Development"), para. 13. See also para 16.

[181] *Idem*, para. 25.

[182] *Idem*, Commitment 7.

[183] Agenda for Development, General Assembly resolution 51/240, adopted 20 June 1997 ("Agenda for Development").

[184] See *idem*, paras. 5-20. See further paras. 183-202.

[185] *Idem*, para. 48.

poorest countries with the most formidable structural problems."[186] This particular group of countries was also the subject of the Paris Declaration, adopted in 1990.[187] According to the declaration, the "refusal to accept the marginalization of the least developed countries [was] an ethical imperative," and "in an increasingly interdependent world, the maintenance or deepening of the gap between the rich and poor nations contain[ed] serious seeds of tension."[188] Thus the international community recognized that there was a moral obligation to give special aid to the least developed nations.[189] Because these obligations were now recognized, developing States actually applied to become members of the "club of the underprivileged," and expressed disappointment when their application was refused.[190]

The Paris Declaration was accompanied by a detailed Programme of Action for the 1990s.[191] The implementation of this programme was the subject of a mid-term review, carried out in 1995, which drew the unfortunate conclusion that "the least developed countries as a group ha[d] not been able to meet many of the objectives of the Programme of Action and [that] their overall socio-economic situation ha[d] continued to deteriorate."[192] Nevertheless, there was a "firm[...] belie[f] that, given political will on the part of the least developed countries, which

---

[186] International Development Strategy for the Fourth United Nations Development Decade, para. 136. The term was used earlier elsewhere. See also W.D. Verwey, "The United Nations and the Least Developed Countries: an Exploration in the Grey Zones of International Law" (1984).

[187] Paris Declaration of the Second United Nations Conference on the Least Developed Countries, held in Paris, on 3 and 4 September 1990, UNDoc. A/Conf.147/18 ("Paris Declaration of the Second United Nations Conference on the Least Developed Countries"). The First United Nations Conference on the Least Developed Countries took place also in Paris, between 1 and 14 September 1981. See Shahid Qadir, "UN Conference on the Least Developed Countries" (1982); and Thomas G. Weiss, "The United Nations Conference on the Least Developed Countries: The Relevance of Conference Diplomacy in Paris for International Negotiations" (1983), for two contrasting impressions (the first highly critical and the other more favourable) of that first conference.

[188] Idem.

[189] One of the more concrete proposals flowing from this ethical imperative was the reaffirmation of the pledge to spend at least 0.15 per cent of the gross national income on this group of least developed countries. Programme of Action for the Least Developed Countries for the 1990s, which can be found in the same report as the Paris Declaration of the Second United Nations Conference on the Least Developed Countries, para. 23. This was actually a pledge that already appeared in the outcome document of the first conference on least developed countries, but it was a pledge that most developed nations failed to implement in reality. See Thomas G. Weiss, "The United Nations Conference on the Least Developed Countries: The Relevance of Conference Diplomacy in Paris for International Negotiations" (1983), p. 650.

[190] The term "club of the underprivileged" was taken from Shahid Qadir, "UN Conference on the Least Developed Countries" (1982), p. 135.

[191] See the Programme of Action for the Least Developed Countries for the 1990s.

[192] Part One, para. (c), Mid-Term Global Review of Progress towards the Implementation of the Programme of Action for the Least Developed Countries for the 1990s, annexed to General Assembly resolution 50/103, adopted 20 December 1995.

have the primary responsibility for their development, and the support of the international community, the least developed countries will be able to enter the next century with better prospects for their peoples."[193]

A new Declaration and Programme of Action for the Least Developed Countries was adopted in 2001, this time in Brussels. The essence of this document was comparable to the previous declarations.[194] In 2006, the implementation of this new Programme was reviewed by the General Assembly, which concluded that some progress had been made, but not much.[195] A Ministerial Conference of Least Developed Countries was therefore convened in Istanbul (2007), and the Istanbul Declaration on Least Developed Countries was adopted, appropriately entitled Time for Action. The Fourth United Nations Conference on the Least Developed Countries also took place there, in 2011.[196] It led to the adoption of the Istanbul Declaration on Renewed and Strengthened Global Partnership for the Development of Least Developed Countries.[197]

## 3.6 The Millennium Declaration

In 2000, at the start of the new millennium, the General Assembly adopted the most ambitious resolution on development in its history: the Millennium Declaration.[198] According to the Preamble, the Assembly saw its "central challenge" as ensuring that "globalization bec[ame] a positive force for all the world's people." [199] The basic premise of the Declaration was that globalization offered great opportunities, but that the benefits of globalization were "very unevenly shared" and its costs

---

[193]*Idem*, para. (g). Part Two contained a detailed assessment of progress in the implementation of the Programme of Action and Part Three consisted of a list of recommendations for the future.

[194] Brussels Declaration and Programme of Action for the Least Developed Countries for the decade 2001-2010, published in the Report of the Third United Nations Conference on the Least Developed Countries, held in Brussels, between 14 and 20 May 2001, UNDoc. A/CONF.191/13.

[195] Declaration of the high-level meeting of the sixty-first session of the General Assembly on the midterm comprehensive global review of the implementation of the Programme of Action for the Least Developed Countries for the Decade 2001-2010, annexed to General Assembly resolution 61/1, adopted 19 September 2006, especially paras. 6 and 7. See also the United Nations Conference on Trade and Development´s Least Developed Countries Report Series, which started in 1996 to report annually.

[196] Programme of Action for the Least Developed Countries for the Decade 2011-2020, General Assembly resolution 65/280, adopted 17 June 2011.

[197] Draft Istanbul Declaration on Renewed and strengthened global partnership for the development of least developed countries, distributed 12 May 2011, UNDoc. A/CONF.219/L.1.

[198] Millennium Declaration, General Assembly resolution 55/2, adopted 8 September 2000 ("Millennium Declaration").

[199] Millennium Declaration, para. 5.

"unevenly distributed."[200] The challenge was therefore to find ways to make the process of globalization "fully inclusive and equitable."[201]

The Declaration listed a number of global values, most of which were directly applicable to development. Together they essentially contained the message that all States, and all individuals, had the right to benefit from globalization, and that all States acting together had the obligation to make that possible. For example, the value of freedom implied that "men and women ha[d] the right to live their lives and raise their children in dignity [and] free from hunger." The value of equality implied that "no individual and no nation must be denied the opportunity to benefit from development." The value of solidarity implied that "global challenges must be managed in a way that distribute[d] the costs and burdens fairly in accordance with basic principles of equity and social justice," and that "those who suffer or who benefit least deserve help from those who benefit most." Finally, the value of shared responsibility implied that the "responsibility for managing worldwide economic and social development [...] must be shared among the nations of the world and should be exercised multilaterally."[202]

The value of global solidarity reveals the basics of global distributive justice. In one of his last speeches as Secretary-General of the United Nations, Kofi Annan spoke about the Millennium Declaration as the practical implementation of the idea of global solidarity. He said: "We are not only all responsible for each other's security. We are also, in some measure, responsible for each other's welfare. Global solidarity is both necessary and possible."[203] He explained that:

> It is necessary because without a measure of solidarity no society can be truly stable, and no one's prosperity truly secure. That applies to national societies – as all the great industrial democracies learned in the 20th century – but it also applies to the increasingly integrated global market economy that we live in today. It is not realistic to think that some people can go on deriving great benefits from globalization while billions of their fellow human beings are left in abject poverty, or even thrown into it. We have to give our fellow citizens, not only within each nation but in the global community, at least a chance to share in our prosperity.[204]

Annan believed it was not "realistic" to think that the global economy could remain unregulated by principles of global social justice. According to Annan, all citizens of the world deserved to get at least a chance to obtain the goods they deserved. If that was impossible in the present international economic order, the rich countries

---

[200] *Idem.*
[201] *Idem.*
[202] *Idem*, para. 7.
[203] United Nations Secretary-General's address at the Truman Presidential Museum and Library, Independence, Missouri (USA), 11 December 2006.
[204] *Idem.*

had a duty to compensate for the unequal outcomes of the global economy. Official development assistance could be seen as a way of complying with this duty to compensate, but according to Annan, even if official development assistance was forthcoming, this was not enough. All countries also had a duty to ensure market access for all States, fair trading agreements, and a non-discriminatory financial system. The world had a duty to correct the global system, not just to pay compensation to those negatively affected by it. It had an obligation to prevent unequal and undeserved results in the allocation of goods. This to ensure that all countries and all individuals[205] could eventually get what they deserved themselves, without having to depend on development assistance.[206]

The rest of the Declaration outlined more specific goals with even more specific targets. The aim was to meet these targets by 2015. These goals and targets included the following:

1. To eradicate extreme poverty and hunger, *i.e.* "to halve […] the proportion of the world's people whose income is less than one dollar a day and the proportion of people who suffer from hunger and, by the same date, to halve the proportion of people who are unable to reach or to afford safe drinking water."[207]
2. To achieve universal primary education, *i.e.* "to ensure that […] children everywhere, boys and girls alike, will be able to complete a full course of primary schooling and that girls and boys will have equal access to all levels of education." [208]
3. "To promote gender equality and the empowerment of women;"[209]
4. To reduce child mortality, *i.e.* "to have reduced […] under-five child mortality by two thirds, of their current rates." [210]

---

[205] The Millennium Development Goals are essentially about improving the lives of individuals, not States. To follow up this idea, Jeffrey Sachs set up the Millennium Villages Project, which aimed to achieve the goals in a number of selected villages. The local government was just one of many participants in these projects; civil society groups, NGOs, and other entities also participated.

[206] This dependency on aid can have negative consequences if it becomes a structural thing. One of the fundamental concerns is that States deliberately refuse to fix their problems because this keeps the aid money flowing. That is one reason why structural aid cannot be the way to repair the injustice of the global economic order.

[207] Millennium Declaration, para. 19.

[208] Idem.

[209] *Idem*, para. 20.

[210] *Idem*, para. 19. See also A World fit for Children, a declaration annexed to General Assembly resolution S-27/2, adopted 10 May 2002. This was a follow-up declaration not only to the Millennium Declaration, but also to the World Declaration on the Survival, Protection and Development of Children, which was adopted at the World Summit for Children on 30 September 1990. UNDoc. A/45/625. The Conference also adopted a Plan of Action for Implementing the World Declaration on the Survival, Protection and Development of Children in the 1990s. Already in the 1990 Declaration (see especially paras. 4-7), we read that children are extremely vulnerable, and are usually the first to suffer from a lack of development, and a lack of basic services.

5. To improve maternal health, *i.e.* "to have reduced maternal mortality by three quarters [...] of their current rates."[211]
6. To combat HIV/AIDS, malaria and other diseases, *i.e.* "to have [...] halted, and begun to reverse, the spread of HIV/AIDS, the scourge of malaria and other major diseases that afflict humanity."[212]
8. To develop a global partnership for development, *i.e.* to make a commitment to "an open, equitable, rule-based, predictable and non-discriminatory multilateral trading and financial system," and to give special attention to the developing countries with special needs.[213]

In addition to the goal of ensuring environmental sustainability (Goal 7), these goals have since become known as the eight Millennium Development Goals (MDGs).[214]

The specific or measurable aspect of the MDGs is a positive thing. The goals are limited in number, they are defined in measurable figures and percentages, and they are bound by time.[215] Therefore it will be quite straightforward to test whether the Goals have been met in 2015. The statistics will merely have to be compared with those of 1990. However, the literature suggests that the MDGs are still not sufficiently specific, and still allow room for fundamentally different interpretations.

These different interpretations can have rather drastic consequences. For example, if the first MDG is achieved, that will be because favourable developments in some parts of Asia, especially in China and India, will compensate for a lack of progress in many other developing countries.[216] It would be inappropriate for the international community to celebrate the achievement of the MDGs in 2015, solely on the basis of the progress made in China and India. After all, those States have received relatively little international development aid. Such a celebration would be based on a misinterpretation of the MDGs. The MDGs must be met in *all* developing nations, not just in the majority. Moreover, if the MDGs are defined in terms of "averages," then they do not take into account a situation in

---

[211] Millennium Declaration, para. 19

[212] *Idem*.

[213] *Idem*, para. 13.

[214] Ensuring environmental sustainability is MDG7. In an effort to assist the Member States in the implementation of their pledges made in the Millennium Declaration, the UN Secretary-General distilled these Millennium Development Goals from the Millennium Declaration. See Road map towards the implementation of the United Nations Millennium Declaration, Report of the Secretary-General, UNDoc. A/56/326, distributed 6 September 2001, paras. 80-163.

[215] According to Alston, it was these three characteristics that made them different from all earlier commitments of the General Assembly. See Philip Alston, "Ships Passing in the Night" (2005), p. 756.

[216] See also Michael A. Clemens, Charles J. Kenny & Todd J. Moss, "Millennium Development Goals, Aid Targets, and the Costs of Over-Expectations" (2005), p. 58 and pp. 59-60. And see the annually published Millennium Development Goals Reports, published by the United Nations Department of Public Information, and available at http://www.un.org/millenniumgoals/.

which a particular minority group in a State does not make any progress, even though the State as a whole does.[217] In short, it makes a great deal of difference whether one measures progress at the global level, at the national level, or at the level of the individual human being.

As Vandemoortele remarked, "global targets are easily set but seldom met."[218] The important question is whether the goals will be achieved by 2015.[219] In the Millennium Development Goals Report of 2007, UN Secretary-General, Ban Ki-Moon, rang all the available alarm bells. He referred in particular to the unwillingness of developed States to increase official development aid as was promised.[220] The rich States of the world had promised to spend 0.7 per cent of their gross domestic product (GDP) on official development assistance, but only five countries had complied up to that point.[221] The question arises whether the failure to achieve the Millennium Development Goals automatically leads to a violation of principles of global social justice. Is it only the result that counts? Clear targets may be the best incentive to act, but they may be achieved by measures that are not based on thinking in terms of global social justice.[222] There may be external causes for failing to reach the targets, such as natural disasters or two global financial crises. In the 2010 report, Ban-Ki Moon noted that "some [of the] hard-won gains [were] being eroded by the climate, food and economic crises."[223] On the other hand, whether or not actual results are achieved can be an indication of the sincerity of the promises and statements made about global social justice.

Another problem with the MDGs was the rather vague allocation of responsibilities. Only the principle of shared responsibility addressed this matter. It stated that "the nations of the world" are jointly responsible. Does that mean that the world as a whole is responsible for achieving the MDGs? As Easterly rightly

---

[217] Jan Vandemoortele, "Are the MDGs Feasible?" (2003), pp. 10-13.

[218] *Idem*, p. 1.

[219] In 2003, little progress was made in achieving the goals, even on the global level. See *idem*, pp. 16-18.

[220] Foreword to The Millennium Development Goals Report 2007, available at http://www.un.org/millenniumgoals.

[221] The idea that a small percentage (initially it was 1 per cent) of the gross national product of rich countries should be reserved for official development assistance can first be found in UN General Assembly Resolution of 15 December 1960, UNDoc. A/RES/1524(XV). The obligation can be found in UN General Assembly Resolution of 24 October 1970, UNDoc. A/RES/2626(XXV). The obligation was reiterated in the 2002 Monterrey Consensus (para. 42), and in the 2005 World Summit Outcome, para. 23. The five countries that did keep their promise were: Denmark (0.84%), Luxembourg (0.81%), Netherlands (0.80%), Norway (0.92%), and Sweden (0.79%). See: http://www.unmillenniumproject.org.

[222] Then again, focusing on "good intent" or "sincere effort" has limited practical value because it provides no incentives to use resources efficiently or to direct them specifically towards achieving the desired results unless the yardstick for effort is very specifically defined.

[223] Foreword to The Millennium Development Goals Report 2010, available at http://www.un.org/millenniumgoals.

pointed out, "if all of us are collectively responsible for a big world goal, then no single agency or politician is held accountable if the goal is not met."[224] On the other hand, the United Nations cannot continue the classical tradition of allocating primary responsibility to developing States themselves, and hold them accountable for a failure to achieve the MDGs for their own citizens.

The Millennium Declaration was not the only declaration on social progress and development adopted in the 2000s. In 2002, a Conference on Financing for Development was held in Monterrey (Mexico). The Monterrey Consensus on Financing for Development was adopted at the end of this.[225] The goal of the conference was ambitious. It was to "eradicate poverty, achieve sustained economic growth and promote sustainable development [through the advancement] of a fully inclusive and equitable global economic system."[226] The Consensus emphasized once again that "each country ha[d] primary responsibility for its own economic and social development, and [that] the role of national policies and development strategies [could not] be overemphasized."[227] At the same time, the Consensus acknowledged that "national development efforts need[ed] to be supported by an enabling international economic environment."[228] In particular, there was a need to attract and facilitate foreign direct investment in *all* the developing nations,[229] to work towards the continued liberalization of trade and towards a "universal, rule-based, non-discriminatory and equitable multilateral trading system,"[230] and to increase official development assistance from the developed States to the developing States to reach the target of 0.7 per cent of the developed States' gross national product.[231] This last aim was specific, as opposed to much of the "empty rhetoric" and "all sorts of lofty ideals" also included in the Consensus, and this became the pledge for which the Monterrey Consensus is best known.[232] The 0.7 per cent figure was not new. It had been included in the Assembly's resolution on

---

[224] William Easterly, "The Utopian Nightmare" (2005), p. 61.

[225] Monterrey Consensus of the International Conference on Financing for Development, published in the Report of the International Conference on Financing for Development, held in Monterrey (Mexico), between 18 and 22 March 2002, UNDoc A/CONF.198/11. For a summary of the Consensus, see Abdel Hamid Bouab, "Financing for Development, the Monterrey Consensus" (2004), pp. 359-368.

[226] *Idem*, para. 1. See further paras. 10-19 of the Consensus.

[227] *Idem*, para. 6.

[228] *Idem*. See also Inaamul Haque & Ruxandra Burdescu, "Monterrey Consensus on Financing for Development" (2004), pp. 241-242.

[229] *Idem*, paras. 20-25. As Haque and Burdescu pointed out, foreign direct investment is focused on a limited group of developing nations, with a relatively stable and reliable economy: China, Brazil, India and Malaysia. See Inaamul Haque & Ruxandra Burdescu, "Monterrey Consensus on Financing for Development" (2004), pp. 245-246.

[230] *Idem*, paras. 26-38. See also paras. 52-67.

[231] *Idem*, paras. 39-46.

[232] See also Nico Schrijver, "The Evolution of Sustainable Development in International Law" (2007), p. 281. The quotes are from Surya P. Subedi, "International Conference on Financing for Development" (2002), p. 53.

the international development strategy of the 1970s.[233] Although it did have some impact, the target failed to motivate all States to increase their official development assistance. This was particularly problematical for a group of least developed States which relied heavily on this formal aid.[234] Sachs suggested that if people in developed countries knew how little aid was transferred by their Governments and thus in their name, to developing nations, they would ask for it to be increased.[235] If people do not believe their own Government is generous enough, they can compensate by giving money themselves, for example, through organizations like Oxfam. However, as Sachs showed, even if such private donations are included in the official development assistance statistics, the United States of America – Sachs' article was exclusively about that State – would still not reach the 0.7 figure.[236]

As the global percentage of official development assistance actually given never reached 0.7 per cent, this figure has been referred to as "the most famous international statistical target ever set and never met."[237] One author called for "a new paradigm for [official development assistance] that will transform it from an uncertain, inadequate, shrinking, and unfocused charity of nations into an adequate, predictable, long-term, focused, and binding obligation of the world community, embedded in international law and aimed at poverty reduction."[238] The Monterrey Consensus, being a non-binding declaration, has not brought about such a paradigm shift.[239]

The true follow-up to the Millennium Declaration was the World Summit Outcome Document adopted in 2005.[240] This Document reaffirmed the pledges made in the Millennium Declaration, and developed concrete measures to realize

---

[233] Jeffrey D. Sachs, "The Development Challenge" (2005), p. 86.

[234] See also Inaamul Haque & Ruxandra Burdescu, "Monterrey Consensus on Financing for Development" (2004), pp. 264-265.

[235] Jeffrey D. Sachs, "The Development Challenge" (2005), pp. 79-80.

[236] *Idem*, p. 80. The article is about the situation in 2005, but according to statistics published on the OECD's website, the situation has not improved since then (see: http://stats.oecd.org). The US has become less and less generous, with 0.23 percent of gross national income used for development assistance in 2005, and only 0.16 per cent in 2007.

[237] Richard Jolly, Louis Emmerij & Thomas G. Weiss, *UN Ideas that Changed the World* (2009), p. 105.

[238] Inaamul Haque & Ruxandra Burdescu, "Monterrey Consensus on Financing for Development" (2004), p. 270.

[239] In 2008, the goals and commitments expressed in the Monterrey Consensus were reaffirmed in the Doha Declaration on Financing for Development, outcome document of the Follow-up International Conference on Financing for Development to Review the Implementation of the Monterrey Consensus, annexed to General Assembly resolution 63/239, adopted 24 December 2008. The Doha Declaration also assessed the implementation of the Monterrey Consensus. In general, the progress in the implementation of the Consensus was mixed. See Doha Declaration, paras. 3 (general assessment), 23 (on foreign direct investment), 31-32 (reform of trading system) and 42-43 (official development assistance).

[240] World Summit Outcome, General Assembly resolution 60/1, adopted 16 September 2005.

the Millennium Development Goals. The values of the Millennium Declaration were reaffirmed in the Document. [241] All States "strongly reiterate[d] [their] determination to ensure the timely and full realization of the development goals and objectives agreed at the major United Nations conferences and summits, including those agreed at the Millennium Summit that are described as the Millennium Development Goals." [242] With regard to building a global partnership for development, the States "reaffirm[ed] that each country must take primary responsibility for its own development and that the role of national policies and development strategies cannot be overemphasized in the achievement of sustainable development" and that "national efforts should be complemented by supportive global programmes, measures and policies aimed at expanding the development opportunities of developing countries." [243] This division of labour and responsibility is based on a recognition, first, that the economic world order harms developing States, and secondly, that developing States have a responsibility themselves to combat local corruption and improve local forms of governance. [244] The Millennium Declaration did not emphasize the primary responsibility of developing States for their own development as strongly as most previous declarations. Thus the 2005 Document was a return to the more traditional approach to development.

## 3.7 Conclusion

The General Assembly's declarations and programmes for action were a response to the needs of developing States. The developing nations never formulated their demands as simple requests for help, and the Assembly's programmes were not "charity programmes." Rather, the developing States demanded that their entitlement to development assistance be acknowledged, and that they should not have to continuously beg for development assistance. They were entitled to international assistance because the present international economic order was unfair and inequitable, and they were the victims of that unfairness and inequity. Therefore there was an obligation for all States to help rectify the consequences of the old order and eventually replace it with a new international economic order that was fair and equitable. As long as this goal was not achieved, the developing States were entitled to compensation for the harm done to them by this unfair system.

At the same time, few of the declarations went so far as to conclude that a system of global distributive justice should be established. An exception is the Millennium Declaration, but the global social justice approach of that declaration

---

[241] *Idem*, para. 4.

[242] *Idem*, para. 17.

[243] *Idem*, para. 22.

[244] Jorg Kustermans, Jacobus Delwaide & Gustaaf Geeraerts, "Global governance en veiligheid" (2007).

was replaced by more traditional ways of thinking only five years later, with the adoption of the World Summit Outcome Document.

It is clear that the General Assembly has continuously stressed the responsibility of States for their own development. The international duties of assistance were secondary to that primary responsibility. Some General Assembly declarations, especially those about the New International Economic Order, aimed to revise the rules of the international economic order. However, these suggestions have not been translated into binding international law. A more modest proposal, *viz.* that the developed States acknowledge the obligation to spend a small part of their gross domestic product on official development assistance, has been more successful in the sense that it was adopted by the General Assembly, although very few States comply with this obligation.

The role of the General Assembly in facilitating and monitoring foreign direct investment has become rather limited now that a system has been set up elsewhere.[245] This means that the declarations of the General Assembly do not give a complete picture of the norms and principles of the international economic order. Many of the fundamental rules, not just those about foreign direct investment, have been made elsewhere. It is true that the United Nations Conference on Trade and Development has played a role with its efforts to integrate developing countries into the global economy,[246] but the World Trade Organization sets out and monitors the main principles of the trading system. The World Bank provides loans, credits and grants to developing countries and also determines the conditions for such loans, credits and grants. The International Monetary Fund ensures financial stability, and the rules on foreign direct investment are set by the Convention on the Settlement of Investment Disputes between States and Nationals of Other States and by a dense network of bilateral investment treaties. The monitoring of that system is partly carried out by the International Centre for Settlement of Investment Disputes. Many of these institutions have some (in)formal links with the United Nations system, but the General Assembly has relatively little influence over them.

## 4    EMERGENCY ASSISTANCE

## 4.1 Introduction

The Assembly has adopted declarations proclaiming principles and frameworks for action in response to immediate threats. These are not primarily based on principles of fairness or global social justice, but rather, on the moral imperative to act

---

[245] See also Richard Jolly, Louis Emmerij & Thomas G. Weiss, *UN Ideas that Changed the World* (2009), p. 101.
[246] See Ian Taylor & Karen Smith, *United Nations Conference on Trade and Development (UNCTAD)*.

whenever fellow human beings are in immediate danger, especially when the costs of acting are not too high.

## 4.2 Natural disasters and other humanitarian emergencies

Whenever an earthquake, a cyclone, or some other natural disaster, hits a particular region, United Nations vehicles appear on television, and UN staff can be seen handing out emergency food supplies. The effect of such emergency relief action is clear. People who would otherwise not have any food or blankets do receive them. The immediate impact of the General Assembly declarations on social progress and development discussed earlier is much less clear.[247]

In 1989, the Assembly adopted the International Framework of Action for the International Decade for Natural Disaster Reduction.[248] The main objective of that Framework was "to reduce through concerted international action, especially in developing countries, the loss of life, property damage and social and economic disruption caused by natural disasters such as earthquakes, windstorms, tsunamis, floods, landslides, volcanic eruptions, wildfires, grasshopper and locust infestations, drought and desertification and other calamities of natural origin."[249] All States were called upon, *inter alia*, "to improve the early international availability of appropriate emergency supplies through the storage or earmarking of such supplies in disaster-prone areas."[250] It was also suggested that the UN Secretary-General establish a special trust fund, and "that voluntary contributions [to that trust fund] from Governments, international organizations and other sources, including the private sector, be strongly encouraged."[251] This Framework was further revised and improved with the adoption of the Yokohama Strategy and Plan of Action for a Safer World, which focused more on the prevention of natural disasters than on the response to such disasters,[252] and the Hyogo Declaration and Framework for Action.[253]

---

[247] Former Secretary-General Boutros-Ghali expressed his concern that this might lead to a focus on short-term projects. See Boutros Boutros-Ghali, "A New Departure on Development" (1995), p. 44.
[248] International Framework of Action for the International Decade for Natural Disaster Reduction, annexed to General Assembly resolution 44/236, adopted 22 December 1989 ("International Framework of Action for the International Decade for Natural Disaster Reduction").
[249] *Idem*, para. 1.
[250] *Idem*, para. 3(g).
[251] *Idem*, para. 15.
[252] Yokohama Strategy and Plan of Action for a Safer World: Guidelines for Natural Disaster Prevention, Preparedness and Mitigation, adopted at the World Conference on Natural Disaster Reduction, held in Yokohama, Japan between 23 and 27 May 1994 ("Yokohama Strategy and Plan of Action").
[253] Hyogo Declaration and Hyogo Framework for Action 2005-2015: Building the Resilience of Nations and Communities to Disasters, both adopted at the World Conference on Disaster Reduction,

One year later (in 1990), the General Assembly adopted a related declaration on the Strengthening of the Coordination of Humanitarian Emergency Assistance of the United Nations.[254] The first principle of that declaration – which reads that "humanitarian assistance is of cardinal importance for the victims of natural disasters and other emergencies" – shows that the concept of humanitarian emergency includes, but is not limited to, natural disasters. The declaration on humanitarian emergencies also proposed the establishment of a special fund financed by voluntary contributions.[255]

The reason for the more generous international assistance provided in response to natural disasters and other humanitarian emergencies might be that States cannot help becoming victims of such immediate disasters and emergencies, while they can be held responsible for failing development policies.

This does not mean that States are not themselves primarily responsible for responding to disasters occurring on their territory. In the Declaration on natural disasters, governments were called upon to "formulate national disaster-mitigation programmes, as well as economic, land use and insurance policies for disaster prevention, and, particularly in developing countries, to integrate them fully into their national development programmes."[256] This suggests that States are primarily responsible for tackling natural disasters occurring within their own territory.[257] The declaration on humanitarian emergencies places an equally strong emphasis on sovereignty, this time both as a source of responsibility and as a source of rights. Regarding the former, it states that "each State has the responsibility first and foremost to take care of the victims of natural disasters and other emergencies occurring on its territory."[258] Regarding the latter, it states that "humanitarian assistance should be provided with the consent of the affected country and in principle on the basis of an appeal by the affected country."[259] When Japan was hit by a disastrous earthquake and tsunami in 2011, it initially did not ask the UN to coordinate the relief efforts. Therefore the UN did not play a leading role.

---

held between 18 and 22 January 2005, in Kobe, Hyogo, Japan. See UNDoc. A/CONF.206/6 ("Hyogo Declaration").

[254] Declaration on the Strengthening of the coordination of humanitarian emergency assistance of the United Nations, annexed to General Assembly resolution 46/182, adopted 19 December 1991.

[255] *Idem*, paras. 21-26.

[256] International Framework of Action for the International Decade for Natural Disaster Reduction, para. 3(a).

[257] The other declarations also stress this point. See *e.g.*, Yokohama Strategy and Plan of Action, principle 10; and the Hyogo Declaration, para. 4.

[258] Declaration on the Strengthening of the coordination of humanitarian emergency assistance of the United Nations, principle 4.

[259] *Idem*, principle 3.

## 4.3 Conclusion

States are more generous in their response to emergencies than in providing structural international development assistance, and the question arises whether this difference can be justified on moral grounds. The idea that all States must act whenever people suffer a disaster and are struggling to survive, meets with almost universal acceptance. However, governments of developed States find it much more difficult to explain to their citizens why a small part of the gross domestic product must be spent on permanent official development assistance.

Nevertheless, the general framework of rights and responsibilities relating to humanitarian aid is not all that different from the more general framework relating to development aid. States remain responsible for repairing the damage caused by a disaster occurring on their territory, and other States only have a duty to assist.

## 5    SUSTAINABLE DEVELOPMENT

## 5.1 Introduction

The UN Charter says little about the protection of the environment.[260] At the San Francisco Conference it was never raised as a topic for discussion.

Nevertheless, there is a link between fair and equitable development and "sustainable" development. Scholars have argued, referring to concepts such as "intergenerational justice" or "intergenerational equity," that one cannot have global social justice without environmental sustainability. [261] After all, future generations also deserve their share of the goods. [262] The protection of the environment can be seen as a way to make social progress and development possible for future generations as well. Although it is problematical, both from a conceptual and a legal point of view, to acknowledge that non-existing entities – future generations – have rights and deserve their fair share of the goods, this has

---

[260] See *e.g.*, Paolo Galizzi, "From Stockholm to New York, via Rio and Johannesburg" (2006), p. 960.

[261] On the cross-fertilization between such theories and the work of the UN, see also *e.g.*, Nico Schrijver, "After us, the deluge? The position of future generations of humankind in international environmental law" (2009); Lothar Gündling, "Our Responsibility to Future Generations" (1990); Edith Brown Weiss, "Our Rights and Obligations to Future Generations for the Environment" (1990); Anthony d"Amato, "Do We Owe a Duty to Future Generations to Preserve the Global Environment?" (1990); Graham Mayeda, "Where Should Johannesburg Take Us" (2004).

[262] See *e.g.*, Edith Brown Weiss, "Our Rights and Obligations to Future Generations for the Environment" (1990), and the various contributions in Andrew Dobson (editor), *Fairness and Futurity: Essays on Environmental Sustainability and Social Justice* (2004).

been the central idea behind sustainable development as introduced by the United Nations.[263]

The United Nations could have chosen a different approach to regulate the relationship between human beings and the earth. The earth could have been considered as something worthy of protection in its own right, rather than as a resource for development by both present and future generations. If the earth were regarded as something of intrinsic value, it would be much more difficult to see the protection of the environment as a way of making development possible for future generations.

Before looking at the major UN declarations on sustainable development, [264] it should be pointed out that the concept of sustainable development is relatively new and has not yet achieved full stature in international law. [265] The concept has not yet inspired the acceptance of *jus cogens*, as is acknowledged both in scholarship[266] and in case law.[267] It is even argued that sustainable development is no more than a "legitimate expectation that actors at the international and domestic levels ought to conduct their affairs to facilitate the realization of [certain] objectives."[268] Sustainable development is an aspect of the UN's work that can be qualified as work in progress, especially when it comes to the codification of the relevant norms. It is itself an emerging norm, slowly but

---

[263] As d'Amato pointed out, there are two difficulties with the argument that we owe something to future generations. First, non-existing entities cannot have rights. Second, by our actions, we significantly change the characteristics of those non-existing entities; we can even make their coming-into-being entirely impossible, for example by destroying the earth entirely. See Anthony d'Amato, "Do We Owe a Duty to Future Generations to Preserve the Global Environment?" (1990).

[264] For an overview of the relevant declarations, see especially Nico Schrijver, "The Evolution of Sustainable Development in International Law" (2007). See also Paolo Galizzi, "From Stockholm to New York, via Rio and Johannesburg" (2006); and Richard Jolly, Louis Emmerij & Thomas G. Weiss, *UN Ideas that Changed the World* (2009), p. 149.

[265] Perhaps sustainability itself should be considered as a global value in international law. See *e.g.*, Nico Schrijver, "The Evolution of Sustainable Development in International Law" (2007), pp. 235-236.

[266] Some authors are more confident. See *e.g.*, André de Hoogh, *Obligations Erga Omnes and International Crimes* (1996), p. 63. The principle of the preservation of the common heritage of mankind is a likely candidate to be considered *jus cogens*. The principle surfaced in General Assembly resolution 2749 (XXV) of 17 December 1970. For a discussion, see Kemal Baslar, *The Concept of the Common Heritage of Mankind in International Law* (1998), p. 363 and further. On this and related concepts, see also Antônio Augusto Cançado Trindade, "International law for humankind: towards a new jus gentium (I)" (2005), p. 365. See also p. 391, where Trindade relates these concepts explicitly with the "basic values of the international community as a whole."

[267] In International Court of Justice, Case concerning the Gabčíkovo-Nagymaros Project (Hungary v. Slovakia), Hungary argued for the *jus cogens* character of the principle of sustainable development (para. 97 of the Judgment of 25 September 1997). The Court did not embrace that view. In a Separate Opinion, Vice-President Weeramantry discussed the legal status of the principle of sustainable development, and attempted to find a balance between the right to development and the protection of the environment. Although he found evidence of universal acceptance of the principle, he did not reach the conclusion that the principle acquired the status of *jus cogens*.

[268] Alhaji B.M. Marong, "From Rio to Johannesburg" (2003), pp. 21-22. See also pp. 56-57, and p. 76.

surely moving towards a value-based principle of international law, from which more specific rules can be derived.

## 5.2 The earth as a resource or as something of intrinsic value?

The earliest resolutions distinguish two different approaches to the topic of development and environmental protection. The earth is either seen as a resource to be used for the benefit and development of mankind, or as something of intrinsic value.

Although some earlier resolutions had already made references to the environment, it really became a new global challenge in the early 1970s.[269] In 1972, a United Nations Conference on the Human Environment took place in Stockholm.[270] It was an ideal opportunity for the UN to show that it could play a crucial role as the commander of "spaceship earth," even in times of Cold War rivalry and the increasing divide between developing and developed nations.[271]

The Declaration on the Human Environment was adopted at the end of that Conference.[272] The Conference also led to the establishment of the United Nations Environment Programme (UNEP). In the Preamble to the resolution establishing this programme, the General Assembly recognized that "environmental problems of broad international significance fall within the competence of the United Nations system," but it did not say on which part of the UN Charter this was based.[273]

The aim of the Declaration on the Human Environment was to come up with a "common outlook and [...] common principles to inspire and guide the peoples of the world in the preservation and enhancement of the human

---

[269] The Declaration on Social Progress and Development (1969), Article 25, already called for "the establishment of legal and administrative measures for the protection and improvement of the human environment. See also Economic development and the conservation of nature, General Assembly resolution 1831(XVII), adopted 18 December 1962. For the prehistory of the concept, see also Nico Schrijver, *Development without Destruction: the UN and Global Resource Management* (2010), pp. 14-33.

[270] On the preparation of the conference, see Maurice Strong, "The Stockholm Conference" (1972).

[271] Richard N. Gardner, "The Role of the UN in Environmental Problems" (1972), p. 254.

[272] Declaration of the United Nations Conference on the Human Environment, adopted 16 June 1972, published in the Report of the United Nations Conference on the Human Environment, held in Stockholm, between 5 and 16 June 1972, UNDoc. A/CONF.48/14/Rev.1 ("Declaration on the Human Environment"). See Louis B. Sohn, "Stockholm Declaration on the Human Environment" (1973), for an extensive commentary. The Conference also adopted an Action Plan for the Human Environment, the implementation of which was qualified as unsatisafctory ten years later by UNEP. The Action Plan was also published in the Report of the Conference. This Action Plan contained 109 recommendations, most of which were addressed to Governments, and some to the United Nations Organization. The Nairobi Declaration can be found in UNEP's Report of the Governing Council on the Work of its 10th Session, 10-18 May 1982, UNDoc. A37/25, Annex II, pp. 49-51.

[273] Institutional and Financial Arrangements for International Environmental Cooperation, General Assembly resolution 2997 (XXVII), adopted 15 December 1972, Preamble.

environment."[274] Or, as Maurice Strong, the Conference's Secretary-General, said prior to the start of the Conference: the aim was to realize the "concept of a planet held in trust for future generations."[275]

The declaration began by noticing that in recent times, "man [had become] both creature and moulder of his environment." This meant that "through the rapid acceleration of science and technology, man ha[d] acquired the power to transform his environment in countless ways and on an unprecedented scale."[276] Man's capacity to control his environment had both good and bad consequences, depending on whether these powers were used responsibly: "man's capability to transform his surroundings, if used wisely, [could] bring to all peoples the benefits of development and the opportunity to enhance the quality of life;" but if "wrongly or heedlessly applied, the same power [could] do incalculable harm to human beings and the human environment."[277] Even in the early 1970s, there were plenty of examples of such harm inflicted on the world: "dangerous levels of pollution," "major and undesirable disturbances to the ecological balance of the biosphere," and "destruction and depletion of irreplaceable resources."[278]

The Declaration focused on the dangers of the misuse of man's powers. The Declaration said nothing about the intrinsic value of the human environment. Instead, the document was full of phrases like "of all things in the world, people are the most precious."[279] The aim was clearly not to preserve the environment for its own sake, but to "defend and improve the human environment for present and future generations."[280]

The 1972 Declaration put forward a set of twenty-six principles on which a common environmental policy should be based. The first principle stated that

> Man has the fundamental right to freedom, equality and adequate conditions of life, in an environment of a quality that permits a life of dignity and well-being, and he bears a solemn responsibility to protect and improve the environment for present and future generations.[281]

It is not very clear whether this was supposed to be interpreted as acknowledging a human right to a healthy or adequate environment or something to that effect. As Sohn rightly remarked, "it would have been an important step forward if the right to an adequate environment were put in the forefront of the statement of principles,

---

[274] Declaration on the Human Environment, Preamble.
[275] Maurice Strong, "The Stockholm Conference" (1972), p. 417.
[276] Declaration on the Human Environment, para. 1.
[277] *Idem*, para. 3.
[278] Idem.
[279] Idem.
[280] *Idem*, para. 6.
[281] *Idem*, principle 1.

thus removing the lingering doubts about its existence."[282] However, if "this phrase [was] meant to convey the existence of the right to an adequate environment, [...] it would have been much better had the draftsmen of the Declaration stated it more clearly." [283]

The Declaration was just as ambiguous about the allocation of duties and responsibilities as it was about the allocation of rights.[284] According to the second part of the principle, "man" has a right to an environment permitting a life of dignity and well-being, and "man" also has the accompanying responsibility to both present and future generations.[285] The same ambiguity can be found in the other principles. Some were addressed to "man," [286] but most were not addressed to anyone. [287] Only a few were addressed to "States." [288] Although the word "sustainable development" did not appear in the Declaration, the main theme was the relationship between the development of the present generation and that of future generations. For example, principle five stated that "the non-renewable resources of the earth must be employed in such a way as to guard against the danger of their future exhaustion and to ensure that benefits from such employment are shared by all mankind."[289]

The most traditional and legalistic principle has also become the best known of all principles. This is principle 21:

> States have, in accordance with the Charter of the United Nations and the principles of international law, the sovereign right to exploit their own resources pursuant to their own environmental policies, and the responsibility to ensure that activities within their jurisdiction or control do not cause damage to the environment of other States or of areas beyond the limits of national jurisdiction.[290]

As Schrijver remarked, that principle "relate[d] exclusively to the transboundary effects and not (or at best in a cursory way) to the management of natural resources

---

[282] Louis B. Sohn, "Stockholm Declaration on the Human Environment" (1973), p. 455.

[283] *Idem*, p. 455. Perhaps the ambiguity was deliberate. After all, Sohn showed, by referring to the *travaux préparatoires*, that many States, and members of the Preparatory Committee, wanted the Declaration to expressly acknoldedge a human right to a "wholesome environment," but that not all States agreed. See p. 429 for the Preparatory Committee, and p. 452 for States.

[284] On the ambiguity as to the addressees of the Declaration, see *idem*, p. 435.

[285] See Declaration on the Human Environment, principle 1.

[286] Provisions addressed to "man" can be found in *idem*, principles 1 and 4.

[287] Provisions addressed to no one can be found in *idem*, principles 2, 3, 5, 6, 8, 9, 10, 12, 14, 15, 16, 17, 18, 19, 20, and 23. Presumably, most of these principles are addressed to States.

[288] Provisions addressed to States can be found in *idem*, principle 7, 11, 13, 21, 22, 24, 25 and 26.

[289] *Idem*, principle 5.

[290] *Idem*, principle 21.

at a national level."[291] Principle 21 can accurately be summarized as the freedom of States to do whatever they want within their own territory, as long as they do not cause transboundary environmental harm.[292] Interpreted in this way, it has little to do with obligations to future generations. As Sohn remarked, "while this provision [did] not go as far as to assert that a state ha[d] unlimited sovereignty over its environment, it [came] quite close to such an assertion."[293] Sohn believed that such an interpretation would not be in accordance with the remainder of the Declaration. Even though principle 21 did not say so, it followed from the Declaration as a whole that

> No state [could] claim an absolute right to ruin its environment in order to obtain some transient benefits. It should think not only of the effect on other peoples but also about the future of its own people. [...] Destruction and depletion of irreplaceable resources [were] clearly condemned by the Declaration, even when there [was] no effect abroad, and a state [could not] engage in such activities behind the shield of misconceived sovereignty.[294]

Some of the ideas of the Stockholm Declaration also ended up in the 1974 Charter of Economic Rights and Duties of States, especially in the part entitled Common Responsibilities Towards the International Community,[295] in which the Assembly proclaimed that "the protection, preservation and enhancement of the environment for the present and future generations [was] the responsibility of all States," and that "all States [should] endeavour to establish their own environment and development policies in conformity with such responsibility."[296]

On 28 October 1982, the General Assembly adopted the World Charter for Nature.[297] This time the earth was no longer treated as a commodity. Bruckerhoff described it as "one of the first legal documents to specifically recognize the intrinsic value of nature."[298] The Assembly now stated that it was "aware that mankind [was] a part of nature," that "civilization [was] rooted in nature," that "living in harmony with nature [gave] man the best opportunities for the development of his creativity," and that it was convinced that "every form of life [was] unique, warranting respect regardless of its worth to man."[299]

---

[291] See Nico Schrijver, "The Evolution of Sustainable Development in International Law" (2007), p. 246. Schrijver added, however, that some other principles were so general that they indirectly addressed also national policies and their potential effect on the environment.

[292] See also Louis B. Sohn, "Stockholm Declaration on the Human Environment" (1973), pp. 485-486.

[293] *Idem*, p. 492.

[294] Idem.

[295] Charter of Economic Rights and Duties of States, Articles 29 and 30.

[296] *Idem*, Article 30.

[297] World Charter for Nature, annexed to General Assembly resolution 37/7, adopted 28 October 1982.

[298] Joshua Bruckerhoff, "Giving Nature Constitutional Protection" (2008), p. 681.

[299] World Charter for Nature, Preamble.

The first principle of the World Charter for Nature proclaimed that "nature shall be respected and its essential processes shall not be impaired."[300] Presumably this principle was addressed to States, but this is not clear.[301] Furthermore, the Charter demands that "natural resources shall not be wasted." Instead, they should be used in a sustainable way.[302] Again it is not clear who is being addressed.

The World Charter for Nature approach has not made all that much impact on international law and international affairs. However, it never disappeared entirely. In 2012, a United Nations Conference on Sustainable Development will be held in Brazil, and the Assembly requested the conference to look at "ways to promote a holistic approach to sustainable development in harmony with nature."[303]

## 5.3 The rise of the three-pillar temple of sustainable development

The United Nations generally sees the earth as a giant natural resource to be enjoyed both by present and future generations. The concept of sustainable development was introduced on the basis of this idea. It was authoritatively defined in "Our Common Future," a report written by the World Commission on Environment and Development, chaired by Gro Harlem Brundtland of Norway, and usually referred to simply as the Brundtland Report.[304]

The main theme of the report was that the global economy and global ecology were "locked together:" they were inseparable.[305] The protection of the environment and the development of States should not be considered as separate issues, and certainly not as opposing interests. After all, the economy is almost entirely dependent on the resources provided by the earth itself, particularly in the developing world. Overexploitation was therefore a threat to the environment and in the long term to the economy itself.[306] The most pressing developmental problems, such as poverty and hunger, and the most pressing environmental problems, such as

---

[300] World Charter for Nature, para. 1.

[301] In *idem*, para. 14, which was about the implementation of the principles, we read that "the principles set forth in the present Charter shall be reflected in the law and practice of each State, as well as at the international level," which indicates that the principles primarily aimed to influence State behavior, especially legislation. However, in para. 24 we read that "each person has a duty to act in accordance with the provisions of the present Charter; acting individually, in association with others or through participation in the political process, each person shall strive to ensure that the objectives and requirements of the present Charter are met." This suggests that the Charter also aimed to influence the behavior of individuals.

[302] See *idem*, para. 13.

[303] Harmony with Nature, General Assembly resolution 65/164, adopted 20 December 2010. As a first step, the Assembly organized an Interactive Dialogue on Harmony With Nature on 20 April 2011.

[304] "Our Common Future": Report of the World Commission on Environment and Development, transmitted to the General Assembly by the Secretary-General on 4 August 1987, UNDoc. A/42/427.

[305] *Idem*, para. 15, on p. 21.

[306] *Idem*, paras. 11-26, on pp. 20-24.

desertification and global warming, were so closely connected that they essentially constituted different sides of the same coin. The problems were all caused by a type of development which was unsustainable, in the sense that it left "increasing numbers of people poor and vulnerable, while at the same time degrading the environment."[307]

At the time the report was published, some of the negative effects of traditional development had not yet occurred, and the present generation had in a sense "borrow[ed] environmental capital from future generations with no intention or prospect of repaying."[308] The negative effects of the unsustainable development would be borne by future generations. The report acknowledged that the present generation has got away with this, as future generations will never be able to reclaim what the present generation has taken away from them. Nevertheless, the report implied that the present generation should find a way of developing that did not compel it to use resources belonging to future generations.[309] The solution to this problem was to make development sustainable, *i.e.* "to ensure that [development] meets the needs of the present [generation] without compromising the ability of future generations to meet their own needs."[310]

The report's description of sustainable development has become the most authoritative definition that the international (legal) order has at its disposal, despite the fact that it is contained in a report, not in a General Assembly resolution, let alone a multilateral treaty.[311]

Most of the report was devoted to showing the potential of sustainable development. The general idea was that the rich should not use all the available natural resources for themselves, leaving nothing for future generations, and that poverty also led to an unsustainable use of natural resources, so that the economic development of the poor would be beneficial to the environment.[312] The report contained numerous recommendations focusing on population control,[313] ensuring a

---

[307] *Idem*, para. 10, on p. 20.

[308] *Idem*, para. 25, on p..24.

[309] *Idem*, paras.25-26.

[310] *Idem*, para. 27.

[311] See also Nico Schrijver, "The Evolution of Sustainable Development in International Law" (2007), p. 231 and p. 373. However, some scholars believe that the Brundtland definition is so vague that it can hardly be labeled as a definition. See Hari M. Osofsky, "Defining Sustainable Development after Earth Summit 2002" (2003).

[312] This approach has been criticized for being inconsistent, since it sees both the rapid economic development of the West and the lack of development of the developing world as a threat to the environment. See James E. Ellis, "Problems and Policies for Planetary Survival" (1988), p. 1308.

[313] See also Key actions for the further implementation of the Programme of Action of the International Conference on Population and Development, annexed to General Assembly resolution S-21/2, adopted 2 July 1999, which sought to implement the Programme of Action of the International Conference on Population and Development, which can be found in the Report of the International Conference on Population and Development, held in Cairo between 5–13 September 1994.

sustainable food supply for all, halting the decreasing diversity of species (plants, animals) and ecosystems,[314] developing and promoting the use of sustainable energy sources, using less polluting forms of technology in global industry, controlling the growth of cities, especially in the developing world and setting up a new legal regime for the management of the "global commons," *i.e.* the oceans, outer space, and Antarctica (the South Pole).[315] Finally, the report discussed the use of the environment as a weapon, as well as the effect of the nuclear arms race on the environment.[316]

A set of Proposed Legal Principles for Environmental Protection and Sustainable Development, adopted by the World Commission on Environment and Development Experts Group on Environmental Law was annexed to the report.[317] The most far-reaching principle was the principle according to which "all human beings ha[d] the fundamental right to an environment adequate for their health and well-being."[318] If adopted by the international community, this principle would remove the obscurities of the Declaration on the Human Environment, and clearly recognize a human right to an enabling environment. Another important principle was the principle on intergenerational equity, according to which "States [should] conserve and use the environment and natural resources for the benefit of present and future generations."[319] This formulation, although inspired by the definition of sustainable development suggested in the Brundtland Report, did not have the

---

[314] This ultimately led to the adoption of the Convention on Biological Diversity, the text of which can be found in United Nations, Treaty Series, vol. 1760, p. 79 and further.

[315] Various treaties have been adopted on the management of the global commons. See *e.g.*, the United Nations Convention on the Law of the Sea, in United Nations, Treaty Series, vol. 1833, p. 3 and further; the Agreement governing the Activities of States on the Moon and Other Celestial Bodies, in United Nations, Treaty Series, vol. 1363, p. 3 and further; The Antarctic Treaty, in United Nations, Treaty Series, vol. 402, p. 70 and futher. See also the Declaration of Principles Governing the Sea-Bed and the Ocean Floor, and the Subsoil Thereof, beyond the Limits of National Jurisdiction, General Assembly resolution 2749(XXV), adopted 17 December 1970.

[316] This was an issue on the General Assembly's agenda from quite early on. See *e.g.*, the Draft Convention on the Prohibition of Action to Influence the Environment and Climate for Military and Other Purposes Incompatible with the Maintenance of International Security, Human Well-Being and Health, annexed to General Assembly resolution 3264(XXIX), adopted 9 December 1974; and the Convention on the Prohibition of Military or Any Other Hostile Use of Environmental Modification Techniques, the text of which was annexed to General Assembly resolution 31/72, adopted 10 December 1976. On the latter Convention, see Erik Koppe, *The use of nuclear weapons and the protection of the environment during international armed conflict* (2008), pp. 124-139.

[317] Summary of Proposed Legal Principles for Environmental Protection and Sustainable Development, adopted by the WCED Experts Group on Environmental Law, published in Our Common Future, pp. 339-342. This group of legal experts was chaired by Robert Munro of Canada, with Johan Lammers of the Netherlands as Rapporteur.

[318] *Idem*, principle 1.

[319] *Idem*, principle 2.

original definition's preference for the interests of the present generation.[320] The remainder of the suggested principles focused on the prohibition of States to cause transboundary damage to the environment.[321]

The Brundtland Report's definition of sustainable development was quickly embraced by the Assembly. A few months after the publication of the report, the General Assembly adopted the Environmental Perspective to the Year 2000 and Beyond, presented as a "broad framework to guide national action and international co-operation on policies and programmes aimed at achieving environmentally sound development."[322] The Environmental Perspective used the definition of sustainable development proposed in the Brundtland Report.[323] The Perspective then distinguished six main issues, and proposed ways to resolve these issues.[324]

The most important declaration on sustainable development was adopted in 1992. The Declaration on Environment and Development was concluded at the end of the United Nations Conference on Environment and Development, held in Rio de Janeiro.[325] The Rio Conference also stimulated the adoption and eventual entry into force of a number of important multilateral treaties relating to the protection of the environment,[326] and adopted a lengthy programme of action called Agenda 21, and a Statement of Principles on All Types of Forests.[327] The implementation of Agenda

---

[320] See also *idem*, principle 3, which suggested that States preserve the world's biological diversity, and respect the principle of the optimum sustainable yield in the use of living natural resources (especially fish).

[321] See *idem*, principles 9-20. See also Nico Schrijver, "The Evolution of Sustainable Development in International Law" (2007), p. 261.

[322] Environmental Perspective to the Year 2000 and Beyond, annexed to General Assembly resolution 42/186, adopted 11 December 1987. The description can be found in para. 2 of that General Assembly resolution. The resolution to which the Environmental Perspective was annexed is itself also worth looking at, since it contains a general description of the consensus at the time, *i.e.* it contains the main "perceptions generally shared by Governments of the nature of environmental problems, and their interrelations with other international problems, and of the efforts to deal with them." See General Assembly resolution 42/186, para. 3.

[323] *Idem*, para. 2.

[324] *Idem*, paras. 5-86. See also General Assembly resolution 42/186, para. 4(a)-(f).

[325] Rio Declaration on Environment and Development, published in the Report of the United Nations Conference on Environment and Development, held in Rio de Janeiro, between 3 and 14 June 1992, UNDoc. A/CONF.151/26/Rev.l (Vol. l) ("Rio Declaration on Environment and Development").

[326] The most important is probably the United Nations Framework Convention on Climate Change. The text of this Convention is published in United Nations, Treaty Series, vol. 1771, p. 107 and further. See also Nico Schrijver, "The Evolution of Sustainable Development in International Law" (2007), p. 263, for an overview of the Conventions adopted at that time.

[327] Agenda 21 and the Non-legally Binding Authoritative Statement of Principles for a Global Consensus on the Management, Conservation and Sustainable Development of All Types of Forests were also published in the Report of the United Nations Conference on Environment and Development, UNDoc. A/CONF.151/26/Rev.l (Vol. l). See also the Non-legally binding instrument on all types of forests, annexed to General Assembly resolution 62/98, adopted 17 December 2007.

21 was assessed five years later and the results were disappointing. In the years following the adoption of the Declaration on Environment and Development, "the state of the global environment ha[d] continued to deteriorate."[328]

The focus here is on the Declaration on Environment and Development, better known simply as the Rio Declaration. The Rio Declaration contained 27 principles on sustainable development. The first principle emphasized the human-centred approach. It stated that "human beings are at the centre of concerns for sustainable development."[329] The second principle reaffirmed principle 21 of the Declaration on the Human Environment.[330] The third principle attempted to reconcile the right to development with the concept of sustainable development, by stating that "the right to development must be fulfilled so as to equitably meet developmental and environmental needs of present and future generations."[331] It is unclear whether this meant that future generations also have a right to development. The fourth principle reflected the gist of the Brundtland Report, *i.e.* that development and the environment were inseparable concepts, and that the new concept of sustainable development had intended to express exactly that. Thus principle four stated that "in order to achieve sustainable development, environmental protection shall constitute an integral part of the development process and cannot be considered in isolation from it."[332] Principles five and six were essentially about intra-generational equity, *i.e.* the equal distribution of natural resources among the States of the present generation. Principle seven introduced the principle of common but differentiated responsibilities. According to this principle, States had different degrees of responsibilities to help "conserve, protect and restore the health and integrity of the Earth's ecosystem (…) in view of the[ir] different contributions to global environmental degradation."[333]

---

[328] See para. 9 (p. 5) of the Programme for the Further Implementation of Agenda 21, adopted by the General Assembly at its nineteenth special session (23-28 June 1997), UNDoc. A/RES/S-19/2, distributed on 19 September 1997, as cited on p. 978 of Paolo Galizzi, "From Stockholm to New York, via Rio and Johannesburg" (2006).

[329] Rio Declaration on Environment and Development, principle 1.

[330]*Idem*, principle 2. As Galizzi pointed out, one difference between Principle 21 of the Stockholm Declaration on the Human Environment and Principle 2 of the Rio Declaration on Environment and Development was that only the latter spoke of the sovereign right of all States to exploit their own resources pursuant to their own environmental and developmental policies. See Paolo Galizzi, "From Stockholm to New York, via Rio and Johannesburg" (2006), p. 973.

[331] *Idem*, principle 3.

[332] *Idem*, principle 4. See also principle 25, which suggested that "peace, development and environmental protection are interdependent and indivisible.".

[333] *Idem*, principle 7, principles 8-19, and also paras. 26 and 27, further elaborated on the responsibilities of States. Principle 15 is particularly interesting, because it introduced the "precautionary approach" principle, according to which the "lack of full scientific certainty [should] not be used as a reason for postponing cost-effective measures to prevent environmental degradation."

The next major declaration on sustainable development, after the Rio Declaration, was the Millennium Declaration. This declaration included in its list of values, the value of respect for nature. This suggests a return to the World Charter for Nature approach to environmental protection. In reality, the Assembly continued to prefer the Declaration on the Human Environment approach, in which the interests of future generations of human beings, and not the interests of nature itself, were the main concern. With regard to respect for nature, the General Assembly stated:

> Prudence must be shown in the management of all living species and natural resources, in accordance with the precepts of sustainable development. Only in this way can the immeasurable riches provided to us by nature be preserved and passed on to our descendants. The current unsustainable patterns of production and consumption must be changed in the interest of our future welfare and that of our descendants.[334]

Section IV of the Millennium Declaration, on "protecting our common environment," elaborated on this value in greater detail. The Assembly pledged to "spare no effort to free all of humanity, and above all our children and grandchildren, from the threat of living on a planet irredeemably spoilt by human activities, and whose resources would no longer be sufficient for their needs."[335] Thus the States resolved to "adopt in all our environmental actions a new ethic of conservation and stewardship." The first elements of this new ethic were then set out in the declaration.[336] The Millennium Development Goals included the goal of ensuring environmental sustainability (MDG7).[337] However, the emphasis of the MDGs was on alleviating poverty in the present generation, and not on the protection of the environment for the benefit of future generations.[338]

The concept of sustainable development was developed in more detail in 2002 during the United Nations Conference on Sustainable Development in

---

[334] Millennium Declaration, para. 6.

[335] *Idem*, para. 21.

[336] *Idem*, para. 23. Then followed some concrete steps, which included support for a number of treaties, including the Kyoto Protocol to the United Nations Framework Convention on Climate Change, published in United Nations, Treaty Series, vol. 2303, p. 148 and further; and the Convention on Biological Diversity, and the United Nations Convention to Combat Desertification in those Countries Experiencing Serious Drought and/or Desertification, Particularly in Africa.

[337] The targets based on MDG7 included the reversal of the loss of environmental resources; to accomplish a significant reduction in the rate of biodiversity loss by 2010; to halve, by 2015, the proportion of people without sustainable access to drinking water; and to improve the lives of the world's slum dwellers.

[338] See Paolo Galizzi, "From Stockholm to New York, via Rio and Johannesburg" (2006), p. 1007. Galizzi thus suggested drafting a set of Millennium Environmental Goals.

Johannesburg, South Africa.[339] A few months before the start of the conference, the International Law Association adopted the New Delhi Declaration of Principles of International Law relating to Sustainable Development. This Declaration clearly and succinctly presented the core legal principles of sustainable development.[340] It was submitted to the General Assembly and had a significant impact on the work of the conference.[341] In the Johannesburg Declaration on Sustainable Development, the States present at the Conference

> Assume[d] a collective responsibility to advance and strengthen the interdependent and mutually reinforcing pillars of sustainable development - economic development, social development and environmental protection - at the local, national, regional and global levels.[342]

The introduction of these three pillars is new, although the Rio Declaration had already hinted at them.[343] The Brundtland Report only referred to the need to combine development and environmental protection in one concept, but did not distinguish between economic and social development.

The fact that only one of the three pillars relates to the environment suggests that the balance between development and the environment, which was established in Rio, was distorted in favour of the former. As Galizzi concluded, "the environment did not have a very good summit at Johannesburg."[344] The developing States are often blamed for this failure, as they focused more on their own immediate developmental problems, rather than on potential developmental problems for future generations. Resources are scarce, and therefore increasing the share of resources for future generations automatically decreases the resources

---

[339] Johannesburg Declaration on Sustainable Development, published in the Report of the World Summit on Sustainable Development, held in Johannesburg (South Africa), between 26 August and 4 September 2002, UNDoc. A/CONF.199/20.

[340] The Declaration was published, with an introduction by Nico Schrijver, in the *Netherlands International Law Review* (2002), pp. 299-305.

[341] See Letter dated 6 August 2002 from Bangladesh and the Netherlands to the United Nations, distributed 31 August 2002, UNDoc. A/57/329.

[342] *Idem*, para. 5.

[343] The Conference also adopted a Plan of Implementation of the World Summit on Sustainable Development, which is published in the Report of the World Summit on Sustainable Development, UNDoc. A/CONF.199/20. In para. 2 of this Plan of Implementation, the three pillars of sustainable development are described; in para. 139, these three pillars are referred to as "dimensions." See also paras. 140(c), 145, and 157.

[344] Paolo Galizzi, "From Stockholm to New York, via Rio and Johannesburg" (2006), p. 990. At best, one can say that the Johannesburg summit mainly served to reiterate commitments towards future generations made in earlier declarations. See also Nico Schrijver, "The Evolution of Sustainable Development in International Law" (2007), p. 282.

available for the present generation.[345] Intergenerational equity comes at the expense of intragenerational equity.

A World Fit for Children deserves a brief mention here. In this declaration the Assembly pledged to "protect the Earth for children," by "safeguard[ing] our natural environment, with its diversity of life, its beauty and its resources, all of which enhance the quality of life, for present and future generations."[346] This could be interpreted as indicating an adjustment in the balance between present and future generations, but the declaration has not had much impact.

In the World Summit Outcome Document of 2005, the General Assembly reaffirmed that "sustainable development [...] constitute[d] a key element of the overarching framework of United Nations activities." It also emphasized that "economic development, social development and environmental protection" constituted the "interdependent and mutually reinforcing pillars" of the concept of sustainable development.[347] Thus it followed the Johannesburg approach, according to which the emphasis of sustainable development should be on the second word, rather than the first.[348] Despite growing concerns about the state of the environment, the Outcome Document mainly reiterated commitments adopted earlier.[349]

## 5.4 Conclusion

The concept of sustainable development was a UN invention. It has become a household concept since it was authoritatively defined by the UN in the 1980s. The central idea is that when we think of development we also bear in mind the interests and needs of future generations. In a way, one has to imagine that these future generations already exist in the moral universe, and that they are entitled to a piece of the pie.[350] The present generation has to put some pie in the freezer, and leave it there for the future generation to defrost. This approach to man's relationship with the environment has been generally accepted, even though some scholars have been critical of the idea that the earth is regarded as no more than a resource for both present and future generations.

---

[345] It appears that Weiss believes that intergenerational equity actually is more important, and that intragenerational equity is a means to intergenerational equity. See Edith Brown Weiss, "Our Rights and Obligations to Future Generations for the Environment" (1990), p. 201.

[346] A world fit for children, annexed to General Assembly resolution S-27/2, adopted 10 May 2002, para. 4.

[347] 2005 World Summit Outcome, paras. 10 and 48. See also paras. 49-56.

[348] See also Paolo Galizzi, "From Stockholm to New York, via Rio and Johannesburg" (2006), pp. 993-1001.

[349] See also Nico Schrijver, "The Evolution of Sustainable Development in International Law" (2007), p. 285.

[350] There is one thing that the pie metaphor overlooks, and that is the fact that the earth, in contrast to the pie, can renew itself to a certain extent, i.e. that it is capable of continuously providing new resources.

Despite its acceptance, the status of sustainable development in international law, as well as its exact content and implications, are as yet unclear. One especially problematical aspect is that the duty to reserve some of the pie for future generations by definition results in less pie for the present generation. This is particularly difficult for developing States, which have been struggling to get their share of the pie for decades.

## 6 THE RIGHT TO DEVELOPMENT

### 6.1 Introduction

In the attempt to create a fair and equitable economic order it is necessary to identify the subjects and objects of that order.[351] Our world is traditionally perceived as a community of sovereign States. Therefore one would initially consider States to be both the object (recipient) and the subject (payer). This was the approach in most of the declarations. They all set out the norms and principles that guide States in their relations with each other, focusing on the relationship between developing States (recipients of aid) and developed States (payers of aid).

It could also be argued that the ultimate recipient of development is the individual human being. This is the approach adopted by many cosmopolitans.[352] The cross-fertilization of the United Nations system, on the one hand, and philosophy, on the other hand, has been much more successful in this approach than it has been when it comes to implementing global justice ideas in the rules and regulations of the State-based international economic order. The fact that the debate on development and social justice is increasingly formulated in terms of human rights, in which individuals formulate claims against their own State and against the international community as a whole, is evidence of the increasing influence of this human-centred approach.[353] The recognition of a universal human right to development and the view of poverty as a human rights violation,[354] as well as the emerging concept of human development to guide United Nations development

---

[351] See on this aspect of the definition of social/distributive justice, Simon Caney, *Justice beyond Borders: A Global Political Theory* (2006), pp. 103-105.
[352] See *e.g.*, Peter Singer, *One World: The Ethics of Globalization* (2002).
[353] Kofi Annan made it his prime task as UN Secretary-General to promote this human-centered approach to basically everything the UN does. See *e.g.*, the Secretary-General's Report: We, the Peoples: the Role of the United Nations in the Twenty-first Century. Distributed 27 March 2000. UNDoc A/54/2000, para. 10.
[354] On the human right to development, one must refer to the UN Human Rights Council's Working Group on the Right to Development. See also Thomas W. Pogge, "Recognized and Violated by International Law: The Human Rights of the Global Poor" (2005).

programmes, are all further evidence of this trend.[355] This trend is a consequence, not so much of changing ideas in the field of development, but rather of changing ideas based on human rights and the promotion of human dignity. These ideas are examined more extensively in the chapter on the value of human dignity. Here, they are examined only to the extent that they relate immediately to development.

The main question is whether in recent times the international community has started to base its ideas in the field of social progress and development on the needs of individuals rather than on the needs of States. Thomas Pogge argued that a duty of global social justice already exists in human rights law.[356] He conducted the debate on development in human rights terms, which led to very interesting results.[357] Thomas Pogge is not alone as regards this approach.[358] Essentially he claimed that poor people have a human right to development and a certain standard of living, and that this human right is violated by the international community. This is because the international community has created and then sustained an international economic order that makes it impossible for many individuals to secure an adequate standard of living.[359]

The easiest way to stop the institutional order from violating this human right to development is to compensate the victims of this violation in some way.[360] This may be easier than creating a perfect international economic order, in which all participants automatically get what they deserve, but such global compensation

---

[355] The term human development was coined by the Nobel Prize winning economist Amartya Sen and the authors of the first Human Development Reports, written for the United Nations Development Programme. For a brief overview of human development ideas, see Richard Jolly, "Human Development" (2007).

[356] The formulation of the problem is inspired by Thomas W. Pogge, "Recognized and Violated by International Law: The Human Rights of the Global Poor" (2005), pp. 717–745.

[357] Pogge's argument can be found in Thomas W. Pogge, "Recognized and Violated by International Law: The Human Rights of the Global Poor" (2005); Pogge, "The International Significance of Human Rights" (2000), pp. 45–69; Pogge, *World Poverty and Human Rights* (2002).

[358] See *e.g.*, Richard Jolly, Louis Emmerij, Dharam Ghai & Frédéric Lapeyre, *UN Contributions to Development Thinking and Practice* (2004). See also Olivier de Frouville, "Article 1, paragraphe 3" (2005), pp. 361-370.

[359] Pogge focused on the negative duty related to the human right of development: he claimed that the current global institutional arrangements as codified in international law constituted a collective human rights violation of enormous proportions to which most of the world's affluent were making uncompensated contributions (Pogge, "Recognized and Violated by International Law" (2005), p. 721). This is different from the argument that the international community is violating the human-rights based claim of the very poor to economic assistance (that would be a neglect of a positive duty). Pogge does not reject this latter claim, but because it is a harder case to make, he leaves it aside, without prejudice (*idem*, p. 720).

[360] Pogge proposes a Global Resources Dividend. See Chapter 8 of Thomas W. Pogge, *World Poverty and Human Rights* (2002). On p. 196, Pogge, explains how it works: "States and their governments shall not have full libertarian property rights with respect to the natural resources in their territory, but can be required to share a small part of the value of any resources they decide to use or sell."

does not currently exist. Pogge's argument is that it should exist, according to already existing international law.

According to Article 55 of the UN Charter, "the United Nations shall promote [..] higher standards of living, full employment, and conditions of economic and social progress and development." An individual cannot base a claim on this rather general provision, but an individual can claim human rights. The international community proclaims the following right in the Universal Declaration of Human Rights:

> Everyone has the right to a standard of living adequate for the health and well-being of himself and of his family, including food, clothing, housing and medical care and necessary social services, and the right to security in the event of unemployment, sickness, disability, widowhood, old age or other lack of livelihood in circumstances beyond his control.[361]

In order to demonstrate that this right can not only be claimed at a national level, but also at the international level, the Declaration stated that "[e]veryone [was] entitled to a social and international order in which the rights and freedoms set forth in this Declaration can be fully realized."[362] Pogge argued that these articles, taken together, establish a duty for the global community to ensure that all individuals within that community can enjoy their right to development.

Reference could be made to binding international treaties which are aimed at guaranteeing the same rights as some of the non-binding declarations, although Pogge did not refer to these. The most relevant is the International Covenant on Economic, Social and Cultural Rights.[363] In Article 2 of this Covenant Member States "undertake[..] to take steps, individually and through international assistance and co-operation, especially economic and technical, to the maximum of its available resources,[[364]] with a view to achieving progressively the full realization

---

[361] Universal Declaration of Human Rights, Part A of International Bill of Human Rights, General Assembly resolution 217(III), adopted 10 December 1948 ("Universal Declaration of Human Rights"), Article 25. See also Chapter VI of this study, especially section 2.3 thereof.

[362] *Idem*, Article 28.

[363] International Covenant on Economic, Social and Cultural Rights, adopted and opened for signature, ratification and accession by General Assembly resolution 2200A (XXI) of 16 December 1966; entry into force 3 January 1976. The United States of America is one of the very few countries that did not ratify the International Covenant on Economic, Social and Cultural Rights. See Thomas W. Pogge, "Recognized and Violated by International Law: The Human Rights of the Global Poor" (2005), p. 719, 720.

[364] See General Comment 3, on the nature of States parties' obligations (Art. 2, para. 1 of the Covenant). This Comment was adopted by the Committee on Economic, Social and Cultural Rights during its Fifth session in 1990. This important General Comment explains that "the phrase [in Article 2] "to the maximum of its available resources"was intended by the drafters of the Covenant to refer to both the resources existing within a State and those available from the international community through international cooperation and assistance."

of the rights recognized in the present Covenant."[365] One of these rights recognized in the Covenant was "the right of everyone to an adequate standard of living for himself and his family, including adequate food, clothing and housing, and to the continuous improvement of living conditions," and "the fundamental right of everyone to be free from hunger." To safeguard the latter right, Member States should take measures "individually and through international co-operation [...] to ensure an equitable distribution of world food supplies in relation to need."[366]

The following sections examine the Assembly resolutions supporting this human-centred, entitlement-based approach to the value of social progress and development. This approach culminated in the Declaration on the Right to Development.

## 6.2 A rights-based approach prior to the Declaration on the Right to Development

In 1969 the General Assembly adopted a Declaration on Social Progress and Development. This resolution is interesting because it is one of the first resolutions that linked social progress to human rights. What was new about the declaration was the idea that individuals had a right to enjoy the fruits of social progress. According to the Assembly, "all peoples and all human beings [...] shall have the right to live in dignity and freedom and to enjoy the fruits of social progress and should, on their part, contribute to it."[367] The question arises what the difference is between human beings having a right to "enjoy the fruits of social progress," and the more old-fashioned approach, according to which social progress is pursued by a State as part of its development policy.[368] In actual fact, the consequences could be far-reaching. If a human rights approach were accepted, it would have the following consequences:

> All human beings in the world are entitled to enjoy the fruits of social progress, and if deprived thereof, they have legal means to demand respect for their right;

---

[365] Member States must try, to the maximum of available resources, to guarantee these rights, individually and collectively. The International Covenant on Civil and Political Rights, adopted by the General Assembly on the 16th of December 1966, entry into force 23 March 1976, requires member States to "respect and to ensure to all individuals within its territory the rights recognized in the present Covenant"(article 2.1), and not just to take steps with a view to progressively realizing the rights.

[366] International Covenant on Economic, Social and Cultural Rights, Article 11.

[367] Declaration on Social Progress and Development, General Assembly resolution 2542(XXIV), adopted 11 December 1969 ("Declaration on Social Progress and Development"), Article 1.

[368] As fruits of social progress, one might think of education, health care, housing, food, and so on.

All States have a legal obligation to ensure that each and every individual within their jurisdiction enjoys the fruits of social progress.[369]

The human rights approach was not so dominant in the declarations adopted in the years following the 1969 Declaration on Social Progress and Development. Nevertheless, sections based on human rights can be found in a few of the general declarations.

For example, the International Development Strategy for the Second United Nations Development Decade of 1970 had a section on human development. This section focused on education, health and adequate housing for individuals.[370] The remainder of the document related solely to the development of developing States, and thus dealt with the individuals residing within those States only indirectly.

The Development Strategy for the Third United Nations Decade added an additional development goal: the promotion of human dignity.[371] As the human rights-based approach is based on a respect for human dignity, this is in line with the human-centred approach to development.

## 6.3 The Declaration on the Right to Development

The Declaration on the Right to Development was adopted by the General Assembly in 1986. The Assembly referred to development not as a policy goal, but as a legal entitlement.[372] None of the earlier declarations had referred explicitly to a human right, or a peoples' right, to development. The Declaration on the Right to Development did exactly that. First, the Declaration on the Right to Development described development as

A comprehensive economic, social, cultural and political process, which aims at the constant improvement of the well-being of the entire population and of all individuals on the basis of their active, free and meaningful participation in development and in the fair distribution of benefits resulting therefrom.[373]

---

[369] See Richard Jolly, Louis Emmerij & Thomas G. Weiss, *UN Ideas that Changed the World* (2009), p. 131. Their reasons were not linked to the Declaration on Social Progress and Development, but to social human rights in general.

[370] International Development Strategy for the Second United Nations Development Decade, paras. 65-72.

[371] *Idem*, para. 8. See also the Guidelines for Consumer Protection, annexed to General Assembly resolution 39/248, adopted 9 April 1985.

[372] See also Bertrand G. Ramcharan, *Contemporary human rights ideas* (2008), pp. 85-97.

[373] Declaration on the Right to Development, General Assembly resolution 41/128, adopted 4 December 1986 ("Declaration on the Right to Development"), Preamble. When the Declaration on the Right to Development was adopted, the United States of America cast the only dissenting vote in the Assembly. See UN Doc. A/41/PV.97.

Then the right to development was defined as

> An inalienable human right by virtue of which every human person and all peoples are entitled to participate in, contribute to, and enjoy economic, social, cultural and political development, in which all human rights and fundamental freedoms can be fully realized.[374]

The right to development was presented as a right to participate in a process called development, and a right to have one's human rights respected while participating in that process.[375] The goal of that process was development, which was itself also defined in terms of the full realization of human rights. Thus there is an overall picture that "using the right to development approach, the objectives of development are set up as entitlements of rights holders, which duty bearers, the individuals, the states, and the international community are expected to fulfil, respect, protect, and promote while respecting international human rights standards."[376]

The beneficiary of the right to development was, first and foremost, the individual. However, it was not enough for the individual to simply wait for this development to take place. The individual also had duties, as an active participant in the process.[377] It was primarily the States who were responsible for making this development possible. As the Assembly said: "States ha[d] the primary responsibility for the creation of national and international conditions favourable to the realization of the right to development."[378] At the international level, this meant that "States ha[d] the duty to take steps, individually and collectively, to formulate international development policies with a view to facilitating the full realization of the right to development."[379] At the national level, it meant that "States should undertake [...] all necessary measures for the realization of the right to development and sh[ould] ensure, *inter alia*, equality of opportunity for all in their access to basic resources, education, health services, food, housing, employment and the fair distribution of income."[380]

Although States, as the key members of the international community, had most of the responsibilities, the Assembly acknowledged in the Declaration that the

---

[374] *Idem*, Article 1.

[375] See Arjun Sengupta, "On the theory and practice of the Right to Development" (2002), pp. 846-852, and 868-876.

[376] *Idem*, p. 852. Schrijver described the right to development as "nothing more and nothing less than the sum of existing human rights." See Nico Schrijver, "The Evolution of Sustainable Development in International Law" (2007), p. 271.

[377] Declaration on the Right to Development, Article 2.

[378] *Idem*, Article 3(1).

[379] *Idem*, Article 4(1).

[380] *Idem*, Article 8(1).

international community did not consist only of States. According to the Universal Declaration of Human Rights, "everyone ha[d] duties to the community in which alone the free and full development of his personality is possible."[381] Inspired by that provision, the Declaration on the Right to Development stated that

> All human beings have a responsibility for development, individually and collectively, taking into account the need for full respect for their human rights and fundamental freedoms as well as their duties to the community, which alone can ensure the free and complete fulfilment of the human being, and they should therefore promote and protect an appropriate political, social and economic order for development.[382]

In 2005, the UN High Commissioner for Human Rights, Louise Arbour pointed out that it made a crucial difference to the poor whether they achieved aid in the form of charity and need-based assistance, or in the form of entitlements:

> The process of development must strive to realize all human rights entitlements of all rights holders. This is particularly relevant for the poor and the marginalized. For them it is necessary that the development process move away from a needs-based exercise in charity and assistance to one that creates and sustains genuine entitlements that span all aspects of their life- economic, social and cultural, as well as the civil and political.[383]

The difference was the entitlement to respect for human dignity and the intrinsic worth of every human being. This meant that, in global partnerships for development, development assistance was no longer based on charity, if it ever was, but rather on legitimate claims made by individuals to those with a duty to provide it. The latter category ultimately included every member of the international community, and thus also individuals themselves. The difference between a needs-based or charity-based approach to development, and that of a rights-based approach, has also been emphasized in much of the literature.[384]

---

[381] Universal Declaration of Human Rights, Article 29. See also Declaration of Human Duties and Responsibilities, adopted by a High-Level Group chaired by Richard J. Goldstone, 1999.

[382] Declaration on the Right to Development, Article 2(2).

[383] Statement by Louise Arbour, UN High Commissioner for Human Rights, to the Working Group on the Right to Development, made in Palais des Nations, Room XVII, in Geneva, on the 15th of February 2005.

[384] See especially Jakob Kirkemann Boesen & Tomas Martin, *Applying a Rights-Based Approach* (2007), pp. 9-13. See also Fateh Azzam, "Reflections on Human Rights Approaches to Implementing the Millennium Development Goals" (2005), p. 24.

When the Declaration on the Right to Development was adopted, the United States of America cast the only negative vote.[385] Eight other countries abstained.[386] One reason for the abstentions was the blurring of the distinction between human rights, peoples' rights, and even the rights of States.[387] This blurring was also a major hurdle, albeit one that was overcome, for many of the States that ultimately voted in favour.[388] They believed that human rights belonged to individuals, and essentially served to protect individuals from the abuse of their own State's power and authority over them. At the same time, this classical approach to human rights does not prevent the consideration of human rights violations committed against an entire group of individuals.[389] This is not the same as giving human rights, traditionally believed to be enjoyed only by individuals, to peoples, or even to States.[390]

## 6.4 A rights-based approach after the Declaration on the Right to Development

The human-centred approach to the value of social progress and development can also be found in resolutions adopted after the Declaration on the Right to Development. In 1991, the Assembly "recogniz[ed] that the elimination of widespread poverty and the full enjoyment of economic, social and cultural rights [were] interrelated goals," and that "extreme poverty [was] a violation of human dignity and could constitute a threat to the right to life."[391] It then affirmed that

---

[385] For a discussion of the US position on the right to development, see Stephen Marks, "The Human Right to Development: Between Rhetoric and Reality" (2004), pp. 137-168.

[386] UN Doc. A/41/PV.97, p. 64. The abstaining States were Denmark, Finland, Germany, Iceland, Israel, Japan, Sweden, and the United Kingdom.

[387] For an explanation of the US dissent, see UN Doc. A/C..3/41/SR.61, p. 32. For the abstentions, see The Federal Republic of Germany (A/C..3/41/SR.61, p. 29-30), Japan (p.31), the United Kingdom (p.33). For Finland, speaking also on behalf of Denmark, Iceland and Sweden, see A/41/PV.97, p. 77.

[388] See, *e.g.*, Norway (A/41/PV.97, p. 57; Norway had voted against the Declaration when it was adopted by the Third Committee of the General Assembly, see A/C..3/41/SR.61, p. 11), Austria (A/C..3/41/SR.61, p. 31), Ireland (A/C..3/41/SR.61, p. 31), Canada (p. 34).

[389] A very helpful brochure on a human rights-based approach to development, published by the Office of the United Nations High Commissioner of Human Rights made this quite clear. It defined human rights as "universal legal guarantees protecting individuals and groups against actions and omissions that interfere with fundamental freedoms, entitlements and human dignity." Office of the United Nations High Commissioner of Human Rights, *Frequently Asked Questions on A Human Rights-Based Approach to Development Cooperation* (2006), p. 1.

[390] *Idem*, pp. 4-5. These debates are examined in more detail in Chapter VI, the chapter on human dignity.

[391] Human rights and extreme poverty, General Assembly resolution 46/121, adopted 17 December 1991, Preamble.

"extreme poverty and exclusion from society constitute[d] a violation of human dignity."[392]

A few years later, the United Nations organized a World Conference on Human Rights, with the specific aim to "examine the relation between development and the enjoyment by everyone of economic, social and cultural rights as well as civil and political rights."[393] In the Vienna Declaration and Programme of Action, the international community reaffirmed that "the right to development, as established in the Declaration on the Right to Development, [was] a universal and inalienable right and an integral part of fundamental human rights," and that it was the duty of the international community to "promote an effective international cooperation for the realization of the right to development and the elimination of obstacles to development."[394] This time the United States joined the consensus.

Reference should also be made to the many commitments in the Copenhagen Declaration on Social Development focusing on the individual and referring to human dignity.[395] Moreover, the Agenda for Development formulated the goal of development almost exclusively in terms of human rights.[396] In particular, the Secretary-General stressed the importance of promoting democracy, respect for human rights and an increased role for civil society within States.[397] In the Millennium Declaration, the world community pledged to "spare no effort to free our fellow men, women and children from the abject and dehumanizing conditions of extreme poverty, to which more than a billion of them are currently subjected."[398] The Assembly then pledged "to mak[e] the right to development a reality for everyone and to free[ing] the entire human race from want."[399] Despite these general references to the right to development, the Millennium Declaration cannot be considered as a continuation of the human rights-based approach, as none of the MDGs is formulated in human rights terms.[400] Nevertheless, it is clear that human rights and the MDGs are at least implicitly linked.[401]

---

[392] *Idem*, para. 1.

[393] General Assembly Resolution 45/155, adopted 18 December 1990. See also Report of the World Conference on Human Rights, A/CONF.157/24.

[394] Vienna Declaration and Programme of Action, UNDoc A/CONF.157/24 ("Vienna Declaration and Programme of Action"), para. 10. See also paras. 25 and 72.

[395] Copenhagen Declaration on Social Development, commitments 2, 3, 5, 6 and 4.

[396] Agenda for Development, para. 44.

[397] See *idem*, paras. 26-32.

[398] Millennium Declaration, para. 11.

[399] *Idem*.

[400] Philip Alston, "Ships Passing in the Night" (2005), p. 757.

[401] See especially Philip Alston, "Ships Passing in the Night" (2005), and Alston, *A Human Rights Perspective on the Millennium Development Goals*, paper written in 2004, as advice for the Millennium Project Task Force on Poverty and Economic Development. See also Millennium Development Goal 8: Indicators for Monitoring Implementation (Note by the Secretariat for second meeting of High-level

To make that link more explicit, Sachs, the director of the Millennium Project, wrote in A Practical Plan to Achieve the Millennium Goals, that

> The Millennium Development Goals (MDGs) are the world's time-bound and quantified targets for addressing extreme poverty in its many dimensions – income poverty, hunger, disease, lack of adequate shelter and exclusion – while promoting gender equality, education, and environmental sustainability. They are also basic human rights – the rights of each person on the planet to health education, shelter, and security as pledged in the Universal Declaration of Human Rights and the UN Millennium Declaration.[402]

Although the Declaration itself did not specifically do so, it is not difficult to translate the MDGs into human rights language.[403] Doing so improves their effectiveness as a trigger for State behaviour, especially as various States have already accepted a legal commitment to promote human rights, whilst the Millennium Declaration is a legally non-binding instrument.[404]

The approach to development from the perspective of legally binding human rights was not accepted by everyone.[405] Every year, the General Assembly adopts a resolution recommending the continued implementation of the right to development with a majority but with a substantial abstaining minority.[406]

The Human Rights Council can help States to implement the right to development. It was mandated by the UN General Assembly to enhance "the promotion and protection of all human rights, civil, political, economic, social and

---

task force on implementation of the right to development), UNDoc. E/CN.4/2005/WG.18/TF/CRP.2, 8 November 2005.

[402] Report by the UN Millennium Project, Investing in Development: A Practical Plan to Achieve the Millennium Development Goals (2005), p. 1.

[403] On efforts to link the MDG's to the human right to development, see "Right to Development", Report of the Working Group on the Right to Development on its seventh session (Geneva, 9-13 January 2006), UNDoc E/CN.4/2006/26.

[404] According to Shetty, "ensuring that the discourse on the [Millennium Development] Goals is continuously anchored within a human rights framework is the only way to ensure that the Goals are achieved in an inclusive and sustainable manner." Salil Shetty, "Millennium Declaration and Development Goals" (2005), p. 8. In the pages immediately thereafter, the author explained how to anchor the MDG's in a human rights framework.

[405] Two years after the adoption of the Millennium Declaration, the US Government made a very controversial reservation to a declaration on food made during the World Food Summit: Five Years Later, held in Rome, between 10 and 13 June 2002. According to the US Government, "the attainment of the right to an adequate standard of living is a goal or aspiration to be realized progressively that does not give rise to any international obligation." The Reservation can be found in Part One of the Report of the World Food Summit: five years later, Rome, 10-13 June 2002, p. 32.

[406] See e.g., A/RES/60/157 (172 in favour to 2 against and 5 abstentions), A/RES/61/169 (134 in favour to 53 against), A/RES/62/161 (136 in favour to 53 against), A/RES/64/172 (133 in favour, 23 against, 30 abstentions), A/RES/65/219 (133 in favour, 24 against, 28 abstentions).

cultural rights, including the right to development."[407] In an address to the Council, Secretary-General Kofi Annan suggested that the Council's most important task was to "mak[e] the 'right to development' clear and specific enough to be effectively enforced and upheld." [408] Following a suggestion of the High-level Task Force on Implementation of the Right to Development,[409] the Working Group on the Right to Development, previously established by ECOSOC but now working for the Human Rights Council, linked Millennium Development Goal 8 (for a global partnership for development) with the realization of the universal human right to development.[410] The Human Rights Council endorsed this view.[411]

In 2006, the Human Rights Council's Sub-Commission on the Promotion and Protection of Human Rights adopted a number of draft guiding principles on extreme poverty and human rights. It defined poverty as "a human condition characterized by sustained or chronic deprivation of resources, capabilities, choices, security and power necessary for the enjoyment of an adequate standard of living and other civil, cultural, economic, political and social rights."[412] It then reiterated the Assembly's opinion referred to earlier, *viz.* that "extreme poverty and exclusion from society constitute[d] a violation of human dignity."[413] It went on to explain that "persons living in extreme poverty are entitled to the full enjoyment of all human rights, including the right to participate in the adoption of decisions which concern them, and to contribute to the well-being of their families, their communities and humankind."[414] This right of the extremely poor to participate in the decision-making processes that concern them, and the prohibition on stigmatizing the poor were further elaborated in the declaration, as well as the way in which all existing human rights should be applied to the extremely poor.[415]

---

[407] General Assembly Resolution of 3 April 2006, UN Doc. A/RES/60/251, para. 4.

[408] Annan, The Secretary-General's address to the Human Rights Council, held in Geneva, Switzerland, on 19 June 2006.

[409] See Report of the High-Level Task Force on the Implementation of the Right to Development on its Third Session, report distributed 13 February 2007, UN Doc. A/HRC/4/WG.2/TF/2, p. 13.

[410] "Right to Development", Report of the Working Group on the Right to Development on its seventh session (Geneva, 9-13 January 2006), UN Doc E/CN.4/2006/26. See also Report of the Working Group on the Right to Development on its eighth session (Geneva, 26 February – 2 March 2007), UN Doc. A/HRC/4/47, distributed 14 March 2007.

[411] UN Human Rights Council Resolution, The right to development (2006/4), adopted on the 30th of June 2006.

[412] Draft guiding principles: "extreme poverty and human rights: the rights of the poor," on pp. 29-38 of the Report of the Sub-Commission on the Promotion and Protection of Human Rights on its Fifty-Eighth Session, UNDoc. A/HRC/Sub.1/58/36, distributed 11 September 2006.

[413] *Idem*, p. 31.

[414] Idem.

[415] See *e.g.*, Draft guidng principles on extreme poverty and human rights, Human Rights Council resolution 12/19, adopted 2 October 2009.

## 6.5 Conclusion

The idea that everyone has a human right to development is gaining popularity and support. In his arguments for the existence of this human right, Pogge referred to the Universal Declaration of Human Rights and subsequent resolutions. Reference can also be made to treaties binding on almost all States, such as the International Covenant on Economic, Social and Cultural Rights, to make a more convincing case. The many resolutions and declarations adopted by the Assembly also serve to strengthen the call for a human rights-based approach to development. With the shift in focus from the State to the individual in international law in general, a human rights approach to development may very well be the natural course to take.[416]

## 7 CONCLUSION

The declarations referred to in this chapter serve as an interpretation and further elaboration of Article 55 of the United Nations Charter. This is the principal article in the Charter that gives the UN a general mandate to realize the value of social progress and development.

No general definition or description of the value of social progress and development was adopted by the General Assembly. The approach was to identify particular things that were lacking, and to find ways to remedy them. Over time, these lacks changed character, and the Assembly changed its strategy accordingly. The same evolution was also influenced by new ways of thinking about social progress and development. These new ideas, which came from UN commissions, world commissions, the academic world and elsewhere, have often had an impact on the Assembly's work in "codifying" the evolution of the value of social progress and development on behalf of all the UN Member States. The inclusion of sustainability in the thinking about development is the clearest example. The human rights-based approach to development can also be referred to as an example of this sort of evolution.

The Assembly's meetings have been as inclusive as is realistically possible, with most States represented there. The fact that even the economically disadvantaged States have had a role in the discussions, had as consequence that the fundamental aspects of the present economic order have been criticized in the Assembly. This inclusiveness has also had an impact on the allocation of responsibilities for implementing these ideas of progress in the real world.

---

[416] The Netherlands delegation at the General Assembly promoted for a while the idea of a new treaty especially on the right to development. See *e.g.*, Nico Schrijver, "The right to development: as fundamental as other human rights?" (2009), and Anna Gouwenberg, *The Legal Implementation of the Right to Development* (2009).

How has the United Nations, and especially the General Assembly, interpreted and implemented its task to promote "higher standards of living, full employment, […] conditions of economic and social progress and development, solutions of international economic, social, health, and related problems and international cultural and educational cooperation"?

The many declarations adopted by the General Assembly on social progress and development contain various strategies and action plans which respond to various threats to the achievement of the value of social progress and development. They all stressed the primary responsibility of States for their own development, and then urged States to assist each other. This chapter has compared these action plans wherever possible, with philosophical ideas about the fair distribution of resources and responsibilities at the global level. The conclusion was that the plans did not aim to put in place a global welfare system, but that they aimed to help developing States to obtain their share of the goods themselves.

But what happens if States cannot get their share of the goods and become increasingly marginalized despite international assistance? What if they cannot even provide the most basic services for their own population? What if they are in immediate need of aid? In that case, the United Nations cannot merely stand aside and watch. Therefore it has adopted various plans specifically aimed at providing immediate aid for immediate emergencies such as natural disasters.

The Assembly also looks after the interests of the unborn. Sustainable development was very much a UN invention, and a very successful invention it has turned out to be. The UN's definition of the concept has also been accepted by scholars. It has served as the basis for many plans seeking to take into account the developmental needs of both present and future generations of humankind.

Finally, the United Nations has played a key role in complementing State-based approaches with human rights-based approaches. This paradigm shift is examined in more general terms in the chapter on human dignity. Above, only its consequences for the interpretation of development and development strategies were examined.

In conclusion, it can be said that there is no lack of declarations and resolutions on the value of social progress and development, but the impact of these resolutions on actual State behaviour, and on the flow of ideas within the academic community, differs significantly per resolution. Some of the declarations and action plans have been ignored, but others, such as the Declaration on the Establishment of a New International Economic Order and the Charter of Economic Rights and Duties of States, did play a major role in the evolution of ideas. These resolutions did not serve as blueprints for global economic policy, but they did greatly influence the scholarly debate on global reform. Another exception is the Millennium Declaration, which has been influential in setting and monitoring targets for development. Some other resolutions have proposed rather drastic changes in the way we think about development. It was the Assembly that suggested using the concept of sustainable development as the basis for a new global developmental policy. It was also the Assembly that promoted a human-centred approach to development. These proposals were embraced, first by scholars, and gradually also by States.

# HUMAN DIGNITY

## 1 INTRODUCTION

The promotion of the value of human dignity is one of the success stories of the United Nations. It has profoundly changed the international legal order and led to a shift in focus in the language of international law. In the past, the State was the principal and almost exclusive participant in the international legal order. States made the rules, and these rules also applied almost exclusively to them. Today individuals are also recognized as participants. If international law is approached from the combined perspective of the State and the individual, the foundations of this language will have to be adapted accordingly. It has already been shown how this shift has affected the UN's work on peace and security and social progress and development.[1] Now this shift is examined in more general terms.

This introduction presents the UN organs which are chiefly responsible for the evolution of the value of human dignity. The most important organ is the former United Nations Commission on Human Rights. In view of its success in promoting the value of human dignity in the past, it is surprising that this Commission is the only UN organ that has ever been abolished and replaced by a new organ, the Human Rights Council. The Commission was most successful in its early days, when it drafted the Universal Declaration of Human Rights. Its successor, the Human Rights Council, still has to prove itself.

The resolutions on human dignity adopted by the General Assembly are examined. The responses of the academic community to these resolutions are also analyzed. The UN's determination to promote human dignity is largely based on the terrible experiences of the Second World War, which has often been characterized as a war – or even a crusade – for human dignity and human rights. After the war the United Nations used the value of human dignity as the foundation of all human rights. The actual list of human rights is examined in detail. The focus is not so much on the judicial interpretation of these rights, but on General Assembly resolutions seeking to promote the value of human dignity through the elaboration of the rights enshrined in the Universal Declaration of Human Rights. The universality of human rights, *i.e.* the idea that human rights are to be enjoyed by all, everywhere, and in all circumstances, is also analyzed.

---

[1] See sections 7 of Chapter IV and 6 of Chapter V, above. For self-determination, see section 6 of Chapter VII.

## 1.1 The role of the Commission on Human Rights and the Human Rights Council

None of the principal organs of the United Nations has a mandate exclusively devoted to the protection of human rights.[2] This is not to say that there was no interest in the international protection of human rights at all in 1945 when the UN Charter was drafted. In Article 68 UN Charter, ECOSOC was asked to set up a commission for the promotion of human rights.[3] On the basis of this provision, the United Nations Commission on Human Rights was established by ECOSOC in 1946. It was mandated to

> Submit [...] proposals, recommendations and reports to [ECOSOC] regarding an international bill of rights; international declarations or conventions on civil liberties, the status of women, freedom of information and similar matters; the protection of minorities [and] the prevention of discrimination on grounds of race, sex, language or religion.[4]

This commission, which Lauterpacht described as the "principal organ of the United Nations for the protection of human rights," was not officially one of the principal organs of the Organization.[5] It was only one of many commissions established by ECOSOC. Nevertheless, until the World Summit of 2005, it was the Human Rights Commission that did most of the work relating to the protection of human dignity and the development of human rights. It has been particularly successful in its main task, the codification and dissemination of human rights.[6] However, as it was only a Commission, it had to rely on ECOSOC, and eventually the General Assembly itself, to ensure that its ideas and declarations were embraced by the international community. Because the Assembly is the only UN organ speaking on behalf of the entire international community, the Assembly resolutions

---

[2] UN Charter, Article 7.

[3] For a brief history of the Commission and a comparison with the Council, see also Nico Schrijver, "The U. N. Human Rights Council: A New 'Society of the Committed'or Just Old Wine in New Bottles?" (2007).

[4] Commission on Human Rights, resolution adopted by the Economic and Social Council on 16 February 1946 (UNDoc. E/20).

[5] Hersch Lauterpacht, "The international protection of human rights" (1947), p. 57 (see also p. 52).

[6] Buergenthal sees the codification of human rights as "the most important contribution of the United Nations to the protection of human rights." See Thomas Buergenthal, "The Evolving International Human Rights System" (2006), p. 791.

are used as the primary documents in this study, not the preparatory work done by the Human Rights Commission.[7]

At the World Summit of 2005 the Members of the United Nations replaced the Human Rights Commission with the Human Rights Council.[8] The Council was formally established one year later.[9] The then Secretary-General Kofi Annan wanted the Council to become one of the principal organs of the United Nations. All global values would then have their own Council: the Security Council for the value of peace and security, the Economic and Social Council for the value of social progress and development, the Trusteeship Council for self-determination, and the Human Rights Council for human dignity. However, the Human Rights Council did not become one of the UN's main organs.[10]

## 2    HUMAN DIGNITY IN SAN FRANCISCO

### 2.1 The Preamble

According to Smuts' first draft of the Preamble, the United Nations was established, *inter alia*, "to re-establish the faith of men and women in fundamental human rights [and] in the sacredness, essential worth and integrity of the human personality."[11] In San Francisco, this was changed into "to reaffirm faith in fundamental human rights, in the dignity and value of every human being, in the equal rights of men and women."[12] One of the more interesting changes was the replacement of the word "re-establish" with "reaffirm." The reason for this change was that, according to the relevant Subcommittee, "that faith [in the dignity and value of every human being] ha[d] never faded," and that it was this faith in human dignity and rights "which moved men and women in all lands to accept the sacrifices by which victory [was]

---

[7] The Assembly's authority to speak on behalf of the entire international community has been most easily accepted in the field of human rights. See also Philip Alston, "Conjuring up New Human Rights: A Proposal for Quality Control" (1984), pp. 608-609. On p. 617, Alston affirmed the conclusion that "a claim is an international human right if the General Assembly says it is."

[8] 2005 World Summit Outcome, paras. 157-160. The establishment of such a Council was already proposed in the early sixties. See Louis B. Sohn, "United Nations Machinery for Implementing Human Rights" (1968), p. 910.

[9] Human Rights Council, General Assembly resolution 60/251, adopted 15 March 2006.

[10] It would have required an amendment of the UN Charter, and that is a most cumbersome process.

[11] Draft Preamble to the Charter of the United Nations Proposed by the Union of South Africa, 26 April, 1945, UNCIO, vol. 3, pp. 474-475. For a slighlty rephrased version, see the Preamble to the Charter of the United Nations Submitted by the South African Delegation in Revision of Draft of April 26, 1945, May 3, 1945, *idem*, pp. 476-477.

[12] Draft Preamble (as Approved by Committee I/1/A), 31 May 1945, UNCIO, vol. 6, p. 694. It is not clear why a reference to human dignity was added at this stage. See also pp. 675-676, Christopher McCrudden, "Human Dignity and Judicial Interpretation of Human Rights" (2008).

achieved."[13] However, "that faith needed reaffirmation in our Charter especially after it ha[d] been trampled upon by Nazism and Fascism in Europe as well as in other instances elsewhere."[14] With one minor change, the subcommittee's formulation was adopted by the Committee and then the Commission.[15]

## 2.2 The Purpose

There was no reference to human rights or human dignity in the Dumbarton Oaks' general list of purposes. However, there was a reference in the document's purpose in disguise.[16] Many States did not think that was enough, and suggested that the promotion of human rights should become a general purpose of the Organization.[17] At the insistence of the US, which was itself inspired by various suggestions by non-State actors and individuals, the sponsors had already remedied the situation even before the San Francisco Conference.[18] They had included in the list of purposes of the revised Dumbarton Oaks proposals the "promotion and

---

[13] Report of Rapporteur, Subcommittee I/1/A, Section 3, to Committee I/1, June 5, 1945, UNCIO, vol. 6, p. 359. See also Report of Rapporteur of Committee 1 to Commission I, UNCIO, vol. 6, p. 392.

[14] *Idem.*

[15] The reference to the dignity and value of the "human being" was changed into that of the "human person", at the request of Smuts. See Report of Rapporteur of Committee 1 to Commission I, UNCIO, vol. 6, p. 461, and the Thirteenth Meeting of Committee I/1, June 5, 1945, *idem*, p. 366, where the Committee adopted the revised text. The Commission also adopted the same text: see First Session of Commission I, June 14, 1945, *idem*, p. 20. See further the Summary Report of Forty-First Meeting, June 25, 1945, UNCIO, vol. 17, p. 380 and the Summary Report of Eleventh Meeting of Steering Committee, June 23, 1945, UNCIO, vol. 5, p. 307, where one last change was made: the deletion of the word "value."

[16] Dumbarton Oaks Proposals for a General International Organization, UNCIO, vol. 3, p. 19.This read as follows: "With a view to the creation of conditions of stability and well-being which are necessary for peaceful and friendly relations among nations, the Organization should [...] promote respect for human rights and fundamental freedoms."

[17] See *e.g.*, Amendments Submitted by Mexico, UNCIO, vol. 3, p. 178; Uruguay, *idem*, p. 34; India, *idem*, p. 527; Venezuela, *idem*, p. 224; Brazil, the Dominican Republic and Mexico (jointly), *idem*, p. 602; Egypt, *idem*, p. 453; Ecuador, *idem*, p. 400; France, *idem*, p. 383. Most of the nations that promoted human rights came from Latin America, and it is clear that they were inspired by the Act of Chapultepec, concluded in Mexico less than two months before the start of the San Francisco Conference.

[18] See Memorandum by the Secretary of State to President Truman, April 19, 1945, in FRUS, *1945, General:* Volume I, p. 354. See also Porter, "Stassen Outlines Our 9 Objectives," in *New York Times* of May 4, 1945, about the importance the US attached to this amendment. Various consultants, representing church bodies and other organizations, urged the US delegation to promote human rights language. See *e.g.*, Minutes of Twenty-sixth Meeting of the United States Delegation, May 2, 1945, in FRUS, *1945, General:* Volume I, p. 532. See also Edward R. Stettinius, "Human Rights in the United Nations Charter" (1946), p. 1; Eibe Riedel, "Article 55(c)" (2002), p. 920; Ruth B. Russell, *A history of the United Nations Charter* (1958), pp. 568-569; Jan Herman Burgers, "The Road to San Francisco" (1992), p.475; John P. Humphrey, "International Protection of Human Rights" (1948), p. 16; Robert C. Hilderbrand, *Dumbarton Oaks* (1990), pp. 91-93.

encouragement of respect for human rights and for fundamental freedoms for all without distinction as to race, language, religion or sex."[19]

In San Francisco, the delegates expressed a "desire to be unstinting and painstaking in formulating a clear and strong statement of purpose" on human rights.[20] At the same time, the human rights purpose could not be formulated *too* strongly, since it was generally believed that "assuring or protecting such fundamental rights [was] primarily the concern of each state;" and that only if "such rights and freedoms were grievously outraged so as to create conditions which threaten peace […] they cease[d] to be the sole concern of each state."[21] Moreover, in view of the US, "it was important to avoid giving the impression that the Organization would deal with individuals," because "[i]ts main function would be to settle disputes between governments and it would be unfortunate to arouse hopes that the Organization would directly help individuals when this could not be realized."[22] The Subcommittee therefore chose not to make too many changes.[23] After some insignificant grammatical changes, the amendment proposal of the sponsors became Article 1(3) of the UN Charter. According to this Article it is one of the Purposes of the United Nations:

> To achieve international co-operation in […] promoting and encouraging respect for human rights and for fundamental freedoms for all without distinction as to race, sex, language, or religion.

There was also a reference to human rights in the purpose in disguise (which became Article 55). Australia suggested, as an amendment only to the purpose in

---

[19] Amendments Submitted by the United States, the United Kingdom, the Soviet Union and China, UNCIO, vol. 3, pp. 622-623. The insertion of this new human rights purpose did not cause the disappearance of the reference to human rights in the purpose-in-disguise (see *idem*, p. 626). The exact wording of this amendment was based on a Russian suggestion. See the Minutes of First Four-Power Consultative Meeting on Charter Proposals, May 2, 1945, in FRUS, *1945, General:* Volume I, p. 551.

[20] Sixth Meeting of Committee I/1, May 14, 1945, UNCIO, vol. 6, p. 296.

[21] Report of Rapporteur, Subcommittee I/1/A, to Committee I/1, June 1, 1945, UNCIO, vol. 6, p. 705.

[22] Minutes of Fifth Meeting of the United States Delegation, April 9, 1945, in FRUS, *1945, General:* Volume I, p. 220.

[23] Text of Chapter I, as Agreed upon by the Drafting Committee of Committee I/1, UNCIO, vol. 6, p. 684. Panama later suggested changing "promotion and encouragement" into "promotion and protection" of human rights. The Delegates of the United Kingdom and the United States objected to the alteration, because they "believed that the amendment would raise the question as to whether or not the Organization should actively impose human rights and freedoms within individual countries, and that it would lead many peoples of the world to expect more of the Organization than it could successfully accomplish." The Panamanian amendment was subsequently rejected. See Tenth Meeting of Committee I/1, June 2, 1945, UNCIO, vol. 6, pp. 324-325. See also Amendments Submitted by Panama, UNCIO, vol. 3, p. 271, and Costa Rica, UNCIO, vol. 3, p. 280 (and 276), and the Statement of Uruguayan Delegation on Its Position with Reference to Chapters I and II as Considered by Committee I/1, UNCIO, vol. 6, p. 628.

disguise, that the Organization should promote the "observance by all members" of human rights, as opposed to promoting only "respect".[24] The difference between promoting "respect" and promoting "observance" of human rights was subtle, and the Coordination Committee had some difficulty understanding it.[25] In the end, the Australian suggestion was adopted, which makes the genuine purpose and the purpose in disguise slightly inconsistent.

A few Latin American States proposed annexing a human rights declaration to the UN Charter.[26] The US was very much in favour of this idea.[27] However, the US explained to the Latin American delegates that some of the other superpowers were opposed to a bill of rights, and thus "[i]t would be extremely difficult to incorporate in the Charter anything approaching a full statement of a bill of rights."[28] In San Francisco the relevant Subcommittee "received the idea with sympathy, but decided that the present Conference, be it only for a lack of time, [could] not proceed to realize such a draft in an international contract," and that it was a good task for the General Assembly.[29] This suggestion was taken over by the Commission.[30] On the last day of the conference, the American President Truman said that "we have good reason to expect an international bill of rights, acceptable to all the nations involved," and that "that bill of rights will be as much a part of international life as our own Bill of Rights is a part of our Constitution."[31] A few years later, the General Assembly adopted the Universal Declaration of Human Rights.[32]

---

[24] Amendments Submitted by Australia, UNCIO, vol. 3, p. 546. See also p. 4, Herbert Vere Evatt, "Economic Rights in the United Nations Charter" (1946).

[25] See Coordination Committee's Summary Report of Seventeenth Meeting, June 13, 1945, UNCIO, vol. 17, pp. 107-108. In the Coordination Committee, it was suggested that only the term "observance" implied an obligation to change the laws of one's own country to implement this article. Another suggestion was that the word "respect" had "the connotation of passive acceptance," while the word "observance," was "intended to imply active implementation."

[26] Amendments Submitted by Cuba, UNCIO, vol. 3, pp. 494-495, and 500-502; Mexico, *idem*, pp. 73-74; Uruguay, *idem*, p. 34 (Uruguay called it a "Charter of Mankind"); Panama, *idem*, pp. 265-266. Uruguay also stressed the need for "a system of effective international juridical guardianship of those rights" (*idem*, p. 35). See also Ecuador, *idem*, p. 423.

[27] See Lawrence E. Davies, "Stettinius Urges World Rights Bill," in *New York Times* of May 16, 1945.

[28] Memorandum of Conversation, by Mr. Leo Pasvolsky, to the Secretary of State, April 21, 1945, in FRUS, *1945, General:* Volume I, p. 357. See also Lawrence E. Davies, "Stettinius Urges World Rights Bill," in *New York Times* of May 16, 1945.

[29] Report of Rapporteur, Subcommittee I/1/A, to Committee I/1, June 1, 1945, UNCIO, vol. 6, p. 705. See also Sixth Meeting of Committee I/1, May 14, 1945, *idem*, p. 296. And see the Report of Rapporteur of Committee 1 to Commission I, *idem*, p. 456, and Fifteenth Meeting of Committee I/1, June 11, 1945, *idem*, p. 423. And see Hersch Lauterpacht, "The international protection of human rights" (1947), p. 74.

[30] Sixth Meeting of Committee I/1, May 14, 1945, UNCIO, vol. 6, p. 296.

[31] Final Plenary Session, June 26, 1945, UNCIO, vol. 1, p. 683.

[32] See next section.

## 2.3 The Universal Declaration of Human Rights

The centrepiece of the United Nations in the field of human rights is a legally non-binding General Assembly resolution, adopted four minutes before midnight on 10 December 1948. It is the Universal Declaration of Human Rights.[33] It was drafted by the Human Rights Commission, chaired by Eleanor Roosevelt.[34] This Declaration initially had very modest aims. It was meant to make all the world's citizens aware of their inalienable rights.[35] Since then, the declaration has done much more than that. It has been the inspiration for all the United Nations resolutions and treaties on human rights that have been adopted since 1948.[36] It also influenced significant changes in the domestic law of various States, and inspired a number of regional treaties.[37] It also directly influenced the philosophical discourse. Beitz, one of today's more prominent philosophers, referred to it as the "founding document of modern human rights doctrine."[38] Soon after its adoption, the Declaration was embraced by "men and women from the streets, from the fields, from the mines, from the factories, from the pampas, and from the sea."[39] This popularity, especially in times of political turmoil, explains the Declaration's success. As Buergenthal remarked, the Declaration has been the starting point for a "worldwide movement that has captured the imagination of human beings yearning to be treated humanely and with dignity."[40] No other UN document, apart from the Charter itself, has been more successful at capturing the imagination.

---

[33] Universal Declaration of Human Rights, Part A of International Bill of Human Rights, General Assembly resolution 217(III), adopted 10 December 1948 ("Universal Declaration of Human Rights"). See John Kenton, "Human Rights Declaration adopted by UN Assembly," in *New York Times* of 11 December 1948; Thomas Buergenthal, "The Evolving International Human Rights System" (2006), p. 787.

[34] For an excellent and detailed account of the drafting history and the debates, see Johannes Morsink, *The Universal Declaration of Human Rights: Origins, Drafting, and Intent* (1999). On pp. 1-12, one can find a brief overview of the drafting stages. See also Roger Normand and Sarah Zaidi, *Human rights at the UN: the political history of universal justice* (2008), pp. 177-182.

[35] See Part D of the Universal Declaration of Human Rights, entitled Publicity to be given to the Universal Declaration of Human Rights, para. 1. See also René Cassin, "Les droits de l'homme" (1974), pp. 3303-331; Johannes Morsink, *Inherent human rights: philosophical roots of the Universal Declaration* (2009), especially pp. 40-46.

[36] See for example the Asian Human Rights Charter, para. 2.2; and the Preamble of the Council of Europe's European Convention on Human Rights, signed in Rome, 4 November 1950; and the preamble of the African Union's African Charter on Human and Peoples' Rights of 1986.

[37] Louis Henkin, "The United Nations and Human Rights" (1965), pp. 506-507.

[38] Charles R. Beitz, "What Human Rights Mean" (2003), p. 36.

[39] René Cassin, "La déclaration universelle et la mise en œuvre des droits de l'homme" (1951), p. 290.

[40] Thomas Buergenthal, "The Evolving International Human Rights System" (2006), p. 807. See also Philip Quincy Wright, "Human Rights and Charter Revision" (1954), pp. 54-55; and Myres S. McDougal & Gerhard Bebr, "Human Rights in the United Nations" (1964), p. 641.

Formally, the Universal Declaration of Human Rights is only a General Assembly resolution. However, it is also an authoritative interpretation of the references to human rights in the UN Charter.[41] There was a close connection between the San Francisco Conference of 1945 and the Universal Declaration of Human Rights, adopted only a few years later. There was not enough time in San Francisco to draft a universal bill of rights to be annexed to the Charter. The Universal Declaration filled that gap. Haimbaugh described the increasing relevance of the declaration in the international legal order as follows:

> What began as mere common aspiration is now hailed both as an authoritative interpretation of the human rights provisions of the United Nations Charter [i.e. Articles 1, 55 and 56] and as established customary law, having the attributes of *jus cogens* and constituting the heart of a global bill of rights.[42]

In any case it is clear that the Universal Declaration has influenced the international legal order in a way that no other General Assembly resolution – and no multilateral treaty except for the UN Charter itself – has ever done.

Throughout the years, the Assembly has made sure that the spotlight remained focused on the declaration. The Assembly proclaimed 10 December as human rights day,[43] and organized various other activities, especially during the thirtieth,[44] thirty-fifth,[45] fortieth,[46] and sixtieth anniversaries of the Universal Declaration.[47] On its sixtieth anniversary, the Assembly referred to the Declaration as the world's "ethical compass," and also stated that for sixty years the Declaration had successfully "empowered women and men around the globe to assert their inherent dignity and rights."[48]

---

[41] Various scholars referred to this argument. See *e.g.*, Louis B. Sohn, "The Improvement of the UN Machinery on Human Rights" (1979), p. 188.

[42] George D. Haimbaugh, "Jus Cogens: Root & Branch (An Inventory)" (1987).

[43] Human rights day, General Assembly resolution 423(V), adopted 4 December 1950.

[44] See the Suggested measures for the celebration of the thirtieth anniversary of the universal declaration of human rights, annexed to Observance of the 30th anniversary of the universal declaration of human rights, General Assembly resolution 32/123, adopted 16 December 1977.

[45] See the Suggested measures for the celebration of the thirty-fifth anniversary of the universal declaration of human rights, annexed to Observance of the 35th anniversary of the Universal Declaration of Human Rights, General Assembly resolution 36/169, adopted 16 December 1981. See also Thirty-five years of the Universal Declaration of Human Rights, General Assembly resolution A/RES/38/57, adopted 9 December 1983.

[46] See Recommended measures for the celebration of the thirtieth anniversary of the universal declaration of human rights, annexed to Fortieth anniversary of the Universal Declaration of Human Rights, General Assembly resolution 41/150, adopted 4 December 1986.

[47] Declaration on the sixtieth anniversary of the Universal Declaration of Human Rights, annexed to Sixtieth anniversary of the Universal Declaration of Human Rights, General Assembly resolution 63/116, adopted 10 December 2008.

[48] *Idem.*

## 2.4 The Principle

During the Dumbarton Oaks conference, the US suggested incorporating a human rights principle in the draft charter. This stated that

> The International Organization should refrain from intervention in the internal affairs of any state, it being the responsibility of each state to see that conditions prevailing within its jurisdiction do not endanger international peace and security and, to this end, to respect the human rights and fundamental freedoms of all its people and to govern in accordance with the principles of humanity and justice.[49]

The UK did not like this new principle, because "such a provision would give rise to the possibility that the organization might engage in criticism of the internal organization of member states."[50] The Soviet Union also opposed it, because "the reference to human rights and basic freedom [was] not germane to the main tasks of an international security organization."[51] Therefore the US withdrew the principle it had proposed.[52] This explains why there was nothing resembling a human rights principle in the Dumbarton Oaks proposals. Following the insistence of the US, a reference to human rights was added to the Dumbarton Oaks proposals, but this reference was not in the section on purposes and principles, nor in the specific mandate of the General Assembly or ECOSOC, but in the general part on Arrangements for International Economic and Social Cooperation.[53]

---

[49] Progress Report on Dumbarton Oaks Conversations – Eighteenth Day, in FRUS, *1944, General:* Volume I, p. 791. This was later rephrased to sound more like a principle. See Progress Report on Dumbarton Oaks Conversations – Twenty-eighth Day, in FRUS, *1944, General:* Volume I, p. 829 (footnote 23). See also Thomas M. Franck, *Recourse to Force* (2002), p. 18; and Ruth B. Russell, *A history of the United Nations Charter* (1958), p. 423. They both cite slightly different versions of this proposal.

[50] *Idem*, p. 789. See also Progress Report on Dumbarton Oaks Conversations – Twenty-seventh Day, *idem*, p. 825.

[51] *Idem*. According to Russell, the Soviet Union was willing to accept the provision if it referred specifically to "fascist States" as the sole violators of human rights obligations. The UK disagreed because there was not yet a universally accepted standard of human rights. See: Ruth B. Russell, *A history of the United Nations Charter* (1958), pp. 423-424.

[52] Progress Report on Dumbarton Oaks Conversations – Twenty-eighth Day, in FRUS, *1944, General:* Volume I, p. 829. When he later met with President Roosevelt in his bedroom, he expressed his disappointment, and told the President that he would "continue to press the matter as hard as we know how." See Meeting in the President's Bedroom with the President and the Secretary, *idem*, p. 834. The result of this pressure was the reference to human rights in the purpose-in-disguise. See also Progress Report on Dumbarton Oaks Conversations – Thirty-fourth Day, *idem*, p. 838. See also *idem*, p. 898, and Dumbarton Oaks Proposals for a General International Organization, UNCIO, vol. 3, p. 19.

[53] See United Nations: Dumbarton Oaks Proposals for a General International Organization, UNCIO, vol. 3, p. 18.

In their amendment proposals, certain States suggested including a general human rights principle.[54] In the relevant Committee in San Francisco, the added value of having a principle in addition to a purpose on human rights was clearly understood. If the UN Charter had only a purpose, then "it would bind only the Organization and would relieve member governments from the obligation to respect the fundamental freedoms of individuals within their own countries."[55] Uruguay sought to remedy this situation by adding a new principle stating that "all members of the Organization should respect the essential rights of mankind." [56] Uruguay explained that its amendment was "based on the premise that the paramount concern of any government should be the essential rights of the human person, and that these rights could be best guaranteed by the united pledge of all nations to respect them."[57] The Committee rejected the Uruguayan suggestion, primarily because it was believed that such a human rights pledge could simply be derived from a combination of the purpose in disguise and the more general pledge successfully proposed by Australia.[58] If the relevant parts of Articles 55 and 56 are combined, the result is a principle stating that "Member States pledge themselves to take joint and separate action in co-operation with the Organization for the promotion of universal respect for, and observance of, human rights." The Committee's view was therefore correct. Ideally, this principle should have been inserted in the list of principles in Article 2, as Uruguay had requested, but the fact that it is to be found in a combination of Articles 55 and 56 does not diminish its legal relevance.

---

[54] See *e.g.*, Amendments Submitted by Uruguay, UNCIO, vol. 3, p. 35, see also Statement of Uruguayan Delegation on Its Position with Reference to Chapters I and II as Considered by Committee I/1, UNCIO, vol. 6, p. 628; Amendments Submitted by New Zealand, UNCIO, vol. 3, p. 486; Chile, *idem*, p. 294; Norway, *idem*, p. 366; Colombia, *idem*, p. 587.

[55] Fifth Meeting of Committee I/1, May 14, 1945, UNCIO, vol. 6, p. 291. This was also pointed out in the Statement of Uruguayan Delegation on Its Position with Reference to Chapters I and II as Considered by Committee I/1, UNCIO, vol. 6, p. 629.

[56] Fourteenth Meeting of Committee I/1, June 7, 1945, UNCIO, vol. 6, p. 381. See also Statement of Uruguayan Delegation on Its Position with Reference to Chapters I and II as Considered by Committee I/1, UNCIO, vol. 6, p. 629.

[57] Fourteenth Meeting of Committee I/1, June 7, 1945, UNCIO, vol. 6, p. 381.

[58] *Idem*. Uruguay was not so pleased with the way in which its proposal was treated. It was especially not pleased with the fact that the discussion just referred to was not mentioned in the Report of the Committee to the Commission. At the request of Uruguay, an Addendum to the Report was circulated. See Addendum to Report of Rapporteur of Committee 1 to Commission I, UNCIO, vol. 6, p. 483. Uruguay also distributed a most interesting statement containing its views. See Statement of Uruguayan Delegation on Its Position with Reference to Chapters I and II as Considered by Committee I/1, UNCIO, vol. 6, p. 632.

## 3   THE CONCEPTUAL BASIS OF HUMAN RIGHTS

### 3.1  Introduction

The drafters of the UN's human rights documents did not want to base their work on one particular philosophy or doctrine, alienating or offending others.[59] They sought a philosophical compromise. This was the use of "human dignity" as a central value, without defining it.[60] The vagueness of the term human dignity has motivated philosophers to come up with their own meaning of this value.[61] Some of these theories are referred to in this section, and are compared with the UN documents.

### 3.2  Prevention of the recurrence of past wrongs

After studying the drafting of the Universal Declaration of Human Rights in great detail, Morsink concluded that "the Holocaust shocked the moral consciousness of all civilized peoples into an increased awareness of the inherent dignity of every human being," and that the Universal Declaration can be seen as an act of protest, a revolutionary document, or "a trumpet call of victory after battle."[62] If the Universal Declaration is the trumpet call, then the references to human rights in the UN Charter were the prelude to it.[63]

It is clear that the human rights movement of the United Nations was a direct consequence of the barbarities of the Second World War.[64] It shares one fundamental characteristic with most national or local human rights movements: it

---

[59] See also Charles R. Beitz, *The idea of human rights* (2009), p. 8, and pp. 20-21.

[60] This does not mean, however, that the drafters of the human rights texts did not have philosophical discussions. They did, especially in the Human Rights Commission, at the time the Universal Declaration of Human Rights was adopted. For a detailed description, see Johannes Morsink, *The Universal Declaration of Human Rights: Origins, Drafting, and Intent* (1999).

[61] As is often pointed out, it was actually the United Nations that ensured a renewed interest of human dignity in philosophical discourse, after it had "been "fading into the past." See *e.g.*, Michael S. Pritchard, "Human Dignity and Justice" (1972), p. 299.

[62] For the first quote, see Johannes Morsink, *Inherent human rights: philosophical roots of the Universal Declaration* (2009), pp. 59-60; for the second, see Johannes Morsink, *The Universal Declaration of Human Rights: Origins, Drafting, and Intent* (1999), p. 38.

[63] Georges Kaeckenbeeck, "La Charte de San-Francisco dans ses rapports avec le droit international" (1948), p. 260.

[64] See *e.g.*, Yehoshua Arieli, "On the Necessary and Sufficient Conditions for the Emergence of the Doctrine of the Dignity of Man and His Rights" (2002), p. 1; Christian Tomuschat, *Human rights: between idealism and realism* (2008), pp. 22-23; René Cassin, "Les droits de l"homme" (1974), pp. 324-325; Thomas Buergenthal, "The Evolving International Human Rights System" (2006), p. 786; Evadné Grant, "Dignity and Equality" (2007), p. 303.

was based not so much on philosophical teachings, but on a shared intuition that the way people had been treated in the (recent) past was fundamentally wrong, and that there was a need for a "revolution."[65] The Second World War has been seen as such a revolution. It has been described as a "war for human rights," even a "crusade for human rights."[66] This international crusade has inspired many domestic revolutions, such as the "revolutions" in Germany, Italy and Japan after the Second World War;[67] in Spain after years of dictatorship;[68] and in South Africa after *apartheid*.[69] The Constitutions of all these States have a reference to human dignity, as if to say: "never again."[70]

The Universal Declaration of Human Rights itself referred to the war, when it stated that

> Disregard and contempt for human rights have resulted in barbarous acts which have outraged the conscience of mankind, and the advent of a world in which human beings shall enjoy freedom of speech and belief and freedom from fear and want has been proclaimed as the highest aspiration of the common people.[71]

The principal aim of the Universal Declaration of Human Rights was therefore to "avoid a return to inhuman ideologies and practices" such as those practised by the Nazis.[72]

---

[65] See John P. Humphrey, "International Protection of Human Rights" (1948), p. 21. See also Jochen Frowein, "Human Dignity in International Law" (2002), pp. 122-123.

[66] The first quote is from John P. Humphrey, "International Protection of Human Rights" (1948), p. 15; the second is from René Cassin, "La déclaration universelle et la mise en œuvre des droits de l"homme" (1951), p. 241. See also Roger Normand and Sarah Zaidi, *Human rights at the UN: the political history of universal justice* (2008), who named one chapter of their book "The Human Rights Crusade in World War II." See also Jean-Pierre Cot & Alain Pellet, "Préambule" (2005), p. 300; they also referred to the Second World War as a "guerre de croisade."

[67] See *e.g.*, Jerzy Zajadlo, "Human dignity and human rights" (1999), p. 19; Evadné Grant, "Dignity and Equality" (2007), p. 307; Christopher McCrudden, "Human Dignity and Judicial Interpretation of Human Rights" (2008), p. 664.

[68] The Spanish constitution, drafted after the death of Dictator Franco, is interesting because it refers explicitly to the Universal Declaration of Human Rights. See Article 10(2). Also cited in Thomas Buergenthal, "The Evolving International Human Rights System" (2006), p. 804.

[69] The Constitution of the Republic of South Africa referred to "human dignity"as founding value of the new society. See Arthur Chaskalson, "The third Bram Fischer lecture" (2000), pp. 195 and 198. See also David Kretzmer and Eckart Klein, *The concept of human dignity in human rights discourse* (2002), p. v; Evadné Grant, "Dignity and Equality" (2007), p. 310. Interestingly, Heyns suggested that the reason why Smuts failed to see that "his" apartheid regime was in violation of the purposes and principles he so strongly supported in San Francisco, was exactly that Smuts himself never suffered from apartheid, whilst he did suffer from the War. Christof Heyns, "The Preamble of the United Nations Charter" (1995), p. 348.

[70] Brenda Hale, "Dignity" (2009), p. 103.

[71] Universal Declaration of Human Rights, Preamble.

[72] Roberto Andorno, "The paradoxial notion of human dignity" (2001), p. 156.

The Nobel Prize winner and one of the survivors of the Auschwitz concentration camps, Elie Wiesel, was asked, during an interview on a Dutch television show, whether there was a connection between his terrible experiences in Auschwitz and his work as a human rights activist. In his affirmative reply, he started by noting that one of the worst things in the concentration camp had been the realization that "nobody was responsible for us," that they were abandoned and all alone. He explained:

> For a victim to be a victim is already bad. And painful. And disrupting. But in addition to that, when a victim feels alone; that's the worst. So one thing I cannot do [as a human rights activist]... Many things I cannot do: I cannot prevent a victim from suffering by others. But I can prevent the victim from feeling alone. And all my activities in the field of human rights [aim to achieve] at least that: I don't want a prisoner of conscience in his or her cell to feel alone. I don't want a child who is hungry somewhere in Africa, and his or her mother, to feel alone.[73]

Essentially, the international protection of human dignity comes down to the duty of the international community as a whole, to protect individuals who have been abandoned by their own State. This duty continues even after the death of individuals. The Assembly "recognizing the importance of promoting the memory of victims of gross and systematic human rights violations and the importance of the right to truth and justice," proclaimed an international day for the right to the truth concerning gross human rights violations and for the dignity of victims.[74]

Similarly, Beitz recently defined "the doctrine of human rights [as] the articulation in the public morality of world politics of the idea that each person is a subject of global concern."[75] There are limits to what the international community can do in cases of terrible abuse, and this will always be the case, but it can make sure that these individuals do not feel alone, abandoned, and entirely dehumanized.

## 3.3  The search for a definition of human dignity

The Universal Declaration contains many references to human dignity.[76] Most importantly, Article 1 of the Declaration stated that "all human beings are born free and equal in dignity and rights [and that] they are endowed with reason and

---

[73] Elie Wiesel interviewed by Chris Kijne in 2006, in the Series Opinie & Gesprek. See also his Nobel lecture of 1986.
[74] Proclamation of 24 March as the International Day for the Right to the Truth concerning Gross Human Rights Violations and for the Dignity of Victims, General Assembly resolution 65/196, adopted 21 December 2010.
[75] Charles R. Beitz, *The idea of human rights* (2009), p. 1. See also p. 12.
[76] Universal Declaration of Human Rights, Preamble. See also Articles 22 and 23 of the Declaration.

conscience and should act towards one another in a spirit of brotherhood."[77] The often intuitive and perhaps even sentimental approach to the value of human dignity makes it even more important for the international community to define it in sufficiently precise terms.

Andorno saw human dignity as "one of the very few common values in our world of philosophical pluralism," and referred to the shared feeling that "human beings have an intrinsic dignity" as the "Standard Attitude."[78] Similarly, Schachter wrote about the dignity of the human person, stating that "no other ideal seems so clearly accepted as a universal social good." [79] Hennette-Vauchez wrote about human dignity that it is "hard to think of other legal concepts as widely consecrated (by norms) and celebrated (by scholars)."[80] One might therefore assume that there is a universally agreed definition of human dignity.[81] But is there such a definition?

One way to begin to understand the meaning of a particular concept is to resort to a dictionary.[82] The Concise Oxford English Dictionary defines dignity as "the state or quality of being worthy of honour or respect."[83] Therefore human dignity is the state or quality of being worthy of honour or respect by virtue of being human.[84] All human beings need to do to deserve to be treated with dignity, is

---

[77] *Idem*, Article 1. This Article, which was included into the Declaration at the request of the French delegate in the Human Rights Commission, was clearly inspired by the French Déclaration des droits de l'homme et du citoyen of 1789, in which we read that "les hommes naissent et demeurent libres et égaux en droits." See Johannes Morsink, *The Universal Declaration of Human Rights: Origins, Drafting, and Intent* (1999), p. 281; Christopher McCrudden, "Human Dignity and Judicial Interpretation of Human Rights" (2008), pp. 676-677.

[78] Roberto Andorno, "The paradoxial notion of human dignity" (2001), p. 151.

[79] Oscar Schachter, "Human Dignity as a Normative Concept" (1983), p. 849.

[80] Stéphanie Hennette-Vauchez, "When Ambivalent Principles Prevail" (2007), p. 3 (footnote 20).

[81] Others were less enthusiastic. For example, Feldman wrote that, although human dignity was generally accepted as an important concept, "the meaning of the word [was] by no means straightforward, and its relationship with fundamental rights [was] unclear." David Feldman, "Human dignity as a legal value - Part I" (1999), p. 682. Even more critical were Mirko Bagaric & James Allan, in their article "The Vacuous Concept of Dignity" (2006), especially pp. 261-268. Sonja Grover then wrote "A response to Bagaric and Allan's 'The Vacuous Concept of Dignity'" (2009), defending the concept.

[82] Many philosophers have used the same strategy. See *e.g.*, David Feldman, "Human dignity as a legal value - Part I" (1999), p. 686; Roberto Andorno, "The paradoxial notion of human dignity" (2001), p. 152. Some authors go much further, and look extensively at the etymology of the word. See *e.g.*, Oscar Schachter, "Human Dignity as a Normative Concept" (1983), p. 849; Carlos Ruiz Miguel, "Human dignity: history of an idea" (2002), pp. 282-283.

[83] See the Concise Oxford English Dictionary, Twelfth edition (2008). The Oxford English Dictionary essentially defines dignity as "the quality of being worthy," or "the state of being worthy of honour or respect." See, respectively, the Oxford English Dictionary, Second edition 1989, and the Oxford Encyclopedic English Dictionary, edition 1996. The Dutch translation of human dignity, "menselijke waardigheid," literally means "human worthiness."

[84] See Roberto Andorno, "The paradoxial notion of human dignity" (2001), p. 153.

simply to be born.[85] Human beings cannot – voluntarily or involuntarily – lose their dignity.[86] This does not mean that all individuals are *actually* treated with dignity and respect from the moment they are born. Certainly, many people "lead a life of abject poverty and indignity."[87] The idea is that no matter how badly they are treated, people never lose the inherent dignity that came with birth.

When a person demands respect for his or her human dignity, he or she is essentially demanding to be considered not as a mere object, but as a human being. He or she demands to be treated with respect, and not to be humiliated, or dehumanized.[88] Such demands can be addressed to the community, but also to oneself. Thus human dignity has two aspects: a "subjective" aspect, *i.e.* human dignity as self-worth, and an "objective" aspect, *i.e.* human dignity as an entitlement for respect from the community.[89] If a person loses his or her self-worth, or is treated by the community as being inferior to other human beings, this does not result in the actual loss of one's dignity, but it does affect one's "sense of dignity."[90] The UN cannot do much to help those who lose their self-worth. The UN focuses on the "objective" aspect. The Organization aims to protect individuals against inhuman treatment by their own community.[91]

If human dignity is understood solely in terms of the entitlements of the individual from his or her State, then it corresponds with the individual's right not to be treated by the State in ways which do not respect the intrinsic worth of the individual. The individual can claim respect for his or her autonomy and freedom. Interpreted in this way, the value of human dignity is closely related to the process of individualization.[92]

---

[85] See also Jack Donnelly, "Human Rights and Human Dignity: An Analytic Critique of Non-Western Conceptions of Human Rights" (1982), pp. 305-306.
[86] Sometimes it looks as if people might lose their dignity. See also Michael S. Pritchard, "Human Dignity and Justice" (1972), p. 305 (about the torture victim who surrenders to his torturers), and p. 307 (about the slave who accepts his fate).
[87] Catherine Dupré, "Unlocking Human Dignity" (2009), p. 193.
[88] See Roberto Andorno, "The paradoxial notion of human dignity" (2001), p. 158; Oscar Schachter, "Human Dignity as a Normative Concept" (1983), pp. 849-850; Gay Moon and Robin Allen, "Dignity Discourse in Discrimination Law" (2006), p. 645; For a critical view, see Daniel Statman, "Humiliation, dignity and self-respect" (2002).
[89] David Feldman, "Human dignity as a legal value - Part I" (1999), pp. 685-686; Gay Moon and Robin Allen, "Dignity Discourse in Discrimination Law" (2006), p. 645. Similarly, Capps interpreted human dignity as a form of "empowerment:" to have dignity means to have the capacity to exercise freedom and autonomy. See Patrick Capps, *Human dignity and the foundations of international law* (2009), especially pp. 108-109..
[90] See also Patrick Lee & Robert George, "The Nature and Basis of Human Dignity" (2008), p. 174.
[91] The UN thus does not have to deal with the difficult issue of someone who voluntarily subjects him or herself to dehumanizing treatment. It is sometimes suggested that such a person might be forced to be treated – and treat him- or herself – with dignity. See also Brenda Hale, "Dignity" (2009), p. 106.
[92] See also Evadné Grant, "Dignity and Equality" (2007), p. 304.

This narrow interpretation of human dignity is not universally acceptable. The individualist aspect is only one part of the respect that the inherent dignity of all human beings requires. As the Constitutional Court of South Africa remarked, "recognizing the unique worth of each person [in the South African Constitution] does not presuppose that a holder of rights is an isolated, lonely and abstract figure possessing a disembodied and socially disconnected self."[93] The individualist aspect reminds one of the life of Diogenes,[94] but the value of human dignity is generally interpreted in more positive terms. Individuals are entitled to live their own lives, and make their own choices, but they are also part of a community of persons who care for each other.[95]

The United Nations deliberately refrained from adopting a particular philosophy of human dignity[96] and did not rely on any particular religious doctrine, for the simple reason that this would mean that it would have to reject others.[97] The UN also refrained from referring to reason or rationality as a basis for human dignity. Although a rationality- based theory would be the least controversial philosophical theory to choose,[98] even that theory has its problematical and controversial aspects.[99] Therefore instead of choosing any particular philosophy as a

---

[93] Opinion Judge Sachs, Constitutional Court of South Africa, National Coalition for Gay and Lesbian Equality and Another v Minister of Justice and Others, Case CCT 11/98, decided on 9 October 1998, para. 117. Cited on p. 313 of Evadné Grant, "Dignity and Equality" (2007).

[94] See section 2.1 of Chapter II, above.

[95] Robert C. Kelman, "The Conditions, Criteria, and Dialectics of Human Dignity" (1977), pp. 531-532. Kelman referred to "individual freedom" as related to the first element, and 'social justice" as related to the second.

[96] When drafting the Universal Declaration of Human Rights, the Commission "agreed to disagree." See Charles R. Beitz, "What Human Rights Mean" (2003), p. 36. See also James Griffin, "The Presidential Address: Discrepancies between the Best Philosophical Account of Human Rights and the International Law of Human Rights" (2001), pp. 5-6.

[97] See Yehoshua Arieli, "On the Necessary and Sufficient Conditions for the Emergence of the Doctrine of the Dignity of Man and His Rights" (2002); Josef L. Kunz, "The United Nations Declaration of Human Rights" (1949), p. 316. However, on p. 299 of this article, the author rightly stressed that human dignity, as used in international human rights instruments, was deliberatedly not based on such doctrines. See also René Cassin, "La déclaration universelle et la mise en œuvre des droits de l'homme" (1951), p. 284.

[98] This Kantian theory is the most objective theory of all. It basically says that to know what is the right thing to do, we must act in such a way that we believe our behavior corresponds with a rule that is suitable to guide the behavior of all. This is very much a law-like way of thinking, and thus is ideally suited as basis for human rights. See George P. Fletcher, "Human Dignity as a Constitutional Value" (1984), especially pp. 174-175.

[99] For example, it could be argued that the theory is biased against non-humans. If "reason" is the basis of human dignity, and it is assumed that animals lack the capacity to reason, then they do not deserve to be treated with dignity. See e.g., Patrick Lee & Robert George, "The Nature and Basis of Human Dignity" (2008), who argue in this way.

basis for human dignity, the United Nations argued that the basis of human dignity is simply its self-evident nature.[100]

It is difficult for the United Nations to use human dignity as a basis for all human rights whilst at the same time refusing to give the value any meaning. The value of human dignity, as used in UN parlance, must have some substance. According to McCrudden, the UN's intention was basically that different philosophers could give substance to the value of human dignity according to their own preferred theories, as long as all these different substances had a common "minimum core," and as long as they all led to essentially the same list of human rights.[101] According to McCrudden, this common core was the idea that "every human being possesse[d] an intrinsic worth, merely by being human," and that "this intrinsic worth should be recognized and respected by others."[102] There was no universally accepted explanation of why all human beings had such an intrinsic worth.[103] McCrudden believed that the UN's theory was controversial in at least one respect, namely that it believed that "recognizing the intrinsic worth of the individual require[d] that the state should be seen to exist for the sake of the individual human being, and not *vice versa*."[104] According to McCrudden, this minimal theory of human dignity was sufficient for the UN to continue its work.[105]

Rather than referring only to this "common core," another option is to admit that the UN had its own, more substantive theory. This is Morsink's view. He referred to the UN's theory of human dignity as the "doctrine of inherent human rights." This was the doctrine which the drafters of the Universal Declaration of Human Rights had chosen in 1948, and which has been followed by the UN ever since. [106] This theory of inherent human rights consisted of theses, the first of which stated that "people everywhere and at all times ha[d] rights that [were] not man-

---

[100] Interestingly, some philosophers go even further in their efforts to "de-philosophize" human rights. For example, Beitz did not even refer to human dignity as the 'source" of human rights. Instead, he believed that it would be better to "approach human rights practically, not as the application of an independent philosophical idea [like human dignity] to the international realm, but as a political doctrine constructed to play a certain role in global political life." Charles R. Beitz, *The idea of human rights* (2009), pp. 48-49 (this is the approach chosen in the entire book).

[101] Christopher McCrudden, "Human Dignity and Judicial Interpretation of Human Rights" (2008), p. 678.

[102] *Idem*, p. 679.

[103] *Idem*, p. 723.

[104] *Idem*, p. 679. As McCrudden rightly emphasized, this did not mean that there was agreement over the choice between an individualistic and a more communitarian conception of human dignity. See *idem*, pp. 699-701.

[105] *Idem*, p. 724. Admittedly, McCrudden did not refer to the UN, but to the international judge.

[106] See Johannes Morsink, *Inherent human rights: philosophical roots of the Universal Declaration* (2009). See also Johannes Morsink, *The Universal Declaration of Human Rights: Origins, Drafting, and Intent* (1999), pp. 284-290, for an overview of the debates in the Human Rights Commission, and pp. 290-302, for a first account of the inherent rights doctrine.

made, but inherent in the human person from the moment of birth."[107] According to the second thesis, "ordinary people in any of the world's villages or cities can come to know in a natural manner – unaided by experts – that people everywhere have the moral birth rights spoken of in the [first] thesis."[108] As this theory relies to a great extent on a globally shared moral intuition, rather than on philosophical doctrine, the interpretation and understanding of the value was left to this intuition, the idea being that everyone can recognize a violation of human dignity without knowing exactly how to define it. This approach, which can be regarded as the UN approach, has many followers. For example, Baroness Hale was convinced that "it should not take anything more than ordinary human empathy to understand that [certain] things are an affront to human dignity and human rights."[109] Similarly, according to Schachter, all people recognize a violation of human dignity when they see it, even though they cannot tell you what human dignity is.[110] In the words of Andorno, "it is easier to understand what is contrary to human dignity than what is in accordance with it [and thus] one of the best ways to explore what human dignity really means, is to start from the experience of indignities suffered by human beings in concrete situations."[111] Admittedly, the reliance on such globally shared moral intuitions alone also has its opponents.[112]

### 3.4 Human dignity as the basis for human rights

According to all UN documents, human rights are based on human dignity. The UN Charter itself already referred, in its Preamble, to the "faith in fundamental human rights [and] in the dignity and worth of the human person."[113] Thus it made a link between human rights and human dignity. This relationship between human rights and human dignity has often been reiterated since 1945. References to human dignity have become commonplace in international human rights declarations and other legal documents.[114] For example, the Vienna Declaration of 1993, adopted at

---

[107] Johannes Morsink, *Inherent human rights: philosophical roots of the Universal Declaration* (2009), p. 17.
[108] *Idem.*
[109] Brenda Hale, "Dignity" (2009), p. 103.
[110] Oscar Schachter, "Human Dignity as a Normative Concept" (1983), p. 849. Henkin spoke of a "common contemporary moral intuition." See Louis Henkin, "The Universality of the Concept of Human Rights" (1989), p. 15.
[111] Roberto Andorno, "The paradoxial notion of human dignity" (2001), pp. 156-157.
[112] See *e.g.*, Patrick Capps, *Human dignity and the foundations of international law* (2009), p. 115.
[113] UN Charter, Preamble.
[114] Christopher McCrudden, "Human Dignity and Judicial Interpretation of Human Rights" (2008), p. 668. For international examples, see *idem*, pp. 668-671. McCrudden also found references to human dignity in separate opinions of judges of the International Court of Justice, but not in actual judgments. See *idem*, pp. 682-683.

the end of the World Conference on Human Rights, states that "all human rights derive from the dignity and worth inherent in the human person," and that they are "the birth right of all human beings."[115] The preamble of the two most important covenants on human rights, states that "these [human] rights derive from the inherent dignity of the human person."[116]

What exactly is the relationship between human dignity and human rights? There is no human right to human dignity. Rather, one must agree with Baroness Hale that it is better to see human dignity as a "value which underlies other more concrete rights."[117] These more concrete rights are the universally recognized human rights, all of which are directly based on the value of human dignity.[118] This link is not entirely uncontroversial. As Schachter rightly pointed out, "the general idea that human rights are derived from the dignity of the person is neither truistic nor neutral."[119] Most cultural traditions embrace human dignity in some form, but this is not always expressed in human rights language.[120] Thus there are alternatives to the view that human dignity is the basis of human rights. A brief explanation of the link between human dignity and rights is provided below.

When individuals claim respect for their human rights, they basically insist on having their dignity respected by the community in which they live.[121] Or in Henkin's words, "the human rights idea declares that every individual has legitimate claims upon his or her own society for certain freedoms and benefits."[122] What are these freedoms and benefits? Essentially, the most complete answer to this question is provided by the entire catalogue of international human rights, and this

---

[115] Vienna Declaration and Programme of Action, adopted at the World Conference on Human Rights, held in Vienna, between 14 and 25 June 1993, UNDoc. A/CONF.157/23, distributed 12 July 1993, Preamble and Article 1. See also Human rights and fundamental freedoms, General Assembly resolution 3222(XXIX), adopted 6 November 1974.

[116] See preamble of both the International Covenant on Civil and Political Rights and the International Covenant on Economic, Social and Cultural Rights, both adopted and opened for signature, ratification and accession by General Assembly resolution 2200A (XXI) of 16 December 1966. Entry into force 1976.

[117] Brenda Hale, "Dignity" (2009), p. 104.

[118] Similarly, Feldman wrote that "there is arguably no human right which is unconnected to human dignity," and Moon & Allen wrote that "human dignity is at the core of all the major human rights texts." See David Feldman, "Human dignity as a legal value - Part I" (1999), p. 690; Gay Moon and Robin Allen, "Dignity Discourse in Discrimination Law" (2006), p. 610. See also Arthur Chaskalson, "The third Bram Fischer lecture" (2000), pp. 197-198.

[119] Oscar Schachter, "Human Dignity as a Normative Concept" (1983), p. 853.

[120] See section on cultural particularities and human rights (5.4 of Chapter VI).

[121] One of the main criticisms of human rights is that it focuses too much on the right to be accepted into a community of care, supposedly ignoring the fact that the same individuals have the corresponding duty to provide such care. However, as Henkin rightly remarked, the language of rights is not inconsistent with the language of duties; it is just one side of the same coin. See Louis Henkin, "The Universality of the Concept of Human Rights" (1989), p. 16.

[122] Louis Henkin, "The Universality of the Concept of Human Rights" (1989), p. 11.

applies to all human beings in this world. All human rights are, by virtue of their foundation in human dignity, universal and inalienable.[123]

Since human dignity is not a legal concept, it has often been argued that individuals have human rights regardless of whether these rights have been recognized by States in international treaties.[124] After all, as all individuals are entitled to respect for their intrinsic dignity, and as human rights are directly derived from that intrinsic dignity and are therefore themselves also inalienable, it would be strange to argue that the existence of human rights nevertheless depended on whether a certain human rights treaty had entered into force. When it comes to gross violations of human dignity, such as torture, slavery, and genocide, it is particularly odd to assume that such grave violations of human rights only became prohibited because of the entry into force of a certain treaty. Similarly, Koskenniemi wondered why "the certainty we have of the illegality of genocide, or of torture [was not] by itself sufficient reason to include those norms in international law."[125]

The main source of inspiration for the human rights catalogue has been the indignities suffered by actual people, especially during the war, and the universal condemnation of the acts concerned.[126] Wrongs which have been perpetrated constitute the foundation of rights, also at the international level.[127] The human rights catalogue cannot be derived entirely from the value of human dignity itself via some philosophical thought experiment, but is the result of a long list of actual violations of human dignity which have subsequently been condemned by the international community as a whole. It could not have been otherwise. After all, the abstract value of human dignity alone is not specific enough as basis for the increasingly detailed category of rights as we know it.[128]

---

[123] See also Klaus Dicke, "The Founding Function of Human Dignity in the Universal Declaration of Human Rights" (2002), pp. 118-120.
[124] See *e.g.*, Hersch Lauterpacht, "The international protection of human rights" (1947), pp. 9-10.
[125] Martti Koskenniemi, "Pull of the Mainstream" (1990), p. 1952.
[126] On the Second World War as source for literally all human rights in the Universal Declaration of Human Rights, see Johannes Morsink, *The Universal Declaration of Human Rights: Origins, Drafting, and Intent* (1999), pp. 36-91; and Johannes Morsink, *Inherent human rights: philosophical roots of the Universal Declaration* (2009), pp. 61-77.
[127] See also Alan Dershowitz, *Rights from Wrongs: A Secular Theory of the Origins of Rights* (2004).
[128] As Beitz pointed out, human rights are thus not "pre-institutional." They depend on the existing institutions of the international society. See Charles R. Beitz, *The idea of human rights* (2009), especially p. 55.

## 3.5 The humanization of international law

The value of human dignity not only served as the foundation for all human rights, but also led to a new way of looking at the international legal order as a whole, and to a new way in which international legal obligations should be phrased.

In the opinion of the judges of the International Criminal Tribunal for former Yugoslavia, "[t]he general principle of respect for human dignity [...] in modern times [...] has become of such paramount importance as to permeate the whole body of international law."[129] Increasingly, international law sees the "worth and the status of the individual as the ultimate unit of all law," and thus focuses on the plight of the individual, wherever he or she may be located.[130] The shift in focus from the State to the individual is often called a paradigm shift.[131] The United Nations has played a leading role in establishing and promoting this shift.[132] This is no coincidence. The "humanization" of international law is a direct consequence of the horrors of the Second World War, in which millions of individuals were left at the mercy of brutal dictators who should have defended and protected their interests.[133] The same War also made the establishment of the United Nations possible.

This process of humanization has had an enormous impact on ethics and ethical theory. Human rights, which are the supreme expression of this humanization of international law, can be found in a series of declarations, of both a legal and a purely moral character. The Universal Declaration of Human Rights of 1948 is the *primus inter pares* of all these declarations.[134] Since that declaration was

---

[129] Prosecutor v. Furundzija, Judgment (Trial Chamber), case no. IT-95-17/1-T, 10 December 1998, para. 183.

[130] The quote is from Hersch Lauterpacht, "The international protection of human rights" (1947), p. 8.

[131] One of the most passionate defenses of this paradigm shift was by Shawcross, the English prosecutor at the Nuremberg Tribunal. See the Trial of the Major War Criminals before the International Military Tribunal Nuremberg (14 November 1945 - 1 October 1946), vol. 19, pp. 471-472 (cited in "The Charter and the Judgment of the Nürnberg Tribunal: History and Analysis", UNDoc. A/CN.4/5, 1949, p. 71).

[132] See *e.g.*, Address by the Secretary-General of the United Nations [Boutros Boutros-Ghali] at the Opening of the World Conference on Human Rights, delivered at Vienna, 14 June 1993, UNDoc. A/CONF.157/22, p. 5.

[133] For the term "humanization", see Theodor Meron, *The Humanization of International Law* (2006), especially pp. 201-207. See also Meron, "International Law in the Age of Human Rights;" Antônio Augusto Cançado Trindade, "International law for humankind: towards a new jus gentium, Part I (2005)," pp. 33- 35; Christian Tomuschat, *Human rights: between idealism and realism* (2008), pp. 22-23.

[134] Besides the UN documents, see the Universal Islamic Declaration of Human Rights: adopted by the Islamic Council in 1980; Cairo Declaration on Human Rights in Islam: adopted at the end of the 19th Islamic Conference of Foreign Ministers in 1990; Declaration toward a Global Ethic: declaration endorsed by the Parliament of the World's Religions in 1993; The Bangkok Declaration: adopted by Ministers and representatives of Asian states in 1993; Asian Human Rights Charter: A People's Charter: Asian Human Rights Commission, 1998. This list is annexed to Will Kymlicka's book, *The*

adopted, the language of human rights, *i.e.* "the rights that one has simply as a human being,"[135] has continued to develop, and has in recent times been extremely successful, functioning as a "global moral vision," [136] a "shared moral touchstone,"[137] the "moral *lingua franca* of our age,"[138] or the "gold standard" of international morality. [139] In the words of one author, "[w]hen someone does something morally wrong one of the most common answers offered today is that 'it is a violation of human rights'."[140] The former UN Secretary-General Boutros-Ghali expressed his hope that "human rights [may] become the common language of all humanity!"[141]

The language of human rights has had an enormous impact on international law. It has influenced all the traditional issues, such as State responsibility, diplomatic protection, the law of treaties, and so on.[142] Moreover, most of the recognized *jus cogens* norms in some way also have a human rights character. This is not surprising when one remembers the moral basis of these rules. After all, morality is more applicable to human beings, who have the capacity to enjoy and to suffer, than to States, which exist only in the abstract. The ILC Rapporteur Fitzmaurice said in 1958 that most of *jus cogens* consisted of "cases where the position of the individual is involved, and where the rules contravened are rules instituted for the protection of the individual."[143] His successor, Waldock, agreed.[144] The French representative made a similar connection between *jus cogens* and the legal protection of the individual, when he said that 'the substance of *jus cogens* was what represented the undeniable expression of the universal conscience, the

---

Globalization of Ethics (2007). For those who believe that the humanist perspective is not represented in this list of declarations, we could refer to the Humanist Manifestos, especially the one of 1973, where the Universal Declaration is also explicitly acknowledged as one of the main sources of inspiration. Humanist Manifesto II, 7th principle.

[135] Jack Donnelly, "Human Rights: Political Aspects" (2004), p. 7025.

[136] Sathirathai, "Renewing Our Global Values: A Multilateralism for Peace, Prosperity, and Freedom," p. 5.

[137] Charles R. Beitz, *The idea of human rights* (2009), p. 44.

[138] Johannes Morsink, *Inherent human rights: philosophical roots of the Universal Declaration* (2009), p. 1.

[139] See, *e.g.*, Will Kymlicka, "Introduction: The Globalization of Ethics" (2007), p. 3. However, the author then lists some counter-arguments, about the so-called Western bias in the approach.

[140] Haule, "Some Reflections on the Foundation of Human Rights – Are Human Rights an Alternative to Moral Values?" p. 369.

[141] Boutros Boutros-Ghali at the Opening of the World Conference on Human Rights, 14 June 1993, UNDoc. A/CONF.157/22, p. 13. See also Charles R. Beitz, *The idea of human rights* (2009), p. 1.

[142] For an excellent overview, see Menno T. Kamminga and Martin Scheinin (editors), *The impact of human rights law on general international law* (2009).

[143] Yearbook of the International Law Commission, 1958, Volume II, p. 40.

[144] Yearbook of the International Law Commission, 1966, Vol. I, Part I, p. 40.

common denominator of what men of all nationalities regarded as sacrosanct, namely, respect for and protection of the rights of the human person."[145]

The United Nations has played a substantial role in promoting a humanized approach to international law. The former Secretary-General Kofi Annan used his two five-year terms in office to promote the value of human dignity, and it became the *Leitmotif* for all of the United Nations' work.[146] The conceptual foundation of this human rights-based approach relies on the work of many individuals and scholars from an impressive range of countries. The United States of America and Europe have always placed great emphasis on the freedom of the individual, and promote individual freedom at the global level.[147] In 1990, the Director of the International Law section of the Institute of State and Law of the Academy of Sciences of the USSR spoke about his own country's approach to human rights and noted that

> I feel that we have hitherto over-emphasized the role of the state, of the nation, and particularly of the classes, forgetting about the human being and humanity. In these times our primary concern should be the interest of humanity as a whole in connection with the global threats to its existence, as well as the rights and freedoms of each human being, for there can be no free society unless every human being who is a member of that society is free.[148]

Efforts are constantly being made to show that other cultures also have a favourable attitude to human rights and a human-centred approach.[149] Recent history shows that representatives of many cultures have made contributions to the development of the human discourse. The main human rights promoters at the San Francisco Conference, where the UN Charter was drafted, were the Latin American countries.[150] The concept of human development was championed by Mahbub ul

---

[145] UNDoc. A/Conf.39/11[A], p. 309. We can also refer to Norway (UNDoc. A/Conf.39/11[A], p. 324), and the United Republic of Tanzania (*idem*, p. 322).

[146] See especially Kofi Annan, *We, the Peoples: the Role of the United Nations in the Twenty-first Century* (2000), para. 10; In larger freedom: towards development, security and human rights for all, Report of the UN Secretary-General, distributed 21 March 2005, UN Doc. A/59/2005, paras. 13 – 15; and Kofi Annan, "Walking the International Tightrope", in the *New York Times* of 19 January 1999.

[147] For the past, see the American Unanimous Declaration of the United States of America (1776), and the French Déclaration des Droits de l'homme et du citoyen (1789). For the (European) present, see *e.g.*, the Declaration on the occasion of the fiftieth anniversary of the signature of the Treaties of Rome, adopted by EU leaders in Berlin, on the 25th of March 2007.

[148] Rein A. Müllerson, "Human Rights and the Individual as Subject of International Law: A Soviet View" (1990).

[149] For Asia, see *e.g.*, Amartya Sen, *Human Rights and Asian Values* (1997); for the Jewish religion, see *e.g.*, Michael Walzer, *Universalism and Jewish Values* (2001); for the Arab world, see *e.g.*, Kevin T. Dwyer, *Arab Voices: The Human Rights Debate in the Middle East* (1991). See also the work of An-Naim, *e.g.*, Abdullahi An-Naim, "Human Rights in the Arab World: A Regional Perspective" (2001).

[150] Ruth B. Russell, *A history of the United Nations Charter* (1958), pp. 568-569.

Haq from Pakistan;[151] "development as freedom" by Amartya Sen from India;[152] "human security" by Amartya Sen, Ramesh Thakur (India), and Sadako Ogata from Japan.[153] Therefore these "human discourses" are truly global. As the United Nations is the only organization that represents the entire world, it is no coincidence that all the above-mentioned scholars have developed their ideas while they were employed by it in some way.[154]

## 3.6 Conclusion

The United Nations has deliberately refrained from adopting a strong position with regard to the conceptual basis of human rights. As the UN represents the entire global community, it could not choose one particular theory over another. Thus this was the only approach available to it. Nevertheless, some ideas have been generally accepted. There is no doubt that the global formulation of human rights was a direct response to the barbarities of the Second World War. Never again should a State be allowed to treat its own citizens in the way that citizens were treated by the Nazi regime. Never again would the international community fail to respond to grave violations of the human dignity of individual people, wherever this took place. There is a universal consensus that human dignity constitutes the basis of all international human rights. However, this does not mean that there is a universally agreed definition of human dignity, or that the relationship between human dignity and rights has been fully understood in any great depth or detail. In general, both the meaning of human dignity and its relationship with human rights are based on generally shared but rather vague intuitions. In addition to serving as the basis for all universally recognized human rights, the value of human dignity also led to a new approach to international law. The State now has to share the stage in the theatre of international law with other actors, including individuals.

---

[151] See Mahbub ul-Haq, *Reflections on Human Development* (1995). See also Richard Jolly, "Human Development" (2007).

[152] Amartya Sen, *Development as Freedom* (1999).

[153] Commission on Human Security, *Human security now* (2003).

[154] See *e.g.*, Richard Jolly, Louis Emmerij, Dharam Ghai & Frédéric Lapeyre, *UN Contributions to Development Thinking and Practice* (2004).

# 4 THE CONTENT OF HUMAN RIGHTS

## 4.1 Introduction

The more concrete and detailed the language of human rights becomes, the harder it is to link it to what it is based on: the value of human dignity. As Ruggie noted, "there is a shared vocabulary endorsing human rights in general, but a cacophony of meanings and preferences concerning the vindication of any particular right."[155] In an attempt to avoid this cacophony, some philosophers have presented their own "best philosophical account" of human rights. These accounts were much more specific and detailed than the intuitive approach of the United Nations. Griffin, for example, presented such an account, and then checked to see whether all universally agreed human rights corresponded with his account.[156] The problem with this sort of academic enterprise is that other philosophers disagree on what is the "best account." Even if the entire world agreed on what is the best account, the list of rights would still not automatically follow from that account; it requires interpretation.[157]

The Assembly's discourse differs from the philosophical discourse in many ways. First of all, the Assembly cannot afford to accept that there is no answer to the question: what are our rights? Secondly, it cannot develop a detailed philosophical account, because that would certainly alienate some of its Member States. Perhaps these differences explain the Assembly's success in coming up with a universally shared and detailed list of human rights. After all, if the details of the philosophical account are not discussed, there is nothing to disagree with. In 1986, the General Assembly recalled, with a considerable sense of pride, "the extensive network of international standards in the field of human rights, which it, other United Nations bodies and the specialized agencies, ha[d] established."[158] It also emphasized the "primacy of the Universal Declaration of Human Rights, the International Covenant on Civil and Political Rights and the International Covenant

---

[155] John G. Ruggie, "Human Rights and the Future International Community" (1983), p. 98.

[156] James Griffin, "The Presidential Address: Discrepancies between the Best Philosophical Account of Human Rights and the International Law of Human Rights" (2001). See also James Griffin, *On human rights* (2008), especially pp. 5-6, 13-14, 51-56, 182-184 and 186-187.

[157] Griffin's account is actually quite original and thus controversial. It focuses on personhood, which requires autonomy, minimum welfare and liberty; and he believes that certain recognized rights are not human rights at all (such as the right to work, and the right to health as defined in international law). See James Griffin, "The Presidential Address: Discrepancies between the Best Philosophical Account of Human Rights and the International Law of Human Rights" (2001), pp. 6-8; and also James Griffin, *On human rights* (2008) (on pp. 32-33 one finds a summary of his theory).

[158] Setting international standards in the field of human rights, General Assembly resolution 41/120, adopted 4 December 1986 ("Setting international standards in the field of human rights"), Preamble.

on Economic, Social and Cultural Rights in this network." [159] The last two documents, referred to by the General Assembly as "the first all-embracing and legally binding international treaties in the field of human rights," [160] were first adopted by the Assembly in 1966, and entered into force ten years later. [161]

The content of human rights is examined below, bearing in mind the central role of the Universal Declaration and the demand that all human rights are derived from human dignity, as the Assembly stated.

## 4.2 The evolution of the contents of human rights

The importance of the Universal Declaration of Human Rights in setting out the world's list of rights has been emphasized already. The question arises whether this list of rights, which was drafted in 1948, is not out of date after more than sixty years.

The short answer is that the Declaration was drafted in such general terms that it allowed for an evolutionary interpretation. Like the UN Charter, the Universal Declaration of Human Rights is a "living document," which can evolve with the times. [162]

None of the human rights treaties adopted after the Universal Declaration contain rights that were not already included in the 1948 document. [163] Whenever a new technology emerged, it soon became clear that the human rights issues relating to this new technology were successfully covered by the terms of the Universal Declaration. For example, the human right of access to the internet is covered by everyone's right to the "freedom to hold opinions without interference and to seek, receive and impart information and ideas through any media and regardless of frontiers." [164] In the United Nations Declaration on Human Cloning, the Assembly

---

[159] *Idem.*

[160] Declaration on the occasion of the 25th anniversary of the adoption of the International Covenants on Human Rights, General Assembly resolution 46/81, adopted 16 December 1991.

[161] International Covenant on Economic, Social and Cultural Rights, International Covenant on Civil and Political Rights and Optional Protocol to the International Covenant on Civil and Political Rights, annexed to General Assembly resolution 2200 (XXI), adopted 16 December 1966. International Covenant on Economic, Social and Cultural Rights, entry into force 3 January 1976, United Nations, Treaty Series, vol. 993, p. 3; International Covenant on Civil and Political Rights, entry into force 23 March 1976, United Nations, Treaty Series, vol. 999, p. 171.

[162] See section 2.5 of Chapter III, on the evolution of the UN Charter.

[163] An exception to this rule is the United Nations Declaration on the Rights of Indigenous Peoples, General Assembly resolution 61/295, adopted 13 September 2007. This Declaration consists mostly of collective rights, which can only be enjoyed – and claimed – by individuals. It may be argued that the right to self-determination is an additional human right. However, it is not clear whether this is a human right at all. For that discussion, see the next chapter.

[164] Universal Declaration of Human Rights, Article 19.

said it was "convinced of the urgency of preventing the potential dangers of human cloning to human dignity," and it therefore "called upon [all States] to prohibit all forms of human cloning inasmuch as they [were] incompatible with human dignity and the protection of human life," but it did not see a reason to add a new human right. [165]

The Assembly explicitly requested that new human rights should accord with the rights that had already been adopted. It "invite[d] Member States and United Nations bodies to bear in mind [certain] guidelines in developing international instruments in the field of human rights." [166] New treaties had to be "consistent with the existing body of international human rights law." All human rights had to be "of fundamental character and derive from the inherent dignity and worth of the human person." They had to be "sufficiently precise to give rise to identifiable and practicable rights and obligations," and they had to "provide, where appropriate, realistic and effective implementation machinery, including reporting systems," and "attract broad international support." [167] These criteria were intended to prevent the Assembly from adopting over-imaginative human rights, such as the "right to sunshine," the "right to a sex break," and the "right to drink oneself to death without interference." [168]

Alston pointed out that "the challenge [was] to achieve an appropriate balance between, on the one hand, the need to maintain the integrity and credibility of the human rights tradition, and on the other hand, the need to adopt a dynamic approach that fully reflect[ed] changing needs and perspectives and respond[ed] to the emergence of new threats to human dignity and well-being." [169] In this context Boutros-Ghali referred to the "dual nature" of human rights. "They should express absolute, timeless injunctions, yet simultaneously reflect a moment in the development of history." [170] They were "both absolute and historically defined." [171] The Assembly has been successful in maintaining the consistency of the human rights tradition, at the same time as ensuring the continued relevance of this tradition.

---

[165] United Nations Declaration on Human Cloning, annexed to General Assembly resolution 59/280, adopted 8 March 2005.
[166] Setting international standards in the field of human rights, para. 4.
[167] *Idem*. See also the guidelines at Philip Alston, "Conjuring up New Human Rights: A Proposal for Quality Control" (1984), pp. 615-617. Since Alston believed such substantive guidelines did not suffice, he also added some procedural guidelines. See *idem*, pp. 619-620.
[168] The examples were taken from Mirko Bagaric & James Allan, "The Vacuous Concept of Dignity" (2006), p. 258.
[169] Philip Alston, "Conjuring up New Human Rights: A Proposal for Quality Control" (1984), p. 609.
[170] Boutros Boutros-Ghali at the Opening of the World Conference on Human Rights, 14 June 1993, UNDoc. A/CONF.157/22, p. 3.
[171] *Idem*.

## 4.3 The categorization of human rights

There are various ways to categorize human rights. McDougal, for example, used a set of rather abstract values, of which respect was the most important.[172] Tomuschat distinguished three different generations of human rights: civil and political rights constituted the first generation, economic and social rights the second, and the more philosophical rights such as the right to peace, belonged to the third generation.[173]

This study uses the categorization presented by René Cassin in his Hague Lecture of 1951.[174] His categorization is followed in this study mainly because Cassin is considered to be one of the fathers of the Universal Declaration. Therefore he is very familiar with that declaration and the various rights in it. This categorization does not in any way suggest that certain rights are more fundamental than others, or that there are different kinds of human rights.[175] Cassin had stressed the "indivisibility" of human rights,[176] and the General Assembly consistently reiterated that "all human rights and fundamental freedoms are indivisible and interdependent,"[177] and that "the promotion and protection of one category of rights can never exempt or excuse States from the promotion and protection of the other rights."[178] Nevertheless, despite the indivisibility of all human rights, it is at least

---

[172] See *e.g.*, Myres S. McDougal & Gerhard Bebr, "Human Rights in the United Nations" (1964), pp. 605-606. The right to participate in government secured, *inter alia*, everyone's share of power (pp. 621-623); the prohibition to discriminate and the right to privacy secured respect for everyone's dignity (pp. 623-624); the right to free speech and to education secured everyone's skill and enlightenment (pp. 624-625 and p. 627); the right to work and to property secured everyone's wealth (pp. 625-626); the right to health, to an adequate standard of living and the prohibition to torture everyone's well-being (pp. 626-627); the right to family everyone's affection (p. 627); the freedom of thought and religion everyone's rectitude (pp. 627-628). For a more extensive account, see Myres S. McDougal, Laswell & Chen, *Human rights and world public order: the basic policies of an international law of human dignity* (1980). See also Robert S. Jordan, "United Nations General Assembly Resolutions as Expressions of Human Values" (1976).
[173] See *e.g.*, Christian Tomuschat, *Human rights: between idealism and realism* (2008), pp. 25-60. The United Nations itself has never adopted this type of categorization.
[174] René Cassin, "La déclaration universelle et la mise en œuvre des droits de l'homme" (1951), p. 278. Beitz also chose to follow Cassin here, but he added a fifth category of peoples' rights, such as the right to self-determination and the right to natural resources. See Charles R. Beitz, *The idea of human rights* (2009), pp. 27-28; and Charles R. Beitz, "Human Rights as a Common Concern" (2001), p. 271.
[175] For some of the pros and cons of establishing a list of fundamental human rights, see Theodor Meron, "On a Hierarchy of International Human Rights" (1986).
[176] See René Cassin, "La déclaration universelle et la mise en œuvre des droits de l'homme" (1951), pp. 285-286. See also Marek Piechowiak, "What are human rights?: the concept of human rights and their extra-legal justification" (1999), p. 9.
[177] Alternative approaches and ways and means within the United Nations system for improving the effective enjoyment of human rights and fundamental freedoms, General Assembly resolution 32/130, adopted 16 December 1977, para. 1(a).
[178] Indivisibility and interdependence of economic, social, cultural, civil and political rights, General Assembly resolution 40/114, adopted 13 December 1985.

intuitively plausible to distinguish certain fundamental rights, such as the prohibition on slavery, torture, genocide and the right to life, from other, less fundamental, rights.[179] The objection to this distinction is that it does not serve any purpose, and that it only degrades the latter category of rights.

## 4.4 Personal freedom

The principal aim of the Universal Declaration of Human Rights was to "liberat[e] individuals from the unjustified oppression and constraint to which they [were] too often subjected."[180] This explains why the human rights that ensure the personal freedom of all individuals figure so prominently in the Declaration.[181]

The most important of these classic rights to freedom is the "right to life, liberty and security of person."[182] The State must not prevent individuals within its jurisdiction from enjoying their personal freedom. The Universal Declaration does not elaborate on this right. That was left to subsequent declarations and treaties.

The most controversial issue with regard to the further elaboration of the right to life was whether it was an absolute right, or whether it allowed for exceptions. One exception to the right to life that is widely recognized, although highly controversial, is the death penalty. In the first draft of the Universal Declaration, the death penalty was expressly acknowledged as a possible exception to the right to life.[183] Since the 1960s, there has been a gradual tendency to prohibit the death penalty. In the Covenant of 1966, the death penalty was still expressly permitted.[184] In 1968, the Assembly invited all States, "desiring to promote further the dignity of man," to impose further restrictions on the imposition of the death penalty.[185] In 1977, it set out as its main objective in this field to "progressively restrict […] the number of offences for which the death penalty may be imposed

---

[179] See Peter R. Baehr, *De rechten van de mens: universaliteit in de praktijk* (1998), pp. 40-53.

[180] Preamble to Part D of the Universal Declaration of Human Rights, entitled Publicity to be given to the Universal Declaration of Human Rights.

[181] Lauterpacht referred to these rights as the "backbone and the origin of national Bills of rights in the past," and thus gave a historic explanation for the focus on these types of rights. See Hersch Lauterpacht, "The international protection of human rights" (1947), p. 86.

[182] Universal Declaration of Human Rights, Article 3. See also Article 6 (right to life), International Covenant on Civil and Political Rights.

[183] The first version read that "every one has the right to life," and that "this right can be denied only to persons who have been convicted under general law of some crime to which the death penalty is attached." Draft outline of international bill of rights, UNDoc. E/CN.4/AC.1/3, distributed 4 June 1947, p. 2.

[184] See International Covenant on Civil and Political Rights, Article 6 (2).

[185] Capital punishment, General Assembly resolution 2393 (XXIII), adopted 26 November 1968.

with a view to [...] abolishing this punishment."[186] With the adoption of an additional protocol in 1989 the General Assembly clearly stated that it aimed at the total abolition of the death penalty.[187]

The right to liberty and security of person is certainly not absolute.[188] The most obvious exception is imprisonment.[189] In contrast to the strong global opposition to the death penalty, there is no global movement calling for the abolition of prisons.[190] Individuals cannot be "subjected to arbitrary arrest, detention or exile."[191] They cannot be imprisoned without a fair trial,[192] but they can be detained for legitimate reasons, and they can be imprisoned after being convicted of a crime by a duly authorized court or tribunal.[193]

When individuals are arrested, detained or imprisoned by law enforcement officials of a State, they are particularly vulnerable to abuse by those officials.[194] The General Assembly has adopted many legal instruments to prevent such abuse, beginning with the Covenant on Civil and Political Rights itself, which proclaims that "all persons deprived of their liberty shall be treated with humanity and with respect for the inherent dignity of the human person."[195] All prisoners are entitled to full respect of their inherent dignity, whatever crime they have committed.[196] In 1978, the Assembly recommended that "in the performance of their duty, law enforcement officials [should] respect and protect human dignity and maintain and

---

[186] Capital punishment, General Assembly resolution 32/61, adopted 8 December 1977. See also Arbitrary or summary executions, General Assembly resolution 35/172, adopted 15 December 1980.

[187] Second Optional Protocol to the International Covenant on Civil and Political Rights, aiming at the abolition of the death penalty, annexed to General Assembly resolution 44/128, adopted 15 December 1989. See also Moratorium on the use of the death penalty, General Assembly resolution 62/149, adopted 18 December 2007.

[188] International Covenant on Civil and Political Rights, Article 9.

[189] See Draft outline of international bill of rights, UNDoc. E/CN.4/AC.1/3, distributed 4 June 1947, Article 6, on p. 4.

[190] The German Federal Constitutional Court refused to accept the argument that life imprisonment without parole was inconsistent with respect for human dignity. See Evadne Grant, "Dignity and Equality" (2007), p. 309.

[191] Universal Declaration of Human Rights, Article 9.

[192] Idem, Article 10 and 11. See also International Covenant on Civil and Political Rights, Articles 14 and 15.

[193] In 1979, the Assembly stressed the importance of the remedy of habeas corpus, i.e. the right to challenge the lawfulness of one's arrest before an impartial tribunal. The right of amparo, habeas corpus or other legal remedies to the same effect, General Assembly resolution 34/178, adopted 17 December 1979.

[194] See generally Human rights in the administration of justice, General Assembly resolution 2858(XXVI), adopted 20 December 1971.

[195] International Covenant on Civil and Political Rights, Article 10.

[196] See Marek Piechowiak, "What are human rights?: the concept of human rights and their extra-legal justification" (1999), p. 6; Roberto Andorno, "The paradoxial notion of human dignity" (2001), p. 160.

uphold the human rights of all persons."[197] The duty of State officials to respect the dignity of all persons involved in criminal proceedings does not apply only to defendants. In 1985, the Assembly rightly emphasized that "victims [of a crime] should be treated with compassion and respect for their dignity" as well.[198] Most resolutions focus on the State's treatment of the (alleged) perpetrator of a crime. In 1988, the Assembly proclaimed that "all persons under any form of detention or imprisonment shall be treated in a humane manner and with respect for the inherent dignity of the human person."[199] Reference should also be made to The Basic Principles for the Treatment of Prisoners, adopted in 1990. The first principle reads that "all prisoners shall be treated with the respect due to their inherent dignity and value as human beings."[200] These declarations serve to remind all States that people who are detained or imprisoned do not cease to be human beings, no matter how horrible the crimes they have (allegedly) committed. Therefore they are at all times entitled to respect for their inherent and inalienable human dignity.

One of the worst violations of the inalienable human worth of detained individuals is the case of enforced disappearance. In 1992, the Assembly stated that "any act of enforced disappearance [was] an offence to human dignity."[201] It also explained that "forced disappearance place[d] the persons subjected thereto outside the protection of the law and inflict[ed] severe suffering on them and their families," and that it constituted a violation of the right to life, liberty and security of person, but also the right to be recognized as a person before the law and the right not to be tortured.[202] In 2006, the Assembly came up with the text of an International Convention for the Protection of All Persons from Enforced Disappearance, which defined enforced disappearance as

---

[197] Code of Conduct for Law Enforcement Officials, General Assembly resolution 34/169, adopted 17 December 1979, Article 2.

[198] Declaration of Basic Principles of Justice for Victims of Crime and Abuse of Power, annexed to General Assembly resolution 40/34, adopted 29 November 1985, para. 4.

[199] Principle 1, Body of principles for the protection of all persons under any form of detention or imprisonment, annexed to General Assembly resolution 43/173, adopted 9 December 1988. This document further included elaborations of the human rights discussed in this paragraph, including the prohibition to torture.

[200] Principle 1, Basic Principles for the Treatment of Prisoners, annexed to General Assembly resolution 45/111, adopted 14 December 1990. See also the United Nations Rules for the Protection of Juveniles Deprived of their Liberty, annexed to General Assembly resolution 45/113, also adopted 14 December 1990. These rules contain various references to the respect for the dignity of such juveniles; see Rules 31, 66, and especially Rule 87. For women prisoners, see the United Nations Rules for the Treatment of Women Prisoners and Non-custodial Measures for Women Offenders, annexed to General Assembly resolution 65/229, adopted 21 December 2010.

[201] Article 1, Declaration on the Protection of All Persons from Enforced Disappearance, annexed to General Assembly resolution 47/133, adopted 18 December 1992, entry into force 23 December 2010.

[202] *Idem*, Article 2.

> The arrest, detention, abduction or any other form of deprivation of liberty by agents of the State or by persons or groups of persons acting with the authorization, support or acquiescence of the State, followed by a refusal to acknowledge the deprivation of liberty or by concealment of the fate or whereabouts of the disappeared person, which place such a person outside the protection of the law.[203]

The worst type of abuse of people held by the State is torture. The Universal Declaration had already proclaimed everyone's right not to be "subjected to torture or to cruel, inhuman or degrading treatment or punishment."[204] Persons detained on the basis of their political opinions and convictions are in particular danger of being tortured.[205] The prohibition on torture was further elaborated upon by the General Assembly in a declaration of 1975, in which the Assembly declared that "torture constitute[d] an aggravated and deliberate form of cruel, inhuman or degrading treatment or punishment," and that it should be defined as

> Any act by which severe pain or suffering, whether physical or mental, is intentionally inflicted by or at the instigation of a public official on a person for such purposes as obtaining from him or a third person information or confession, punishing him for an act he has committed or is suspected of having committed, or intimidating him or other persons.[206]

Such acts should be considered as "an offence to human dignity," and as a violation of the purposes of the UN Charter and the Universal Declaration of Human Rights.[207] As philosophers have sometimes pointed out, the whole idea of torture is to make people lose their self-worth and sense of dignity. The aim is to break them so they will do anything just to stop the pain and humiliation.[208] The Human Rights Commission was asked to prepare a convention on torture based on the general

---

[203] Article 2, International Convention for the Protection of All Persons from Enforced Disappearance, annexed to General Assembly resolution 61/177, adopted 20 December 2006.

[204] Article 5, Universal Declaration of Human Rights. See also Article 7, International Covenant on Civil and Political Rights.

[205] Protection of the human rights of certain category of prisoners, General Assembly resolution 32/121, adopted 16 December 1977. See also Protection of persons detained or imprisoned as a result of their struggle against apartheid, racism and racial discrimination, colonialism, aggression and foreign occupation and for self-determination, independence and social progress for their people, General Assembly resolution 32/122, adopted 16 December 1977, and Protection of the human rights of arrested or detained trade union activists, General Assembly resolution 33/169, adopted 20 December 1978.

[206] Article 1, Declaration on the Protection of All Persons from Being Subjected to Torture and Other Cruel, Inhuman or Degrading Treatment or Punishment, annexed to General Assembly resolution 3452(XXX), adopted 9 December 1975.

[207] *Idem*, Article 2.

[208] Michael S. Pritchard, "Human Dignity and Justice" (1972), pp. 301-302. Simultaneously, torture also constitutes a violation of the dignity of the State on whose behalf the torture is committed, and possibly also of humanity's dignity as a whole. See David Feldman, "Human dignity as a legal value - Part I" (1999), p. 685.

definition quoted above. Until this convention entered into force, States were asked to make unilateral declarations against torture.[209] The Assembly adopted the text of the Convention against Torture in 1984.[210] It entered into force a few years later.[211] The Assembly has consistently held the view that torture can never be justified, *i.e.* "that freedom from torture [was] a non-derogable right that must be protected under all circumstances."[212] In 1982, the Assembly expressly prohibited health personnel from being involved in acts of torture.[213]

Another right that should be included in the category of personal freedom rights is the right not to be "held in slavery or servitude."[214] In the first draft of the Universal Declaration, slavery was held to be "inconsistent with the dignity of man," but this phrase was removed in the final version.[215] The Covenant on Civil and Political Rights broadened the scope of this right by also prohibiting "forced or compulsory labour," but expressly excluded "hard labour in pursuance of a sentence to [...] punishment by a competent court" from the reach of this prohibition.[216] Slavery still occurs in various parts of the world, and the prohibition on slavery is therefore as relevant and urgent as ever.[217]

The right not to be "subjected to arbitrary interference with his privacy, family, home or correspondence, nor to attacks upon his honour and reputation" also fits in this category of human rights protecting personal freedom.[218] This is essentially the right to privacy. It has not been the subject of many Assembly resolutions since it was adopted in the Universal Declaration of 1948.

---

[209] See Draft convention against torture and other cruel, inhuman or degrading treatment or punishment, General Assembly resolution 32/62, adopted 8 December 1977, and Unilateral declarations by member states against torture and other cruel, inhuman or degrading treatment or punishment, General Assembly resolution 32/64, also adopted on 8 December 1977.

[210] Convention against Torture and Other Cruel, Inhuman or Degrading Treatment or Punishment, General Assembly resolution 39/46, adopted 10 December 1984.

[211] Convention against Torture and Other Cruel, Inhuman or Degrading Treatment or Punishment, entry into force on 26 June 1987, United Nations, Treaty Series, vol. 1465, p. 85.

[212] Torture and other cruel, inhuman or degrading treatment or punishment, General Assembly resolution 62/148, adopted 18 December 2007. According to Article 2 of the Torture Convention, "no exceptional circumstances whatsoever, whether a state of war or a threat or war, internal political instability or any other public emergency, may be invoked as a justification of torture."

[213] Principles of Medical Ethics relevant to the role of health personnel, particularly physicians, in the protection of prisoners and detainees against torture, and other cruel, inhuman or degrading treatment or punishment, annexed to General Assembly resolution 37/194, adopted 18 December 1982.

[214] Article 4, Universal Declaration of Human Rights

[215] Draft outline of international bill of rights, UNDoc. E/CN.4/AC.1/3, distributed 4 June 1947, p. 4.

[216] Article 8, International Covenant on Civil and Political Rights.

[217] See also Claude Emerson Welch, "Defining Contemporary Forms of Slavery: Updating a Venerable NGO" (2009).

[218] Article 12, Universal Declaration of Human Rights. See also Article 17, International Covenant on Civil and Political Rights.

## 4.5 The freedom to associate with others

Included in this category are all those rights that allow individuals to freely associate with other individuals, without unwanted interference by the State.

The largest and most abstract group is the international community itself. The Universal Declaration proclaimed that everyone has "the right to recognition everywhere as a person before the law." [219] This does not grant individuals *international* legal personality, but it ensures that they are treated as a legal person in any jurisdiction they find themselves in. There are no legal black holes where individuals are legally irrelevant. [220] This right is most relevant for individuals who do not enjoy the nationality of the State in which they reside. In 1985, the Assembly stressed that aliens, individuals who were not nationals of the State where they lived, were entitled to enjoy most of the human rights that ordinary citizens enjoyed. [221]

The right to belong to a particular nation, *i.e.* "the right to a nationality," [222] is a more specific right. According to the Declaration, "no one shall be arbitrarily deprived of his nationality nor denied the right to change his nationality." [223] This right has been the main inspiration for the Convention on the Nationality of Married Women, adopted in 1957. [224] The main problem with regard to securing this right is the existence of individuals without a nationality, or stateless individuals. To combat this phenomenon, the International Law Commission proposed a Draft Convention on the Elimination of Future Statelessness and a Draft Convention on the Reduction of Future Statelessness. [225] The Assembly then convened a world conference, [226] which chose the less demanding of the two drafts. [227]

---

[219] Article 6, Universal Declaration of Human Rights. See also Article 16, International Covenant on Civil and Political Rights.

[220] See Ralph Wilde, "Legal "Black Hole"?: Extraterritorial state action and international treaty law on civil and political rights" (2005).

[221] Declaration on the human rights of individuals who are not nationals of the country in which they live, General Assembly resolution 40/144, adopted 13 December 1985.

[222] Article 15, Universal Declaration of Human Rights. See also Human rights and arbitrary deprivation of nationality, Human Rights Council resolution 7/10, adopted 27 March 2008.

[223] Idem.

[224] Convention of the Nationality of Married Women, annexed to General Assembly resolution 1040(XI), adopted 29 January 1957.

[225] The two drafts can be found at the Report of the International Law Commission to the General Assembly, in the Yearbook of the International Law Commission, vol. II, pp. 143-147.

[226] Elimination or reduction of future statelessness, General Assembly resolution 896(IX), adopted 4 December 1954.

[227] Convention on the Reduction of Statelessness. Entry into force, 13 December 1975. United Nations, Treaty Series, vol. 989, p. 175. See also the Convention relating to the Status of Stateless Persons. Entry into force on 6 June 1960. United Nations, Treaty Series, vol. 360, p.117. Entry into force on 6 June 1960.

For individuals who are mistreated in their country of nationality, the Universal Declaration proclaimed the right to leave their country, but not a right to be welcomed in any other country.[228] The only right recognized in the Universal Declaration was a "right to seek and to enjoy in other countries asylum from persecution."[229] People fleeing their own country to seek asylum elsewhere posed a major problem immediately after the end of the Second World War. In 1946, the Assembly established the International Refugee Organization,[230] which was originally intended to be non-permanent. Its main objective was "to bring about a rapid and positive solution of the problem of *bona fide* refugees and displaced persons."[231] Generally speaking, refugees were asylum seekers who fulfilled particular legal criteria. The International Refugee Organization had a rather limited definition of refugees. It assisted only those individuals who had become refugees as a direct result of the Nazi regime, the Spanish Civil War, or those who had already been refugees before the start of the war.[232] "Persons who evidently assisted the enemy," such as traitors, quislings and war criminals, were denied the status of refugees.[233] Also excluded were persons who aimed to overthrow their own government after the war, and most controversially, basically all "persons of German ethnic origin."[234]

In 1950, the Assembly created the Office of the United Nations High Commissioner for Refugees, which eventually replaced the International Refugee Organization.[235] In 1950, the Assembly also adopted the first Article of a Draft Convention relating to the Status of Refugees, in which the term "refugee" was defined in more general terms than was the case in the Statute of the International Refugee Organization.[236]

---

[228] Article 13, Universal Declaration of Human Rights. See also Article 12, International Covenant on Civil and Political Rights.

[229] *Idem*, Article 14. The Declaration adds that "this right may not be invoked in the case of prosecutions genuinely arising from non-political crimes or from acts contrary to the purposes and principles of the United Nations." See also Article 13, International Covenant on Civil and Political Rights.

[230] Constitution of the International Refugee Organization, annexed to Refugees and displaced persons, General Assembly 62 (I), adopted 15 December 1946. See also United Nations, Treaty Series, vol. 18, p. 3.

[231] *Idem*, Article 1(a), Definitions, Annex I..

[232] *Idem*, Article 1, Part I, Section A.

[233] See Sir Arthur Rucker, "The Work of the International Refugee Organization" (1949), p. 66.

[234] Article 1 and 6, Part II, and also Article 1(c), Annex I, Constitution of the International Refugee Organization. Article 14(2) of the Universal Declaration aimed to say the same thing. See Sibylle Kapferer, "Article 14(2) of the Universal Declaration of Human Rights and Exclusion from International Refugee Protection" (2008).

[235] Statute of the Office of the United Nations High Commissioner for Refugees, General Assembly resolution 428 (V), adopted 14 December 1950.

[236] Draft Convention relating to the Status of Refugees, General Assembly resolution 429 (V), adopted 14 December 1950.

Based on the Assembly's draft, a convention was drawn up by the United Nations Conference of Plenipotentiaries on the Status of Refugees and Stateless Persons, organized in Geneva in July 1951.[237] Although the Convention referred to both the UN Charter and the Universal Declaration of Human Rights, it is not a human rights convention in the strict sense, because it does not explicitly grant people, or even the select category of refugees, the right to asylum. It does, however, prohibit States from sending refugees back to "the frontiers of territories where [the refugee's] life or freedom would be threatened."[238]

Since 1951, the international community has continued to be rather vague about the existence of an actual right to enjoy asylum, as proclaimed in the Universal Declaration. In the Declaration on Territorial Asylum, the Assembly referred to Article 14 of the Universal Declaration, but did not reiterate the right to enjoy asylum.[239] It mainly dealt with the practicalities that States had to deal with after deciding to grant asylum. It recommended, *inter alia*, that "when a State finds difficulty in granting or continuing to grant asylum, States individually or jointly through the United Nations shall consider, in a spirit of international solidarity, appropriate measures to lighten the burden on that State."[240] The next step was to draft a convention on the topic.[241] A Conference was convened, but the participating States were unable to adopt a convention. Since the adoption of the Universal Declaration, no general human right to asylum has been added to the list.[242]

Once individuals belong to a particular State, they also have various rights to become actively involved in the social life of that State. They have "the right to take part in the government of their country, directly or through freely chosen representatives," and "the right of equal access to public service in their country."[243] There is also a right to vote, which is described as follows:

> The will of the people shall be the basis of the authority of government; this will shall be expressed in periodic and genuine elections which shall be by universal and

---

[237] Convention relating to the Status of Refugees, United Nations, Treaty Series, vol. 189, p. 137. It entered into force on 22 April 1954.

[238] *Idem*, Article 33.

[239] This right to asylum also did not make in into the International Covenant on Civil and Political Rights.

[240] Declaration on territorial asylum, General Assembly resolution 2312 (XXII), adopted 14 December 1967.

[241] Elaboration of a draft convention on territorial asylum, General Assembly resolution 3456 (XXX), adopted 9 December 1975.

[242] See also Ranjana Khanna, "Representing Culture" (2006), p. 474.

[243] Article 21, Universal Declaration of Human Rights. See also Article 25, International Covenant on Civil and Political Rights.

equal suffrage and shall be held by secret vote or by equivalent free voting procedures.[244]

The Universal Declaration suggested that the right to vote required a democratic form of government, without explicitly stating this. In 1988, while avoiding the word "democracy," the Assembly "stresse[d] its conviction that periodic and genuine elections are a necessary and indispensable element of sustained efforts to protect the rights and interests of the governed and that, as a matter of practical experience, the right of everyone to take part in the government of his or her country is a crucial factor in the effective enjoyment by all of a wide range of other human rights." [245] In 1993, the Vienna Declaration linked human rights and democracy, although it did not state that all individuals had a right to democracy. The Declaration described democracy as a form of governance "based on the freely expressed will of the people to determine their own political, economic, social and cultural systems and their full participation in all aspects of their lives."[246] The international community stated a clear preference for one particular form of domestic politics (democracy) over all others, as the most obvious means to realize certain political human rights. In 1995, the Assembly referred to the "indissoluble links between the principles enshrined in the Universal Declaration of Human Rights and the foundations of any democratic society," and urged States and the Organization to assist new democracies.[247] In 2000, the Assembly "call[ed] upon States to promote and consolidate democracy," and suggested various means to do so.[248] In 2004, the Assembly produced an interesting list of "essential elements of democracy." These included "respect for human rights," especially the freedom of association, the freedom of expression, the right to be elected to public office and the right to vote. [249] But democracy was about more than just human rights. Other elements listed by the Assembly included the existence of a "pluralistic system of political parties and organizations, respect for the rule of law, the separation of powers, the independence of the judiciary, transparency and accountability in public administration, and free, independent and pluralistic media."[250] This detailed list describes a particular form of democracy.

---

[244] *Idem.*

[245] Enhancing the effectiveness of the principle of periodic and genuine elections, General Assembly resolution 43/157, adopted 8 December 1988.

[246] Para. 8, Vienna Declaration and Programme of Action.

[247] Support by the United Nations System of the efforts of Governments to promote and consolidate new or restored democracies, General Assembly resolution 50/133, adopted 20 December 1995.

[248] This list was extremely lengthy and not very focused, which indicates that the Assembly might not have had a very clear idea of what democracy entailed exactly. Promoting and consolidating democracy, General Assembly resolution 55/96, adopted 4 December 2000.

[249] Enhancing the role of regional, subregional and other organizations and arrangements in promoting and consolidating democracy, General Assembly resolution 59/201, adopted 20 December 2004.

[250] *Idem.*

At the same time, the Assembly categorically refused to admit that one form of democracy prevalent in one region of the world should be promoted at a global level as a means to realize certain human rights. The Assembly explicitly "recogniz[ed] that there [was] no single political system or single model for electoral processes equally suited to all nations and their peoples, and that political systems and electoral processes [were] subject to historical, political, cultural and religious factors."[251] This should not be interpreted to mean that the United Nations believed that democracy was not suitable for all nations, but rather that "there [was] no universal model of democracy."[252] Moreover, the Assembly believed that democracy should not be imposed upon all States in the world. "There [was] no universal need for the United Nations to provide electoral assistance to Member States, except in special circumstances."[253]

Besides political participation, individuals also have the "the right freely to participate in the cultural life of the community, to enjoy the arts and to share in scientific advancement and its benefits."[254] In 2009, the Committee on Economic, Social and Cultural Rights adopted a General Comment on cultural rights.[255] This stressed that "[t]he full promotion of and respect for cultural rights is essential for the maintenance of human dignity and positive social interaction between individuals and communities in a diverse and multicultural world."[256] As the Committee acknowledged, the right to participate in cultural life obliges States to allow all citizens to enjoy their particular culture, and it requires States to take certain actions to ensure that all citizens can freely enjoy this right.[257] The Committee tried to define the term "culture". It referred to culture, first in general terms, as "a broad, inclusive concept encompassing all manifestations of human existence."[258] As examples of such manifestations, the Committee referred to

---

[251] Respect for the principles of national sovereignty and non-interference in the internal affairs of States in their electoral process, General Assembly resolution 49/180, adopted 23 December 1994. See also General Assembly resolution 44/147, adopted 15 December 1989.
[252] Promoting and consolidating democracy, General Assembly resolution 55/96, adopted 4 December 2000.
[253] These special circumstances included "decolonization, in the context of regional or international peace processes or at the request of specific sovereign States, by virtue of resolutions adopted by the Security Council or the General Assembly in each case, in strict conformity with the principles of sovereignty and non-interference in the internal affairs of States." See Respect for the principles of national sovereignty and non-interference in the internal affairs of States in their electoral process, General Assembly resolution 49/180, adopted 23 December 1994.
[254] Article 27, Universal Declaration of Human Rights. See also Article 15, International Covenant on Economic, Social and Cultural Rights.
[255] Right of everyone to take part in cultural life, General comment No. 21, adopted by the Committee on Economic, Social and Cultural Rights, distributed 21 December 2009, UNDoc E/C.12/GC/21.
[256] Idem, para. 1.
[257] Idem, para. 6. See also paras. 44-72. Most of the Comment dealt with State obligations to promote and respect the right.
[258] Idem, para. 11.

> Ways of life, language, oral and written literature, music and song, non-verbal communication, religion or belief systems, rites and ceremonies, sport and games, methods of production or technology, natural and man-made environments, food, clothing and shelter and the arts, customs and traditions through which individuals, groups of individuals and communities express their humanity and the meaning they give to their existence, and build their world view representing their encounter with the external forces affecting their lives.[259]

This description can be characterized as a brave attempt to define a term that is actually indefinable, and is therefore often left undefined. It is too soon to tell whether this description has been accepted as the authoritative legal interpretation of the term.

People can also form their own group within a State. They have the right "to freedom of peaceful assembly and association."[260] People may choose to join any society they want, and "no one may be compelled to belong to an association." [261]

The most concrete association of individual people protected by human rights law is the family. The General Assembly declared that all "men and women of full age, without any limitation due to race, nationality or religion, have the right to marry and to found a family."[262] In the Assembly's view, "the family [was] the natural and fundamental group unit of society and [was] entitled to protection by society and the State."[263] The Assembly not only sought to protect the family against outside oppression, but also emphasized that the decision to found a family had to be based on free choice and consent. The Convention on Consent to Marriage, Minimum Age for Marriage and Registration of Marriages, adopted in 1962, states that "no marriage shall be legally entered into without the full and free consent of both parties," and that States must specify a minimum age for marriage.[264] This minimum age was not specified in the Convention itself. A few years later, the Assembly adopted a recommendation on this matter, in which it *did*

---

[259] *Idem*, para. 13.

[260] Article 20, Universal Declaration of Human Rights. See also Article 22, International Covenant on Civil and Political Rights.

[261] *Idem*.

[262] *Idem*, Article 16. The Declaration adds that all individuals "are entitled to equal rights as to marriage, during marriage and at its dissolution," and that "marriage shall be entered into only with the free and full consent of the intending spouses." See also Articles 23 and 24, International Covenant on Civil and Political Rights.

[263] *Idem*. See also Article 10, International Covenant on Economic, Social and Cultural Rights.

[264] Articles 1 and 2, Convention on Consent to Marriage, Minimum Age for Marriage and Registration of Marriages, annexed to General Assembly resolution 1763 A (XVII), adopted 7 November 1962. The Convention entered into force 9 December 1964. See United Nations, Treaty Series, vol. 521, p. 231.

specify an absolute global minimum age for marriage, which was set at fifteen years.[265]

## 4.6 Spiritual freedom

The core of this category of rights had been included in the Universal Declaration, which states that "everyone has the right to freedom of thought, conscience and religion."[266] The relationship with human dignity was explicitly mentioned in later resolutions. For example, in 2000, the Assembly reaffirmed that "freedom of thought, conscience, religion and belief [was] a human right derived from the inherent dignity of the human person."[267]

The Universal Declaration regarded religion as a matter of personal choice. The Universal Declaration was very progressive in this respect. According to the Declaration, "this right include[d] freedom to change [one's] religion or belief, and freedom, either alone or in community with others and in public or private, to manifest [one's] religion or belief in teaching, practice, worship and observance."[268]

As Franck pointed out, for a person convinced of the invincible truth of his own beliefs, it is very difficult to tolerate – let alone respect – people who have different beliefs.[269] Therefore it is extremely important to teach people to appreciate (religious) beliefs that differ from their own. In 1981, the Assembly demanded that children be taught "respect for freedom of religion or belief of others."[270] However, the problem of religious intolerance only increased in intensity. In 2005, the Assembly "expresse[d] deep concern at the negative stereotyping of religions and manifestations of intolerance and discrimination in matters of religion or belief still in evidence in some regions of the world."[271] This became an explosive issue because of the increasing frequency of acts of terrorism motivated by religion. On

---

[265] Principle II, Recommendation on Consent to Marriage, Minimum Age for Marriage and Registration of Marriages, annexed to General Assembly resolution 2018 (XX), adopted 1 November 1965.

[266] Article 18, Universal Declaration of Human Rights. See also Article 18, International Covenant on Civil and Political Rights.

[267] Article 1, Elimination of all forms of religious intolerance, General Assembly resolution 55/97, adopted 4 December 2000. See also Article 3, Declaration on the Elimination of All Forms of Intolerance and of Discrimination Based on Religion or Belief, General Assembly resolution 36/55, adopted 25 November 1981, in which the Assembly determined that "discrimination between human beings on grounds of religion or belief constitute[d] an affront to human dignity."

[268] Article 18, Universal Declaration of Human Rights. This is nowadays also the view of the Human Rights Council. See Freedom of Religion or Belief, Human Rights Council resolution 16/13, adopted 24 March 2011.

[269] Thomas M. Franck, "Is Personal Freedom a Western Value?" (1997), especially p. 626.

[270] Article 5, Declaration on the Elimination of All Forms of Intolerance and of Discrimination Based on Religion or Belief.

[271] Combating defamation of religions, General Assembly resolution 60/150, adopted 16 December 2005.

the one hand, this development showed how some people abused religion to carry out acts of violence, while others were motivated to link a particular religion with such violence in general terms. The Assembly warned against this way of thinking, by "reaffirming that terrorism cannot and should not be associated with any religion, nationality, civilization or ethnic group."[272]

Spiritual freedom is not limited to what goes on inside one's own mind. It also includes the right to influence the opinion of others. The Universal Declaration added that "everyone has the right to freedom of opinion and expression," a right which includes the "freedom to hold opinions without interference and to seek, receive and impart information and ideas through any media and regardless of frontiers."[273] The Covenant limited this freedom of expression by declaring that "any propaganda for war shall be prohibited by law," and the same applied to "any advocacy of national, racial or religious hatred that constitutes incitement to discrimination, hostility or violence."[274]

## 4.7 The freedom to secure for oneself an adequate standard of living

All individuals also have socio-economic rights.[275] The most important of these rights is the "right to a standard of living adequate for the health and well-being of himself and of his family." [276] This right includes the right to adequate "food, clothing, housing and medical care and necessary social services," as well as "the right to security in the event of unemployment, sickness, disability, widowhood, old age or other lack of livelihood in circumstances beyond his control."[277] As the Assembly explained in 1970, the basic idea was not so much to guarantee a life of luxury for all human beings, but rather to "ensure a minimum standard of living consistent with human dignity."[278]

Some of the elements included in the right to an adequate standard of living were treated separately. Most importantly, in the Covenant on Economic, Social and Cultural Rights, the Assembly defined the right to an adequate standard of

---

[272] Protection of human rights and fundamental freedoms while countering terrorism, General Assembly resolution 62/159, adopted 18 December 2007.

[273] Article 19, Universal Declaration of Human Rights. See also Articles 19, International Covenant on Civil and Political Rights.

[274] *Idem*, Article 20.

[275] *Idem*, Article 22. Both this article and the Covenant on Economic, Social and Cultural Rights are more careful in the description of the duties of States when compared to the International Covenant on Civil and Political Rights.

[276] *Idem*, Article 25. See also Article 11, International Covenant on Economic, Social and Cultural Rights.

[277] Idem.

[278] Para. 9, Declaration on the occasion of the twenty-fifth anniversary of the United Nations, General Assembly resolution 2627 (XXV), adopted 24 October 1970.

living and the right to the enjoyment of the highest attainable standard of physical and mental health as two separate rights.[279] The latter right was the subject of a number of General Assembly resolutions. In 2003, the Assembly reaffirmed that the right to health was a human right and "that such right derive[d] from the inherent dignity of the human person."[280] It defined health as "a state of complete physical, mental and social well-being and not merely the absence of disease or infirmity." [281] In 1991, the Assembly adopted a declaration specifically on mental illness, in which it proclaimed that "all persons with a mental illness, or who are being treated as such persons, shall be treated with humanity and respect for the inherent dignity of the human person." This meant that they enjoyed all the other human rights, and that they "ha[d] the right to live and work, to the extent possible, in the community."[282]

There are other examples in which one aspect of the right to an adequate standard of living was isolated from the other aspects. For example, the right to housing was the subject of the Vancouver and Istanbul Declarations on Human Settlements, and the Declaration on Cities and Other Human Settlements in the New Millennium. [283] The Assembly also adopted a number of resolutions specifically on the right to food, stating that "hunger constitute[d] an outrage and a violation of human dignity."[284] Extreme poverty was also seen as "a violation of

---

[279] See Article 12, International Covenant on Economic, Social and Cultural Rights, for the latter right.

[280] The right of everyone to the enjoyment of the highest attainable standard of physical and mental health, General Assembly resolution 58/173, adopted 22 December 2003.

[281] *Idem.*

[282] Principles for the Protection of Persons with Mental Illness and for the Improvement of Mental Health Care, annexed to The protection of persons with mental illness and the improvement of mental health care, General Assembly resolution 46/119, adopted 17 December 1991.

[283] Vancouver Declaration on Human Settlements, contained in the report of Habitat: United Nations Conference on Human Settlements, a conference held in Vancouver, Canada, between 31 May and 11 June 1976; Istanbul Declaration on Human Settlements, included in the Report of the United Nations Conference on Human Settlements (Habitat II), a conference held in Istanbul, between 3 and 14 June 1996, UNDoc. A/CONF.165/14, distributed 7 August 1996;. Declaration on Cities and Other Human Settlements in the New Millennium, annexed to General Assembly resolution S-25/2, adopted 9 June 2001.

[284] The right to food, General Assembly resolution 56/155, adopted 19 December 2001, para. 1. In that resolution, the Assembly also welcomed a General Comment of the Committee on Economic, Social and Cultural right in which it affirmed that "the right to adequate food is indivisibly linked to the inherent dignity of the human person and is indispensable for the fulfilment of other human rights" (para. 13). See also the Universal Declaration on the Eradication of Hunger and Malnutrition, adopted on 16 November 1974 by the World Food Conference (the declaration was later endorsed by the General Assembly, in General Assembly resolution 3348(XXIX), adopted 17 December 1974); the Rome Declaration on World Food Security, published in Food and Agriculture Organization of the United Nations, Report of the World Food Summit, 13-17 November 1996 (WFS 96/REP); World Food Summit Plan of Action, published in Food and Agriculture Organization of the United Nations, Report of the World Food Summit, 13-17 November 1996 (WFS 96/REP); Declaration of the World Food Summmit: Five Years Later, annexed to a Letter dated 21 October 2002 from the Permanent

human dignity."[285] As these declarations ended up referring to all the other aspects of the right to an adequate standard of living as well, they show how difficult it is to isolate just one aspect of this right.[286] A more useful approach is to focus the attention of the international community on particular problems relating to this right, such as the problematic situation of the world's homeless.[287]

In addition to the right to an adequate standard of living and the sub-rights included in this, these socio-economic rights also include "the right to work, to free choice of employment, to just and favourable conditions of work and to protection against unemployment,"[288] and "the right to rest and leisure, including reasonable limitation of working hours and periodic holidays with pay."[289]

This list also includes the "right to education."[290] According to the General Assembly, elementary education must be free and compulsory. This is not the case for higher forms of education.[291] The Assembly also gave some suggestions for subjects to be included in the curriculum. In its view, "education [should] be directed to the full development of the human personality and to the strengthening of respect for human rights and fundamental freedoms." [292] In the Covenant, the Assembly added that education should also be aimed at developing a "sense of [the child's] dignity" to the full. [293] Since then, the Assembly has often reiterated the importance of educating people about their rights and of making them aware of their intrinsic dignity and rights.[294] In 2011, the Human Rights Council adopted the

---

Representative of Italy to the United Nations addressed to the Secretary-General, UNDoc. A/57/499. See also para. 19, Millennium Declaration..

[285] Vienna Declaration and Programme of Action, para. 25. See also Second United Nations Decade for the Eradication of Poverty (2008-2017), General Assembly resolution 65/174, adopted 20 December 2010, where the Assembly underlined that "the eradication of poverty and hunger [was] an ethical, social, political and economic imperative of humankind."

[286] In a resolution on the right to adequate housing, for example, the necessity is stressed to take measures to "promote the right of all persons to an adequate standard of living for themselves and their families, including adequate housing." Para. 2, Realization of the right to adequate housing, General Assembly resolution 41/146, adopted 4 December 1986.

[287] See International Year of Shelter for the Homeless, General Assembly resolution 36/71, adopted 4 December 1981.

[288] Article 23, Universal Declaration of Human Rights. See also Articles 6 and 7, International Covenant on Economic, Social and Cultural Rights.

[289] *Idem*, Article 24.

[290] *Idem*, Article 26.

[291] *Idem*. The article states that "technical and professional education shall be made generally available and higher education shall be equally accessible to all on the basis of merit."

[292] *Idem*. Education should further "promote understanding, tolerance and friendship among all nations, racial or religious groups, and [it should] further the activities of the United Nations for the maintenance of peace."

[293] Article 13, International Covenant on Economic, Social and Cultural Rights.

[294] See *e.g.*, Vienna Declaration and Programme of Action, para. 33 and paras. 78-82.

United Nations Declaration on Human Rights Education and Training, with the same purpose in mind.[295]

## 4.8 Conclusion

The Assembly used its authority to adopt declarations to elaborate on the rights already recognized in its Universal Declaration of 1948. It did not operate in an *ad hoc* manner, adding rights according to the latest fashion. All of the Assembly's human rights declarations were part of a particular project: to codify the continuing evolution of universal human rights. In its work, the Assembly made sure that it complied with the conditions it had set out for itself.[296] One of these conditions was that all human rights had to be derived from the value of human dignity. The Assembly has been faithful to this condition. One cannot help but notice the many explicit references to human dignity as the basis for all human rights. Another condition was that the rights were "sufficiently precise to give rise to identifiable and practicable rights and obligations." The Assembly has also achieved this. Many of the rights have been fleshed out further, without becoming so detailed that they are too rigid to be applied in different contexts and situations. The condition that they attract "broad international support" has also been observed, as most of the treaties referred to in this section have been widely ratified. The question arises whether the Assembly will ever finish its task of identifying and defining international human rights. As time passes, the precise application of human rights leads to various new problems. At the same time, no entirely new rights have been added to the list of 1948. The Universal Declaration provides a stable foundation which is able to cope with changing times, conditions, and even attitudes.

## 5    THE WORLDWIDE, CONTINUOUS AND EQUAL APPLICATION OF HUMAN RIGHTS

### 5.1 Introduction

According to King Hassan II of Morocco, the "concept of human rights [...] is universal and can in no way be departed from or called into question."[297] Human

---

[295] United Nations Declaration on Human Rights Education and Training, Human Rights Council resolution 16/1, adopted 23 March 2011.

[296] See Setting international standards in the field of human rights, para. 4.

[297] Verbatim Records of the 3046th meeting of the Security Council, 31 January 1992, UNDoc. S/PV.3046, p. 41.

rights can and should be enjoyed by all people in all societies.[298] They "create a global safety net of rights applicable to all persons, everywhere."[299] This safety net literally covers the entire world. No exceptions to the universal and equal protection of human rights are allowed. This idea, that human rights are universally applicable, without any distinction, has frequently been emphasized by the United Nations.

It all begins with the UN Charter. Article 1 states that it is one of the purposes of the United Nations to "promot[e] and encourag[e] respect for human rights and for fundamental freedoms for all without distinction as to race, sex, language, or religion." The Universal Declaration reiterates the universal application of human rights. Article 2 of that Declaration declares that "everyone is entitled to all the rights and freedoms set forth in this Declaration, without distinction of any kind, such as race, color, sex, language, religion, political or other opinion, national or social origin, property, birth or other status."[300] In 1993, the world adopted the Vienna Declaration on Human Rights, which stated that "the universal nature of these rights and freedoms is beyond question," and that "all human rights are universal, indivisible and interdependent and interrelated."[301] The mandate of the newly established High Commissioner for Human Rights also emphasized the universal application of human rights, [302] as did the mandate of the Human Rights Council.[303] To celebrate the sixtieth anniversary of the Universal Declaration, all States reaffirmed their "commitment towards the full realization of all human rights for all, which are universal, indivisible, interrelated, interdependent and mutually reinforcing."[304] These are only a few examples of statements which reiterated the universality of human rights.

This universality is directly derived from the fact that all human rights are based on human dignity. If all human beings have rights just because they have an inherent worth as human beings, it is hard to justify that some people are "more

---

[298] Charles R. Beitz, *The idea of human rights* (2009), p. 59.

[299] Thomas M. Franck, "Are Human Rights Universal?" (2001), p. 193.

[300] The Universal Declaration of Human Rights adds that "no distinction shall be made on the basis of the political, jurisdictional or international status of the country or territory to which a person belongs, whether it be independent, trust, non-self-governing or under any other limitation of sovereignty."

[301] Vienna Declaration and Programme of Action, paras. 1 and 5. See also para. 32, in which "the importance of ensuring "the universality, objectivity and non-selectivity of the consideration of human rights issues" was reaffirmed.

[302] High Commissioner for the promotion and protection of all human rights, General Assembly resolution 48/141, adopted 7 January 1994, Preamble and para. 3(b).

[303] Human Rights Council, General Assembly resolution 60/251, adopted 15 March 2006, para. 4.

[304] Declaration on the sixtieth anniversary of the Universal Declaration of Human Rights, annexed to Sixtieth anniversary of the Universal Declaration of Human Rights, General Assembly resolution 63/116, adopted 10 December 2008.

worthy" than others. [305] The United Nations has combated various forms of discrimination based on the unequivocal rejection of the idea that some individuals are more worthy than others. In particular, the Assembly has condemned all forms of racial discrimination, and discrimination based on gender. It has also rejected any suggestions that human rights only apply in times of peace. Even during the most challenging of times, human rights continue to regulate the relationship between the State and all the individuals within its jurisdiction.

## 5.2 Equal rights and dignity for all

The UN Charter itself prohibited all distinctions based on "race, sex, language, or religion." [306] In 1948, the Universal Declaration broadened the list of categories significantly. In addition to the prohibited distinctions included in the Charter, a distinction based on "political or other opinion, national or social origin, property, birth or other status" was also prohibited. [307] The difference between them is not problematic, since the Charter's enumeration of prohibited distinctions was never intended to be exhaustive in any way.

The General Assembly has always related equality to respect for human dignity. It adopted a number of declarations to condemn and combat various forms and manifestations of discrimination, and in doing so it frequently referred to such discrimination as a violation of the respect for human dignity.

In combating prohibited distinctions, the Assembly focused on combating racial discrimination. In 1960, the Assembly expressed the principle "that the United Nations is duty bound to combat these manifestations [and therefore] resolutely condemn[ed] all manifestations and practices of racial, religious and national hatred." [308] In this way it accepted the duty to actively combat racist ideologies. As usual, one of the means to do so was to prepare a declaration, followed by a multilateral treaty. [309]

---

[305] See Marek Piechowiak, "What are human rights? The concept of human rights and their extra-legal justification" (1999), p. 5 and pp. 6-7. See also Christian Tomuschat, *Human rights: between idealism and realism* (2008), p. 69.

[306] Article 1(3), UN Charter. See also Article 55(c).

[307] Article 2, Universal Declaration of Human Rights. See also Article 7.

[308] Manifestations of racial and national hatred, General Assembly resolution 1510 (XV), adopted 12 December 1960.

[309] And thus, in 1962, "deeply disturbed by the manifestations of discrimination based on differences of race, colour and religion still in evidence throughout the world," and "emphasizing that each State ought to take all the necessary action to put an end to these violations, which infringe human dignity," the Assembly requested the Human Rights Commission to prepare a first draft. Preparation of a draft declaration and a draft convention on the elimination of all forms of racial discrimination, General Assembly resolution 1780 (XVII), adopted 7 December 1962.

In 1963, the United Nations adopted the Declaration on the Elimination of All Forms of Racial Discrimination, in which it proclaimed that "discrimination between human beings on the ground of race, colour or ethnic origin [was] an offence to human dignity."[310] The Declaration also called upon all States not to discriminate, and to actively combat discriminatory policies anywhere in the world, especially policies of racial segregation and *apartheid*.[311] In addition, it called upon States to condemn racist propaganda and to punish any acts of violence aimed against any race or group of persons of another colour or ethnic origin.[312] Although mainly addressing States in more traditional language, there was one article in the declaration which read like a true human rights provision. It guaranteed the right to an "effective remedy and protection against any discrimination."[313]

In 1965, the Assembly adopted the text of a Convention on the Elimination of All Forms of Racial Discrimination.[314] Racial discrimination was broadly defined as "any distinction, exclusion, restriction or preference based on race, colour, descent, or national or ethnic origin which ha[d] the purpose or effect of nullifying or impairing the recognition, enjoyment or exercise, on an equal footing, of human rights."[315] All States prepared to sign the Convention were "convinced that any doctrine of superiority based on racial differentiation is scientifically false, morally condemnable, socially unjust and dangerous" and "condemn[ed] racial discrimination and undert[ook] to pursue by all appropriate means and without delay a policy of eliminating racial discrimination in all its forms and promoting understanding among all races."[316]

The adoption of the Convention did not stop the Assembly from adopting further declarations on the topic of racial discrimination. For decades, most of these declarations focused on combating the *apartheid* policies of South Africa. In 1973, the Assembly adopted a Programme for the Decade for Action to Combat Racism and Racial Discrimination. The ultimate goal of this Programme was to "promote human rights and fundamental freedom for all, without distinction of any kind on

---

[310] Article 1, United Nations Declaration on the Elimination of All Forms of Racial Discrimination, General Assembly resolution 1904 (XVIII), adopted 20 November 1963.

[311] *Idem*, Articles 2-6.

[312] *Idem*, Article 9.

[313] *Idem*, Article 7.

[314] International Convention on the Elimination of All Forms of Racial Discrimination, General Assembly resolution 2106 (XX), adopted 21 December 1965. The Convention entered into force on 4 January 1969. United Nations, Treaty Series, vol. 660, p. 195.

[315] *Idem*, Article 1. It is well-known that the Assembly labeled "zionism" as a form of racism in its resolution 3379 (XXX), adopted 10 November 1975. This resolution was revoked in General Assembly resolution 46/86, adopted 16 December 1991. This is the only resolution in the Assembly's history that was ever revoked by a subsequent resolution.

[316] *Idem*, Article 2.

grounds of race, colour, descent or national or ethnic origin."[317] One of the key events of this first decade was a world conference on racism held in 1978, at which all States expressed their determination to eradicate racism and *apartheid*, referred to as "evils perpetrated against the dignity of the human being."[318] The main theme of the decade was certainly the fight against *apartheid*. As early as 1973, the Assembly adopted the text of an International Convention on the Suppression and Punishment of the Crime of Apartheid.[319] The idea was that such a convention would "make it possible to take more effective measures at the international and national levels with a view to the suppression and punishment of the crime of *apartheid*."[320] The Convention criminalized *apartheid*, labelling it a "crime against humanity."[321] It defined *apartheid* by enumerating certain "inhuman acts," such as the infringement of the freedom or dignity of a certain racial group, "committed for the purpose of establishing and maintaining domination by one racial group of persons over any other racial group of persons and systematically oppressing them." [322] The year 1978, when the first global anti-racism conference was organized, was also proclaimed as anti-*apartheid* year. The purpose of this proclamation was to "make world opinion fully aware of the inhumanity of *apartheid*."[323] Mindful of the "gross indignities" that South Africa inflicted on its foreign workers, most of whom came from neighbouring countries, the Assembly "endorsed" a Charter of Rights for Migrant Workers in Southern Africa in the same year (1978), which addressed the "gross indignities" inflicted on the foreign workers by the country's migratory labour system.[324]

---

[317] Programme for the Decade for Action to Combat Racism and Racial Discrimination, annexed to General Assembly resolution 3057 (XXVIII), adopted 2 November 1973. It also called upon the eradication of racist policies and ideologies. See also the Programme of activities to be undertaken during the second half of the Decade for Action to Combat Racism and Racial Discrimination, annexed to General Assembly resolution 34/24, adopted 15 November 1979.

[318] Declaration, included in the Report of the World Conference to Combat Racism and Racial Discrimination, held at Geneva, between 14 and 25 August 1978, UNDoc. A/CONF.92/40, p. 10.

[319] International Convention on the Suppression and Punishment of the Crime of Apartheid, General Assembly resolution 3068 (XXVIII), adopted 30 November 1973. The treaty entered into force on 18 July 1976. See United Nations, Treaty Series, vol. 1015, p. 243.

[320] *Idem*, Preamble.

[321] *Idem*, Article 1.

[322] *Idem*, Article 2. The Convention applied to all forms of apartheid now and in the future, and was thus not applicable exclusively to the apartheid of South AfricaSouth Africa.

[323] Programme for the International Anti-Apartheid Year, annexed to Policies of apartheid of the Government of South Africa, General Assembly resolution 32/105, adopted 14 December 1977, para. 1(a).

[324] This Charter of Rights for Migrant Workers in Southern Africa was initially adopted at a Conference on Migratory Labour, which took place on 7 April 1978, in South AfricaSouth Africa. The text of the Charter was annexed to Migratory Labour in Southern Africa, General Assembly resolution 33/162, adopted 20 December 1978.

Apartheid was also the main theme of the second anti-racism decade, which started with the second world conference on racism, organized in 1983. At that conference, apartheid was described as "an institutionalized form of racism [and] a deliberate and totally abhorrent affront to the conscience and dignity of mankind, a crime against humanity and a threat to international peace and security."[325] The programme for the second decade to combat racism also focused on condemning and combating South Africa's apartheid policies.[326] The same decade also saw the adoption, in 1985, of the text of an International Convention against Apartheid in Sports.[327] Finally, in 1989 the Assembly adopted the Declaration on Apartheid and its Destructive Consequences in Southern Africa, in which the Assembly reminded the world that apartheid had sought, inter alia, to "dehumanize entire peoples."[328] In the last years of the decade, the Assembly foresaw the end of apartheid through negotiated settlement, and that is what happened.[329] The global value of human dignity figured prominently in the new Constitution of South Africa. Equality was defined in the Constitution, and also in the case law of the Court, in terms of equality of dignity.[330]

In 1993, the Assembly proclaimed the Third Decade to Combat Racism and Racial Discrimination. Despite the end of the apartheid regime in South Africa, the Assembly saw the previous two decades largely as failures and simply adopted the list of ultimate goals of the first decade as the ultimate goals for the third decade.[331] In 1994, one year after the first free elections in South Africa, the

---

[325] Declaration, included in the Report of the Second World Conference to Combat Racism and Racial Discrimination, held in Geneva, between 1 and 12 August 1983, UNDoc. A/CONF.119/26, para. 6. Most of the other paragraphs in the Declaration also focused on South Africa; some of them addressed racist propaganda, neo-Nazism, minorities, migrants and refugees.

[326] Programme of Action for the Second Decade to Combat Racism and Racial Discrimination, annexed to General Assembly resolution 38/14, adopted 22 November 1983. It did, however, also address more general issues, such as education, propaganda, and the protection against racism of minority groups, indigenous peoples, and migrants.

[327] International Convention against Apartheid in Sports, annexed to Policies of apartheid of the Government of South Africa, General Assembly resolution 40/64, Part G, adopted 10 December 1985. Earlier, General Assembly resolution 32/105, adopted 14 December 1977, already annexed to it an International Declaration against Apartheid in Sports. The Convention entered into force on 3 April 1988. See United Nations, Treaty Series, vol. 1500, p. 161.

[328] Preamble, Declaration on Apartheid and its Destructive Consequences in Southern Africa, annexed to General Assembly resolution S-16/1, adopted 14 December 1989.

[329] Idem.

[330] See Evadne Grant, "Dignity and Equality" (2007).

[331] Programme of Action for the Third Decade to Combat Racism and Racial Discrimination (1993-2003), annexed to General Assembly resolution 48/91, adopted 20 December 1993, para. 1. In the Preamble of this resolution, the Assembly "not[ed] with grave concern that despite the efforts of the international community, the principal objectives of the two Decades for Action to Combat Racism and Racial Discrimination have not been attained and that millions of human beings continue to this day to be the victims of varied forms of racism, racial discrimination and apartheid."

Assembly adopted a revised version of the programme.[332] With *apartheid* dealt with, the Assembly now focused on racial hatred and the "ethnic cleansing" practised during the armed conflict in the former Yugoslavia in the 1990s.[333] The Assembly referred to ethnic cleansing and racial hatred as "totally incompatible with universally recognized human rights and fundamental freedoms."[334]

A World Conference against Racism took place in South Africa in 2001.[335] Compared with the earlier declarations, the Declaration adopted at this conference sounded much more positive.[336] For example, instead of simply condemning racism – which it did – it also affirmed the importance of "tolerance, pluralism and respect for diversity" and the "values of solidarity, respect, tolerance and multiculturalism," referring to these values as "the moral ground and inspiration for [the] worldwide struggle against racism."[337]

### 5.3 Equal rights and dignity for men and women

The Preamble of the UN Charter states that the United Nations is determined "to reaffirm faith in [...] the equal rights of men and women." Article 1 one states that it is one of the purposes of the Organization to "achieve international co-operation in [...] promoting and encouraging respect for human rights and for fundamental freedoms for all without distinction as to [...] sex." This last phrase is repeated in Article 55 UN Charter. Despite all these references, the Assembly concluded in

---

[332] The section on apartheid consisted of just one paragraph, which basically called for the repair of the damage done in the past. Revised Programme of Action for the Third Decade to Combat Racism and Racial Discrimination (1993-2003), annexed to General Assembly resolution 49/146, adopted 23 December 1994, para. 3.

[333] Third Decade to Combat Racism and Racial Discrimination, General Assembly resolution 49/146, adopted 23 December 1994, para. 1.

[334] "Ethnic cleansing"and racial hatred, General Assembly resolution 47/80, adopted 16 December 1992, para. 3.

[335] Report of the World Conference against Racism, Racial Discrimination, Xenophobia and Related Intolerance, held in Durban (South AfricaSouth Africa), between 31 August and 8 September 2001. UNDoc. A/CONF.189/12 ("Report of the World Conference against Racism").

[336] Admittedly, not all paragraphs in the declaration were as positive. Most of the Declaration was more traditional. It consisted of a long list of various forms of discrimination, and ways to address them. See further the Outcome Document of the Durban Review Conference, adopted at the Durban Review Conference, which took place between 20 and 24 April 2009 in Geneva, UNDoc. A/CONF.211/8; and The fight against racism, racial discrimination, xenophobia and related intolerance and the comprehensive implementation of and follow-up to the Durban Declaration and Programme of Action, General Assembly resolution 57/195, adopted 18 December 2002, and subsequent such resolutions.

[337] Declaration, included in the Report of the World Conference against Racism, paras. 5 and 6. See also *idem*, para. 32. Much earlier, the General Conference of the United Nations Educational, Scientific and Cultural Organization (UNESCO) already adopted a declaration in which the positive aspects of the rich diversity was celebrated. See Declaration on Race and Racial Prejudice, adopted by UNESCO, 27 November 1978, UNDoc. E/CN.4/Sub.2/1982/2/Add.1.

1946, that "certain Member States ha[d] not yet granted to women, political rights equal to those granted to men," and therefore it "recommend[ed] that all Member States, which ha[d] not already done so, adopt[ed] measures necessary to fulfil the purposes and aims of the Charter in this respect by granting to women the same political rights as to men."[338] In 1952, the Assembly went one step further and adopted a Convention on the Political Rights of Women, proclaiming the rights of women to vote, to be eligible for election to all publicly elected offices, and to exercise all public functions.[339]

This Convention was only about political equality between men and women, and therefore there was still a need for a more comprehensive declaration, or preferably a convention. The first step in this direction was taken by the Assembly in 1967, when it adopted the Declaration on the Elimination of Discrimination against Women. [340] In this Declaration, the Assembly considered that discrimination against women was "an obstacle to the full development of the potentialities of women in the service of their countries and of humanity."[341] Discrimination based on sex was also considered to be "fundamentally unjust and constitute[d] an offence against human dignity."[342] The Declaration urged States to abolish all laws which violated this principle of equality, and to replace them with laws affirming such equality. In 1970, the Assembly suggested that the United Nations Organization should "set an example" by ensuring equal opportunities for men and women in the employment of its own staff.[343]

In 1975, another step was taken with the adoption of the Declaration of Mexico on the Equality of Women and Their Contribution to Development and Peace. [344] This Declaration proclaimed that "equality between women and men means equality in their dignity and worth as human beings as well as equality in their rights, opportunities and responsibilities." [345] This declaration called for

---

[338] Political rights of women, General Assembly resolution 56 (I), adopted 11 December 1946.

[339] Convention on the Political Rights of Women, annexed to General Assembly resolution 640 (VII), adopted 20 December 1952. The treaty entered into force on 7 July 1954. See United Nations, Treaty Series, vol. 193, p. 135.

[340] Declaration on the Elimination of Discrimination against Women, General Assembly Resolution 2263(XXII), adopted 7 November 1967.

[341] *Idem*, Preamble.

[342] *Idem*, Article 1.

[343] Employment of qualified women in senior and other professional positions by the secretariats of organizations in the United Nations system, General Assembly resolution 2715(XXV), adopted 15 December 1970. It also adopted a Programme of concerted international action for the advancement of women, annexed to General Assembly resolution 2716 (XXV), adopted on the same day.

[344] Declaration of Mexico on the Equality of Women and Their Contribution to Development and Peace, adopted at the World Conference of the International Women's Year, held in Mexico City, between 19 June and 2 July 1975, UNDoc E/CONF.66/34, distributed 2 July 1975.

[345] *Idem*, para. 1.

equality in all situations and circumstances, both in society and in the family.[346] The inviolability of the human body, as well as the right of every woman to decide freely whether to marry – or not to marry – were explicitly connected to human dignity.[347]

In 1979, the General Assembly, "recalling that discrimination against women violates the principles of equality of rights and respect for human dignity," adopted the text of a Convention on the Elimination of All Forms of Discrimination against Women.[348] The Convention defined discrimination based on sex in very broad terms, as

> Any distinction, exclusion or restriction made on the basis of sex which has the effect or purpose of impairing or nullifying the recognition, enjoyment or exercise by women, irrespective of their marital status, on a basis of equality of men and women, of human rights and fundamental freedoms in the political, economic, social, cultural, civil or any other field.[349]

In addition to ensuring that the domestic laws were in accordance with the principle of equality,[350] the Convention also urged States, *inter alia*, to "take all appropriate measures to modify the social and cultural patterns of conduct of men and women, with a view to achieving the elimination of prejudices and customary and all other practices which are based on the idea of the inferiority or the superiority of either of the sexes or on stereotyped roles for men and women."[351] This was the most difficult and ambitious goal set out in the Convention, *i.e.* to change these conventional ideas, prevalent in almost all societies in the world, about the traditional roles specifically assigned to men and women in society. The Committee on the Elimination of Discrimination against Women was established to assist States to strive for the common goals outlined in the Convention.[352]

Although the Convention in a sense completed the Assembly's work on promoting the idea of equality between the sexes, it continued to adopt declarations

---

[346] *Idem*, see especially para. 5.

[347] *Idem*, paras. 11 and 13.

[348] Convention on the Elimination of All Forms of Discrimination against Women, annexed to General Assembly resolution 34/180, adopted 18 December 1979. The Convention entered into force on 3 September 1981. United Nations, Treaty Series, vol. 1249, p. 13. The quote is from the preamble of the Convention.

[349] *Idem*, Article 1.

[350] The largest part of the Convention contained ways in which the equality of rights played out for specific rights, such as the right to work, the right to education, etc.

[351] Article 5, Convention on the Elimination of All Forms of Discrimination against Women.

[352] The Committee can receive individual complaints, after the entry into force, on 22 December 2000, of the Optional Protocol to the Convention on the Elimination of All Forms of Discrimination against Women, attached to General Assembly resolution 54/4, adopted 6 October 1999, UNDoc. A/RES/54/4. See United Nations, Treaty Series, vol. 2131, p. 83 et seq.

emphasizing particular problems and aspects. Examples include the Declaration on the Protection of Women and Children in Emergency and Armed Conflict,[353] the Geneva Declaration for Rural Women, which was adopted by the wives of heads of State and Government,[354] a resolution on women migrant workers,[355] the Declaration on the Elimination of Violence against Women,[356] and other more general declarations.[357] One of the most difficult tasks was to combat traditional practices in which the man played the dominant role in society, and which were therefore practices that were inconsistent with equal rights. Over the years the Assembly became increasingly confident in this respect. For example, in the declaration on the fight against domestic violence of 1990, the Assembly still felt it was necessary to state that it was "conscious that the complex problem of domestic violence [was] viewed differently in various cultures of different countries and that at the international level it must be addressed with sensitivity to the cultural context in each country."[358] Three years later, the Assembly proclaimed that "States should condemn violence against women and should not invoke any custom, tradition or religious consideration to avoid their obligations with respect to its elimination."[359]

## 5.4 Cultural particularities and human rights

Most religions and cultural traditions have embraced the value of human dignity in some way, but not all these traditions have used the language of human rights to put

---

[353] Declaration on the Protection of Women and Children in Emergency and Armed Conflict, General Assembly resolution 3318 (XXIX), adopted 14 December 1974. This Declaration was thus adopted prior to the adoption of the Convention.

[354] Geneva Declaration for Rural Women, adopted at the Summit on the Economic Advancement of Rural Women, held in Geneva, on 25 and 26 February 1992, UNDoc. A/47/308, distributed 2 July 1992. See also Summit on the Economic Advancement of Rural Women, General Assembly resolution 47/174, adopted 22 December 1992.

[355] Migrant women workers, General Assembly resolution 47/96, adopted 16 December 1992. In this resolution, the Assembly "expresse[d] grave concern over the plight of migrant women workers who become victims of physical, mental and sexual harassment and abuse."

[356] Declaration on the Elimination of Violence against Women, General Assembly resolution 48/104, adopted 20 December 1993. See also the Model Strategies and Practical Measures on the Elimination of Violence against Women in the Field of Crime Prevention and Criminal Justice, annexed to General Assembly resolution 52/86, adopted 12 December 1997.

[357] See especially the Beijing Declaration and Platform for Action, adopted at the Fourth World Conference on Women, which was held in Beijing between 4 and 15 September 1995, UNDoc. A/CONF.177/20/Rev.1, pp. 2-5, and the Political Declaration, General Assembly resolution S-23/2, adopted 10 June 2000. See also the Declaration on the Participation of Women in Promoting International Peace and Cooperation, annexed to General Assembly resolution 37/63, adopted 3 December 1982.

[358] Domestic violence, General Assembly resolution 45/114, adopted 14 December 1990.

[359] Article 4, Declaration on the Elimination of Violence against Women, General Assembly resolution 48/104, adopted 20 December 1993.

this value into practice. Most cultural traditions, notably those with strong religious foundations, have focused on the human *duties* towards the local community, not the human *rights* granted by that community to all individuals.[360] The emphasis on human *rights* is therefore a particular approach to ethics which is not universally shared. Objections are supported by the claim that the human rights discourse, as recognized in international law, has a particular rather than a global origin.[361]

In response, it could be argued that the language of human rights has *become* a global language, as revealed by the fact that human rights treaties have been universally ratified.[362] The few States that have failed to ratify the human rights treaties are bound anyway, as these norms have become customary international law.[363] This has been a slow and gradual development. Before 1948, there was probably not a single State that acted in accordance with the human rights proclaimed in the Universal Declaration.[364] Initially it was certainly not seen as the codification of existing State practice. However, societies have evolved since 1948, using the Declaration as their source of inspiration. By embracing human rights, and by adjusting State practice accordingly, States have adopted an approach which was entirely "new," in the most general sense of the term.

The universality of the internationally recognized catalogue of human rights is also questioned. According to the Assembly, all international human rights are based on a shared intuitive understanding of human dignity. In his opening

---

[360] See *e.g.*, Jack Donnelly, "Human Rights and Human Dignity: An Analytic Critique of Non-Western Conceptions of Human Rights" (1982); Rhoda E. Howard and Jack Donnelly, "Human Dignity, Human Rights, and Political Regimes" (1986), an article which was discussed in Neil Mitchell, Rhoda E. Howard, and Jack Donnelly, "Liberalism, Human Rights, and Human Dignity" (1987); John D'Arcy May, "Human Dignity, Human Rights, and Religious Pluralism: Buddhist and Christian Perspectives" (2006).

[361] Many attempts have been made to find one or more drafters of the Universal Declaration of Human Rights. Eleanor Roosevelt, who chaired the Commission, and Charles Malik, who was the Commission's Rapporteur, and René Cassin, who received the Nobel Peace Prize in 1968 and claimed to be the principal drafter himself, are often considered as the "masterminds" behind the declaration. Less often does one hear the name of John Humphrey, who was responsible for a first draft from the UN Secretariat. In reality, it was not the work of one person, but a collective effort. See *e.g.*, Mary Ann Glendon, "John P. Humphrey and the drafting of the Universal Declaration of Human Rights" (2000); Christopher McCrudden, "Human Dignity and Judicial Interpretation of Human Rights" (2008), pp. 676-677; and Andrew Woodcock, "Jacques Maritain, Natural Law and the Universal Declaration of Human Rights" (2006), pp. 246-248. Normand and Zaidi wished to point out that the Declaration was based almost entirely on "Western sources." See Roger Normand and Sarah Zaidi, *Human rights at the UN: the political history of universal justice* (2008), p. 195.

[362] Beitz also used this as "proof" of the universal acceptance of the link between human dignity and human rights. See Charles R. Beitz, "What Human Rights Mean" (2003), p. 45. Admittedly, some regions focus more on peoples' rights as opposed to individual human rights, but at the same time they do ratify all the relevant international treaties. See Jack Donnelly, "Human Rights and Human Dignity: An Analytic Critique of Non-Western Conceptions of Human Rights" (1982), pp. 311-313.

[363] Thomas Buergenthal, "The Evolving International Human Rights System" (2006), p. 790.

[364] See also Thomas M. Franck, "Are Human Rights Universal?" (2001), pp. 198-200.

statement to the Vienna Conference on Human Rights in 1993, the then UN Secretary-General Boutros Boutros-Ghali emphasized that the list of internationally recognized human rights was not a list of rights that all cultures almost accidentally or coincidentally found acceptable. Instead, the idea was to find what united us as human beings:

> Thus the human rights that we proclaim and seek to safeguard can be brought about only if we transcend ourselves, only if we make a conscious effort to find our common essence beyond our apparent divisions, our temporary differences, our ideological and cultural barriers. In sum, what I mean to say, with all solemnity, is that the human rights we are about to discuss here at Vienna are not the lowest common denominator among all nations, but rather what I should like to describe as the "irreducible human element," in other words, the quintessential values through which we affirm together that we are a single human community![365]

The Assembly has attempted to follow the same approach, basing all human rights directly on the value of human dignity. This is also what makes all human rights universally applicable, not the accidental fact that a particular right happens to be recognized globally.

The universality of human rights is still occasionally disputed.[366] Criticisms usually come from Governments which feel burdened by the formidable task of securing respect for and observance of the human rights of all their citizens. The universality of human rights is never disputed by those citizens themselves, as they mainly benefit from (international) human rights protection.[367] As Franck wrote, "it often turns out that oppressive practices defended by leaders of a culture, far from being pedigreed, are little more than the current self-interested preferences of a power elite."[368] Such Governments do not even bother to explain what the purpose would be of disregarding human rights. Instead, they simply refer to what they perceive as the particular values and traditions of the culture they claim to represent, and maintain that, in any case, all States have "a sovereign right to be let alone and not be judged by international human rights standards."[369]

---

[365] Boutros Boutros-Ghali at the Opening of the World Conference on Human Rights, 14 June 1993, UNDoc. A/CONF.157/22, p. 3.
[366] For a discussion, see *e.g.*, Christian Tomuschat, *Human rights: between idealism and realism* (2008), pp. 69-96; Peter R. Baehr, *De rechten van de mens: universaliteit in de praktijk* (1998), pp. 27-39; Robert C. Kelman, "The Conditions, Criteria, and Dialectics of Human Dignity" (1977), pp. 542-547.
[367] See Bertrand G. Ramcharan, *Contemporary human rights ideas* (2008), pp. 1-2. Ramcharan believed that it was mostly "dictators and social scientists" who criticized the universality of human rights. See *idem*, pp. 53-54. The quote is from a speech by a Senator of the Philippines, as cited in Ramcharan's book.
[368] Thomas M. Franck, "Are Human Rights Universal?" (2001), p. 197.
[369] *Idem*, p. 192.

To settle the universality debate once and for all, Ramcharan simply argued for a "democratic test of universality." The idea is simple, at least in theory: we just ask every single person in the world – instead of the officials who claim to represent them – if he or she would like to enjoy human rights, *i.e.* to live, to be free from torture, slavery, and genocide, to freely choose his or her religion, have an adequate standard of living, etc. The answer to all these questions is likely to be a resounding and consistent "yes." [370]

Such a global human rights referendum has not yet been organized. Thus politicians can continue the debate on the universality of human rights. The solution is in the form of a compromise: we distinguish a "hard core" of human rights, based directly on human dignity, and then leave the details to be filled in locally, in accordance with local customs and traditions. Li Peng, the Premier of the State Council of the People's Republic of China, explained in 1992 that "[t]he human rights and fundamental freedoms of all mankind should be universally respected," but he immediately added that "[i]n essence, the issue of human rights falls within the sovereignty of each country," and that "[a] country's human rights situation should not be judged in total disregard of its history and national conditions," and therefore that "[i]t is neither appropriate nor workable to demand that all countries measure up to the human rights criteria or models of one country or a small number of countries." [371] The way forward was "to engage in discussion and cooperation with other countries on an equal footing on the question of human rights on the basis of mutual understanding, mutual respect and seeking consensus, while reserving differences," and not to "interfere[…] in the internal affairs of other countries using the human rights issue as an excuse."[372]

The UN is not unsympathetic to this Chinese approach. The international community acknowledged the importance of local particularities in the Vienna Declaration, when it stated that "the significance of national and regional particularities and various historical, cultural and religious backgrounds must be borne in mind." At the same time, it was "the duty of States, regardless of their political, economic and cultural systems, to promote and protect all human rights and fundamental freedoms."[373]

In other resolutions, the Assembly called upon States to appreciate the cultural diversity in the world, and not to see this cultural diversity solely as a potential danger to the universal application of human rights. For example, in 1999

---

[370] Bertrand G. Ramcharan, *Contemporary human rights ideas* (2008), pp. 59 and 61.
[371] Verbatim Records of the 3046th meeting of the Security Council, 31 January 1992, UNDoc. S/PV.3046, pp. 92-93.
[372] *Idem*, pp. 92-93.
[373] Vienna Declaration and Programme of Action, para. 5. This was also the message of para. 1(d), Alternative approaches and ways and means within the United Nations system for improving the effective enjoyment of human rights and fundamental freedoms, General Assembly resolution 32/130, adopted 16 December 1977.

the Assembly "recognize[d] that respect for cultural diversity and the cultural rights of all" could "advanc[e] the application and enjoyment of universally accepted human rights across the world."[374] In 2001, it proclaimed the "promotion and protection of all human rights and fundamental freedoms and enrichment of common understanding of human rights" as one of the objectives of the global dialogue among civilizations.[375] As long as respect for cultural differences does not require actual violations of the internationally recognized human rights to be condoned, or require the rejection of certain categories of rights, the UN does not object.[376]

The debate about the universality of human rights is far from over. It is essentially about balancing respect for cultural and religious traditions and particularities, and respect for universally recognized human rights. Therefore Morsink was right when he wrote that "it is inevitable that a document like the Universal Declaration of Human Rights should raise questions about the possibility of there being universal values," and that "this questioning started before the document was even finished, has continued to this day, and will never end."[377]

## 5.5 Human rights in difficult times

It is in times of crisis that the protection of human rights is most crucial, but also the most difficult. Generally speaking, human rights cannot be set aside in such difficult times. At the same time, there is room for some flexibility. Most human rights are not absolute. They do not apply fully in time of "public emergency which threatens the life of the nation."[378] The principal exceptions to this general rule include the inherent right to life, the prohibition of torture and slavery, and the right to freedom of thought and religion.[379]

---

[374] Human rights and cultural diversity, General Assembly resolution 54/160, adopted 17 December 1999, para. 2.

[375] Article 2, Global Agenda for Dialogue among Civilizations, General Assembly resolution 56/6, adopted 9 November 2001. See also Promotion of religious and cultural understanding, harmony and cooperation, General Assembly resolution 58/128, adopted 19 December 2003.

[376] See also Bertrand G. Ramcharan, *Contemporary human rights ideas* (2008), p. 56. Beitz's view was different. He distinguished certain rights that constituted a "common core" of global morality, or a more or less accidental "overlapping consensus" of all the cultural traditions in this world, from the remaining human rights. However, he believed that even the remaining rights, which were by definition partisan, could be promoted on the global level, as long as this was done through international institutions (the UN). See Charles R. Beitz, "Human Rights as a Common Concern" (2001).

[377] Johannes Morsink, *The Universal Declaration of Human Rights: Origins, Drafting, and Intent* (1999), p. ix.

[378] See Article 4(1), International Covenant on Civil and Political Rights.

[379] See *idem*, Article 4(2).

One of the most dramatic public emergencies is a state of armed conflict. It is true that humanitarian law protects individuals who find themselves in the middle of an armed conflict.[380] Nevertheless, the Assembly has consistently held that humanitarian law was not intended to replace human rights law in times of armed conflict. In a resolution entitled Respect for Human Rights in Armed Conflicts adopted in 1968, the Assembly affirmed the following three basic humanitarian principles:

> That the right of the parties to a conflict to adopt means of injuring the enemy is not unlimited;

> That it is prohibited to launch attacks against the civilian populations as such;

> That a distinction must be made at all times between persons taking part in the hostilities and members of the civilian population to the effect that the latter be spared as much as possible.[381]

These principles did not contain any reference to human rights, and thus the resolution itself did not do justice to its title. The opposite applies to a resolution entitled Basic Principles for the Protection of Civilian Populations in Armed Conflicts, adopted in 1970.[382] Although the title did not refer to human rights, the first basic principle stated that "fundamental human rights, as accepted in international law and laid down in international instruments, continue to apply fully in situations of armed conflict."[383] It could not be put more simply than that.

This approach was further elaborated upon in subsequent resolutions and declarations. For example, in the Assembly's Declaration on the Protection of Women and Children in Emergency and Armed Conflict, the Assembly emphasized that "women and children belonging to the civilian population and finding themselves in circumstances of emergency and armed conflict [...] shall not be deprived of shelter, food, medical aid or other inalienable [human] rights."[384] Much later, in 1999, the Security Council also stressed in general terms, the need for

---

[380] Since the United Nations has not played a major role in the development of humanitarian law, this will not be discussed extensively in this study.

[381] Respect for Human Rights in Armed Conflicts, General Assembly resolution 2444 (XXIII), adopted 19 December 1968.

[382] Basic Principles for the Protection of Civilian Populations in Armed Conflicts, General Assembly resolution 2675 (XXV), adopted 9 December 1970.

[383] *Idem*, Principle 1.

[384] Declaration on the Protection of Women and Children in Emergency and Armed Conflict, General Assembly resolution 3318 (XXIX), adopted 14 December 1974, para. 6. The rights explicitly referred to were all human rights, *i.e.* they were those contained in the Universal Declaration of Human Rights, the International Covenant on Civil and Political Rights, the International Covenant on Economic, Social and Cultural Rights, and the Declaration of the Rights of the Child.

States engaged in armed conflict, to continue to respect the human rights of the civilian population trapped in that armed conflict.[385] In 2008, the Council adopted a resolution on sexual violence during armed conflict.[386] In that resolution, the Council "recogniz[ed] that States bear primary responsibility to respect and ensure the human rights of their citizens, as well as all individuals within their territory as provided for by relevant international law."[387]

Another public emergency posing a threat to human rights protection is the fight against terrorism. In order to remind all States that this fight did not allow them to disregard human rights law, the Assembly adopted a number of resolutions on the relationship between human rights and terrorism. In a resolution of 1993, the Assembly "unequivocally condemn[ed] all acts, methods and practices of terrorism in all its forms and manifestations, wherever and by whomever committed, as activities aimed at the destruction of human rights."[388] It also "call[ed] upon States, in accordance with international standards of human rights, to take all necessary and effective measures to prevent, combat and eliminate terrorism."[389] Terrorism itself was seen as an attack on human rights. At the same time, certain ways of combating terrorism were also considered as attacks on human rights. As the fight against terrorism increased in intensity, the latter aspect was increasingly emphasized. For example, in a resolution adopted in 1995, the Assembly added, in the preamble, that "all measures to counter terrorism must be in strict conformity with international human rights standards."[390] In 2002, one year after the terrorist attacks on the World Trade Center and the Pentagon, the Assembly focused almost exclusively on the latter aspect. The warning referred to above was promoted from the preamble to the principal paragraph of the resolution, and the High Commissioner for Human Rights was asked to examine the protection of human rights in the fight against terrorism.[391] In 2005, the Assembly, "deeply deploring the occurrence of violations of human rights and fundamental freedoms in the context of the fight against terrorism," "reaffirm[ed] that it [was] imperative that all States work to uphold and

---

[385] Security Council resolution 1265 (1999), adopted 17 September 1999. On 23 December 2006, the Security Council also adopted resolution 1738 (2006), on the protection of journalists during armed conflict.

[386] Security Council resolution 1820 (2008), adopted 19 June 2008.

[387] *Idem*, Preamble. See also Security Council resolution 1960 (2010), adopted 16 December 2010.

[388] Human rights and terrorism, General Assembly resolution 48/122, adopted 20 December 1993, para. 1.

[389] *Idem*, para. 2.

[390] Preamble, General Assembly resolution 50/186, adopted 22 December 1995.

[391] See Protecting human rights and fundamental freedoms while countering terrorism, General Assembly resolution 57/219, adopted 18 December 2002, para. 1. One year later, the Security Council adopted a declaration on combating terrorism, which focused more on finding means to effectively fight terrorism than on human rights protection in the process, but it did refer – only once - to States' obligations to respect human rights. Para. 6, Declaration on the issue of combating terrorism, annexed to Security Council resolution 1456 (2003), adopted 20 January 2003.

protect the dignity of individuals and their fundamental freedoms [...] while countering terrorism."[392] In 2007, the Assembly expressed its concern about certain measures that it believed were inconsistent with human rights. These measures included the detention of alleged terrorists in places outside the protection of the law, and the return of alleged terrorists to countries without assessing whether this would put them at risk of being tortured. The Assembly urged States to stop using such measures in the fight against terrorism.[393]

The Organization itself, and especially the Security Council, has also been criticized for the way it deals with the terrorist threat.[394] Most importantly, the Council was blamed for imposing economic sanctions against individuals believed to be involved in terrorist activities, but these individuals had no possibility to challenge this determination. Various corrective measures were adopted by the United Nations Security Council in response to such criticism. These include a delisting procedure for individuals who object to the Council's conclusion that they are supporting terrorist activities, and the appointment of an Ombudsperson.[395]

## 5.6 Conclusion

Human rights are universal. They provide a legal safety net covering all the world's citizens, wherever they are, in whatever situation they find themselves. The Assembly has explicitly prohibited all forms of discrimination based on race and sex. Any such discrimination is considered, by definition, to be a violation of the duty to promote and respect the human rights of all individuals. This part of the universality thesis is generally unchallenged.

The universality thesis has been questioned when it comes to particular rights in the human rights catalogue. It has been suggested that some rights are not universal, or that the emphasis on individual *rights* – as opposed to *duties* towards the community – does not correspond well with all cultural traditions. In response, it is argued that all human rights flow directly from the value of human dignity itself, and that this value is, in various ways, embraced by all cultural traditions. It is also argued that the catalogue of human rights is flexible enough to allow room for a context-dependent interpretation, and that the core of all human rights norms

---

[392] Protection of human rights and fundamental freedoms while countering terrorism, General Assembly resolution 60/158, adopted 16 December 2005.

[393] Protection of human rights and fundamental freedoms while countering terrorism, General Assembly resolution 62/159, adopted 18 December 2007.

[394] See *e.g.*, Nico Schrijver & Larissa van den Herik, "Leiden Policy Recommendations on Counter-Terrorism and International Law" (2010); Nico Schrijver & Larissa van den Herik, "Eroding the Primacy of the UN System of Collective Security: the Judgment of the European Court of Justice in the Cases of Kadi and Al Barakaat" (2008).

[395] See Security Council resolution 1904, adopted 17 December 2009, UNDoc S/RES/1904 (2009).

corresponds well with all of the world's cultural traditions. In other words, "universality does not mean uniformity."[396]

Finally, there was an examination of the resolutions and declarations dealing with the argument that in times of crisis human rights protection should be set aside. Generally speaking, the Assembly has rejected such arguments, even as regards the situation of armed conflict or the fight against terrorism. Thus the Assembly has sought to protect the universality of human rights, also in times of crisis. Human rights apply at all times, in all circumstances.

## 6    HUMAN RIGHTS OF PARTICULARLY VULNERABLE GROUPS

### 6.1 Introduction

Individuals with relatively little power to stand up for their own rights are the most vulnerable to abuse.[397] To avoid such abuse, the Assembly wanted to ensure "the protection of the rights and the assuring of the welfare of children, the aged and the disabled," and "the provision of protection for the physically or mentally disadvantaged."[398] The following sections examine the protection of the human dignity and rights of these most vulnerable groups. The general idea is that like all other human beings, individuals belonging to such vulnerable groups are entitled to all human rights. They do not have more or fewer rights than other individuals. However, to enjoy the same rights as everyone else, they need – and are entitled to – extra protection.

### 6.2 Children and elderly people

In the first year of its existence, the General Assembly established an International Children's Emergency Fund (UNICEF), to be "utilized for the benefit of children and adolescents of countries which were the victims of aggression."[399] UNICEF soon extended its operations to aiding all children in need.[400]

---

[396] See *e.g.*, Advisory Council on International Affairs of the Netherlands, *Universality of Human Rights: Principles, Practice and Prospects* (2008), p. 19.

[397] See also Roberto Andorno, "The paradoxial notion of human dignity" (2001), p. 159.

[398] Article 11, Declaration on Social Progress and Development, General Assembly resolution 2542 (XXIV), adopted 11 December 1969.

[399] Establishment of an International Children's Emergency Fund, General Assembly resolution 57(I), adopted 11 December 1946. UNICEF got the Nobel Peace Prize in 1965.

[400] See Continuing needs of children, General Assembly resolution 417 (V), adopted 1 December 1950, and United Nations Children's Fund, General Assembly resolution 802 (VIII) , adopted 6 October 1953.

The Universal Declaration stated that "childhood [was] entitled to special care and assistance," and that "all children, whether born in or out of wedlock, [should] enjoy the same social protection."[401]

In 1959, the Assembly adopted the Declaration of the Rights of the Child.[402] In this declaration, it acknowledged that "the child, by reason of his physical and mental immaturity, need[ed] special safeguards and care, including appropriate legal protection." The Assembly proclaimed that "the child shall enjoy special protection, and shall be given opportunities and facilities, by law and by other means, to enable him to develop physically, mentally, morally, spiritually and socially in a healthy and normal manner and in conditions of freedom and dignity." [403] The Declaration also stated that a child needed "love and understanding," and that, generally, his own parents were the best people to provide this.[404] The Declaration did not go so far as to proclaim a right of the child to a family. The Draft Declaration on Social and Legal Principles relating to the Protection and Welfare of Children states that "every child has a right to a family," preferably the biological family. In cases where this is not possible for some reason, adoption by another family, or temporary placement in a foster family, is also considered a possibility.[405] This sentence was removed from the final version of the declaration.[406]

In 1989, the Assembly, "convinced that an international convention on the rights of the child [...] would make a positive contribution to protecting children's rights and ensuring their well-being," adopted the text of the Convention on the Rights of the Child.[407] Although the text of the Convention is long and detailed, many of the key issues have not been resolved. For example, children were defined as "human being[s] below the age of eighteen years unless under the law applicable to the child, majority is attained earlier." [408] Therefore there was no universal agreement about when a child ceases to be a child. The Assembly also avoided the

---

[401] Article 25, Universal Declaration of Human Rights.

[402] Declaration of the Rights of the Child, General Assembly resolution 1386 (XIV), adopted 20 November 1959.

[403] *Idem*, Principle 2.

[404] *Idem*, Principle 6.

[405] Draft Declaration annexed to General Assembly resolution 36/167, adopted 16 December 1981, para. 7.

[406] Declaration on Social and Legal Principles relating to the Protection and Welfare of Children, with Special Reference to Foster Placement and Adoption Nationally and Internationally, annexed to General Assembly resolution 41/85, adopted 3 December 1986.

[407] Convention on the Rights of the Child, annexed to General Assembly resolution 44/25, adopted 20 November 1989. The Convention entered into force on 2 September 1990. United Nations, Treaty Series, vol. 1577, p. 3.

[408] *Idem*, Article 1.

problematic question of when a child comes into being,[409] and refrained from explicitly proclaiming the child's right to a family. It was, however, very explicit about prohibiting the imposition of the death penalty for offences committed by persons below the age of eighteen, regardless of whether such persons were considered to be children according to domestic law.[410]

Since the adoption of the Convention, the United Nations has continued to adopt declarations to keep the world's attention focused on the rights of the child. The General Assembly has been assisted in this task by a number of world conferences organized by the UN, resulting in declarations such as the World Declaration on the Survival, Protection and Development of Children.[411] Reference could also be made to A World Fit for Children, a declaration in which the world pledged to "respect the dignity and to secure the well-being of all children."[412] Others focused on particular situations, such as the plight of street children,[413] child prostitution and pornography,[414] and children in armed conflict.[415] The Security Council has adopted a few general resolutions on this last issue.[416]

Old age is a matter of concern at the other end of life. This became a hot topic especially in the 1990s.[417] In 1991, the Assembly adopted the United Nations

---

[409] See also Philip Alston, "Unborn Child and Abortion under the Draft Convention on the Rights of the Child" (1990).

[410] Article 37, Convention on the Rights of the Child.

[411] World Declaration on the Survival, Protection and Development of Children, adopted at the World Summit for Children, held in New York on 30 September 1990, UNDoc. A/45/625, distributed 18 October 1990. The aim was essentially to work together in order to "to give every child a better future" (para. 1). According to the declaration, "the children of the world [were] innocent, vulnerable and dependent," and "their time should be one of joy and peace, of playing, learning and growing" (para. 2). To accomplish this, the States committed themselves to a list of very generally formulated tasks.

[412] A world fit for children, annexed to General Assembly resolution S-27/2, adopted 10 May 2002, para. 4. See also the objective to "leave no child behind," which is defined as: "each girl and boy is born free and equal in dignity and rights; therefore, all forms of discrimination affecting children must end" (para. 7). See also the Declaration of the commemorative high-level plenary meeting devoted to the follow-up to the outcome of the special session on children, General Assembly resolution 62/88, adopted 13 December 2007, in which various commitments were reaffirmed.

[413] Plight of street children, General Assembly resolution 47/126, adopted 18 December 1992.

[414] Need to adopt efficient international measures for the prevention of the sale of children, child prostitution and child pornography, General Assembly resolution 48/156, adopted 20 December 1993. This ultimately led to the Optional Protocol to the Convention on the Rights of the Child on the sale of children, child prostitution and child pornography, annexed to General Assembly resolution 54/263, adopted 25 May 2000. It entered into force on 18 January 2002.

[415] Protection of children affected by armed conflicts, General Assembly resolution 48/157, adopted 20 December 1993. This ultimately led to the Optional Protocol to the Convention on the Rights of the Child on the involvement of children in armed conflict, also annexed to General Assembly resolution 54/263, adopted 25 May 2000. This protocol entered into force on 12 February 2002.

[416] Security Council resolution 1261 (1999), adopted 25 August 1999. The Council usually deals with specific conflicts, not general and abstract issues.

[417] In 1982, the Assembly already "endorsed" the Vienna International Plan of Action on Ageing. See Question of aging, General Assembly resolution 37/51, adopted 3 December 1982.

Principles for Older Persons.[418] Aware of the fact that "in all countries, individuals are reaching an advanced age in greater numbers and in better health than ever before," it encouraged States to incorporate certain principles in their domestic policy to ensure the independence of the elderly, their continued participation and integration in the community, their access to health care and other forms of care, their access to resources and opportunities for their continued development, and respect for their inherent dignity. With regard to dignity, the principles stated that "older persons should be able to enjoy human rights and fundamental freedoms when residing in any shelter, care or treatment facility, including full respect for their dignity, beliefs, needs and privacy and for the right to make decisions about their care and the quality of their lives," and that they "should be able to live in dignity and security and be free of exploitation and physical or mental abuse."[419]

In 1992, the Assembly adopted a Proclamation on Ageing.[420] In this resolution, it used very strong words to stress the acute nature of the problem. For example, it referred to the "unprecedented ageing of populations taking place throughout the world," and the "revolutionary change in the demographic structure of societies," which required a "fundamental change in the way in which societies organize their affairs."[421] As part of the solution, it urged the international community, *inter alia*, to support national initiatives on ageing so that, among many other goals, "older persons [were] viewed as contributors to their societies and not as a burden."[422]

## 6.3 Persons with disabilities

In 1971, the Assembly proclaimed that "the mentally retarded person ha[d], to the maximum degree of feasibility, the same rights as other human beings."[423] The general aim of the Declaration on the Rights of Mentally Retarded Persons was to emphasize the "necessity of assisting mentally retarded persons to develop their abilities in various fields of activities and of promoting their integration as far as possible in normal life."[424] Therefore they had a right to medical care, to a decent

---

[418] United Nations Principles for Older Persons, annexed to Implementation of the International Plan of Action on Ageing and related activities, General Assembly resolution 46/91, adopted 16 December 1991.

[419] *Idem*, paras. 14 and 17. Para. 18 added that "older persons should be treated fairly regardless of age, gender, racial or ethnic background, disability or other status, and be valued independently of their economic contribution."

[420] Proclamation on Ageing, annexed to General Assembly resolution 47/5, adopted 16 October 1992.

[421] *Idem*, Preamble.

[422] *Idem*, Article 2(d).

[423] Para. 1, Declaration on the Rights of Mentally Retarded Persons, General Assembly resolution 2856 (XXVI), adopted 20 December 1971. The Declaration did not define the term "mentally retarded."

[424] *Idem*, Preamble.

standard of living, and a right to work as far as their capabilities allowed them to do so.[425]

In 1991, the Assembly adopted the Principles for the Protection of Persons with Mental Illness and the Improvement of Mental Health Care.[426] It proclaimed that "all persons with a mental illness, or who are being treated as such persons, shall be treated with humanity and respect for the inherent dignity of the human person."[427] The Assembly also emphasized that persons with a mental illness had the right to exercise all internationally recognized human rights, and had the right to "live and work, to the extent possible, in the community."[428]

The Assembly did not limit itself to mentally retarded persons and people suffering from mental illness. In 1975, the General Assembly adopted a Declaration on the Rights of Disabled Persons.[429] The term "disabled person" was defined

As any person unable to ensure by himself or herself, wholly or partly, the necessities of a normal individual and/or social life, as a result of deficiency, either congenital or not, in his or her physical or mental capabilities.[430]

Thus it also included the category of *mentally* retarded persons. According to the Declaration, "disabled persons ha[d] the inherent right to respect for their human dignity," which meant in practice that "disabled persons, whatever the origin, nature and seriousness of their handicaps and disabilities, ha[d] the same fundamental rights as their fellow-citizens of the same age, which implie[d] first and foremost the right to enjoy a decent life, as normal and full as possible."[431]

In 1993, serious steps had already been taken towards drawing up a convention on disabilities. Initially, the proposal for this convention failed to materialize because "in the opinion of many representatives, existing human rights documents guaranteed persons with disabilities the same rights as other persons."[432] Therefore as a first step, the Assembly adopted a set of Standard Rules on the Equalization of Opportunities for Persons with Disabilities.[433] These rules were not legally binding as such, but the idea was that they would become customary

---

[425] See *idem*, Articles 2 and 3.
[426] Principles for the protection of persons with mental illness and the improvement of mental health care, General Assembly resolution 46/119, adopted 17 December 1991.
[427] *Idem*, Principle 1(2).
[428] *Idem*, Principle 1(5) and 3.
[429] Declaration on the Rights of Disabled Persons, General Assembly resolution 3447 (XXX), adopted 9 December 1975.
[430] *Idem*, Article 1.
[431] *Idem*, Article 3.
[432] Para. 9, Standard rules on the equalization of opportunities for persons with disabilities, annexed to General Assembly resolution 48/96, adopted 20 December 1993.
[433] *Idem*.

international law.[434] The purpose of the rules was "to ensure that girls, boys, women and men with disabilities, as members of their societies, may exercise the same rights and obligations as others."[435] This purpose could be achieved through the equalization of opportunities, a process which was described as "the process through which the various systems of society and the environment, such as services, activities, information and documentation, are made available to all, particularly to persons with disabilities."[436]

Despite the initial hesitations, the Assembly adopted the Convention on the Rights of Persons with Disabilities in 2006.[437] The purpose of this Convention was to "promote, protect and ensure the full and equal enjoyment of all human rights and fundamental freedoms by all persons with disabilities, and to promote respect for their inherent dignity."[438] Unlike many other human rights conventions, this Convention elaborated on human dignity, by declaring as one of the general principles the "respect for inherent dignity, individual autonomy including the freedom to make one's own choices, and independence of [all] persons."[439] The Convention did not contain a definition of "disability." It mainly consisted of a list of already recognized human rights, such as the right to be free from torture, the right to life, liberty, and security of person, the right to education, health, work, and an adequate standard of living, all of which were adapted to the special needs of disabled people. A Committee on the Rights of Persons with Disabilities was established to monitor the promotion and respect of the rights contained in the Convention.[440]

The category of disabled persons is substantial. In 1982, the Assembly estimated that "no less than five hundred million persons are estimated to suffer from disability of one form or another, of whom four hundred million are estimated to be in developing countries."[441] About ten years later, the Assembly noted that "the number of persons with disabilities in the world [was] large and [was] growing."[442] This is still the case, approximately fifteen years later. In 2009, the

---

[434] *Idem*, para. 14.
[435] *Idem*, para. 15. In para. 16, disabled persons were defined as people suffering from various "functional limitations."
[436] *Idem*, para. 24.
[437] Convention on the Rights of Persons with Disabilities, annexed to General Assembly resolution 61/106, adopted 13 December 2006.
[438] *Idem*, Article 1.
[439] *Idem*, Article 3(a).
[440] Optional Protocol to the Convention on the Rights of Persons with Disabilities, attached to General Assembly resolution 61/106, adopted 13 December 2006, UNDoc. A/RES/61/106. The protocol entered into force 3 May 2008, and allows the Committee to receive individual complaints.
[441] Preamble, World Programme of Action concerning Disabled Persons, General Assembly resolution 37/52, adopted 3 December 1982.
[442] Standard rules on the equalization of opportunities for persons with disabilities, annexed to General Assembly resolution 48/96, adopted 20 December 1993, para. 1.

World Health Organization estimated that there were about 650 million people with disabilities in the world, which is approximately ten per cent of the world's population.[443] 80 per cent of these people live in developing countries.[444]

## 6.4 Migrants, minorities and indigenous peoples

Some individuals are vulnerable to human rights abuses because they are part of a particular group. This applies especially for foreign migrants, and individuals belonging to a minority or an indigenous population. The Assembly regarded the protection of these individuals as essentially a human rights issue, meaning that the protection granted to these groups was granted, not just to the group itself, but above all to the individuals in that group. Essentially this meant that individual migrants, individuals of minority groups, and individuals of the indigenous population were granted special protection. As soon as a minority group or a group of indigenous people can be qualified as a "people," such groups have a right of self-determination. In that sense, the protection of such groups goes beyond the protection of the human dignity of the individuals comprising that group.[445]

In 1990, the Assembly signalled a need to "ensure the human rights and dignity of all migrant workers and their families." It adopted the International Convention on the Protection of the Rights of all Migrant Workers and Members of Their Families.[446] The Convention defined a "migrant worker" as a person "engaged in a remunerated activity in a State of which he or she is not a national."[447] The Convention not only emphasized that migrants had human rights just like anyone else, but it also sought to provide special protection for such individuals.[448]

---

[443] See World Health Organization's World Report on Disability and Rehabilitation, available on its website: http://www.who.int/disabilities/publications/concept_note_2009.pdf.

[444] Realizing the Millennium Development Goals for persons with disabilities through the implementation of the World Programme of Action concerning Disabled Persons and the Convention on the Rights of Persons with Disabilities, General Assembly resolution 63/150, adopted 18 December 2008.

[445] This will be discussed in Chapter VII on self-determination of peoples, section on minority groups (4.5).

[446] International Convention on the Protection of the Rights of all Migrant Workers and Members of Their Families, General Assembly resolution 45/158, adopted 18 December 1990. Already in the 1970s, the Assembly adopted resolutions on the violation of the human dignity of foreign immigrants, in Europe and elsewhere. See *e.g.*, Exploitation of labour through illicit and clandestine trafficking, General Assembly resolution 2920 (XXVII), adopted 15 November 1972; and, specifically on migrant workers, Measures to improve the situation and ensure the human rights and dignity of all migrant workers, General Assembly resolution 32/120, adopted 16 December 1977.

[447] Article 2, International Convention on the Protection of the Rights of all Migrant Workers.

[448] It thus listed the already recognized human rights, but described them as they applied to the particular situation of the migrant worker. In doing so, the Convention made a distinction between migrants that were "authorized to enter, to stay and to engage in a remunerated activity in the State of

The Assembly's concern with the plight of minorities ultimately led to the adoption in 1992 of a Declaration on the Rights of Persons Belonging to National or Ethnic, Religious or Linguistic Minorities. [449] According to this declaration, "persons belonging to national or ethnic, religious and linguistic minorities [had] the right to enjoy their own culture, to profess and practice their own religion, and to use their own language, in private and in public, freely and without interference or any form of discrimination."[450] This Declaration followed the provision in the International Covenant on Civil and Political Rights, which stated that "in those States in which ethnic, religious or linguistic minorities exist, persons belonging to such minorities shall not be denied the right, in community with the other members of their group, to enjoy their own culture, to profess and practice their own religion, or to use their own language."[451]

In 2007, the Assembly adopted the United Nations Declaration on the Rights of Indigenous Peoples. [452] Although the Assembly had referred to the plight of indigenous peoples in earlier resolutions, the adoption of this Declaration in 2007 showed the increased interest there had been in the issue in recent years. [453] Like any other human rights declaration, the Declaration stressed that indigenous peoples had a right to have their dignity respected, and that they were entitled to enjoy their human rights just like anyone else. [454] Although the declaration described its own provisions as "minimum standards for the survival, dignity and well-being of the indigenous peoples of the world," the declaration was rather extensive and went much further than merely the protection of the human rights of the individuals belonging to such indigenous peoples. [455] It provided all kinds of special rights and

---

employment" and those that were not so authorized. Although the former group had some more extensive rights, the most basic human rights applied to all migrant workers. Compare Part IV: Other Rights of Migrant Workers and Members of their Families who are Documented or in a Regular Situation with Part III: Human Rights of All Migrant Workers and Members of their Families of the International Convention on the Protection of the Rights of all Migrant Workers

[449] Declaration on the Rights of Persons Belonging to National or Ethnic, Religious or Linguistic Minorities, annexed to General Assembly resolution 47/135, adopted 18 December 1992.

[450] *Idem*, Article 2.

[451] International Covenant on Civil and Political Rights, Article 27.

[452] United Nations Declaration on the Rights of Indigenous Peoples, General Assembly resolution 61/295, adopted 13 September 2007 ("Declaration on the Rights of Indigenous Peoples").

[453] Apart from paragraphs in more general resolutions about racism and racial discrimination, the International Year for the World's Indigenous People, General Assembly resolution 46/128, adopted 17 December 1991, can also be referred to, to which was annexed the Programme of Activities for the International Year for the World's Indigenous People; International Decade of the World's Indigenous People, General Assembly resolution 48/163, adopted 21 December 1993, and the Programme of activities for the International Decade of the World's Indigenous People, annexed to General Assembly resolution 50/157, adopted 21 December 1995. See also para. 20, Vienna Declaration and Programme of Action.

[454] See Declaration on the Rights of Indigenous Peoples, especially Articles 1, 2, and 15.

[455] *Idem*, Article 43.

privileges to indigenous peoples as a group so that they could maintain their traditional way of life and develop their cultural heritage.[456]

## 6.5 Conclusion

Certain groups are particularly vulnerable to human rights abuses, and are in particular need of assistance to enable them to enjoy their human rights. This applies to children and elderly people, but also to persons with disabilities. The Disabilities Convention in particular made an explicit link with the global value of human dignity. The special protection of various groups of individuals who were particularly vulnerable to human rights abuses was also examined, including migrants, minorities and indigenous peoples. The special protection of all vulnerable groups gives extra meaning to the value of human dignity by emphasizing the universal applicability of the value, and by showing that the implementation of this value requires different actions, depending on the vulnerability of the individuals concerned to attacks on their human dignity.

Various declarations and conventions appear to grant certain human rights only to one particular group of persons. Such a selective approach is in conflict with the idea that all human beings have the same entitlements. A closer look at the description of the rights granted to specific groups in these documents shows that the vulnerable groups are not granted any new rights at all. What is new is the obligation of States to make an extra effort to ensure that persons belonging to vulnerable groups can enjoy their human rights, just like everyone else. The child has the right to be part of a family, but so do adults. The difference is that the child is much more vulnerable, and needs special care. The elderly have the right to healthcare, but so do young people. The disabled have the right to an adequate standard of living, but so does everyone else. And persons belonging to ethnic minorities have the right to enjoy their own culture, just like persons belonging to the ethnic majority. Most importantly, all vulnerable groups have the right to respect for their intrinsic human dignity, just like everyone else. The difference is that States must make an extra effort to ensure such respect for particularly vulnerable persons.

---

[456] The Declaration on the Rights of Indigenous Peoples listed a number of human rights, most of which were collective rights, which can be enjoyed only by the group of indigenous people, not by indigenous individuals acting in isolation. This makes it an unusual human rights declaration. Even the Declaration on the Rights of Persons Belonging to National or Ethnic, Religious or Linguistic Minorities does not share this characteristic.

## 7 CONCLUSION

A world in which the intrinsic human dignity of all the world's citizens is respected and secured is a better world for all. During the Second World War, entire groups of people were dehumanized, and this showed the importance of universal respect for the global value of human dignity. Just after the war, there was some dispute about the exact interpretation of the value, and there were heated debates about the best way to secure its promotion and respect. But there was no objection to the value itself. The basic idea, that all human beings had to be treated with dignity, precisely because they were human beings, was universally accepted.

At the same time, without further elaboration, the idea that human beings have to be treated with dignity seems rather meaningless. Therefore the United Nations took it upon itself to draw up a list of specific entitlements based on the value of human dignity: a list of human rights. In San Francisco, it was decided to postpone the task of codifying a list of universal rights. Once the General Assembly had been established it started to work on this grandiose task. It began by listing the entitlements that arise from the value of human dignity. It used its resolutions to issue declarations, listing the human rights that can be derived directly from the value of human dignity. These declarations have almost all been transformed into multilateral treaties, which significantly increased their capacity to motivate action. These human rights have proved to be flexible enough to cope with the changing times.

The development and codification of the catalogue of human rights and the promotion of universal respect for human dignity have been one of the biggest success stories of the United Nations, when it comes to promoting and developing ideas. Initially the main source of these ideas was the United Nations Commission on Human Rights. Its ideas were often adopted by the international community as a whole through Assembly resolutions, and even international treaties. After several successful years in which the Commission focused on the codification of human rights, it was much less successful at promoting compliance with these rights, and it was subsequently abolished and replaced by the Human Rights Council.

The main aim of this chapter was to show that the value of human dignity, albeit without explicit definition, was used as the foundation for all human rights. This has been the approach of the Assembly since the very beginning, and it has also been embraced in scholarly (philosophical) literature.

The catalogue of human rights was first presented in the Universal Declaration of Human Rights adopted in 1948, and was elaborated in more detail by the Assembly as time progressed. Human rights were divided into four separate subcategories: personal freedom, the freedom to associate with others, spiritual freedom, and the freedom to secure for oneself an adequate standard of living. What all these rights had in common was their foundation in human dignity.

Furthermore, it was shown that the fact that human rights could be derived from the value of human dignity, also had as a logical consequence that human rights were universal, in the sense that they applied to all human beings, everywhere, and in all situations. This in turn led to the conclusion that no distinction could be made on the basis of race or gender, and that human rights continued to apply, even in situations of armed conflict, and even during the fight against terrorism. Nevertheless, it was suggested that some room should be provided for local cultures to integrate human rights in their particular policies, and that local communities should have some flexibility in doing so. The slogan "universality does not mean uniformity" is often used in this context. It does not follow from the universality of human rights that there cannot be any differences whatsoever in the practical implementation of these rights.[457]

Finally, this chapter looked at the work of the Assembly in promoting special protection for particularly vulnerable groups, such as children, the elderly and disabled people. The Assembly based the need of these groups for special protection explicitly on human dignity. The same can be said for the special protection of various groups of individuals who are particularly vulnerable to human rights abuses, such as migrants, minorities and indigenous peoples.

Although the UN General Assembly never defined the value of human dignity, the frequent references to it have provided sufficient ammunition for some scholars to work with. The UN has made it clear that it regards human dignity as something inherent. All human beings are automatically entitled to universal respect for their inherent dignity. The Assembly also related the value of human dignity to individual autonomy, the freedom of individual people to make choices that determine the course of their own lives. As early as 1948, the Assembly stated that all human beings were born free and equal in dignity. The list of rights provides further hints of exactly what the UN believed the value of human dignity to entail. All in all, the Assembly has been relatively outspoken on the subject of human dignity. Some scholars have used these UN documents as the basis for their reflections on human dignity and human rights. The UN can use this scholarly work for a better understanding of the value it helped to create, and to guarantee coherence in the expansion of the human rights catalogue. The cross-fertilization between the UN and scholarship on the value of human dignity can encourage the UN to become more outspoken in its treatment of the other values. Scholarly discussion of a particular value, both within and outside the UN assembly halls, could also contribute to the UN's more practical work. It can improve the coherence of the many action plans, and guarantee a certain unity in the Organization's daily work.

---

[457] See *e.g.*, Advisory Council on International Affairs of the Netherlands, *Universality of Human Rights: Principles, Practice and Prospects* (2008), p. 19.

# THE SELF-DETERMINATION OF PEOPLES

## 1 INTRODUCTION

The United Nations is established, *inter alia*, to "develop friendly relations among nations based on respect for the principle of equal rights and self-determination of peoples."[1] This is one of the most ambiguously formulated purposes in the UN Charter. It has served as the constitutional basis for all the UN's work on promoting the value of self-determination of peoples.

Most of this chapter takes that phrase as its starting point, and then discusses General Assembly resolutions and other international legal instruments that describe the principle of equal rights and self-determination of peoples in more detail. The resolutions on the process of decolonization are examined first. This is where the principle has been applied most frequently and most successfully.

Secondly, the application of the right to self-determination to *all* peoples is examined. It is here that the need for philosophical guidance is most urgent, especially with regard to the definition of the word "peoples." Applying the right to self-determination to their own situation, various minorities have claimed "internal" self-determination, *i.e.* a democratic system in which they can play a meaningful role, and "external" self-determination, *i.e.* a right to secede from their State, and begin their own State. Philosophers have followed this trend in international law since the early 1990s, and the controversial issue of secession quickly changed from a "forgotten problem of political philosophy" into one of the more popular topics for philosophers to think about. The same happened to the philosophical thinking about self-determination in general.[2]

The principle of self-determination can also be applied to States, and be used as the basis of the principle of sovereign independence. The claim that the right to self-determination of peoples should be considered as a human right is also discussed.

---

[1] Article 1(2), UN Charter. This phrase is repeated in Article 55.
[2] The quote is from Harry Beran, "A liberal theory of secession" (1984), p. 21. See p. 23 for self-determination itself. His article was one of the earlier ones. Most other articles appeared after the dissolution of the Soviet Union and Yugoslavia, in the 1990s. See *e.g.*, Allen E. Buchanan, "Toward a Theory of Secession" (1991), which also noted the lack of philosophical interest in the issue, even by the classical philosophers (see especially p. 323).

## 2  THE SELF-DETERMINATION OF PEOPLES IN SAN FRANCISCO

### 2.1  The self-determination of peoples

*2.1.1 The Preamble*

There is nothing about self-determination, self-government, or independence of peoples in the Preamble. Since Smuts was not only the mastermind behind the Preamble, but also a highly influential politician in South Africa at a time when *apartheid* rule was being introduced, this is not all that surprising.

*2.1.2  The Purpose*

In the initial Dumbarton Oaks proposals, there was no reference to the self-determination or self-government of all the world's peoples, even though it did appear in earlier documents, most notably in the Atlantic Charter of 1941.[3] None of the smaller States suggested that this should be changed.[4] Nevertheless, at the insistence of the Soviet Union, the revised Dumbarton Oaks proposals contained a reference to the self-determination of peoples in the provision on "friendly relations."[5] It seems that this amendment was not intended to refer to the right to self-determination of peoples as it is currently interpreted.[6]

According to the Soviet amendment, respect for the principle of self-determination of peoples was a means to develop friendly relations among nations. The question arises what self-determination of *peoples* has to do with developing friendly relations among *nations*. As Belgium pointed out, the amendment was based on a confusion between "peoples" and "States."[7] This confusion was not

---

[3] See also Antonio Cassese, *Self-determination of peoples: a legal reappraisal* (1995), p. 38.

[4] That is surprising, since a few of the States that participated in the conference were not yet considered as independent States, and one might thus expect that they would fight hard to make sure that the right to self-determination was included. Examples of such States were Syria, Lebanon, India, the Ukraine and Belarus. See William C. Johnstone, "The San Francisco Conference" (1945), p. 224.

[5] Amendments Submitted by the United States, the United Kingdom, the Soviet Union and China, UNCIO, vol. 3, p. 622. This exact same phrase was repeated in the article on the socioeconomic purposes. See *idem*, p. 626. This amendment was adopted by the relevant Committee (see Report of the Rapporteur Committee II/3, Approved by Committee II/3, June 8, 1945, UNCIO, vol. 10, p. 270), and ended up in the Charter. See also Grigory I. Tunkin, "The legal nature of the United Nations" (1969), pp. 15-16; Jean-François Dobelle, "Article 1, paragraphe 2" (2005), p. 339.

[6] See also Hans Kelsen, "The Preamble of the Charter - A Critical Analysis" (1946), pp. 150-151.

[7] Belgian Delegation Amendment to Paragraph 2 of Chapter I, UNCIO, vol. 6, p. 300. Belgium explains: "Surely one could use the word 'peoples' as an equivalent for the word 'state', but in the expression 'the peoples' right of self-determination' the word 'peoples' means the national groups which do not identify themselves with the population of a state." See also Antonio Cassese, *Self-

purely academic, because the promotion of a peoples' right to self-determination could lead to unwanted interference in the domestic affairs of States, and would therefore not necessarily help develop friendly relations between States. To avoid such confusion, Belgium suggested changing the phrase to "to strengthen international order on the basis of respect for the essential rights and equality of the States, and of the peoples' right of self-determination."[8] The Belgian suggestion was rejected, and the Soviet provision was eventually adopted.[9]

The provision does not clearly state that it is one of the general purposes of the Organization to promote the self-determination of peoples. Nor does it explain what rights and duties can be derived from the right to self-determination of peoples.[10] In the relevant Committee in San Francisco there was some disagreement on this question. During one of the Committee's meetings, "it was strongly emphasized on the one side that this principle [of self-determination] corresponded closely to the will and desires of peoples everywhere and should be clearly enunciated in the Chapter [but] on the other side, it was stated that the principle conformed to the purposes of the Charter only insofar as it implied the right of self-government of peoples and not the right of secession."[11] In the end, the Committee concluded that "the principle of equal rights of peoples and that of self-determination were two complementary parts of one standard of conduct," and that "an essential element of the principle in question [was] a free and genuine expression of the will of the people, which avoid[ed] cases of the alleged expression of the popular will, such as those used for their own ends by Germany and Italy in later years."[12] This explanation raised more questions than it answered. Even after this statement was made, a member of the Coordination Committee still wondered whether the right of self-determination meant "the right *of a state* to have its own democratic institutions" or whether it meant that all peoples had "the right of secession."[13] The Coordination Committee suggested that the Committee that came

---

*determination of peoples: a legal reappraisal* (1995), pp. 38-39; Satpal Kaur, "Self-determination in international law" (1970), pp. 484-485.

[8] *Idem.*

[9] See Report of Rapporteur, Subcommittee I/1/A, to Committee I/1, June 1, 1945, UNCIO, vol. 6, p. 704; Text of Chapter I, as Agreed upon by the Drafting Committee, UNCIO, vol. 6, p. 684. See also Second Meeting of Commission I, June 15, 1945, UNCIO, vol. 6, p. 65.

[10] See also Antonio Cassese, *Self-determination of peoples: a legal reappraisal* (1995), pp. 38-43.

[11] Sixth Meeting of Committee I/1, May 14, 1945, UNCIO, vol. 6, p. 296. See also Antonio Cassese, *Self-determination of peoples: a legal reappraisal* (1995), p. 40.

[12] Report of Rapporteur of Committee 1 to Commission I, June 13, 1945, UNCIO, vol. 6, p. 455.

[13] Twenty-Second Meeting, June 15, 1945, UNCIO, vol. 17, p. 143. Another member wondered "whether self-determination might mean the capacity of peoples to govern themselves, and secondly whether the phrase suggested the right of secession on the part of peoples, within a state." Twenty-Second Meeting, June 15, 1945, UNCIO, vol. 17, p. 143. Yet another member believed that "the right of self-determination meant that a people may establish any regime which they may favour." Summary Report of Twenty-Fourth Meeting, June 16, 1945, UNCIO, vol. 17, p. 163.

up with the provision should provide the necessary clarification, but this never happened.[14]

The chapter on the international trusteeship system should also be examined here.[15] This chapter is unusual in that the Organization can promote the purposes listed there only with regard to the trust territories, of which there were no more than eleven.[16] The Dumbarton Oaks proposals did not have a chapter on trusteeships, and therefore all the drafting and negotiating took place in San Francisco, more or less at the end of the conference.[17] All of the sponsors – as well as France and Australia – came up with their own draft chapter on trusteeships.[18] According to an American draft which was used as the basis for discussion in San Francisco, one of the "basic objectives of the trusteeship" was "to promote the political, economic, and social advancement of the trust territories and their inhabitants and their progressive development toward self-government in forms appropriate to the varying circumstances of each territory."[19] The most important debate was whether a reference to independence should be included here. In the UK's opinion, "[w]hat the dependent peoples wanted was an increasing measure of self-government" and that "independence would come, if at all, by natural development."[20] In response, the delegate from the Soviet Union reminded the other superpowers that they had already included the "self-determination of peoples" among the general purposes of the Organization, and that therefore it "could hardly be omitted from the trusteeship chapter."[21] In response to these objections, the US

---

[14] Twenty-Second Meeting, June 15, 1945, UNCIO, vol. 17, p. 143.

[15] For an overview of the *travaux préparatoires* of the chapter on the trusteeship system, see also James N. Murray, *The United Nations trusteeship system* (1957), pp. 23-45.

[16] Ten of those territories were former League of Nations mandates, and one was a former colony of Italy (Somaliland). All of those territories have since become independent, so that the list of purposes currently applies to no territory at all. See Ralph Wilde, "Trusteeship Council" (2007), p. 151.

[17] James B. Reston, "Conference Turns to Final Problems," in *New York Times* of May 17, 1945. See also George Thullen, *Problems of the trusteeship system: a study of political behavior in the United Nations* (1964), pp. 40-51; Huntington Gilchrist, "Colonial Questions at the San Francisco Conference" (1945), p. 983.

[18] For the ultimate purpose of that system, which differed per Major Power, see Amendments Submitted by France, UNCIO, vol. 3, pp. 604-605; USA, *idem*, p. 607; China, *idem*, p. 615; Soviet Union, *idem*, p. 618; and the UK, *idem*, p. 609. See also Australia, *idem*, p. 548; Mexico, *idem*, p. 172. The drafts suggested some prior consultations. Austriala's draft was very similar to that of the UK; and the Chinese, French and American drafts were also similar. See Charmian Edwards Toussaint, *The trusteeship system of the United Nations* (1956), p. 18-35; ; Huntington Gilchrist, "Colonial Questions at the San Francisco Conference" (1945), p. 985.

[19] Proposed Working Paper for Chapter on Dependent Territories and Arrangements for International Trusteeship, UNCIO, vol. 10, p. 678.

[20] Fourth Meeting of Committee II/4, May 14, 1945, UNCIO, vol. 10, p. 440. The Mexican delegate suggested that 'self-government was a desirable goal," but that "independence should be conceded whenever a self-governing people had unmistakably expressed its wish for complete liberation." Fifth Meeting of Committee II/4, May 15, 1945, UNCIO, vol. 10, p. 446.

[21] *Idem*, p. 441.

suggested an amendment which was unanimously adopted, that referred to the "progressive development toward self-government or independence as may be appropriate to the particular circumstances of each territory and its peoples and the freely expressed wishes of the peoples concerned, and as may be provided in the trusteeship arrangement."[22]

## 2.1.3    The Principle

No principle was ever added to the Charter obliging all States to promote and respect the right to self-determination of all the world's peoples. Reference can be made here to Chapter XI, which comes closest to this, and contains the Declaration Regarding Non-Self-Governing Territories. This declaration was essentially based on a suggestion made by the UK. As an amendment, the UK suggested that "States Members of the United Nations which have responsibilities for the administration of dependent territories inhabited by peoples not yet able to stand by themselves under the strenuous conditions of the modern world" would have the duty "to promote to the utmost the well-being of the inhabitants of these territories within the world community." [23] This emphasis on the interests of the inhabitants themselves was later referred to by the executive officer of the relevant Commission as "the most enlightened thinking on the subject."[24] In any case, this duty, or "sacred trust of civilization" - the term used by the UK - included "the development of self-government in forms appropriate to the varying circumstances of each territory."[25] This duty applied to all colonial powers, and was thus much more broadly applicable than the purposes promoted through the trusteeship system. This more general application made it a unique declaration. As Evatt pointed out, it was "the first joint declaration in history by the major colonial Powers of principles applicable to all their non-self-governing territories."[26]

The relevant Subcommittee made a few changes to the UK draft. First of all, the UK´s reference to the dependent territories, which was reminiscent of the League of Nations Covenant, was replaced by a more modern version.[27] Then the

---

[22] Thirteenth Meeting of Committee II/4, June 8, 1945, UNCIO, vol. 10, pp. 513-514. See also the Working Paper for Chapter on Dependent Territories and Arrangements for International Trusteeship, as of June 9, 1945 (as Approved Provisionally, with Amendments), UNCIO, vol. 10, p. 526. China also actively promoted this compromise. See Charmian Edwards Toussaint, *The trusteeship system of the United Nations* (1956), pp. 33 and 57.

[23] Amendments Submitted by United Kingdom, UNCIO, vol. 3, p 609. This formulation is based on Article 22 of the Covenant of the League of Nations. See also Australia, *idem*, p. 548.

[24] Huntington Gilchrist, "Colonial Questions at the San Francisco Conference" (1945), p. 986.

[25] Amendments Submitted by United Kingdom, UNCIO, vol. 3, p 609.

[26] Herbert Vere Evatt, *The United Nations* (1948), p. 32.

[27] See Proposed Text for Chapter on Dependent Territories and Arrangements for International Trusteeship (as Far as Approved by Drafting Subcommittee II/4/A, June 11, 1945), UNCIO, vol. 10, p.

US suggested some more substantial changes, which were all adopted.[28] No reference to independence or self-determination was ever included. The purposes are restricted to the promotion of self-government. A delegate of the Philippines believed that the phrase "to assist [the dependent peoples] in the progressive development of their free political institutions," added at the request of the US, could also mean independence, depending on the wishes of the dependent peoples themselves.[29] The executive officer of the relevant Commission later openly wondered about the meaning of the term "self-government" if it did not at least include "potential independence?"[30] Despite the fact that in subsequent practice and scholarship the provisions were generally interpreted in this way,[31] the Report of the Rapporteur clearly shows that this interpretation was not shared by most delegates.[32] When the entire provision was about to be adopted, the Dutch delegate referred to some "grievances which were acutely felt by dependent peoples," including "forced labour" and "the humiliation caused by the assertion of racial superiority," and asked the US whether these grievances were dealt with in the provision as redrafted by the US.[33] The US affirmed that in the draft there was an implicit "moral obligation to endeavour to overcome these [...] evils."[34]

In San Francisco the Declaration on the relationship between the colonial powers and their colonies was qualified as "a unilateral declaration of member states, each for itself, which stated the principles they recognized in carrying responsibilities which they had or might have."[35] Qualifying it as a declaration should not be interpreted to mean that this part of the Charter was somehow less binding than the rest. By signing this declaration, which formed an integral part of the UN Charter, certain States, *i.e.* the colonizers, accepted certain fundamental

---

533. See also Draft Report of the Rapporteur of Committee II/4, UNCIO, vol. 10, p. 575, and Report of the Rapporteur of Committee II/4, UNCIO, vol. 10, p. 608.

[28] First, some minor changes were made. See Working Paper for Chapter on Dependent Territories and Arrangements for International Trusteeship, as of June 9, 1945 (as Approved Provisionally, with Amendments), UNCIO, vol. 10, p. 525, Proposed Text for Chapter on Dependent Territories and Arrangements for International Trusteeship (as Far as Approved by Drafting Subcommittee II/4/A, June 11, 1945), UNCIO, vol. 10, p. 533. But then the US proposed a whole list of more substantial changes. See the Fifteenth Meeting of Committee II/4, June 18, 1945, UNCIO, vol. 10, pp. 561-563. See also Redraft of Working Paper, Section A, UNCIO, vol. 10, p. 570.

[29] Fifteenth Meeting of Committee II/4, June 18, 1945, UNCIO, vol. 10, p. 562.

[30] Huntington Gilchrist, "Colonial Questions at the San Francisco Conference" (1945), p. 987.

[31] See Charmian Edwards Toussaint, *The trusteeship system of the United Nations* (1956), p. 58. See also the subsequent resolutions of the General Assembly.

[32] Report of the Rapporteur of Committee II/4, UNCIO, vol. 10, p. 609 (see also p. 576).

[33] Fifteenth Meeting of Committee II/4, June 18, 1945, UNCIO, vol. 10, p. 563. See also Annex B to the Report of the Rapporteur of Committee II/4, UNCIO, vol. 10, p. 619 (see also p. 586), where one can find a written version of the three questions.

[34] *Idem.*

[35] Coordination Committee's Summary Report of Thirty-Seventh Meeting, June 20, 1945, UNCIO, vol. 17, pp. 307-308.

legal duties and responsibilities towards their colonies.[36] As the principle stated in the Declaration applied to all colonial powers, while the purpose applied only to the trust territories, the principle and the purpose are not entirely consistent in their scope of application. Their content also differs substantially. Most importantly, the principle refers to the duty of colonial powers to promote "self-government" of basically all dependent peoples in the world, while the purpose refers to the role of the Organization in promoting "self-government or independence" only of the trust territories.[37]

## 2.2 The self-determination of peoples organized as a State (sovereignty)

### 2.2.1 The Preamble

Do peoples continue to have a right to self-determination after they have successfully gained their sovereign independence? A State's claim to sovereign independence is nowadays considered more of a hindrance to the promotion of values than a value-based claim.[38] This section examines the San Francisco documents to find out whether this was already the dominant view in 1945. The Preamble does not say much about sovereignty. It only contains a reference to equality of States, not to their independence.[39]

### 2.2.2 The Purpose

The Dumbarton Oaks proposals did not see the promotion of respect for the equality or independence of States as one of the Organization's purposes. Various States suggested that it should be a purpose of the Organization to promote the juridical

---

[36] See also Charmian Edwards Toussaint, *The trusteeship system of the United Nations* (1956), p. 230. One of those colonizers, the Netherlands, saw no problem with this declaration, because it "corresponded strikingly with the Dutch views regarding the overseas territories of the Kingdom." See the Dutch Government's "Memorie van Toelichting bij de Goedkeuringswet van het Handvest der Verenigde Naties," in Handelingen der Staten-Generaal, Tweede Kamer, Bijlagen Tijdelijke Zitting 1945, Bijlage no. 3, p. 24.
[37] See Articles 73 and 76 of the UN Charter, respectively. The difference between the principle and the purpose was pointed out during the Eleventh Meeting of Committee II/4, May 31, 1945, UNCIO, vol. 10, pp. 496-497.
[38] See *e.g.*, Robert McCorquodale, "An Inclusive International Legal System" (2004), p. 484.
[39] Draft Preamble to the Charter of the United Nations Proposed by the Union of South Africa, 26 April, 1945, UNCIO, vol. 3, pp. 474-475. According to Smuts' first draft of the Preamble, the United Nations was established, *inter alia*, to re-establish the faith "in the equal rights of [...] of individual nations large and small." This paragraph got an awkward place: it was attached to the paragraph on respect for human rights, somewhat as an appendix. The phrase was never really commented upon, and, after a small modification, ended up in the Charter.

equality of States.[40] The Philippines believed this to be a matter relating to racial discrimination. It suggested that the Organization should have a mandate to develop "the spirit of brotherhood and racial equality among nations,"[41] and that this should be a purpose. At the request of the Soviet Union, the sponsors added a reference to equality in the provision on "friendly relations."[42] The idea was that this provision should state that the "[e]quality of rights [...] extends in the Charter to States, nations, and peoples."[43] This was the only change made to the provision in San Francisco.[44] The provision does not give the Organization the mandate to promote the equality of States, nations and peoples. Even though the positions of the State flags, flying from the flagpoles in front of the San Francisco conference centre, "were being changed daily to guard against any complaints of inequality," the Organization did not have a general purpose to promote the equal rights of States.[45]

More or less the same is true for the independence of States. The Dumbarton Oaks did not see the promotion of respect for sovereign independence as a purpose of the Organization. Many States suggested that this purpose should be added.[46] Even Poland, which did not participate in the San Francisco Conference but nevertheless submitted a list of amendment proposals to the US Government, suggested that the Organization should afford "to all nations the means of dwelling within their own boundaries in freedom from fear and want."[47] Despite the popularity of this purpose, especially among the smaller States, it never made it into the Charter. Is this because it would be contradictory to oblige the United Nations to promote the sovereign independence of States when the *raison d'être* of the organization was to promote the increasing interdependence of States? Or maybe the purpose was so obvious that there was no need to state it explicitly. In Schachter's view, "one of [the UN's] primary aims, if not its *raison d'être*, was to preserve and promote the independence and integrity of States."[48] If that is true, it is

---

[40] See *e.g.*, Amendments Submitted by Panama, UNCIO, vol. 3, p. 273; Cuba, *idem*, p. 497; Honduras, *idem*, p. 349.

[41] Amendments Submitted by the Philippines, UNCIO, vol. 3, p. 535. See also Haiti, *idem*, p. 52, and Sixth Plenary Session, May 1, 1945, UNCIO, vol. 1, p. 443.

[42] Amendments Submitted by the United States, the United Kingdom, the Soviet Union and China, UNCIO, vol. 3, p. 622.

[43] See Text of Chapter I, as Agreed upon by the Drafting Committee, UNCIO, vol. 6, p. 684.

[44] See section 5.4 of Chapter VII.

[45] See "Charter for Peace," an editorial that appeared in the *New York Times* of May 20, 1945.

[46] This was one of the most important amendment proposals. See *e.g.*, Amendments Submitted by New Zealand, UNCIO, vol. 3, p. 486; Mexico, *idem*, p. 179; Ecuador, *idem*, p. 399; Iran, *idem*, p. 554; Honduras, *idem*, p. 349; Peru, *idem*, p. 596; Panama, *idem*, pp. 265 and 273; Cuba, *idem*, pp. 494-497.

[47] The proposals are not included in the UNCIO collection, but they are cited in James B. Reston, "Poles in London Ask Oaks Revision," in *New York Times* of February 11, 1945. Poland did not attend the conference, because there was a dispute as to who should represent Poland.

[48] Oscar Schachter, "The charter's origins in today's perspective" (1995), p. 45.

remarkable that this primary aim cannot be found in the UN Charter itself.

### 2.2.3    The Principle

The first principle, according to the Dumbarton Oaks proposals, was "the principle of the sovereign equality of all peace-loving states."[49] There was wide support for this equality principle.[50] At the same time, many States were concerned that the rest of the UN Charter did not do justice to this principle because it gave such a prominent role to the major powers.[51] These States considered that there were good reasons for the prominent position of the most powerful. However, the problem was that the balance between the effectiveness of the Organization, especially in the maintenance of international peace and security, and respect for the equality of States, had been lost.[52] On the final day of the Conference, President Truman (US) tried to reassure these States, when he said that the great powers were given great responsibilities rather than great privileges. He explained that "the responsibility of great States [was] to serve, and not to dominate the peoples of the world."[53]

Some States believed that the same provision also intended to oblige States to respect the sovereign independence of all other States.[54] The majority were not very convinced, and suggested including in the list of principles an explicit reference to the obligation to respect other States' independence.[55] Mexico was one

---

[49] Dumbarton Oaks Proposals for a General International Organization, UNCIO, vol. 3, p. 3.

[50] See *e.g.*, Amendments Submitted by Uruguay, UNCIO, vol. 3, p. 35; Chile, *idem*, p. 283; Paraguay, *idem*, p. 347; Ecuador, *idem*, pp. 398-399; Colombia, *idem*, p. 587.

[51] When the principle of sovereign equality of nations was discussed in the Committee, one delegate said that, since "states members of the world Organization would not receive equal treatment," the use of the words "sovereign equality" was "somewhat ironic." Seventh Meeting of Committee I/1, May 16, 1956, UNCIO, vol. 6, p. 304. See also Eleventh Meeting of Committee I/1, June 4, 1945, UNCIO, vol. 6, p. 332.

[52] See *e.g.*, Amendments Submitted by Colombia, UNCIO, vol. 3, p. 587, Panama, *idem*, pp. 260-261, Netherlands, *idem*, p. 315.

[53] Verbatim Minutes of Opening Session, April 25, 1945, UNCIO, vol. 1, p. 113. In the same speech, President Truman referred to the premise of "might makes right" as the "fundamental philosophy of our enemies", and as a premise that must certainly be denied. Senator Vandenberg later reffered to "might makes right" as a "jungle-creed." See Vandenberg, "Vandenberg's Plea for Charter as the Only Hope of Averting Chaos in World."

[54] See *e.g.*, Amendments Submitted by the Dominican Republic, UNCIO, vol. 3, p. 564. And see section 5.4 of Chapter VII of this study.

[55] This was by far the most popular amendment proposal. See *e.g.*, Amendments Submitted by Uruguay, UNCIO, vol. 3, pp. 30 and p. 35; Chile, *idem*, p. 283; Brazil, *idem*, p. 246; Mexico, *idem*, pp. 65-66; Ecuador, *idem*, pp. 398-399; Egypt, *idem*, p. 454; Ethiopia, *idem*, p. 558; Panama, *idem*, p. 270; Paraguay, *idem*, p. 347; Honduras, *idem*, p. 350; Czechoslovakia, *idem*, p. 467; Cuba, *idem*, p. 497; Bolivia, *idem*, pp. 582-583; Colombia, *idem*, p. 588; Documentation for Meetings of Committee I/1, UNCIO, vol. 6, pp. 542 and 563 (Iran).

of those States. In support of its non-intervention amendment, Mexico quoted from an American-Canadian Technical Plan, drafted by a group of individual experts. This stated that "each of the States which form the Community of States must be responsible for the conduct of its own household, [which implies] that in its internal affairs each State must be free from interference by other States acting on their own authority."[56] Panama believed that "[e]ach State ha[d] a legal duty to refrain from intervention in the internal affairs of any other State."[57] At the same time, Panama proposed that "[e]ach State ha[d] a legal duty to see that conditions prevailing within its own territory d[id] not menace international peace and order, and to this end it must treat its own population in a way which will not violate the dictates of humanity and justice or shock the conscience of mankind."[58] Bearing in mind the legal duty of States not to intervene proclaimed by Panama, the question is what happens when a State fails to comply with Panama's "legal duty" not to mistreat its own citizens. This issue later resurfaced in San Francisco, when the obligation of the Organization itself not to intervene in the internal affairs of its Members was discussed.

Despite the fact that many States suggested adding a genuine non-intervention principle, the relevant Subcommittee in San Francisco did not make any changes to the Dumbarton Oaks draft.[59] The prohibition on intervention was believed to be "explicitly or implicitly contained in other provisions of the Charter, particularly under Purposes and Principles."[60] However, no other purpose or principle springs to mind.[61] Thus the obligation of non-intervention must be derived from the sovereign equality principle. It was agreed that the term "sovereign equality" implied that "states are juridically equal," "that they enjoy the rights inherent in their full sovereignty," "that the personality of the state is respected, as well as its territorial integrity and political independence," and "that the state should, under international order, comply faithfully with its international duties and

---

[56] Amendments Submitted by Mexico, UNCIO, vol. 3, p. 67. This non-intervention principle was not aimed at the Organization, only at other Member States acting individually. See *idem*, p. 68. See also Uruguay, *idem*, p. 30.
[57] *Idem*, p. 270.
[58] Amendments Submitted by Panama, UNCIO, vol. 3, p. 269. See also Chile, *idem*, p. 293. On p. 54 of Louis B. Sohn, "The issue of self-defense and the UN Charter" (1995), it is suggested that this was an American formulation.
[59] There is no such provision in the Text of Chapter II, as Agreed upon by the Drafting Committee, UNCIO, vol. 6, p. 687.
[60] Report of Rapporteur of Subcommittee I/1/A, to Committee I/1, UNCIO, vol. 6, p. 717.
[61] One might think of the prohibition to use force. But, as Peru rightly remarked, "[w]hen the ideas of sovereignty and territorial integrity are dealt with only in relation to the use of force, there is not the absolute respect which in other cases would have been established." Second Meeting of Commission I, June 15, 1945, UNCIO, vol. 6, p. 68.

obligations."[62] Rolin, the Belgian President of the Committee, felt that "if we have succeeded in expressing these four concepts in two words, 'sovereign equality,' we have broken the record for conciseness."[63] Not all the delegates were equally impressed by this conciseness. Peru was particularly insistent on having all these elements – and duties – arising from the sovereignty of States explicitly mentioned in the Charter, rather than implied in the term sovereign equality.[64] But the majority believed that this was not necessary.[65]

The sovereign equality principle does not explain how States ought to behave in order to respect the sovereign equality of all States. Australia remarked that this makes the principle rather an "empty phrase."[66] The principle also says little, if anything at all, about sovereign independence. The UN Charter thus does not contain an explicit prohibition on States intervening in the domestic affairs of other States, even though this is one of the most important – and most widely supported – norms of all.[67] It was certainly widely supported in Latin America.[68] Their big brother, the United States of America, was much less enthusiastic. It even opposed any references to non-intervention in the Charter.[69] This US strategy

---

[62] Report of Rapporteur of Subcommittee I/1/A, to Committee I/1, UNCIO, vol. 6, p. 718. See also Eighth Meeting of Committee I/1, May 17, 1945, UNCIO, vol. 6, p. 311; Report of Rapporteur of Committee 1 to Commission I, UNCIO, vol. 6, p. 457.

[63] *Idem*, p. 70.

[64] Second Meeting of Commission I, June 15, 1945, UNCIO, vol. 6, pp. 67-69, and Report of Rapporteur of Commission I, UNCIO, vol. 6, p. 230. See also Eleventh Meeting of Committee I/1, June 4, 1945, UNCIO, vol. 6, pp. 331-332.

[65] The Rapporteur of the Subcommittee insisted once more that all this was implied in the term "sovereign equality." See Second Meeting of Commission I, June 15, 1945, UNCIO, vol. 6, p. 69.

[66] See remark of Australian delegate during the First Plenary Session, April 26, 1945, UNCIO, vol. 1 p. 173.

[67] Reference is sometimes made to Article 2(7) UN Charter. However, as Nolte rightly emphasized, that provision "protects only against acts of the United Nations [Organization] and not against acts of other States." Georg Nolte, "Article 2(7)" (2002), p. 151. On the place of the notion of sovereignty in the UN Charter, see also Nico Schrijver, "The Changing Nature of State Sovereignty" (1999).

[68] Latin American delegates constantly defended the principle of sovereign equality and independence. See *e.g.*, Venezuela (Seventh Plenary Session, May 1, 1945, UNCIO, vol. 1, p. 517), Amendments Submitted by Honduras, UNCIO, vol. 3, p. 349; Brazil, *idem*, p. 236; Mexico, *idem*, pp. 65-66 and 179. See also Sixteenth Meeting of Committee I/1, June 13, 1945, UNCIO, vol. 6, p. 495. These States referred to regional legal documents in which the non-intervention principle was included, such as the Convention of Montevideo on the Rights Duties of States (whose definition of a State, by the way, must be regarded as incorporated in the Charter), the Protocol of Buenos Aires relative to Non-Intervention, the Declaration of Lima, and the Constitution of their regional security arrangement, only a month old at the time: the Act of Chapultepec (Mexico). Human rights protection was also emphasized there. See Jan Herman Burgers, "The Road to San Francisco" (1992), p. 476.

[69] See especially the formal decision of the entire US Delegation to "oppose reference to non-intervention anywhere in the Charter." Minutes of Forty-first Meeting of the United States Delegation, May 16, 1945, in FRUS, *1945, General:* Volume I, p. 751. See also *e.g.*, Minutes of the Fourteenth Meeting of the United States Delegation, April 24, 1945, in FRUS, *1945, General:* Volume I, pp. 374-375.

explains why there is no general non-intervention principle in the UN Charter. Another explanation could be that States interpreted the word "force" in the prohibition on the use of force – Article 2(4) UN Charter – so broadly that it became a general non-intervention principle.[70]

The lack of such a principle also explains why the United Nations does not have any specific means at its disposal to ensure respect by States for the sovereign equality and independence of other States. The United Nations can protect a State against military interventions by other States. That was, after all, the main reason that the Organization was established. The prohibition on the use of military force is certainly covered by Article 2(4) UN Charter. However, the Organization does not have any specific powers to protect States against non-military intervention by other States in their domestic affairs.[71]

In sharp contrast to its opposition to a principle obliging States to respect the sovereign independence of other States, the US was a big supporter of a principle obliging the Organization to respect the sovereign independence of its Member States.[72] The original Dumbarton Oaks proposals had not contained such a general principle. There was only a non-intervention provision in the chapter on the settlement of disputes, which obliged the Organization not to interfere in the domestic affairs of States when settling international disputes.[73] To emphasize the importance of respect for the sovereign independence of States, the sponsors promoted this non-intervention provision from the chapter on the settlement of disputes to the list of general principles.[74] This promotion, which was not suggested by any of the smaller States, survived the San Francisco Conference.[75] It became Article 2(7) UN Charter, which reads as follows:

---

[70] See section 4 of Chapter IV, above.

[71] Uruguay suggested that this ought to be a possibility: "The Uruguayan Government desires that there be confirmed, expressly, the guarantee of the independence and subsistence of the nations, and that there be established categorically for the associates of the international organization, the obligation of maintaining, even by armed force, the integrity of the rights and the frontiers of the countries threatened or attacked." Position of the Government of Uruguay Respecting the Plans of Postwar International Organization for the Maintenance of Peach and Security in the World, UNCIO, vol. 3, p. 30.

[72] See John H. Crider, "Stress Autonomy in Domestic Field," in *New York Times* of May 25, 1945.

[73] Dumbarton Oaks Proposals for a General International Organization, UNCIO, vol. 3, p. 13.

[74] See Amendments Submitted by the United States, the United Kingdom, the Soviet Union and China, UNCIO, vol. 3, p. 623 (the new principle) and p. 625 (deletion of the non-intervention principle in the chapter describing the collective security arrangement). See also Sixteenth Meeting of Committee I/1, June 13, 1945, UNCIO, vol. 6, p. 494-499. The reason why there was no such principle in the Dumbarton Oaks proposals is that the issue of "domestic jurisdiction" became entangled with the question on human rights. See Ruth B. Russell, *A history of the United Nations Charter* (1958), p. 463.

[75] The smaller nations only wanted more international law inserted into the provision. They wanted the distinction between the domestic and the international to be determined by law, and they wanted the International Court to make such a determination. For a discussion of the complete drafting history of Article 2(7), see *e.g.*, Lawrence Preuss, "Article 2, paragraph 7 of the Charter of the United Nations and

> Nothing contained in the present Charter shall authorize the United Nations to intervene in matters which are essentially within the domestic jurisdiction of any state or shall require the Members to submit such matters to settlement under the present Charter; but this principle shall not prejudice the application of enforcement measures under Chapter VII.

When asked to explain the need for such a general non-intervention principle for the Organization, the US explained that the constant broadening of the UN's purposes raised the question whether "the Organization [would] deal with the governments of the member states," or whether it would "penetrate directly into the domestic life and social economy of the member states." [76] The general non-intervention principle for the Organization, as suggested by the sponsors, made it clear that the Organization would deal only with governments in the promotion of its purposes. [77]

Because the non-intervention principle, as applied to the Organization, basically prohibits the United Nations from taking certain actions, it cannot come as a surprise that this principle has been the main inspiration for a great number of limitations and constraints on the functions and powers allotted to the Organization for the promotion of the other global values.

For example, the suggestion that only "democratic" States would qualify for UN membership was rejected, because it "would imply an undue interference with internal arrangements." [78] Furthermore, the distinction between non-self-governing territories and trust territories was based on respect for State sovereignty. As the UK pointed out, "[t]he compulsory application of the trusteeship system to existing colonies [...] would amount to interference with the internal affairs of

---

matters of domestic jurisdiction' (1950). See also "Dulles Wins Plea to Bar League from Meddling in Domestic Issues," in the *New York Times* of June 16, 1945.

[76] Seventeenth Meeting of Committee I/1, June 14, 1945, UNCIO, vol. 6, p. 508.

[77] *Idem.* See also Report of Rapporteur of Committee 1 to Commission I, UNCIO, vol. 6, p. 486 (the Rapporteur agreed). According to the revised Dumbarton Oaks proposal, the only exception to the non-intervention principle was the action of the Security Council taken under Chapter VIII, Section B, of the Dumbarton Oaks proposals, which eventually became Chapter VII of the UN Charter. Australia believed that this exception was too wide, and suggested to narrow it down to "enforcement measures". See Amendment by the Australian Delegation to Proposed Paragraph 8 of Chapter II (Principles), UNCIO, vol. 6, pp. 436-440. The US also accepted this solution. See Minutes of Sixty-third Meeting of the United States Delegation, June 4, 1945, in FRUS, *1945, General:* Volume I, p. 1142. Norway objected with convincing arguments to this Australian proposal. See Sixteenth Meeting of Committee I/1, June 13, 1945, UNCIO, vol. 6, p. 498, and Statement by the Norwegian Delegation on Paragraph 8, Chapter II, June 12, 1945, *idem*, p. 430. But the Committee nonetheless adopted the provision as amended by Australia. See Seventeenth Meeting of Committee I/1, June 14, 1945, *idem*, p. 513, and the Report of Rapporteur of Committee 1 to Commission I, *idem*, pp. 488-489.

[78] Sixth Meeting of Committee I/2, May 14, 1945, UNCIO, vol. 7, p. 36.

member states."[79] Therefore the Trusteeship Council was allowed to deal only with a few trust territories, and not with all colonies, which significantly diminished the Council's relevance.[80] The Rapporteur had to make it explicitly clear that "nothing in this Chapter [on the Trusteeship system] of the Charter shall be construed in or of itself to alter in any manner any rights whatsoever of any states or any peoples or the terms of existing international instruments to which member states may respectively be parties."[81]

When the functions and powers of the General Assembly were discussed, the Soviet Union considered that there was a danger that the Organization could interfere in the domestic affairs of States, and that the Charter should explicitly forbid the Assembly from doing so. The Dominican Republic made the same point in a separate statement.[82] In response, Evatt, the Australian delegate, referred to the general non-intervention principle cited above.[83] In his view, "the general prohibition of intervention in domestic affairs which is contained in the Charter is an overriding principle or limitation and controls each and every organ and body of

---

[79] Fourth Meeting of Committee II/4, May 14, 1945, UNCIO, vol. 10, p. 440. Other colonial powers shared this view. See *e.g.*, Belgian Delegation Amendment to Paragraph 2 of Chapter I, UNCIO, vol. 6, p. 300. When the trusteeship system was being discussed, France "called attention to the principle [...]" of nonintervention in the domestic affairs of member states." Third Meeting of Committee II/4, May 11, 1945, UNCIO, vol. 10, p. 433. France even issued a statement to this effect. See the Report of Rapporteur of Commission I, UNCIO, vol. 10, p. 622 (the text of the declaration), and Sixteenth Meeting of Committee II/4, June 20, 1945, UNCIO, vol. 10, p. 602 (introduction of this declaration). The Netherlands said, about the Trusteeship Chapter, that "[i]n this chapter we find far-reaching obligations and responsibilities but nobody need fear, as a consequence, interference in domestic affairs, since such interference has been expressly excluded in the Chapter on Principles." Third Meeting of Commission II, June 20, 1945, UNCIO, vol. 8, p. 129. Interestingly, the Netherlands also believed that "[t]he superimposition of [the trusteeship] system would be a backward step from the point of view of the more advanced colonial territories,"and thus the Netherlands "could not agree to its universal application." Third Meeting of Committee II/4, May 11, 1945, UNCIO, vol. 10, p. 433. Australia believed that "[t]here would be no interference with sovereignty," because "[a]ll that would be done [by the trusteeship system] would be to treat the welfare of dependent peoples as a matter not only of local but of international concern." First Plenary Session, April 26, 1945, UNCIO, vol. 1, p. 178. South Africa believed that "in drawing up general principles [relating to non-selfgoverning territories], that the terms of existing mandates could not be altered without the consent of the mandatory power." Fourth Meeting of Committee II/4, May 14, 1945, UNCIO, vol. 10, p. 439.
[80] According to Article 77 of the UN Charter, "[t]he trusteeship system shall apply to such territories in the following categories as may be placed thereunder by means of trusteeship agreements: a. territories now held under mandate; b. territories which may be detached from enemy states as a result of the Second World War; and c. territories voluntarily placed under the system by states responsible for their administration." There are no examples of the latter category.
[81] Revised Report of the Rapporteur of Commission II to the Plenary Session, UNCIO, vol. 8, p. 271.
[82] Statement Made by the Delegate of the Dominican Republic at the Fourteenth Meeting of Committee II/2, UNCIO, vol. 9, p. 102.
[83] Summary Report of Ninth Meeting of Executive Committee, June 17, 1945, UNCIO, vol. 5, pp. 524-525.

the Organization, of which the General Assembly is one."[84] The Soviet Union was not convinced, and the description of the Assembly's powers was changed to appease it.[85]

Certain States were worried that with the expansion of the Organization's socio-economic purposes, the UN would acquire the right to interfere in domestic affairs.[86] The new article proposed by Australia (the so-called pledge), obliging all States to take joint and separate action to promote these socio-economic purposes, did not help to reassure these States. Australia explained that the obligation to take separate action, *i.e.* the obligation of all States to "pursue the objectives of [Article 55] by its own action in its own way," did not imply that the Organization could interfere in the domestic affairs of States to ensure that they promoted the socio-economic purposes at a national level.[87] Belgium, supporting the Australian amendment, remarked that "[s]eparate action might imply interference with domestic affairs," but that the delegates need not be concerned, because "adequate protection [was] given elsewhere in the Charter."[88] The Belgian delegate was referring here to the general prohibition on the Organization intervening in domestic affairs, which became Article 2(7) UN Charter.[89] However, according to the US, this general "safeguarding clause [was] not sufficient since a pledge of the type adopted by Australia would make internal affairs matters of international concern." Thus they would cease to fall "essentially within the domestic jurisdiction," and therefore the safeguarding clause would not apply.[90] To avoid any ambiguity, the US delegate proposed including a statement in the records, which made it clear that the Organization could not interfere in domestic affairs when promoting the socio-economic purposes.[91] This declaration was unanimously adopted.[92]

---

[84] Summary Report of Tenth Meeting of Executive Committee, June 18, 1945, UNCIO, vol. 5, p. 535. See also Summary Report of Eighth Meeting of Steering Committee, June 18, 1945, UNCIO, vol. 5, p. 272.

[85] See section 3.5 of Chapter III, above.

[86] For example, Liberia remarked that "in connection with the working out of details of whatever economic, social or other humanitarian problems, as may be projected at the Conference, care should be taken to see that definite and specific means be set out therefore; as otherwise unjustifiable interference in the internal affairs of nations might occur." Memorandum of the Liberian Government on the Dumbarton Oaks Proposals, UNCIO, vol. 3, p. 464. Uruguay was more open to the Organization's "interference." See New Uruguayan Proposals on Dumbarton Oaks Proposals, UNCIO, vol. 3, p. 43.

[87] Twelfth Meeting of Committee II/3, May 25, 1945, UNCIO, vol. 10, p. 100. See also the Fifteenth Meeting of Committee II/3, May 30, 1945, UNCIO, vol. 10, pp. 139-141.

[88] See Fifteenth Meeting of Committee II/3, May 30, 1945, UNCIO, vol. 10, p. 139.

[89] That is Article 2(7) UN Charter.

[90] Fifteenth Meeting of Committee II/3, May 30, 1945, UNCIO, vol. 10, p. 140.

[91] Eleventh Meeting of Committee II/3, May 24, 1945, UNCIO, vol. 10, p. 83. The proposed statement was as follows: "The members of Committee 3 of Commission II are in full agreement that nothing contained in Chapter IX can be construed as giving authority to the Organization to intervene in the domestic affairs of member states." It was adopted unanimously.

The most problematic was the apparent conflict between the obligation for the Organization to respect the sovereign independence of States and the obligation for the Organization to promote universal respect for human dignity and human rights. For the US, the biggest supporter of the non-intervention principle, intervention for the promotion of human dignity was acceptable. Even during the Dumbarton Oaks deliberations the US already wanted to include in the Charter an article making the principle of non-intervention dependent on the requirement that a State respect the human rights and fundamental freedoms of all its people and that it should govern in accordance with the principles of humanity and justice.[93] This suggestion was withdrawn even before the Dumbarton Oaks text was sent to the other States.

In an amendment, France made a similar suggestion:

> The provisions [in the Charter] should not apply to situations or disputes arising out of matters which by international law are solely within the domestic jurisdiction of the state concerned, unless the clear violation of essential liberties and of human rights constitutes in itself a threat capable of compromising peace.[94]

France explained that "experience of recent years had made it desirable that the Organization should intervene to protect certain minorities."[95] In response, Australia proposed that, by concluding a multilateral treaty on the topic of minorities, the community of States could in the future make the basic respect for minority rights – and human rights – within a certain country, a matter of international concern.[96] France, apparently convinced by the arguments put forward by Australia, withdrew its amendment.[97] However, until such a convention was concluded, Uruguay pointed out that a "dictatorial government could raise

---

[92] The concerns were primarily of the USA (see the Ninth Meeting of Committee II/3, May 21, 1945, UNCIO, vol. 10, p. 52, and the Tenth Meeting of Committee II/3, May 22, 1945, UNCIO, vol. 10, p. 57), but others expressed them too. During the Eleventh Meeting of Committee II/3, May 24, 1945, UNCIO, vol. 10, p. 83, the American statement was adopted unanimously.

[93] See section 2.3 of Chapter VII.

[94] Comments of the French Ministry of Foreign Affairs, UNCIO, vol. 3, p. 386. This amendment resurfaced when Australia suggested considering only the Security Council's enforcement measures to maintain international peace and security as excluded from the non-intervention principle. See Sixteenth Meeting of Committee I/1, June 13, 1945, UNCIO, vol. 6, p. 498.

[95] Sixteenth Meeting of Committee I/1, June 13, 1945, UNCIO, vol. 6, p. 498.

[96] Amendment by the Australian Delegation to Proposed Paragraph 8 of Chapter II (Principles), UNCIO, vol. 6, p. 439. Belgium had some objections. See Belgian complaint at the Seventeenth Meeting of Committee I/1, June 14, 1945, UNCIO, vol. 6, p. 511. Already in 1947, this solution was defended in scholarship. See, *e.g.*, Clark M. Eichelberger, "The United Nations Charter: A Growing Document" (1947), p. 102.

[97] Sixteenth Meeting of Committee I/1, June 13, 1945, UNCIO, vol. 6, p. 499.

exceptions of 'domestic jurisdiction' to any interference by the Organization, with respect to its internal arbitrary rule."[98]

In the end, no human rights exception to the non-intervention principle was inserted in the UN Charter. This means that the UN cannot, against the sovereign will of its Member States, intervene in their essentially domestic affairs, not even to promote respect for human rights. Respect for the sovereign independence of States required this absolute prohibition. As soon as States voluntarily authorize the Organization to promote human rights at the national level as well, for example, by ratifying a human rights treaty, this argument will no longer form an obstacle to the Organization.

The conclusion is that the UN Charter does not contain an explicit prohibition on States intervening in the domestic affairs of other States. The United Nations Organization also has no clear mandate to promote the sovereign independence of States, and prevent one State intervening in the affairs of another. However, the Charter does contain a prohibition on the United Nations Organization itself intervening in the domestic affairs of its Member States. An explanation of this surprising fact is that the US had far less difficulty with the idea of States interfering in other States' domestic affairs than with the idea that the Organization could interfere in the affairs of Member States.

## 3    THE UN CHARTER SYSTEM

### 3.1 Introduction

The UN Charter devoted three chapters to the plight of a specific group of peoples who did not enjoy any form of self-government or independence, *i.e.* colonial peoples. To ensure their advancement, the UN set up the trusteeship system, and inserted a declaration into the Charter on the treatment of colonies. Self-determination is not mentioned even once in those chapters.

The UN's work related to these specific parts of the Charter is discussed below. Its objectives regarding colonial peoples quickly became much more ambitious than those set out in the Charter itself. The outline of those more ambitious goals is dealt with in the following section (4).

### 3.2 The Trusteeship Council and the trust territories

The Trusteeship system of the United Nations was set up to introduce emerging nations to adult statehood. In Toussaint's words: "Even as the education and

---

[98] Statement of Uruguayan Delegation on Its Position with Reference to Chapters I and II as Considered by Committee I/1, UNCIO, vol. 6, p. 632.

guidance of youth to take its place in the national society is recognized as of vital concern to the modern State government [...] so is the education and guidance of youthful nations to take their places as adult members of the international society of vital concern to a present-day comprehensive international organization."[99] This comparison is unfortunate in many ways, but it does accurately reflect the way of thinking in the early days.

According to Article 76 of the UN Charter, one of the basic objectives of the trusteeship system was

> To promote the political, economic, social, and educational advancement of the inhabitants of the trust territories, and their progressive development towards self-government or independence as may be appropriate to the particular circumstances of each territory and its peoples and the freely expressed wishes of the peoples concerned, and as may be provided by the terms of each trusteeship agreement.[100]

The tortuous language of this paragraph can be explained by the disagreement among the major powers about the ultimate purpose of the trusteeship system. It was a compromise, and this compromise did not allow for an explicit reference to the self-determination of peoples. Thus "advancement" rather than "independence" was the ultimate objective of the trusteeship system.[101]

It is now generally agreed that the UN Charter is a "living document," and that its interpretation evolves with the evolution of the international community.[102] As well as looking at the Council's mandate, it is also important to look at its actual accomplishments.

What are the accomplishments of the trusteeship system? The trusteeship system of the United Nations was supervised by the Trusteeship Council. Despite being one of the principal organs of the United Nations, the Trusteeship Council actually operated under the authority of the General Assembly, just like the Economic and Social Council.[103] The Trusteeship Council has been very active from the very beginning. Because it had a limited task and a limited membership, its work was not as politicized as that of the General Assembly.[104]

On 13 December 1946, the General Assembly approved the first set of Trusteeship Agreements in accordance with Article 85 of the UN Charter.[105] Only

---

[99] Charmian Edwards Toussaint, *The trusteeship system of the United Nations* (1956), p. vii.
[100] Article 76(b), UN Charter.
[101] Dietrich Rauschning, "Article 76" (2002), p. 1107.
[102] See section 2.4 of Chapter III.
[103] Articles 7 and 85, UN Charter.
[104] Annette Baker Fox, "The United Nations and Colonial Development" (1950), pp. 203 and 214.
[105] According to Article 85(1), "[t]he functions of the United Nations with regard to trusteeship agreements for all areas not designated as strategic, including the approval of the terms of the trusteeship agreements and of their alteration or amendment, shall be exercised by the General Assembly."

then could the Trusteeship Council be established and the Chapters on the Trusteeship Council become fully operational.[106] These agreements related to the following territories: New Guinea, Ruanda-Urundi, Cameroon, Togoland, Western Samoa and Tanganyika.[107] In the same resolution the Assembly appointed Australia, Belgium, France, New Zealand, and the United Kingdom as the Administering Authorities of these territories.[108] This automatically made them members of the Trusteeship Council, together with the remaining members of the Security Council, plus two elected members: Mexico and Iraq.[109] In 1947, certain Pacific Islands and Nauru were added to the list of trust territories,[110] followed in 1950 by Somalia.[111] The islands had the United States of America as the Administering Authority, Somaliland fell under the responsibility of Italy. No new territories have been added to the list since 1950. During the time of the League of Nations, a Mandate for Palestine was entrusted to the United Kingdom. Even though the United States called for a temporary trusteeship arrangement for Palestine in 1948, it never became a United Nations trusteeship.[112]

The Trusteeship Council was most apparent when it went on mission visits, interviewing the local inhabitants in the trust territories, and when it received petitions from those local inhabitants.[113] In some cases cultural conflicts occurred when the Trusteeship Council came to visit. For example, in the more traditional societies of the trust territories, a general rule applied that wisdom came with old age. Thus when a UN mission consisted mainly of young international civil servants and diplomats, this often had a negative effect on the respect shown to them by the local population.[114] Moreover, the United Nations was not well known as an organization in the colonial territories. In the early days, at least, "the peoples of the

---

[106] Charmian Edwards Toussaint, *The trusteeship system of the United Nations* (1956), pp. 34-35.
[107] Approval of Trusteeship Agreements, General Assembly resolution 63(I), adopted 13 December 1946. For a list of trust territories, see Dietrich Rauschning, "Article 75" (2002), pp. 1104-1105.
[108] *Idem.*
[109] See Article 86 UN Charter, and Establishment of the Trusteeship Council, General Assembly resolution 64(I), adopted 14 December 1946.
[110] Trusteeship of strategic areas, Security Council resolution 21, adopted 2 April 1947; Proposed Trusteeship Agreement for Nauru, General Assembly resolution 140(III), adopted 1 November 1947. The reason that the Pacific Islands were the concern of the Council, and not the Assembly, was because these islands were considered strategic areas in the sense of Article 83 UN Charter.
[111] Trusteeship Agreement for the Territory of Somaliland under Italian administration, General Assembly resolution 442 (V), adopted 2 December 1950.
[112] See the Minutes of the Security Council meeting of 19 March 19 1948, UNDoc. S/P. V. 271, which contain the discussions in the Security Council on the adoption and further implementation of Security Council resolution 42 (1948), adopted 5 March 5 1948. In recent times, it has been suggested once again to turn Palestine into a US-supervised trusteeship. See *e.g.*, Martin Indyk, "A trusteeship for Palestine?" (2003).
[113] John Fletcher-Cooke, "Some Reflections on the International Trusteeship System" (1959), pp. 425-429.
[114] *idem*, p. 427.

trust territories ha[d] only the vaguest impression of what the United Nations [was] all about."[115] This made it difficult to earn their trust and confidence.

Be that as it may, whenever a UN mission arrived in a particular territory – this happened once every three years – the locals saw it as a "heaven-sent opportunity to ventilate [their] grievances," and this they frequently did.[116] These grievances then ended up in the Council's reports, and the administering territory had to respond to them. The petition system was also quite successful. At first, very few petitions made it to the UN Headquarters in New York.[117] However, since 1949 the number of petitions has "widened to a torrent."[118] Some of these petitions, especially those containing more general complaints, also ended up in the Council's reports.

Unlike the Security Council and the Economic and Social Council, the Trusteeship Council actually finished its work, although this does not make it the most successful of the three councils. The Trusteeship Council had a limited task: to assist eleven territories on their way to "advancement." With the independence in 1994 of the last Pacific Island (Palau), all the trust territories have become independent, and the Trusteeship Council therefore now finds itself essentially with nothing to do.[119]

## 3.3 Non-self-governing territories

In addition to the category of trust territories, the UN Charter also recognized a category of non-self-governing territories. These were defined as "territories whose peoples have not yet attained a full measure of self-government."[120] As the General Assembly later stated, "the authors of the Charter of the United Nations had in mind that Chapter XI [of the UN Charter] should be applicable to territories which were then known to be of the colonial type."[121] Strictly speaking, the eleven trust territories were also colonial territories, and thus also non-self-governing territories.

---

[115] Sherman S. Hayden, "The Trusteeship Council" (1951), p. 232.
[116] John Fletcher-Cooke, "Some Reflections on the International Trusteeship System" (1959), p. 428.
[117] Sherman S. Hayden, "The Trusteeship Council" (1951), p. 232.
[118] *Idem*, p. 228.
[119] Recently, two major books were published which both claimed that the trusteeship-idea never really disappeared from the scene. See Carsten Stahn, *The law and practice of international territorial administration: Versailles to Iraq and beyond* (2008), and Ralph Wilde, *International territorial administration: how trusteeship and the civilizing mission never went away* (2008).
[120] See Article 73, and generally the Declaration regarding non-self-governing territories, which constituted chapter XI of the UN Charter.
[121] Principles which should guide Members in determining whether or not an obligation exists to transmit the information called for in Article 73(e) of the Charter of the United Nations, annexed to General Assembly resolution 1541(XV), adopted 15 December 1960 ("Principles for Article 73(e)"), principle 1.

This meant that the objectives for the non-self-governing territories also applied to the trust territories, but not the other way round.[122]

As not all the colonial powers were prepared to submit their colonial territories to the supervision of the Trusteeship Council, a much larger group of colonial territories remained which were not labelled as trust territories, but which were also considered to lack "a full measure of self-government." In 1945, these territories were found over almost the entire globe. The group included the Belgian and French Congo, South West Africa, Indo-China, the Netherlands Indies, Morocco, Tunisia, Greenland and Alaska. At some point all these territories, and many others, had been considered to be non-self-governing territories. [123] The Trusteeship Council was not entrusted with any particular supervisory role for the non-self-governing territories, except for the eleven trust territories,[124] but at least colonial issues were no longer considered a domestic matter for the colonial powers. The chapter emphasized that "colonial problems should be considered as international problems and not merely problems of individual colonial powers,"[125] and that the international community recognized colonial territories as separate entities in international law.[126]

The ultimate objective for this gigantic group of non-self-governing territories was not "their progressive development towards self-government or independence as may be appropriate," as was the case for the trust territories, but a much more modest objective:

> To develop self-government, to take due account of the political aspirations of the peoples, and to assist them in the progressive development of their free political institutions, according to the particular circumstances of each territory and its peoples and their varying stages of advancement.[127]

The most important difference between the trust territories and the other non-self-governing territories was the difference in the ultimate objective: "self-government

---

[122] See also Charmian Edwards Toussaint, *The trusteeship system of the United Nations* (1956), pp. 53 and 229.

[123] The Belgian and French Congo both became independent in 1960, and are now the Democratic Republic of the Congo and the Republic of the Congo. South West Africa became independent in 1990, as Namibia. Indo-China became independent in the 1940s and 1950s, as Laos, Vietnam and Cambodia. The Netherlands Indies became independent in 1949, as Indonesia. Morocco and Tunisia both became independent in 1956. Greenland and Alaska did not become independent, and are now an autonomous country within the Kingdom of Denmark and one of the United States of America, respectively.

[124] See Article 88, UN Charter.

[125] Huntington Gilchrist, "Colonial Questions at the San Francisco Conference" (1945), p. 982.

[126] Ulrich Fastenrath, "Article 73" (2002), p. 1090.

[127] Article 73(b), UN Charter.

or independence" for the trust territories, and "self-government" only for the other non-self-governing territories.[128]

This difference in the ultimate objective had to some extent already been "corrected" by the Assembly in 1952. The Assembly then proclaimed a list of "factors indicative of the attainment of independence or of other separate systems of self-government." [129] In this way the Assembly attempted to determine more specifically when a non-self-governing territory could be considered to be self-governing. It was important to determine this, because as soon as the territory concerned could be considered to be self-governing, the specific obligations relating to these territories, included in the Charter's declaration on non-self-governing territories, ceased to apply. [130] As factors indicative of the attainment of independence, the Assembly referred to a territory's capacity to assume international responsibility for both internal and external sovereign acts, its eligibility for UN membership, and the territory's capacity to enter into relations with other governments. The Assembly also referred to the existence within such territories of a separate government, acting without control or interference from other States, and based on the principle of "complete freedom of the people of the territory to choose the form of government which they desire."[131] This last criterion can be considered to be very strict, especially for its time. The question even arises whether all the States that were already recognized as independent and sovereign States at the time actually fulfilled this last criterion.[132]

In 1960, the Assembly declared that a "Non-Self-Governing Territory can be said to have reached a full measure of self-government by emergence as a sovereign independent State, free association with an independent State, or integration with an independent State." [133] The Assembly did not elaborate on the first option. Presumably, what was meant by becoming a sovereign State was self-evident. With regard to the second option, free association, the Assembly stressed that such an association could only come about on the basis of the "free and voluntary choice by the peoples of the territory concerned expressed through informed and democratic processes."[134] Similarly, integration "should be on the basis of complete equality

---

[128] Compare Articles 76 and 73, UN Charter. See also Ulrich Fastenrath, "Article 73" (2002), p. 1090. Other differences, such as the explicit reference to human rights only in the chapter on trust territories were soon "interpreted away" by the Assembly. See already Racial discrimination in Non-Self-Governing Territories, General Assembly resolution 644(VII), adopted 10 December 1952.

[129] Factors which should be taken into account in deciding whether a Territory is or is not a Territory whose people have not yet attained a full measure of self-government, General Assembly resolution 648(VII), adopted 10 December 1952 ("Factors").

[130] See especially the reporting obligation of Article 73(e), UN Charter. See also principles II and X-XII, Principles for Article 73(e).

[131] Factors, First Part, Section B.

[132] See also Clyde Eagleton, "Excesses of Self-Determination" (1953), p. 600.

[133] Principles for Article 73(e), principle VI.

[134] *Idem*, principle VII.

between the peoples of the erstwhile Non-Self-Governing Territory and those of the independent country with which it is integrated," and be the result of the "freely expressed wishes of the territory's peoples [...] their wishes having been expressed through informed and democratic processes."[135] This leads to the conclusion that there was a presumption that peoples wanted to become States, and that if they chose otherwise, it had to be crystal clear that this was a free choice, arrived at without any outside pressure or coercion.[136] Both free association and integration were considered a suspect category, in the sense that some form of outside coercion was almost automatically presumed when a non-self-governing territory preferred either of these two options to independence.[137] Almost all of the non-self-governing territories have become independent States, and chose not to become associated or integrated with an existing State.[138]

## 3.4 Conclusion

Despite the careful language in the Charter, the Assembly explicitly expressed a preference for independence over other forms of self-government, and this is what happened with most of the non-self-governing territories.[139] Almost all of them ended up, in a relatively short time, as independent States.

It is difficult to see this process of decolonization, and the UN's role in this, as being based on, or inspired by, the chapters in the UN Charter about non-self-governing territories. First of all, the UN Charter did not see immediate independence as the desirable goal for all these territories. In fact, one could go even further and argue that the emphasis on independence as a goal for all non-self-governing territories was a deviation from the UN Charter's chapter on these territories, as the general "advancement" of the colonial peoples could be hindered by granting them independence too soon. The swiftness of the decolonization process was considered a problem by some commentators. For example, Eagleton reminded the United Nations that its duty to "guard the welfare of the whole community appear[ed] to be in direct conflict with the supposed obligation to produce more and more infant states and turn them loose upon the streets."[140] However, once the process of decolonization started, there was no way back.

---

[135] *Idem*, principles VIII and IX.
[136] See also Hurst Hannum, "Rethinking self-determination" (1993), p. 14, and pp. 40-41.
[137] See also James Crawford, "The Right of Self-Determination in International Law" (2001), p. 17.
[138] Some territories did not become independent States. Netherlands New Guinea, Hong Kong, the Cameroons, Togoland, Alaska and Hawaii all joined another State. There are still 16 non-self-governing territories, most of which are islands in the Atlantic, Pacific and Indian Oceans, and the Caribbean Sea.
[139] See *e.g.*, Progress achieved in Non-Self-Governing Territories, General Assembly resolution 1535 (XV), adopted 15 December 1960.
[140] Clyde Eagleton, "Excesses of Self-Determination" (1953), pp. 601-602.

This quest for independence cannot be based on the chapters in the UN Charter discussed up to now. There is another version of the story, not based on the three chapters on trust and non-self-governing territories in the UN Charter, but rather on the value of self-determination of peoples. This story is the subject of the remainder of this chapter.

## 4    THE RIGHT OF PEOPLES TO SELF-DETERMINATION

### 4.1 Introduction

Article 1(2) of the UN Charter lists as one of the purposes of the United Nations:

> To develop friendly relations among nations based on respect for the principle of equal rights and self-determination of peoples.

Respect for the principle of self-determination of peoples was seen in the UN Charter as a basis for the development of friendly relations among nations. Thus it was not seen as a purpose on its own.

However, as Cassese noted, "in the decades immediately following the Second World War, the principle [of self-determination] embedded in article 1(2) of the United Nations Charter evolved in a manner which those who drafted it could not have foreseen."[141] Most importantly, the value of self-determination became detached from the goal of developing friendly relations among nations, so that "self-determination has become an independent and absolute value."[142]

This process, which was led by the Assembly, started very early on.[143] After detaching self-determination of peoples from the purpose of developing friendly relations among States, the Assembly turned the principle of self-determination into a revolutionary principle, in exactly the same way as the principle of the universal protection of human rights. The principle of self-determination became a legal instrument, not to develop friendly relations among States, but to support the liberation struggles of the colonial peoples and other oppressed groups of people. This revolution often jeopardized, rather than "developed," the friendly relations among nations, as the Belgian delegate had already foreseen in San Francisco.[144]

---

[141] Antonio Cassese, *Self-determination of peoples: a legal reappraisal* (1995), p. 44. See also Rosalyn Higgins, *Problems and process* (1994), pp. 111-112.

[142] Antonio Cassese, "Political self-determination" (1979), p. 147.

[143] See *e.g.*, Recommendations concerning international respect for the right of peoples and nations to self-determination, General Assembly resolution 1188 (XII), adopted 11 December 1957.

[144] See section 2.2 of Chapter VII.

The first part of this section looks for a general definition of the word "people," as used in the value of self-determination of peoples. This is followed by an examination of the application of the principle of self-determination to three different types of "peoples": colonial peoples, the entire population of a State, and minority peoples within a State.

## 4.2 Definition of peoples entitled to self-determination

Initially, only colonial peoples were recognized as having a right to self-determination. As it was clear what was meant by colonial peoples, there was no need to look for a definition of "peoples". Very soon, the colonial powers started to complain about what they perceived to be an arbitrary application of a general legal principle to a select group of peoples. They believed that it was unfair that their administration of colonial peoples was subject to international supervision, while the administration by States of other distinct peoples was not. The UN Charter clearly distinguished colonial peoples from all other peoples by devoting three chapters to the former category, and not a word to the plight of peoples residing within the metropolitan areas of a State (minorities). This distinction was followed in practice, even though its justification was not always clear.[145] Belgium was particularly outspoken in its criticism.[146] It proposed what came to be known as the "Belgian thesis," according to which the Declaration on non-self-governing territories should be applicable to all non-self-governing peoples, including indigenous peoples and other minorities residing within a State.[147] This thesis was rejected by the majority of Member States.

As time progressed and the United Nations was "dredging the bottom of the colonial reservoir," the principle of the self-determination of peoples – though not the Charter's chapters on non-self-governing territories – was also applied beyond the colonial context.[148] The first time that a general provision on the self-determination of peoples was included in a legal instrument, after the adoption of the UN Charter, was in the 1950s, when the classic human rights covenants were drafted.[149] The Article on the self-determination of peoples reads as follows:

---

[145] See Article 74, UN Charter.

[146] Charmian Edwards Toussaint, *The trusteeship system of the United Nations* (1956), pp. 233-234.

[147] See Patrick Thornberry, "Self-determination, minorities, human rights" (1989), pp. 873-875.

[148] Elmer Plischke, "Self-Determination" (1977), p. 47.

[149] Admittedly, it took a long time (until 1976) before these covenants actually entered into force.

All peoples have the right of self-determination. By virtue of that right they freely determine their political status and freely pursue their economic, social and cultural development.[150]

As Franck later pointed out, the *travaux* of this Article showed that even in the 1950s, "the majority [of delegates] utterly rejected the notion that the entitlement applied only to colonial 'peoples,' declaring, rather, that if included [in the human rights covenants], it must apply to peoples everywhere."[151] The universal application of the right to self-determination made the need for a general definition of peoples more urgent than ever, but the human rights covenants did not define "people" at all.

In the search for a general definition of "peoples," the suggestion that the term is applicable only to individuals with a common religion, language, culture and/or ethnic origin must be rejected. Such a definition gives the impression that only homogeneous groups are entitled to self-determination. States do not have homogeneous populations consisting solely of individuals of the same ethnic, linguistic, and religious group. If the word "people" is interpreted as referring to a group of individuals united by shared ethnic, linguistic and religious characteristics, the entire population of a State cannot be referred to as a people. As Chowdhury explained, there is not a single State comprised of a "people" in that sense.[152] It has never been the goal to establish States with homogeneous populations. If all people with a shared language, ethnic origin etc. were granted their own State, then State borders would have to be redrawn, and most States would fall apart into several new States.[153] Individuals with a mixed heritage would have to live in different States simultaneously. This would not only be a tremendous operation, but as Falk rightly pointed out, "nurturing the dream of statehood for the several thousand distinct peoples in the world will provide continual fuel for strife."[154]

---

[150] Article 1 of the International Covenant on Civil and Political Rights, annexed to General Assembly resolution 2200A (XXI), adopted 16 December 1966, entry into force 23 March 1976); and Article 1 of the International Covenant on Economic, Social and Cultural Rights, annexed to the same General Assembly resolution, entry into force 3 January 1976.

[151] Thomas M. Franck, "The Emerging Right to Democratic Governance" (1992), p. 58. See also Alexandre Kiss, "The peoples' right to self-determination" (1986), p. 174.

[152] S.K. Roy Chowdhury, "The status and norms of self-determination in contemporary international law" (1977), pp. 75-76. See also Robert McCorquodale, "Self-determination: a human rights approach" (1994), p. 866.

[153] Buchanan referred to this idea that all "people" deserve their own State as the "Nationalist Principle." See Allen E. Buchanan, "The right to self-determination: analytical and moral foundations" (1991), p. 46.

[154] See also Richard A. Falk, "Self-determination under international law" (2002), p. 31. See also p. 36.

There is no reason whatsoever to adopt such a narrow definition of the concept of a "people."[155] Most importantly, contrary to what some philosophers believe, the General Assembly never adopted such a definition.[156] Moreover, there are good reasons for not defining "people" in this way. What makes the concept valuable is that it allows a certain group of individuals to complain *as a group* – and thus not as isolated individuals – against outside oppression aimed *at the group*.[157] In colonial times, the so-called "colonial peoples" did not constitute a homogenous group. Far from it. They often comprised individuals of different ethnic tribes with a wide variety of religious beliefs. What united them, and what made them a "people," was the fact that they were oppressed by a colonial power. Or, to use the words of the Declaration on the Granting of Independence to Colonial Countries and Peoples, they were united by being subjected to alien subjugation, domination and exploitation.[158] The same applies for the entire population of a State – and for minority groups – who are oppressed by their own government. Therefore it is the oppression that alienates the oppressed from the oppressor. If the term "people" is interpreted in this way, *i.e.* as defining a group of individuals united in their struggle against outside oppression, the concept of "people" can be applied to colonial peoples, the entire population of a State, and minority peoples.[159]

---

[155] Efforts were also made to define "people" in less substantive terms. For example, Cristescu suggested that a "people" could be identified with the help of the following elements: "the term 'people' denotes a social entity possessing a clear identity and its own characteristics," and "it implies a relationship with a territory, even if the people in question has been wrongfully expelled from it and artificially replaced by another population." Cristescu, Special Rapporteur of the UN Sub-Commission on Prevention of Discrimination and Protection of Minorities, *The Right to Self-Determination: Historical and Current Development on the Basis of United Nations Instruments*, a study published in 1981, UNDoc. E/CN.4/Sub.2/404/Rev. 1, para. 279. Cristescu added a third element, which was that "a people should not be confused with ethnic, religious or linguistic minorities, whose existence and rights are recognized in article 27 of the International Covenant on Civil and Political Rights." Some scholars, most notably Higgins, do believe that the issue of minority rights can be dealt with exclusively through Article 27, and that they should thus not be regarded as a "people." See Rosalyn Higgins, *Problems and process* (1994), pp. 124-125.

[156] Allen E. Buchanan, "Toward a Theory of Secession" (1991), pp. 328-329. Buchanan believed that using self-determination of peoples as basis for secession meant dividing the world into peoples, defined in the narrow terms just rejected.

[157] This comes very close to the argument made in Daniel Philpott, "In Defense of Self-Determination" (1995), pp. 364-366. He suggested that a group more or less identifies itself as such, when it starts to make claims and rebels against what it considers to be an oppressive "foreign" domination. However, Philpott did not believe some form of oppression was required to justify any claim to secession or statehood (see especially pp. 366-369). See also Margaret Moore, "On National Self-Determination" (1997), pp. 905-907.

[158] See section 4.3 of Chapter VII.

[159] See also Robert McCorquodale, "Self-determination beyond the colonial context and its potential impact on Africa" (1992).

## 4.3 The self-determination of colonial peoples

Initially the right to self-determination of peoples was used as a "convenient weapon against colonialism."[160] It was applied mainly with regard to the colonial peoples struggling for liberation. The fundamental questions relating to the self-determination of peoples – who? what? how? – all had relatively straightforward answers. According to the "colonial version" of the principle of self-determination, "the populations of colonies, within their existing frontiers, should receive full independence at the earliest opportunity and the metropolitan powers had the duty to carry this out."[161] Although each of these answers to the who?, what? and how? questions is a matter of debate, the process of decolonization did take place along these lines.

In 1952, the Assembly recommended that all States should "recognize and promote the realization of the right of self-determination of the peoples of Non-Self-Governing and Trust Territories."[162] Thus it linked the value of the self-determination of peoples to the Charter's chapters on trusteeship and on the non-self-governing territories. The Charter itself did not make this link.[163] With a single resolution, the Assembly changed the objective of "advancement" into that of "self-determination," overruling the tortuous compromise reached after the difficult discussions in San Francisco.[164] Furthermore, the States responsible for the administration of the non-self-governing territories were required to report on the "extent to which the right of peoples and nations to self-determination [was] exercised by the peoples of those Territories."[165] This reporting duty was based on Article 73(e) of the UN Charter, but there was nothing in that article about self-determination. According to the article on the right to self-determination contained in both classic human rights covenants: "The States [...] having responsibility for the administration of Non-Self-Governing and Trust Territories, shall promote the realization of the right of self-determination, and shall respect that right, in conformity with the provisions of the Charter of the United Nations."[166] The end of the sentence suggests that the obligation to promote the self-determination of the

---

[160] Satpal Kaur, "Self-determination in international law" (1970), p. 482.

[161] Sally Healy, "The principle of self-determination still alive and well" (1981), p. 17.

[162] The right of peoples and nations to self-determination, General Assembly resolution 637(VII), adopted 16 December 1952, Section A.

[163] The UN's role in the transformation of the non-self-governing territories into sovereign States, and the UN's role in promoting the right to self-determination of colonial peoples, are discussed separately in this study only to improve the clarity of the examinations.

[164] See section 2.1 of Chapter VII, above.

[165] The right of peoples and nations to self-determination, General Assembly resolution 637(VII), adopted 16 December 1952, Section B.

[166] Article 1(3), International Covenant on Civil and Political Rights and International Covenant on Economic, Social and Cultural Rights.

dependent territories was based on the UN Charter. However, the UN Charter did not oblige these States to promote self-determination, and the Assembly and the human rights covenants had therefore considerably changed the colonial powers' obligations.[167]

To remove all possible doubts, the Assembly adopted the most important resolution on decolonization a few years later. This was the Declaration on the Granting of Independence to Colonial Countries and Peoples.[168] Nirmal referred to it as "a milestone in the crusade against colonialism."[169] Whether or not "crusade" is a particularly fortunate choice of words, one must surely agree with Nirmal that this resolution marked the "acceptance of self-determination as an appropriate idiom for the process of decolonization."[170] It clearly and definitively replaced the more carefully phrased objectives regarding the non-self-governing territories in the UN Charter with the objective of self-determination. The Assembly, recognizing the "passionate yearning for freedom in all dependent peoples," declared that "all peoples ha[d] the right to self-determination [and that] by virtue of that right they freely determine their political status and freely pursue their economic, social and cultural development."[171]

The principal idea of the Declaration on the Granting of Independence to Colonial Countries and Peoples was that the colonized peoples were entitled to their own sovereign State. Hannum stated that the thrust of the resolution could be summarized in just one sentence: "All colonial territories have the right of independence."[172] The Assembly urged that immediate steps be taken for all "territories which have not yet attained independence, to transfer all powers to the peoples of those territories, without any conditions or reservations, in accordance with their freely expressed will and desire, without any distinction as to race, creed or colour, in order to enable them to enjoy complete independence and freedom."[173]

Many resolutions have been adopted since to monitor and encourage the implementation of the Declaration on the Granting of Independence to Colonial Countries and Peoples. These resolutions were particularly addressed to the most

[167] See also Antonio Cassese, *Self-determination of peoples: a legal reappraisal* (1995), p. 58.
[168] Declaration on the Granting of Independence to Colonial Countries and Peoples, General Assembly resolution 1514 (XV), adopted 14 December 1960 ("Declaration on the Granting of Independence to Colonial Countries and Peoples"). One year later, the Assembly established a Special Committee on Decolonization to oversee the implementation of the declaration. See The Situation with regard to the Implementation of the Declaration on the Granting of Independence to Colonial Countries and Peoples, General Assembly resolution 1654 (XVI), adopted 27 November 1961.
[169] B. C. Nirmal, *The right to self-determination in international law* (1999), p. 42.
[170] Sally Healy, "The principle of self-determination still alive and well" (1981), p. 17.
[171] Declaration on the Granting of Independence to Colonial Countries and Peoples, para. 2. This formulation was an exact copy of Article 1 of the two human rights covenants, an article which was drafted already in 1955, but which took a long time to enter into force.
[172] Hurst Hannum, "Rethinking self-determination" (1993), p. 12.
[173] Declaration on the Granting of Independence to Colonial Countries and Peoples, para. 5.

persistent colonizers. In the beginning, no specific countries were mentioned,[174] but later on, the Assembly named Portugal and South Africa as "colonial Powers" that "refuse[d] to recognize the right of colonial peoples to independence."[175]

The means available to colonial peoples to fight for their independence was a particularly problematic issue. In 1965, the Assembly "recognize[d] the legitimacy of the struggle by the peoples under colonial rule to exercise their right to self-determination and independence and invite[d] all States to provide material and moral assistance to the national liberation movements in colonial Territories."[176] These "national liberation movements" were later also referred to as "freedom fighters,"[177] or "fighters for freedom and self-determination."[178]

This issue of the legality of (armed) resistance to colonialism was revisited when the Friendly Relations Declaration was being drafted.[179] During the second session of the drafting committee, more delegates from developing nations were invited to participate.[180] The result was immediately apparent.[181] It was suggested that the Charter prohibited the use of force in international relations, that the relationship between a colonial power and the colonial territories was such an "international relation," and that therefore the use of force by colonial powers against their colonial peoples was prohibited under Article 2(4) UN Charter.[182] Others suggested that Article 2(4) was strictly about the use of force between sovereign States, and that it therefore said nothing about the relationship between colonial powers and their colonial territories.[183]

---

[174]See *e.g.*, The Situation with regard to the Implementation of the Declaration on the Granting of Independence to Colonial Countries and Peoples, General Assembly resolution 1810 (XVII), adopted 17 December 1962, para. 5.

[175] Implementation of the Declaration on the Granting of Independence to Colonial Countries and Peoples, General Assembly resolution 2105 (XX), adopted 20 December 1965.

[176] *Idem*, para. 10. One year later, the Assembly went as far as to "declare[..] that the continuation of colonial rule threaten[ed] international peace and security." See Implementation of the Declaration on the Granting of Independence to Colonial Countries and Peoples, General Assembly resolution 2189 (XXI), adopted 13 December 1966, para. 6.

[177] Programme of action for the full implementation of the Declaration on the Granting of Independence to Colonial Countries and Peoples, General Assembly resolution 2621 (XXV), adopted 12 October 1970, para. 6(a).

[178]Basic Principles of the Legal Status of the Combatants Struggling Against Colonial and Alien Domination and Racist Regimes, General Assembly resolution 3103 (XXVIII), adopted 12 December 1973.

[179] See section 5.5 of Chapter III.

[180] Consideration of principles of international law concerning friendly relations and co-operation among states in accordance with the Charter of the United Nations, General Assembly resolution 2103 (XX), adopted 20 December 1965.

[181] See also Bert V.A. Röling, "International Law and the Maintenance of Peace" (1973).

[182] Special Committee on Principles of International Law concerning Friendly Relations and Co-operation among States, Report, A/6230, adopted 27 June 1966 ("Second Report"), para. 113.

[183] Special Committee, Second Report, paras. 114.

It was also suggested that under Article 51 UN Charter, colonial peoples had a right to defend themselves against colonial oppression by using armed force.[184] Opponents of this interpretation of the Charter suggested that Article 51 only recognized the inherent right of States to defend themselves, and that colonial peoples did not have their own State.[185] During the third session of the drafting committee, the right of self-defence for colonial peoples against colonial domination was once again proclaimed – and denied – by various States represented in the Committee.[186] During the fourth session, the right of colonial peoples to use armed force to defend themselves against colonial domination was referred to as a "sacred right." At the same time, it was suggested that if such an exception to the prohibition on the use of force were accepted, any rebel group could call itself a "liberation group" and refer to the opponent as a "neo-colonialist" power, in this way legalizing its use of force.[187] At the end of the discussions of the drafting committee's fifth session, the only serious disagreement that remained, and the only reason that no final text could be adopted, was the suggested right of colonial peoples to use armed force to defend themselves against colonial domination.[188] According to many representatives, such a right was inconsistent with the UN Charter, which gave only States a right to self-defence, and in any case no system of law could possibly establish a legal right of revolution, whatever the cause of such revolution. The same was said of minorities within a State. It was suggested that if grave discrimination occurred against any ethnic minority inside an independent State, that minority would have the right to rebel, but that it would be a purely domestic matter.[189]

In the end, no exception for colonial liberation struggles was inserted in the provision on the prohibition on the use of force finally adopted by the Committee.[190] What was included was the duty of every State to refrain from any use of force which deprived peoples of their right to self-determination. This duty was reiterated under the heading of self-determination, and followed by a paragraph stating that, in their actions to resist such armed actions, these peoples were entitled

---

[184] Special Committee, Second Report, paras. 136-147. See also Vekateshwara Subramanian Mani, *Basic principles of modern international law* (1993), pp. 40-48.

[185] Special Committee, Second Report, paras. 151. Sohn had a big influence on the text of Article 51, as he himself later claimed. See Louis B. Sohn, "The issue of self-defense and the UN Charter" (1995).

[186] Special Committee on Principles of International Law concerning Friendly Relations and Co-operation among States, Report, A/6799 ("Third Report"), paras. 100-106.

[187] Special Committee on Principles of International Law concerning Friendly Relations and Co-operation among States, Report, A/7326, adopted 30 September 1968 ("Fourth Report"), paras. 102-110.

[188] Special Committee on Principles of International Law concerning Friendly Relations and Co-operation among States, Report, A/7619, adopted 19 September 1969 ("Fifth Report"), p. 40.

[189] Special Committee, Fifth Report, paras. 111-116, and paras. 166-168, and 177 (on self-determination).

[190] See also Gaetano Arangio-Ruiz, "The normative role of the General Assembly" (1972), p. 569.

to receive foreign support.[191] This does sound like an internationally recognized right of colonial peoples to self-defence.

A few years later, the Assembly proclaimed certain basic principles determining the legal status of "freedom fighters" fighting for liberation from colonial powers. The most important of these principles was that "the struggle of peoples under colonial and alien domination and racist regimes for the implementation of their right to self-determination and independence [was] legitimate and in full accordance with the principles of international law."[192] The Assembly also proclaimed, *inter alia*, that "the armed conflicts involving the struggle of peoples against colonial and alien domination and racist regimes [were] to be regarded as international armed conflicts."

As time passed, many colonies became independent, with or without the use of armed force. On the twenty-fifth anniversary of the Declaration on the Granting of Independence to Colonial Countries and Peoples, the Assembly was pleased to note that in the past twenty-five years, approximately one hundred States had emerged into "sovereign existence," and that "the process of national liberation [was thus] irresistible and irreversible."[193]

In 1990, all that was required was to "remove the last vestiges of colonialism in all regions of the world."[194] Apart from the thorny issue of the Western Sahara and East-Timor, the only colonies left in the world were some small islands. Referring to those remaining colonies, the Assembly "declare[d] that exercise of the right to self-determination should be carried out freely and without outside pressure, in a form reflecting authentic interests and aspirations of the peoples."[195] Options other than independence were available to these islands. These other options (integration or association with an existing State) particularly appealed to them, as many were too small to function as an independent State.[196]

In 2010, The Assembly celebrated the fiftieth anniversary of the Declaration on the Granting of Independence to Colonial Countries and Peoples. It

---

[191] Special Committee on Principles of International Law concerning Friendly Relations and Co-operation among States, Report, A/8018, adopted 1 May 1970 ("Sixth Report"), p. 43.

[192] Basic Principles of the Legal Status of the Combatants Struggling Against Colonial and Alien Domination and Racist Regimes, General Assembly resolution 3103 (XXVIII), adopted 12 December 1973, Principle 1.

[193] Twenty-fifth anniversary of the Declaration on the Granting of Independence to Colonial Countries and Peoples, General Assembly resolution 40/56, adopted 2 December 1985.

[194] Thirtieth anniversary of the Declaration on the Granting of Independence to Colonial Countries and Peoples, General Assembly resolution 45/33, adopted 20 November 1990, para. 3.

[195] International Decade for the Eradication of Colonialism, General Assembly resolution 46/181, adopted 19 December 1991, para. 3.

[196] In 2010, the General Assembly was "deeply concerned about the fact that, fifty years after the adoption of the Declaration, colonialism has not yet been totally eradicated." The mission was thus not yet completed. See Fiftieth anniversary of the Declaration on the Granting of Independence to Colonial Countries, General Assembly resolution 65/118, adopted 10 December 2010.

"recogniz[ed] the significant and commendable role played by the United Nations, since its very inception, in the field of decolonization, and not[ed] the emergence, during this period, of more than one hundred States into sovereign existence."[197]

## 4.4 The self-determination of entire populations of an independent State

Cassese pointed out that the word "peoples," as used in Article 1 of the human rights covenants, also applied to "entire populations living in independent and sovereign States."[198] Initially not much attention was devoted to this application, as there was a lack of political urgency.[199] The application was simply assumed.[200] Whenever the meaning of the word "people" was discussed, the dominant question was always whether it referred solely to colonial peoples – a suggestion explicitly denied in the legal instruments referred to above[201] – or whether it also applied to minority groups within a State. Other applications, such as the application to the entire population of a State, were not extensively discussed.

An exception to this general rule is the Friendly Relations Declaration, adopted in 1970. In that Declaration there is one notorious paragraph about the right to self-determination of the entire population of a State:

> Nothing in the foregoing paragraphs [on the self-determination of peoples should] be construed as authorizing or encouraging any action which would dismember or impair, totally or in part, the territorial integrity or political unity of sovereign and independent States conducting themselves in compliance with the principle of equal rights and self-determination of peoples and thus possessed of a government representing the whole people belonging to the territory without distinction as to race, creed or colour.[202]

---

[197] Fiftieth anniversary of the Declaration on the Granting of Independence to Colonial Countries and Peoples, General Assembly resolution 65/118, adopted 10 December 2010.

[198] Antonio Cassese, *Self-determination of peoples: a legal reappraisal* (1995), pp. 59-62. Cassese explicitly rejects this view. According to Higgins, the entire population of a State was the only group, besides colonial peoples, to which the label "people" was applicable. See Rosalyn Higgins, *Problems and process* (1994), p. 124.

[199] During the drafting of the human rights covenants, this type of self-determination did not get much attention. The few references to the right to self-determination of "majorities" as oppsed to "minorities" might point in the direction of a right to self-determination of the entire peoples. However, it is not quite the same. See, *e.g.*, Greece's remark at General Assembly's Third Committee, 647th Meeting, 28 October 1955, UNDoc. A/C.3/SR.647, or the remark at Special Committee, Third Report, para. 194.

[200] This only changed when it was "discovered" that the right to self-determination of peoples could actually be used against the government of a State. This will be discussed in the next section.

[201] For the Friendly Relations Declaration, see also C. Don Johnson, "Toward self-determination" (1973), p. 152.

[202] Friendly Relations Declaration.

This clause was reiterated in some of the most important declarations, in particular the Vienna Declaration and Programme of Action (1993),[203] and the Declaration on the Occasion of the Fiftieth Anniversary of the United Nations (1995).[204] In both these documents the phrase "without distinction as to race, creed or colour" was replaced by "without distinction of any kind," to emphasize that the list of prohibited distinctions in the Friendly Relations Declaration was not exhaustive.[205]

Although it reads like a savings clause, it is in reality much more than that.[206] It described the essence of the right to self-determination as being applicable to the entire population of a State. Rosenstock, who played a principal part in the drafting of the clause, considered that "a close examination of its text [would] reward the reader with an affirmation of the applicability of the principle [of self-determination] to peoples within existing states and the necessity for governments to represent the governed."[207] The clause suggests that respect for the right to self-determination of the entire population of a State requires that the entire population is represented in some way by the government of that State. According to Higgins, the right should be interpreted as requiring that "a free choice be afforded to the peoples, on a continuing basis, as to their system of government, in order that they [could] determine their economic, social, and cultural development."[208] It was the right of the entire population to control its own destiny.

This interpretation of the principle of self-determination would be consistent with that of the drafters of the UN Charter. In 1945 it had already been agreed that "an essential element of the principle in question [was] a free and genuine expression of the will of the people, which avoid[ed] cases of the alleged expression of the popular will, such as those used for their own ends by Germany

---

[203] Vienna Declaration and Programme of Action, para. 2.

[204] Declaration on the Occasion of the Fiftieth Anniversary of the United Nations, General Assembly resolution 50/6, adopted 24 October 1995, para. 1.

[205] See also James Crawford, "The Right of Self-Determination in International Law" (2001), p. 56. Antonio Cassese, *Self-determination of peoples: a legal reappraisal* (1995), pp. 112-118, believed that the list of prohibited distinctions in the Friendly Relations Declaration was exhaustive. He basically suggested that only religious and racial (minority) groups were protected by the savings clause.

[206] See also Antonio Cassese, *Self-determination of peoples: a legal reappraisal* (1995), pp. 108-125, who focuses almost entirely on this "savings clause" in his discussion of internal self-determination.

[207] Robert Rosenstock, "The Declaration of Principles of International Law Concerning Friendly Relations" (1971), p. 732.

[208] Rosalyn Higgins, *Problems and process* (1994), pp. 119-120. Thornberry simply defined self-determination as "the right of all peoples to govern themselves." Patrick Thornberry, "The principle of self-determination" (1994), p. 175. Plischke defined it as "the continuing exercise of free choice by peoples respecting their own political destiny." Elmer Plischke, "Self-Determination" (1977), p. 46. Similarly, Brownlie believed that the "core [of the principle of self-determination of peoples] consists in the right of a community which has a distinct character to have this character reflected in the institutions of government under which it lives." Ian Brownlie, "The Rights of Peoples in Modern International Law" (1988), p. 5.

and Italy in later years."[209] Any dictatorial government, comparable to the German and Italian governments during the Second World War, constituted a violation of the right to self-determination of the oppressed peoples. The principle basically called for some form of "representative government" in which "all the elements of the population of the territory [were] represented in the appropriate – representative – institutions."[210]

The link between the right to self-determination of peoples and representative government has often been reiterated in the literature, especially by liberal lawyers and philosophers. Franck, one of the most influential lawyers in the former category, was one of the first to argue for an "emerging right to democratic government," largely based on the right to self-determination.[211] According to Franck, self-determination could be seen as the "historic root from which the democratic entitlement grew."[212] This view was also supported by liberal philosophers, who argued that participation in a democratic community came closest to the liberal ideal, a world where all individuals live in the society in which they choose to live.[213]

A distinction is made between self-determination as applied to the relationship between peoples and their "own" rulers, and the relationship between peoples and oppressive forces "from outside." The former is referred to as "internal" and the latter as "external" self-determination.[214] Thornberry described this distinction most succinctly, when he referred to external self-determination as "casting off alien rule," and internal self-determination as "putting forward the people as the ultimate authority within the State."[215] The problem with this distinction is that it is highly artificial. What is a question of "internal" self-determination from the point of view of the oppressing government is often a matter

---

[209] Report of Rapporteur of Committee 1 to Commission I, June 13, 1945, UNCIO, vol. 6, p. 455. See also Antonio Cassese, "Political self-determination" (1979), pp. 138-139, who has a slightly different interpretation of the UNCIO statement.

[210] See also Gaetano Arangio-Ruiz, "The normative role of the General Assembly" (1972), p. 570. In Hurst Hannum, "Rethinking self-determination" (1993), p. 17, it is pointed out that "representative government" is not a synonym of "democracy."

[211] Thomas M. Franck, "The Emerging Right to Democratic Governance" (1992), especially pp. 52-56.

[212] *Idem*, p. 52. Other scholars later agreed that self-determination, if applied to the entire population of a State, essentially came down to a claim for "democratic government." See Antonio Cassese, "The International Court of Justice and the right of peoples to self-determination" (1996), p. 352, who simply equated "internal self-determination" with "democratic government."

[213] Harry Beran, "A liberal theory of secession" (1984), pp. 24-25.

[214] Cassese is generally credited for having "invented" this distinction. See Antonio Cassese, "Political self-determination" (1979), p. 137. See also Rosalyn Higgins, *Problems and process* (1994), p. 117; Allan Rosas, "Internal self-determination" (1993), especially p. 232; Alexandre Kiss, "The peoples' right to self-determination" (1986), pp. 170-171; Frank Przetacznik, "The basic collective human right to self-determination of peoples and nations as a prerequisite for peace" (1990), pp. 54-55; Robert McCorquodale, "Self-determination: a human rights approach" (1994), pp. 863-864.

[215] Patrick Thornberry, "Self-determination, minorities, human rights" (1989), p. 869.

of "external" self-determination from the point of view of the oppressed peoples themselves.[216] This applies particularly to oppressed minority groups, who consider what might officially be their "own" government to be an oppressor "from outside."

It is not clear what the implications are of an entitlement to representative government. Does it mean that other States or the international community as a whole can interfere in the domestic affairs of a non-democratic State to assist the entire population of that State in securing its right to self-determination? The most obvious way to do so would be to remove the non-representative government from power and replace it with a democratically elected government. However, the principle of sovereign independence, itself also based on the value of the self-determination of peoples, prevents such action.[217] Only when the right to democratic governance, as based on self-determination, prevails over the principle of sovereign independence, can such interference be justified.[218]

## 4.5 The self-determination of minority peoples

The term "people" is not restricted to the entire population of a State or to colonial territories.[219] As Moore remarked, to grant a right to self-determination only to those categories would be "inconsistent and ethically problematic."[220] Indigenous peoples and other minority peoples also have a right to self-determination.

The term "minority peoples" is used to refer to a particular kind of "peoples," *i.e.* a particular group of individuals entitled to self-determination as a group. Minority peoples are groups of individuals who constitute an identifiable minority within a particular State. It is not the meaning of the term "minority" that is a matter of concern here, but the meaning of the term "people."

Be that as it may, it is still useful to say a few words about minorities here, in order to explain what is meant by the term "minority people." A "minority" is sometimes defined simply in a mathematical sense. In that case it is a distinct group of individuals living in a society where they constitute a relatively small part of the

---

[216] And thus Rosas was entirely correct when he remarked that "even in its 'external' dimension, self-determination cannot be completely detached from the idea of democracy." Allan Rosas, "Internal self-determination" (1993), especially p. 235.

[217] See section 5 of Chapter VII, below.

[218] See also Pieter Hendrik Kooijmans, "Tolerance, sovereignty and self-determination" (1996), p. 212; and Ved P. Nanda, "Self-determination and secession under international law" (2001), p. 310.

[219] This view was highly criticized in Clyde Eagleton, "Excesses of Self-Determination" (1953). Eagleton point out that it is not easier to distinguish a colonial people than it is to distinguish a minority people. Most so-called "colonial peoples" were probably not homogenous groups at all. See also David Makinson, "Rights of peoples" (1988), p. 74.

[220] Margaret Moore, "On National Self-Determination" (1997)," p. 902. Moore actually believed this restricted view was the view of the UN. See also S. Prakash Sinha, "Has self-determination become a principle of international law today?" (1974), p. 347 and pp. 359-360.

general population.[221] A minority has also been defined in a more substantive sense. In that case the term refers to a group of people whose "ethnic, religious or linguistic traditions or characteristics [...] differ from those of the rest of the population."[222] Individuals belonging to a minority as defined in that sense have been granted special protection and certain privileges. See Article 27 of the International Covenant on Civil and Political Rights,[223] and the Declaration on the Rights of Persons Belonging to National or Ethnic, Religious and Linguistic Minorities.[224] This special protection has little to do with any right to the self-determination of the minority. It simply stresses that individuals in a minority group need special protection to safeguard their individual human rights, which are identical to the individual human rights of the majority.[225] Minorities are perceived as yet another particularly vulnerable group of people, who find it difficult to have their human rights recognized and adequately protected.[226] The reason why the substantive definition of a minority has been rejected in the context of self-determination was precisely because it "eliminate[ed] from the definition certain national groups which should be given special protection."[227] An overemphasis on ethnic, religious and linguistic traditions would also label certain groups as a

---

[221] In this sense, the term minority is used as a relational term; it simply means that there are less individuals of one group (minority) than there are of another group (majority). See also David Makinson, "Rights of peoples" (1988), p. 73.

[222] Definition proposed by the Sub-Commission on Prevention of Discrimination and Protection of Minorities, UNDoc. E/CN.4/Sub.2/149, para. 26, as cited at Capotorti, Study on the Rights of Persons belonging to ethnic, religious and linguistic minorities, UNDoc. E/CN.4/SUB.2/384/REV.1, p. 5. On pp. 1-12 of the Study, one finds an excellent overview of attempts to define "minority."

[223] Article 27 reads as follows: "In those States in which ethnic, religious or linguistic minorities exist, persons belonging to such minorities shall not be denied the right, in community with the other members of their group, to enjoy their own culture, to profess and practise their own religion, or to use their own language." On the relationship between Article 1 and 27, see Patrick Thornberry, "Self-determination, minorities, human rights" (1989), pp. 877-881.

[224] Declaration on the Rights of Persons Belonging to National or Ethnic, Religious and Linguistic Minorities, annexed to General Assembly resolution 47/135, adopted 18 December 1992.

[225] See also Human Rights Committee, General Comment no. 23 on the rights of minorities (Art. 27), adopted 8 April 1994, UNDoc. CCPR/C/21/Rev.1/Add.5. There, the Committee noted that "this article establishes and recognizes a right which is conferred on individuals belonging to minority groups" (para. 1). The Committee explicitly separates this approach from the people's-approach of Article 1 (para. 3.1) These rights are therefore discussed in Chapter VI on human dignity. See also Rosalyn Higgins, *Problems and process* (1994), pp. 126-127; James Crawford, "The Right of Self-Determination in International Law" (2001), pp. 23-24, and Philip Alston, "Peoples' Rights: Their Rise and Fall" (2001), p. 274. Some authors are very convinced that minorities are generally excluded from the peoples with a right to self-determination. See *e.g.*, Jean Salmon, "internal aspects of the right to self-determination" (1993), especially p. 256.

[226] See section 6.4 of Chapter VI.

[227] Francesco Capotorti, Study on the Rights of Persons belonging to ethnic, religious and linguistic minorities, UNDoc. E/CN.4/SUB.2/384/REV.1, p. 6. See also James Crawford, "The Right of Self-Determination in International Law" (2001), pp. 64-65.

minority, though they should not be labelled as such. An example could be the Chinese living in Chinatown, New York.[228] Such minority groups are not entitled to autonomy or secession, but they are in need of special protection to guarantee their individual human rights.

In this chapter, the term "minority" does not refer to a group of people who are vulnerable to human rights violations because of their particular ethnic, religious or linguistic characteristics. Here, the term simply refers to a group of a relatively small number of individuals residing in a particular State. The way in which the minority can be distinguished from the majority differs in each case, and is left open. When considering whether such minority groups have the right to self-determination, the question is whether they can be considered as a "people." As Ryngaert and Griffioen pointed out, "minorities and peoples are not mutually exclusive terms;"[229] the one category ("people") does not by definition include the other ("minority").

The *travaux* of the common Article 1 in the human rights covenants provide an authoritative reflection of the views of various States on the question whether minorities could qualify as a "people." According to Venezuela the term "peoples" did not apply to "racial, religious, or other groups or minorities."[230] Greece suggested that the principle applied, not to minorities but only to "national majorities living in their own territory but unable freely to determine their political status."[231]

On the other hand, the delegate of the UK believed that "the concept of self-determination could not be whittled down to exclude minorities," because "its great force lay precisely in the fact that it was all embracing."[232] Thus it was necessary to carefully consider the consequences of granting minorities a right to self-determination. [233] Similarly the Soviet Union suggested that its own implementation of the right should be seen as exemplary. It recognized the right of all Soviet nations, as yet without statehood, to "free self-determination even to the extent of secession and the establishment of independent States."[234]

---

[228] See also Frank Przetacznik, "The basic collective human right to self-determination of peoples and nations as a prerequisite for peace" (1990), p. 52.

[229] *Idem*, p. 578.

[230] General Assembly's Third Committee, 646th Meeting, 27 October 1955, UNDoc. A/C.3/SR.646.

[231] General Assembly's Third Committee, 647th Meeting, 28 October 1955, UNDoc. A/C.3/SR.647.

[232] General Assembly's Third Committee, 642nd Meeting, 24 October 1955, UNDoc. A/C.3/SR.642.

[233] General Assembly's Third Committee, 652nd Meeting, 4 November 1955, UNDoc. A/C.3/SR.652.

[234] General Assembly's Third Committee, 646th Meeting. However, some authors suggest that – at least in practice - the Soviet Union intended to apply the principle of self-determination exclusively to the colonies. See Antonio Cassese, "Political self-determination" (1979), p. 140; Frank Przetacznik, "The basic collective human right to self-determination of peoples and nations as a prerequisite for peace" (1990), p. 108; Robert McCorquodale, "Self-determination beyond the colonial context and its potential impact on Africa" (1992), pp. 596-599.

A literal reading of Article 1, as it was initially proposed, is consistent with the view that minority groups were not excluded from the definition of a "people." All the paragraphs of the initial draft of the Human Rights Commission applied to *all* peoples, not just colonial peoples. The provision read as follows:

> All States, including those having responsibility for the administration of Non-Self-Governing and Trust Territories and *those controlling in whatsoever manner the exercise of that right by another people*, shall promote the realization of that right in all their territories, and shall respect the maintenance of that right in other States, in conformity with the provisions of the United Nations Charter.[235]

This provision applied to all peoples, albeit with a special reference to the responsibilities of States responsible for colonial territories. It therefore obliged all States to promote the self-determination of any people within its territory.

To prevent such a universal application, the provision was redrafted to make it applicable only to colonial territories.[236] India defended the new discriminatory provision, stating that "the colonial problem was the most pressing," and that "the problems of other groups might be tackled later."[237] Iraq was more categorical. It believed that "the right of self-determination applied to a people under foreign domination, whether it could be defined as a nation or not, but not to a separatist movement within a sovereign State."[238] These two States were thinking of the treatment of their own minority groups. Many former colonies were faced with similar issues with regard to minorities within their State borders. As Thornberry remarked, such issues were largely concealed from international scrutiny in colonial times, but after decolonization, minorities in former colonies had good reason to fear that the "inter-ethnic solidarity in the face of a common alien oppressor may be ruptured and replaced by a more intimate, local and knowing oppression."[239] In general, it can be said that the Western States favoured the universal application of the right to self-determination, while "the new States

---

[235] Emphasis added. Commission on Human Rights, Report of the Tenth Session, 23 February—16 April 1954, UNDoc. E/2573, p. 62.
[236] Although all peoples were granted a right to self-determination, the Working Party (a drafting commission) changed the paragraph on obligations (para. 2 in the initial proposal cited above and para. 3 in the Working Party's draft) in such a way that only States responsible for Trust Territories and Non-Self-Governing Territories had a responsibility to promote the realization of the right in territories under their jurisdiction. See UNDoc. A/C.3/L.489. As Belgium rightly pointed out, in this way the right and the obligation were inconsistent, the former being universal and the latter applicable only to colonial peoples. General Assembly's Third Committee, 669th Meeting, 23 November 1955, UNDoc. A/C.3/SR.669.
[237] General Assembly's Third Committee, 671st Meeting, 25 November 1955, UNDoc. A/C.3/SR.671. During the same meeting, Pakistan expressed an identical view.
[238] *Idem*.
[239] Patrick Thornberry, "Self-determination, minorities, human rights" (1989), p. 867.

which had won independence under the banner of self-determination were not at all prepared to concede this right to their own minorities." [240] The discriminatory redraft was soon "undone" at the request of Yugoslavia in particular, but with the approval of most States. [241] Thus the provision which was finally adopted once again fully applied to all peoples, including minority peoples. [242]

With the recognition of minorities as "peoples" entitled to self-determination, the consequences of this right also had to be discussed. Sweden immediately came to the point, when its delegate stated that "it was problematical [...] whether every minority should be deemed to have the right to sever its connexion with the political entity to which it belonged." [243] The key problem was whether minority peoples had a right to secede and start their own State. According to China, this question had already been settled in San Francisco in 1945, when it was decided that "the principle [of self-determination] conformed to the purposes of the Charter only insofar as it implied the right of self-government of peoples and not the right of secession." [244] The Netherlands delegate believed that the provision as it was first drafted could be read to mean that "every group which regarded itself as a nation was entitled to form a State of its own, irrespective of whether it had previously been part of another State or had been ruled by another State." [245] This would also apply to minority peoples. Canada, whose population included various indigenous peoples and other minority peoples, believed that the preferences and interests of such minority peoples should not automatically prevail over those of the State as a whole. A balance had to be found, and the automatic right to secession of minority peoples lacked sufficient flexibility. [246] Australia, where there were also

---

[240] Sally Healy, "The principle of self-determination still alive and well" (1981), p. 18. See also Jean-François Dobelle, "Article 1, paragraphe 2" (2005), p. 340.

[241] General Assembly's Third Committee, 669th Meeting. Yugoslavia submitted an amendment, to make the application universal once more: A/C.3/L.489. Many States supported the amendment. See Denmark, General Assembly's Third Committee, 669th Meeting; UK, Costa Rica, General Assembly's Third Committee, 670th Meeting, 24 November 1955, UNDoc. A/C.3/SR.670; Netherlands, Iraq, General Assembly's Third Committee, 671st Meeting.

[242] Unfortunately, India preferred to maintain its position that the right only applied to colonial peoples, and especially not to minority groups within a State. See the Declaration made by India at the time of its accession to the International Covenant on Economic, Social and Cultural Rights, on 10 April 1979, and the objection made by the Netherlands on 12 January 1981, both available at http://treaties.un.org. See also Allan Rosas, "internal self-determination" (1993), p. 242; Patrick Thornberry, "Self-determination, minorities, human rights" (1989), p. 879; Hurst Hannum, "Rethinking self-determination" (1993), pp. 25-26; See also James Crawford, "The Right of Self-Determination in International Law" (2001), pp. 28-29.

[243] General Assembly's Third Committee, 641st Meeting, 21 October 1955, UNDoc. A/C.3/SR.641.

[244] Sixth Meeting of Committee I/1, May 14, 1945, UNCIO, vol. 6, p. 296. See also Colombia, Saudi Arabia, General Assembly's Third Committee, 648th Meeting, 31 October 1955, UNDoc. A/C.3/SR.648. See also Antonio Cassese, *Self-determination of peoples: a legal reappraisal* (1995), p. 40.

[245] General Assembly's Third Committee, 642nd Meeting.

[246] General Assembly's Third Committee, 645th Meeting, 27 October 1955, UNDoc. A/C.3/SR.645.

various indigenous peoples, similarly believed that it would be unfortunate if the human rights covenants suggested that "any minority [was allowed] freely to determine its own status," rather than stating that "minorities should have equal rights with majorities within a State."[247]

Other States also believed that it would be enough if the rights and interests of minority peoples were sufficiently represented in government. For example, Greece stressed that the right to self-determination of peoples was a "corollary of the democratic principle of government with the consent of the governed."[248] If the question could be settled by allowing minority peoples meaningful participation in domestic politics, then the Netherlands foresaw a more practical problem. It believed that it was not always clear how a minority could express itself in domestic government, as there was often no official representative of minority groups.[249]

The debate on this topic was not definitively settled in the Committee. The text of the covenant is ambiguous – or silent – on exactly what "peoples," especially minority peoples, are entitled to. This is not surprising, considering that there was no generally agreed definition of either "people" or "minority" in the first place. Thus it may be concluded that the precise application of the right to self-determination is almost entirely dependent on the context.[250]

After 1955, when the drafting of the common Article 1 was finished, the Assembly adopted various other resolutions on a more general right of peoples to self-determination. The Declaration on the Granting of Independence to Colonial Countries and Peoples of 1960 proclaimed the right to self-determination of colonial peoples, but said little about minorities.[251] One of the most important resolutions is the Friendly Relations Declaration adopted in 1970 at a time when the "substantial work of decolonization was already over."[252]

As the Friendly Relations Declaration is such an important resolution on the right to self-determination of minority peoples, it is worth looking in more detail at the *travaux préparatoires*. During the second session of the Special Committee responsible for drafting it, a number of newly independent States were invited to join the debate.[253] From that second session onwards, the Committee started to

---

[247] General Assembly's Third Committee, 647th Meeting.

[248] *Idem.* See also Denmark, General Assembly's Third Committee, 644th Meeting, 26 October 1955, UNDoc. A/C.3/SR.644.

[249] General Assembly's Third Committee, 642nd Meeting. See also Belgium, in General Assembly's Third Committee, 643rd Meeting, 25 October 1955, UNDoc. A/C.3/SR.643. See also David Makinson, "Rights of peoples" (1988), pp. 77-78.

[250] Richard A. Falk, "Self-determination under international law" (2002), p. 47.

[251] Declaration on the Granting of Independence to Colonial Countries and Peoples, General Assembly resolution 1514 (XV), adopted 14 December 1960.

[252] B. C. Nirmal, *The right to self-determination in international law* (1999), p. 43. See also p. 152,

[253] Consideration of principles of international law concerning friendly relations and co-operation among states in accordance with the Charter of the United Nations, General Assembly resolution 2103 (XX), adopted 20 December 1965.

work on the principle of equal rights and the self-determination of peoples.[254] It was suggested that this principle, as proclaimed in Article 1(2) UN Charter, should apply both to States and to peoples, and possibly even to individuals,[255] but that it was currently most relevant in the colonial context.[256] According to this principle, peoples under colonial rule – and possibly also other peoples – had a right to independence, and a right to freely choose their political system.[257]

It is interesting to point out that it was once again the new States that suggested that the principle should apply, first and foremost, to colonial peoples. This caused Houben, the Dutch delegate at the Committee, to remark that it was "seriously distressing that the majority of the United Nations membership [was] so little interested in the universal application of the principle of self-determination," which he considered "a blatant example of the supremacy of narrow self-interest over the demands of world-wide justice." [258] This remark was not entirely inappropriate, since it was mainly the Western States that called for the universal application of the right to self-determination, and the "new" States that called for a "discriminatory" application.[259]

One of the main problems in defining the principle of self-determination, as acknowledged during the third session of the Special Committee, was to determine the beneficiaries of this right. It was suggested that all peoples had a right to self-determination, but others objected that this would motivate minority groups within States to claim "people" status and then to secede. Therefore it was suggested that the principle applied only to a majority within a generally accepted political unit.[260] According to India, the principle's application should be even more restricted. In the Indian delegate's view, it "was applicable only to peoples under alien subjugation or colonial rule, but not to parts of existing States." [261] This suggestion that the principle applied, as a special privilege, exclusively to colonial peoples, which India also brought forward when the human rights covenant was

---

[254] Special Committee, Second Report. As noted in Edward McWhinney, "The 'New' Countries and the 'New' International Law" (1966), p. 2, the influence of the small countries on the work of the Special Committee was already visible during the first session, but this influence only increased in subsequent sessions.

[255] The link with human rights was made from the very beginning. See Special Committee, Second Report, paras. 464 and 489.

[256] Special Committee, Second Report, paras. 464, 477-479.

[257] Special Committee, Second Report, paras. 480-481.

[258] Piet-Hein Houben, "Principles of International Law Concerning Friendly Relations and Co-Operation Among States" (1967), p. 724.

[259] No agreement was reached during this session of the Committee. Special Committee, Second Report, para. 519.

[260] Special Committee, Third Report, para. 194.

[261] Vekateshwara Subramanian Mani, *Basic principles of modern international law* (1993), p. 230.

drafted, was rejected.[262] Thus there was a general consensus that the right to self-determination was "a universal right of *all* peoples."[263]

The principle of self-determination was also discussed extensively during the Special Committee's fourth session. One of the first issues brought to the table was whether reference should be made to a right of all peoples to self-determination, or to a principle of self-determination which entailed certain duties for States.[264] This is a very important point, because if self-determination is considered as a principle, there is no immediate need to consider peoples as separate entities, with their own rights and duties in international law. As Rosenstock remarked in the Special Committee, there was a "split between those who accepted a right of self-determination of peoples and the duty of states to grant it, and those who argued that under international law only states could have rights or be the beneficiaries of rights."[265] One representative preferred the latter option, as it was still difficult to determine exactly who would have the right of self-determination, if this were to be proclaimed as a right.[266]

During the fifth session, many of the debates of the previous session continued. The idea that the principle applied to all peoples gained some ground.[267] It was suggested that the application of the principle to "multinational States" would strengthen rather than weaken this application, as "the right was the very foundation of a voluntary association among the peoples."[268] At the same time, some representatives suggested that granting each tribal, racial, ethnic and religious group a right to self-determination would carry the principle to an "absurd extreme."[269] Ethnic minorities subject to grave forms of discrimination had the right to rebel, but this was not considered an international issue.[270]

In the end, the Friendly Relations Declaration does not explicitly exclude or include minorities, or any other group, in its definition of "peoples." It merely stated that

---

[262] Special Committee, Third Report, paras. 195-196, 198. See also Gaetano Arangio-Ruiz, "The normative role of the General Assembly" (1972), p. 565.

[263] Robert Rosenstock, "The Declaration of Principles of International Law Concerning Friendly Relations" (1971), p. 731.

[264] Special Committee on Principles of International Law concerning Friendly Relations and Co-operation among States, Report, A/7326, adopted 30 September 1968 ("Fourth Report"), paras. 154-160.

[265] Robert Rosenstock, "The Declaration of Principles of International Law Concerning Friendly Relations" (1971), p. 730.

[266] Special Committee, Fourth Report, para. 157.

[267] Special Committee, Fifth Report, para. 156.

[268] *Idem*, para. 176.

[269] *Idem*, para. 157.

[270] *Idem*, para. 177.

> By virtue of the principle of equal rights and self-determination of peoples enshrined in the Charter of the United Nations, all peoples have the right freely to determine, without external interference, their political status and to pursue their economic, social and cultural development, and every State has the duty to respect this right in accordance with the provisions of the Charter.[271]

The consequences of accepting the right to self-determination of minority peoples were also discussed. Some delegates believed that only by becoming a sovereign State could peoples be regarded as being able to successfully exercise this right. Others believed that what mattered was that peoples achieved some form of self-government through their own free choice. If they chose a free association with an existing State, or integration into an existing State, that would be just as acceptable as the choice to become an independent State. [272] What was important was that it was up to the peoples themselves. They always had the option of becoming an independent State.[273]

Those were the general rules. But did they also apply to minority peoples? The most thorny issue was the right to secession.[274] Secession essentially meant independence. The word "secession" was never used in reference to the liberation, or road to independent statehood, of colonial peoples, but it quickly became the key word in the discussions about the rights of minority peoples. According to Emerson, this difference was easy to explain, as "the transition from colonial status to independence" [was] seen as "the 'restoration' of a rightful sovereignty of which the people ha[d] been illegitimately deprived by the colonial Power." [275] The situation was entirely different with respect to minority peoples, or so it was suggested.[276]

It was believed that the principle of self-determination of all peoples should not be formulated in such a way that it entailed "the right of any group of disaffected people to break away at their pleasure from the State to which they presently belong[ed] and establish a new State closer to their hearts' desire," *i.e.*

---

[271] Friendly Relations Declaration. However, when one looks at the description of the exact obligations that flow from the right to self-determination as so defined, there are good reasons to include minorities into the definition.

[272] Special Committee, Third Report, paras. 211-213. See also Vekateshwara Subramanian Mani, *Basic principles of modern international law* (1993), pp. 243-244.

[273] Christian Tomuschat, "Self-determination in a post-colonial world" (1993), p. 12.

[274] On secession, including this thorny issue, see also Marcelo G. Kohen (editor), *Secession: international law perspectives* (2006).

[275] Emerson, "Self-Determination" (1971), p. 465.

[276] Of course, one can object to this. Indigenous peoples (*e.g.*, Indians, Inuits), for example, must by definition be seen as the original owners of the land they live on, and the remainder of the population effectively occupied this land.

motivating all kinds of secessionist movements.[277] However, if minority peoples were not entitled to secession, what exactly were they entitled to? The right to self-determination was closely linked to the right of all individuals – including individuals of minority peoples – to have the chance of meaningful political influence. The right to self-determination called for a democratic form of government, or at least a government which "derive[d] its existence and powers from a certain minimum of consent of the peoples under its control."[278]

Some last minute discussions about the problem of secessionist movements took place during the sixth and final session of the Special Committee.[279] The question of secession was the most difficult unresolved question at that time. It was suggested that the right to secession of minority peoples was not a right under international law, but rather an issue to be regulated by domestic constitutional law. The international principle of non-intervention would ensure that a State could deal with the issue independently of other States. In response, it was suggested that all peoples – and not just colonial peoples – had a right to self-determination under international law. This meant that minority peoples were a separate entity in international law, precisely because they could be defined as a "people." In that case, the exercise of the right to self-determination by such a minority would by definition be an international issue, and not an issue of essentially domestic concern.[280]

In the end the Assembly solemnly proclaimed that "all peoples have the right freely to determine, without external interference, their political status and to pursue their economic, social and cultural development."[281] This was a right to be promoted and respected by all States, and States owed this duty directly to all peoples.[282] Furthermore, the Assembly explained that "the establishment of a sovereign and independent State, the free association or integration with an independent State or the emergence into any other political status freely determined by a people constitute[d] modes of implementing the right of self-determination by that people."[283] The choice was up to the peoples themselves.[284] These modes of implementation were available to all peoples, not just colonial peoples.

---

[277] Special Committee, Fourth Report, paras. 163-164. The description is taken from Satpal Kaur, "Self-determination in international law" (1970), p. 491. The author strongly rejected that secession could be based on the right to self-determination (see *idem*, p. 493).

[278] *Idem*, paras. 185-188. During the fifth session, the link between self-determination and democracy was once again acknowledged. The principle of self-determination was even referred to as "one of the fundamental elements of modern democracy." Special Committee on Principles of International Law concerning Friendly Relations and Co-operation among States, Report, A/7619, adopted 19 September 1969 ("Fifth Report"), para. 147.

[279] Special Committee, Sixth Report.

[280] Special Committee, Fifth Report, pp. 52-53.

[281] Friendly Relations Declaration.

[282] See also Gaetano Arangio-Ruiz, "The normative role of the General Assembly" (1972), pp. 564-565.

[283] *Idem*.

There is good reason to suggest that the drafters did *not* intend to grant minority peoples a right to secede. The "savings clause" in the Friendly Relations Declaration supports this conclusion. This clause suggests that as long as all individuals, including individuals that are in some way identifiable as a minority group, are represented by their own government in some way and are not suppressed by the majority, no issues following from the right to self-determination of peoples will arise.[285] In Crawford's words, peoples are not "non-self-governing" in a State with a representative government: since they are represented in government, they are self-governing.[286] This implies that minorities residing within a State do not, at least not in all circumstances, have the option of becoming a separate State.[287] The rule is that secession is prohibited, and any group wanting to secede therefore has to present arguments showing why its case is exceptional. The most important exceptional circumstance, as implied in the "savings clause," is political exclusion and oppression of the minority by the majority.

This issue came up recently in a case before the International Court of Justice.[288] In 2008, the General Assembly of the United Nations asked the International Court of Justice to give legal advice on the following question:

> Is the unilateral declaration of independence by the Provisional Institutions of Self-Government of Kosovo in accordance with international law?[289]

Although the question was not directly about Kosovo's claim to statehood, or about the right of the people of Kosovo to self-determination and secession from Serbia, this was clearly the underlying issue. The question then, was whether any claim to secession by Kosovo, and possibly international assistance to the people of Kosovo in enforcing that claim, would constitute a violation of Serbia's sovereign independence. If the general rules outlined above are followed, the people of

---

[284] S.K. Roy Chowdhury, "The status and norms of self-determination in contemporary international law" (1977), p. 81.

[285] As is often pointed out, this might mean that a "pure" democracy is not good enough, since it might prevent certain small minorities from having their particular interests taken care of. See S.K. Roy Chowdhury, "The status and norms of self-determination in contemporary international law" (1977), pp. 77-78; Hurst Hannum, "Rethinking self-determination" (1993), pp. 60-61; James Crawford, "The Right of Self-Determination in International Law" (2001), p. 26, and p. 65; Harry Beran, "A liberal theory of secession" (1984), pp. 26-28.

[286] James Crawford, *The creation of states in international law* (2006), p. 127.

[287] See also Patrick Thornberry, "The democratic or internal aspect of self-determination" (1993), p. 116.

[288] Before this case, the Court never had to deal with self-determination outside the colonial context in any great detail. See also Antonio Cassese, "The International Court of Justice and the right of peoples to self-determination" (1996); James Crawford, "The Right of Self-Determination in International Law" (2001), p. 36.

[289] Request for an Advisory Opinion, transmitted to the International Court of Justice pursuant to General Assembly resolution 63/3, adopted 8 October 2008.

Kosovo are entitled to secession from Serbia only if Serbia makes it impossible for the people of Kosovo to participate in Serbian politics, and if the Kosovo people are otherwise isolated and discriminated against *as a people*.

In their pleadings, the Netherlands suggested this application of the principle of self-determination to the situation in Kosovo. The Netherlands distinguished two "substantive conditions" for secession:

> A right to external self-determination [i.e. secession] only arises in the event of a serious breach of either [..] the obligation to respect and promote the right to self-determination due to the absence of a government representing the whole people belonging to the territory, or the denial of fundamental human rights to a people; or [...] the obligation to refrain from any forcible action which deprives people of this right.[290]

There was also a procedural condition. According to the Netherlands, secession was only an option in the case that "all effective remedies [were] exhausted in the pursuit of a settlement."[291] This meant that "all avenues must have been explored to secure the respect for and the promotion of the right to self-determination through available procedures, including bilateral negotiations, the assistance of third parties and, where agreed or accessible, recourse to domestic or indeed international courts and arbitral tribunals."[292] This view, *i.e.* that secession is a "qualified right," in the sense that it is available to minority groups only in exceptional circumstances as a measure of last resort, is generally shared in both the legal and philosophical literature.[293] The advisory opinion was issued by the International Court, but little was said about the extent of the rights of minorities to self-determination.[294]

---

[290] Verbatim record of the public sitting held on Thursday 10 December 2009, at 10 a.m., at the Peace Palace, on the Accordance with International Law of the Unilateral Declaration of Independence by the Provisional Institutions of Self-Government of Kosovo, available at http://www.icj-cij.org, p. 9.

[291] *Idem.*

[292] *Idem.*

[293] See *e.g.*, Dietrich Murswiek, "The issue of a right of secession – reconsidered" (1993), pp. 26-27; Patrick Thornberry, "The democratic or internal aspect of self-determination" (1993), p. 116; Cedric Ryngaert & Christine Griffioen, "The Relevance of the Right to Self-Determination in the Kosovo Matter" (2009), pp. 575-576, and p. 579; Allen E. Buchanan, "Toward a Theory of Secession" (1991), p. 342.

[294] The direct answer to the question actually posed by the Assembly was that international law had nothing to say about declarations made by individuals claiming to represent minorities residing within a particular State. See International Court of Justice, Accordance with Accordance with international law of the unilateral declaration of independence in respect of Kosovo, Advisory Opinion of 22 July 2010.

## 4.6 Arguments about various peoples' claims to self-determination

The States and the United Nations did not manage to define the term "people." They also failed to clearly define the content of any people's right to self-determination. The conceptual confusion resulting from this indecision inspired many scholars to endeavour to establish conceptual clarity.

According to Beran, Philpott and other liberal philosophers, all peoples had a *prima facie* right to secession. Such a right could be based directly on the liberal idea, that as far as possible, people were free to live in the society of their choice.[295] Any restrictions on this freedom had to be justified.[296] This was the case for both colonial and minority peoples.

For both lawyers and philosophers, it is unacceptable if one and the same principle is applied differently in identical situations. The principle of self-determination of peoples has to be applied "coherently."[297] It is necessary to explain why secession was the rule in the case of colonial peoples and other options were considered "suspect," while secession was the exception in the case of minority peoples.

One explanation is that the implementation of any people's right to self-determination must be balanced against the principle of the sovereign independence of the State, or as Buchanan put it, the right of the larger community to "preserve itself."[298] The effect on the State's sovereignty is more substantial if it is a metropolitan area that is at stake.[299] Another much more convincing argument is to see colonialism itself as a special circumstance. The argument is that the oppression of minority peoples generally does not reach the level of oppression used by

---

[295] Since personal choice and autonomy constituted the core of this argument, one possible argument to resist secession was the prevention of the emergence of a dictatorship. If the whole idea is that secession would benefit individual people's autonomy, and if secession would mean changing a democracy run by "foreigners" by a local dictatorship, this would not mean progress. See Allen E. Buchanan, "Toward a Theory of Secession" (1991), pp. 335-336; Daniel Philpott, "In Defense of Self-Determination" (1995), pp. 371-375.

[296] See Harry Beran, "A liberal theory of secession" (1984), especially pp. 30-31; Christopher H. Wellman, "A Defense of Secession and Political Self-Determination," (1995), especially p. 161; Daniel Philpott, "In Defense of Self-Determination" (1995). It must be pointed out that Philpott does not talk about secession, but about any actualization of self-determination. At the end of his article, he actually argues that "a presumption against secession should be adopted" and a "more benign form" of exercising one's right to self-determination must be found (*idem*, pp. 381-382), since secessionist movements lead to much bloodshed.

[297] See Martti Koskenniemi, "National Self-Determination Today" (1994), p. 242.

[298] Allen E. Buchanan, "Toward a Theory of Secession" (1991), pp. 332-335.

[299] See also James Crawford, "The Right of Self-Determination in International Law" (2001), p. 7; Cedric Ryngaert & Christine Griffioen, "The Relevance of the Right to Self-Determination in the Kosovo Matter" (2009), p. 575.

colonial powers to dominate colonial peoples.[300] It has to stop somewhere, otherwise all kinds of peoples, not treated entirely according to their own wishes, would be entitled to secede. In the end, this would lead to a situation in which "everyman's yard [is] his country."[301]

Some philosophers concluded from the above that a people's right to secession was *not* a *prima facie* right, but that it should be granted only in special circumstances.[302] The burden of proof was on the seceding people.[303] This should not be interpreted to mean that the existence of oppression alone *is* a justification for secession. The claim to self-determination is still based on the principle of autonomy, but taking other considerations into account, any claim to autonomy prevails over competing claims only in the case of oppression.[304] History actually reflects philosophy on this particular issue. Over the years, the actual desire for secession of minority peoples has not in general been based solely on claims for autonomy. In fact, as Higgins pointed out, "the desire of ethnic groups to break away [was] most noticeable when they [were] oppressed."[305]

International law has also adopted the latter view. Because the interests of the larger group (the State) and that of the international community have to be taken into account, secession can only be considered an option if the oppression reaches a certain level of gravity. This balancing act allows for the conclusion that it is only when the oppression of minority peoples approaches a level of gravity reminiscent of colonial times, that minority peoples have a right to secede. Minority peoples

---

[300] Hurst Hannum, "Rethinking self-determination" (1993), pp. 41-49. Hannum did not believe there actually was a right to remedial secession, but discussed various reasons why there ought to be such a right.

[301] Allen E. Buchanan, "Toward a Theory of Secession" (1991), pp. 337-338.

[302] Based on the idea that the exercise of the right to self-determination by one people – Rawls did not really differentiate between States and peoples - might affect the enjoyment of that same right by another people, John Rawls in his *Law of Peoples* (1999), especially p. 38, presented the right to self-determination as a conditional right. It could only be exercised with respect for the rights of other peoples and individuals.

[303] Allen E. Buchanan, "Toward a Theory of Secession" (1991), pp. 337-338. The most important ground for secession was "discriminatory redistribution," *i.e.* the situation where a minority is discriminated against when it comes to the distribution of the State's goods. The other group of philosophers did not deny the importance of historic and present grievances and oppression, but believed those to be supporting arguments, not necessary arguments. See Daniel Philpott, "In Defense of Self-Determination" (1995), pp. 375-378.

[304] As was pointed out in Alan Patten, "Democratic Secession from a Multinational State" (2002), especially pp. 559-561, the outcome of both competing theories ("a right to secession with lots of exceptions" versus "a right to secession only in special circumstances") was generally identical. Still, he tried to find a third way. In his view, secession was allowed only "when the State has failed to introduce meaningful constitutional arrangements that recognize the distinct national identity of (some) members of the secessionist group" (p. 563).

[305] Rosalyn Higgins, *Problems and process* (1994), p. 124.

have a right to what Crawford termed "remedial secession," but only "in extreme cases of oppression."[306]

This is how the savings clause of the Friendly Relations Declaration has generally been interpreted. [307] Thus secession was implicitly authorized in the savings clause of the Friendly Relations Declaration, but only as an *ultimum remedium*. In Kooijmans' words, the right to secession was the "avenging angel for the persistent denial of the right of (internal) self-determination of a minority group."[308] However, the focus should be on meaningful participation. As Franck pointed out, if this was the correct interpretation of the right to self-determination, it "stopped being a principle of exclusion (secession) and became one of inclusion: the right to participate."[309] In the view of the Canadian delegate speaking in the Committee which drafted the Friendly Relations Declaration, this was the correct approach, as "there would [...] be no danger that some might be misled in attempting to invoke the principle to justify the dislocation of a State within which various communities had been co-habiting successfully and peacefully for a considerable time."[310]

---

[306] James Crawford, *The creation of states in international law* (2006), p. 119. In the literature, the legality/desirability of "remedial secession" has received more attention than any issue relating to self-determination. See *e.g.*, Patrick Thornberry, "Self-determination, minorities, human rights" (1989), p. 876; Allen E. Buchanan, "Toward a Theory of Secession" (1991), pp. 330-332 and p. 342; Cedric Ryngaert & Christine Griffioen, "The Relevance of the Right to Self-Determination in the Kosovo Matter" (2009), p. 575; Margaret Moore, "On National Self-Determination" (1997), p. 902; Robert McCorquodale, "Self-determination beyond the colonial context and its potential impact on Africa" (1992), pp. 603-604; Robert McCorquodale, "Self-determination: a human rights approach" (1994), pp. 862 and 880 and 883. In the latter article (especially on p. 883), it is suggested that the right to self-determination only applies in cases of oppression. This is incorrect, however. The idea, rather, is that it always applies to a "people," but that secession is only a consequence of its application in cases of serious oppression. Hurst Hannum, "The right of self-determination in the twenty-first century" (1998), pp. 776-777, believed that the oppression-exception to the prohibition to secede was lex ferenda.

[307] For the sake of convenience, the savings clause will be repeated here: "Nothing in the foregoing paragraphs shall be construed as authorizing or encouraging any action which would dismember or impair, totally or in part, the territorial integrity or political unity of sovereign and independent States conducting themselves in compliance with the principle of equal rights and self-determination of peoples as described above and thus possessed of a government representing the whole people belonging to the territory without distinction as to race, creed or colour." Friendly Relations Declaration.

[308] Pieter Hendrik Kooijmans, "Tolerance, sovereignty and self-determination" (1996), p. 215. See also Ved P. Nanda, "Self-determination and secession under international law" (2001), p. 314; Cedric Ryngaert & Christine Griffioen, "The Relevance of the Right to Self-Determination in the Kosovo Matter" (2009), p. 581. Not everybody agreed. See *e.g.*, Johan D. van der Vyver, "The Right to Self-Determination and its Enforcement" (2004), pp. 427-430.

[309] Thomas M. Franck, "The Emerging Right to Democratic Governance" (1992), p. 59.

[310] Special Committee, Sixth Report, para. 177. Later on, the Canadian Supreme Court explicitly accepted the right to remedial secession, but denied it to the people of Quebec. See James Crawford, *The creation of states in international law* (2006), pp. 119-120.

The most authoritative example of this balancing act can be found in a judgment of the Canadian Supreme Court. The case before the Court was about the legal entitlements of the Quebecois. Because many of the most influential scholars on the topic were involved in the case, the Canadian Court became, at least for a short while, a pseudo-International Court of Justice.[311] In its judgment, the Court stated that

> A right to secession only arises under the principle of self-determination of peoples at international law where "a people" is governed as part of a colonial empire; where "a people" is subject to alien subjugation, domination or exploitation; and possibly where "a people" is denied any meaningful exercise of its right to self-determination within the state of which it forms a part. In other circumstances, peoples are expected to achieve self-determination within the framework of their existing state. A state whose government represents the whole of the people or peoples resident within its territory, on a basis of equality and without discrimination, and respects the principles of self-determination in its internal arrangements, is entitled to maintain its territorial integrity under international law and to have that territorial integrity recognized by other states.[312]

For minority peoples the right to form their own State (to secede) is unavailable, as long as they find themselves in a State providing them sufficient means to be represented in the government of that State.

This general rule also applies to a particular kind of minority: indigenous peoples. According to the United Nations Declaration on the Rights of Indigenous Peoples, "indigenous peoples have the right to self-determination," and "by virtue of that right they freely determine their political status and freely pursue their economic, social and cultural development."[313] It may be concluded from this general language, reminiscent of Article 1 of the human rights covenants, that indigenous peoples are a "people." The Declaration does not grant them a right to secede. Instead, the Assembly proclaimed that "indigenous peoples, in exercising their right to self-determination, have the right to autonomy or self-government in

---

[311] Abi-Saab, Franck, Pellet, Shaw, and Crawford all participated in some way. See James Crawford, "The Right of Self-Determination in International Law" (2001), footnote 105, on p. 47.

[312] Supreme Court of Canada, Reference re Secession of Quebec, judgment delivered 20 August 1998, para. 154. See also paras. 130 and 138. The judgment has been cited very frequently in the self-determination literature, since it is basically the only post-colonial self-determination judgment available. See in particular James Crawford, "The Right of Self-Determination in International Law" (2001), pp. 57-63. See also e.g., Ved P. Nanda, "Self-determination and secession under international law" (2001), pp. 316-317; Cedric Ryngaert & Christine Griffioen, "The Relevance of the Right to Self-Determination in the Kosovo Matter" (2009), p. 582.

[313] Article 3, Declaration on the Rights of Indigenous Peoples. As Thornberry rightly pointed out, indigenous peoples are almost by definition minorities. See Patrick Thornberry, "Self-determination, minorities, human rights" (1989), p. 869.

matters relating to their internal and local affairs, as well as ways and means for financing their autonomous functions;"[314] and that "indigenous peoples have the right to maintain and strengthen their distinct political, legal, economic, social and cultural institutions, while retaining their right to participate fully, if they so choose, in the political, economic, social and cultural life of the State."[315] Thus they have a right to participate in the government of the State in which they live, and to a certain degree of autonomy. But what if these rights and political privileges are not granted to them? What if indigenous peoples are gravely discriminated against, and what if they are completely barred from exercising any governmental functions?[316] The Declaration is silent on these matters. It was no accident that secession was not mentioned in the declaration as one of the options available to these peoples, but it is always difficult to interpret the meaning of silence.[317] Presumably, since indigenous peoples are minority peoples, the general rule also applies to them. Thus the extent of their rights as peoples depends only on the gravity of the oppression to which they are subjected by the majority.

## 4.7 Conclusion

Initially the principle of self-determination of peoples was used to dismantle the colonial empires. The United Nations has been very successful in convincing the colonial powers that their colonial possessions were immoral, in the sense that they violated the respect for the self-determination of the colonial peoples. The principle of self-determination of peoples therefore required that all colonial territories, whether they were trust territories or non-self-governing territories, had the right to complete independence. This is exactly what happened.

So far everything was relatively clear, calm, and uncontroversial. As Koskenniemi noted, it was during the period of decolonization that "we were able to contain [the principle's] potentially explosive nature by applying it principally to the relationships between old European empires and their overseas colonies."[318] With decolonization largely completed, the bomb burst. The consequences of the

---

[314] *Idem*, Article 4.

[315] *Idem*, Article 5.

[316] According to Margaret Moore, "An historical argument for indigenous self-determination" (2003), when answering these questions, past forms of injustice should also be taken into account, together with the present consequences of that past oppression (see especially p. 97). Although the past is very similar to that of the colonies, the present situation of many indigenous peoples is much better than the situation of the colonies when they all became independent States, and thus the indigenous peoples' claims may not be identical to those of the colonial peoples. See especially *idem*, p. 104. See also Allen E. Buchanan, "Toward a Theory of Secession" (1991), pp. 329-330.

[317] See Alfredsson, "The right of self-determination and indigenous peoples," who gives an overview of the debates on this matter (the article was published before the resolution was finally adopted). See also Christian Tomuschat, "Self-determination in a post-colonial world" (1993), p. 13.

[318] Martti Koskenniemi, "National Self-Determination Today" (1994), p. 241.

application of the principle of self-determination outside the colonial context, *i.e.* to *all* peoples, including the entire population of independent States and minority peoples within a State, was confusing and unclear, and there was a general lack of philosophical thinking about what "peoples" are. This lack of clarity led some scholars to extrapolate far-reaching consequences from the principle. Others argued that the principle did not even apply outside the colonial context.[319] It is hard to justify, in the language of international law, why one and the same principle should be applied in one way in the colonial situation and differently in all other situations. Therefore an attempt has been made to come up with a general theory and general criteria for the application of the principle to all peoples.

These were not that difficult to find. All claims based on self-determination have one thing in common: they are responses to oppression. As Falk rightly noted, "the whole history of the right of self-determination is, for better and worse, the story of adaptation to the evolving struggles of peoples variously situated to achieve effective control over their own destinies, especially in reaction to circumstances that are discriminatory and oppressive."[320] In this sense, there is nothing unique about the colonial form of oppression. Only the gravity of the oppression and the openness with which it was practised are unique.

A general rule was distilled on the basis of this history: if the oppression of a people reaches the level of oppression of "colonial times," or more in general, of flagrant and mass violations of human rights, the right to independence of such peoples should not be denied.[321] This rule, which can be referred to as the rule on remedial secession, can just as easily be applied to the oppression by local dictators as it can be applied to colonial rule.[322]

In post-colonial situations, independence was seen as an *ultimum remedium*. A preferable way for a State to respect the right to self-determination of its entire population, and that of minority peoples within it, was to grant them a right to meaningful political participation. This solution was unimaginable for the colonial peoples, but it is available in other situations. As long as this right was

---

[319] Cassese believed Article 1 of the human rights covenants only applied to "entire populations living in independent and sovereign States," "entire populations of territories that have yet to attain independence," and "populations living under foreign military occupation." Antonio Cassese, *Self-determination of peoples: a legal reappraisal* (1995), pp. 59-62.

[320] Richard A. Falk, "Self-determination under international law" (2002), p. 48.

[321] *Idem* (about indigenous peoples). Margaret Moore, "An historical argument for indigenous self-determination" (2003), pp. 90-91, also suggests that the mistreatment of indigenous peoples often reached the level of oppression in colonial times.

[322] See also James Crawford, *The creation of states in international law* (2006), p. 127. As Philpott phrased it, "just as self-governing people ought to be unchained from kings, nobles, churches, and ancient custom, self-determining peoples should be emancipated from outside control – imperial power, colonial authority, Communist domination." See Daniel Philpott, "In Defense of Self-Determination" (1995), pp. 352-353. International lawyers would probably say it the other way around, since the issue of secession started in colonial times.

granted, peoples had no right to secede. "Internal" self-determination comes first. "External" self-determination is only an option in extreme cases, when "internal" self-determination is frustrated.[323] In this sense, the self-determination of peoples was, in Hannum's words, "both a shield that protect[ed] a State (in most cases) from secession and a spear that pierce[d] the governmental veil of sovereignty behind which undemocratic or discriminatory regimes attempt[ed] to hide."[324]

The UN never took a clear position in the "peoples" debate. There is as yet no universal agreement about the application of the right to self-determination of peoples to *all* peoples. These uncertainties will not disappear in the near future. Nevertheless, the right to self-determination of peoples is now firmly established in international law, and the United Nations can congratulate itself for having played a crucial role in this.[325] It is often suggested that the principle should be recognized as having the status of *jus cogens*,[326] especially in relation to the struggle against the colonial domination of the 1960s.[327] This enthusiasm is in contrast with the lack of agreement about what the principle entails exactly, and what States should do to respect it. Another question is whether general rules and principles can be objectively applied. The United Nations quickly recognized the Republic of South Sudan, but has much more difficulty in reaching a common position on Kosovo or the Palestinian territories.[328]

---

[323] See also para. 138, Supreme Court of Canada, Reference re Secession of Quebec, judgment delivered 20 August 1998.

[324] Hurst Hannum, "Rethinking self-determination" (1993), p. 32.

[325] The International Court of Justice referred to the principle of self-determination of peoples as "one of the essential principles of contemporary international law." See Case Concerning East Timor (Portugal v. Australia), Judgment of 30 June 1995, para. 29, and the caselaw referred to there. See also International Court of Justice, Legal Consequences of the Construction of a Wall in the Occupied Palestinian Territory, Advisory Opinion of 9 July 2004, para. 155.

[326] Afghanistan, UNDoc. A/Conf.39/5 (Vol. II), p. 288; Bulgaria, p. 298, Cyprus, p. 303, Czechoslovakia, p. 304, Pakistan, p. 312, Peru, p. 313, Poland, p. 315, Ukraine, p. 319, USSR, p. 321; USSR, p. 294 of UNDoc. A/Conf.39/11[A], Sierra Leone, p. 300, Ghana, p. 301, Cyprus, p. 306. See also Hector Gros Espiell, "Self-determination and jus cogens" (1979); Alexandre Kiss, "The peoples' right to self-determination" (1986), p. 174; McCorquodale, "Self-determination beyond the colonial context and its potential impact on Africa," p. 594 and literature referred to there in footnote 8.

[327] Byelorussian Soviet Socialist Republic, p. 307 of UNDoc. A/Conf.39/11[A]; Ukraine, p. 322. See also Draft articles on Responsibility of States for Internationally Wrongful Acts, with commentaries, as included in the Yearbook of the International Law Commission, 2001, vol. II, Part Two, p. 85.

[328] Admission of the Republic of South Sudan to membership in the United Nations, General Assembly resolution 65/308, adopted 14 July 2011, without vote.

## 5    THE RIGHT OF STATES TO SELF-DETERMINATION

### 5.1  Introduction

History shows that the principle of self-determination of peoples has been used essentially to liberate peoples from governments that oppress them. This has been the case for all colonial peoples. It is also the case for minorities ruled by majority governments. It is equally true for the entire population of a State dominated by a dictatorial regime. But the same value of self-determination of peoples can also be used as the basis for State sovereignty. It can provide the moral basis for all States' claims for protection against unwanted interference from *other* States.

Statehood is the most comprehensive realization of the self-determination of peoples. Most peoples, especially the colonial peoples, saw statehood as their ultimate aim. Becoming an independent State was the ultimate expression or consequence of a people's right to self-determination, autonomy and responsibility for its own future. This sovereign independence was not a given once it was successfully achieved. It had to be continuously defended. The value of self-determination of peoples continued to serve as the value inspiring the on-going struggle for the sovereign independence of all peoples.

The principles of sovereign independence and equality of States are considered here as ways to protect the self-determination of peoples, organized in the form of a State, from outside oppression and coercion. As Crawford pointed out, it is only because this theory does not always work in practice, *i.e.* because so many peoples are ruled by governments that exploit rather than represent them, that it was necessary to distinguish "peoples" and States.[329] In the ideal situation, the State and its peoples are essentially one and the same thing.[330] In that case at least, the principle of self-determination of peoples and the principle of sovereign independence are, as Kooijmans said, "two sides of the same coin."[331] There are many States in the world where the actual situation comes close to the ideal. In such cases, the international community's obligation to respect the right to self-determination of the State, and its obligation to respect the self-determination of the State's entire population, are essentially identical.

The sovereign equality and independence of States is seen by States themselves as one of the most valuable principles of international law. It is something to cherish and defend. When the international community of States drafted the Vienna Convention on the Law of Treaties, and included a definition of

---

[329] James Crawford, "The rights of peoples" (1988), p. 56. See also pp. 166-167. See further Pieter Hendrik Kooijmans, "Tolerance, sovereignty and self-determination" (1996), p. 217.
[330] Obivously, this is not a factual statement. It is always possible to distinguish a group of people from the abstract concept we call State. See also David Makinson, "Rights of peoples" (1988), p. 73.
[331] Pieter Hendrik Kooijmans, "Tolerance, sovereignty and self-determination" (1996), p. 217.

*jus cogens* in that Convention, two of the most popular examples of *jus cogens* norms were the sovereign equality of states[332] and the non-intervention principle.[333] Those States that most strongly supported the concept of *jus cogens*, and the underlying idea that certain norms aiming to protect certain fundamental common interests overruled other norms of international law, were also the States that most strongly supported respect for sovereign independence and the non-intervention principle, granting both the status of *jus cogens*.[334]

The popularity of the principles of sovereign independence and equality can be explained by saying that governments, especially those which oppress their own population, prefer to be left alone. This argument has nothing to do with morality, and it has nothing to do with values. However, if sovereignty is linked to self-determination, to the right of peoples to live in freedom and be considered as equal to other peoples, to develop their own political system and to exploit their own natural resources, it becomes something that *can* be morally defended.

Sovereignty is examined below not as a factual given or a necessary evil, but as a value-based concept, something worth defending in law and in scholarship.

## 5.2 The self-determination of peoples organized in a State

Some scholars have interpreted the references to self-determination in the UN Charter – Articles 1 and 55 – as essentially referring to the self-determination *of States*. At the same time, just as many scholars have rejected this view, arguing instead that it applies to peoples.[335] Because of its ambiguity, the text of the UN Charter cannot serve as conclusive evidence of either of these approaches.

---

[332] Bulgaria, UNDoc. A/Conf.39/5 (Vol. II), p. 298; Cyprus, p. 301, Czechoslovakia, p. 304, Ethiopia, p. 306: "the inalienable right of States to live in independence and dignity", Ukraine, p. 319, USSR, p. 321; USSR, p. 294 of UNDoc. A/Conf.39/11[A], Ghana, p. 301, Cyprus, p. 306, Byelorussian Soviet Socialist Republic, p. 307, Italy, p. 311, Czechoslovakia, p. 318.

[333] Bulgaria, p. 298 of UNDoc. A/Conf.39/5 (Vol. II), Cyprus, p. 301, Czechoslovakia, p. 304, Peru, p. 313, Poland, p. 315, Ukraine, p. 319, USSR, p. 321; USSR, p. 294 of UNDoc. A/Conf.39/11[A]). Some states also mentioned the norm invalidating unequal or "leonine" treaties, where one party is the lion and the other the prey, or, in less metaphorical terms: where a powerful state, often the (former) colonizer, imposes a treaty on the powerless (the colonized). Algeria, p. 288 of UNDoc. A/Conf.39/5 (Vol. II); Byelorussian Soviet Socialist Republic, p. 299; Ukraine, p. 319; USSR, pp. 320-321; Cyprus, p. 306 of UNDoc. A/Conf.39/11[A]).; Finland objected to this example by remarking that the *jus cogens* article "started from the hypothesis that the partners had freely concluded the treaty but had violated some peremptory norm of jus cogens which harmed the interests of the international community, of a third State, or of individuals", p. 295.

[334] This was already pointed out by Virally in Michel Virally, "Réflexions sur le « jus cogens »" (1966), pp. 12-13.

[335] See Eyassu Gayim, *The principle of self-determination: a study of its historical and contemporary legal evolution* (1989), pp. 21-23. On pp. 23-26, he lists writers and primary sources suggesting the exact opposite, but this, as Gayim implicitly admits, cannot be based on a strict reading of the Charter's text or *travaux*. G. S. Swan, "Self-Determination and the United Nations Charter" (1982), p. 273, also

The *travaux préparatoires* of the UN Charter contain an interesting discussion about the differences between the terms "State," "nation," and "people," as used in the UN Charter.[336] According to the drafters, the word "State" was used "to indicate a definite political entity."[337] The word was compared with the word "nation," as follows:

> The word "nation" [was] used […] for the most part in a broad and non-political sense, *viz.,* "friendly relations among nations." In this non-political usage, "nation" would seem preferable to "State" since the word "nation" [was] broad and general enough to include colonies, mandates, protectorates, and quasi-states as well as states. It also ha[d] a poetical flavour that [was] lacking in the word "State."[338]

If this is the correct interpretation of the word "nation," it is a much broader term than "State."[339] This interpretation of the word "nation" comes close to that of a "people." As the UN is an organization of sovereign States and not peoples, the name "United Nations" is inappropriate. Moore's suggestion that to be precise the "United Nations Organization" should be renamed the "Assembly of Sovereign States"[340] deserves some sympathy.

After dealing with the terms "State" and "nation," the drafters turned to the word "people." This word was used in different ways. First of all, it was used "whenever the idea of 'all mankind' or 'all human beings' [was] to be emphasized," as it was, for example, in the Preamble.[341] What is more interesting is the use of the term in relation to self-determination. According to the drafters, "the phrase 'self-determination of peoples' [was] in such common usage that no other word seem[ed] appropriate."[342] That does not help much. The answer to the question raised by the drafters, as to whether "the juxtaposition of 'friendly relations among nations' and 'self-determination of peoples' [was] proper" was more enlightening.[343] In response, it was suggested that "there appear[ed] to be no difficulty in this juxtaposition since 'nations' [was] used in the sense of all political entities, states

suggests that the drafters did not intend to apply the principle only to States. See also S. Prakash Sinha, "Has self-determination become a principle of international law today?" (1974), p. 334, who points out that the *travaux* do not provide the answer (p. 336).

[336] Coordination Committee, Memorandum on a List of Certain Repetitive Words and Phrases in the Charter, UNCIO vol. 18, pp. 654-658. See also Patrick Thornberry, "Self-determination, minorities, human rights" (1989), p. 871.

[337] Coordination Committee, Memorandum on a List of Certain Repetitive Words, p. 657.

[338] *Idem.*

[339] Some authors have a different opinion, and believe that "State" and "nation," as used in the UN Charter, have an identical meaning. See Hurst Hannum, "Rethinking self-determination" (1993), p. 11.

[340] Margaret Moore, "On National Self-Determination" (1997), p. 901.

[341] Coordination Committee, Memorandum on a List of Certain Repetitive Words, p. 658.

[342] *Idem.*

[343] *Idem.*

and non-states, whereas 'peoples' refer[red] to groups of human beings who may, or may not, comprise states or nations."[344] Thus "nations" were defined as groups of human beings, *i.e.* "peoples" organized as a political entity, such as a State or colony. Groups of human beings without any political organization were still "peoples," but not "nations," let alone "States."

According to Article 1 of the human rights covenants, which contains the most authoritative definition of self-determination available since the entry into force of the UN Charter, the right applies to all peoples, irrespective of whether they are organized as a "nation," "State," or not organized at all. This definition is as follows:

> All peoples have the right of self-determination. By virtue of that right they freely determine their political status and freely pursue their economic, social and cultural development.[345]

What is interesting for present purposes is that initially the Human Rights Commission referred to the right to self-determination of peoples *and* nations.[346] This led to a debate about the exact meaning of these two terms, "peoples" and "nations." The delegates who discussed the difference between self-determination of peoples and self-determination of nations pointed out that the two words were not identical and that, as Australia stated, "a people was not necessarily a nation and a nation was not necessarily one people."[347] This is consistent with the views presented in 1945, according to which nations were politically organized peoples, and it is possible that two or more peoples unite in one nation.

A few other States also tried to explain the difference between peoples and nations. The UK's explanation was the most straightforward. Its delegate explained that "peoples" meant "peoples who were not independent," and "nations" meant "sovereign States."[348] This view seems incorrect. In any case it is much more restrictive than that of the drafters in San Francisco. The UK basically said that "nation" and "State" were synonymous. The Syrian delegate disagreed. In his view, a nation was not necessarily the same as a State. He considered that "a nation should be comprised of people belonging to the same ethnic group," "the land on which the nation was settled should be delimited," and "the individuals concerned

---

[344] *Idem.*

[345] Article 1, International Covenant on Civil and Political Rights/International Covenant on Economic, Social, and Cultural Rights.

[346] In 1955, the Third Committee had before it the following draft of the Human Rights Commission: "All peoples and all nations shall have the right of self-determination, namely, the right freely to determine their political economic, social and cultural status." Commission on Human Rights, Report of the Tenth Session, 23 February—16 April 1954, UNDoc. E/2573, p. 62.

[347] General Assembly's Third Committee, 647th Meeting.

[348] General Assembly's Third Committee, 652nd Meeting, 4 November 1955, UNDoc. A/C.3/SR.652.

should show a collective will to live together."[349] This is yet another approach, which is difficult to reconcile with the approach chosen in San Francisco.

Although interesting, the correct interpretation of the word "nation," as used in the first draft of the right to self-determination, is of little relevance anymore, since the word was soon removed from the article.[350] If the San Francisco approach is followed, this makes little difference, as the word "people" refers both to politically organized peoples, *i.e.* "nations" and "States," and to non-politically organized peoples, including minority peoples. That appears to be the correct interpretation. After all, when the USSR asked whether the remaining concept of "peoples" included the deleted concept of "nations," it got an affirmative reply.[351] Presumably then, "nations" and "States" are included in the definition of "peoples."[352]

Although most agreed with the deletion of the word "nations," Pakistan was not so happy with this change. Its delegate suggested that "in its revised form [*i.e.* with the word "nations" deleted], the paragraph was more likely to harm sovereign States than to help colonial peoples," as it "would apply to all national minorities everywhere, no matter how small, and might lead to the disintegration of existing States."[353] This objection had little to do with the deletion of the word "nations," but more with the interpretation of the word "peoples." Belgium neatly summarized the debate by stating that the deletion of the word "nations" had not made the meaning of the word "peoples" clearer in any way.[354]

When the Friendly Relations Declaration was drafted, little was said about the application of the principle of self-determination to nations or States. At one point, it was suggested that the right to external independence and internal autonomy of peoples, organized as an independent State, could be based on the principle of self-determination.[355]

---

[349] General Assembly's Third Committee, 648th Meeting. In an ambitious attempt to clarify the applicability of the principle, the delegate of Lebanon distinguished six categories to which the principle applied. See General Assembly's Third Committee, 649th Meeting.

[350] It was removed by the Working Party, which was basically a drafting committee. Their version of the provision was almost identical to the one that ended up in the Covenants. See UNDoc. A/C.3/L.489. See also General Assembly's Third Committee, 668th Meeting, 22 November 1955, UNDoc. A/C.3/SR.668.

[351] General Assembly's Third Committee, 668th Meeting.

[352] And, as Hannum pointed out, Article 1 as finally adopted could easily be applied even to States. Hurst Hannum, "Rethinking self-determination" (1993), p. 19.

[353] General Assembly's Third Committee, 671st Meeting.

[354] General Assembly's Third Committee, 669th Meeting. But it did in a way remove the term 'nation' from the discourse about self-determination. In order for a people to have a right to self-determination, it need not be a nation. As a consequence, the literature about the nation and nationalism, such as the work by Ernest Gellner and Benedict Anderson, is not dealth with in great detail in this study. See Ernest Gellner, *Nations and nationalism* (2008), esp. pp. 1-7; and Benedict Richard O'Gorman Anderson, *Imagined communities* (2006, original of 1983), esp. pp. 6-7.

[355] Special Committee, Third Report, paras. 197 and 228-229.

Do States have a right to self-determination? They do, but it is difficult to base such a right to self-determination of States on either the UN Charter or common Article 1 of the human rights covenants. The subsequent sections will show that the concept of "sovereignty" rather than "self-determination" is used as the basis of the claim that States are entitled to respect for their independence and equality. But the link with self-determination is still there.

### 5.3 The independence of States and the prohibition of inter-State intervention

The principle of non-intervention, based on the self-determination of the State, is examined below. There is enormous disagreement regarding this principle in the literature. According to some, it is a non-derogable principle of international law (*jus cogens*) which constitutes the basis of the entire international legal order. According to others, the principle does not even exist. [356] The two views could not be further removed from each other.

When Article 1 of the human rights covenants was being drafted, various delegates believed that the non-intervention principle could be derived from the right to self-determination. For example, according to the Dutch delegate, the "external" aspect of self-determination consisted of "the right of a nation already constituted as a State to choose its own form of government and freely to determine its own policies."[357] The word "freely" meant without any outside interference. This shows the clear links between self-determination and non-intervention. This link has been affirmed in scholarship. For example, Crawford wrote that when the principle is applied to existing States, "the principle of self-determination normally takes the well-known form of the rule preventing intervention in the internal affairs of a State, a central element of which is the right of the people of the State to choose for themselves their own form of government."[358]

---

[356] Lowe believed that "the most interesting question regarding the principle of non-intervention in international law is why on earth anyone should suppose that it exists." Vaughan Lowe, "The principle of non-intervention" (1994), p. 67.
[357] General Assembly's Third Committee, 642nd Meeting. Colombia had a slightly different interpretation of the distinction, see General Assembly's Third Committee, 648th Meeting, 31 October 1955, UNDoc. A/C.3/SR.648.
[358] James Crawford, *The creation of states in international law* (2006), pp. 126 and 128.

## 5.4 Self-determination as the basis for the principle of non-intervention

### 5.4.1 Introduction

The prohibition of one State to intervene in the affairs of another follows directly from the principle of sovereign independence of States.[359] This principle is in turn a "continuation" of the principle of self-determination of peoples.[360] That last link is the least obvious. There is some disagreement in the literature on whether such a link can be made at all. Some of the most renowned scholars see self-determination as a "justification" for State sovereignty and the sovereign independence that comes with it.[361] Others believe the link to be "unnecessary."[362]

In any case, the link was particularly evident – and essential – from the perspective of the socialist countries, as well as the "new" countries, established after liberating themselves from colonialism. The former believed that the right to self-determination of peoples changed into the right to non-intervention as soon as a newly formed State was generally recognized.[363] The latter believed that the principle of non-intervention protected their sovereign independence from any future attempts at colonization. Thus it served as a principle complementing that of self-determination.[364]

The problem with this argument was that the prohibition on intervening in the affairs of States could also be used to block any international assistance for people still suffering from colonization to liberate themselves from their oppressor. As Koskenniemi rightly pointed out, this showed the "ambiguous relationship" between statehood and self-determination: it could be used to justify statehood, but also to challenge it.[365]

---

[359] Hans Kelsen, "The Draft Declaration on Rights and Duties of States" (1950), p. 268.

[360] The Assembly has often assumed the two principles are closely connected, without, however explaining the connection in any great detail. See Declaration on the Inadmissibility of Intervention in the Domestic Affairs of States and the Protection of Their Independence and Sovereignty, General Assembly resolution 2131 (XX), adopted 21 December 1965, para. 6; Report of the Sixth Committee, UNDoc, A/5671, adopted 13 December 1963, para. 83.

[361] In *The Law of Peoples* (1999), John Rawls essentially described all peoples as having their own State. In such an ideal world, self-determination can of course be used as foundation for the non-intervention principle. Another example is Martti Koskenniemi, "National Self-Determination Today" (1994), p. 245.

[362] See, *e.g.*, Hurst Hannum, "Rethinking self-determination" (1993), p. 36, footnote 146; James Crawford, "The Right of Self-Determination in International Law" (2001), p. 41.

[363] Antonio Cassese, *Self-determination of peoples: a legal reappraisal* (1995), p. 45.

[364] See also Edward McWhinney, "The 'New' Countries and the 'New' International Law" (1966), p. 23.

[365] Martti Koskenniemi, "National Self-Determination Today" (1994), pp. 248-249. See also Jean-François Dobelle, "Article 1, paragraphe 2" (2005), pp. 345-346.

This problem was generally solved by the small States themselves, by recognizing a "colonial exception" to the non-intervention principle, which meant that the principle did not apply to the relations between a colonial people and the colonial power.[366] To prevent any further appeals to self-determination, many of the resolutions on the topic contained what Higgins termed an "anxious refrain," stressing that the right to self-determination should never lead to threats to the territorial integrity of States.[367] This only made the conflict between sovereign independence and the right to self-determination of peoples more evident. It did not solve any of the doctrinal difficulties with the relationship between statehood and self-determination in any way.

After the process of decolonization was largely completed, the non-intervention principle became more and more absolute. What disappeared into the background was the idea, very much at the basis of self-determination as applied to States, that it included the right of peoples to control their own destiny. It is only in the last few decades that these origins of the non-intervention principle have been taken seriously once again, in the sense that it has been suggested that governments do not deserve to be protected from international interference if they blatantly refuse to act on behalf of (all) the State's peoples.

### 5.4.2    Absolute prohibition on all forms of inter-State intervention

The non-intervention principle is not explicitly mentioned in the UN Charter anywhere. This was deliberate. Although the drafters of the United Nations Charter did refer to the self-determination of peoples in the list of purposes, they deliberately refrained from including the promotion of respect for the sovereign independence of States in that list. They also refrained from including the prohibition of inter-State intervention in the list of principles.

Although the efforts to include a non-intervention principle in the Charter failed, it is useful to look more closely at these efforts.[368] In San Francisco, Cuba suggested that a Declaration of the Duties and Rights of Nations be annexed to the Charter.[369] Panama proposed simply using the Declaration of the Rights and Duties of Nations, adopted by the American Institute of International Law in 1916, for this purpose.[370] Both declarations contained an explicit right to independence for all States. The Panamanian declaration states that

---

[366] Edward McWhinney, "The 'New' Countries and the 'New' International Law" (1966), p. 24.
[367] Rosalyn Higgins, *Problems and process* (1994), p. 121.
[368] See section 2.1 Of Chapter VII.
[369] See Seven Proposals on the Dumbarton Oaks Proposals Submitted by the Delegation of Cuba, UNCIO, vol. 3, pp. 495-499.
[370] See the Additional Amendments proposed by Panama, UNCIO, vol. 3, pp. 265, 266, and, for the text of the Declaration, pp. 272-273. The Netherlands also suggested annexing a similar declaration, but it

Every nation has the right to independence in the sense that, it has a right to the pursuit of happiness and is free to develop itself without interference or control from other states, provided that in so doing it does not interfere with or violate the rights of other states.[371]

Similarly, according to Article I of the Cuban Declaration,

A state has the right [...] to defend its integrity and independence, to provide for its maintenance and prosperity, to organize itself as it sees fit, to legislate on its interests, to administer its services, and to determine the jurisdiction and qualification of its courts [ and] the exercise of these rights has no other limits than respect for the rights of other states, in conformity with international law.[372]

Cuba later explained that it did not wish to insist on the inclusion of its Declaration in the Charter, but rather that "note should be taken of the fact that the Cuban Delegation had made these specific suggestions and [that it] hoped that the Assembly of the world Organization would give them due consideration."[373]

This is exactly what happened. A first draft of a Declaration on Rights and Duties of States was drawn up by the International Law Commission, and presented to the world by the Assembly in 1949. [374] The word "independence" was predominant in the ILC's declaration. According to Article 1, "every State has the right to independence and hence to exercise freely, without dictation by any other State, all its legal powers, including the choice of its own form of government."[375] Article 3 proclaims that "every State has the duty to refrain from intervention in the internal or external affairs of any other State." [376] The Assembly largely ignored the Declaration, and no further work was done on it. Kelsen's conclusion that the ILC's Declaration "ha[s] no legal importance whatsoever," therefore quickly turned out to be entirely correct.[377]

---

did not actually propose a first draft of such a declaration. See Amendments submitted by the Netherlands Delegation to the San Francisco Conference, UNCIO, vol. 3, p. 323.

[371] Additional Amendments proposed by Panama, UNCIO, vol. 3, p. 273.

[372] Seven Proposals on the Dumbarton Oaks Proposals Submitted by the Delegation of Cuba, UNCIO, vol. 3, p. 496.

[373] Seventh Meeting of Committee I/1, May 17, 1945, UNCIO, vol. 6, p. 304.

[374] Draft Declaration on Rights and Duties of States, annexed to General Assembly resolution 375 (IV), adopted 6 December 1949. The ILC's Declaration was almost identical to a Panamanian draft presented to it.

[375] *Idem*, Article 1.

[376] *Idem*, Article 3.

[377] Hans Kelsen, "The Draft Declaration on Rights and Duties of States" (1950), p. 260.

The story continued twenty years later, with the adoption of the Friendly Relations Declaration.[378] The non-intervention principle was discussed in some detail during the first session of the Declaration's drafting committee.[379] The principle of non-intervention was mainly promoted by the small Latin American nations which did not appreciate the constant interventions of their big brother, the United States of America, in their internal affairs.[380] Consistent with its position in San Francisco, the "big brother" claimed that only the use of military force was prohibited, not other types of inter-State intervention.[381] The Latin American States wanted to separate the prohibition on the use of force and the general prohibition on intervention.[382] In their view, any form of intervention by one State in either the internal or external affairs of another State, was illegal. As this would make international cooperation difficult,[383] it was suggested that only *coercive* intervention should be prohibited.[384] As was often suggested, the basis of the principle of non-intervention was respect for the self-determination of peoples.[385] However, it was also pointed out that, strictly speaking, the non-intervention principle prohibited interventions in the internal affairs of States, and this was not always in the interest of the peoples concerned.[386]

Because an extensive interpretation of the word "force" would transform the prohibition on the use of force essentially into a general non-intervention principle, it is interesting to link the debates on the meaning of the word "force," as used in the provision prohibiting the use of force, to the debate about the legal consequences of the lack of a general principle of non-intervention.[387] According to some delegates, this lack of a general non-intervention principle in the UN Charter was not an accidental omission. Therefore it should be concluded that, at least according to the UN Charter, the only inter-State intervention that was not permitted was intervention by military force, as defined in Article 2(4) of the Charter.[388] However, according to others, a more general non-intervention principle

---

[378] See also section 5.5 of Chapter III.

[379] Special Committee on Principles of International Law concerning Friendly Relations and Co-operation among States, Report, A/5746, adopted 16 november 1964 ("First Report"), paras. 211-291.

[380] See also Gaetano Arangio-Ruiz, "The normative role of the General Assembly" (1972), p. 549; Piet-Hein Houben, "Principles of International Law Concerning Friendly Relations and Co-Operation Among States" (1967), p. 735.

[381] See proposals of the USA, Special Committee, First Report, paras. 211-291.

[382] See also Gaetano Arangio-Ruiz, "The normative role of the General Assembly" (1972), p. 560.

[383] As was pointed out frequently by some delegations. See Special Committee, First Report, paras. 252 and 264.

[384] Special Committee, First Report, paras. 240-241.

[385] *idem*, paras. 257.

[386] *idem*, paras. 260.

[387] The prohibition to use force can be found in Article 2(4), UN Charter, and is discussed extensively in this study's chapter on peace and security (Chapter IV).

[388] *Idem*, para. 219. See also Vekateshwara Subramanian Mani, *Basic principles of modern international law* (1993), pp. 59-61; Vaughan Lowe, "The principle of non-intervention" (1994), p. 68.

was implied, by the principle prohibiting the use of force itself, as well as the principle of sovereign equality, Article 2(1) UN Charter.[389] Article 2(7) was also mentioned, but generally rejected as it was about the *Organization's* duties to respect the non-intervention principle, not the duty of *States* themselves.[390]

During its second session, the discussion of the Special Committee on the non-intervention principle was heavily influenced by the Declaration on the Inadmissibility of Intervention and Interference in the Internal Affairs of States, adopted in 1965.[391] Even though there was general agreement that the Inadmissibility Declaration was not "sacrosanct" for the Committee, it chose to adopt the definition of the non-intervention principle contained in that resolution as a *fait accompli*.[392] The Dutch representative later complained about the way in which the Eastern European countries in particular used the General Assembly declaration as a general discussion killer.[393] This did not mean that there were no interesting discussions during the second session at all. It was suggested once again that the basis of non-intervention was the recognition of an inalienable right of all peoples to freely determine their own destiny, free from outside interference.[394] This linked non-intervention to the principle of self-determination of peoples, a link which was especially obvious for new States, which had just gained their independence through decolonization.[395] Moreover, it was suggested that when a colonial power violated a peoples' right to self-determination, it was violating the non-intervention principle, and other States could assist these peoples.[396] According to the more traditional view, which considered the relations between a colonial power and its colonies as a "domestic affair," such third State assistance would actually violate the non-intervention principle. But in the Committee's view, peoples, as separate entities in international law, were also protected by the non-intervention principle.

---

[389] Article 2(1), UN Charter. See Special Committee, First Report, para. 216. This was also the view of Mani, who wrote that "although the principle of non-intervention is not specifically referred to in the U.N. Charter, it has been generally recognized to be embedded in the Charter system." Vekateshwara Subramanian Mani, *Basic principles of modern international law* (1993), p. 57.

[390] Special Committee, First Report, paras. 216, 219-220, and paras. 286-291.The USA was particularly outspoken in its defense of a literal and thus restricted interpretation of Article 2(7), UN Charter. See Robert Rosenstock, "The Declaration of Principles of International Law Concerning Friendly Relations" (1971), p. 726.

[391] Special Committee on Principles of International Law concerning Friendly Relations and Co-operation among States, Report, A/6230, adopted 27 June 1966 ("Second Report"), paras. 292-300.

[392] Gaetano Arangio-Ruiz, "The normative role of the General Assembly" (1972), p. 560.

[393] Piet-Hein Houben, "Principles of International Law Concerning Friendly Relations and Co-operation Among States" (1967), pp. 716-718.

[394] Special Committee, Second Report, para. 289.

[395] *Idem*, para. 289.

[396] *Idem*, paras. 321-324.

When the non-intervention principle was discussed during the third session, one superpower (USSR) remarked that the other (USA) had recently assumed the function of an international policeman, and was practising open and systematic intervention in the affairs of other States.[397] Such behaviour motivated the smaller States to call for a complete prohibition on all forms of inter-State intervention. The use of military force was also discussed in this context as the most intrusive form of such intervention.[398] This makes perfect sense, but the Assembly had already chosen to treat the prohibition on the use of inter-State force as a separate principle.[399] Less intrusive forms, such as coercive economic measures, were also considered to be prohibited.[400] Mani, the delegate from India, later proposed the following general definition of unlawful forms of intervention:

> An impugned act of intervention generally consists of two elements: first, the act in question must at least be an attempt to coerce another State; second, such coercion must be directed towards producing a desired effect, namely, to obtain the subordination of the sovereign will of the victim State, or secure from it advantages of any kind.[401]

The delegate of the United Kingdom, who proposed a similar definition, referred to the first element as the element of "intent," and the second as the element of "effect."[402] This definition used "coercion" as the central notion of unlawful forms of intervention, an approach consistent with that of most delegates of the Special Committee. Other States were more cautious, and remarked that it was hard to make a distinction between coercive measures, and the legitimate persuasion and bargaining with which States usually sought to influence each other.[403]

In the end, the definition of the non-intervention principle in the Friendly Relations Declaration adopted by the General Assembly in 1970 was an exact copy of that contained in the Declaration on the Inadmissibility of Intervention in the Domestic Affairs of States and the Protection of Their Independence and

---

[397] Special Committee on Principles of International Law concerning Friendly Relations and Co-operation among States, Report, A/6799, adopted 26 September 1967 ("Third Report"), para. 311. The USA later complained that such accusations should not be made in a Special Committee, and should not be mentioned in the Reports. See Special Committee, Third Report, para. 476.

[398] Special Committee, Third Report, paras. 349-350.

[399] In this study, the same approach was chosen. The prohibition to use force has been discussed in section 4 of Chapter IV.

[400] Special Committee, Third Report, para. 352.

[401] Vekateshwara Subramanian Mani, *Basic principles of modern international law* (1993), p.67.

[402] Vaughan Lowe, "The principle of non-intervention" (1994), p. 67.

[403] Special Committee, Third Report, para. 353.

Sovereignty.[404] As the Friendly Relations Declaration is generally considered to be more authoritative, the non-intervention principle as it was defined there is used as reference here.[405]

In the Friendly Relations Declaration, the Assembly prohibited all forms of inter-State intervention. It solemnly proclaimed the "principle concerning the duty not to intervene in matters within the domestic jurisdiction of any State."[406] This principle was described in the strictest sense, as follows:

> No State or group of States has the right to intervene, directly or indirectly, for any reason whatever, in the internal or external affairs of any other State.

This was followed by a list of every kind of imaginable type of intervention. Direct armed intervention, armed assistance to rebel groups operating in another State, economic measures as a means of coercion, and various forms of political interference were all prohibited.

The United Kingdom made an interesting "reservation" to this broad definition of the non-intervention principle. It reiterated a remark it had made earlier, which stated that:

> In considering the scope of "intervention," it should be recognized that in an interdependent world, it is inevitable and desirable that States will be concerned with and will seek to influence the actions and policies of other States, and that the objective of international law is not to prevent such activity but rather to ensure that it is compatible with the sovereign equality of States and self-determination of their peoples.[407]

The extensive definition of intervention was also highly criticized in the literature mainly for the same reasons given by the UK in its reservation. Arangio-Ruiz, for example, believed that it "condemn[ed] indiscriminately undesirable and innocent (or even useful) conduct."[408] The only way to discriminate between undesirable and innocent inter-State interventions was to read into it a sort of a bad intent requirement. The prohibition would then be confined to "evildoing interference," or

---

[404] Declaration on the Inadmissibility of Intervention in the Domestic Affairs of States and the Protection of Their Independence and Sovereignty, General Assembly resolution 2131 (XX), adopted 21 December 1965.
[405] Only para. 6 of the Declaration on the Inadmissibility of Intervention in the Domestic Affairs of States was not copied into the Friendly Relations Declaration. This paragraph was about the right to self-determination and independence of peoples and nations.
[406] Friendly Relations Declaration.
[407] Special Committee on Principles of International Law concerning Friendly Relations and Co-operation among States, Report, A/8018, adopted 1 May 1970 ("Sixth Report"), para. 231. See also Special Committee, First Report, paras. 264, and p. 116 (original statement).
[408] Gaetano Arangio-Ruiz, "The normative role of the General Assembly" (1972), p. 555.

"bad faith interference," or "unjustified interference."[409] However, the absolute formulation of the non-intervention principle does not have such a bad intent requirement.

The adoption of this very extensive prohibition on intervention did not stop certain States from continuing their attempts to influence the domestic organization of other States. In 1976, the Assembly "not[ed] with great concern that several Member States ha[d] been subjected to various forms of interference, pressure and organized campaigns of vilification and intimidation designed to deter them from pursuing their united and independent role in international relations."[410] It therefore "reaffirmed the inalienable sovereign right of every State to determine freely, and without any form of interference, its political, social and economic system and its relations with other States and international organizations," and "denounce[d] any form of interference, overt or covert, direct or indirect, including recruiting and sending mercenaries, by one State or group of States and any act of military, political, economic or other form of intervention in the internal or external affairs of other States."[411]

A few years later, the Assembly adopted a resolution on the inadmissibility of the policy of hegemonism in international relations.[412] The word "hegemonism" was defined as the "manifestation of the policy of a State, or a group of States, to control, dominate and subjugate, politically, economically, ideologically or militarily, other States, peoples or regions of the world."[413] As past examples of hegemonism, the Assembly referred to imperialism, colonialism, neo-colonialism and racism. In the Assembly's view, it was the "common desire of all peoples to oppose hegemonism and to preserve the sovereignty and national independence of States," and therefore it "reject[ed] all forms of domination, subjugation, interference or intervention and all forms of pressure, whether political, ideological, economic, military or cultural, in international relations." [414]

In 1981, the Assembly adopted a Declaration on the Inadmissibility of Intervention and Interference in the Internal Affairs of States.[415] The Declaration declared that "no State or group of States ha[d] the right to intervene or interfere in any form or for any reason whatsoever in the internal and external affairs of other States."[416] It then provided a long list of specific rights that followed from this

---

[409] *Idem*, p. 558.

[410] Preamble, Non-interference in the internal affairs of States, General Assembly resolution 31/91, adopted 14 December 1976.

[411] *Idem*, paras. 1 and 3.

[412] Inadmissibility of the policy of hegemonism in international relations, General Assembly resolution 34/103, adopted 14 December 1979.

[413] *Idem*, Preamble.

[414] *Idem*, Preamble and para. 3.

[415] Declaration on the Inadmissibility of Intervention and Interference in the Internal Affairs of States, annexed to General Assembly resolution 36/103, adopted 9 December 1981.

[416] *Idem*, Article 1.

principle. The Assembly proclaimed, *inter alia*, the "sovereign and inalienable right of a State freely to determine its own political, economic, cultural and social system, to develop its international relations and to exercise permanent sovereignty over its natural resources, in accordance with the will of its people, without outside intervention, interference, subversion, coercion or threat in any form whatsoever."[417] This was followed by an equally long list of prohibitions, including essentially all imaginable forms of interference. For example, the Assembly proclaimed that all States had a duty "to refrain from the exploitation and the distortion of human rights issues as a means of interference in the internal affairs of States."[418] At the same time, the Assembly proclaimed "the right and duty of States [...] to work for the elimination of massive and flagrant violations of the rights of nations and peoples, and in particular, for the elimination of *apartheid* and all forms of racism and racial discrimination."[419]

In 1983, the Assembly adopted a resolution on economic measures as a means of political and economic coercion against developing countries.[420] In an understatement, the Assembly "consider[ed] that coercive measures ha[d] a negative effect on the economies of the developing countries and their development efforts and [did] not help to create a climate of peace and friendly relations among States." [421] Thus it "reaffirm[ed] that developed countries should refrain from threatening or applying trade restrictions, blockades, embargoes and other economic sanctions [...] against developing countries as a form of political and economic coercion which affects their economic, political and social development."[422]

### 5.4.3    The prohibition on intervention by the United Nations

In the resolutions referred to in the previous section, the prohibition on inter-State intervention was presented as a fundamental principle of international law, respect for which was considered essential, especially by the new and small States.[423] As the international community focused on prohibiting more and more forms of

---

[417] *Idem*, Aricle I(b).

[418] *Idem*, Article II(l).

[419] *Idem*, Article III(c).

[420] Economic measures as a means of political and economic coercion against developing countries, General Assembly resolution 38/197, adopted 20 December 1983. See also Elimination of coercive economic measures as a means of political and economic compulsion, General Assembly resolution 51/22, adopted 27 November 1996, and Unilateral economic measures as a means of political and economic coercion against developing countries, General Assembly resolution 52/181, adopted 18 December 1997.

[421] *Idem*, Preamble.

[422] *Idem*, Preamble and para. 3.

[423] See also Separate Opinion of President Nagendra Singh to International Court of Justice, Case Concerning Military and Paramilitary Activities in and against Nicaragua (Nicaragua v. United States of America), Merits, Judgment of 27 June 1986, p. 156.

intervention, it lost sight of the justifications or roots of the principle. The principle can only be justified morally to protect of the value of self-determination of peoples – not governments – against foreign oppression and coercion.[424]

Admittedly, some of the earlier resolutions did already acknowledge that the prohibition on inter-State intervention had its limits. The savings clause of the Friendly Relations Declaration can be referred to here.[425] When promoting the right to self-determination of peoples, this clause prohibited States from engaging in any form of intervention in the affairs of States, on condition that "States conduct[ed] themselves in compliance with the principle of equal rights and self-determination of peoples [...] and thus possessed of a government representing the whole people belonging to the territory without distinction as to race, creed or colour."[426] If the latter condition was not fulfilled, intervention that was intended to promote the right to self-determination of non-represented people would be permitted. As Chowdhury said, "a State not possessed of a representative government [...] cannot claim immunity by relying on the principle of non-intervention."[427] The most important question now is who will be the judge? Who will decide when a State violates the right to self-determination of peoples within its jurisdiction? And who decides what to do in the case that a Government abuses the prohibition on inter-State intervention, and treats "its" peoples as it likes? Since States are prohibited from intervening in the affairs of other States, only the United Nations Organization can play this role.

However, according to Article 2(7) of the UN Charter, the Organization cannot intervene in the internal affairs of its Member States:

> Nothing contained in the present Charter shall authorize the United Nations to intervene in matters which are essentially within the domestic jurisdiction of any state or shall require the Members to submit such matters to settlement under the present Charter; but this principle shall not prejudice the application of enforcement measures under Chapter VII.

As the last part of this provision already indicates, there are exceptions to the rule that the Organization cannot intervene. The most explicitly formulated exception relates to the Organization's work in promoting the value of peace and security. The idea that this exception was also applicable in cases of the abuse of sovereign rights was developed in more detail with the introduction of the responsibility to

---

[424] See also Nico Schrijver, "The Changing Nature of State Sovereignty" (1999).

[425] See section 4.4 of Chapter VII.

[426] Friendly Relations Declaration. See also S.K. Roy Chowdhury, "The status and norms of self-determination in contemporary international law" (1977), p. 80.

[427] S.K. Roy Chowdhury, "The status and norms of self-determination in contemporary international law" (1977), p. 84.

protect.[428] It is a matter of dispute how "new" the responsibility to protect is. It can easily be traced back at least to the San Francisco Conference, where the following principle was proposed:

> It is the duty of each member of the Organization to see to it that conditions prevailing within its jurisdiction do not endanger international peace and security and, to this end, to respect the human rights and fundamental freedoms of all its people and to govern in accordance with the principles of humanity and justice. Subject to the performance of this duty the Organization should refrain from intervention in the internal affairs of any of its members.[429]

Such a principle never made it into the list of principles of the UN Charter. The idea of conditional sovereignty, which constitutes the basis of the responsibility to protect, has experienced a revival in recent times. The concept can best be seen as the expression of a change in attitudes brought about by the end of the Cold War. It was during the first high-level Security Council meeting of 1992 organized to celebrate the end of the Cold War that the Belgian representative made the following statement:

> My country believes that the *raison d'être* of the principle of non-interference is to allow States to foster in freedom the well-being of their peoples. However, no Government should use that principle as a legal argument to condone abuses of human rights.[430]

The principle of non-intervention was therefore seen as a principle with a specific purpose, *viz.* to secure the freedom of peoples. Abuse of this principle, which the Belgian representative described in terms of human rights violations, should not be condoned. This could be called the modern, conditional version of the non-intervention principle.

The representative of China, on the other hand, provided an excellent summary of the "old" thinking about non-intervention. According to China, international affairs were governed by five principles of peaceful coexistence, *viz.* the principles of mutual respect for sovereignty and territorial integrity, mutual non-

---

[428] The literature on the concept is overwhelming. See *e.g.*, James Pattison, *Humanitarian intervention and the responsibility to protect* (2010); Ekkehard Strauss, *The emperor's new clothes?* (2009); Alex J. Bellamy, *Responsibility to protect* (2009); Gareth Evans, *The responsibility to protect* (2008); Ramesh Thakur, *The United Nations, Peace and Security* (2006), pp. 244-264.

[429] See also sections 2.1 of Chapter VII and 2.4 of Chapter VI. This suggestion is very similar to Principle 2 of the Principles for the International Law of the Future, published in *the American Journal of International Law*, Vol. 38, No. 2, Apr., 1944 (Supplement: Official Documents). See also the interesting commentary which was published together with the Principle.

[430] Verbatim Records of the 3046th meeting of the Security Council, 31 January 1992, UNDoc. S/PV.3046, p. 73.

aggression, non-interference in each other's internal affairs, equality, and mutual benefit. [431] As China also explained, "[t]he core of these principles is non-interference in each other's internal affairs."[432]

In the post-Cold War period, it was the Belgian view that prevailed. In December 2001, the non-governmental International Commission on Intervention and State Sovereignty (ICISS) published a report introducing the responsibility to protect. The concept can be defined by the following two basic principles:

> State sovereignty implies responsibility, and the primary responsibility for the protection of its people lies with the state itself.
>
> Where a population is suffering serious harm, as a result of internal war, insurgency, repression or state failure, and the state in question is unwilling or unable to halt or avert it, the principle of non-intervention yields to the international responsibility to protect.[433]

The responsibility to protect was embraced by the General Assembly in 2005. According to the Assembly, "each individual State ha[d] the responsibility to protect its populations from genocide, war crimes, ethnic cleansing and crimes against humanity." If a State failed to do so, "the international community, through the United Nations" had the responsibility to "help to protect populations from genocide, war crimes, ethnic cleansing and crimes against humanity." [434] The Assembly stressed that such international action had to be taken in accordance with the UN Charter, in particular in accordance with its rules on the use of force. The Assembly was very careful about the words it chose, but at least it accepted the *rationale* behind the concept, *i.e.* the conditionality of the non-intervention principle and the prohibition of its abuse.

In 2009, the General Assembly discussed the concept extensively. [435] It gathered to discuss the Secretary-General's report on the implementation of the responsibility to protect. [436] The report distinguished three pillars. First, the primary responsibility of each State to protect its own population from genocide, war

---

[431] *Idem*, p. 92.

[432] *Idem*.

[433] See the Synopsis of International Commission on Intervention and State Sovereignty (ICISS), *Responsibility to Protect*.

[434] 2005 World Summit Outcome, resolution adopted by the General Assembly on 16 September 2005, UNDoc, 60/1, paras. 138-139.

[435] On 18 April 2008, the Pope addressed the General Assembly, and focused his speech on embracing the responsibility to protect.

[436] Report of the Secretary-General, Implementing the responsibility to protect, distributed 12 January 2009. UNDoc. A/63/677. For a commentary, see Advisory Council on International Affairs of the Netherlands, *The Netherlands and the Responsibility to Protect: The Responsibility to Protect People from Mass Atrocities*, Advisory report no 70, published June 2010.

crimes, ethnic cleansing and crimes against humanity. Secondly, the complementary responsibility of the international community to assist States in carrying out their national obligations. And thirdly, the commitment of the international community to take timely and decisive action, in accordance with the UN Charter, whenever a State was manifestly failing to meet its responsibilities.

The 63$^{rd}$ President of the General Assembly, d'Escoto-Brockmann of Nicaragua, who was not the most enthusiastic supporter of the concept, opened a special discussion on the topic. He understood the responsibility to protect to mean that "people ha[d] the right to get rid of their government when it oppresse[d] them and ha[d] thereby failed in its responsibility to them."[437] This was the general idea behind the concept. In his view, this showed why – even though the concept was only introduced in 2001 – "the great anti-colonial struggles and the anti-*apartheid* struggles […] were the greatest application of responsibility to protect in world history."[438] On the other hand, at the time some of the colonial powers actually used arguments similar to those on which the responsibility to protect was based in order to defend their intervention in the colonies. D'Escoto-Brockmann explained that it was therefore precisely those "recent and painful memories related to the legacy of colonialism [that gave] developing countries strong reasons to fear that laudable motives [could] end up being misused, once more, to justify arbitrary and selective interventions against the weakest states."[439]

After d'Escoto-Brockmann, a number of experts took the floor. This was one of the opportunities for experts to address the delegates of the General Assembly directly and be asked questions afterwards. This approach can be applauded for being a most original and direct means of connecting the scholarly community and the political community of the UN.

Most of the experts focused on the potential and past abuse of the language used to justify the responsibility to protect. According to Chomsky: "Virtually every use of force in international affairs ha[d] been justified in terms of [the responsibility to protect], including the worst monsters."[440] As examples, Chomsky referred to Japan's attack on Manchuria, Italy's invasion of Ethiopia, and Hitler's occupation of Czechoslovakia. Similarly, Bricmont reminded the international community that the (traditional) barbarities in a particular society were often

---

[437] Office of the 63$^{rd}$ President of the General Assembly, *Concept note on responsibility to protect populations from genocide, war crimes, ethnic cleansing and crimes against humanity* ("*Concept note on responsibility to protect*"), p. 2. This note was used as basis for the Interactive Thematic Dialogue of the United Nations General Assembly on the Responsibility to Protect, held on 23 July 2009, at United Nations Headquarters.

[438] *Concept note on responsibility to protect*, p. 1.

[439] D'Escoto-Brockmann, Statement at the Opening of the Thematic Dialogue of the General Assembly on the Responsibility to Protect, UN Headquarters, New York, 23 July 2009.

[440] Chomsky's untitled statement to the United Nations General Assembly Thematic Dialogue on the Responsibility to Protect.

replaced by the barbarities of military intervention. This was especially the case during the colonial age, but some more recent military interventions also qualified as this sort of barbaric response to barbarities.[441] All these statements focused on reminding the international community of the enormous potential for abuse of the concept, to justify all sorts of military interventions by one State in the affairs of another. In response, the delegate of Ghana rightly remarked that all principles were susceptible to abuse, and that the principle of non-interference was certainly no exception.[442] Although explicitly addressed to him, Chomsky did not respond to this verbal intervention.

Evans, the principal author of the ICISS Report, made a more positive contribution to the debate. He summarized the idea of the responsibility to protect as follows:

> The issue is not the "right" of big States to do anything, including throwing their weight around militarily, but the "responsibility" of all States to protect their own people from atrocity crimes, and to assist others to do so by all appropriate means. The core responsibility is that of the individual sovereign State itself, and it is only if it is unable or unwilling to do so that the question arises of other States' responsibility to assist or engage in some way.[443]

In Evans's view, the whole idea of the concept was to achieve a "conceptual shift from 'the right to intervene' to 'the responsibility to protect'," *i.e.* to emphasize not the foreign military intervention, but the reinterpretation of sovereignty, and the principle of non-intervention.[444] This had been understood by the General Assembly in 2005, when it committed itself to the responsibility to protect. Earlier, the UN Secretary-General had already suggested that this was a "universal and irrevocable commitment."[445] What was needed now was agreement on ways of implementing the responsibility to protect.[446]

---

[441] Bricmont, *A More Just World and the Responsibility to Protect*, Statement to the United Nations General Assembly Interactive Thematic Dialogue on the Responsibility to Protect. See also Ngugi's Statement entitled *Uneven Development is the Root of Many Crimes*. He emphasized the increasing gap between the "haves" and "have nots" in the world.

[442] Delegates seek to end global paralysis in face of atrocities as General Assembly holds interactive dialogue on responsibility to protect, UNDoc. GA/10847.

[443] Evans, *Implementing the responsibility to protect*, Statement to United Nations General Assembly Informal Interactive Dialogue on the Responsibility to Protect.

[444] *Idem*.

[445] General Assembly, 96th plenary meeting of the sixty-third session, held 21 July 2009, UNDoc. A/63/PV.96.

[446] Luck, the Secretary-General's adviser, also suggested that the participants focus on the implementation of the responsibility to protect. See Edward C. Luck, Special Adviser to the Secretary-General, Remarks to the General Assembly on the Responsibility to Protect, New York. 23 July 2009.

After the experts had spoken, all the delegates gathered in the General Assembly had an opportunity to respond.[447] Formally, the Secretary-General's report on the implementation of the responsibility to protect served as the basis of the Assembly's discussion. Despite this, the debate focused just as much on the concept itself as it did on its implementation. The Swedish delegate, who spoke on behalf of all the member States of the European Union and some associated States, explained that "the basic principle of State sovereignty is and should remain undisputed," but that "it should also be recognized that State sovereignty implie[d] not only rights, but also responsibilities and obligations under international law, including the protection of human rights as an essential element of responsible sovereignty." Therefore sovereignty was not a right to be left alone, but a responsibility to care for one's population: a "responsible sovereignty." The most important responsibility flowing from sovereignty was the responsibility of every State "to protect the populations within its own borders." If a State failed to carry out this responsibility, the international community had to intervene, but always in accordance with international law. Sweden and the rest of Europe agreed with the Secretary-General that the challenge for the immediate future was the effective implementation of the concept. There was a need to turn the "authoritative and enduring words of the 2005 World Summit Outcome […] into doctrine, policy and, most importantly, deeds."[448]

According to the Egyptian delegate, who spoke on behalf of an even larger group, the non-aligned States, it was undoubtedly true that "each individual State had the responsibility to protect its populations." At the same time, the group had some hesitations about the concept, especially because of the potential of "misusing it to legitimize unilateral coercive measures or intervention in the internal affairs of States."[449] Thus, as usual, the new and smaller States stressed the need for absolute respect of their sovereign independence and the principle of non-intervention.

After these two collective statements, representatives of individual States shared their views with their fellow delegates. Although these mainly repeated the two collective statements, occasionally there were some interesting additional thoughts.

With regard to the first pillar about the primary responsibility of States to care for their own population, one group, mostly Western States, saw the responsibility to protect as a sign of a new interpretation of sovereignty, *i.e.* responsible sovereignty.[450] Although most other States agreed that sovereignty

---

[447] D'Escoto-Brockmann also opened the Assembly's plenary on the topic. See General Assembly, 97th plenary meeting of the sixty-third session, held 23 July 2009, UNDoc. A/63/PV.97.
[448] General Assembly, 97th plenary meeting of the sixty-third session, pp. 4-5.
[449] *Idem*, p. 5.
[450] For the UK, see General Assembly, 97th plenary meeting of the sixty-third session, p. 7; France, p. 9; Belgium, p. 18; Korea, p. 19; Costa Rica, p. 23; Czech Republic, 98th plenary meeting of the sixty-third

entailed responsibilities, they were hesitant to accept the conclusions drawn by the Western group, that whenever a government manifestly failed to carry out its sovereign responsibilities, the non-intervention principle could be set aside and the international community could intervene. For example, Malaysia agreed that the sovereignty-as-responsibility approach actually "strengthened the principle of sovereignty by making the State responsible for the protection of its population," in the sense that it showed that "the population [was] guaranteed safety and protection in return for granting legitimate power to the State and its machinery."[451] However, it could not accept that States would lose some of their sovereign rights whenever they failed to protect their own population from genocide, crimes against humanity, war crimes or ethnic cleansing.[452]

Because of these and similar concerns, another group stressed that the responsibility to protect could never be interpreted as altering the principle of non-intervention in any way, especially not by allowing the always controversial "humanitarian interventions."[453] The representative of Guatemala spoke on behalf of many of the "new" and relatively small States, when he remarked that "for countries like mine that greatly value the principle of non-intervention in the internal affairs of sovereign States, there is a lingering suspicion that the responsibility to protect can, in specific moments or situations, be invoked as a pretext for improper intervention."[454]

Regarding the second pillar on international assistance, many developing States stressed the importance of development aid as a form of international assistance.[455] Some developed countries agreed, but added that such aid should also

---

session, held 24 July 2009, UNDoc. A/63/PV.98, p. 22. For Ireland, see General Assembly, 99th plenary meeting of the sixty-third session, held 24 July 2009, UNDoc. A/63/PV.99, p. 1; Romania, p. 9; Slovenia, p. 11; Croatia, p. 15. For Sri Lanka, see General Assembly, 100th plenary meeting of the sixty-third session, held 28 July 2009, UNDoc. A/63/PV.100, p. 2; East-Timor, p. 15; Panama, p. 16; Tanzania, p. 28.

[451] General Assembly, 101st plenary meeting of the sixty-third session, held 28 July 2009, UNDoc. A/63/PV.101, p. 4.

[452] *Idem.*

[453] About humanitarian interventions, see especially the remarks by Argentina, at General Assembly, 101st plenary meeting of the sixty-third session, pp. 10-11. According to Argentina, it was clear that "the concept of the responsibility to protect equal[ed] humanitarian intervention." See also Serbia (*idem*, p. 13), who reminded fellow delegates of the humanitarian intervention in Kosovo in 1999, which he believed was evidence that "paths paved with good intentions can sometimes lead to unjustifiable actions."

[454] General Assembly, 97th plenary meeting of the sixty-third session, p. 15. For Pakistan, see 98th plenary meeting of the sixty-third session, p. 3; Ecuador, p. 9; Chile, p. 11; Colombia, p. 14; Uruguay, p. 18. For Venezuela, see General Assembly, 99th plenary meeting of the sixty-third session, pp. 5-6; Bolivia, p. 9; Luxembourg, p. 17. For Iran, see General Assembly, 100th plenary meeting of the sixty-third session, p. 10; Nicaragua, p. 13; North Korea, pp. 17-18. Argentina, General Assembly, 101st plenary meeting of the sixty-third session, pp. 10-11.

[455] See *e.g.*, Brazil, at General Assembly, 97th plenary meeting of the sixty-third session, p. 13; Denmark and Costa Rica, p. 23. For Pakistan, see 98th plenary meeting of the sixty-third session, p. 3;

be used to improve good governance and democracy within developing States. For example, France suggested that "development aid, by promoting democratic governance and respect for the rule of law, play[ed] a major role in implementing the responsibility to protect."[456] This was based on the idea, explicitly expressed by Chile, that "democracies, despite their imperfections, tend[ed] not to commit atrocities such as the four mass crimes."[457] As this suggested that aid could be accompanied by various conditions and interference in domestic affairs, such remarks worried some of the developing States. For example, Ecuador stressed that "the issue of development assistance [should not be] linked to possible conditionalities with regard to the responsibility to protect."[458] Some States were concerned that the implementation of the responsibility to protect would not lead to more development assistance, but that it would take away some of the resources used for development assistance. For example, the delegate of the Philippines warned that "the United Nations resources to be used for [the responsibility to protect] should not affect other activities undertaken in the context of other legal mandates, such as development assistance."[459]

Some States suggested that, with regard to the third pillar which dealt with international intervention in case of abuse of sovereignty, the list of situations calling for international intervention should be broadened, and include more than the categories recognized in the World Summit Outcome Document: *i.e.* war crimes, crimes against humanity, ethnic cleansing and genocide. For example, France pledged to

> Remain vigilant to ensure that natural disasters, when combined with deliberate inaction on the part of a Government that refuses to provide assistance to its population in distress or to ask the international community for aid, do not lead to human tragedies in which the international community can only look on helplessly.[460]

This suggested that the responsibility to protect could also be violated by a State in the case of a government's unwillingness to act and come to the aid of its people. The Assembly only saw a violation of the responsibility to protect in certain

---

South Africa, p. 16. Ireland, 99th plenary meeting of the sixty-third session, p. 2; for Swaziland, see General Assembly, 100th plenary meeting of the sixty-third session, p. 21; Benin, pp. 24-25.

[456] General Assembly, 97th plenary meeting of the sixty-third session, p. 10.

[457] General Assembly, 98th plenary meeting of sixty-third session, held 24 July 2009, UNDoc. A/63/PV.98, p. 11.

[458] *Idem*, p. 9. See also Malaysia, at General Assembly, 101st plenary meeting of the sixty-third session, p. 5.

[459] General Assembly, 97th plenary meeting of the sixty-third session, p. 12.

[460] *Idem*, p. 9.

specific and deliberate attacks by a Government on its own population.[461] That was enough for almost all the delegates. Immediately after the French delegate had spoken, the delegate of the Philippines stressed that the concept's application "should be limited to those four crimes and applied only to them," and that "any attempt to enlarge its coverage [might] diminish its value or devalue its original intent and scope." [462]

For present purposes, it is relevant to point out that the responsibility to protect, as adopted in the World Summit Outcome Document, has great potential in the sense that it protects the population of States from certain forms of oppression by their own government. Thus it helps to solve the above-mentioned problem that the principle of self-determination can be invoked both by a dictatorial government to prevent other States from interfering, and by (parts of) the population of that very same State to demand international assistance to achieve their right to self-determination. However, the applicability of the responsibility to protect as a trump card to overrule non-intervention is extremely limited. As yet it does not include a duty of the international community to intervene whenever a State fails to represent its entire population. Furthermore, the responsibility to protect, as formulated in the World Summit Outcome Document of 2005, emphasizes the importance of collective responses. It does not allow States, acting unilaterally or in small groups, to intervene in the affairs of other States, not even to prevent genocide, war crimes, crimes against humanity, or ethnic cleansing from being committed. The United Nations, especially its Security Council, continues to be the only "judge" that can authorize such interventions. Therefore it is important that the Council has already applied the responsibility to protect a number of times since its adoption in the World Summit Outcome Document of 2005.[463]

## 5.5  Introduction

In this section the value of self-determination of peoples was used as the foundation for the principle of the sovereign independence of States, and the non-intervention principle. The popularity of the latter principle among State representatives can be easily explained. Government officials have good reason to defend the view that

---

[461] These specific acts were genocide, war crimes, ethnic cleansing and crimes against humanity. See quotation from the 2005 World Summit Outcome document above.

[462] General Assembly, 97th plenary meeting of the sixty-third session, p. 11. Similarly, the Brazilian delegate stressed that "attempts to expand the responsibility to protect to cover other calamities, such as HIV/AIDS, climate change or the response to natural disasters, would undermine the 2005 consensus and stretch the concept beyond recognition or operational utility." *Idem*, p. 12. See also Pakistan, at General Assembly, 98th plenary meeting of the sixty-third session, p. 3.

[463] See *e.g.*, Security Council 1973 (2011), adopted 17 March 2011, and Resolution 1975 (2011), adopted by the Security Council on 30 March 2011.

other States, headed by other governments, should not interfere with their work. However, to justify the existence of the non-intervention principle by stating that it has always been there and that it protects governments from unwanted interference is not a valid moral argument. In this section, the moral justification of the non-intervention principle was sought and found in the value of self-determination of peoples, as organized in a State. This grounding of sovereign independence in the self-determination of peoples clearly explains why the principle of non-intervention does not leave States, and their governments, entirely free to act. As soon as a government ceases to represent its people, the link between the sovereign independence of the State and the self-determination of its people ceases to exist, and in that case a government can no longer invoke the non-intervention principle.

## 6    THE HUMAN RIGHT TO SELF-DETERMINATION

## 6.1 Introduction

It is sometimes argued that the self-determination of peoples is not a value in and of itself, but that it is ultimately based on the value of human dignity. This was Waldron's view.[464] He argued that, "if we were asked to give an account of the dignity of an institution or a nation, we might well answer in terms that focused mostly on the contribution the entity makes to the well-being and rights and dignity of the individuals who live under it," and thus "it is not clear [...] that we are getting to any idea of a foundational or inherent dignity of groups when we talk of the dignity of the nation-state or the dignity of this or that institution or community."[465] This is a common argument in liberal philosophy: any claim to self-determination is a claim to "self-rule," a demand to be responsible for one's own choices and destiny. A claim to self-determination of peoples, both the external (non-interference) and internal element (representative government), is ultimately based on the individual's entitlement to autonomy.[466]

However, the fact that the self-determination of peoples ultimately protects the dignity of the individuals of those peoples does not mean there is nothing intrinsic about the value of peoples' claims to self-determination. The two values of human dignity and peoples' claims to self-determination are merely very closely related.

So can the value of self-determination of peoples be defined independently from human dignity? As was the case for all other global values, the value of self-

---

[464] See also p. 163, C. Don Johnson, "Toward self-determination" (1973).
[465] Jeremy Waldron, "The Dignity of Groups" (2008), p. 8.
[466] See *e.g.*, Daniel Philpott, "In Defense of Self-Determination" (1995), especially pp. 355-362.

determination of peoples shows itself most clearly when it is trampled upon. In colonial times, certain groups of individuals were seen as being "backward." Although this had direct consequences with regard to the respect for the dignity of the individuals concerned, it was above all an insult to the group as such. Therefore it was the group as such, and not the individuals constituting the group, that felt a need to defend itself by upholding its right to freedom, autonomy, and self-determination. In Waldron's words,

> If a dignitary slur on a[n] individual is based wholly or partly on contempt for the group to which that individual belongs as a collective entity, then perhaps nothing less than an assertion or a reassertion of its dignity as an entity, its equal foundational dignity as a group, will succeed in combating or rebutting such prejudice.[467]

This is exactly what happened. The principle of self-determination of peoples has been used primarily to assist groups, mainly colonial peoples, in their efforts to liberate themselves from oppression aimed at the group. Although both the principle of self-determination of peoples and the entire body of human rights are thus legal tools to fight oppression, they are responses to two fundamentally different kinds of oppression, with differing targets.[468] One kind of oppression is aimed at the group, another at individual people. Thus the legal tools aim to protect different values. One aims to protect the dignity and self-determination of peoples from oppression. The other aims to protect the dignity and autonomy of individuals, or human dignity. The principle of self-determination of peoples thus serves a function which is conceptually separable from any norms protecting human dignity.

This section examines what the UN has made of this debate. It looks at the relationship between self-determination of peoples and human dignity and human rights.

The most authoritative definition of the right to self-determination of peoples can be found in common Article 1 of the two classical human rights covenants. Therefore one is tempted to conclude that on the basis of this fact alone, it must be regarded as a human right, like the other rights in those covenants. The right to self-determination does have a lot in common with these other human rights. As Crawford pointed out, like human rights, "the primary impact of [the right to self-determination of peoples] is against the government of the State in question, and one of its main effects is to internationalize key aspects of the relationship between the people concerned and that State, represented by its government."[469] It turns what used to be a national matter into an international

---

[467] Jeremy Waldron, "The Dignity of Groups" (2008), p. 19.
[468] Robert McCorquodale, "Self-determination: a human rights approach" (1994), p. 872, believed that the oppression was essentially identical.
[469] James Crawford, The Rights of Peoples (1988), p. 164.

matter, *i.e.* the relationship between the State and (parts of) its own population. Moreover, in resolutions of the Assembly, human rights and self-determination are often interrelated. For example, in 1980, "the subjection of peoples to alien domination" was not only labelled as a threat to international peace and security, but also as "a denial of fundamental human rights."[470]

Despite the many interrelations, there are good reasons not to go down the road of equating human rights and self-determination. As a brief examination of the *travaux préparatoires* of the human rights covenants shows, the right to self-determination ended up in the covenants because the "new" States believed it to be a good opportunity to achieve wide recognition of the right in a multilateral treaty. Even the most enthusiastic supporters did not consider the right to self-determination to be a human right *per se*. There are many good reasons to agree with this assessment. First of all, the right to self-determination of nations and peoples does not pertain to individuals, as do all other human rights. Secondly, the right to self-determination of nations and peoples is not directly based on the value of human dignity, but rather on the value of the dignity and self-determination of peoples.

## 6.2 Article 1 of the Covenants

The Universal Declaration of Human Rights does not say anything about any human right to self-determination. Two years after the adoption of the Universal Declaration, the Assembly, initially at the initiative of the Soviet Union, "call[ed] upon the Economic and Social Council to request the Commission on Human Rights to study ways and means which would ensure the right of peoples and nations to self-determination."[471] A few months later, the Soviet Union suggested the first version of an article on national self-determination and minorities, to be included in any future human rights covenant.[472]

---

[470] Preamble, Plan of Action for the Full Implementation of the Declaration on the Granting of Independence to Colonial Countries and Peoples, General Assembly resolution 35/118, adopted 11 December 1980. This was reiterated in Twenty-fifth anniversary of the Declaration on the Granting of Independence to Colonial Countries and Peoples, General Assembly resolution 40/56, adopted 2 December 1985.

[471] Draft international covenant on human rights and measures of implementation: future work of the commission on human rights, General Assembly resolution 421 D(V), adopted 4 December 1950. See also Antonio Cassese, *Self-determination of peoples: a legal reappraisal* (1995), p. 48. See also Note by the Secretary-General, on section D of resolution 421 (V) of the General Assembly, concerning the right of peoples and nations to self-determination, UNDoc. E/CN.4/516.

[472] USSR's Proposal for additional articles, printed on p. 26, Report of the Commission on Human Rights, Sixth Session (27 March - 19 May 1950), UNDoc. E/1681. See also the Proposal by the Union of Soviet Socialist Republics, UNDoc. A/C.3/L.96, printed on p. 35, Report of the Commission on Human Rights, Seventh Session (16 April - 19 May 1951), UNDoc. E/1992.

As the Human Rights Commission did not have enough time to fulfil the Assembly's request in 1950, the Assembly decided to do the work itself two years later, and proposed the text of a provision on self-determination to be included in any forthcoming covenant(s) on human rights, stating that "all peoples shall have the right to self-determination."[473] The adoption of this resolution embracing the human right to self-determination had an enormous impact on all future developments, but it did not mean that the debate on the legal character of the right to self-determination was finally settled. In particular, it did not mean that there was universal agreement that the right belonged in a human rights covenant, let alone that it should be considered as a human right in and of itself. In the same year the Assembly saw "the right of peoples and nations to self-determination [as] a prerequisite to the full enjoyment of all fundamental rights," and thus presumably not as a human right, but as a necessary condition for the realization of human rights.[474]

Some serious discussions took place on the legal nature of the right to self-determination three years later, especially in the Third Committee of the General Assembly. The culmination of these debates was the General Assembly's session of 1955, at the end of which the final text on the right to self-determination was adopted, as it appeared in both of the classic human rights covenants.[475] These debates are examined below, insofar as they relate to the human rights character of the right to self-determination.[476]

At the very beginning of the debates, the Egyptian delegate reminded States that the provision on the right to self-determination was the only provision in the covenants explicitly requested by the General Assembly itself.[477] He – and many other delegates with him – concluded from this that the Third Committee was obliged to include a provision on the right to self-determination in the human rights covenants, and could no longer choose to reject it entirely.[478]

---

[473] Inclusion in the International Covenant or Covenants on Human Rights of an article relating to the right of peoples to self-determination, General Assembly resolution 545(VI), adopted 5 February 1952.
[474] The right of peoples and nations to self-determination, General Assembly resolution 637(VII), adopted 16 December 1952.
[475] As the representative of Lebanon rightly pointed out, it was during the 1955 session that "the [General Assembly's Third] Committee was discussing the question of self-determination more thoroughly than it had ever done before." General Assembly's Third Committee, 649th Meeting, 1 November 1955, UNDoc. A/C.3/SR.649.
[476] See also Antonio Cassese, *Self-determination of peoples: a legal reappraisal* (1995), pp. 49-52; Marc J. Bossuyt, *Guide to the "travaux préparatoires"of the International Covenant on Civil and Political Rights* (1987), pp. 19-48.
[477] General Assembly's Third Committee, 641st Meeting, 21 October 1955, UNDoc. A/C.3/SR.641. Reference was made to General Assembly resolution 545(VI).
[478] For Egypt, Ukraine, Afghanistan, see General Assembly's Third Committee, 641st Meeting. For Poland, see General Assembly's Third Committee, 643rd Meeting, 25 October 1955, UNDoc. A/C.3/SR.643. For Czechoslovakia, El Salvador, Iran, see General Assembly's Third Committee, 645th Meeting, 27 October 1955, UNDoc. A/C.3/SR.645.; Philippines, see General Assembly's Third

Other delegations did not feel bound by the Assembly's resolution. They suggested deleting the entire article. For example, the Swedish delegate believed that self-determination, as codified in the Charter, was more of a "guiding principle" than a (human) right, and that "the notion of self-determination did not come within the sphere of human rights covered in the draft covenants, and that the adoption of [an article on self-determination] might even jeopardize the covenants."[479] The Swedish delegate explained that the right to self-determination of peoples and nations "was not, like the other rights stated in the draft covenants, an individual right or a right coming within the domestic jurisdiction of States."[480] Thus it was a "mistake to mention it in the covenants."[481] Similarly, the Netherlands believed the article to be "entirely unacceptable," because it related "not to an individual right, but to a collective right, to be exercised by peoples and nations," and therefore it had "no place in the covenants."[482] Together with Australia and the UK, the Netherlands formally proposed to delete the entire article.[483]

In response to these objections, many supporters of the article spoke eloquently about the importance of the liberation of colonial and other suppressed peoples, and wondered why anyone would be against their liberation.[484] These statements were misleading, as those rejecting the article did not do so – or at least did not do so formally – because they were opposed to self-determination. They rejected the provision because they did not consider it a (human) right.[485] New Zealand reminded fellow delegates that it was "futile" to "approach the problem in a violently anti-colonialist frame of mind."[486]

Even some of the most fervent supporters of the right to self-determination of peoples did not see it as a human right. They referred to it as a "prerequisite" for the enjoyment of fundamental human rights, exactly as the Assembly had done

---

Committee, 646th Meeting, 27 October 1955, UNDoc. A/C.3/SR.646; Guatemala, General Assembly's Third Committee, 647th Meeting, 28 October 1955, UNDoc. A/C.3/SR.647.

[479] General Assembly's Third Committee, 641st Meeting. Similarly, the UK referred to it as a "political principle," as opposed to a right. See General Assembly's Third Committee, 642nd Meeting, 24 October 1955, UNDoc. A/C.3/SR.642.

[480] *Idem.*

[481] *Idem.* See also UK, in General Assembly's Third Committee, 641st Meeting.

[482] General Assembly's Third Committee, 642nd Meeting. See also UK, in General Assembly's Third Committee, 641st Meeting; Belgium (who made the same objection but did not believe it was reason enough to delete the right entirely), in General Assembly's Third Committee, 643rd Meeting; Denmark, in General Assembly's Third Committee, 644th Meeting, 26 October 1955, UNDoc. A/C.3/SR.644; Canada, in General Assembly's Third Committee, 645th Meeting.

[483] See amendment proposal A/C.3/L.460, p. 3.

[484] See *e.g.*, Syria, General Assembly's Third Committee, 648th Meeting, 31 October 1955, UNDoc. A/C.3/SR.648; Bolivia, General Assembly's Third Committee, 651st Meeting, 3 November 1955, UNDoc. A/C.3/SR.651.

[485] See also remark by Australia, in General Assembly's Third Committee, 647th Meeting.

[486] General Assembly's Third Committee, 649th Meeting.

previously. The Final Communiqué, adopted at the Asian-African Conference which took place between 18 and 24 April 1955 in Bandung, Indonesia also referred to it in this way.[487] Some scholars also adopted this view.[488]

Brazil most explicitly rejected this "prerequisite" argument. It admitted that human rights and self-determination "were closely linked and even to some extent interdependent," but it also argued that "it did not follow [from this close link] that self-determination must be regarded as a prerequisite of the exercise of the other rights," as "experience showed that a society could be master of its destiny without its members necessarily enjoying the individual rights enunciated in the draft covenants."[489] The idea that respect for the dignity of individual human beings required something other than respect for the value of self-determination of peoples, was the most important challenge to the position that the realization of the self-determination of peoples was necessarily a sufficient foundation for respect for more traditional human rights. As Waldron argued, "if we accord dignity to groups, it is possible that we may be dignifying the very structures of rank and privilege that egalitarian dignity-talk aims to transcend." In doing so, "we may be undermining the transvaluation that lies at the heart of the association of dignity with human rights."[490]

Other States did not directly challenge the "prerequisite" argument, but pointed out that the right to self-determination had to be promoted differently from the more traditional human rights. The inclusion of the right to self-determination in the human rights covenants would not do justice to this difference. For example, the delegate of the UK pointed out that "the various delegations [...] had been so carried away by their enthusiasm and their desire to affirm an important principle that they had failed to give due consideration to the legal and political effects of converting a principle into a universal right."[491] To do so would mean, as the UK delegate pointed out, that the right to self-determination of nations and peoples

---

[487] For the Assembly, see General Assembly resolution 637(VII), adopted 16 December 1952. Many States referred to the Bandung document. For some background about this conference, see Roland Burke, "Compelling Dialogue of Freedom" (2006). For statements calling the right to self-determination a "prerequisite," see for Egypt, the Ukraine, and Saudi Arabia, General Assembly's Third Committee, 641st Meeting. For Belarus and Indonesia, see 644th Meeting. For Czechoslovakia and Iran, see 645th Meeting. For Greece, see 647th Meeting; for India, see 651st Meeting. Similarly, Poland believed that "the right of self-determination was the very basis of the individual rights, and that no man could be free unless his people were free" (643rd Meeting). Belarus made similar remarks (644th Meeting); and so did Chile (645th Meeting). The USSR believed self-determination was the "primary condition for the exercise of all the other human rights" (646th Meeting). See also Yugoslavia (647th Meeting).
[488] See e.g., Antonio Cassese, "Political self-determination" (1979), p. 142; Alexandre Kiss, "The peoples' right to self-determination" (1986), p. 174; Robert McCorquodale, "Self-determination: a human rights approach" (1994), p. 872.
[489] General Assembly's Third Committee, 650th Meeting, 2 November 1955, UNDoc. A/C.3/SR.650.
[490] Jeremy Waldron, "The Dignity of Groups" (2008), p. 25.
[491] General Assembly's Third Committee, 642nd Meeting.

would become subject to the same supervisory mechanism as all the other more traditional human rights. This meant, *inter alia*, that States had the obligation to ensure respect for the right to self-determination of peoples and nations within their territories, and allow complaints about potential violations.[492] The UK could not go into detail, because the exact obligations regarding the promotion and protection of all human rights in the covenants were not known at the time that the article on the right to self-determination was discussed.[493]

The most important problem with the "prerequisite" argument was that it did not respond to the objections made by the Netherlands and many other Western States, that there was no room for such a so-called "collective right" as the right to self-determination of peoples in a covenant which proclaimed individual human rights. Some States did come up with a direct response to this Dutch objection. Generally, their response was that the distinction between collective rights and individual rights was artificial. For example, the delegate of the Soviet Union suggested that, "depending upon the angles from which they were regarded, rights appeared as both individual and collective," in the sense that "it was individuals who enjoyed them, but they had a meaning only because individuals lived in a society."[494] The delegate of El Salvador reminded delegates that the French Declaration of the Rights of Man of 1789 was considered to be one of the first examples of a document containing individual human rights, but "it included the right to resist oppression among its most important provisions," and "that right might be described as collective on the same grounds as the right of self-determination." In other words, the "distinction could be misleading, since the so-called collective rights constituted the expression of individual will through collective methods."[495] Another case in point was the right to vote, which was meaningless if perceived as the isolated right of one individual to write a name on a piece of paper.[496] The act of casting a vote only had meaning in a collective institution called democracy, but this did not mean the right to vote was not a human right.

Instead of arguing that the distinction between collective and individual rights was flawed, other States suggested that it was a good idea to place greater emphasis on collective rights, because they were also rights enjoyed by individual human beings. For example, Mexico believed that the covenants should not treat the

---

[492] *Idem.*

[493] Lebanon made a big point of this, and wondered whether what was to become Article 2 of the Covenants actually applied to Article 1. See General Assembly's Third Committee, 668th Meeting, 22 November 1955, UNDoc. A/C.3/SR.668.

[494] General Assembly's Third Committee, 646th Meeting. See also remark by Greece, in General Assembly's Third Committee, 647th Meeting.

[495] General Assembly's Third Committee, 645th Meeting. See also Egypt, General Assembly's Third Committee, 651st Meeting.

[496] See also remark by Greece, in General Assembly's Third Committee, 647th Meeting.

human being as an "isolated unit but as a member of his family and social group, and the intention was to stipulate [..] a right which, though applying to the community, was essentially an attribute of the individual."[497] The delegate of Costa Rica explained that "the right of self-determination was pre-eminently a human right, since it could not be exercised through a Government or a representative organ, but pertained exclusively to each of the individuals who comprised a people," and "it was the sum of individual wills that constituted the will of a people."[498] Yugoslavia came up with a very original, but unworkable suggestion. The Yugoslav delegate suggested that "if the inclusion of the article were approached from the point of view that every individual had the right to decide the status of his people, the whole problem became quite simple."[499] This solution would only work if all the individuals constituting a people would choose the same status of the people they belonged to. In the end, all these counter-arguments may not convince everyone, but at least they were direct responses to the question posed by so many Western States, *i.e.,* why a peoples' right should be included in a treaty about individual rights.

Some States attempted to answer the Western States' question by connecting the right to self-determination to more traditional human rights. [500] India, for example, reminded fellow delegates that, even though there was no explicit right to self-determination in the Universal Declaration of Human Rights, it was closely linked to the remark to be found in Article 21(3) of the Universal Declaration, that "the will of the people shall be the basis of the authority of government." [501] This link between the right to self-determination of peoples, especially its internal aspect, and human rights, especially the civil and political rights of the individuals which together constitute those peoples, is often made in the literature.[502] Taken together, they amount to what can only be called a right to live in a political system representing the rights and interests of all people, peoples, and individuals.[503]

The Western States were not convinced and maintained their position that the right to self-determination did not have a place in a covenant listing individual

---

[497] General Assembly's Third Committee, 646th Meeting.

[498] General Assembly's Third Committee, 649th Meeting.

[499] General Assembly's Third Committee, 647th Meeting.

[500] No State ever suggested that the right to self-determination was an individual human right. However, in the literature this argument has been made. See Matej Accetto, "The Right to Individual Self-Determination" (2004).

[501] General Assembly's Third Committee, 651st Meeting. See also Special Committee on Principles of International Law concerning Friendly Relations and Co-operation among States, Report, A/6799, adopted 26 September 1967 ("Third Report"), para. 218-222.

[502] Antonio Cassese, *Self-determination of peoples: a legal reappraisal* (1995), pp. 53-55. Cassese concluded that self-determination ultimately requires a democratic form of government, in order to secure the rights of all individuals, including minorities, to meaningful political participation.

[503] Allan Rosas, "Internal self-determination" (1993), especially p. 241.

human rights. Some States put forward a compromise solution. Brazil suggested dealing with "the human rights proper in the covenants and with the right of peoples to self-determination in a supplementary protocol."[504] Because it believed that "the right to self-determination fell into a different category from the other rights recognized in the draft covenants," China suggested that a third multilateral treaty be drawn up, specifically about the right to self-determination.[505] As the Chinese delegate explained: "While it could not be denied that the right of self-determination belonged to peoples and nations, and not to individuals, it had been argued that every individual belonging to a people or nation had to exercise the right individually."[506] The latter view was unacceptable to China, as the right to self-determination was "one of a people or nation in relation to other peoples and nations, while all the other rights recognized in the draft covenants were rights of persons in relation to other persons or to the State."[507] Because of the "unique nature" of the right, China therefore suggested a separate treaty, and many other delegates agreed with this proposal.[508]

The Chinese suggestion was withdrawn, and the right to self-determination did end up in the human rights covenants. It is difficult to conclude from this that the right to self-determination of peoples can therefore be regarded as a "basic collective human right," in the words of Przetacznik.[509]

The general comment on the right to self-determination of peoples adopted by the Human Rights Committee in 1984 must also be discussed briefly. This comment, which interpreted Article 1 of the covenants, saw the right to self-determination as "an essential condition for the effective guarantee and observance of individual human rights and for the promotion and strengthening of those rights."[510] This is certainly reminiscent of the "prerequisite" argument, *i.e.,* that respect for self-determination of peoples constitutes a *conditio sine qua non* for the

---

[504] See General Assembly's Third Committee, 648th Meeting and 650th Meeting.
[505] General Assembly's Third Committee, 642nd Meeting. Similarly, Brazil suggested a protocol about self-determination. See General Assembly's Third Committee, 648th Meeting.
[506] Idem.
[507] *Idem.*
[508] *Idem.* See *e.g.,* Israel (643rd Meeting); Honduras (647th Meeting); Costa Rica (649th Meeting); Egypt (651st Meeting); Sweden, Denmark (669th Meeting).
[509] Frank Przetacznik, "The basic collective human right to self-determination of peoples and nations as a prerequisite for peace" (1990), p. 50. Hurst Hannum, "The right of self-determination in the twenty-first century" (1998), pp. 773-774, also believed it was a collective human right.
[510] General Comment No. 12: The right to self-determination of peoples (Art. 1), adopted by the Human Rights Committee on 13 March 1984. The Committee added that "it is for that reason that States set forth the right of self-determination in a provision of positive law in both Covenants and placed this provision as article 1 apart from and before all of the other rights in the two Covenants."

respect of human rights, but that it is not a human right itself.[511] This conclusion is largely supported by the *travaux*.

## 6.3 Conclusion

The close connection between human rights and the right to self-determination of peoples is acknowledged by all States. Whether the right to self-determination should be seen as a human right in and of itself, whether it should be "deconstructed" into more traditional human rights, or whether it ought to be perceived as a "prerequisite" for the enjoyment of human rights, are more controversial issues.

All three positions were defended, and with good arguments. The "prerequisite" argument appears to be the most popular, but there are some dissenting opinions. The Brazilian delegate explained why respect for human rights and respect for the principle of self-determination could lead to inconsistent obligations.[512] This suggests that the right to self-determination of peoples and more traditional human rights ultimately aim to protect different values. There is a good explanation for this. The legal language of human rights and that of self-determination respond to different types of oppression and humiliation. The former aims to preserve the dignity of individuals against inhuman and degrading treatment, while the latter aims to preserve the dignity of peoples against degrading treatment of peoples as such.

## 7 CONCLUSION

The term "self-determination" appears only twice in the UN Charter, in a very ambiguous sense. The chapters in the UN Charter on the non-self-governing territories do not contain any explicit link with the right to self-determination of peoples. Nevertheless, the United Nations played an immensely important role in the road to independent statehood of virtually all colonial territories. The Organization also played a major role in protecting the sovereign independence of all its Member States, including that of the States that were the proud result of a

---

[511] Similarly, when the Friendly Relations Declaration was drafted, it was suggested that respect for the self-determination of peoples should be seen as the "foundation" of human rights. Special Committee on Principles of International Law concerning Friendly Relations and Co-operation among States, Report, A/6799, adopted 26 September 1967 ("Third Report"), para. 191. The link with human rights was made from the very beginning. See Special Committee, Second Report, paras. 464 and 489. However, at the World Conference on Human Rights (1993), "the denial of the right of self-determination [was considered] as a violation of human rights." Para. 2, Vienna Declaration and Programme of Action.

[512] General Assembly's Third Committee, 650th Meeting, 2 November 1955, UNDoc. A/C.3/SR.650.

colonial people's successful struggle for self-determination. After the waves of decolonization in the 1960s and 1970s, the United Nations began to play a principal part in the "modernization" – or "evolution" – of this age-old concept of sovereignty, in an attempt to reconnect it to its roots: the self-determination of peoples.

The story of the self-determination of peoples shares many characteristics with the story of the other global values. The value became prominent only after those peoples who did not enjoy it were able to come to the fore and have their voices heard as recognized participants in the global discussions taking place in the United Nations. Initially, the peoples who did not have a right to control their own destinies were the colonial peoples. When the UN Charter was drafted, they could not participate in the global discussions. This explains why there are so few references to the value of self-determination in the Charter. The General Assembly, where the value-based authoritative decision making continued after San Francisco, did much better. When the debate in the Assembly became more and more inclusive with the admission of more and more liberated peoples, the value of self-determination was taken more and more seriously.

Despite the success of the decolonization process, the value of self-determination has not been fully and finally realized. The story of the value of self-determination is the same as the story of all other values: instead of ever achieving the full realization of this global value, it serves to motivate the world to continuously improve itself. Admittedly the Trusteeship Council has not had all that much work to do since the last trust territory became independent, but the value of self-determination of peoples continues to serve as a guiding value in the relationship between people, however defined, and those who rule over them. Any kind of oppression constitutes a violation of a people's right to freely determine its own future. There is no reason to claim that such oppression must be "foreign" in some way before it can be considered as a hindrance to the enjoyment of the self-determination of a people. As the recent wave of popular uprisings in the Middle East and elsewhere has shown, this struggle against oppression did not come to an end with decolonization.[513] It will never end, just as the quest for peace and security, respect for human dignity, and universal social progress and development will never end.

What about the place of this value in international law, the language which motivates action *par excellence*? The UN also helped to establish the right to self-determination of peoples firmly as an international legal principle. The problems

---

[513] Reference is made here to the popular uprisings of 2011 in Tunisia, Egypt, Libya, Syria and elsewhere in the Arab world. Both the Security Council and the Assembly responded quickly in the case of Libya. See Resolution 1970 (2011), adopted by the Security Council on 26 February 2011, and subsequent resolutions. And Suspension of the rights of membership of the Libyan Arab Jamahiriya in the Human Rights Council, General Assembly resolution 65/265, adopted 1 March 2011.

are in the details. These problems mainly started to arise when the principle was applied outside the colonial context. In the process of decolonization the international community could work with a shared "instinct" of what constituted a colonial people. Now that minorities and other peoples have begun to claim a right to self-determination, the need for a more conceptual definition has become increasingly urgent. What are "peoples"? How can they be defined? And what exactly are they entitled to? These questions remain largely unanswered. What is clear is that the value of self-determination becomes relevant when a certain group of individuals experiences a particular form of oppression directed at the group. This leaves the group without any control over its own destiny. This is what happened to colonial peoples, whose oppressor was always relatively easy to identify. The colonial peoples could therefore be identified, despite the fact that the individuals within these groups were often of mixed ethnic and religious origin. However, oppression has also been experienced by certain minority peoples, including indigenous peoples, and by the entire populations of dictatorial States. There too, the oppression united the oppressed individuals in their desire to determine their own future, *i.e.* to enjoy their right to self-determination.

More conceptual or philosophical thinking on the subject is necessary. Nevertheless, there is no controversy about the status of self-determination of peoples as a value and as a principle of international law. This results in a situation where, as Crawford said, there is a right which is generally admitted to exist, even though no one knows what exactly is meant by it.[514] Thus it is unique in the sense that the principle – or is it a right? – of self-determination has been qualified as both *jus cogens* and *jus obscura*.[515]

The value of self-determination of peoples was also applied to States. It was suggested that as long as the government of a State represented the interests of its people, it could rely on self-determination as the basis for its claims to sovereign independence. The non-intervention principle protects States from outside oppression by prohibiting interference in the group's internal affairs. However, as soon as a State starts oppressing its own population, outside interference against the wishes of the oppressing Government is acceptable, provided that the interference responds to the demands for international assistance by the oppressed peoples themselves. The relationship between the value of self-determination of peoples and the prohibition for States and the Organization to intervene in the affairs of States is therefore a rather complex relationship. This relationship was examined in more detail in the discussion about the responsibility to protect, a concept which allows

---

[514] James Crawford, "The Right of Self-Determination in International Law" (2001), p. 10. See also Jean-François Dobelle, "Article 1, paragraphe 2" (2005), p. 355.

[515] For the former label, see *e.g.*, Hector Gros Espiell, "Self-determination and jus cogens" (1979). For the latter label, see James Crawford, "The Right of Self-Determination in International Law" (2001), p. 38.

for certain exceptions to the non-intervention principle, thereby obliging States to use their sovereign powers responsibly.

Finally, a human rights version of the value of self-determination of peoples was examined, as was done for all other values. It was noted that the right to self-determination had found a prominent place in the two classic human rights covenants, but that this did not mean that self-determination should itself be considered as a human right. There were essentially three possibilities: self-determination could be seen as a human right in and of itself, as essentially replaceable by certain more traditional human rights, or as something distinct from human rights. It was suggested that the right to self-determination of peoples was based on the value of peoples' self-determination. Traditional human rights, on the other hand, are based on the value of human dignity.

Despite the cautious language of the UN Charter, and despite many legal uncertainties, the value of self-determination of peoples has found its place in the language of international law. Thus Hannum's suggestion that the issue of self-determination was "too important to be left to lawyers" has not proved to be correct.[516]

---

[516] Hurst Hannum, "The right of self-determination in the twenty-first century" (1998), p. 779.

In 1945, the world had to reinvent itself. After the devastations of the Second World War, the international order had to be reconstructed almost from scratch. This was the purpose of the international gathering in San Francisco, where representatives of approximately fifty States came together, united in their fight against a common enemy, to draft a blueprint for a new world order. This blueprint was published in a small blue booklet, the United Nations Charter. All the States in the world have now subscribed to the values, purposes and principles contained in the Charter. Since 1945, the UN Charter has continued to inspire the international community to continuously improve itself in a never-ending attempt to realize certain fundamental values.

The role of the United Nations in the evolution of global values was the central theme of this study. The following questions were posed:

How and to what extent have moral points of view, defined in the language of values, determined the founding of the United Nations and the evolution of its purposes, principles and policies?

How has the United Nations influenced these moral views through its own contributions to the debate on values, as well as its contributions to the "translation" of these values into the language of international law, particularly by adopting general resolutions, declarations, treaties and other legally relevant texts?

The United Nations started to play its part in the evolution of global values immediately after the Second World War. This war had shown the importance of respect for and the realization of certain core values in international life. These values found their way into the UN Charter in one way or another. A world dominated by war, in which human beings were treated as objects, in which peoples were subjected to dictatorial and foreign rule, in which individuals and peoples could not achieve a basic standard of living, was not a world worth living in. A set of purposes for a new world order was identified, based on these collective experiences of fundamental lacks. Above all, the world needed to

Avoid the catastrophic wars of the past by maintaining international peace and security;

Avoid extreme poverty by promoting social progress and development;

447

Avoid the inhuman treatment of individuals anywhere in the world by universally promoting respect for human rights;

Avoid the exploitation and oppression of entire peoples by promoting the self-determination of all peoples.

These became the general purposes of the United Nations Organization. They are listed in Article 1 of its Charter, as follows:

To maintain international peace and security [...]

To develop friendly relations among nations based on respect for the principle of equal rights and self-determination of peoples,

To achieve international co-operation in solving international problems of an economic, social, cultural, or humanitarian character,

And [to achieve international co-operation] in promoting and encouraging respect for human rights and for fundamental freedoms for all without distinction as to race, sex, language, or religion [...]

Normally, the text and *travaux préparatoires* of the UN Charter, as well as the General Assembly's resolutions interpreting the Charter, are not examined as contributions to a global debate about values. Instead, the focus is on the immediate impact of the UN's work on particular disputes and emergencies, or on the binding character of the norms proclaimed by the UN and the effectiveness of the UN's measures to ensure compliance with these norms. This is unfortunate, because the importance of a continuous and global discourse about values and ideas cannot be overestimated. The power of values may be more difficult to measure than the power of particular compliance and enforcement mechanisms, but it is clear that universal agreement on where the world should be heading is crucial, also when specific challenges need to be addressed.

The role of the United Nations in the evolution of global values has been essential. As Pronk pointed out, the United Nations is not merely an organization established to urge all States to respect and comply with their international obligations. The United Nations is, above all, a "value community."[1] Since 1945, the organization has organized an on-going international dialogue which has resulted in a more or less global consensus on shared values, purposes, principles, and norms. This process has not received the attention it deserves. That is why Pronk called for the history of the United Nations to be written from the perspective

---

[1] Jan Pronk, "Een nieuwe jas voor de Verenigde Naties" (2007).

of values.[2] Writing this history requires an approach to the documents of the United Nations that is different from a strictly political or legal approach. It means looking in detail at the minutes of the discussions that preceded the adoption, both of the United Nations Charter itself, but also of all subsequent declarations based on the Charter. It also means that the Assembly's declarations have to be read as part of a larger story, as stepping stones in the continuous evolution and crystallization of a discourse on values. The research into the discussions, and especially the declarations that were the products of these discussions, must examine not so much whether States can be "bound" by statements made by their representatives during a specific meeting, or whether States have to abide by certain provisions in a particular declaration. Instead, the research must examine the substance of the provision itself, its context and relationship with other provisions, the arguments made in support of that provision, and the objections made against these arguments. Instead of analysing the power politics – which have certainly had an influence on the debates – it is necessary to see what happened to a particular line of argument. Why did one argument "defeat" another? What was the relationship between one argument and another, possibly made in a different context? These are the questions which arise when writing a history of ideas.

To write this history of UN values it was necessary to start at the very beginning. The first step was to come up with a suitable definition of the term "global value". In international law scholarship, there are many references to global values and the fundamental norms derived from them.[3] At the same time, very few scholars of international law have attempted to define the term "value," as though its meaning were self-evident. It seems Walzer's suggestion to "never define your terms" was followed; in his view, defining one's terms was unnecessary, and would only lead to trouble.[4] Although the importance of definitions should not be overemphasized, this study attempted to define global values. Scholars of various other disciplines – sociology, psychology, philosophy – have made earnest attempts to define the concept of "value." Although they were operating in a different context, largely defined by the basic principles of their own particular discipline,

---

[2] *Idem.*

[3] This is especially in the case of *jus cogens* norms, which supposedly are all value-based norms. See *e.g.*, Takeshi Minagawa, "Essentiality and reality of international jus cogens," (1984), p. 4; Andreas L. Paulus, "Jus Cogens in a Time of Hegemony and Fragmentation: an Attempt at a Re-appraisal," (2005), p. 299; Jochen Frowein, "Jus Cogens" (1997), p. 67; Antonio Gómez Robledo, "Le *Ius Cogens* International : Sa Genèse, Sa Nature, Ses Fonctions", (1981), p. 93. Kolb, who does not fully agree with the suggestion that *jus cogens* norms are by definition value-based norms, has gathered an impressive series of references to values/interests as basis of *jus cogens*. See Robert Kolb, *Théorie du ius cogens international: Essai de relecture du concept* (2001), pp. 73-74, and continued on pp. 74-75 in footnote 224. For more recent examples (since 2001), see Santiago Villalpando, *L'émergence de la communauté internationale dans la responsabilité des Etats* (2005), p. 89 (see also the page long footnote 299, on p. 89, with a list of literature relating values to *jus cogens*.)

[4] See Marcel Becker, "In gesprek met Michael Walzer" (2008), p. 36.

their findings have helped define the concept of value as used in this study. Based on this interdisciplinary exploration, a definition was found, derived mainly from the work of Rokeach, a well-known social psychologist. In this study, global values have been defined as

> A set of enduring, globally shared, beliefs that a specific state of the world, which is possible, is socially preferable, from the perspective of the life of all human beings, to the opposite state of the world.

Some of the most important elements in this definition required closer examination. For example, the definition presents "value" as a relative notion. It does not refer to an ideal world, but to a preferable world. The principal role of the discourse on values is to inspire the international community to continuously improve itself. Even though these efforts cannot be characterized as a Sisyphean endeavour, it is clear that they will never be completed. Perhaps the world is making progress, but it is not moving towards a clear and stable ideal. It is not only the world, but the discourse on values itself that is continuously evolving. Thus values serve as a carrot dangling just in front of the donkey, and urging it to continuously move forward. However, the carrot does not lead the donkey towards any previously determined final destination. And there is no chance that the donkey will ever grab the carrot, eat it and lose all motivation to continue its perpetual march.

Another important element in the definition was the idea that global values were globally shared beliefs, and that such beliefs should be defined from the perspective of the life of all human beings. This suggests that there are certain beliefs that all human beings subscribe to. These beliefs do not overlap simply by chance. They overlap because all human beings have something in common. The realization of these common beliefs is in everyone's interests. This presupposes that despite the existence of groups with competing desires, values and interests, international society is looking for more than ways and principles which allow these groups to coexist together. It presupposes that all individuals in this world together constitute a single body. This body could be referred to as the global community. The question remains how literally this idea of a global community, or global neighborhood, should be taken. Clearly, people do not actually interact with all the other individuals in this world. But that is equally impossible in all States, even in most cities. The important thing is that people feel the need to justify their behaviour at a global level, and there are signs that this is happening. Cosmopolitan theories were used to explain and justify this sentiment. Moral imperatives follow from this need for the global justification of particular behaviour, and also aim for a global reach. According to Singer, as "the revolution in communications has created a global audience [we] feel a need to justify our behavior to the whole world."[5] One

---

[5] Peter Singer, *One World: The Ethics of Globalization* (2002), p. 12.

cannot justify one's behaviour if there is no common moral language in which to do so. This study suggests that the common moral language is the language of global values.

Thus the assumption is that the inhabitants of this global community all share certain values, certain beliefs about a preferable world. The only way to discover these beliefs is through a global gathering of that community, a "town meeting of the world." Only a continuous discussion, in particular a discussion between people from different ways of life, will reveal which values are universally shared, and which are not.[6] Any process that can define the world's values, defined as globally shared beliefs, has to be sufficiently inclusive: it has to include the views of all the individuals of the world in some way. There is no better place for the evolution of global values than in a deliberative organ where the views of all the world's citizens are represented. Apart from the inclusive character of the discussion, two further conditions which any value-defining process had to meet were added. These conditions together ensure the relevance for global decision making of the global discussion about values. First, any meaningful discussion about global values must be a genuine discussion. It should not consist of continuously conflicting value systems and interests. Instead, all the participants must bear the global interest in mind, and show consideration not only for themselves and for their own lives, but also for others, ultimately for the global community as a whole. This should not be understood to mean that, as soon as all the participants have the global interest in mind, there will be no more conflicts about values. Practice shows that the opposite is true. In addition to the challenge of reconciling the global language of values with the language of all the local communities of this world – with their own culture, traditions and language of values – there is an equally formidable challenge of resolving the conflicts between the *global* values themselves. These conflicts are probably unavoidable; they constitute "an intrinsic, irremovable element in human life."[7] The challenge, which was beyond the scope of this study, is therefore to find an "uneasy equilibrium" between conflicting global values, an equilibrium that is "constantly threatened and in constant need of repair."[8] The global discussion about values must also be action-oriented. It must be able to motivate the international community to act, to make certain short-term sacrifices in order to realize more ambitious goals in the long

---

[6] Kwame Anthony Appiah, *Cosmopolitanism: Ethics in a World of Strangers* (2006), p xxi.

[7] Isaiah Berlin, *Liberty: Incorporating Four Essays on Liberty* (2002, original of 1969) p. 213.

[8] Isaiah Berlin, "On the Pursuit of the Ideal" (1988). Although these clashes between global values themselves have not been analyzed in detail in this study, some clashes have been uncovered, such as the clash between the promotion of the value of self-determination of peoples organized as a State and the promotion of the respect for human dignity of individuals within that State. See section 2.2 of Chapter VII.

term. The potential of international law as the language in which the values and ensuing obligations are expressed, was analyzed in this context.

Does such a process of value-based, authoritative decision making exist already? Is there a value-making process which is sufficiently inclusive, genuine and action-motivating? This study sees the United Nations as the most suitable candidate to provide such a process of value-based, authoritative decision making. The San Francisco Conference of 1945 and the annual meetings of the General Assembly are qualified in this study as global discussions about values. Do the United Nations and especially its General Assembly have a formal mandate to facilitate a global discussion about values? Did the "founding fathers" gathered in San Francisco grant it that role? Even though the word "value" was mentioned only a few times in San Francisco, and did not end up in the UN Charter, it is not far-fetched to qualify the discussions about the reconstruction of the international (legal) order as value-based discussions. According to the UN Charter, the Organization and its Member States have to act in accordance with certain principles or rules of action in their pursuit of certain common purposes, or aims of action. Although the Charter does not make this explicit, all of the purposes are without exception defined as the realization of a particular value. As Part II of this study showed, the Assembly has in actual fact played the role of facilitating a global discussion about values since it was established.

With regard to the inclusive character of the UN's discussions, it is true that representatives of colonial peoples, the Axis powers, and those States that refused to declare war against these Axis powers, were all absent in San Francisco. However, this lack of inclusiveness was corrected in subsequent years, when all States ratified the UN Charter, thereby adhering to the UN purposes, principles and values. The most fundamental "flaws" in the Charter were amended in practice later on. The cursory references to human rights and self-determination, for example, were interpreted broadly and flexibly, allowing the Charter to also play a key role in those fields which had been largely neglected by the "founding fathers" in 1945. These examples also show the practical importance of the inclusive character of the debates: it was only when the developing States became Members that the Assembly concentrated intensively on international development assistance. And it was only when some of the liberated peoples were admitted, that the Organization became seriously engaged in the decolonization process.

Once the Charter had entered into force and the United Nations Organization was established, the global discussion about values continued in the General Assembly. Every year, all the world's States send their representatives to the UN Headquarters in New York to collectively seek global solutions for global challenges. The UN Charter is used as the constitutional framework. This explains the central role played in those Assembly discussions by the values and value-based norms defined in that document. As regards the genuine character of the discussion, it must be acknowledged that the sincerity of the statements made in the Assembly is often questioned. Do they really mean what they say? Do they act accordingly? Are those grandiose statements not examples of hypocrisy? How does the United Nations ensure that States are actually encouraged to do more than pay lip service to the norms and values mentioned in the General Assembly's declarations? There are various ways in which promises made in Assembly resolutions can have consequences. First of all, the United Nations invests a great deal of energy and many resources in publishing its work. Various non-governmental organizations and the global media closely scrutinize what is going on in the Assembly. It is increasingly difficult for any State representative to make a promise in the Assembly, and assume that no one has heard it or cares about it. In 1951, the instrument of "naming and shaming" had already been described by the President of the International Court of Justice as being more powerful than most legalistic methods of "enforcement"; and this is even more the case sixty years later.[9]

With regard to the capacity of the UN's discussion to motivate action, the emphasis has been placed on the many multilateral treaties that have resulted from the Assembly's work. But Assembly declarations which have not been translated into the language of multilateral treaty law have been just as effective in influencing State policy.[10] These declarations have had such a significant effect precisely because they are seen as authoritative interpretations of the norms contained in the UN Charter. These norms themselves are binding on all States. As the Charter norms are formulated in general and often ambiguous terms, their authoritative interpretation by the Assembly can in fact amount to legislation. The General Assembly is ideally suited to interpret these norms and principles on behalf of all States party to the UN Charter. At the same time, the declarations of the Assembly can serve as "evidence" of the development of customary international law. This is particularly the case if States act in accordance with the norms they have proclaimed in the resolutions adopted by the General Assembly. Thus the Assembly is much more than a debating society: there are various ways of ensuring the legal and political relevance of the value-making process taking place in the General Assembly of the United Nations.

When the role of the Assembly is characterized in this way – as a global discussion about values – various possibilities can be suggested to strengthen the

---

[9] See Alvarez, Separate Opinion in the ICJ's Reservations to the Genocide Convention Advisory Opinion, 28 May 1951, p. 52.

[10] For the value of peace and security, reference can be made to the Declaration on Principles of International Law concerning Friendly Relations and Cooperation among States in Accordance with the Charter of the United Nations, General Assembly resolution 2625 (XXV), adopted on 24 October 1970; for the self-determination of peoples the Declaration on the Granting of Independence to Colonial Countries and Peoples, General Assembly resolution 1514 (XV), adopted 14 December 1960; for social progress and development we can refer to the United Nations Millennium Declaration; and for human dignity the Universal Declaration of Human Rights, General Assembly resolution 217 (III), adopted on 10 December 1948.

capacity of the Assembly. For example, the Assembly could be made more democratic to improve the inclusive character of the debates. The Assembly delegates could be selected on the basis of popular elections, similar to the European Parliament. Possibly larger countries, such as China, could be given more votes than smaller States, such as Nauru. To prevent States from preaching one thing in the Assembly, and practising an entirely different policy back home, the "legal force" of Assembly declarations could be clarified. For example, in its declarations the Assembly could explicitly note when it intends to interpret a UN Charter principle. Assembly declarations containing rules which derive directly from Charter principles constitute an authoritative interpretation of those principles. Therefore they are binding, not only on the Assembly itself, but also on Member States. Such clarity would increase not only the genuine character of the discussion, but also the capacity of Assembly declarations to motivate action. Moreover, as there is still uncertainty about whether the Assembly can interpret the Charter, not only on its own behalf but also on behalf of the Member States, this "power of interpretation" of Assembly declarations could be acknowledged formally and explicitly by the Member States themselves.

After examining the term "global value" and describing the role of the United Nations in the evolution of these values, Part II analyzed the actual evolution of the global values through the normative work of the United Nations. The documents of the San Francisco Conference, the UN Charter itself, and the Charter-based Assembly resolutions were extensively studied to write a history of the United Nations as a community of values. The intention was to find reflections of a global consensus in those documents, regarding the continuously evolving meaning of the values indirectly outlined in the UN Charter itself: peace and security, social progress and development, human dignity, and the self-determination of peoples. These are the most fundamental global values referred to in the United Nations Charter, and therefore the values analyzed in this study.

The cross-fertilization between the work of the United Nations and the debate on values taking place in scholarship was a major theme in this study. Some examples of fruitful cooperation were described, and some potential examples uncovered. To facilitate further development in this direction, a summary is provided here of some of the major ideas developed by the UN and presented in this study, which can be explored in the literature in more detail. In addition, some of the ideas explored in the scholarship are presented which the UN can use in its future work. All these suggestions together also provide a brief summary of Part II of this study.

The value of peace and security was discussed first. The United Nations has made some attempts to define peace in general terms, for example, by referring to the culture of peace. From the start, the problem with such positive definitions of peace was that they ended up describing a peaceful world as a perfect world, thus making the value of peace and security indistinguishable from other values. It is perhaps for that reason that the United Nations mainly busied itself identifying various specific threats to and breaches of international peace and security. A peaceful world, then, is a world without such threats, *i.e.* without inter-State and civil wars, without attacks by mercenaries and terrorists, and without the arms race and the development of various weapons of mass destruction. These have all been labelled by the UN Security Council and the Assembly as direct threats to international peace and security. Climate change, diseases of mass destruction and poverty also affect peace and security, but they do so indirectly. To label them as threats to the peace would, once again, lead to a value of peace which lacks conceptual clarity. Thus the United Nations preferred to refer to them as "root causes" of threats to the peace. As with all values, the UN has also promoted a human rights-based approach to peace and security. The UN has suggested that peace must be defined from the perspective of individual human beings, and not only from a State perspective. This change of perspective, if adopted by the international community, would drastically alter the definition of peace and security. From a State-centred perspective, it is possible to distinguish the root causes of threats to the peace from the threats themselves. But poverty poses just as much of an immediate threat to the life of an individual as the development of an atomic bomb, or the start of an inter-State war. How should a threat to human security then be defined, taking into account that threats to human security should somehow be distinguishable from other types of threats? This new approach has not yet been fully explored. The concept of "human security" was first introduced in the Human Development Report of 1994, as requiring both "safety from such chronic threats as hunger, disease and repression" and "protection from sudden and hurtful disruptions in the patterns of daily lives."[11] Since 1994, human security has been discussed extensively in the literature. Perhaps this will one day lead to a coherent theory which the UN can implement in its work.

The second value is social progress and development. The Assembly has adopted more resolutions on this value than on any other value. In those resolutions, the UN focused largely on international programmes and plans for development, rather than on defining the notion of development itself. The aim of all these plans and programmes was to engage in collective action in order to improve the international economic order by tackling the rising inequalities in the world, as well as by responding to the marginalization and absolute lack of development in certain parts of the world. The Assembly has consistently stressed the primary responsibility of States for their own development. But it has also recognized the duty of all States, especially the developed ones, to assist developing States in their development. These plans and programmes have been compared, wherever possible, with scholarly theories of global social and distributive justice. The main

---

[11] Mahbub ul-Haq, *New dimensions of human security* (Human development report 1994), p. 23.

question then was: "Who is entitled to what?" The developing States, which have a strong majority in the Assembly, claim that they suffer because of the international economic order set up by the developed States. They ask for that order to be corrected, and until the corrections have been made, for compensation for the damage caused to them by the existing order. These demands are clearly based on principles of distributive justice, especially the basic principle that all participants deserve an equal share of the goods, unless there are convincing moral reasons to justify a different arrangement. In the scholarship, a distinction is made between claims based on (distributive) justice and claims based on an absolute duty for those capable of doing so to come to the aid of those in dire need. Following this distinction, the UN's efforts to coordinate emergency relief aid and those to improve the system for the provision of official development assistance have been treated separately. Apart from calling for an equitable distribution of the goods among the present generation, the United Nations also acknowledged that future generations already have a claim to some of the same goods. One of the success stories has been the UN's role in promoting the idea of "sustainable development," defined as development that meets the needs of the present generation without compromising the ability of future generations to meet their own needs. This definition has been embraced both in scholarship and by the UN and its specialized agencies. The UN has also concerned itself with a human rights based approach to development. The Assembly has proclaimed a right to development, defined as an inalienable human right by virtue of which every human person and all peoples are entitled to participate in, contribute to, and enjoy economic, social, cultural and political development, in which all human rights and fundamental freedoms can be fully realized. However, it is as yet unclear whether the (human) right to development has been unambiguously embraced, either in UN parlance or in the scholarship.

The third value is human dignity. The development of this value, in the language of human rights, has been the biggest success story of the United Nations. The Assembly has been very consistent and explicit in its use of human dignity as the source of all human rights. It started with the adoption of the Universal Declaration of Human Rights in 1948, which stated that "all human beings are born free and equal in dignity and rights." The idea that human dignity constitutes a universally shared foundation of the human rights movement has also been accepted in the literature. But what is human dignity? The concept is often given a religious connotation, but this option is not available to the United Nations, which does not adhere to any particular religion. The UN uses a highly intuitive approach to human dignity. All individuals in this world have inherent rights, which do not depend on their recognition by others. Individuals have these rights simply by virtue of being human. This claim has universal validity: all human beings, wherever they are, whoever they are, and in whatever circumstances they find themselves, are entitled to respect for their intrinsic dignity and the rights that derive from it. The same intuitive approach is used to derive human rights from this value of human dignity. All human beings are able to tell which specific rights constitute the core of rights derived directly from human dignity. Because we are all human beings, the core of the catalogue of rights does not depend on one's background, religion or culture. From the very beginning the Assembly busied itself defining this core of universally valid human rights norms based on human dignity. Some philosophers have proposed other less intuitive theories. The work of Beitz and Griffin, in particular, comes to mind.[12] Griffin used the UN's work as a starting point, and then criticized the Assembly's application of its own theory. He believed that some universally recognized human rights should not be recognized as such, because they could not be based on human dignity. Such discussions are fruitful in developing the potential for cross-fertilization between philosophers and the UN.

The last value on the list is the value of the self-determination of peoples. The importance of this value is largely due to the UN's success in overseeing the process of decolonization. When the value was applied to the colonies, not much conceptual thinking was needed. It was clear who the colonial peoples were, and who the colonial powers. The conceptual challenges started to emerge when the principle was applied outside the colonial context. There appears to be a consensus in the United Nations that the principle of self-determination protects peoples against all forms of oppression. There is no reason to suggest that the principle applies only when the oppression is in some ways "foreign," as was the case in the colonial context. A group of individuals can just as easily be targeted, as a group, by its own leader. There are minority peoples, including indigenous peoples, who suffer from being oppressed by the majority. Or an entire population can be oppressed by its own dictatorial Government. Interpreted in this way, the value has not only motivated calls for secession, but it has also inspired the participatory processes in many States in a positive way. When a people has realized its right to control its own destiny with the creation of its own independent State, there is still a danger that other States could come and oppress it by interfering in the group's internal affairs. Challenges to the sovereign independence of States thus also challenge the full enjoyment of the right to self-determination of peoples. Despite many debates and resolutions, it is still unclear what "peoples" are, and exactly what they are entitled to. The UN has provided a wealth of ideas and possible applications of the value, but it has made very few of the hard choices that have to be made. The UN proposed a human rights approach to the value of self-determination of peoples. Article 1 of both classic human rights covenants proclaims that all peoples have the right of self-determination, and that by virtue of that right they may freely determine their political status and freely pursue their economic, social and cultural development. The inclusion of this right in the human

---

[12] Charles R. Beitz, *The idea of human rights* (2009); James Griffin, *On human rights* (2008).

rights covenants has led to extensive discussion, both in the United Nations and in the literature. Is it a human right? Or is the right to self-determination a prerequisite for the enjoyment of human rights? The debate is far from over.

It is interesting to compare the different approaches used by the UN in its work on the continued evolution of these four global values. The UN mainly developed a long list of (potential) threats to peace and security. It left the value itself largely undefined, although it has come up with some highly influential new concepts and ideas, such as "human security." With regard to social progress and development, the General Assembly focused on drafting a long series of action plans, comprising various commitments to assist developing nations in their development. As the UN did not provide a substantial definition of the value itself, it is not always easy to understand what the ultimate goal of all these plans is. Thus they mainly served as ammunition for economists, who could discuss and criticize specific policy elements. Because there was no ultimate goal, moral philosophers, on the other hand, had little to work with. The UN's work on the value of human dignity has yet another character. There, the UN did not restrict itself to defining a list of threats to dignity, nor did it limit itself to designing various action plans to promote human dignity globally. The UN produced a long list of human rights which States must respect to promote the value of human dignity. The UN has given various "hints" about the meaning of the value itself and has consequently significantly influenced scholarly debate. Self-determination is probably the vaguest of all four values. We do not even know who is entitled to self-determination, and what they are entitled to exactly, and in what circumstances. All we know is that it is based on the desire of various communities to freely control their own destiny, without any outside oppression. Here, the UN is in need of some help from the scholarly community.

In the research into the history of the United Nations as a community of values, one is struck by an unusual characteristic of the United Nations debates. The debates, both in San Francisco and in the Assembly, all have a highly abstract and philosophical character. This in itself distinguishes the debates from the usual political discourse, where a concrete global challenge has emerged and State representatives urgently come together to collectively find a solution and divide the tasks. At the same time, the San Francisco and Assembly debates are not purely philosophical debates. Those participating in the debates all represent a particular State, with its own special interests, and its own cultural peculiarities and historical traditions. Many of the representatives receive instructions from home, and merely read out the statement prepared and approved beforehand at the Assembly. This makes actual interaction rather difficult, but it allows the other States – and researchers – to get an impression of a State's opinion on a specific point. The UN debates examined in this study were always organized for a particular purpose: the drafting of fundamental principles or norms. Each and every time, the main aim of all the representatives was therefore to find a global compromise. This was the case in San Francisco in 1945, and it has been the case for the Assembly since its establishment. In a way, what the representatives ought to do is reflect the general spirit prevailing in their State, and try very hard to ensure that this spirit is in turn reflected, as far as possible, in the treaty text and the declarations that are ultimately adopted. Of course, whether representatives genuinely attempt to reflect this general spirit differs per country. Because of the consistency of their positions on various issues on the Assembly's agenda, many states have acquired a certain personality, rather like individual persons. At the same time, there is no reason why States, like individuals, cannot change their minds. The UN documents are examined as reflections of these global conversations, they contain a wealth of information and a wealth of arguments. Even when at key moments, the result of these discussions is an empty compromise – many of the most important issues have been left undecided – the road leading to this empty compromise can be interesting to examine.

Furthermore, when the importance of the debates themselves is acknowledged, it becomes even more interesting to think of ways to improve the quality of the debates themselves. One way would be to exploit the potential of the cross-fertilization between the UN and the academic community further. This could be done, first of all, by publishing and promoting the UN documents, especially the San Francisco proceedings and the Assembly's resolutions and debates. The proceedings of the debates resulting in the most important declarations and legal texts of the international community could be disseminated and then studied widely. The United Nations has already realized the importance of the wide dissemination of its work. It is investing a great deal of energy and resources in facilitating this process. It has made many of its documents available online free of charge, and it has developed various ways – mainly online – to present the key documents in the field of peace and security, development, and human rights, in an accessible way. It has also devoted a section of its website to the promotion of the UN's values and ideas through the language of international law. Increasingly, the Organization makes use of the internet to link scholarship to the work of the United Nations. The Audio-visual Library of International Law is an example of this.[13] All these developments are promising, and will increase the exposure of the work of the United Nations, facilitating the cross-fertilization between the UN and the academic community, increasing its relevance, and ensuring that all the world's citizens can identify better with the work done in New York. Hammarskjold, the second UN Secretary-General, famously compared the United Nations Organization with a painting. In his view, everything would be all right if the world's people would stop thinking of the United Nations as "a weird Picasso abstraction and see it as a drawing they made themselves." The world population has to identify with the

---

[13] See http://www.un.org/law/avl/.

values and purposes, first proclaimed in the UN Charter, and then developed in more detail, on their behalf, by the General Assembly. This has been the aim since 1945. For example, even during the San Francisco Conference, Gildersleeve of the US delegation had already suggested that the preamble "should be hung up in every peasant's cottage throughout the world," as a source of inspiration.[14]

The process of cross-fertilization between the United Nations and the international community, especially researchers and specialists, should also be "institutionalized" in some way. Ideally, the most influential individuals in the public debate could be invited to participate in the debates at the General Assembly. The delegates of all the States in the world can then ask these experts for their opinion, and they can choose to adopt a certain idea or theory, or not. In this way, the global consensus reached at the Assembly will be firmly based on ideas developed in scholarship, as well as on political compromise. That would be the ideal. Such debates have taken place. The debate on the responsibility to protect comes to mind.[15] Unfortunately, instead of showing the potential of such debates, that debate mainly revealed the pitfalls. First of all, the initiative could be criticized for a lack of sincerity. After all, the debate was organized by a strong and outspoken opponent of the idea which was to be discussed, and the discussion was organized to raise doubts about the universal agreement reached earlier. Secondly, the scholars and experts who had been invited strongly disagreed with each other. This is the norm in essentially any debate in scholarship. One wonders how the international community, as represented in the Assembly, can learn from scholars if they disagree so fundamentally with each other. Thirdly, it showed that the Assembly did not need a fully-fledged definition of a particular concept. It needed only an intuitive understanding of a particular concept that was sufficiently profound to be able to inspire action. These experiences and pitfalls make one wonder whether the continued evolution and codification of global values in the language of international law actually benefits from a bigger role for experts. Ultimately, only practice will provide an answer to this question, by proving or disproving the strength of ideas that have been fully worked out. Past experiences of cross-fertilization between the UN and the academic world could be used to improve and perfect the model. The present problems might turn out to be no more than teething troubles, obstacles that can be overcome in the future.

This study has examined how moral values determined the founding of the United Nations Organization in 1945, and the evolution of its purposes, principles and policies since then. A detailed examination of the *travaux préparatoires* of the United Nations Conference on International Organization has shown that the

---

[14] Minutes of Twenty-First Meeting of the United States Delegation, April 27, 1945, in FRUS, *1945, General:* Volume I, p. 478. See also First Session of Commission I, June 14, 1945, UNCIO, vol. 6, p. 19.
[15] See section 5.3 of Chapter VII.

drafting of the United Nations Charter was significantly influenced by global moral values, *i.e.* globally shared beliefs distinguishing right from wrong, good from bad, the current from a preferable state of the world. A common desire to eradicate war, poverty, inhuman treatment, and the exploitation of peoples, have led to an affirmation of the values of peace and security, social progress and development, human dignity and the self-determination of all peoples. All these values ended up in the UN Charter. This study also analyzed how the United Nations continued to influence global morality through its own contributions to the debate on values, and its contributions to the "translation" of these values into the language of international law. It has been demonstrated that, since 1945, moral values have continued to influence the work of the United Nations, especially that of the General Assembly. By interpreting the values embedded in the Charter in its many declarations, the Assembly has guided the evolution of these values. The Assembly's declarations taken together, with the UN Charter as their backbone, constitute a particular system of values and principles of conduct, distinguishing between the current world and a "better world." In this way, they are clear examples of contributions to a moral discourse. Their link with the UN Charter also gives them legal significance, and the fact that they are the result of inter-State negotiations gives them a political foundation as well.

In a position somewhere between high-flown moral principles, legal norms, and down to earth political compromise, Assembly declarations are rather like giraffes. As Thomas Franck explained, this animal shows that it is "perfectly possible to have one's head in the clouds while keeping one's feet firmly planted on the ground."[16] All the General Assembly's declarations together constitute the last wild herd of giraffes, leading us through the dusty desert to the nearest oasis. Just like giraffes, there is always a danger that Assembly declarations relate mainly to each other, ignoring the obstacles on the ground. Lowe warned the Assembly not to use its declarations to build a castle in the sky. The search for "coherence with other principles" should not be considered more important than a real link with State practice and policy.[17] Otherwise the Assembly would engage in an exercise of UN Charter exegesis, focusing on explaining the "meaning and significance of earlier 'authoritative' texts" while becoming more and more detached from political reality.[18]

Clearly one of the most formidable challenges for the future is to find ways to compel all States to take the value-based declarations of the Assembly more seriously. States should be motivated to acknowledge that the Assembly's words need to be translated into concrete action, *i.e.* meaningful financial and political commitments, robust enforcement mechanisms, and so on. In order to succeed, the

---

[16] See Thomas M. Franck, "Tribute to Professor Louis B. Sohn" (2007), p. 24.
[17] Vaughan Lowe, "The principle of non-intervention" (1994), p. 73.
[18] *Idem.*

Assembly must restrict itself to tackling the global challenges, and to providing common responses to them. It should not set out to replace the colourful diversity of local traditions and policies in the world with a single global culture and policy. Like any truly cosmopolitan institution the Assembly's powers are limited: it can go only as far as to promote an abstract ethic – a set of values – and norms based on these. It can never provide a real and concrete "refuge" for people. This is something which only local communities can provide.[19] If the Assembly overreaches itself, if the discourse on global values is dominated too much by cosmopolitan (and benign) elites, and if the opposing forces are ignored, a counter-reaction could continue to grow, and the world could witness a rise of local values and a growing tendency for people to define their political identity in terms of their connection to a particular ethnic or religious group rather than on the basis of modern constitutional citizenship.

---

[19] The formulation is based on Martha C. Nussbaum, "Patriotism and Cosmopolitanism" (1994), as cited in section 2.3 of Chapter II of this study.

# DE VERENIGDE NATIES, DE EVOLUTIE VAN MONDIALE WAARDEN EN INTERNATIONAAL RECHT (NEDERLANDSE SAMENVATTING)

## 1 INLEIDING

Een man liep langs het bouwterrein van een nieuwe kathedraal. Hij vroeg een van de werklieden wat hij aan het doen was, en deze antwoordde: "Ik ben stenen aan het breken." Een tweede bouwvakker zei: "Ik ben mijn salaris aan het verdienen." En een derde, aan wie de man opnieuw dezelfde vraag stelde, draaide zijn ogen, vol religieuze hartstocht, in de richting van de half afgewerkte kathedraal, en antwoordde: "Ik ben een kathedraal aan het bouwen."[1]

Met deze parabel beschreef de Luxemburgse afgevaardigde tijdens de San Francisco Conferentie de wederopbouw waarmee de internationale gemeenschap na afloop van de Tweede Wereldoorlog was begonnen. Hij herinnerde zijn collega's aan het grote belang van de taak die zij gezamenlijk probeerden te verwezenlijken. De kathedraal in aanbouw was de Verenigde Naties. De blauwdruk van deze Organisatie-in-oprichting, het Handvest, werd door de afgevaardigden van vijftig landen in San Francisco getekend op 26 juni 1945.

Dit onderzoek gaat over dat Handvest. Het beschrijft welke mondiale waarden aan de basis stonden van dit document en wat er met die waarden is gebeurd in de afgelopen zesenzestig jaar. De ontstaansgeschiedenis van deze "grondwet van de wereld," zoals het Handvest ook wel wordt omschreven, is allereerst onderzocht. Hoewel de *travaux préparatoires* van het Handvest al eerder zijn bestudeerd, is dat nooit gedaan vanuit een mondiale waardenperspectief. De verdere evolutie van die waarden, door de Verenigde Naties, wordt eveneens geanalyseerd. De nadruk ligt op de resoluties van de Algemene Vergadering, omdat de Vergadering het meest geschikte hoofdorgaan van de Organisatie is om met gezag een dergelijke mondiale discussie over waarden te leiden.

---

[1] Verenigde Naties, *Documents of the United Nations Conference on International Organization* (22 volumes), vol. 1, p. 504.

## 2 PROBLEEMSTELLING

De Verenigde Naties wordt meestal beschouwd als een politieke organisatie, een samenwerkingsverbond van Staten met een aantal diverse en zeer ambitieuze taken. Meestal richt het onderzoek zich op de manier waarop de VN heeft getracht deze taken te realiseren, onder meer door haar lidstaten, via het internationaal recht, te verplichten zich te houden aan tal van normen en beginselen. In deze studie ligt de nadruk op de ontwikkeling van ideeën, of meer specifiek: op de definitie en de verdere evolutie van een beperkt aantal mondiale waarden in het werk van de Verenigde Naties.

Het nut van het schrijven van een dergelijke VN-ideeëngeschiedenis werd al eerder ingezien. Zo constateerde Jan Pronk, prominent Nederlands politicus en speciale vertegenwoordiger van de VN Secretaris-Generaal in de Soedan, dat er behoefte was aan een "geschiedenis" van de Verenigde Naties als waardengemeenschap:

> De [Verenigde Naties] is meer dan een internationaal overlegorgaan [...], meer ook dan een organisatie die door de samenbundeling van macht op consensusbasis kan ingrijpen als de internationale vrede en veiligheid worden bedreigd, meer ook dan een samenstel van organisaties die programma's uitvoeren ten gunste van vrede, ontwikkeling en armoedebestrijding. De Verenigde Naties is ook een waardegemeenschap. Door middel van intensief en continue internationaal overleg, is wereldwijde consensus bewerkstelligd over beginselen, normen en waarden. De resultaten zijn vastgelegd in charters, verdragen en resoluties. Zonder dit alles had de Verenigde Naties nooit effectief kunnen optreden, noch bij de uitvoering van programma's, noch wanneer internationaal ingrijpen gewenst wordt geacht. Er kan een geschiedenis van de Verenigde Naties worden geschreven vanuit deze optiek: de ontwikkeling van waarden om aldus de uitdagingen gezamenlijk beter het hoofd te kunnen bieden. De basis is vastgelegd in het Handvest van de Verenigde Naties en in de Verklaring van de Rechten van de Mens. In deze teksten gaat het om vrede, mensenrechten, de menselijke waardigheid, internationale economische en sociale samenwerking, respect voor het beginsel van gelijke rechten en zelfbeschikking van alle volken, territoriale integriteit van alle staten en andere basiswaarden.[2]

Er zijn drie belangrijke redenen voor het beschrijven van de evolutie van mondiale waarden in het werk van de Verenigde Naties. In de eerste plaats is de VN-bijdrage aan de evolutie van waarden en ideeën ondergewaardeerd. Een tweede reden is dat een dergelijke beschrijving kan laten zien hoe invloedrijk ideeën kunnen zijn in de mondiale politiek. De nadruk op het falen van de VN in specifieke gevallen –zoals bij de volkerenmoord in Rwanda en Srebrenica in de jaren negentig - doet geen recht aan het succes van de VN in de ontwikkeling van nieuwe, en zeer

---

[2] Jan Pronk, 'Een nieuwe jas voor de Verenigde Naties' (2007), p. 187.

464

invloedrijke, ideeën. Deze ideeën hebben grote invloed gehad op de praktijk, bijvoorbeeld op het proces van dekolonisering en de bevordering van mensenrechten. Ten derde, recentelijk hebben meerdere invloedrijke politici gebruikgemaakt van het mondiale waarden-discours om de doelstellingen van hun buitenlands beleid te beschrijven. Mondiale waarden zijn mede daarom uitgegroeid tot een populair object van studie, vooral in de disciplines van het internationale recht, de politieke wetenschappen en de wijsbegeerte. Veel internationale juristen vragen zich af of de internationale rechtsorde is veranderd van een in wezen waardevrij samenwerkingsverband tussen soevereine en onafhankelijke Staten, in een meer kosmopolitische rechtsorde, gebaseerd op gedeelde universele waarden en gemeenschappelijke belangen. Kosmopolitische filosofen hebben sinds de Oudheid al gepleit voor een door gemeenschappelijke belangen en waarden gekenmerkte wereldorde. Mede vanwege de globalisering kent het kosmopolitisme in de afgelopen jaren een sterke opmars: in plaats van een theoretische utopie, lijkt een kosmopolitische visie op de wereld, waarin verschillende volkeren uiteindelijk een eenheid vormen, steeds meer een mogelijke beschrijving te worden van de actuele werkelijkheid. De Verenigde Naties speelt een centrale rol in deze ontwikkeling.

## 3 ONDERZOEKSVRAAG

Het doel van deze studie is om de documenten van de Verenigde Naties te bestuderen vanuit een waardenperspectief. Allereerst wordt een beschrijving gegeven van de "geboorte" van de belangrijkste naoorlogse waarden in 1945. Vervolgens wordt de evolutie van deze fundamentele waarden onderzocht. Deze studie beperkt zich niet tot het geven van een beschrijving van deze evolutie. De invloed van de VN op het wetenschappelijke – en dan vooral filosofische - waardendiscours is ook geanalyseerd, en, *vice versa*, de invloed van wetenschappelijke theorieën op de VN. De onderzoeksvraag luidt als volgt:

> Op welke manier en in welke mate hebben morele standpunten, gedefinieerd in de taal van mondiale waarden, de oprichting van de Verenigde Naties en vervolgens de evolutie van haar doelstellingen, beginselen en beleid mede bepaald? Hoe heeft de Verenigde Naties op haar beurt deze morele opvattingen beïnvloed door middel van haar eigen bijdragen aan het waarden-debat, en door haar bijdragen aan de vertaling van deze mondiale waarden in de taal van het internationale recht, in het bijzonder door middel van de adoptie van algemene resoluties, verklaringen, en verdragsteksten?

Om antwoord te geven op deze onderzoeksvraag, zijn de archieven van de Verenigde Naties bestudeerd. De mondiale waarden die de geboorte van de Verenigde Naties bepaald hebben zijn geïdentificeerd. Ook wordt beschreven hoe

465

deze waarden in de loop der tijd zijn mee veranderd met de veranderende wereld, vooral door middel van de verklaringen van de Algemene Vergadering.

Deze historische beschrijving wordt voorafgegaan door een aantal meer theoretische bespiegelingen over de relatie tussen mondiale waarden, het internationaal recht en de Verenigde Naties. Dit heeft niet alleen tot doel de centrale rol van de Algemene Vergadering in dit onderzoek te rechtvaardigen, maar ook om het potentieel van de Verenigde Naties als een "waarden producerende machine" te laten zien.

## 4 METHODOLOGIE

In de eerste hoofdstukken zijn enkele centrale begrippen vanuit een algemene, abstracte benadering bekeken. Allereerst is de literatuur over mondiale waarden geanalyseerd. Verschillende definities van het begrip "waarde" zijn onderzocht die als inspiratie hebben gediend bij het formuleren van een definitie die het object van deze studie omschrijft en bepaalt.

Nadat een definitie van mondiale waarden is geformuleerd, wordt een van de belangrijkste aannames van dit onderzoek getoetst: dat een mondiaal plenair orgaan de leidende rol zou moeten spelen in de evolutie van mondiale waarden. Verschillende theorieën, vooral van een kosmopolitisch karakter, worden geanalyseerd. Deze theorieën staan aan de basis van het idee dat er geen betere plek voor de ontwikkeling van mondiale waarden is dan een overlegorgaan waarin, op de een of andere manier, de mening van alle burgers in de wereld vertegenwoordigd is.

De volgende stap is om te bepalen of een dergelijk orgaan bestaat, of dat er een orgaan bestaat dat het in zich heeft uit te groeien tot mondiaal overlegorgaan. De Algemene Vergadering van de Verenigde Naties wordt voorgesteld als kandidaat. Primaire bronnen en wetenschappelijke literatuur worden geanalyseerd om te bepalen wat de oprichters van de VN precies van plan waren met de Algemene Vergadering, en wat er geworden is van deze plannen. Essentieel hierbij is de vraag hoe de vertegenwoordigers van de lidstaten zelf hun rol in de Algemene Vergadering interpreteren. Zien zij de jaarlijkse bijeenkomsten in New York als een bron van nieuwe ideeën, of slechts als een instrument voor politieke samenwerking? Het een sluit het ander natuurlijk niet uit.

Deel II vormt het beschrijvende gedeelte van deze studie. De nadruk ligt op de bestudering van de primaire bronnen, voornamelijk VN-documenten, en verslagen van VN-besprekingen. De methodologie is identiek in de vier hoofdstukkengewijd aan de bespreking van een mondiale waarde. Allereerst worden de *travaux préparatoires* van het VN Handvest onderzocht. Vervolgens worden de resoluties van de Algemene Vergadering als de ruggengraat van de beschrijving van de verdere evolutie van elk van de mondiale waarden nader bestudeerd. Hierbij is een selectie gemaakt van de meest relevante resoluties, zoals resoluties waarin de Vergadering algemene beginselen heeft geproclameerd. Dergelijke resoluties zijn meestal "verklaringen" genoemd, door de Algemene Vergadering zelf, om hun bijzondere karakter te benadrukken. Veel verklaringen zijn vergezeld van een actieprogramma, waarvan de uitvoering het onderwerp van opvolgende resoluties is, die elk jaar opnieuw worden aangenomen. Omdat deze studie gaat over de evolutie van de waarden zelf worden deze uitvoeringsresoluties niet in detail besproken.

De mondiale waarden-benadering vereist een methode bij de bestudering van de documenten van de Verenigde Naties, die anders is dan wanneer voor een strikt politieke of juridische benadering gekozen wordt. Omdat de resoluties als verslag van de mondiale ideeëngeschiedenis beschouwd worden, is het belangrijk ook naar de notulen van de bijbehorende discussies te kijken. Dit geldt uiteraard ook voor de discussies die aan de basis stonden van het Handvest zelf. De resoluties en notulen moeten gelezen worden als onderdeel van een groter geheel, als hoofdstukken uit het verhaal van de voortgaande evolutie van het mondiale waarden-discours. Bij het onderzoek naar beraadslagingen en daaruit resulterende resoluties ligt het accent op de inhoud van de resolutiezelf, en op de relatie met andere resoluties. Op welke manier past een bepaalde verklaring in het grotere geheel? Dat is in dit kader steeds de kernvraag. Ook moet gekeken worden naar de argumenten ter ondersteuning van essentiële bepalingen in de resoluties – grotendeels ongeacht welke Staat met deze argumenten gekomen is - en de tegenargumenten. In plaats van de machtspolitiek –waarvan de invloed op het debat zeker niet onderschat wordt – is bestudeerd wat er gebeurt met een bepaalde argumentatie. Waarom "verliest" een idee het van een ander? Is de onderliggende argumentatie van het ene idee consistent met de argumentatie waarop een ander idee, wellicht in een andere context, gebaseerd is? Bij het schrijven van een geschiedenis van ideeën, komen dergelijke vragen op de voorgrond te staan.

De bestudering van de wetenschappelijke literatuur dient om de wetenschappelijke behandeling van die waarde te vergelijken met de manier waarop dezelfde waarde is geïnterpreteerd in de documenten van de Algemene Vergadering. Wanneer de kruisbestuiving tussen de ideeën van de VN en die uit de wetenschap succesvol geweest is, of wanneer nog niet benutte mogelijkheden kunnen worden geïdentificeerd, wordt deze kruisbestuiving uitvoeriger behandeld.

Het doel van dit onderzoek is niet om een volledig overzicht te geven van de rechtsnormen op het gebied van elke afzonderlijke mondiale waarde. Het doel is bescheidener, in die zin dat alleen de bijdrage van de Verenigde Naties is onderzocht. Rechtsnormen van buiten het VN-systeem worden slechts zijdelings behandeld. Aan de andere kant is het werkterrein van deze studie uitgebreider, aangezien bij de bestudering van het VN-systeem niet alleen documenten worden behandeld die als internationale rechtsbronnen gezien moeten worden, maar ook overige documenten die een rol hebben gespeeld in het waarden-debat. De resoluties van de Algemene Vergadering hebben een belangrijke invloed op de ontwikkeling van het internationaal recht, in die zin dat (een deel van) bepaalde resoluties is omgevormd tot multilateraal verdrag, of doordat de resolutie gewoonterecht verwoordt, of omdat de resolutie gezien wordt als juridisch bindende interpretatie van artikelen uit het VN Handvest zelf. Maar ook resoluties die geen directe invloed hebben gehad op de ontwikkeling van nieuwe rechtsnormen worden behandeld, wanneer ze een rol hebben gespeeld in het waarden-debat. Om dezelfde reden worden invloedrijke VN-rapporten bestudeerd, en worden de *travaux préparatoires* van het VN-Handvest uitgebreid bekeken, hoewel deze, volgens het Verdrag van Wenen inzake het Verdragenrecht, hooguit mogen worden gebruikt als hulpmiddel bij de interpretatie van een verdrag.

Dit alles suggereert wellicht dat de evolutie van mondiale waarden en de evolutie van de normen van het internationale recht twee gescheiden werelden zouden zijn. Dat is zeker niet het geval. Al in het eerste deel van de studie wordt aangetoond dat mondiale waarden alleen kunnen dienen als richtlijn voor de internationale betrekkingen en samenwerking als iemand of iets verantwoordelijk gehouden kan worden voor het verwezenlijken en voor het bevorderen van respect voor deze mondiale waarden. De ideale taal waarin dergelijke verantwoordelijkheden vastgelegd en verdeeld kunnen worden is de taal van het internationaal recht. Daarmee valt de bestudering van de rol van de Verenigde Naties bij de toewijzing van verantwoordelijkheden voor de continue bevordering en eerbiediging van mondiale waarden en de hierop gebaseerde normen binnen het onderzoeksterrein van deze studie. Maar het moge duidelijk zijn dat sommige niet-bindende - of 'politieke' - verklaringen net zo effectief zijn in het bevorderen van respect voor mondiale waarden als sommige multilaterale verdragen.

## 5 SAMENVATTING PER HOOFDSTUK

### 5.1 Inleiding

In de inleiding wordt de onderzoeksvraag, probleemstelling en methodologie uiteengezet.

### 5.2 Mondiale waarden

In het tweede hoofdstuk wordt de volgende definitie van een mondiale waarde voorgesteld:

> Een mondiale waarde is een volgehouden en wereldwijd gedeelde overtuiging dat een specifieke toestand van de wereld, die realiseerbaar is, de voorkeur verdient,

vanuit het perspectief van het leven van alle mensen, boven een tegengestelde toestand van de wereld.

Deze definitie is het resultaat van een pragmatische zoektocht naar een werkdefinitie, die als doel heeft het onderwerp van deze studie te verduidelijken en te begrenzen. Enkele elementen van deze definitie zijn nader geanalyseerd. Zo wordt uitgelegd waarom mondiale waarden niet alleen dienen te worden omschreven vanuit het perspectief van Staten, maar ook vanuit het perspectief van het collectief van alle individuele mensen. Ook is een geschikte methode voor het vinden van een lijst van mondiale waarden voorgesteld.

## 5.3 De Verenigde Naties en mondiale waarden

Als de Conferentie van San Francisco begint in de lente van 1945, is de Tweede Wereldoorlog bijna voorbij. Een belangrijke uitdaging van de overwinnende Staten, verenigd onder de noemer van "de Verenigde Naties," is om ook na het verslaan van de gemeenschappelijke vijand verenigd te blijven. In de studie wordt aangetoond dat, in de naoorlogse periode, mondiale waarden alle Staten in de wereld hebben weten te verenigen.

De belangrijkste inspiratie voor de lijst van mondiale waarden uit het VN-Handvest was een lijst van "kwaden" die het wereldtoneel domineerden in de zwarte jaren vóór 1945. De verwoestende oorlog inspireerde de deelnemers aan de Conferentie van San Francisco om te streven naar vrede en veiligheid. De onmenselijke behandeling van grote groepen mensen tijdens diezelfde oorlog stond aan de basis van het streven naar universeel respect voor menselijke waardigheid. De koloniale onderdrukking van vele volkeren werd in 1945 nog niet gezien, althans niet door alle Verenigde Naties, als een van de grote kwaden. Een bescheiden voorloper van het recht op zelfbeschikking van alle volkeren vond desondanks een plek in het Handvest. Tot slot vormde de behoefte aan armoedebestrijding, werkgelegenheid voor iedereen, sociale vooruitgang en ontwikkeling de basis voor de laatste waarde, al werd ook deze waarde – ontwikkeling en sociale vooruitgang - maar terloops genoemd in het Handvest. Het element duurzaamheid stond zelfs helemaal niet in het Handvest vermeld.

Deze vier waarden vonden hun plek in artikel 1 van het Handvest. Het Handvest gebruikt echter niet het begrip "waarde," maar begrippen als "doelstelling" en "beginsel," die meer gebruikelijk zijn voor verdragsteksten. De beginselen worden gedefinieerd als "regels van actie," en de doelstellingen als "doel van actie." Het verband tussen de begrippen die in het Handvest gebruikt worden en het begrip "waarde" zoals gedefinieerd in deze studie wordt als volgt uitgelegd: als de doelstellingen gezamenlijk het "doel van actie" vormen, dan is de "verwezenlijking en bevordering van respect voor mondiale waarden" te omschrijven als dat doel. Als bijvoorbeeld menselijke waardigheid een mondiale

469

waarde is, dan is het bevorderen van respect voor menselijke waardigheid een doelstelling, en vormt de verplichting om mensenrechten te respecteren het bijbehorende beginsel, dat vervolgens weer wordt uitgewerkt in een uitgebreide verzameling specifieke rechtsnormen die wij kennen als de mensenrechten.

Deze studie laat zien dat de Algemene Vergadering de discussie over mondiale waarden, die gestart is in San Francisco, heeft voortgezet. Omdat een dergelijke kwalificatie van het werk van de Algemene Vergadering niet vanzelfsprekend is, wordt kritisch gekeken naar enkele kenmerken van de Vergadering. Is de Algemene Vergadering daadwerkelijk de "wereldgemeenteraad" geworden die de oprichters voor ogen hadden? In dit onderzoek wordt deze vraag bevestigend beantwoord.

## 5.4 Vrede en veiligheid

In deel II wordt de rol die de Verenigde Naties gespeeld heeft in de ontwikkeling van mondiale waarden onderzocht. Vrede en veiligheid - de twee worden altijd als één begrip gebruikt - is de eerste mondiale waarde die wordt behandeld. Overigens betekent dit niet automatisch dat dit ook de belangrijkste waarde is. De Verenigde Naties heeft geen rangorde aangebracht in het viertal mondiale waarden dat in deze studie wordt behandeld.

Toch is aan vrede en veiligheid, vooral in het begin, een belangrijke plaats toegekend. Het is niet verrassend dat onmiddellijk na de Tweede Wereldoorlog een gewapend conflict tussen Staten beschouwd werd als het grootste kwaad, en vrede en veiligheid daaromals de belangrijkste mondiale waarde. Diezelfde oorlogservaring verklaart ook waarom vrede en veiligheid in eerste instantie gezien werd als de beschrijving van een wereld zonder interstatelijke oorlogen.

De Verenigde Naties heeft enkele pogingen ondernomen om de waarde van vrede en veiligheid te definiëren in positieve zin. Zo is, vooral door UNESCO, geprobeerd om een "cultuur van vrede" te omschrijven. Het probleem met dergelijke positieve definities en omschrijvingen was echter dat ze uiteindelijk neerkwamen op de beschrijving van een perfecte wereld in plaats van een vreedzame en veilige wereld, waardoor de waarde van vrede en veiligheid niet meer te onderscheiden was van andere waarden. Daarom werd vrede en veiligheid door de Verenigde Naties aanvankelijk vooral gedefinieerd in negatieve termen, dat wil zeggen als een situatie zonder internationale conflicten, burgeroorlogen, aanvallen van huurlingen en terroristen, en zonder de wapenwedloop en de ontwikkeling van massavernietigingswapens. Deze zaken zijn door de Veiligheidsraad en/of de Algemene Vergadering bestempeld als directe bedreigingen voor de internationale vrede en veiligheid. Ook zogeheten massavernietigingsziekten en extreme armoede zijn van invloed op de vrede en veiligheid. Deze worden daarom door de Verenigde Naties omschreven als onderliggende oorzaken van bedreigingen van vrede en veiligheid, maar niet als een directe bedreiging.

Enkele recente rapporten van de Verenigde Naties hebben gesuggereerd dat vrede en veiligheid ook moet worden gedefinieerd vanuit het perspectief van de individuele mens, en niet alleen vanuit een Statenperspectief. Een dergelijke verschuiving van perspectief vereist een drastische verandering van de definitie van vrede en veiligheid. Soms wordt wel van de noodzaak van een paradigmaverschuiving gesproken. Armoede, bijvoorbeeld, is net zozeer een onmiddellijke bedreiging voor het leven van een individu als een interstatelijke oorlog. Om het ene als bedreiging van de menselijke ontwikkeling te beschouwen en het andere als bedreiging van de vrede en veiligheid lijkt dan niet logisch. In deze verschuiving van perspectief ligt de nadruk op de introductie en verdere uitwerking van het begrip 'menselijke veiligheid.'

## 5.5 Sociale vooruitgang en ontwikkeling

De tweede mondiale waarde is sociale vooruitgang en ontwikkeling. De Algemene Vergadering heeft verschillende strategieën en actieplannen voor ontwikkeling opgesteld en aangenomen. Het uiteindelijke doel hiervan was om de lidstaten ertoe aan te sporen gezamenlijk de internationale economische orde te verbeteren, in het bijzonder door het aanpakken van de toenemende ongelijkheid, maar ook door de marginalisering en het absoluut gebrek aan ontwikkeling in bepaalde delen van de wereld tegen te gaan. De Algemene Vergadering benadrukt consequent de primaire verantwoordelijkheid van de lidstaten voor hun eigen ontwikkeling. Maar tegelijkertijd wordt erkend dat alle Staten, en in het bijzonder de ontwikkelde landen, de plicht hebben om ontwikkelingslanden te ondersteunen in hun ontwikkeling.

In deze studie zijn dergelijke plannen en programma's vergeleken met wetenschappelijke theorieën over sociale en verdelende rechtvaardigheid op wereldschaal. De belangrijkste vraag is dan, "wie heeft recht op wat en waarom?" De ontwikkelingslanden, met een meerderheid in de Algemene Vergadering, beweren dat ze het slachtoffer zijn van een internationale economische orde waarvan de regels bepaald zijn door - en in het voordeel werken van - de ontwikkelde landen. Ze vragen om veranderingen die deze orde eerlijker en rechtvaardiger moeten maken. Totdat de hervormingen zijn voltooid, zou er een verplichting bestaan tot vergoeding van de vanwege deze oneerlijkheid geleden schade. Dergelijke eisen zijn gebaseerd op principes van verdelende rechtvaardigheid, in het bijzonder het uitgangspunt dat iedereen recht heeft op een gelijk deel van de goederen, tenzij er overtuigende morele redenen zijn om een andere regeling te rechtvaardigen.

In de wetenschap wordt veelal een onderscheid gemaakt tussen claims gebaseerd op beginselen van (verdelende) rechtvaardigheid, en claims op basis van een absolute plicht, voor degenen die daartoe in staat zijn, om mensen in grote nood te hulp te schieten. Naar aanleiding van dit onderscheid worden de inspanningen om officiële ontwikkelingshulp te garanderen en de economische orde te hervormen, aan de ene kant, en inspanningen van de Verenigde Naties om noodhulp te bieden bij rampen, aan de andere kant, afzonderlijk behandeld.

Een deel van dit hoofdstuk is gewijd aan een bespreking van het begrip "duurzame ontwikkeling." De Verenigde Naties heeft erkend dat de toekomstige generaties aanspraak kunnen maken op een deel van dezelfde goederen waar de huidige generatie nu al gebruik van maakt. De promotie van het idee van duurzame ontwikkeling is een van de succesverhalen uit de ideeëngeschiedenis van de Verenigde Naties. Duurzame ontwikkeling wordt zowel in de wetenschap als binnen de VN gedefinieerd als een vorm van ontwikkeling die aansluit op de behoeften van de huidige generatie zonder het vermogen van toekomstige generaties om in hun eigen behoeften te voorzien in gevaar te brengen.

Tot slot wordt gekeken naar de "humanisering" van deze mondiale waarde, in het bijzonder door het definiëren van een recht op ontwikkeling. Ook hier heeft de VN een leidende rol gespeeld. De Algemene Vergadering heeft een recht op ontwikkeling omschreven als een recht op grond waarvan ieder individu en alle volkeren aanspraak kunnen maken op de mogelijkheid om bij te dragen aan, en de voordelen te genieten van, economische, sociale, culturele en politieke ontwikkeling, waarbij de rechten van de mens en de fundamentele vrijheden ten volle kunnen worden gerealiseerd.

## 5.6 Menselijke waardigheid

De derde mondiale waarde is menselijke waardigheid. De bevordering van respect voor deze waarde, en de verdere ontwikkeling ervan in de taal van de mensenrechten, is wellicht het grootste succesverhaal uit de ideeëngeschiedenis van de Verenigde Naties. Vanaf het allereerste begin heeft de VN de waarde van menselijke waardigheid expliciet als bron en basis bestempeld van alle mensenrechten. Het begon allemaal in 1948, met de afkondiging van de Universele Verklaring van de Rechten van de Mens, waarin werd gesteld dat ieder mens vrij geboren wordt en gelijk is en blijft in waardigheid en rechten. Het idee dat de menselijke waardigheid een universeel gedeeld fundament van de mensenrechtenbeweging vormt is ook algemeen geaccepteerd in de literatuur.

Maar wat is menselijke waardigheid nu eigenlijk? Om universele acceptatie van deze waarde en de daaruit afgeleide mensenrechten te garanderen, heeft de Algemene Vergadering bewust nagelaten om de waarde van menselijke waardigheid in algemene termen te omschrijven. Dit biedt een mooie gelegenheid aan de wetenschap om een dergelijke omschrijving te formuleren. Vaak wordt aan menselijke waardigheid een religieuze connotatie meegegeven. Maar deze optie is niet beschikbaar voor de Verenigde Naties, omdat deze zich niet als geloofsgemeenschap kan presenteren, laat staan als aanhanger van één specifiek geloof. De VN maakt daarom liever gebruik van een meer intuïtieve benadering van menselijke waardigheid. Alle personen in deze wereld hebben inherente rechten, zo leert de VN ons, die niet afhankelijk zijn van erkenning door anderen. Individuen hebben dus mensenrechten eenvoudigweg op grond van hun mens-zijn. Deze claim heeft universele geldigheid: alle mensen, waar ze ook zijn, wie ze ook zijn en in welke omstandigheden zij zich ook mogen bevinden, hebben recht op respect voor hun intrinsieke waardigheid en de rechten die hieruit voortvloeien. Dezelfde intuïtieve benadering wordt gebruikt bij het afleiden van de mensenrechten uit de waarde van menselijke waardigheid. En omdat we allemaal mensen zijn, is de kern van de mensenrechtencatalogus niet afhankelijk van iemands achtergrond, religie of cultuur.

## 5.7 Zelfbeschikking van volkeren

De laatste te bespreken waarde is zelfbeschikking van alle volkeren. In 1945was de wereld nog grotendeels blind voor de onderdrukking en uitbuiting van volkeren door buitenlandse overheersing. Het Handvest was dus aarzelend bij de vaststelling van het alternatief voor dit kwaad, namelijk het zelfbeschikkingsrecht van alle volkeren.

Zodra de VN deze omissie gecorrigeerd had, werd de Organisatie juist een van de leidende krachten bij de mondiale promotie en verwezenlijking van deze waarde. Resoluties van de Algemene Vergadering hebben een belangrijke rol gespeeld in het proces van dekolonisatie. Zolang de waarde werd toegepast op de koloniën, was niet veel conceptueel denken nodig. Het was duidelijk wie de koloniale volkeren waren, en wie de koloniale machten.

Dit proces is nu grotendeels afgerond, en daarmee is behoefte ontstaan aan een meer algemene definitie van het zelfbeschikkingsrecht van volkeren. Er lijkt voorzichtig een consensus te ontstaan, mede gevormd door de Algemene Vergadering, dat de zelfbeschikking van volkeren een waarde is die volkeren beschermt tegen alle mogelijke vormen van onderdrukking. Er is immers geen reden om te suggereren dat de waarde alleen van toepassing is wanneer de onderdrukking in wat voor opzicht dan ook "vreemd" of "buitenlands" is, zoals het geval was in de koloniale context. Een volk kan evenzeer worden onderdrukt, als groep, door de eigen leider. Men kan hierbij denken aan minderheden, waaronder inheemse bevolkingsgroepen, die lijden onder de onderdrukking door de meerderheid. Of aan de gehele bevolking van een bepaald land, onderdrukt door de eigen dictatoriale regering. Nu de waarde op deze manier wordt opgevat, biedt ze niet alleen een basis voor het uitoefenen van een recht op externe zelfbeschikking, dat wil zeggen afscheiding van een volk van de Staat waarin het zich bevindt door de vorming van een nieuwe eigen Staat. De waarde biedt vooral een vruchtbare basis voor een recht op interne zelfbeschikking. Dat recht beoogt het ontstaan van participatieve processen binnen lidstaten te bevorderen, waaraan het gehele volk kan deelnemen. Wanneer een volk het lot in eigen handen heeft, bestaat nog altijd de mogelijkheid dat andere Staten ingrijpen in de interne aangelegenheden van dit volk. Vandaar dat de garantie van respect voor de soevereine onafhankelijkheid van Staten ook gebaseerd wordt op de mondiale waarde van zelfbeschikking.

Veel over de exacte betekenis van de waarde van zelfbeschikking van volkeren, en de consequenties ervan, staat nog ter discussie. Ondanks vele debatten en resoluties, is er nog altijd geen consensus over wat een volk precies is, en waar een volk nu precies recht op heeft. De VN biedt een rijkdom aan ideeën en mogelijke toepassingen van de waarde aan, maar tegelijkertijd worden moeilijke keuzes tot nog toe dikwijls uit de weg gegaan.

De Verenigde Naties heeft ook een humanisering van deze waarde voorgesteld, dat wil zeggen een mensenrechtelijke benadering van de waarde van zelfbeschikking van de volkeren. De artikelen 1 van beide klassieke mensenrechtenverdragen verkondigen dat alle volkeren het recht op zelfbeschikking hebben, en dat ze op grond van dat recht vrijelijk hun politieke status kunnen bepalen evenals hun economische, sociale en culturele ontwikkeling. De opname van dit recht in de mensenrechtenverdragen heeft geleid tot voortdurende discussies, zowel bij de Verenigde Naties als in de literatuur, over de vraag of zelfbeschikking nu een mensenrecht is.

## 6 CONCLUDERENDE OPMERKINGEN EN EEN BLIK IN DE TOEKOMST

Deze studie wordt afgesloten met een beoordeling van de rol van de VN bij de evolutie van mondiale waarden, en met een korte blik in de toekomst. Het doel van dit onderzoek was te onderzoeken hoe en in welke mate mondiale waarden de oprichting van de Verenigde Naties en de evolutie van haar doelstellingen, beginselen en beleid mede bepaald hebben. Voorts is gekeken of de Verenigde Naties en de wetenschap elkaar hebben aangevuld en beïnvloed bij het interpreteren en verder ontwikkelen van mondiale waarden als vrede en veiligheid, duurzame ontwikkeling en sociale vooruitgang, menselijke waardigheid, en zelfbeschikking van volkeren.

Bij wijze van algemene conclusie zijn de verschillende benaderingen vergeleken die de VN heeft gebruikt bij het uitwerken van de vier mondiale waarden. De waarde van vrede en veiligheid is door de VN vooral ontwikkeld door het vaststellen van een lijst potentiële bedreigingen van de vrede en veiligheid. Als het gaat om sociale vooruitgang en ontwikkeling, heeft de Algemene Vergadering zich geconcentreerd op het opstellen van een lange reeks van actieplannen en ontwikkelingsprogramma's, met daarin toezeggingen van de internationale gemeenschap om ontwikkelingslanden te helpen bij hun ontwikkeling. Het werk van de VN betreffende de mondiale waarde van menselijke waardigheid heeft weer een geheel ander karakter. Daar heeft de VN zich niet beperkt tot het definiëren van een lijst van bedreigingen van de waardigheid – zoals bij vrede en veiligheid - of tot het ontwerpen van diverse actieplannen om de menselijke waardigheid wereldwijd te bevorderen – zoals bij ontwikkeling. In plaats hiervan heeft de VN vooral gewerkt aan een imposante lijst van mensenrechten, die alle lidstaten van de Organisatie dienen te respecteren. Omdat de VN verschillende aanwijzingen heeft gegeven aangaande de betekenis van menselijke waardigheid zelf, is hier het meest expliciet sprake van kruisbestuiving tussen de wetenschap en de VN. Zelfbeschikking is waarschijnlijk de meest dubbelzinnige van de vier mondiale waarden. Er is enige consensus over dat het zelfbeschikkingsrecht gebaseerd is op de wens van verschillende gemeenschappen om controle over het eigen lot te hebben, zonder enige externe onderdrukking. Maar over vragen als wie recht heeft op zelfbeschikking, en waarop men precies recht heeft, en in welke omstandigheden, is nog altijd geen overeenstemming bereikt.

Ter afsluiting van de studie worden enkele opmerkingen gemaakt over het karakter van de debatten over mondiale waarden. Bij het onderzoek naar de ideeëngeschiedenis van de Verenigde Naties, valt het geheel eigen karakter op van de beraadslagingen van de San Francisco Conferentie en de Algemene Vergadering. Sommige debatten, zowel in San Francisco als in de Vergadering, hebben een abstract en welhaast filosofisch karakter. Dit onderscheidt hen van de gebruikelijke interstatelijke en politieke bijeenkomsten, die veel meer een praktijkgericht karakter hebben. Toch zijn de debatten in San Francisco en de Algemene Vergadering niet louter filosofische debatten. De deelnemers zijn geen onafhankelijke wetenschappers, maar vertegenwoordigers van een bepaalde Staat, met eigen belangen en eigen culturele en historische tradities. De meeste vertegenwoordigers beperken zich tot het voorlezen aan de Algemene Vergadering van de verklaring die vooraf is goedgekeurd als de officiële visie van de betreffende Staat. Dit maakt betekenisvolle communicatie over en weerlastig. Maar het maakt het wel mogelijk voor andere Staten - en onderzoekers - om een beeld te krijgen van de "mening" van een Staat op een bepaald punt. Toch blijft het niet hierbij, want anders zou er nooit een resolutie aangenomen worden. Er moet worden onderhandeld, gediscussieerd, Staten moeten van gedachten worden veranderd. De resolutie, vooral wanneer ze bij consensus aangenomen zijn, bevatten dikwijls een compromis.

Wanneer de verklaringen van de Algemene Vergadering worden gezien als "codificatie" van het mondiale waarden-discours, is het interessant een blik in de toekomst te werpen, en te denken aan manieren om de kwaliteit van de debatten zelf te verbeteren. Een manier om dit te doen is door het potentieel van de kruisbestuiving tussen de VN en de academische gemeenschap meer te benutten. Dit zou kunnen gebeurendoor het publiceren en het algemeen verspreiden van de VN-documenten, in het bijzonder de San Francisco documenten en de resolutie en verslagen van de beraadslagingen van de Algemene Vergadering. De Verenigde

Naties doet dit al, gebruik makend van de nieuwe media. Ook het organiseren van debatten, waarin de Algemene Vergadering door experts wordt toegesproken, is een mogelijkheid. Idealiter zou een dergelijk proces van kruisbestuiving tussen de Verenigde Naties en wetenschapper toe kunnen bijdragen dat de wereldwijde consensus die bereikt wordt in de Algemene Vergadering ook nog eens stevig verankerd is in wetenschappelijk gefundeerde ideeën en theorieën. De toekomst zal uitwijzen of dit in de alledaagse praktijk van de internationale betrekkingen een wenselijk en vooral haalbaar idee is.

# CURRICULUM VITAE

OTTO SPIJKERS

Born in Voorburg, Netherlands, on December 7, 1979

Education
- Diplôme Approfondi de Langue Française, 2011.
- Hague Academy of International Law, 2009.
- LL.M., International Law, University of Amsterdam, including one semester at New York University Law School, 2006.
- MA, Philosophy, University of Amsterdam, including one year at the University of Malta, 2006.
- Propaedeusis in International Relations, University of Sussex, 1999.
- Gymnasium Diploma, Gymnasium Haganum, 1998.

Professional experience
- Head Reading Room & Public Services Coordinator, Peace Palace Library, since 2010.
- Consultant of the United Nations International Law Fellowship Programme, 2010.
- PhD Candidate, Grotius Centre for International Legal Studies, Leiden University, 2006-2010.

Memberships & Activities
- Participant and co-founder of the Dutch International Commission of Jurists' working group on Sustainable Development, since 2007.
- Reporter for the study groups on the Responsibility of International Organizations and United Nations Reform, 74th Biennial Conference of the International Law Association in The Hague (August 2010).
- Intern at the Office of Legal Affairs (Codification Division) of United Nations Headquarters, New York, USA, 2008.
- Intern at the Appeals Chamber Support Unit of the International Criminal Tribunal for Rwanda, and assistant to a judge of the Appeals Chamber, 2005.
- Volunteer, Rechtswinkel Amsterdam, 2003-2004.

- Creator, editor and blogger of the Invisible College Blog (www.invisiblecollegeblog.com), official blog of the Netherlands School of Human Rights Research.

Selected publications
- 'What's running the world: global values, international law, and the United Nations,' *Interdisciplinary Journal of Human Rights Law*, vol. 4 (2009-2010), no. 1, pp. 67-87.
- 'The immunity of the United Nations in relation to the genocide in Srebrenica in the eyes of a Dutch District Court,' *Journal of International Peacekeeping*, vol. 13 (2009), no. 1-2, pp. 197-219.
- 'Legal mechanisms to establish accountability for the genocide in Srebrenica,' *Human Rights & International Legal Discourse*, vol. 1 (2007), no. 2, pp. 231-265.
- 'De notie van wereldrecht vóór, tijdens, en na de oprichting van de Verenigde Naties,' *Nederlands Juristenblad*, special issue '65 Jaar Wereldrecht,' NJB, vol. 85 (2010), pp. 12-15.
- Book review of Mazower's No Enchanted Palace, in the *Leiden Journal of International Law*, vol. 24 (2011), no. 1, pp. 261-266.

# BIBLIOGRAPHY

- Georges Abi-Saab, "Cours général de droit international public," in *Recueil des cours*, Volume 207 (1987-VII).
- Georges Abi-Saab, "Whither the international community?" in the *European journal of international law*, vol. 9 (1998), no 2.
- Matej Accetto, "The Right to Individual Self-Determination," in the *Slovenian Law Review*, no.1 (2004).
- Advisory Council on International Affairs of the Netherlands, *Universality of Human Rights: Principles, Practice and Prospects*, Advice no. 63, published November 2008.
- Gudmundur Alfredsson, "The right of self-determination and indigenous peoples," in Tomuschat (editor), *Modern law of self-determination*. Nijhoff, 1993.
- Aligarh Muslim University (Directorate of General Education Reading Material Project), *Man, Reality, and Values*. Asia Publishing House, 1964.
- Sabina Alkire, *A Conceptual Framework for Human Security (CRISE Working Paper)*. University of Oxford, 2003.
- Philip Alston, "Conjuring up New Human Rights: A Proposal for Quality Control," in the *American Journal of International Law*, Vol. 78 (1984), No. 3.
- Philip Alston, "Unborn Child and Abortion under the Draft Convention on the Rights of the Child," in the *Human Rights Quarterly*, volume 12 (1990).
- Philip Alston, "Peoples' Rights: Their Rise and Fall," in Alston (editor), *Peoples' rights*. Oxford University Press, 2001.
- Philip Alston, "Ships Passing in the Night: The Current State of the Human Rights and Development Debate Seen through the Lens of the Millennium Development Goals," in the *Human Rights Quarterly*, Volume 27 (2005).
- Philip Alston, *A Human Rights Perspective on the Millennium Development Goals*. Paper prepared as a contribution to the work of the Millennium Project Task Force on Poverty and Economic Development, available at http://www2.ohchr.org/english/issues/millenium-development/resources.htm.
- José E. Alvarez, "Judging the Security Council," in the *American Journal of International Law*, Vol. 90, No. 1 (January 1996), p. 1-39.
- José E. Alvarez, "Legal Perspectives," in Weiss & Daws (eds.), *The Oxford Handbook on the United Nations*. Oxford University Press, 2007.
- American Humanist Association, *Humanist Manifesto* (1933), *Humanist Manifesto II* (1973), and *Humanist Manifesto III* (2003) (available online at www.americanhumanist.org).

- Benedict Richard O'Gorman Anderson, *Imagined communities: reflections on the origin and spread of nationalism*. Verso, 2006 (original of 1983).
- Roberto Andorno, "The paradoxial notion of human dignity," in *Rivista internazionale di diritto filosofia del diritto*, vol. 78 (2001), no. 2.
- Abdullahi An-Naim, "Human Rights in the Arab World: A Regional Perspective," in *Human Rights Quarterly*, vol. 23 (2001), no. 3.
- Kofi Annan, "Walking the International Tightrope," in the *New York Times* of 19 January 1999.
- Kofi Annan, "Two concepts of sovereignty," *The Economist*, 18 September 1999.
- Kofi Annan, *"We the peoples": the role of the United Nations in the 21st century*. Department of Public Information, United Nations, 20. Also distributed on 27 March 2000, as UNDoc A/54/2000.
- Kofi Annan, *Dag Hammarskjöld and the 21st Century (The Fourth Dag Hammarskjöld Lecture)*, delivered in Uppsala, Sweden, 6 September 2001.
- Kofi Annan, *Global Values: The United Nations and the Rule of Law in the 21st Century*. Singapore: Institute of South-East Asian Studies, 2000. Annan, Nobel Lecture, Oslo, December 10, 2001 (available online at nobelprize.org).
- Kofi Annan, "Do we still have Universal Values?," Third Global Ethic Lecture, delivered at Tübingen University, Germany, 12 December 2003 (available online at www.valuescaucus.org).
- Kofi Annan, *In larger freedom: towards development, security and human rights for all*. United Nations, 2005. Also distributed on 21 March 2005, as UN Doc. A/59/2005.
- Kofi Annan, "How We Envy the World Cup," *Bild am Sonntag*, 04 June 2006.
- Kwame Anthony Appiah, *Cosmopolitanism: Ethics in a World of Strangers*. Norton, 2006.
- Gaetano Arangio-Ruiz, "The normative role of the General Assembly of the United Nations and the Declaration of Principles of Friendly Relations," in *Recueil des cours*, Volume 137 (1972-III).
- Yehoshua Arieli, "On the Necessary and Sufficient Conditions for the Emergence of the Doctrine of the Dignity of Man and His Rights," in Klein & Kretzmer, *The concept of human dignity in human rights discourse*. Kluwer Law International , 2002.
- Fateh Azzam, "Reflections on Human Rights Approaches to Implementing the Millennium Development Goals," in *SUR – International Journal on Human Rights*, Volume 2 (2005).
- Peter R. Baehr, *De rechten van de mens: universaliteit in de praktijk*. Boom, 1998.
- Mirko Bagaric & James Allan, "The Vacuous Concept of Dignity," in the *Journal of Human Rights*, volume 5 (2006).
- Annette Baker Fox, "The United Nations and Colonial Development," in *International Organization*, Vol. 4 (1950), No. 2.
- John Banville, "Beyond dentistry (Book review of Heresies: Against Progress and Other Illusions by John Gray)," in *the Guardian* of September 4, 2004.
- Michael Barnett and Martha Finnemore, *Rules for the World: International Organizations in Global Politics*. Cornell University Press, 2004.

- Kemal Baslar, *The Concept of the Common Heritage of Mankind in International Law*. Martinus Nijhoff Publishers, 1998.
- Marcel Becker, "In gesprek met Michael Walzer" [transl.: "A conversation with Michael Walzer"], in Walzer, *Oorlog en Dood: Over de Rechtvaardige Oorlog in Onze Tijd* [transl.: *War and Death: On Just War in Our Time*]. Damon, 2008.
- Mohammed Bedjaoui, "Article 1," in Cot & Pellet, *La Charte des Nations Unies: commentaire article par article*, vol. 1 (2005).
- Charles R. Beitz, *Political Theory and International Relations*. Princeton University Press, 1999.
- Charles R. Beitz, "Human Rights as a Common Concern," in the *American Political Science Review*, Vol. 95 (2001), no. 2.
- Charles R. Beitz, "What Human Rights Mean," in *Daedalus*, Vol. 132 (2003), No. 1.
- Charles R. Beitz, *The idea of human rights*. Oxford University Press, 2009.
- Alex J. Bellamy, *Responsibility to protect: the global effort to end mass atrocities*. Polity, 2009.
- Harry Beran, "A liberal theory of secession," in *Political Studies*, Vol. 32 (1984), no. 1.
- Sir Carl Berendsen, "The United Nations and international law," in *American Society of International Law Proceedings*, vol. 41 (1947).
- Louis René Beres, "Reordering the Planet: the Four Phases of World Order Design," in Beres & Targ, *Planning Alternative World Futures: Values, Methods, and Models*. Praeger Publishers, 1975.
- Isaiah Berlin, "On the Pursuit of the Ideal," essay published in the *New York Review of Books*, Volume 35, no.4, 17 March 1988.
- Tony Blair, "Clash about Civilizations," speech 21 March 2006 (www.pm.gov.uk/output).
- Tony Blair, "PM's foreign policy speech: third in a series of three," 26 May 2006. (www.pm.gov.uk/output).
- Tony Blair, "A Battle for Global Values," in *Foreign Affairs*, January/February 2007.
- Samuel A. Bleicher, "The Legal Significance of Re-Citation of General Assembly Resolutions," in the *American Journal of International Law*, Vol. 63 (1969).
- Niels Blokker, "The Crime of Aggression and the United Nations Security Council," in the *Leiden Journal of International Law*, vol. 20 (2007).
- Jakob Kirkemann Boesen & Tomas Martin, *Applying a Rights-Based Approach: An Inspirational Guide for Civil Society*, Danish Institute for Human Rights, 2007.
- James Bohman & Matthias Lutz-Bachmann (editors), *Perpetual Peace: Essays on Kant's Cosmopolitan Ideal (Studies in Contemporary German Social Thought)*. Massachusetts Institute of Technology, 1997.
- Marc J. Bossuyt, *Guide to the "travaux préparatoires" of the International Covenant on Civil and Political Rights*. Nijhoff, 1987.

- Abdel Hamid Bouab, "Financing for Development, the Monterrey Consensus: Achievements and Prospects," in the *Michigan Journal of International Law*, Volume 26 (2004).
- Evgheny V. Bougrov, The United Nations and the maintenance of international peace and security. Nijhoff, 1987
- Jane Boulden & Thomas G. Weiss, *Terrorism and the UN: before and after September 11*. Indiana University Press, 2004.
- Boutros Boutros-Ghali, *An Agenda for Peace: Preventive diplomacy, peacemaking and peace-keeping, Report of the Secretary-General pursuant to the statement adopted by the Summit Meeting of the Security Council on 31 January 1992*, published 17 June 1992, UNDoc. A/47/277.
- Boutros Boutros-Ghali, "A New Departure on Development," in *Foreign Policy*, No. 98 (1995).
- Boutros Boutros-Ghali, *Unvanquished: A U.S. - U.N. Saga*. Random House, 1999.
- Alan Boyle, "The principle of co-operation: the environment," in Lowe (editor), *The United Nations and the principles of international law: essays in memory of Michael Akehurst*. Routledge, 1994.
- Lennert Breuker, "The Judgment of the ICJ in the Genocide Case: 'the state as perpetrator of genocide'," in *Griffin's View*, Volume 8, Number 2.
- James Leslie Brierly, "The Covenant and the Charter," in the *British Yearbook of International Law*, Volume 23 (1946).
- Bengt Broms, "The definition of aggression," in *Recueil des cours*, vol. 154 (1977).
- Ian Brownlie, "The Rights of Peoples in Modern International Law," in Crawford (editor), *The Rights of Peoples*. Clarendon Press, 1988.
- Joshua Bruckerhoff, "Giving Nature Constitutional Protection: A Less Anthropocentric Interpretation of Environmental Rights," in *Texas Law Review*, Volume 86 (2008).
- Koos van der Bruggen, *Mondiale moraal: rechten en plichten op wereldschaal*. Available at www.law.leiden.edu/organisation/publiclaw/publicinternationallaw.
- Allen E. Buchanan, "The right to self-determination: analytical and moral foundations," in the *Arizona journal of international and comparative law*, vol. 8 (1991), no. 2.
- Allen E. Buchanan, "Toward a Theory of Secession," in *Ethics*, Vol. 101 (1991), No. 2.
- Thomas Buergenthal, "The Evolving International Human Rights System," in the *American Journal of International Law*, Vol. 100 (2006), No. 4.
- Hedley Bull, *The Anarchical Society: A Study of Order in World Politics*, Macmillan Press, 1977.
- Jan Herman Burgers, "The Road to San Francisco: The Revival of the Human Rights Idea in the Twentieth Century," in *Human Rights Quarterly*, vol. 14 (1992).
- Roland Burke, "Compelling Dialogue of Freedom: Human Rights at the Bandung Conference," in *Human Right Quarterly*, vol. 28 (2006).
- Michael Byers, "Conceptualising the Relationship between *Jus Cogens* and *Erga Omnes* Rules," in *Nordic journal of international law*, vol. 66 (1997), no. 2-3.

- Simon Caney, *Justice beyond Borders: A Global Political Theory*. Oxford University Press, 2006.
- Patrick Capps, *Human dignity and the foundations of international law*. Hart, 2009.
- Antonio Cassese, *Self-determination of peoples: a legal reappraisal*. Cambridge University Press, 1995.
- Antonio Cassese, "The International Court of Justice and the right of peoples to self-determination," in Lowe & Fitzmaurice (editors), *Fifty years of the International Court of Justice: essays in honor of Sir Robert Jennings*. Cambridge University Press, 1996.
- Antonio Cassese, *International law* (2nd ed). Oxford University Press, 2005.
- René Cassin, "La déclaration universelle et la mise en œuvre des droits de l'homme," in *Recueil des cours*, Volume 79 (1951).
- René Cassin, "Les droits de l'homme," in *Recueil des cours*, vol. 140 (1974).
- Jorge Castaneda, "Valeur juridique des résolutions des Nations Unies," in the *Recueil des cours,* vol. 129 (1970).
- Christine Cerna (Rapporteur), "The Charter of Economic Rights and Duties of States," in *American Society of International Law Proceedings*, volume 69 (1975).
- Mintauts Chakste, "Justice and Law in the Charter of the United Nations," in the *American Journal of International Law*, Vol. 42 (1948).
- Arthur Chaskalson, "The third Bram Fischer lecture: human dignity as a foundational value of our constitutional order," in the *South African Journal on Human Rights*, vol. 16 (2000), no. 2.
- S. K. Chatterjee, "The Charter of Economic Rights and Duties of States: An Evaluation after 15 Years," in the *International Comparative Law Quarterly*, vol. 40 (1991).
- Regis Chemain & Alain Pellet (editors), *La Charte des Nations Unies, constitution mondiale?* Pedone, 2006.
- Simon Chesterman, Thomas M. Franck & David M. Malone, *Law and practice of the United Nations: documents and commentary*. Oxford University Press, 2008.
- B.S. Chimni, "Third World Approaches to International Law: A Manifesto," in *International Community Law Review*, Volume 8 (2006), No. 1.
- S.K. Roy Chowdhury, "The status and norms of self-determination in contemporary international law," in the *Netherlands international law review*, vol. 24 (1977).
- Grenville Clark & Louis Sohn, *World peace through world law*. Harvard University Press, 1958.
- Michael A. Clemens, Charles J. Kenny & Todd J. Moss, "Millennium Development Goals, Aid Targets, and the Costs of Over-Expectations," in *Sustainable Development Law & Policy*, Volume 6 (2005).
- Commission on Global Governance, *Our Global Neighborhood*, Oxford University Press, 1995.
- Commission on Human Security, *Human Security Now*. Communications Development Incorporated, 2003.
- Commission to Study the Organization of Peace, *The United Nations and the organization of peace: third report*. League of Nations Union, 1943.

- Benedetto Conforti, "Le rôle de l'accord dans le système des Nations Unies," in *Recueil des cours*, vol. 142 (1974).
- Andrew F. Cooper and John English, "International Commissions and the mind of Global Governance," in Thakur, Cooper & English (editors), *International Commissions and the Power of Ideas*. United Nations University Press, 2005.
- Jean-Pierre Cot & Alain Pellet, "Préambule," in Cot & Pellet, *La Charte des Nations Unies: commentaire article par article*, vol. 1 (2005).
- Alexis C. Coudert, "Hope for World Peace," in *New York Times* of April 22, 1945.
- Robert W. Cox, "Ideologies and the New International Economic Order: Reflections on Some Recent Literature," in *International Organization*, Vol. 33 (1979), No. 2.
- James Crawford, "The rights of peoples: 'peoples' or 'governments'?" in Crawford (editor), *The Rights of Peoples*. Clarendon Press, 1988.
- James Crawford, "The Right of Self-Determination in International Law: Its Development and Future," in Alston (editor), *Peoples' rights*. Oxford University Press, 2001.
- James Crawford, *Argument and Change in World Politics: Ethics, Decolonization, and Humanitarian Intervention*. Cambridge Studies in International Relations, Cambridge University Press, 2002.
- James Crawford, "Multilateral Rights and Obligations in International Law," in *Recueil des cours*, Volume 319 (2006).
- James Crawford, *The creation of states in international law*. Clarendon Press, 2006.
- John H. Crider, "Stress Autonomy in Domestic Field," in *New York Times* of May 25, 1945.
- John H. Crider, "World Economic Council Emerging," in *New York Times* of May 27, 1945.
- John H. Crider, "Assembly to Act as "Town Meeting,"" in *New York Times* of May 30, 1945.
- John H. Crider, "Parley to Set Body for Human Rights," in *New York Times* of June 3, 1945.
- John H. Crider, "Egyptian Proviso on Police Defeated," in *New York Times* of June 15, 1945.
- Anthony D'Amato, "Do We Owe a Duty to Future Generations to Preserve the Global Environment?," in the *American Journal of International Law*, Vol. 84 (1990), No. 1.
- Jean d'Aspremont, *Contemporary International Rulemaking and the Public Character of International Law*, International Law and Justice Working Paper 2006/12. Institute for International Law and Justice of New York University School of Law, 2006.
- Roméo Dallaire, with Brent Beardsley, *Shake Hands with the Devil: The Failure of Humanity in Rwanda*. Random House of Canada, 2003.
- Daniëlla Dam-de Jong, "International Law and Resource Plunder: The Protection of Natural Resources during Armed Conflict," in Fauchald, Hunter, & Xi (editors), *Yearbook of International Environmental Law*. Oxford University Press, 2009.

- Gennady M. Danilenko, "International Jus Cogens: Issues of Law-Making," in *European Journal of International Law*, Vol. 2 (1991) No. 1.
- John D'Arcy May, "Human Dignity, Human Rights, and Religious Pluralism: Buddhist and Christian Perspectives," in *Buddhist-Christian Studies*, Vol. 26 (2006).
- Lawrence E. Davies, "Ask World Rights to Raw Materials," in *New York Times* of May 27, 1945.
- Lawrence E. Davies, "Small Nations Set Goals for Parley," in *New York Times* of April 29, 1945.
- Lawrence E. Davies, "Stettinius Urges World Rights Bill," in *New York Times* of May 16, 1945.
- Lawrence E. Davies, "Historic Plenary Session Approves World Charter," in *New York Times* of June 26, 1945.
- Lawrence E. Davies, "Nation after Nation Sees era of Peace in Signing Charter," in *New York Times* of June 26, 1945.
- Lawrence E. Davies, "Charter is Flown to Washington," in *New York Times* of June 29, 1945.
- Betty Jane Davis, *Charter for Tomorrow: the San Francisco Conference*. Bulletin No. 6 of the Bureau of International Relations, University of Washington, 1946.
- Fernand Dehousse, *Cours de politique internationale: le plan de Dumbarton Oaks: la conférence de San Francisco : la charte des Nations Unies avec les principaux textes originaux.* Lebègue, 1945.
- Department of External Affairs (Canada), *Report on the United Nations conference on international organization: held at San Francisco, 25th April-26th June 1945*. Cloutier, 1945.
- Department of State (USA), *Dumbarton Oaks documents on international organization*. United States Government Printing Office, 1944.
- Alan Dershowitz, *Rights from Wrongs: A Secular Theory of the Origins of Rights*. Basic Books, 2004.
- Klaus Dicke, "The Founding Function of Human Dignity in the Universal Declaration of Human Rights," in Klein & Kretzmer, *The concept of human dignity in human rights discourse*. Kluwer Law International , 2002.
- Diogenes, *The Lives and Opinions of Eminent Philosophers*. Tranlation: Yonge. London,: G. Bell & sons, 1891.
- Jean-François Dobelle, "Article 1, paragraphe 2," in Cot & Pellet, *La Charte des Nations Unies: commentaire article par article*, vol. 1 (2005).
- Andrew Dobson (editor), *Fairness and Futurity: Essays on Environmental Sustainability and Social Justice*. Oxford University Press, 2004.
- Jack Donnelly, "Human Rights and Human Dignity: An Analytic Critique of Non-Western Conceptions of Human Rights," in *American Political Science Review*, Vol. 76 (1982), No. 2.
- Jack Donnelly, "Human Rights: Political Aspects," in the *International Encyclopedia of the Social & Behavioral Sciences*. Elsevier, 2004 (available online at www.sciencedirect.com)

- John F. Dorsey, "Preferential Treatment: A New Standard for International Economic Relations," in the *Harvard International Law Journal*, vol. 18 (1977).
- Michael W. Doyle, "The UN Charter: a Global Constitution?" in *Ruling the world?: constitutionalism, international law, and global governance*. Cambridge University Press, 2009.
- Elizabeth Monroe Drews and Leslie Lipson, *Values and Humanity*. St Martin's Press, 1971.
- John Foster Dulles, "The United Nations: A Prospectus (The General Assembly)," in *Foreign Affairs*, Volume 24 (1945).
- Alexandre Dumas, *Les Trois Mousquetaires*. Meline, Cans et Compagnie, 1844.
- René-Jean Dupuy, *La communauté internationale entre le mythe et l'histoire*. Economica/UNESCO, 1986.
- Pierre-Marie Dupuy, "The Constitutional Dimension of the Charter of the United Nations Revisited," in *Max Planck Yearbook of United Nations Law* 1997.
- Pierre-Marie Dupuy, "L'unité de l'ordre juridique international: cours général de droit international public," in *Recueil des cours*, Volume 297 (2002).
- Jean Dupuy, *San Francisco et la Charte des Nations Unies*. Office français d'édition, 1945.
- Dutch Government, "Memorie van Antwoord bij de Goedkeuringswet van het Handvest der Verenigde Naties," in *Handelingen der Staten-Generaal: Bijlagen tijdelijke zitting 1945*.
- Dutch Government, "Memorie van Toelichting bij de Goedkeuringswet van het Handvest der Verenigde Naties," in *Handelingen der Staten-Generaal: Bijlagen tijdelijke zitting 1945*.
- Kevin T. Dwyer, *Arab Voices: The Human Rights Debate in the Middle East*. Routledge, 1991.
- Clyde Eagleton, "The Charter Adopted at San Francisco," in the *American Political Science Review*, Volume 39, No. 5 (1945).
- Clyde Eagleton, "Excesses of Self-Determination," in *Foreign Affairs*, Vol. 31 (1953), No. 4.
- William Easterly, "The Utopian Nightmare," in *Foreign Policy*, September/October 2005.
- Clark M. Eichelberger, "The United Nations Charter: A Growing Document," in the *Annals of the American Academy of Political and Social Science*, Vol. 252 (1947).
- Björn Elberling "The *ultra vires* character of legislative action by the Security Council," in the *International organizations law review*, vol. 2 (2005).
- Taslim Olawale Elias, "Scope and meaning of article 2(4) of the United Nations Charter," in *Contemporary problems of international law* (1988).
- James E. Ellis, "Problems and Policies for Planetary Survival," in *Ecology*, Volume 69 (1988), No. 4.
- Rupert Emerson, "Self-Determination," in the *American Journal of International Law*, Vol. 65 (1971), No. 3.

- Héctor Gros Espiell, "Self-determination and jus cogens," in Cassese (editor), *U.N. law/fundamental rights: two topics in international law*. Sijthoff & Noordhoff, 1979.
- Gareth Evans, Mohamed Sahnoun *et al.*, *The responsibility to protect: report of the International Commission on Intervention and State Sovereignty*. International Development Research Centre, 2001.
- Gareth Evans, *The responsibility to protect: ending mass atrocity crimes once and for all*. Brookings Institution Press, 2008
- Herbert Vere Evatt, "Economic Rights in the United Nations Charter," in the *Annals of the American Academy of Political and Social Science*, Vol. 243 (1946).
- Herbert Vere Evatt, *The United Nations*. Harvard university press, 1948.
- Richard A. Falk, "Toward a New World Order," in Mendlovitz, *On the Creation of a Just World Order*. The Free Press, 1975.
- Richard A. Falk, *A Study of Future Worlds*. North-Holland Publishing Company, 1975.
- Richard A. Falk, "Contending Approaches to World Order," in Falk, Kim & Mendlovitz (editors), *Toward a Just World Order* (vol. 1 of the *Studies on a Just World Order*). Westview Press, 1982.
- Richard A. Falk, Samuel S. Kim & Saul H. Mendloovitz, "General Introduction," in Falk, Kim & Mendlovitz (editors), *Toward a Just World Order* (vol. 1 of the *Studies on a Just World Order*). Westview Press, 1982.
- Richard A. Falk, Samuel S. Kim & Saul H. Mendlovitz, "Voices of the Oppressed," in Falk, Kim & Mendlovitz (editors), *Toward a Just World Order* (vol. 1 of the *Studies on a Just World Order*). Westview Press, 1982.
- Richard A. Falk, Friedrich Kratchowil, & Saul H. Mendlovitz (editors), *International law: a Contemporary Perspective* (vol. 2 of the *Studies on a Just World Order*). Westview Press, 1985.
- Richard A. Falk, Samuel S. Kim, Donald McNemar & Saul H. Mendlovitz, *The United Nations and a Just World Order* (vol. 3 of the *Studies on a Just World Order*). Westview Press, 1991.
- Richard A. Falk, *On Humane Governance: Toward a New Global Politics*. Polity Press, 1995.
- Richard A. Falk, "Self-determination under international law: the coherence of doctrine versus the incoherence of experience," in Danspeckgruber (editor), *The self-determination of peoples: community, nation and state in an interdependent world*. Lynne Rienner, 2002.
- Bardo Fassbender, "The United Nations Charter as Constitution of the International Community," in *Columbia Journal of Transnational Law*, vol. 36 (1998).
- Bardo Fassbender & Albert Bleckmann, "Article 2(1)," in Simma (editor), *The Charter of the United Nations: A Commentary* (2nd edition). Oxford University Press, 2002.
- Ulrich Fastenrath, "Article 73," in Simma (editor), *The Charter of the United Nations: a commentary* (2nd edition), Oxford University Press, 2002.
- David Feldman, "Human dignity as a legal value - Part I," in *Public law*, 1999.

- Clarence Clyde Ferguson, "The Politics of the New International Economic Order," in the *Proceedings of the Academy of Political Science*, Vol. 32 (1977), No. 4.
- George A. Finch, "The United Nations Charter," in the *American Journal of International Law*, Volume 39, No. 3 (1945).
- George P. Fletcher, "Human Dignity as a Constitutional Value," in the *University of Western Ontario Law Review*, vol. 22 (1984).
- John Fletcher-Cooke, "Some Reflections on the International Trusteeship System, with Particular Reference to its Impact on the Governments and Peoples of the Trust Territories," in *International Organization*, Vol. 13 (1959), No. 3.
- Ann Florini, "The Evolution of International Norms," in *International Studies Quarterly*, Vol. 40, No. 3, Special Issue: Evolutionary Paradigms in the Social Sciences. (Sep., 1996).
- Maurice Flory, "International Development Strategy for the Third United Nations Development Decade," in the *Journal of African Law*, vol. 26 (1982).
- Foreign Relations Committee (US Senate), "Foreign Relations Committee's Report Urging Ratification of the United Nations Charter," in *New York Times* of July 17, 1945.
- William T.R. Fox, "The Super-Powers at San Francisco," in *The Review of Politics*, Volume 8, No. 1 (1946).
- Thomas M. Franck, *The Power of Legitimacy among Nations*. Oxford University Press, 1990.
- Thomas M. Franck, "The "Powers of Appreciation": Who is the Ultimate Guardian of UN Legality?," in *The American Journal of International Law*, Vol. 86, No. 3 (July 1992).
- Thomas M. Franck, "The Emerging Right to Democratic Governance," in the *American Journal of International Law*, Vol. 86 (1992), No. 1.
- Thomas M. Franck, *Fairness in International Law and Institutions*. Clarendon Press, 1995.
- Thomas M. Franck, "Is Personal Freedom a Western Value?," in the *American Journal of International Law*, Vol. 91 (1997), No. 4.
- Thomas M. Franck, "Are Human Rights Universal?" in *Foreign Affairs*, vol. 80 (2001).
- Thomas M. Franck, *Recourse to Force: State Action against Threats and Armed Attacks*. Cambridge University Press, 2002.
- Thomas M. Franck, "Is the UN Charter a Constitution?," in Frowein, Scharioth, Winkelmann & Wolfrum (editors), *Verhandeln für den Frieden - Negotiating for Peace: Liber amicorum Tono Eitel (Beiträge zum ausländischen öffentlichen Recht und Völkerrecht) Liber Amicorum Tono Eitel*, 2003.
- Thomas M. Franck, "Tribute to Professor Louis B. Sohn," in the *Harvard international law journal*, Volume 48, issue 1 (2007).
- Thomas L. Friedman, *The World Is Flat: a Brief History of the Twenty-first Century*. Farrar/Straus/Giroux, 2005.

- Carl J. Friedrich, "The Ideology of the United Nations Charter and the Philosophy of Peace of Immanuel Kant 1795-1945," in the *Journal of Politics*, Vol. 9, No. 1 (1947).
- Olivier de Frouville, "Article 1, paragraphe 3," in Cot & Pellet, *La Charte des Nations Unies: commentaire article par article*, vol. 1 (2005).
- Jochen Frowein, "Reactions by not directly affected states to breaches of public international law," in *Recueil des cours*, Volume 248 (1994-IV).
- Jochen Frowein, "Jus Cogens," in Vol. 3 (from Jan Mayen to Pueblo incident) of Bernhardt, Bindschedler, & Macalister-Smith, *Encyclopedia of public international law (published under the auspices of the Max Planck Institute for Comparative Public Law and International Law under the dir. of Rudolf Bernhardt)*, Elsevier, 1997.
- Jochen Frowein, "Human Dignity in International Law," in Klein & Kretzmer, *The concept of human dignity in human rights discourse*. Kluwer Law International, 2002.
- Paolo Galizzi, "From Stockholm to New York, via Rio and Johannesburg: Has the Environment Lost Its Way on the Global Agenda," in the *Fordham International Law Journal*, Volume 29 (2006).
- Toma Galli, "The Conference on Disarmament: its Glorious History, Non-existent Present and Uncertain Future," in Budislav Vukas and Trpimir Šošić (editors), *International law: new actors, new concepts, continuing dilemmas: liber amicorum Božidar Bakotić*. Brill, 2010.
- Francisco V. García-Amador y Rodríguez, "Proposed New International Economic Order: A New Approach to the Law Governing Nationalization and Compensation," in the *Lawyer of the Americas*, vol. 12 (1980).
- Richard N. Gardner, "The Role of the UN in Environmental Problems," in *International Organization*, Vol. 26 (1972), No. 2.
- Eyassu Gayim, *The principle of self-determination: a study of its historical and contemporary legal evolution*. The Norwegian Institute of Human Rights, 1989.
- Willem van Genugten, Kees Homan, Nico Schrijver & Paul de Waart, *The United Nations of the Future: Globalization with a Human Face*. KIT Publishers, 2006.
- Elisabeth Gerle, *In Search of a Global Ethics: Theological, Political, and Feminist Perspectives based on a Critical Analysis of JPIC and WOMP*. Lund University Press, 1995
- Ernest Gellner, *Nations and nationalism*. Cornell University Press, 2008.
- Karol N. Gess, "Permanent Sovereignty over Natural Resources," in the *International and Comparative Law Quarterly*, volume 13 (1964).
- Pankaj Ghemawat, "Why the World Isn't Flat," in *Foreign Policy*, March/April 2007
- Christopher L. Gilbert & David Vines (editors), *The World Bank: Structure and Policies*. Cambridge University Press, 2006.
- Huntington Gilchrist, "Colonial Questions at the San Francisco Conference," in the *American Political Science Review*, Vol. 39 (1945), No. 5.
- Emile Giraud, "La revision de la Charte des Nations Unies," in *Recueil des cours*, Volume 90 (1956-II).

- Mary Ann Glendon, "John P. Humphrey and the drafting of the Universal Declaration of Human Rights," in the *Journal of the History of International Law*, vol. 2 (2000), no. 2.
- Michael J. Glennon, "De l'absurdité du droit impératif (*Jus cogens*)," in the *Revue générale de droit international public*, vol. 110 (2006), no. 3.
- Antonio Gómez Robledo, "Le *Ius Cogens* International : Sa Genèse, Sa Nature, Ses Fonctions," in *Recueil des cours*, vol 172, no. 1981-III (1981).
- Leland M. Goodrich, Edvard Hambro, *Charter of the United Nations: Commentary and Documents*. World Peace Foundation, 1946.
- Leland M. Goodrich, *The United Nations and the maintenance of international peace and security*. The Brookings Institution, 1955.
- Leland M. Goodrich, "San Francisco in retrospect," in the *International journal*, vol. 25 (1969-1970).
- Mikhail Gorbachev, "The Third Pillar of Sustainable Development," in Corcoran (editor), *Toward a Sustainable World: The Earth Charter in Action*. Amsterdam: KIT Publishers, 2005.
- Branislav Gosovic and John G. Ruggie, "On the Creation of a New International Economic Order: Issue Linkage and the Seventh Special Session of the UN General Assembly," in *International Organization*, Vol. 30 (1976), No. 2.
- Anna Gouwenberg, *The Legal Implementation of the Right to Development: A Study of the Grotius Centre for International Legal Studies Leiden University*. Grotius Centre for International Legal Studies, 2009.
- Vera Gowlland-Debass, "The Relationship Between the International Court of Justice and the Security Council in the Light of the Lockerbie Case," in the *American Journal of International Law*, Vol. 88 (1994), No. 4.
- Vera Gowlland-Debbas, "Judicial insights into fundamental values and interests of the international community," in Muller, Raic & Thuránszky (editors), *The International Court of Justice : its future role after fifty years*. Martinus Nijhoff, 1997.
- Evadné Grant, "Dignity and Equality," in *Human Rights Law Review*, vol. 7 (2007), no. 2.
- John N. Gray, *Heresies: Against Progress and Other Illusions*. Granta Publications, 2004.
- Wilhelm G. Grewe & Daniel-Erasmus Khan, "Drafting History," in Simma (editor), *The Charter of the United Nations: A Commentary* (2nd edition). Oxford University Press, 2002.
- James Griffin, "The Presidential Address: Discrepancies between the Best Philosophical Account of Human Rights and the International Law of Human Rights," in the *Proceedings of the Aristotelian Society*, Vol. 101 (2001).
- James Griffin, *On human rights*. Oxford University Press, 2008.
- Sonja Grover, "A response to Bagaric and Allan's 'The Vacuous Concept of Dignity'," in the *International Journal of Human Rights*, vol. 13 (2009), no. 4.
- Lothar Gündling, "Our Responsibility to Future Generations," in the *American Journal of International Law*, Vol. 84 (1990), No. 1.

- Jürgen Habermas, *Theorie des kommunikativen Handelns*. Suhrkamp, 1981 (Transl: *The theory of communicative action* by MacCarthy). Beacon, 1984.
- Jürgen Habermas, *The Postnational Constellation: Political Essays*, translated, edited, and with an introduction by Max Pensky. MIT Press, 2001.
- G. W. Haight, "New International Economic Order and the Charter of Economic Rights and Duties of States," in the *International Lawyer*, volume 9 (1975).
- George D. Haimbaugh, "Jus Cogens: Root & Branch (An Inventory)," in *Touro Law Review*, vol. 3 (1987).
- Brenda Hale, "Dignity," in the *Journal of Social Welfare and Family Law*, vol. 31 (2009), no. 2.
- Fred Halliday, "Global Governance : Prospects and Problems," in *Citizenship Studies*, vol. 4, no. 1 (2000).
- Loek Halman, Ruud Luijkx and Marga van Zundert, *Atlas of European Values*. 2005: Universiteit Tilburg and Brill Publishers (See also www.atlasofeuropeanvalues.com).
- Sir Keith Hancock & Jean van der Poel (editors), *Selections from the Smuts Papers, Volume IV: November 1918 – August 1919*. Cambridge University Press, 1966.
- Lauri Hannikainen, *Peremptory Norms (jus cogens) in International Law: Historical Development, Criteria, Present Status* (study). Lakimiesliiton Kustannus, 1988.
- Hurst Hannum, "Rethinking self-determination," in the *Virginia journal of international law*, vol. 34 (1993), no. 1.
- Hurst Hannum, "The right of self-determination in the twenty-first century," in the *Washington and Lee law review*, vol. 55 (1998), no. 4.
- Mahbub ul-Haq, *People's participation: human development report 1993*. Oxford University Press, 1993.
- Mahbub ul-Haq, *New dimensions of human security: human development report 1994*. Oxford University Press, 1994.
- Mahbub ul-Haq, *Reflections on Human Development*. Oxford University Press, 1995.
- Inaamul Haque & Ruxandra Burdescu, "Monterrey Consensus on Financing for Development: Response Sought from International Economic Law," in the *Boston College International and Comparative Law Review*, Volume 27 (2004).
- Keith Harper, "Does the United Nations have the competence to act as Court and Legislature?," in the *New York University journal of international law and politics*, vol. 27 (1994).
- Romuald R. Haule, "Some Reflections on the Foundation of Human Rights – Are Human Rights an Alternative to Moral Values?," in *Max Planck United Nations Year Book*, vol. 10 (2006).
- Sherman S. Hayden, "The Trusteeship Council: Its First Three Years," in the *Political Science Quarterly*, Vol. 66 (1951), No. 2.
- Tim Hayward, "Thomas Pogge's Global Resources Dividend: A Critique and an Alternative," *in Journal of Moral Philosophy* 2.3 (2005).

- Sally Healy, "The principle of self-determination still alive and well," in *Millennium: journal of international studies*, vol. 10 (1981).
- Georg Wilhelm Friedrich Hegel, *Elements of the philosophy of right*, Original Title: *Grundlinien der Philosophie des Rechts,* 1821 (Translation: Hegel, *Elements of the philosophy of right (Cambridge texts in the history of political thought)*. Wood (editor), Nisbet (translation). Cambridge University Press, 1991.
- David Held, "Law of States, Law of Peoples," in *Legal Theory*, vol. 8 (2002).
- David Held, *Global Covenant: The Social Democratic Alternative to the Washington Consensus*. Polity Press, 2004.
- Louis Henkin, "The United Nations and Human Rights," in *International Organization*, Vol. 19 (1965), No. 3.
- Louis Henkin, *How Nations Behave: Law and Foreign Policy*. Columbia University Press, 1979.
- Louis Henkin, "International law: politics, values and functions (general course on public international law)," in *Recueil des cours*, Volume 216 (1989-IV).
- Louis Henkin, "The Universality of the Concept of Human Rights," in the *Annals of the American Academy of Political and Social Science*, Vol. 506 (1989).
- Stéphanie Hennette-Vauchez, "When Ambivalent Principles Prevail: Leads for Explaining Western Legal Orders' Infatuation with the Human Dignity Principle." European University Institute, *EUI LAW Series*, report no. 2007/37.
- Larissa Jasmijn van den Herik, *The contribution of the Rwanda Tribunal to the development of international law*. Nijhoff, 2005.
- Christof Heyns, "The Preamble of the United Nations Charter: the contribution of Jan Smuts," in the *African journal of international and comparative law*, vol. 7 (1995).
- Steven V. Hicks, *International Law and the Possibility of a Just World Order*. Rodopi, 1999.
- Rosalyn Higgins, *The development of international law through the political organs of the United Nations*. Oxford University Press, 1963.
- Rosalyn Higgins, "International Law and the Avoidance, Containment and Resolution of Disputes (General course on Public International Law)," in the *Recueil des cours*, Volume 230 (1991-V).
- Rosalyn Higgins, *Problems and process: international law and how we use it*. Clarendon Press, 1994.
- Rosalyn Higgins, "Human Rights in the International Court of Justice," *Leiden Journal of International Law*, vol. 20 (2007).
- High-level Panel on Threats, Challenges and Change, *A more secure world: Our shared responsibility*, 2 December 2004, UNDoc. A/59/565
- Robert C. Hilderbrand, *Dumbarton Oaks: the origins of the United Nations and the search for postwar security*. University of North Carolina Press, 1990.
- Christian Hillgruber, "The Right of Third States to Take Countermeasures," in Tomuschat & Thouvenin, *The Fundamental Rules of the International Legal Order: Jus Cogens and Obligations Erga Omnes*. Martinus Nijhoff, 2006.
- Fred Hirsch, "Is there a New International Economic Order?," in *International Organization*, Vol. 30 (1976), No. 3.

- Thomas Hobbes, *Leviathan* (1651).
- André de Hoogh, *Obligations Erga Omnes and International Crimes: A Theoretical Inquiry into the Implementation and Enforcement of the International Responsibility of States.* Kluwer International Law, 1996.
- Linus A. Hoskins, "The New International Economic Order: A Bibliographic Essay," in the *Third World Quarterly*, Vol. 3 (1981), No. 3.
- Piet-Hein Houben, "Principles of International Law Concerning Friendly Relations and Co-Operation Among States," in the *American Journal of International Law*, Vol. 61 (1967), No. 3.
- Michel Houellebecq, *Plateforme: au milieu du monde.* Flammarion, 2001.
- Rhoda E. Howard and Jack Donnelly, "Human Dignity, Human Rights, and Political Regimes," in the *American Political Science Review*, Vol. 80 (1986), No. 3.
- Human Security Centre, *Human Security Report 2005: War and Peace in the 21st Century*, Oxford University Press, 2005
- John P. Humphrey, "International Protection of Human Rights," in the *Annals of the American Academy of Political and Social Science,* Vol. 255 (1948).
- Samuel P. Huntington, *The Clash of Civilizations and the Remaking of World Order.* Simon & Schuster, 1996.
- G. John Ikenberry and Anne-Marie Slaughter, *Forging A World Of Liberty Under Law: U.S. National Security In The 21st Century.* Final Paper of the Princeton Project on National Security, September 2006.
- Independent International Commission on Kosovo, *Kosovo Report: Conflict, International Response, Lessons Learned.* Oxford University Press 2000
- Martin Indyk, "A trusteeship for Palestine?," in *Foreign affairs*, vol. 82 (2003), no. 3.
- Ronald Inglehart (editor), *Human Beliefs and Values: A Cross-Cultural Sourcebook Based on the 1999-2002 Values Surveys.* Siglo XXI, 2004.
- International Commission on Intervention and State Sovereignty (ICISS), *Responsibility to Protect.* International Development Research Centre, 2001
- James, "Wilson Forgotten at San Francisco," in *New York Times* of April 30, 1945.
- Philip C. Jessup, "Parliamentary diplomacy: an examination of the legal quality of the rules of procedure of organs of the United Nations," in the *Recueil des cours*, vol. 89 (1957).
- Eduardo Jiménez de Aréchaga, "State Responsibility for the Nationalization of Foreign Owned Property," in *New York University Journal of International Law and Politics*, volume 11 (1978).
- Roben Johansen, "The Elusiveness of a Humane World Community," in Falk, Kim & Mendlovitz (editors), *Toward a Just World Order* (vol. 1 of the *Studies on a Just World Order*). Westview Press, 1982.
- Robert C. Johansen, *The National Interest and the Human Interest: An Analysis of U.S. Foreign Policy.* Princeton University Press, 1980.
- C. Don Johnson, "Toward self-determination: a reappraisal as reflected in the declaration on friendly relations," in *Georgia journal of international and comparative law*, vol. 3 (1973).

- Ian Johnstone, "Legislation and adjudication in the UN Security Council: bringing down the deliberative deficit," in *American Journal of International Law*, Vol 102 (2008), no. 2.
- William C. Johnstone, "The San Francisco Conference," in *Pacific Affairs*, Vol. 18, No. 3 (1945).
- Richard Jolly, Louis Emmerij, Dharam Ghai & Frédéric Lapeyre, *UN Contributions to Development Thinking and Practice,* United Nations Intellectual History Project Series. Indiana University Press, 2004.
- Richard Jolly, "Human Development," in Weiss & Daws (eds.), *The Oxford Handbook on the United Nations*. Oxford University Press, 2007.
- Richard Jolly, Louis Emmerij & Thom Weiss, *UN Ideas that Changed the World*. Indiana University Press, 2009.
- Robert S. Jordan, "United Nations General Assembly Resolutions as Expressions of Human Values," in the *International Studies Quarterly*, Vol. 20 (1976).
- Emmanuelle Jouannet, "Les travaux préparatoires de la Charte des Nations Unies," in Cot & Pellet, *La Charte des Nations Unies: commentaire article par article*, vol. 1 (2005).
- Christopher C. Joyner, "U.N. General Assembly resolutions and international law: rethinking the contemporary dynamics of norm-creation," in the *California Western international law journal*, vol. 11 (1981).
- Georges Kaeckenbeeck, "La Charte de San-Francisco dans ses rapports avec le droit international," in *Recueil des cours*, vol. 70 (1948).
- Mary Kaldor, "The idea of global civil society," in *International Affairs*, 79, 3 (2003).
- Menno T. Kamminga and Martin Scheinin, *The impact of human rights law on general international law*. Oxford University Press, 2009.
- Keith R. Kane, "The United Nations: A Prospectus (The Security Council)," in *Foreign Affairs*, Volume 24 (1945).
- Immanuel Kant, *Grundlegung zur Metaphysik der Sitten*, 1785 (transl.: Ellington, *Grounding for the Metaphysics of Morals*, Hackett Publishing, 1993).
- Immanuel Kant, *Zum Ewigen Frieden: Ein philosophischer Entwurf*, 1795.
- Immanuel Kant, *Anthropologie in pragmatischer Hinsicht*, 1798 (transl.: Gregor, *Anthropology from a Pragmatic Point of View*. Martinus Nijhoff, 1974).
- Sibylle Kapferer, "Article 14(2) of the Universal Declaration of Human Rights and Exclusion from International Refugee Protection," in the *Refugee Survey Quarterly*, Vol. 27 (2008), No. 3.
- Matthias Kaufmann, "Kantian Ethics and Politics," in the *International Encyclopedia of the Social & Behavioral Sciences*. Elsevier, 2004 (available online at www.sciencedirect.com)
- Johan Kaufmann, *United Nations Decision Making*. Sijthoff & Noordhoff, 1980.
- Satpal Kaur, "Self-determination in international law," in the *Indian journal of international law*, vol. 10 (1970).
- John Kekes, *The Morality of Pluralism*. Princeton University Press, 1993.
- Kevin W. Kelley, *The Home Planet*. Mir Publishers, 1988.

- Robert C. Kelman, "The Conditions, Criteria, and Dialectics of Human Dignity," in *International Studies Quarterly*, vol. 21 (1977), no. 3.
- Hans Kelsen, "The Old and the New League: The Covenant and the Dumbarton Oaks Proposals," in the *American Journal of International Law*, Volume 39 (1945).
- Hans Kelsen, "The Preamble of the Charter – A Critical Analysis," in the *Journal of Politics*, Vol. 8 (1946), No. 2.
- Hans Kelsen, "The Draft Declaration on Rights and Duties of States," in the *American Journal of International Law*, Vol. 44 (1950), No. 2.
- Hans Kelsen, *The Law of the United Nations: A Critical Analysis of its Fundamental Problems*. Stevens & Sons, 1950.
- Hans Kelsen, *Pure Theory of Law*. University of California Press, 1967.
- Paul Kennedy, *The Parliament of Man: The Past, Present, and Future of the United Nations*. Random House, 2006.
- John Kenton, "Human Rights Declaration adopted by UN Assembly," in *New York Times* of 11 December 1948.
- Ranjana Khanna, "Representing Culture, Translating Human Rights Symposium, Panel III: Asylum," in the *Texas International Law Journal*, volume 41 (2006).
- Samuel S. Kim, *The Quest for a Just World Order*. Westview Press, 1984.
- Grayson Kirk & Lawrence H. Chamberlain, "The Organization of the San Francisco Conference," in *Political Science Quarterly*, Vol. 6 (1945), No. 3.
- Alexandre Kiss, "The peoples' right to self-determination," in the *Human rights law journal*, vol. 7 (1986), no. 2-4.
- Jan Klabbers, "Constitutionalism Lite," in *International Organizations Law Review*, volume 1 (2004).
- Eelco N. van Kleffens, "The United Nations and Some Main Trends of Our Time," in the *Annals of the American Academy of Political and Social Science*, Vol. 252 (1947).
- David Kretzmer and Eckart Klein, *The concept of human dignity in human rights discourse*. Kluwer Law International , 2002.
- Pierre Klein, "Responsibility for Serious Breaches of Obligations Deriving from Peremptory Norms of International Law and United Nations Law," in the *European journal of international law*, vol. 13 (2002), issue 5.
- Pauline Kleingeld, "Kant's Cosmopolitan Law: World Citizenship for a Global Order," in *Kantian Review*, Volume 2 (1998).
- Pauline Kleingeld, "Six Varieties of Cosmopolitanism in Late Eighteenth-Century Germany," in *Journal of the History of Ideas* 60.3 (1999).
- Pauline Kleingeld, "Approaching Perpetual Peace: Kant's Defence of a League of States and his Ideal of a World Federation," in *European Journal of Philosophy*, 12:3 (2004).
- Pauline Kleingeld, "Wereldburgers in eigen land: Over kosmopolitisme en patriottisme," inaugural lecture delivered on 30th of September 2005 at Leiden.
- Pauline Kleingeld, *Cosmopolitanism: entry for the Internet Stanford Encyclopedia of Philosophy* (available online at plato.stanford.edu/entries/cosmopolitanism/).

- Florence Rockwood Kluckhohn and Fred L. Strodtbeck, *Variations in Value Orientations*. Row, 1961.
- Alexandra Knight, "Global Environmental Threats: Can the Security Council protect our Earth?," in *New York University Law Review*, vol. 80 (2005), no. 5.
- Bert Koenders, *Van Vollenhovenlezing "Rule of Law, Good Governance and Development Cooperation in Turbulent Times,"* speech delivered in Leiden, on 17 September 2007 (available online at www.minbuza.nl).
- Marcelo G. Kohen (editor), *Secession: international law perspectives*. Cambridge University Press, 2006.
- Robert Kolb, *Théorie du ius cogens international: Essai de relecture du concept*. Presses universitaires de France, 2001.
- Borris M. Komar, "A Code of World Law Now," in *Nordisk Tidsskrift for International Ret*, Vol. 36 (1966).
- Pieter Hendrik Kooijmans, "Tolerance, sovereignty and self-determination," in the *Netherlands international law review*, vol. 43 (1996), no. 2.
- Erik Koppe, *The use of nuclear weapons and the protection of the environment during international armed conflict*. Hart, 2008.
- Martti Koskenniemi, "The Politics of International Law," *European Journal of International Law*, Vol. 1 (1990) No. 1/2.
- Martti Koskenniemi, "Pull of the Mainstream," in *Michigan Law Review*, vol. 88 (1990).
- Martti Koskenniemi, "National Self-Determination Today: Problems of Legal Theory and Practice," in the *International and Comparative Law Quarterly*, vol. 43 (1994).
- Martti Koskenniemi, "The police in the Temple: order, justice and the UN, a dialectical view," in the *European journal of international law*, vol. 6 (1995).
- Martti Koskenniemi, "Solidarity measures: state responsibility as a new international order?," in *The British Yearbook of International Law*, vol. 72 (2001).
- Martti Koskenniemi, *The Gentle Civilizer of Nations : The Rise and Fall of International Law 1870-1960*. Cambridge University Press, 2001.
- Martti Koskenniemi, "'The Lady Doth Protest Too Much': Kosovo, and the Turn to Ethics in International Law," in the *Modern Law Review*, Volume 65 (2002), No. 2.
- Martti Koskenniemi, "By their acts you shall know them... (and not by their legal theories)," *European Journal of International Law*, vol. 15 (2004), No. 4.
- Martti Koskenniemi, "International law in Europe: between tradition and renewal," in the *European Journal of International Law*, Vol. 16 (2005), No. 1.
- Martti Koskenniemi, *From Apology to Utopia: The Structure of International Legal Argument*. Cambridge University Press, 2005 (original is of 1989).
- Martti Koskenniemi, *Fragmentation of international law: difficulties arising from the diversification and expansion of international law (Report of the Study Group of the International Law Commission)*, 13 April 2006, UN Doc. A/CN.4/L.682.
- Rajni Kothari, "World Politics and World Order: The Issue of Autonomy," in Mendlovitz, *On the Creation of a Just World Order*. The Free Press, 1975.

- Walter M. Kotschnig, "The United Nations as an Instrument of Economic and Social Development," in *International Organization*, Vol. 22 (1968), No. 1.
- Keith Krause, "Disarmament," in Thomas G. Weiss and Sam Daws (editors), *The Oxford handbook on the United Nations*. Oxford University Press, 2007.
- Anne O. Krueger, "Whither the World Bank and the IMF?," in Journal of Economic Literature, vol. 36 (1998).
- Thomas Kuhn, *The Structure of Scientific Revolutions*. University of Chicago Press, 1962.
- Hans Küng, *Declaration toward a Global Ethic*, declaration adopted at the Parliamant of the World's Religions, Chicago 1993 (available online at www.weltethos.org).
- Hans Küng, *Towards a Common Civilization: Public Lectures by Hans Kueng and Mohd Kamal Hassan*. Institute of Islamic Understanding Malaysia, 1997.
- Kunstenaar, "Revised Morals Urged," in *New York Times* of April 22, 1945.
- Josef L. Kunz, "The United Nations Declaration of Human Rights," in the *American Journal of International Law*, Vol. 43 (1949), no. 2.
- Andrew Kuper, "Rawlsian Global Justice: Beyond a Law of Peoples to a Cosmopolitan Law of Persons," in *Political Theory* 28:5, 2000.
- Jorg Kustermans, Jacobus Delwaide & Gustaaf Geeraerts, "Global governance en veiligheid," in Vrede en Veiligheid 36 (2007).
- Will Kymlicka, "Introduction: The Globalization of Ethics," in Sullivan & Kymlicka, *The Globalization of Ethics: Religious and Secular Perspectives*. Cambridge University Press, 2007.
- Manfred Lachs, "Article 1, paragraphe 1," in Cot & Pellet, *La Charte des Nations Unies: commentaire article par article*, vol. 1 (2005).
- Anne Lagerwall, "Article 53," in Corten & Klein (eds.), *Les Conventions de Vienne sur le droit des traités: Commentaire article par article*. Bruylant, 2006.
- Anne Lagerwall, "Article 64," in Corten & Klein (eds.), *Les Conventions de Vienne sur le droit des traités: Commentaire article par article*. Bruylant, 2006.
- Julian Lamont, "The Concept of Desert in Distributive Justice," in the *Philosophical Quarterly*, vol. 44 (1994), No. 174.
- Bart Landheer, "Ethical Values in International Decision-making: Remarks around the Conference," in Landheer, van der Molen *et al* (editors), *Ethical Values in International Decision-making: The Conference of June, 16-20, 1958*. Martinus Nijhoff, 1960.
- Hersch Lauterpacht, "The international protection of human rights," in *Recueil des cours*, Volume 70 (1947).
- Patrick Lee & Robert George, "The Nature and Basis of Human Dignity," in *Ratio Juris*, Vol. 21 (2008), no. 2.
- Bernard-Henri Levy, "'Europe Has Lost Confidence': Interview with French Philosopher Bernard-Henri Levy," in the *Spiegel Online*, March 23, 2007.
- Yuen-li Liang, "The Progressive Development of International Law and its Codification under the United Nations," in the *American Society of International Law Proceedings*, vol. 24 (1947).

497

- Yuen-li Liang, "The General Assembly and the Progressive Development and Codification of International Law," in the *American Journal of International Law*, Vol. 42 (1948).
- David R. Lindskog, "The New International Economic Order," in the *International Financial Law Review*, vol. 5, issue 11 (1986).
- Frances Livingstone, "Withdrawal from the United Nations: Indonesia," in *The International and Comparative Law Quarterly*, Vol. 14 (1965), No. 2.
- Vaughan Lowe, "The principle of non-intervention: use of force," in Lowe (editor), *The United Nations and the principles of international law: essays in memory of Michael Akehurst*. Routledge, 1994.
- Vaughan Lowe (editor), *The United Nations Security Council and war: the evolution of thought and practice since 1945*. Oxford University Press, 2008.
- Evan Luard, *A History of the United Nations, Volume 1*. Macmillan Press, 1982.
- R. St. John Macdonald, "Solidarity in the Practice and Discourse of Public International Law," in the *Pace International Law Review*, volume 8 (1996).
- Ronald Macdonald, "The Charter of the United Nations in constitutional perspective," in the *Australian Year Book of International Law*, vol. 20 (1999).
- S. Neil MacFarlane and Yuen Foong Khong, *Human Security and the UN: A Critical History (United Nations Intellectual History Project)*. Indiana University Press, 2006.
- MacLean, Swift, and Blair, "Commentaries," in the *Virginia Journal of International Law*, vol. 16 (1975-1976).
- Marie-France Major, "Mercenaries and international law," in the *Georgia Journal of International and Comparative Law*, vol. 22 (1992), no. 1
- David Makinson, "Rights of peoples: point of view of a logician," in Crawford (editor), *The Rights of Peoples*. Clarendon Press, 1988.
- Vekateshwara Subramanian Mani, *Basic principles of modern international law: a study of the United Nations debates on the principles of international law concerning friendly relations and co-operation among states*. Lancers Books, 1993.
- Vekateshwara Subramanian Mani, "The Friendly Relations Declaration and the International Court of Justice," in Anghie & Sturgess (editors), *Legal visions of the 21st century: essays in honor of Judge Christopher Weeramantry*. Kluwer Law International, 1998.
- Kenneth Marvin Manusama, *The United Nations Security Council in the post-cold war era: applying the principle of legality*. Nijhoff, 2006.
- Ronald A. Manzer, "The United Nations Special Fund," in *International Organization*, Vol. 18 (1964), No. 4.
- Henry Margenau, *Facts and Values*. Brown University Papers Number XXXI, 1955.
- Stephen Marks, "The Human Right to Development: Between Rhetoric and Reality," in *Harvard Human Rights Journal*, Vol. 17 (2004).
- Alhaji B.M. Marong, "From Rio to Johannesburg: Reflections on the Role of International Legal Norms in Sustainable Development," in the *Georgetown International Environmental Law Review*, Volume 16 (2003).

- Axel Marschik, "The Security Council as World Legislator?: Theory, Practice and Consequences of an Expanding World Power," *IILJ Working Paper*, No. 2005-18.
- Marshal, "Smuts And The Preamble To The UN Charter," in *The Round Table*, Volume 358 (2001), No. 1.
- Larry May, *Aggression and crimes against peace*. Cambridge University Press, 2008.
- Graham Mayeda, "Where Should Johannesburg Take Us - Ethical and Legal Approaches to Sustainable Development in the Context of International Environmental Law," in the *Colorado Journal of International Environmental Law and Policy*, volume 15 (2004).
- Timothy L.H. McCormack, "H.V. Evatt at San Francisco: a lasting contribution to international law," in *Australian Year Book of International Law*, vol. 13 (1990).
- Anne O'Hare McCormick, "San Francisco: Battlefield for Peace," in *New York Times* of May 6, 1945.
- Anne O'Hare McCormick, "San Francisco: Voice of Europe is Muted at Conference," in *New York Times* of May 14, 1945.
- Robert McCorquodale, "Self-determination beyond the colonial context and its potential impact on Africa," in the *African journal of international and comparative law*, vol. 4 (1992).
- Robert McCorquodale, "Self-determination: a human rights approach," in the *international and comparative law quarterly*, vol. 43 (1994), no. 4.
- Robert McCorquodale, "An Inclusive International Legal System," in *Leiden Journal of International Law*, vol. 17 (2004).
- Christopher McCrudden, "Human Dignity and Judicial Interpretation of Human Rights," in the *European Journal of International Law*, Vol. 19 (2008), no. 4.
- Myres S. McDougal, "Law School of the Future: From Legal Realism to Policy Science in the World Community," in the *Yale Law Journal*, volume 56 (1947).
- Myres S. McDougal & Gerhard Bebr, "Human Rights in the United Nations," in the *American Journal of International Law*, Vol. 58 (1964), No. 3.
- Myres S. McDougal, Laswell & Chen, *Human rights and world public order: the basic policies of an international law of human dignity*. Yale University Press, 1980.
- Myres S. McDougal, *Studies in World Public Order*. New Haven Press, 1987.
- Dominic McGoldrick, "The principle of non-intervention: human rights," in Lowe (editor), *The United Nations and the principles of international law: essays in memory of Michael Akehurst*. Routledge, 1994.
- McNeil, "New Security Charter Seems to be Assured," in *New York Times* of May 20, 1945.
- McNeil, "A New Kind of League, a New Kind of World," in *New York Times* of June 24, 1945.
- Edward McWhinney, "The 'New' Countries and the 'New' International Law: The United Nations' Special Conference on Friendly Relations and Co-Operation Among States," in the *American Journal of International Law*, vol. 60 (1966), no. 1.
- Saul Mendlovitz, *On the Creation of a Just World Order*. The Free Press, 1975.

- Saul Mendlovitz and Thomas Weiss, "The Study of Peace and Justice: Toward a Framework for Global Discussion," in Beres & Targ, *Planning Alternative World Futures: Values, Methods, and Models*. Praeger Publishers, 1975.
- Falk, Kim & Mendlovitz (editors), *Toward a Just World Order* (vol. 1 of the *Studies on a Just World Order*). Westview Press, 1982.
- Theodor Meron, "On a Hierarchy of International Human Rights," in the *American Journal of International Law*, Vol. 80 (1986), No. 1.
- Theodor Meron, *The Humanization of International Law*. Martinus Nijhoff, 2006.
- Carlos Ruiz Miguel, "Human dignity: history of an idea," in the *Jahrbuch des öffentlichen Rechts der Gegenwart*, vol. 50 (2002).
- Mill, *Utilitarianism*. Oxford University Press, 1998 (first printed in 1863).
- David Miller, "Reasonable Partiality Towards Compatriots," in *Ethical Theory and Moral Practice*, Volume 8 (2005), Nos. 1-2.
- David Miller, *Social Justice*. Oxford: Clarendon Press, 1979.
- Lynn H. Miller, *Global Order: Values and Power in International Politics*. Westview Press, 1990
- Takeshi Minagawa, "Essentiality and reality of international jus cogens," in *Hitotsubashi journal of law and politics*, vol. 12 (1984).
- Ministère des affaires ètrangères (Canada), *Rapport sur les travaux de la conférence des Nations Unies sur l'"organisation internationale tenue à San-Francisco du 25 avril au 26 juin 1945* . Cloutier, 1945.
- Ministerie van Buitenlandse Zaken (Netherlands), *Het ontstaan der Verenigde Naties : San Francisco, 25 april - 25 juni 1945*.  Staatsdrukkerij- en Uitgeverijbedrijf, 1950.
- Neil Mitchell, Rhoda E. Howard, and Jack Donnelly, "Liberalism, Human Rights, and Human Dignity," in the *American Political Science Review*, Vol. 81 (1987), No. 3.
- Darrel Moellendorf, *Cosmopolitan Justice*. Westview Press, 2002
- Gay Moon and Robin Allen, "Dignity Discourse in Discrimination Law: A Better Route to Equality?," in the *European Human Rights Law Review*, vol. 11 (2006).
- Margaret Moore, "An historical argument for indigenous self-determination," in Macedo & Buchanan, *Secession and self-determination*.  New York University Press, 2003.
- Margaret Moore, "On National Self-Determination," in *Political Studies*, vol. 45 (1997).
- Barrington Moore, *Reflections on the Causes of Human Misery and upon Certain Proposals to Eliminate Them*. Beacon, 1973.
- Hans J. Morgenthau, *Politics among Nations: The Struggle for Power and Peace*. McGraw-Hill, 1948.
- Hans J. Morgenthau, "The New United Nations and the Revision of the Charter," in the *Review of Politics*, Vol. 16 (1954).
- Johannes Morsink, *The Universal Declaration of Human Rights: Origins, Drafting, and Intent.* University of Pennsylvania Press, 1999.
- Johannes Morsink, *Inherent human rights: philosophical roots of the Universal Declaration*. University of Pennsylvania Press, 2009.

- Rein A. Müllerson, "Human Rights and the Individual as Subject of International Law: A Soviet View," in *European Journal of International Law*, Vol. 1 (1990) , no. 1/2.
- James N. Murray, *The United Nations trusteeship system*. University of Illinois press, 1957.
- Dietrich Murswiek, "The issue of a right of secession – reconsidered," in Tomuschat (editor), *Modern law of self-determination*. Nijhoff, 1993.
- Thomas Nagel, *Equality and Partiality*. Oxford University Press, 1991.
- Thomas Nagel, "The Problem of Global Justice," Philosophy & Public Affairs, Vol. 33 (2005), no. 2.
- Ved P. Nanda, "Self-determination and secession under international law," in the *Denver journal of international law and policy*, vol. 29 (2001), no. 3-4.
- Netherlands Scientific Council for Government Policy in their report on *Waarden, normen en de last van het gedrag* [values, norms and the burden of behavior], Amsterdam University Press, 2003 (available online at www.wrr.nl)
- New York Times, "Transcript of Molotoff Interview," in *New York Times* of April 27, 1945.
- New York Times, "Jewish Group Asks World Rights Bill," in *New York Times* of April 30, 1945.
- New York Times, "Conference Talks Stress Unity Plea," in *New York Times* of May 2, 1945.
- New York Times, "Widen Definition of Human Rights," in *New York Times* of May 18, 1945.
- New York Times, "Charter for Peace," in *New York Times* of May 20, 1945.
- New York Times, "'Old League' Chief Quits Conference," in *New York Times* of May 27, 1945.
- New York Times, "General Assembly Powers Voted: It Loses Rigid Rule over Council," in *New York Times* of May 27, 1945.
- New York Times, "Human Rights Seen Safe in Conference," in *New York Times* of June 4, 1945.
- New York Times, "Dulles Wins Plea to Bar League from Meddling in Domestic Issues," in *New York Times* of June 16, 1945.
- New York Times, "UNCIO's Charter: The Final Tasks," in *New York Times* of June 17, 1945.
- New York Times, "Success at San Francisco," in *New York Times* of June 22, 1945.
- B. C. Nirmal, *The right to self-determination in international law: evolution, U.N. law and practice, new dimensions*. Deep & Deep, 1999.
- André Nollkaemper, *Kern van het Internationaal Publiekrecht*. Boom Juridische Uitgevers, 2007.
- Georg Nolte, "Article 2(7)," in Simma (editor), *The Charter of the United Nations: A Commentary* (2nd edition). Oxford University Press, 2002.
- Roger Normand and Sarah Zaidi, *Human rights at the UN: the political history of universal justice*. Indiana University Press, 2008

501

- Martha C. Nussbaum, "Patriotism and Cosmopolitanism," in *Boston Review*, Vol. 19 (1994), No. 5.
- Martha C. Nussbaum, "Kant and Stoic Cosmopolitanism," in *The Journal of Political Philosophy*, Vol. 5 (1997), No 1.
- Office of the United Nations High Commissioner of Human Rights, *Frequently Asked Questions on A Human Rights-Based Approach to Development Cooperation* (HR/PUB/06/8 ). United Nations, 2006.
- Sadako Ogata, *State Security – Human Security (Fridtjof Nansen Memorial Lecture 2001)*. United Nations University, 2001.
- Lassa Francis Lawrence Oppenheim, *The Future of International Law*. The Clarendon Press, 1921.
- Hari M. Osofsky, "Defining Sustainable Development after Earth Summit 2002," in *Loyola of Los Angeles International and Comparative Law Review*, Volume 26 (2003).
- David Owen, "The United Nations Expanded Program of Technical Assistance - A Multilateral Approach," in the *Annals of the American Academy of Political and Social Science,* Vol. 323 (1959)
- Daphna Oyserman, "Values: Psychological Perspectives," in the *International Encyclopedia of the Social & Behavioral Sciences*. Elsevier, 2004 (available at www.sciencedirect.com)
- Roland Paris, "Human Security: Paradigm Shift or Hot Air?" in *International Security*, Vol. 26 (2001).
- Alan Patten, "Democratic Secession from a Multinational State," in *Ethics*, Vol. 112 (2002).
- James Pattison, *Humanitarian intervention and the responsibility to protect: who should intervene?*. Oxford University Press, 2010
- Andreas L. Paulus, "Jus Cogens in a Time of Hegemony and Fragmentation: an Attempt at a Re-appraisal," in the *Nordic journal of international law*, vol. 74 (2005), no. 3-4.
- Paxman (rapporteur), "Discussion," in the *Virginia Journal of International Law*, vol. 16 (1975-1976).
- Alain Pellet, "La formation du droit international dans le cadre des Nations Unies," in *European Journal of International Law*, vol 6 (1995).
- Alain Pellet, "Between Codification and Progressive Development of the Law: Some Reflections from the ILC," in *International Law Forum du droit international*, vol. 6 (2004).
- Christopher K. Penny, *Climate change and the Security Council: a preliminary framework for implementing remedial measures through Chapter VII of the UN Charter*. Centre for International Sustainable Development Law (CISDL), 2007.
- M. J. Peterson, *The General Assembly in World Politics*. Allen & Unwin, 1986.
- M. J. Peterson, "General Assembly," in Weiss & Daws (eds.), *The Oxford Handbook on the United Nations*. Oxford University Press, 2007.
- Daniel Philpott, "In Defense of Self-Determination," in *Ethics*, vol. 105 (1995).

- Daniel Philpott, "Global Ethics and the International Law Tradition," in Sullivan & Kymlicka, *The Globalization of Ethics: Religious and Secular Perspectives.* Cambridge University Press, 2007.
- Marek Piechowiak, "What are human rights?: the concept of human rights and their extra-legal justification," in Hanski & Suksi, *An introduction to the international protection of human rights: a textbook.* 2$^{nd}$ edition. Åbo Akademi University, 1999.
- Roland Pierik, Wouter Werner, "Cosmopolitism, Global Justice, and International Law," in *Leiden Journal of International Law*, 18 (2005).
- Burton Yale Pines (editor), *A World Without a U.N.: what would happen if the United Nations shut down.* Heritage Foundation, 1984.
- Elmer Plischke, "Self-Determination: Reflections on a Legacy," in *World Affairs*, vol. 140 (1977).
- Plutarch, *De Fortuna Alexandri.*
- Jean van der Poel (editor), *Selections from the Smuts Papers, Volume VI: December 1934 – August 1945.* Cambridge University Press, 1973.
- Thomas W. Pogge, *Realizing Rawls.* Cornell University Press, 1989.
- Thomas W. Pogge, "An Egalitarian Law of Peoples," in *Philosophy and Public Affairs*, 23:3, 1994.
- Thomas W. Pogge, "Priorities of Global Justice," in *Metaphilosophy* 32 (issue 1&2).
- Thomas W. Pogge, "The International Significance of Human Rights," in *The Journal of Ethics*, Volume 4 (2000), Nos. 1-2.
- Thomas W. Pogge, *World Poverty and Human Rights: Cosmopolitan Responsibilities and Reforms.* Polity, 2002.
- Thomas W. Pogge, "Recognized and Violated by International Law: The Human Rights of the Global Poor," in the *Leiden Journal of International Law*, vol. 18 (2005).
- Hambro Pollux, "The Interpretation of the Charter," in the *British Yearbook of International Law*, volume 23 (1946).
- Porter, "Stassen Outlines Our 9 Objectives," in *New York Times* of May 4, 1945.
- Porter, "Smaller Countries Rush Amendments," in *New York Times* of May 5, 1945.
- Porter, "Soviet Action Hit," in *New York Times* of May 6, 1945.
- Porter, "Gromyko Insists on Big Power Unity," in *New York Times* of May 29, 1945.
- Porter, "Economic Council is Key Peace Aid," in *New York Times* of June 12, 1945.
- Porter, "Charter Stronger than Expected," in *New York Times* of June 17, 1945.
- Samantha Power, *"A problem from hell": America and the age of genocide.* Basic Books, 2002.
- Lawrence Preuss, "Article 2, paragraph 7 of the Charter of the United Nations and matters of domestic jurisdiction," in the *Recueil des cours*, vol. 74 (1950).

- Michael S. Pritchard, "Human Dignity and Justice," in *Ethics*, vol. 82 (1972), no. 4.
- Jan Pronk, "Een nieuwe jas voor de Verenigde Naties," in *Vrede & Veiligheid*, vol. 36 (2007), no. 2.
- Frank Przetacznik, "The basic collective human right to self-determination of peoples and nations as a prerequisite for peace," in the *New York Law School Journal of Human Rights*, vol. 8 (1990), no. 1.
- Hilary Putnam, *The Collapse of the Fact/Value Dichotomy and Other Essays*. Harvard University Press, 2002.
- Shahid Qadir, "UN Conference on the Least Developed Countries: Neither Breakthrough nor Breakdown," in the *Third World Quarterly*, Volume 4 (1982).
- Peter Railton, "Ethics and Values," in the *International Encyclopedia of the Social & Behavioral Sciences*. Elsevier, 2004 (available online at www.sciencedirect.com).
- Bertrand G. Ramcharan, *Human Rights and Human Security*. Martinus Nijhoff, 2002.
- Bertrand G. Ramcharan, *Contemporary human rights ideas*. Routledge, 2008.
- Albrecht Randelzhofer, "Article 2," in Simma (editor), *The Charter of the United Nations: A Commentary* (2nd edition). Oxford University Press, 2002.
- Albrecht Randelzhofer, "Article 2(4)," in Simma (editor), *The Charter of the United Nations: A Commentary* (2nd edition). Oxford University Press, 2002.
- Dietrich Rauschning, "Article 75," in Simma (editor), *The charter of the United Nations: a commentary*. Oxford University Press, 2002.
- Dietrich Rauschning, "Article 76," in Simma (editor), *The charter of the United Nations: a commentary*. Oxford University Press, 2002.
- John Rawls, *A Theory of Justice (Revised Edition)*. Oxford University Press, 1999 (original of 1971).
- John Rawls, *The Law of Peoples*. Harvard University Press, 1999.
- Nicholas Rescher, *Introduction to Value Theory*. Prentice-Hall, 1969.
- Georg Ress, "Interpretation," in Simma (editor), *The Charter of the United Nations: A Commentary* (2nd edition). Oxford University Press, 2002.
- James B. Reston, "Dutch Oppose Idea of Oaks Big 5 Veto," in *New York Times* of February 8, 1945.
- James B. Reston, "Light on Foreign Policy Awaited," in *New York Times* of February 11, 1945.
- James B. Reston, "Poles in London Ask Oaks Revision," in *New York Times* of February 11, 1945.
- James B. Reston, "Pacific War Role for Soviet Hinted," in *New York Times* of February 13, 1945.
- James B. Reston, "Mexico Talks Designed to Link Hemisphere to Dumbarton Oaks," in *New York Times* of February 19, 1945.
- James B. Reston, "American Nations Seek Council Post," in *New York Times* of February 23, 1945.
- James B. Reston, "Hemisphere Peace Sought at Parley," in *New York Times* of February 24, 1945.

- James B. Reston, "Parley Near Crisis on Security Steps," in *New York Times* of February 28, 1945.
- James B. Reston, "Chapultepec Plan to Keep Peace in Americas Seen Sure to Pass," in *New York Times* of March 3, 1945.
- James B. Reston, "U.S. Retains Right to Alter Oaks Plan," in *New York Times* of April 7, 1945.
- James B. Reston, "Six Problems Facing Security Conference," in *New York Times* of April 15, 1945.
- James B. Reston, "Molotoff Coming to Conference; Stalin Acts at Truman's Request," in *New York Times* of April 15, 1945.
- James B. Reston, "Dumbarton 'Gaps' Big Parley Issue," in *New York Times* of April 16, 1945.
- James B. Reston, "Party Ship is Sent to Parley by Soviet," in *New York Times* of April 21, 1945.
- James B. Reston, "Changes Offered in Oaks Proposals," in *New York Times* of April 23, 1945.
- James B. Reston, "Dutch to Ask Veto for Small Nations," in *New York Times* of April 24, 1945.
- James B. Reston, "France Lining up with Big Powers," in *New York Times* of April 25, 1945.
- James B. Reston, "46 Nations Ready to Organize Peace; Only Poles Absent," in *New York Times* of April 25, 1945.
- James B. Reston, "Italians Protest Parley Exclusion," in *New York Times* of April 26, 1945.
- James B. Reston, "Justice Put First," in *New York Times* of April 26, 1945.
- James B. Reston, "Oaks Amendments Speed New Charter," in *New York Times* of May 6, 1945.
- James B. Reston, "Attack is Opened on Big 5 Veto Right," in *New York Times* of May 10, 1945.
- James B. Reston, "Conference Turns to Final Problems," in *New York Times* of May 17, 1945.
- James B. Reston, "U.S. Avoids Pledge to Free Colonies; Veto Plan Stands," in *New York Times* of May 18, 1945.
- James B. Reston, "U.S Foreign Policy Set by Stettinius for Secure Peace," in *New York Times* of May 29, 1945.
- James B. Reston, "Russians Demand Curb on Assembly or They Won't Sign," in *New York Times* of June 18, 1945.
- James B. Reston, "Truce is Offered by Soviet on Issue of Assembly Talk," in *New York Times* of June 20, 1945.
- Gerard Reve, *Op weg naar het einde*. van Oorschot, 1963.
- Emery Reves, *The Anatomy of Peace*. Harper & Brothers, 1945.
- Rodilf Rezsohazy, "Sociology of Values," in the *International Encyclopedia of the Social & Behavioral Sciences*. Elsevier, 2004 (available online at www.sciencedirect.com)

- António Sousa Ribeiro, "Cosmopolitanism," in the *International Encyclopedia of the Social & Behavioral Sciences*. Elsevier, 2004 (available online at www.sciencedirect.com)
- Eibe Riedel, "Article 55(c)," in Simma (editor), *The Charter of the United Nations: A Commentary* (2nd edition). Oxford University Press, 2002.
- Thomas Risse and Kathryn Sikkink, "The socialization of international human rights norms into domestic practices: an introduction," in Risse, Ropp & Sikkink (eds), *The Power of Human Rights: International Norms and Domestic Change*. Cambridge University Press, 1999.
- Thomas Risse, "Global Governance and Communicative Action," in *Government and Opposition*, Vol. 39 (2004), No. 2.
- Jacob Robinson, "Metamorphosis of the United Nations," in *Recueil des cours*, vol. 94 (1958).
- Richard Robinson, *An Atheist's Values*. Clarendon Press, 1964.
- Milton Rokeach, *The Nature of Human Values*. Free Press, 1973.
- Bert V.A. Röling, "International Law and the Maintenance of Peace," in the *Netherlands Yearbook of International Law,* vol. 4 (1973).
- Bert V. A. Röling, "On the prohibition of the use of force," in Anthony. R. Blackshield (editor), *Legal change: essays in honour of Julius Stone*. Butterworth, 1983.
- Allan Rosas, "internal self-determination," in Tomuschat (editor), *Modern law of self-determination*. Nijhoff, 1993.
- James N. Rosenau, "Governance, Order, and Change in World Politics," in Rosenau & Czempiel (editors), *Governance without Government: Order and Change in World Politics*. Cambridge University Press. 1992.
- Robert Rosenstock, "The Declaration of Principles of International Law Concerning Friendly Relations: A Survey," in the *American Journal of International Law*, vol. 65 (1971), No. 4.
- Gert Rosenthal, "Economic and Social Council," in Weiss & Daws (eds.), *The Oxford Handbook on the United Nations*. Oxford University Press, 2007.
- Nicholas Rostow, "International Law and the Use of Force: a Plea for Realism," in the *Yale Journal of International Law*, vol. 34 (2009), no. 2
- Emma Rothschild, "What is security?," in *Daedalus*, Summer 1995.
- Charles E. Rousseau, *Droit International Public*. Sirey, 1970.
- Samuel Rozemond, *Kant en de Volkenbond*, study at the University of Amsterdam, 1930.
- Eduard Rozental, "Charter of Economic Rights and Duties of States and the New International Economic Order," in the *Virginia Journal of International Law*, vol. 16 (1975-1976).
- Alfred P. Rubin, "The Charter of Economic Rights and Duties of States: Remarks," in the *American Society of International Law Proceedings*, vol. 69 (1975).
- Sir Arthur Rucker, "The Work of the International Refugee Organization," in *International Affairs*, Vol. 25 (1949), No. 1.
- John G. Ruggie, "Human Rights and the Future International Community," in *Daedalus*, Vol. 112 (1983), No. 4.

- Ruth B. Russell, *A history of the United Nations Charter: The role of the United States, 1940-1945*. Brookings Institution (The Brookings series on the United Nations), 1958.
- Richard Ryder, "All beings that feel pain deserve human rights: Equality of the species is the logical conclusion of post-Darwin morality," in *the Guardian*, 6 August 2005.
- Cedric Ryngaert & Christine Griffioen, "The Relevance of the Right to Self-Determination in the Kosovo Matter," in the *Chinese journal of international law*, vol. 8 (2009), no. 3.
- Jeffrey D. Sachs, "The Development Challenge," in *Foreign Affairs*, Volume 84 (2005).
- Milan Sahović, "Codification des principes du droit international des relations amicales et de la coopération entre les Etats," in *Recueil des cours*, vol. 137 (1974).
- Yoshikazu Sakamoto, "Toward Global Identity," in Mendlovitz, *On the Creation of a Just World Order*. The Free Press, 1975.
- Jean Salmon, "Internal aspects of the right to self-determination," in Tomuschat (editor), *Modern law of self-determination*. Nijhoff, 1993.
- Surakiart Sathirathai, "Renewing Our Global Values: A Multilateralism for Peace, Prosperity, and Freedom," in *Harvard Human Rights Journal*, vol 19 (2006).
- Oscar Schachter, "The relation of law, politics and action in the United Nations," in *Recueil des cours*, vol. 109 (1964).
- Oscar Schachter, "International law in theory and practice (general course in public international law)," in *Recueil des cours*, Volume 178 (1982-V).
- Oscar Schachter, "Human Dignity as a Normative Concept," in the *American Journal of International Law*, Vol. 77 (1983), No. 4.
- Oscar Schachter, "United Nations law," in the *American journal of international law*, vol. 88 (1994).
- Oscar Schachter, "The charter's origins in today's perspective," in the *American Society of International Law Proceedings*, vol. 89 (1995).
- Oscar Schachter, "The UN Legal Order: An Overview," in Schachter & Joyner (editors), *United Nations Legal Order*. Cambridge University Press, 1995.
- F. B. Schick, "Towards a living constitution of the United Nations," in the *International Law Quarterly*, vol. 2 (1948).
- Stephen C. Schlesinger, *Act of Creation: The Founding of the United Nations: A Story of Superpowers, Secret Agents, Wartime Allies and Enemies, and Their Quest for a Peaceful World*. Westview Press, 2003.
- Schneider Report, *A la recherche d'une sagesse pour le monde: quel rôle pour les valeurs éthiques dans l'éducation?*, written for UNESCO/Club of Rome, 1987 (available at unesdoc.unesco.org)
- Nico Schrijver, "International Organization for the Management of Interdependence: Alternative Ideas in Pursuit of Global Decision Making," in the *Bulletin of Peace Proposals*, vol. 19 (1988).
- Nico Schrijver, "International Organization for Environmental Security,'" *Bulletin of Peace Proposals*, 20 (1989).

- Nico Schrijver, *Sovereignty over natural resources: balancing rights and duties*. Cambridge University Press, 1997.
- Nico Schrijver, "The Changing Nature of State Sovereignty," in *British Yearbook of International Law*, Volume 70 (1999).
- Nico Schrijver, "Article 2, paragraphe 4," in Cot & Pellet, *La Charte des Nations Unies: commentaire article par article*, vol. 1 (2005).
- Nico Schrijver, "Les valeurs fondamentales et le droit des Nations Unies," in Chemain & Pellet (editors), *La Charte des Nations Unies, constitution mondiale?* Pedone, 2006.
- Nico Schrijver, "The Future of the Charter of the United Nations," in *Max Planck Yearbook of United Nations Law* (2006).
- Nico Schrijver, *Na ons de zondvloed: de positie van toekomstige generaties in het volkenrecht*. Boom Juridische Uitgevers, 2006.
- Nico Schrijver, "The U. N. Human Rights Council: a New "Society of the Committed" or Just Old Wine in New Bottles?," in *Leiden journal of international law*, vol. 20 (2007), no. 4
- Nico Schrijver, "De Verenigde Naties in de 21ste eeuw," in Jansen *et al* (editors), *Burgers en barbaren: over oorlog tussen recht en macht*. Boom Tijdschriften, 2007.
- Nico Schrijver, "The Evolution of Sustainable Development in International Law: Inception, Meaning and Status," in *Recueil des cours*, volume 329 (2007).
- Nico Schrijver, "Unravelling State Sovereignty: the Controversy on the Right of Indigenous Peoples to Permanent Sovereignty over their Natural Wealth and Resources," in Boerefijn, Goldschmidt & Flinterman, *Changing perceptions of sovereignty and human rights: essays in honor of Cees Flinterman*. Intersentia, 2008.
- Nico Schrijver & Larissa van den Herik, "Eroding the Primacy of the UN System of Collective Security: the Judgment of the European Court of Justice in the Cases of Kadi and Al Barakaat," in the *International Organizations Law Review*, vol. 5 (2008), no. 2.
- Nico Schrijver, "After us, the deluge? The position of future generations of humankind in international environmental law," in M. A. Mohamed Salih (editor), *Climate Change and Sustainable Development: New Challenges for Poverty Reduction*. Edward Elgar Publishing, 2009.
- Nico Schrijver, "The right to development: as fundamental as other human rights?," in Piet de Klerk, Jeroen Steeghs, Jean-Pierre Kempeneers & Bartjan Wegter (editors), *A Majoor Boost for the United Nations: A collection of essays on the occasion of the departure of Frank Majoor from New York*. Netherlands Mission to the United Nations, 2009.
- Nico Schrijver, *Development without destruction: the UN and global resource management*. Indiana University Press, 2010.
- Nico Schrijver & Larissa van den Herik, "Leiden Policy Recommendations on Counter-Terrorism and International Law," in the *Netherlands International Law Review*, vol. 57 (2010), no. 3.

- Stephen M. Schwebel, "The Story of the U.N.'s Declaration on Permanent Sovereignty over Natural Resources," in the *American Bar Association Journal*, volume 49 (1963).
- Stephen M. Schwebel, "Aggression, intervention and self-defense in modern international law," in *Recueil des cours*, vol. 136 (1972).
- Egon Schwelb, "Withdrawal from the United Nations: The Indonesian Intermezzo," in *The American Journal of International Law*, Vol. 61 (1967), No. 3.
- Secretariat of the International Military Tribunal, *Trial of the Major War Criminals before the International Military Tribunal Nuremberg (14 November 1945 - 1 October 1946)*, 42 volumes, published by the Secretariat of the Tribunal, 1947 (available online: http://www.loc.gov).
- Secretary of state for foreign affairs (UK), *A commentary on the Dumbarton Oaks proposals for the establishment of a general international organisation : presented by the secretary of state for foreign affairs to Parliament by command of His Majesty, November 1944*. Stationery office, 1944.
- Secretary of state for foreign affairs (UK), *A commentary on the charter of the United Nations signed at San Francisco on the 26th June, 1945 : presented by the secretary of state for foreign affairs to Parliament by command of His Majesty*. His Majesty's Stationery Office, 1945.
- Sectie Voorlichting van het Militair Gezag (Netherlands), *Nederland en Dumbarton Oaks: de voorstellen der conferentie van Dumbarton Oaks voor het Statuut eener Wereldorganisatie en de Nota der Nederlandsche Regeering houdende aanbevelingen ter zake dezer voorstellen*. Sectie Voorlichting van het Militair Gezag, 1945.
- Amartya Sen, *Human Rights and Asian Values (Sixteenth Morgenthau Memorial Lecture on Ethics & Foreign Policy)*. Carnegie Council on Ethics and International Affairs, 1997.
- Amartya Sen, *Development as Freedom*. Random House, 1999.
- Arjun Sengupta, "On the theory and practice of the Right to Development," in *Human Rights Quarterly*, Vol. 24 (2002).
- Salil Shetty, "Millennium Declaration and Development Goals: Opportunities for Human Rights," in *SUR – International Journal on Human Rights*, volume 7 (2005).
- Bruno Simma and Andreas L. Paulus, "The 'International Community': Facing the Challenge of Globalization," in the *European Journal of International Law*, Vol. 9 (1998).
- Bruno Simma, "From bilateralism to community interest in international law," in *Recueil des cours*, Volume 250 (1994-VI).
- Bruno Simma, "The contribution of Alfred Verdross to the theory of international law," in the *European journal of international law*, vol. 6 (1995), no. 1.
- Sir Ian Sinclair, "The Significance of the Friendly Relations Declaration," in Lowe (editor), *The United Nations and the principles of international law: essays in memory of Michael Akehurst*. Routledge, 1994.
- Hans W. Singer, "The New International Economic Order: An Overview," in *the Journal of Modern African Studies*, Vol. 16 (1978), No. 4.

- Peter Singer, *One World: The Ethics of Globalization*. Yale University Press, 2002.
- S. Prakash Sinha, "Has self-determination become a principle of international law today?," in the *Indian journal of international law*, vol. 14 (1974).
- Krzysztof Skubiszewski, "Remarks on the interpretation of the United Nations Charter," in Mosler & Bernhardt (editors), *Völkerrecht als Rechtsordnung, Internationale Gerichtsbarkeit, Menschenrechte: Festschrift für Hermann Mosler*. Springer-Verlag, 1983.
- Anne-Marie Slaughter, *A New World Order*. Princeton University Press, 2004
- Blaine Sloan, "The binding force of a 'recommendation' of the General Assembly of the United Nations," in the *British Yearbook of International Law*, vol. 25 (1948).
- Blaine Sloan, "The United Nations charter as a constitution," in the *Pace yearbook of international law*, vol. 1 (1989).
- Jan Christiaan Smuts, *The League of Nations: A Practical Suggestion*. Nation Press, 1919.
- Louis B. Sohn, *Cases and other materials on world law: the interpretation and application of the charter of the United Nations and of the constitutions of other agencies of the world community*. The Foundation Press, 1950.
- Louis B. Sohn, "The impact of the United Nations on international law," in the *Proceedings of the American Society of International Law*, vol. 46 (1952).
- Louis B. Sohn, "United Nations Machinery for Implementing Human Rights," in the *American Journal of International Law*, vol. 62 (1968), no. 4.
- Louis B. Sohn, "Stockholm Declaration on the Human Environment," in the *Harvard International Law Journal*, Volume 14 (1973).
- Louis B. Sohn, "The Improvement of the UN Machinery on Human Rights," in the *International Studies Quarterly*, Vol. 23 (1979), No. 2.
- Louis B. Sohn, "The issue of self-defense and the UN Charter," in the *American Society of International Law Proceedings*, vol. 89 (1995).
- Max Sørensen, "Principes de droit international public," in *Recueil des cours*, vol. 101 (1961).
- Soviet Union, *Soviet Union at the San Francisco Conference*. Soviet News Booklet Series, 1945.
- Otto Spijkers, "Legal Mechanisms to Establish Accountability for the Genocide in Srebrenica," in *Human Rights & International Legal Discourse*, vol. 2 (2007).
- Otto Spijkers, "What's running the world: global values, international law, and the United Nations," in the *Interdisciplinary Journal of Human Rights Law*, vol. 4 (2010).
- Otto Spijkers, "De notie van wereldrecht vóór, tijdens en na de oprichting van de Verenigde Naties," in the *Nederlands juristenblad*, vol. 85 (2010).
- Carsten Stahn, *The law and practice of international territorial administration: Versailles to Iraq and beyond*. Cambridge University Press, 2008.
- Daniel Statman, "Humiliation, dignity and self-respect," in Klein & Kretzmer, *The concept of human dignity in human rights discourse*. Kluwer Law International, 2002.

- Edward R. Stettinius, *Charter of the United Nations: report to the President on the results of the San Francisco conference by the chairman of the United States delegation, the secretary of state*. Government printing office, 1945.
- Edward R. Stettinius, *United Nations will write charter for World Organization (address of April 6, 1945)*. United States Government Printing Office, 1945.
- Edward R. Stettinius, "Text of the Statement by Stettinius to Senate Hearing on the Charter of the United Nations," in *New York Times* of July 10, 1945.
- Edward R. Stettinius, "Human Rights in the United Nations Charter," in the *Annals of the American Academy of Political and Social Science*, Vol. 243 (1946).
- Ekkehard Strauss, *The emperor's new clothes? The United Nations and the implementation of the responsibility to protect*. Nomos, 2009
- Maurice Strong, "The Stockholm Conference," in the *Geographical Journal*, Vol. 138 (1972), No. 4.
- Surya P. Subedi, "International Conference on Financing for Development, Monterrey, Mexico, 18-22 March 2002," in *International Law FORUM Du Droit International*, Volume 4 (2002).
- Sutterlin, "Interview with Alger Hiss (February 13 and October 11, 1990)," in *United Nations Oral History Project Interview Transcripts*. Manuscripts and Archives, Yale University Library.
- Erik Suy, "Article 53," in Corten & Klein (eds.), *Les Conventions de Vienne sur le droit des traités :Commentaire article par article*. Bruylant, 2006.
- G. S. Swan, "Self-Determination and the United Nations Charter," in the *Indian journal of international law*, vol. 22 (1982).
- Paul C. Szasz, "The Security Council Starts Legislating," in the *American Journal of International Law*, Vol. 96, No. 4 (Oct., 2002),.
- Sandra Szurek, "La Charte des Nations Unies constitution mondiale?," in Cot & Pellet, *La Charte des Nations Unies: commentaire article par article*, vol. 1 (2005).
- Harry R. Targ, "Constructing Models of Presents, Futures, and Transitions: an Approach to Alternative World Futures," in Beres & Targ, *Planning Alternative World Futures: Values, Methods, and Models*. Praeger Publishers, 1975.
- Kok-Chor Tan, *Justice Without Borders: Cosmopolitanism, Nationalism, and Patriotism*. Cambridge University Press, 2004.
- Kok-Chor Tan, "The Boundary of Justice and the Justice of Boundaries: Defending Global Egalitarianism," in *Canadian Journal of Law and Jurisprudence*, Vol. 19, no. 2 (July 2006).
- Task Force on the United Nations, United States Institute of Peace, *American Interests and UN Reform*, 2005 (available online at http://usinfo.state.gov).
- Ian Taylor & Karen Smith, *United Nations Conference on Trade and Development (UNCTAD)*. Routledge, 2007.
- Fernando R. Tesón, *Humanitarian Intervention: An Inquiry into Law and Morality* (Third Edition). Transnational Publishers, 2005 (original is of 1988).
- John Tessitore, "The UN at 60: Still Misunderstood," in *Providence Journal*, January 11, 2007.
- Ramesh Thakur, Andrew F. Cooper & John English, *International Commissions and the Power of Ideas*. United Nations University Press, 2005.

- Ramesh Thakur, *The United Nations, peace and security: from collective security to the responsibility to protect*. Cambridge University Press, 2006.
- United Nations, *The United Nations conference on international organization, San Francisco, California, April 25 to June 26, 1945: selected documents*. United States Printing office, 1946.
- Patrick Thornberry, "Self-determination, minorities, human rights: a review of international instruments," in the *international and comparative law quarterly*, vol. 38 (1989).
- Patrick Thornberry, "The democratic or internal aspect of self-determination," in Tomuschat (editor), *Modern law of self-determination*. Nijhoff, 1993.
- Patrick Thornberry, "The principle of self-determination," in Lowe (editor), *The United Nations and the principles of international law: essays in memory of Michael Akehurst*. Routledge, 1994.
- Jean-Marc Thouvenin, "Article 103," in Cot & Pellet, *La Charte des Nations Unies: commentaire article par article*, vol. 1 (2005).
- George Thullen, *Problems of the trusteeship system: a study of political behavior in the United Nations*. Droz, 1964.
- S. Azadon Tiewul, "The United Nations Charter of Economic Rights and Duties of States," in the *Journal of international law and economics*, vol. 10 (1975).
- Jan Tinbergen, "International Economic Planning," in *Daedalus*, Vol. 95 (1966), No. 2.
- Frederick S. Tipson, "The Laswell-McDougal Enterprise: Toward a World Public Order of Human Dignity," in the *Virginia Journal of International Law*, vol. 14 (1973), no. 3.
- Christian Tomuschat, "Obligations arising for states without or against their will," in *Recueil des cours*, Volume 241 (1993-IV).
- Christian Tomuschat, "Self-determination in a post-colonial world," in Tomuschat (editor), *Modern law of self-determination*. Nijhoff, 1993.
- Christian Tomuschat, "Die internationale Gemeinschaft," in *Archiv des Völkerrechts*, vol. 33 (1995).
- Christian Tomuschat, "Foreword," in Tomuschat (editor), *The United Nations at Age Fifty: A Legal Perspective*. Kluwer Law International, 1995.
- Christian Tomuschat, "International law: ensuring the survival of mankind on the eve of a new century (general course on public international law)," in *Recueil des cours*, Volume 281 (1999).
- Christian Tomuschat, "Article 2(3)," in Simma (editor), *The Charter of the United Nations: A Commentary* (2nd edition). Oxford University Press, 2002.
- Christian Tomuschat, *Human rights: between idealism and realism*. 2nd edition. Oxford University Press, 2008.
- David Tothill, "Evatt and Smuts in San Francisco," in *The round table: a quarterly review of the politics of the British Empire*, vol. 96 (2007).
- Charmian Edwards Toussaint, *The trusteeship system of the United Nations*. Stevens & Sons, 1956.

- Antônio Augusto Cançado Trindade, "International law for humankind: towards a new jus gentium (II): general course on public international law," in *Recueil des cours*, Volume 317 (2005).
- Antônio Augusto Cançado Trindade, "International law for humankind: towards a new jus gentium (I): general course on public international law," in *Recueil des cours*, Volume 316 (2005).
- Harry S. Truman, *Address in San Francisco at the Closing Session of the United Nations Conference*, June 26th, 1945, in Woolley and Peters, *The American Presidency Project* [online].
- Grigory I. Tunkin, "The legal nature of the United Nations," in *Recueil des cours*, vol. 119 (1969).
- Grigory I. Tunkin, "International law in the international system," in *Recueil des cours*, Volume 147 (1975-IV).
- Grigory I. Tunkin, "Politics, law and force in the interstate system," in *Recueil des cours*, Volume 219 (1989-VII).
- United Nations Information Organisation, *An introduction to the United Nations*. United Nations Information Organisation, 1945.
- United Nations, "Report of the Committee on the Progressive Development of International Law and its Codification on the Methods for Encouraging the Progressive Development of International Law and its Eventual Codification," in the *American Journal of International Law*, Vol. 41 (1947), Supplement.
- United Nations (Department of public information), *Guide to the United Nations charter*. United Nations (Department of public information), 1947.
- United Nations Development Programme (UNDP), *Human Development Report 1994: New dimensions of human security*, Oxford University Press, 1994.
- United Nations Centre for Disarmament Affairs, *The United Nations and disarmament since 1945*. United Nations, 1996.
- United Nations High-level Panel on Threats, Challenges, and Change, *A more secure world: our shared responsibility: report of the High-level Panel on Threats, Challenges and Change*. United Nations, 2004. Also distributed on 2 December 2004, as UNDoc. A/59/565.
- United Nations Millennium Project, *Investing in Development: A Practical Plan to Achieve the Millennium Development Goals*. United Nations Development Programme, 2005.
- Francis Aimé Vallat, "Voting in the General Assembly of the United Nations," in the *British Yearbook of International Law*, vol. 31 (1954).
- Francis Aimé Vallat, "The competence of the United Nations General Assembly," in *Recueil des cours*, Volume 97 (1959-II).
- Peter Vallentyne, "Desert and Entitlement: An Introduction," in Vallentyne (Editor), *Equality and Justice, Volume Six (Desert and Entitlement)*. Routledge, 2003.
- Van der Goes van Naters, Beaufort, Terpstra, Joekes & Krijger, "Voorlopig Verslag," in *Handelingen der Staten-Generaal: Bijlagen tijdelijke zitting 1945*.
- Johan D. van der Vyver, "The Right to Self-Determination and its Enforcement," in the *ILSA Journal of International & Comparative Law*, vol. 10 (2004), no. 2.

- Jan Vandemoortele, "Are the MDGs Feasible?," in the *Development Policy Journal*, Volume 3 (2003).
- Arthur Vandenberg, "Vandenberg's Plea for Charter as the Only Hope of Averting Chaos in World (Text of Senator's Report to Congress)," in *New York Times* of June 30, 1945.
- Alfred Verdross, "Le fondement du droit international," in *Recueil des cours*, Volume 16 (1927-I).
- Alfred Verdross, "Idées directrices de l'Organisation des Nations Unies," in *Recueil des cours*, vol. 83 (1955).
- Maxime Verhagen, Norbert Schmelzer lecture, 18 April 2007, The Hague (available online at www.minbuza.nl).
- Jonathan M. Verschuuren, *Principles of environmental law: the ideal of sustainable development and the role of principles of international, European, and national environmental law*. Nomos, 2003.
- W.D. Verwey, "The United Nations and the Least Developed Countries: an Exploration in the Grey Zones of International Law," in Jerzy Makarczyk & Manfred Lachs (editors), *Essays in International Law in Honour of Judge Manfred Lachs*. M. Nijhoff, 1984.
- Santiago Villalpando, *L'émergence de la communauté internationale dans la responsabilité des Etats*. Presses universitaires de France, 2005.
- Michel Virally, "Réflexions sur le « *jus cogens* »," in the *Annuaire français du droit international*, vol. 12 (1966).
- Gerrit Jan de Voogd & Cornelis Willem van Santen, *Volkenbond en Vereenigde Naties*. Nederlands Genootschap voor Internationale Zaken, 1946.
- Jeremy Waldron, "The Dignity of Groups," in *Acta Juridica* (2008), NYU School of Law, Public Law Research Paper No. 08-53 (2008).
- Kenneth Waltz, *Theory of International Politics*. McGraw-Hill, 1979.
- Michael Walzer, *Just and Unjust Wars: A Moral Argument with Historical Illustrations* (Fourth Edition). Basic Books, 2006 (original is of 1977).
- Michael Walzer, *Spheres of Justice: A Defense of Pluralism and Equality*. Basic Nooks, 1983.
- Michael Walzer, *Thick and Thin: Moral Argument at Home and Abroad*. University of Notre Dame Press, 1994.
- Michael Walzer, *International Society: What is the Best that We Can Do?*, June 2000, Paper number 8 in the Occasional Papers Series of School of Social Science at the Institute for Advanced Study (www.sss.ias.edu)
- Michael Walzer, *Universalism and Jewish Values (Twentieth Annual Morgenthau Memorial Lecture on Ethics & Foreign Policy)*, Carnegie Council on Ethics and International Affairs, 2001.
- Thomas G. Weiss, "The United Nations Conference on the Least Developed Countries: The Relevance of Conference Diplomacy in Paris for International Negotiations," in *International Affairs*, Volume 59 (1983), No. 4.
- Thomas G. Weiss & Sam Daws, "World Politics: Continuity and Change since 1945," in Weiss & Daws (eds.), *The Oxford Handbook on the United Nations*. Oxford University Press, 2007.

- Thomas G. Weiss, David P. Forsythe, Roger A. Coate & Kelly-Kate Pease, *The United Nations and Changing World Politics*. Westview Press, 2009.
- Edith Brown Weiss, "Our Rights and Obligations to Future Generations for the Environment," in *American Journal of International Law*, Vol. 84 (1990), No. 1.
- Guenter Weissberg, "United Nations movements toward world law," in the *international and comparative law quarterly*, vol. 24 (1975).
- Carl-Friedrich von Weizsäcker, "A Sceptical Contribution," in Mendlovitz, *On the Creation of a Just World Order*. The Free Press, 1975.
- Claude Emerson Welch, "Defining Contemporary Forms of Slavery: Updating a Venerable NGO," in the *Human Rights Quarterly*, vol. 31 (2009).
- Marc Weller, "The international response to the dissolution of the Socialist Federal Republic of Yugoslavia," in the *American journal of international law*, vol. 86 (1992), no. 3
- Sumner Welles, *The United Nations: their creed for a free world*. United States Government Printing Office, 1942.
- Christopher H. Wellman, "A Defense of Secession and Political Self-Determination," in *Philosophy and Public Affairs*, Vol. 24 (1995), No. 2.
- Alexander E. Wendt, *Social Theory of International Politics*. Cambridge University Press, 1999.
- Burns H. Weston, "Charter of Economic Rights and Duties of States and the Deprivation of Foreign-Owned Wealth," in the *American Journal of International Law*, volume 75 (1981).
- G. White, "A New International Economic Order?," in the *Virginia Journal of International Law*, vol. 16 (1975-1976).
- Robin C. A. White, "New International Economic Order," in *International & Comparative Law Quarterly*, vol. 24 (1975).
- Nigel D. White, *Keeping the peace: the United Nations and the maintenance of international peace and security*. Manchester University Press, 1997.
- Nigel D. White, *The United Nations system: Toward International Justice*. Lynne Rienner Publishers, 2002.
- Cees Wiebes, "De oprichting van de Verenigde Naties: 50 jaar geleden. Het dagboek van Minister Eelco van Kleffens over de conferentie in San Francisco, 11 april – 7 juni 1945," in *Jaarboek Buitenlandse Zaken*, 1995. SDU Publishers, 1995
- Elie Wiesel, interviewed by Kijne in 2006, in *Opinie & Gesprek*, produced by NRC-*Handelsblad* and *VPRO*.
- Ralph Wilde, "Legal 'Black Hole'? Extraterritorial state action and international treaty law on civil and political rights," in the *Michigan Journal of International Law*, vol. 26 (2005), no. 3.
- Ralph Wilde, "Trusteeship Council," in Weiss & Daws (eds.), *The Oxford Handbook on the United Nations*. Oxford University Press, 2007.
- Ralph Wilde, *International territorial administration: how trusteeship and the civilizing mission never went away*. Oxford University Press, 2008.
- Bernard Williams, "Consistency and Realism," in Williams, *Problems of the Self: Philosophical Papers (1956-1972)*. Cambridge University Press, 1973.

- Witenberg, "New Set of Rules Acceptable to All Nations is Proposed," in *New York Times* of May 13, 1945.
- Rüdiger Wolfrum, "Preamble," in Simma (editor), *The Charter of the United Nations: A Commentary* (2<sup>nd</sup> edition). Oxford University Press, 2002.
- Rüdiger Wolfrum, "Purposes and Principles," in Simma (editor), *The Charter of the United Nations: A Commentary* (2<sup>nd</sup> edition). Oxford University Press, 2002.
- Rüdiger Wolfrum, "Article 56," in Simma (editor), *The Charter of the United Nations: A Commentary* (2<sup>nd</sup> edition). Oxford University Press, 2002.
- Andrew Woodcock, "Jacques Maritain, Natural Law and the Universal Declaration of Human Rights," in the *Journal of the History of International Law*, vol. 8 (2006).
- World Bank (Post-Conflict Unit, led by Colletta), *Security, Poverty Reduction and Sustainable Development: Challenges for the New Millennium*. World Bank, 1999.
- Philip Quincy Wright, "Human Rights and Charter Revision," in the *Annals of the American Academy of Political and Social Science*, Vol. 296 (1954).
- Philip Quincy Wright, *The Study of International Relations*. Appleton, Century, Crofts, 1955.
- Alan Zaitchik, "On Deserving to Deserve," in *Philosophy and Public Affairs*, Vol. 6, No. 4 (1977).
- Jerzy Zajadło, "Human dignity and human rights," in Hanski & Suksi, *An introduction to the international protection of human rights: a textbook*. 2<sup>nd</sup> edition. Åbo Akademi University, 1999.

# SCHOOL OF HUMAN RIGHTS RESEARCH SERIES

The School of Human Rights Research is a joint effort by human rights researchers in the Netherlands. Its central research theme is the nature and meaning of international standards in the field of human rights, their application and promotion in the national legal order, their interplay with national standards, and the international supervision of such application. The School of Human Rights Research Series only includes English titles that contribute to a better understanding of the different aspects of human rights.

Published titles within the Series:

1. Brigit C.A. Toebes, *The Right to Health as a Human Right in International Law*
   ISBN 90–5095–057–4

2. Ineke Boerefijn, *The Reporting Procedure under the Covenant on Civil and Political Rights. Practice and Procedures of the Human Rights Committee*
   ISBN 90–5095–074–4

3. Kitty Arambulo, *Strengthening the Supervision of the International Covenant on Economic, Social and Cultural Rights. Theoretical and Procedural Aspects*
   ISBN 90–5095–058–2

4. Marlies Glasius, *Foreign Policy on Human Rights. Its Influence on Indonesia under Soeharto*
   ISBN 90–5095–089–2

5. Cornelis D. de Jong, *The Freedom of Thought, Conscience and Religion or Belief in the United Nations (1946–1992)*
   ISBN 90–5095–137–6

6.  Heleen Bosma, *Freedom of Expression in England and under the ECHR: in Search of a Common Ground. A Foundation for the Application of the Human Rights Act 1998 in English Law*
    ISBN 90–5095–136–8

7.  Mielle Bulterman, *Human Rights in the External Relations of the European Union*
    ISBN 90–5095–164–3

8.  Esther M. van den Berg, *The Influence of Domestic NGOs on Dutch Human Rights Policy. Case Studies on South Africa,Namibia, Indonesia and East Timor*
    ISBN 90–5095–159–7

9.  Ian Seiderman, *Hierarchy in International Law: the Human Rights Dimension*
    ISBN 90–5095–165–1

10. Anna Meijknecht, *Towards International Personality: the Position of Minorities and Indigenous Peoples in International Law*
    ISBN 90–5095–166-X

11. Mohamed Eltayeb, *A Human Rights Approach to Combating Religious Persecution. Cases from Pakistan, Saudi Arabia and Sudan*
    ISBN 90–5095–170–8

12. Machteld Boot, *Genocide, Crimes Against Humanity, War Crimes: Nullum Crimen Sine Lege and the Subject Matter Jurisdiction of the International Criminal Court*
    ISBN 90–5095–216-X

13. Corinne Packer, *Using Human Rights to Change Tradition. Traditional Practices Harmful to Women's Reproductive Health in sub-Saharan Africa*
    ISBN 90–5095–226–7

14. Theo R.G. van Banning, *The Human Right to Property*
    ISBN 90–5095–203–8

15. Yvonne M. Donders, *Towards a Right to Cultural Identity?*
    ISBN 90–5095–238–0

16. Göran K. Sluiter, *International Criminal Adjudication and the Collection of Evidence: Obligations of States*
    ISBN 90–5095–227–5

17. Nicola Jägers, *Corporate Human Rights Obligations: in Search of Accountability*
    ISBN 90–5095–240–2

18. Magdalena Sepúlveda, *The Nature of the Obligations under the International Covenant on Economic, Social and Cultural Rights*
    ISBN 90–5095–260–7

19. Mitsue Inazumi, *Universal Jurisdiction in Modern International Law: Expansion of National Jurisdiction for Prosecuting Serious Crimes under International Law*
    ISBN 90–5095–366–2

20. Anne-Marie L.M. de Brouwer, *Supranational Criminal Prosecution of Sexual Violence: The ICC and the Practice of the ICTY and the ICTR*
    ISBN 90–5095–533–9

21. Jeroen Gutter, *Thematic Procedures of the United Nations Commission on Human Rights and International Law: in Search of a Sense of Community*
    ISBN 90–5095–557–6

22. Hilde Reiding, *The Netherlands and the Development of International Human Rights Instruments*
    ISBN 978–90–5095–654–3

23. Ingrid Westendorp, *Women and Housing: Gender Makes a Difference*
    ISBN 978–90–5095–669–7

24. Quirine A.M. Eijkman, *We Are Here to Serve You! Public Security, Police Reform and Human Rights Implementation in Costa Rica*
    ISBN 978–90–5095–704–5

25. Antoine Ch. Buyse, *Post-conflict Housing Restitution. The European Human Rights Perspective with a case study on Bosnia and Herzegovina*
    ISBN 978–90–5095–770–0

26. Gentian Zyberi, *The Humanitarian Face of the International Court of Justice. Its Contribution to Interpreting and Developing International Human Rights and Humanitarian Law Rules and Principles*
    ISBN 978–90–5095–792–2

27. Dragoş Cucereanu, *Aspects of Regulating Freedom of Expression on the Internet*
    ISBN 978–90–5095–842–4

28. Ton Liefaard, *Deprivation of Liberty of Children in Light of International Human Rights Law and Standards*
    ISBN 978–90–5095–838–7

29. Laura van Waas, *Nationality Matters. Statelessness under International Law*
    ISBN 978–90–5095–854–7

30. Jeroen Denkers, *The World Trade Organization and Import Bans in Response to Violations of Fundamental Labour Rights*
    ISBN 978–90–5095–855–4

31. Irene Hadiprayitno, *Hazard or Right? The Dialectics of Development Practice and the Internationally Declared Right to Development, with Special Reference to Indonesia*
    ISBN 978–90–5095–932–2

32. Michał Gondek, *The Reach of Human Rights in a Globalising World: Extraterritorial Application of Human Rights Treaties*
    ISBN 978–90–5095–817–2

33. Jeff Handmaker, *Advocating for Accountability: Civic-State Interactions to Protect Refugees in South Africa*
    ISBN 978–90–5095–910–0

34. Anna Oehmichen, *Terrorism and Anti-Terror Legislation: The Terrorised Legislator? A Comparison of Counter-Terror Legislation and Its Implications on Human Rights in the Legal Systems of the United Kingdom, Spain, Germany and France*
    ISBN 978–90–5095–956–8

35. Simon Walker, *The Future of Human Rights Impact Assessments of Trade Agreements*
    ISBN 978–90–5095–986–5

36. Fleur van Leeuwen, *Women's Rights Are Human Rights: The Practice of the United Nations Human Rights Committee and the Committee on Economic, Social and Cultural Rights*
    ISBN 978–90–5095–980–3

524

37. Eva Rieter, *Preventing Irreparable Harm. Provisional Measures in International Human Rights Adjudication*
    ISBN 978–90–5095–931–5

38. Desislava Stoitchkova, *Towards Corporate Liability in International Criminal Law*
    ISBN 978–94–000–0024–7

39. Paulien Muller, *Scattered Families. Transnational Family Life of Afghan Refugees in the Netherlands in the Light of the Human Rights-Based Protection of the Family*
    ISBN 978–94–000–0021–6

40. Bibi van Ginkel, *The Practice of the United Nations in Combating Terrorism from 1946 to 2008. Questions of Legality and Legitimacy*
    ISBN 978–94–000–0076–6

41. Christophe Paulussen, *Male captus bene detentus? Surrendering suspects to the International Criminal Court*
    ISBN 978–94–000–0100–8

42. Brianne McGonigle Leyh, *Procedural Justice? Victim Participation in International Criminal Proceedings*
    ISBN 978-1-78068-020-0

43. Maria Ventegodt Liisberg, *Disability and Employment. A Contemporary Disability Human Rights Approach Applied to Danish, Swedish and EU Law and Policy*
    ISBN 978-1-78068-028-6

44. Tarlach McGonagle, *Minority Rights, Freedom of Expression and of the Media: Dynamics and Dilemmas*
    ISBN 978-94-000-0215-9

45. Marloes van Noorloos, *Hate Speech Revisited. A comparative and historical perspective on hate speech law in the Netherlands and England & Wales*
    ISBN 978-1-78068-032-3

46. Hanneke Senden, *Interpretation of Fundamental Rights in a Multilevel Legal System. An analysis of the European Court of Human Rights and the Court of Justice of the European Union*
    ISBN 978-1-78068-027-9